DRAMA
for Students

Advisors

Jayne M. Burton is a teacher of secondary English and an adjunct professor for Northwest Vista College in San Antonio, TX.

Klaudia Janek is the school librarian at the International Academy in Bloomfield Hills, Michigan. She holds an MLIS degree from Wayne State University, a teaching degree from Rio Salado College, and a bachelor of arts degree in international relations from Saint Joseph's College. She is the IB Extended Essay Coordinator and NCA AdvancEd co-chair at her school. She is an IB workshop leader for International Baccalaureate North America, leading teacher training for IB school librarians and extended essay coordinators. She has been happy to serve the Michigan Association for Media in Education as a board member and past president at the regional level, advocating for libraries in Michigan schools.

Greg Bartley is an English teacher in Virginia. He holds an M.A.Ed. in English Education from Wake Forest University and a B.S. in Integrated Language Arts Education from Miami University.

Sarah Clancy teaches IB English at the International Academy in Bloomfield Hills, Michigan. She is a member of the National Council of Teachers of English and Michigan Speech Coaches, Inc. Sarah earned her undergraduate degree from Kalamazoo College and her Master's of Education from Florida Southern College. She coaches the high-ranking forensics team and is the staff adviser of the school newspaper, *Overachiever*.

Karen Dobson is a teen/adult librarian at Plymouth District Library in Plymouth, Michigan. She holds a Bachelor of Science degree from Oakland University and an MLIS from Wayne State University and has served on many committees through the Michigan Library Association.

Tom Shilts is the youth librarian at the Okemos branch of Capital Area District Library in Okemos, Michigan. He holds an MSLS degree from Clarion University of Pennsylvania and an MA in U.S. History from the University of North Dakota.

DRAMA
for Students

Presenting Analysis, Context, and Criticism
on Commonly Studied Dramas

VOLUME 34

Kristin Mallegg, Project Editor

Foreword by Carole L. Hamilton

GALE
CENGAGE Learning·

Farmington Hills, Mich • San Francisco • New York • Waterville, Maine
Meriden, Conn • Mason, Ohio • Chicago

GALE
CENGAGE Learning®

Drama for Students, Volume 34

Project Editor: Kristin B. Mallegg

Rights Acquisition and Management: Ashley Maynard

Composition: Evi Abou-El-Seoud

Manufacturing: Rita Wimberley

Imaging: John Watkins

Digital Content Production: Edna Shy

For product information and technology assistance, contact us at
Gale Customer Support, 1-800-877-4253.
For permission to use material from this text or product,
submit all requests online at **www.cengage.com/permissions.**
Further permissions questions can be emailed to
permissionrequest@cengage.com

While every effort has been made to ensure the reliability of the information presented in this publication, Gale, a part of Cengage Learning, does not guarantee the accuracy of the data contained herein. Gale accepts no payment for listing; and inclusion in the publication of any organization, agency, institution, publication, service, or individual does not imply endorsement of the editors or publisher. Errors brought to the attention of the publisher and verified to the satisfaction of the publisher will be corrected in future editions.

Gale
27500 Drake Rd.
Farmington Hills, MI, 48331-3535

ISBN-13: 978-1-4103-2832-8
ISSN 1094-9232

This title is also available as an e-book.
ISBN-13: 978-1-4103-2834-2
Contact your Gale, a part of Cengage Learning sales representative for ordering information.

Printed in Mexico
1 2 3 4 5 6 7 21 20 19 18 17

Table of Contents

The Study of Drama

We study drama in order to learn what meaning others have made of life, to comprehend what it takes to produce a work of art, and to glean some understanding of ourselves. Drama produces in a separate, aesthetic world, a moment of being for the audience to experience, while maintaining the detachment of a reflective observer.

Drama is a representational art, a visible and audible narrative presenting virtual, fictional characters within a virtual, fictional universe. Dramatic realizations may pretend to approximate reality or else stubbornly defy, distort, and deform reality into an artistic statement. From this separate universe that is obviously not "real life" we expect a valid reflection upon reality, yet drama never is mistaken for reality—the methods of theater are integral to its form and meaning. Theater is art, and art's appeal lies in its ability both to approximate life and to depart from it. For in intruding its distorted version of life into our consciousness, art gives us a new perspective and appreciation of life and reality. Although all aesthetic experiences perform this service, theater does it most effectively by creating a separate, cohesive universe that freely acknowledges its status as an art form.

And what is the purpose of the aesthetic universe of drama? The potential answers to such a question are nearly as many and varied as there are plays written, performed, and enjoyed.

Dramatic texts can be problems posed, answers asserted, or moments portrayed. Dramas (tragedies as well as comedies) may serve strictly "to ease the anguish of a torturing hour" (as stated in William Shakespeare's *A Midsummer Night's Dream*)—to divert and entertain—or aspire to move the viewer to action with social issues. Whether to entertain or to instruct, affirm or influence, pacify or shock, dramatic art wraps us in the spell of its imaginary world for the length of the work and then dispenses us back to the real world, entertained, purged, as Aristotle said, of pity and fear, and edified—or at least weary enough to sleep peacefully.

It is commonly thought that theater, being an art of performance, must be experienced—seen—in order to be appreciated fully. However, to view a production of a dramatic text is to be limited to a single interpretation of that text—all other interpretations are for the moment closed off, inaccessible. In the process of producing a play, the director, stage designer, and performers interpret and transform the script into a work of art that always departs in some measure from the author's original conception. Novelist and critic Umberto Eco, in his *The Role of the Reader: Explorations in the Semiotics of Texts* (Indiana University Press, 1979), explained, "In short, we can say that every performance offers us a complete and satisfying version of the work, but at the same time makes it incomplete for us, because it cannot simultaneously give all the other artistic solutions which the work may admit."

Thus Laurence Olivier's coldly formal and neurotic film presentation of Shakespeare's *Hamlet* (in which he played the title character as well as directed) shows marked differences from subsequent adaptations. While Olivier's Hamlet is clearly entangled in a Freudian relationship with his mother Gertrude, he would be incapable of shushing her with the impassioned kiss that Mel Gibson's mercurial Hamlet (in director Franco Zeffirelli's 1990 film) does. Although each of performances rings true to Shakespeare's text, each is also a mutually exclusive work of art. Also important to consider are the time periods in which each of these films was produced: Olivier made his film in 1948, a time in which overt references to sexuality (especially incest) were frowned upon. Gibson and Zeffirelli made their film in a culture more relaxed and comfortable with these issues. Just as actors and directors can influence the presentation of drama, so too can the time period of the production affect what the audience will see.

A play script is an open text from which an infinity of specific realizations may be derived. Dramatic scripts that are more open to interpretive creativity (such as those of Ntozake Shange and Tomson Highway) actually require the creative improvisation of the production troupe in order to complete the text. Even the most prescriptive scripts (those of Neil Simon, Lillian Hellman, and Robert Bolt, for example), can never fully control the actualization of live performance, and circumstantial events, including the attitude and receptivity of the audience, make every performance a unique event. Thus, while it is important to view a production of a dramatic piece, if one wants to understand a drama fully it is equally important to read the original dramatic text.

The reader of a dramatic text or script is not limited by either the specific interpretation of a given production or by the unstoppable action of a moving spectacle. The reader of a dramatic text may discover the nuances of the play's language, structure, and events at their own pace. Yet studied alone, the author's blueprint for artistic production does not tell the whole story of a play's life and significance. One also needs to assess the play's critical reviews to discover how it resonated to cultural themes at the time of its debut and how the shifting tides of cultural interest have revised its interpretation and impact on audiences. And to do this, one needs to know a little about the culture of the times which produced the play as well as the author who penned it.

Drama for Students supplies this material in a useful compendium for the student of dramatic theater. Covering a range of dramatic works that span from 442 BCE to the 1990s, this book focuses on significant theatrical works whose themes and form transcend the uncertainty of dramatic fads. These are plays that have proven to be both memorable and teachable. *Drama for Students* seeks to enhance appreciation of these dramatic texts by providing scholarly materials written with the secondary and college/university student in mind. It provides for each play a concise summary of the plot and characters as well as a detailed explanation of its themes. In addition, background material on the historical context of the play, its critical reception, and the author's life help the student to understand the work's position in the chronicle of dramatic history. For each play entry a new work of scholarly criticism is also included, as well as segments of other significant critical works for handy reference. A thorough bibliography provides a starting point for further research.

This series offers comprehensive educational resources for students of drama. *Drama for Students* is a vital book for dramatic interpretation and a valuable addition to any reference library.

Sources

Eco, Umberto, *The Role of the Reader: Explorations in the Semiotics of Texts*, Indiana University Press, 1979.

Carole L. Hamilton
Author and Instructor of English at Cary
Academy, Cary, North Carolina

Introduction

Purpose of the Book

The purpose of *Drama for Students* (*DfS*) is to provide readers with a guide to understanding, enjoying, and studying dramas by giving them easy access to information about the work. Part of Gale's "For Students" literature line, *DfS* is specifically designed to meet the curricular needs of high school and undergraduate college students and their teachers, as well as the interests of general readers and researchers considering specific plays. While each volume contains entries on "classic" dramas frequently studied in classrooms, there are also entries containing hard-to-find information on contemporary plays, including works by multicultural, international, and women playwrights. Entries profiling film versions of plays not only diversify the study of drama but support alternate learning styles, media literacy, and film studies curricula as well.

The information covered in each entry includes an introduction to the play and the work's author; a plot summary, to help readers unravel and understand the events in a drama; descriptions of important characters, including explanation of a given character's role in the drama as well as discussion about that character's relationship to other characters in the play; analysis of important themes in the drama; and an explanation of important literary techniques and movements as they are demonstrated in the play.

In addition to this material, which helps the readers analyze the play itself, students are also provided with important information on the literary and historical background informing each work. This includes a historical context essay, a box comparing the time or place the drama was written to modern Western culture, a critical essay, and excerpts from critical essays on the play. A unique feature of *DfS* is a specially commissioned critical essay on each drama, targeted toward the student reader.

The "literature to film" entries on plays vary slightly in form, providing background on film technique and comparison to the original, literary version of the work. These entries open with an introduction to the film, which leads directly into the plot summary. The summary highlights plot changes from the play, key cinematic moments, and/or examples of key film techniques. As in standard entries, there are character profiles (noting omissions or additions, and identifying the actors), analysis of themes and how they are illustrated in the film, and an explanation of the cinematic style and structure of the film. A cultural context section notes any time period or setting differences from that of the original work, as well as cultural differences between the time in which the original work was written and the time in which the film adaptation was made. A film entry concludes with a critical overview and critical essays on the film.

To further help today's student in studying and enjoying each play or film, information on audiobooks and other media adaptations is provided (if available), as well as suggestions for works of fiction, nonfiction, or film on similar themes and topics. Classroom aids include ideas for research papers and lists of critical and reference sources that provide additional material on each drama. Film entries also highlight signature film techniques demonstrated, as well as suggesting media literacy activities and prompts to use during or after viewing a film.

Selection Criteria

The titles for each volume of *DfS* are selected by surveying numerous sources on notable literary works and analyzing course curricula for various schools, school districts, and states. Some of the sources surveyed include: high school and undergraduate literature anthologies and textbooks; lists of award-winners, and recommended titles, including the Young Adult Library Services Association (YALSA) list of best books for young adults. Films are selected both for the literary importance of the original work and the merits of the adaptation (including official awards and widespread public recognition).

Input solicited from our expert advisory board—consisting of educators and librarians—guides us to maintain a mix of "classic" and contemporary literary works, a mix of challenging and engaging works (including genre titles that are commonly studied) appropriate for different age levels, and a mix of international, multicultural and women authors. These advisors also consult on each volume's entry list, advising on which titles are most studied, most appropriate, and meet the broadest interests across secondary (grades 7–12) curricula and undergraduate literature studies.

How Each Entry Is Organized

Each entry, or chapter, in *DfS* focuses on one play. Each entry heading lists the full name of the play, the author's name, and the date of the play's publication. The following elements are contained in each entry:

Introduction: a brief overview of the drama which provides information about its first appearance, its literary standing, any controversies surrounding the work, and major conflicts or themes within the work. Film entries identify the original play and provide understanding of the film's reception and reputation, along with that of the director.

Author Biography: in play entries, this section includes basic facts about the author's life, and focuses on events and times in the author's life that inspired the drama in question.

Plot Summary: a description of the major events in the play. Subheads demarcate the play's various acts or scenes. Plot summaries of films are used to uncover plot differences from the original play, and to note the use of certain film angles or techniques.

Characters: an alphabetical listing of major characters in the play. Each character name is followed by a brief to an extensive description of the character's role in the play, as well as discussion of the character's actions, relationships, and possible motivation. In film entries, omissions or changes to the cast of characters of the film adaptation are mentioned here, and the actors' names—and any awards they may have received—are also included.

Characters are listed alphabetically by last name. If a character is unnamed—for instance, the Stage Manager in *Our Town*—the character is listed as "The Stage Manager" and alphabetized as "Stage Manager." If a character's first name is the only one given, the name will appear alphabetically by the first name.

Variant names are also included for each character. Thus, the nickname "Babe" would head the listing for a character in *Crimes of the Heart,* but below that listing would be her less-mentioned married name "Rebecca Botrelle."

Themes: a thorough overview of how the major topics, themes, and issues are addressed within the play. Each theme discussed appears in a separate subhead. While the key themes often remain the same or similar when a play is adapted into a film, film entries demonstrate how the themes are conveyed cinematically, along with any changes in the portrayal of the themes.

Style: this section addresses important style elements of the drama, such as setting, point of view, and narration; important literary devices used, such as imagery, foreshadowing, symbolism; and, if applicable, genres to which the work might have belonged, such as Gothicism or Romanticism. Literary terms are explained within the entry, but can also be found in the Glossary. Film entries cover how the director conveyed the meaning, message, and mood of the work using film in comparison to the author's use of language, literary device, etc., in the original work.

Historical Context: in play entries, this section outlines the social, political, and cultural climate in which the author lived and the play was created. This section may include descriptions of related historical events, pertinent aspects of daily life in the culture, and the artistic and literary sensibilities of the time in which the work was written. If the play is a historical work, information regarding the time in which the play is set is also included. Each section is broken down with helpful subheads. Film entries contain a similar Cultural Context section, because the film adaptation might explore an entirely different time period or culture than the original work, and may also be influenced by the traditions and views of a time period much different than that of the original author.

Critical Overview: this section provides background on the critical reputation of the play or film, including bannings or any other public controversies surrounding the work. For older plays, this section includes a history of how the drama or film was first received and how perceptions of it may have changed over the years; for more recent plays, direct quotes from early reviews may also be included.

Criticism: an essay commissioned by *DfS* which specifically deals with the play or film and is written specifically for the student audience, as well as excerpts from previously published criticism on the work (if available).

Sources: an alphabetical list of critical material used in compiling the entry, with full bibliographical information.

Further Reading: an alphabetical list of other critical sources which may prove useful for the student. It includes full bibliographical information and a brief annotation.

Suggested Search Terms: a list of search terms and phrases to jumpstart students' further information seeking. Terms include not just titles and author names but also terms and topics related to the historical and literary context of the works.

In addition, each entry contains the following highlighted sections, set apart from the main text as sidebars:

Media Adaptations: if available, a list of audiobooks and important film and television adaptations of the play, including source information. The list may also include such variations on the work as musical adaptations and other stage interpretations.

Topics for Further Study: a list of potential study questions or research topics dealing with the play. This section includes questions related to other disciplines the student may be studying, such as American history, world history, science, math, government, business, geography, economics, psychology, etc.

Compare and Contrast: an "at-a-glance" comparison of the cultural and historical differences between the author's time and culture and late twentieth century or early twenty-first century Western culture. This box includes pertinent parallels between the major scientific, political, and cultural movements of the time or place the drama was written, the time or place the play was set (if a historical work), and modern Western culture. Works written after 1990 may not have this box.

What Do I Read Next?: a list of works that might give a reader points of entry into a classic work (e.g., YA or multicultural titles) and/or complement the featured play or serve as a contrast to it. This includes works by the same author and others, works from various genres, YA works, and works from various cultures and eras.

The film entries provide sidebars more targeted to the study of film, including:

Film Technique: a listing and explanation of four to six key techniques used in the film, including shot styles, use of transitions, lighting, sound or music, etc.

Read, Watch, Write: media literacy prompts and/or suggestions for viewing log prompts.

What Do I See Next?: a list of films based on the same or similar works or of films similar in directing style, technique, etc.

Other Features

DfS includes "The Study of Drama," a foreword by Carole Hamilton, an educator and author who specializes in dramatic works. This essay examines the basis for drama in societies and what drives people to study such work. The essay also discusses how *DfS* can help teachers show students how to enrich their own reading/viewing experiences.

A Cumulative Author/Title Index lists the authors and titles covered in each volume of the *DfS* series.

A Cumulative Nationality/Ethnicity Index breaks down the authors and titles covered in each volume of the *DfS* series by nationality and ethnicity.

A Subject/Theme Index, specific to each volume, provides easy reference for users who may be studying a particular subject or theme rather than a single work. Significant subjects from events to broad themes are included.

Each entry may include illustrations, including photo of the author, stills from stage productions, and stills from film adaptations, if available.

Citing Drama for Students

When writing papers, students who quote directly from any volume of *DfS* may use the following general forms. These examples are based on MLA style; teachers may request that students adhere to a different style, so the following examples may be adapted as needed.

When citing text from *DfS* that is not attributed to a particular author (i.e., the Themes, Style, Historical Context sections, etc.), the following format should be used in the bibliography section:

> "*Candida.*" *Drama for Students.* Ed. Sara Constantakis. Vol. 30. Detroit: Gale, Cengage Learning, 2013. 1–27. Print.

When quoting the specially commissioned essay from *DfS* (usually the first piece under the "Criticism" subhead), the following format should be used:

> O'Neal, Michael J. Critical Essay on *Candida. Drama for Students.* Ed. Sara Constantakis. Vol. 30. Detroit: Gale, Cengage Learning, 2013. 12–15. Print.

When quoting a journal or newspaper essay that is reprinted in a volume of *DfS*, the following form may be used:

> Lazenby, Walter. "Love and 'Vitality' in *Candida.*" *Modern Drama* 20.1 (1977): 1–19. Rpt. in *Drama for Students.* Ed. Sara Constantakis. Vol. 30. Detroit: Gale, Cengage Learning, 2013. 18–22. Print.

When quoting material reprinted from a book that appears in a volume of *DfS*, the following form may be used:

> Phelps, William Lyon. "George Bernard Shaw." *Essays on Modern Dramatists.* New York: Macmillan, 1921. 67–98. Rpt. in *Drama for Students.* Ed. Sara Constantakis. Vol. 30. Detroit: Gale, Cengage Learning, 2013. 26. Print.

We Welcome Your Suggestions

The editorial staff of *Drama for Students* welcomes your comments and ideas. Readers who wish to suggest dramas to appear in future volumes, or who have other suggestions, are cordially invited to contact the editor. You may contact the editor via e-mail at: **ForStudentsEditors @cengage.com.** Or write to the editor at:

Editor, *Drama for Students*

Gale

27500 Drake Road

Farmington Hills, MI 48331-3535

Literary Chronology

1905: John Patrick is born on May 17 in Louisville, Kentucky.

1912: Lucille Fletcher is born on March 28 in Brooklyn, New York.

1924: James Baldwin is born on August 2 in Harlem, New York.

1926: Peter Shaffer is born on May 15 in Liverpool, United Kingdom.

1929: Ira Levin is born on August 27 in New York, New York.

1938: John Guare is born on February 5 in New York, New York.

1941: The play *Lift Every Voice and Sing* is produced.

1951: The play *The Curious Savage* is produced.

1954: John Patrick is awarded the Pulitzer Prize for Drama for *The Teahouse of the August Moon.*

1959: Yasmina Reza is born on May 1 in Paris, France.

1964: The play *Blues for Mister Charlie* is produced.

1965: Diana Son is born in Philadelphia, Pennsylvania.

1969: John Cariani is born on July 23 in Brocton, Massachusetts.

1972: Prince Gomolvilas is born on August 28 in Indianapolis, Indiana.

1975: Julia Cho is born in Los Angeles, California.

1978: The play *Deathtrap* is produced.

1980: The play *Amadeus* is produced.

1984: The film *Amadeus* is released.

1985: *Amadeus* wins the Academy Awards for best picture, best director, best actor, best adapted screenplay, best sound, best art direction, best costume design, and best makeup.

1987: James Baldwin dies of stomach cancer on December 1 in Saint-Paul-de-Vence, France.

1995: John Patrick dies of interrupted respiration on November 7 in Delray Beach, Florida.

1998: The play *Stop Kiss* is produced.

1998: Yasmina Reza is awarded the Tony Award for Best Play for *Art.*

2000: Lucille Fletcher dies of a stroke on August 31 in Langhorne, Pennsylvania.

2002: The play *The Theory of Everything* is produced.

2004: The play *Almost, Maine* is produced.

2005: The play *BFE* is produced.

2006: The play *God of Carnage* is produced.

2007: Ira Levin dies of a heart attack on November 12 in New York, New York.

2009: Yasmina Reza is awarded the Tony Award for Best Play for *God of Carnage.*

2009: Matthew Warchus is awarded the Tony Award for Best Director of a Play for *God of Carnage.*

2009: Marcia Gay Harden is awarded the Tony Award for Best Actress in a Play for *God of Carnage*.

2010: The play *A Free Man of Color* is produced.

2016: Peter Shaffer dies on June 6 in County Cork, Ireland.

Acknowledgements

The editors wish to thank the copyright holders of the excerpted criticism included in this volume and the permissions managers of many book and magazine publishing companies for assisting us in securing reproduction rights. We are also grateful to the staffs of the Detroit Public Library, the Library of Congress, the University of Detroit Mercy Library, Wayne State University Purdy/Kresge Library Complex, and the University of Michigan Libraries for making their resources available to us. Following is a list of the copyright holders who have granted us permission to reproduce material in this volume of DfS. Every effort has been made to trace copyright, but if omissions have been made, please let us know.

COPYRIGHTED EXCERPTS IN DfS, VOLUME 32, WERE REPRODUCED FROM THE FOLLOWING PERIODICALS:

American Theatre, October 2004. Copyright © Theatre Communications Group. —*Broadway World*, March 27, 2013. Copyright © Broadway World. —*Daily Herald*, June 9, 2004. Copyright © Daily Herald. Reproduced by permission of the publisher. —*Fast Company*, March 16, 2015. Copyright © Fast Company. Reproduced by permission of the publisher. —*Independent*, December 3, 1995. Copyright © Independent Print Ltd. —*Islands Sounder*, February 18, 2011. Copyright © Black Press. Reproduced by permission of the publisher. —*LA Weekly*, May 15, 2013. Copyright © Los Angeles Weekly (LA Weekly). —*Los Angeles Times*, November 11, 2014. Copyright © Los Angeles Times. —*Los Angeles Times*, March 22, 2009. Copyright © Los Angeles Times. —*New Yorker*, June 13, 2005. Copyright © Conde Nast Publications. Reproduced by permission of the publisher. —*Playbill*, March 19, 2016. Copyright © Playbill Incorporated. Reproduced by permission of the publisher. —*The Seattle Times*, February 28, 2008. Copyright © The Seattle Times. Reproduced by permission of the publisher. —*Stage*, May 1, 2011. Copyright © Stage Magazine. Reproduced by permission of the publisher. —*Theatre Journal*, June 13, 2008. Copyright © Johns Hopkins University Press. Reproduced by permission of the publisher. —*Theatre Journal*, 2011. Copyright © Johns Hopkins University Press. Reproduced by permission of the publisher. —*Variety*, November 13, 2000. Copyright © Reed Business Information. Reproduced by permission of the publisher. —*Variety*, June 6, 2005. Copyright © Reed Business Information. Reproduced by permission of the publisher. —*Variety*, November 18, 2010. Copyright © Reed Business Information. Reproduced by permission of the publisher.

COPYRIGHTED EXCERPTS IN DfS, VOLUME 32, WERE REPRODUCED FROM THE FOLLOWING BOOKS:

Giguere, Amanda. From *The Plays of Yasmina Reza on the English and American Stage*.

Copyright © 2010 Amanda Giguere. Reproduced by permission of McFarland Kael, Pauline. From *Taking It All In*. Copyright © 1984 Curtis Brown. Reproduced by permission of the publisher. —McDonough, Carla J. From *Staging Masculinity: Male Identity in Contemporary American Drama*. © 2006 [1997] Carla J. McDonough. Reproduced by permission of McFarland Mitchell, Charles P. From The *Great Composers Portrayed on Film, 1913 through 2002*. Copyright © 2010 [2004] Charles P. Mitchell. Reproduced by permission of McFarland Molette, Carlton W. From *James Baldwin: A Critical Evaluation*. Copyright © 1977 Howard University Press c/o The Permissions Company. Reproduced by permission of the publisher. —Plunka, Gene A. From *The Black Comedy of John Guare*. Copyright © 2002 Associated University Press. Reproduced by permission of the publisher. —Pratt, Louis H. From *James Baldwin*. Copyright © 1978 The Gale Group. —Rosefeldt, Paul. From *The Absent Father in Modern Drama*. Copyright © 1995 Peter Lang. Reproduced by permission of the publisher. —Younkins, Edward W. From *Exploring Capitalist Fiction: Business through Literature and Film*. Copyright © 2014 Rowman & Littlefield. Reproduced by permission of the publisher.

COPYRIGHTED EXCERPTS IN *DfS*, VOLUME 32, WERE REPRODUCED FROM THE FOLLOWING WEBSITES:

DCTheatreScene.com, November 3, 2015. Copyright © DCTheatreScene.com. —*Talkin Broadway.com*. Copyright © Talkin' Broadway. —*TheaterMania.com*, May 31, 2005. Copyright © TheaterMania.com. —*ThinkProgress.com*, October 16, 2014. Courtesy of Think Progress. —*WNYC.com*, March 28, 2012. Copyright © WNYC.

Contributors

Susan K. Andersen: Andersen is a writer and teacher with a PhD in English literature. Entry on *Almost, Maine*. Original essay on *Almost, Maine*.

Bryan Aubrey: Aubrey holds a PhD in English. Entries on *Blues for Mister Charlie* and *A Free Man of Color*. Original essays on *Blues for Mister Charlie* and *A Free Man of Color*.

Kristen Sarlin Greenberg: Greenberg is a freelance writer and editor with a background in literature and philosophy. Entry on *Amadeus*. Original essay on *Amadeus*.

Michael Allen Holmes: Holmes is a writer with existential interests. Entries on *The Curious Savage* and *The Theory of Everything*. Original essays on *The Curious Savage* and *The Theory of Everything*.

Amy L. Miller: Miller is a graduate of the University of Cincinnati. Entries on *The God of Carnage* and *Stop Kiss*. Original essays on *The God of Carnage* and *Stop Kiss*.

Michael J. O'Neal: O'Neal holds a PhD in English. Entry on *Deathtrap*. Original essay on *Deathtrap*.

Jeffrey Eugene Palmer: Palmer is a scholar, freelance writer, and teacher of high school English. Entry on *The Hitch-Hiker*. Original essay on *The Hitch-Hiker*.

April Paris: Paris is a freelance writer with a background in academic writing. Entry on *BFE*. Original essay on *BFE*.

William Rosencrans: Rosencrans is a writer and copy editor. Entry on *Glengarry Glen Ross*. Original essay on *Glengarry Glen Ross*.

Almost, Maine

JOHN CARIANI

2004

It is hard to find critical material on John Cariani's play *Almost Maine*, but it has entered the popular mainstream, much performed in regional theaters and high schools since its premiere in 2004. In the contemporary theater scene, Cariani's plays do not stand up to the intellectual rigor of an Edward Albee or a Tony Kushner, but that is not his ambition. He prefers a theater of the heart to a theater of ideas, he has said. An actor turned playwright to produce material he wanted to perform for auditions and comedy skits, he has written plays that are widely regarded in the country and throughout the world, even if they are not studied critically. He is an actor attuned to audience response, a comedian who has mastered rhythm and pause and comic puns.

His first and most popular of four plays, *Almost, Maine*, is a tribute to his hometown of Presque Isle, Maine. This play has a lot in common with Shakespeare's *A Midsummer Night's Dream*. *Almost, Maine*, Cariani says in his production notes, is a winter's night dream, with lovers finding each other in the magic of a Maine winter night, under the auspices of an aurora borealis. It is composed of nine skits of two-person dialogues, a cross section of couples in the mythical town of Almost, Maine, caught at the same moment of 9:00 p.m. on a Friday winter night. Some are ice-skating or snowmobiling, some are at the local Moose Paddy bar, and some are out looking at the stars. This play is so popular today it competes with *A Midsummer Night's Dream* and *Our Town*

John Cariani (© *Roy Rochlin* / *Getty Images*)

in high school drama departments and regional theaters. Cariani's connection to Shakespeare continued in his hit role in the Broadway musical *Something Rotten!*, in which he plays Nigel Bottom, a rival playwright to Shakespeare.

AUTHOR BIOGRAPHY

John Edward Cariani was born on July 23, 1969, in Brockton, Massachusetts, but moved with his family when he was eight to Presque Isle, Maine, the model for Almost, Maine, in his play. In Presque Isle High School he was involved in music and theater, amazed that he could make people laugh, thus beginning his interest in comedy. He graduated in 1987 and then went on to Amherst College, where he sang with the Zumbyes, an a cappella group, and with the glee club. He graduated in 1991 with a major in history. In Springfield, Massachusetts, he did an internship with StageWest to learn acting and directing. A move to New York began his acting

career with the Hudson Valley Shakespeare Festival (1997–1999), where he played comic roles in *As You Like It*, *The Winter's Tale*, *Much Ado about Nothing*, and *Twelfth Night*. He was also in off-Broadway shows, such as *It's My Party (and I'll Die If I Want To*, with actor F. Murray Abraham (1999).

After small film roles in *Kissing Jessica Stein* (2001); *Scotland, PA* (2001); *Shaft* (2001); and *Showtime* (2002), he found his famous television role as Julian Beck, forensic expert, on *Law & Order*, from 2002 to 2007. As Motel the Tailor, Cariani won a Tony nomination in a Broadway production of *Fiddler on the Roof* in 2004, with Alfred Molina as the lead.

Cariani acted in episodes for TV series such as *Numb3rs* as physicist Otto Bahnoff (2009) and as Michael Falk, Autistic Reporter, on *Onion News Network* (2011–2012). He also appeared on Showtime's *Homeland* (2012), *The Good Wife* (2014), and *The Blacklist* (2016). Other films Cariani has to his credit include *Robot Stories* (2003), *The Reunion* (2004), *High Street Plumbing* (2008), *Certainty* (2011), *Henry* (2011) *Elephant Sighs* (2012), *Deliver Us from Evil* (2014), and *Paper Dreams* (2015). As Nigel Bottom in the successful Broadway musical *Something Rotten!* (2015–2016), in which Cariani plays a rival playwright to Shakespeare, he has been nominated for an Outer Critics Circle Award for outstanding featured actor.

Cariani became a playwright almost by accident—from an actor's point of view. He ran out of audition material and began to write his own comedy skits, some of which he performed with friends at NBC's Performance Space. There, director Gabriel Barre saw the skits and asked Cariani if he had more. He did. After Barre read them, he encouraged Cariani to make a play out of them, and that was the genesis of *Almost, Maine*, workshopped in 2002 and finally premiered with the Portland Stage Company in 2004. The New York production in 2006 did not go over as well, closing after a month. Cariani has said he was disappointed in that production, which made the play into fluff when there is actually a lot of heartache in the characters. His second play, *cul-de-sac*, about suburban couples trying to keep up with the Joneses, was produced off Broadway in 2006 by Transport Group, with Cariani as Joe Jones. It is still unpublished as Cariani revises it. His third play, *Last Gas*, premiered at Portland

Stage Company in 2010 and has been seen at the Stonington Opera House, Maine, in 2013 and in Rochester, New York, in 2014. Cariani's fourth play, *Love/Sick*, premiered in 2010 and played at Portland Stage Company in 2013 and Hartford TheaterWorks in 2014. *Almost, Maine* came back to New York in triumph in 2014, put on by the Transport Group with Cariani in the cast. That production was filmed for the Theatre on Film and Tape Library Archive of the New York Public Library for the Performing Arts at Lincoln Center. Cariani is described by other actors as authentic and caring. That is the way he comes across in interviews and in his compassion for his characters.

PLOT SUMMARY

Playwright's Notes

The playwright gives directions that are part of the play and telling of the story. The dialogue is overlapping, with characters speaking over each other's lines. Almost, Maine, is a fictitious town in northern Maine in the middle of nowhere. It is very cold, with a long winter. The northern lights can be seen and are used in the play as a reminder of love's magic. Each of the nine plays has a magical moment of love. It is to be understood that all these moments are happening at the same time, 9:00 p.m. on the same Friday winter night. The people of this place are ordinary, hardworking, and not cynical. They are not stupid country people; they speak from the heart. The play is sweet but should not be overplayed as cute.

Prologue

It is a cold winter night in the mythical town of Almost, Maine. The backdrop is a field of stars. Pete and Ginette have just started dating. They sit on a bench in Pete's yard looking at the stars. They do not sit close to each other. Ginette keeps trying to say, "I love you," but other words come out. Finally, she blurts out that she loves him. He looks away and says nothing. Now both are uncomfortable in a long silence. Finally, he says he loves her too. She goes on to say she feels very close to him as she edges over, intimating she would like to be even closer.

Pete contradicts her, saying she is as far from him as she can get if she sits next to him. He makes a snowball and shows her that logically, the distance from one to the other around

MEDIA ADAPTATIONS

- Act 1, scene 4 of Cariani's *Almost, Maine*, "Getting It Back," the story of Gayle and Lendall, is presented as a short, stand-alone video online at *Vimeo.com* by Ivan Salinas. Starring Adam Meredith and Shantelle Szyper, it was filmed at AAU Theatre, San Francisco, on October 23, 2014, and is available at https://vimeo.com/109878843.

- Cariani gives a short talk on YouTube on the value of Shakespeare (https://www.youtube.com/watch?v=dZZ1x_0HJQI), perhaps because in his Broadway musical role in *Something Rotten!* he had to sing a duet called "I Hate Shakespeare."

- Beth Stevens interviewed Cariani at *Broadway.com* for *One on One* on May 23, 2016, about his Broadway role as a rival playwright to Shakespeare in *Something Rotten!* (https://www.youtube.com/watch?v=91mBphr3Cdw).

the circle of the globe makes them at the farthest distance from each other right now. Ginette is trying to make sense of this logical paradox but is disheartened, thinking he does not want to be with her. Now she moves away, and Pete is surprised that his interesting theory is not having the right effect. She moves away, and he says, according to his theory, that she is actually getting closer. She starts to leave. As she moves away, he keeps saying that she is getting closer and closer, until she finally exits, and he is alone.

Act 1

SCENE 1: HER HEART

A woman is standing in the front yard of an old farmhouse, clutching a small paper bag. A man comes out of the house, slamming the door. He has on an overcoat over his pajamas. He says hello and asks the woman if he can do something for her; he saw her from the window. She says she just wants to look at the northern lights. He sees she has pitched a tent. The woman pulls out a brochure about Maine that explains Maine people are neighborly and let campers and skiers stay for free in their yards. She asks if it is true. She goes on talking without waiting for answers, saying she is farther away from home than she has ever been. He haltingly assents, and she rushes to him and hugs him, squishing the paper bag between their bodies.

She turns around to look at the northern lights but then realizes she does not have her bag. He gives her back her bag. He tries to explain that she does not know when the northern lights will happen. In their small talk, he suddenly kisses her, and now he has the paper bag again. He says he loves her. She says she is not there for that but to say good-bye to her husband, who just died, and the northern lights are the torches of the recently departed. The man apologizes and says his name is East; she is called Glory. Glory asks where she is, and East says, "Almost, Maine," which is not on any map. The town never got organized. Glory starts panting and says East is holding her heart (the paper bag). He gives it back. She explains it is her heart that her husband broke when he ran off with someone else. She shakes the bag full of pieces of slate. At the hospital, they took out her heart, which had turned to slate, and gave her an artificial heart. When her husband tried to get her back, she could not respond, and he died of grief. East kisses Glory and says he loves her. He will fix her broken heart, because he is a repairman. He opens the bag and begins to repair it. The northern lights appear.

SCENE 2: SAD AND GLAD

Jimmy is sitting alone in the local cafe, the Moose Paddy, and sees Sandrine walk by. They awkwardly greet each other and keep repeating the same thing over and over—that they are doing well. Jimmy mentions he has not seen her for months, since that morning when he woke up and she was gone. The waitress comes to take their order, but they explain they are not together. In strained conversation, Jimmy tries to get Sandrine to talk to him. He mentions he has taken over his father's heating-and-cooling business. She has heard this. He brags about how hard he is working. He mentions that he is alone. East is one of his workers. His brother and sister left town, so he is alone. His mother and father retired and left town, and he is alone. His dog also died. He asks her if she would like to come over and hang out with him. She hesitates.

The waitress enters to tell them about the Friday special; there are free drinks if you are sad. Sandrine says she cannot come over; she has to get back to her group of girls in the front. Then she confesses that she has another guy. This is her bachelorette party; she is getting married. Jimmy receives these blows as they both just say yeah and wow to each other. He asks who it is, and she says it is Martin Laferriere. Jimmy says that is the ranger from Ashland; he is a legend. Jimmy starts hollering and raising his arms to call the waitress back for a drink. Sandrine sees a black mark on Jimmy's arm. It is a tattoo that says "Villian." She asks who that is. He says he misspelled "Villain." He says he wrote it on his arm to punish himself for losing her, so girls would stay away from him. He asks if he can kiss her; she kisses him on the cheek.

The waitress comes back from having served the party of girls with Sandrine and says she is happy that there is no free drink for those who are glad, because those girls are very glad. The waitress suddenly understands Jimmy is sad and tells him if he says he is sad, he will get a free drink. Jimmy does not respond. She says to call her if he needs anything; her name is "Villian." Struck by the magic coincidence of her name and his tattoo, he perks up and tells her he is not sad; he wants another Bud. The scene ends with an aurora borealis.

SCENE 3: THIS HURTS

A woman is ironing a man's clothes in Ma Dudley's Boarding House in Almost, Maine. A man is sitting near her on a bench. The woman starts to fold the man's clothes but then instead crumples them all up and takes the iron, burning herself on it. The man sees this and writes "iron" in a book called "Things That Can Hurt You." As the woman folds up the ironing board she accidentally hits the man in the head with it. The woman keeps apologizing, but he says he cannot feel pain. Ironing boards are not on his list of things that can hurt you. He shows her the book he is making with his brother, Paul. He tries to prove his point by smashing her in the head with the ironing board. She hollers and asks him why he did that. He asks, did that hurt? She says yes, so he adds it to his list. He picks up another book, called "Things to Be Afraid Of." He asks her if he should be afraid of ironing boards. She says no, because it is not meant to be used that way. He continues that an ironing board must be the opposite of God. His brother tells him that

God will not hurt him, but he should "fear" him. He is confused. It takes a lot to learn what does or does not hurt and what to be afraid of and not to be afraid of.

The woman says he is talking crazy, but the man insists he has congenital analgesia—he cannot feel pain. He starts hitting himself with things. He tells her to try it. She refuses. He says okay, she can just go away and leave him, like everyone else. He has recently put himself on his list of things to be afraid of.

The woman decides to try to give him a hit on the head. He says he is fine because there is no blood or discoloration. She tells him that some things that hurt do not bruise or bloody. They introduce themselves to each other as Marvalyn and Steve. She lives with her boyfriend, Eric. Steve tells her that his brother, Paul, has to teach him what hurts because his body does not feel. He has on his list bears, guns, knives, himself, and pretty girls. Marvalyn is surprised, but Steve tells her he has to be afraid of love. Fortunately, he is so messed up that he probably will not have to deal with it.

Marvalyn begins kissing him. Finally, he kisses back. He feels his lips and asks if there is any blood. She says no, but she has to go now. Eric will be upset at her absence. She takes the ironing board and accidentally hits Steve in the head. He hollers "OW." They look at each other in surprise at his sudden ability to feel pain as the aurora borealis lights go off.

SCENE 4: GETTING IT BACK

Lendall is awakened and going to the door of his house as Gayle is pounding on the door, calling his name. She bursts in, saying she wants it back. She wants all the love she gave him; she has his in the car. She does not want it anymore. Lendall says he does not want it back. She returns with huge red bags full of love. She dumps them on the floor. Lendall is amazed and notes that it is a lot. He says he does not know if he has room. She insists that he give her back the love she gave him. He says okay and returns with a tiny bag. He said it was all he could find.

She says they are through. She asked him in December if they were going to get married, and he was quiet. Marvalyn told her that meant he did not want to. She has tried to make him love her by giving him every bit of her love, and now she has none left for herself. She needs to get away. All she has right now is his love, and she

cannot give that to other people. They should give back their love and call it even. (She looks at her pitifully small bag.) She asks if he lost her love, because surely she gave him more than that. He tells her to take what she came for and exits the room. She opens the small bag and asks what is in the bag. Lendall answers from offstage that it is an engagement ring. She asks but where is the love she gave him? He says it is concentrated right there in the ring—eleven years' worth of her love. She can have it back. They kiss under the aurora borealis.

Interlogue

Returning to the first couple, Ginette and Pete from the prologue, Pete is still sitting alone on the bench with the snowball next to him, wondering what happened to Ginette.

Act 2

SCENE 5: THEY FELL

Two country boys are hanging out in a potato field, drinking beers. Randy is trying to tell Chad that he had a bad time with a girl. Chad interrupts him and says his time was worse. Sally Dunleavy told Chad he smelled and she could not go out with him. Randy tells him he does not mind the way he smells. Chad says he has had worse experience in love and so he gets to pick what they will do tomorrow—bowling. Randy says he is not the winner. His girl's face broke. He was dancing with Yvonne LaFrance at the rec center, and he threw her up and over, and she landed on her face. She went to the emergency room. She asked him to call her old boyfriend, who told Randy to leave. Chad says, okay, he wins. Randy says he chooses bowling for tomorrow.

They drink their beers and crush their cans. Chad does not know why he tries to date when he could spend his time with someone he likes, like Randy. There is so much in the world that does not make sense, and there is only one thing that makes him feel good—spending time with his friend Randy. The two stop, trying to figure this out. Chad says he will pick Randy up after three tomorrow. Randy starts to leave. Chad suddenly crumples to the ground, a visual metaphor for falling in love. Randy rushes back. Chad explains he just fell in love with Randy. Randy says Chad is his best friend and he does not know what he is talking about, but he admits that Chad is the only one who makes him feel good; however, he is crossing a line with what he just said. Then Randy falls down. They look at each other and try to reach each other across the stage but keep falling down as the aurora borealis comes up.

SCENE 6: WHERE IT WENT

Phil and Marci have been ice-skating on Echo Pond. They undo their skates and put on boots. Phil has hockey skates, while Marci has figure skates. She has one shoe on and one skate. Phil and Marci talk over each other, Phil wishing Marci was not mad and she protesting she is not, though she wishes he would pay more attention. He admits he had fun skating, but they keep arguing about little things. He had to work; she cannot find her shoe. She reminds him they got away from the kids for a Friday night by themselves. They used to come here to Echo Pond. Phil shakes off Marci's touch. Marci sees a shooting star and makes a wish. They continue to quibble, but she cannot find her shoe. (This is a reference to "waiting for the other shoe to drop." She is trying to tell him something.)

Phil makes a wish on a star too and invites Marci to wish with him. She tells him that he is wishing on a planet, on Saturn. She finally tells him it is their anniversary. Phil blames his negligence on overwork. They need the money. She complains that she is lonely and that he is missing the children's birthdays and activities. He accuses her of lying and of being absent in their marriage long before he was. They both admit they did not have fun skating. Suddenly, Marci's other shoe drops out of the sky. She takes the keys and leaves Phil alone. He sees a shooting star, and the aurora borealis comes up, as scene 7 begins.

SCENE 7: STORY OF HOPE

There is a sound of a car approaching, a car door slamming, and the car driving away. A woman stands on a front porch of a small home, carrying a suitcase. The story is one of loss, so the man has to be short or thin and look like loss. The man is half what he used to be. The man answers the door in his bathrobe.

The woman speaks furiously that she is all alone in the world and scared and she knew there was one place she could come. Then she stops, because the man is not who she thought he would be. She apologizes and asks if Daniel Harding lives here. She asks if he knows where he is. She thought he would always be there—a big, tall guy who played basketball. She carries on a monologue, not allowing the man to answer. She mentions she used to live here, and Daniel was one of those who stayed in the town. She was one who left. He comments that most people do leave. She says regretfully that you have to hold on to people or you lose them. She mentions she took a taxi from Bangor, over a hundred miles away. The man asks why she did that, and she answers that she came to answer a question he once asked her. She never answered him. He asked her to marry him. She was going off to college and said she would have to think about it. She left him without an answer. Now she knows that was not right to do, especially to someone you love. He asks, you loved him? She says yes, and she still does.

The man now goes on about how she probably did not really hurt the man, because they were young. By not answering at all, she only killed hope the long, slow way. He says goodbye, using her name, "Hope." She realizes he is Danny, after all. Just then, a woman calls him from within. He tells the woman, Hope, that he hopes she finds her place in the world. After he leaves, she gives the answer she came to give him, now too late: "Yes."

SCENE 8: SEEING THE THING

Two snowmobiles approach (known by the sound) and park offstage, with only their headlights seen. There is a small shack in the wilderness but still within the city limits. Rhonda and Dave enter in snowmobile suits. He has a wrapped painting behind his back as a present. She tells him it is a first to have someone at her house. She is going to let him only on the winterized porch. He says what a good time he had on the snowmobiles, eating at the Snowmobile Club and then having beers at the Moose Paddy. He mentions they have been friends for years, and now he gives her a present. She unwraps the painting (the audience does not see it), but does not seem to know what it is. He admits he painted it, but she does not know what to make of it. He says it is the kind of painting you stare at until you see the thing, done in dots (a style called pointillism). She has to step back to see it. She has to figure it out. She has to look but cannot try to see something. He tells her to trick it, look at it sideways, until she sees it. He tries to talk her into going into the house and having a couple of beers while she figures it out. She objects. She keeps staring at the painting and says that it is roadkill, or a dead raccoon in the road. Or a dead deer in the road. Or a dead moose. He says he will give her a hint. He kisses her on the mouth. She is mad and tells him never to do that again. She goes into the house.

He stands outside and says that people say she is hung up and that he should be persistent. Dan and Suzzette told him that. Marci and Phil say it, and Randy and Chad, and Lendall and Gayle, Marvalyn and Eric, Jimmy, Sandrine, and East. He wants a kiss back, but she says she does not know how. She only knows how to arm wrestle. He keeps kissing her until she can see the painting. She does not say what it is but only that she can see it now. Now she kisses him back and asks what next. He unzips her snowsuit, and they remove layers and layers of winter clothes until they are in their long underwear. Now Rhonda calls Dave into the house, and he leaves the painting so the audience can see: a big red heart. There is an aurora borealis.

Epilogue

Pete is still sitting on his bench with the snowball, looking to where Ginette left. Suddenly, she appears from the opposite direction, and, using the snowball, he asks nonverbally if she has been all around the world; she nods yes, but now she is back and "close." They hug as the aurora borealis lights flash.

CHARACTERS

Chad

Chad is one of the country boys (in act 2, scene 5, "They Fell") who hangs out in the fields with his buddy Randy, drinking beer. He tells Randy that his date, Sally, said she did not like the way he smelled. Randy has an even worse story of his date with Yvonne. Chad realizes that the only thing in the world that makes him feel good is his buddy Randy. He has a moment of revelation that he is actually falling in love with Randy and literally cannot stand up.

Dan

See Daniel Harding.

Dave

Dave is the snowmobiler (in act 2, scene 8, "Seeing the Thing") who is Rhonda's buddy. Though she treats him as if they are just two guys hanging out, he is trying to turn her attention to a romantic attachment. He makes a painting of a heart to show her his intent, but it is done in a pointillistic style, with many dots, so it can be interpreted in various ways. She does not understand what he means until he kisses her and explains that they should move on with their relationship. All of their friends are rooting for the friendship to blossom into a romance. She sees the heart in the painting after he kisses her, and then she gets turned on, becoming passionate and inviting him into her house.

Sally Dunleavy

Sally Dunleavy was the date that Chad almost had in act 2, scene 5, until she refused to go out with him because he smelled bad. Sally Dunleavy and Yvonne LaFrance represent the unsuccessful relationships with women that send Chad and Randy into each other's arms.

East

East is the man on the farm (in act 1, scene 1, "Her Heart") who sees Glory from his window and falls in love with her. He lets her camp on his land so she can see the aurora borealis. He explains that he is a repairman and can fix her broken heart, as he removes a piece of slate from the bag where she carries her heart.

Eric

Eric is the current difficult boyfriend of Marvalyn in "This Hurts" (act 1, scene 3). She lives with him upstairs in the boarding house, while she falls in love with Steve in the basement doing laundry. He mentions that he hears her fighting with Eric. Eric seems to be domineering, for Marvalyn is anxious he will be angry at her absence.

Gayle

Gayle is the angry woman (in act 1, scene 4, "Getting It Back") who demands that her boyfriend, Lendall, give back her love. She says she will return his, which she dumps on his floor in huge bags. He is confused by her anger, but it comes out that they have gone together for eleven years and when she asked if they would ever marry, he was silent. Thinking he meant no, she wants to call it off. She has given away all her love for nothing, she says, and now she has none left for herself or anyone else. She is shocked when he produces a tiny bag representing the love she gave him. Inside is an engagement ring, mending the argument and showing that her love was not in vain.

Ginette

Ginette is in love with Pete in the prologue and epilogue, but she is shy. Once she admits she loves Pete, she tries to get closer to him on the bench. She wants to get closer to him physically and emotionally. Although he seems to return her love, he takes the conversation in a different direction, telling her that far is near. Confused, she leaves. They are split up for the whole play and reunite only after she has circumnavigated the globe to be near him. These are physical representations of what lovers go through to be "close." They misread each other but somehow find a way to be together.

Glory

Glory is the widow (in act 1, scene 1, "Her Heart") who shows up at the farm of East with a broken heart, carried in a bag. In her marriage, first her husband broke her heart by running off with someone else, and then she broke his when he wanted to come back and she had no love to give him. He ran out and had a car accident. She feels guilty, as though she was responsible. She asks East if she can camp out on his farm so she can see the aurora borealis, for she knows the newly dead are there, bearing torches. She wants to say good-bye to him. Instead, she finds East to mend her heart. He takes her broken heart in a bag and fixes it.

Daniel Harding

Daniel Harding is the man who lost his true love in "Story of Hope" (act 2, scene 7). When a woman called Hope knocks on his door, he listens while she explains that she ran off after their high school romance to go to college and did not bother to answer him when he proposed marriage. Now she is back after all these years to say "yes." Before she can say this, however, Daniel's current girlfriend calls him back into the house. It is too late. Love's loss is registered physically in Daniel's shriveled body, which makes him literally half the man he used to be.

Hope

Hope (in act 2, scene 7, "Story of Hope") is an aggressive and desperate woman who has come a long way to find her lost love and give the answer to his marriage proposal of many years before, which she rudely ignored. She gives all the excuses—that she was going off to her own life in the world, and though she promised to give an answer by dawn, she left. Now she hardly

recognizes Daniel but wants to tell him yes, before dawn. It is too late, as he is called into the house by his current wife or girlfriend. Hope is played as a real woman and as though the loss is hers, but her name makes her perhaps a symbol of *his* hope, his fantasy, that she will come back some day. His body shows he has wasted away waiting for her answer.

Jimmy

Jimmy is the "sad" character in "Sad and Glad" (act 1, scene 2). He sits in the local bar, the Moose Paddy, drinking beer, and runs into his old girlfriend, Sandrine, whom he awkwardly tries to make up with. It is a painful scene, as he explains how lonely he is since he woke up one day and she was gone. He invites her to come over, but she reluctantly explains she is at her bachelorette party with her girlfriends, for she is getting married tomorrow. Jimmy absorbs this shock, trying to pretend to be glad for her. He is obviously measuring his own lack compared with her strong and masculine fiancé, a park ranger. She sees the tattoo on his arm that says, "Villian," and asks who that is. He says he misspelled "Villain," trying to brand himself on his arm for losing her. When Sandrine leaves, the waitress says he can have a free drink if he is sad; he should just call her. Her name is "Villian." In happy wonder at this coincidence, he orders another beer, saying he is not sad but glad.

Martin Laferriere

Martin Laferriere is a big, strong ranger from Ashland in "Sad and Glad" (act 1, scene 2). Martin is the one engaged to Sandrine, Jimmy's former girlfriend, whom he meets on the night before her wedding to Martin. Jimmy seems a bit jealous and intimidated because Martin is big, courageous, handsome, and heroic.

Yvonne LaFrance

Yvonne LaFrance in "They Fell" (act 2, scene 5) is Randy's disastrous date to a dance in which he picked her up and threw her over his head, and she fell on her face and went to the emergency room.

Lendall

Lendall is the man (in act 1, scene 4, "Getting It Back," whose girlfriend, Gayle, is angry with him. He listens patiently while she tries to return his love in large bags and asks for her love, which she gave him back again because she wants to call it off. She is pleasantly surprised when he gives her back her love in the form of an engagement ring.

Marci

Marci is the wife (in act 2, scene 6, "Where It Went") who is trying to smother her constant disappointment as she and husband, Phil, go skating on Echo Pond. He knows she is unhappy about something, and it finally comes out, using the metaphor gimmick of "dropping the other shoe." She cannot find her shoe as they take off their skates. They begin to argue, and she accuses him of being absent in their marriage, of forgetting things, like the kids' games and birthdays. He does not even remember that this is their anniversary. When he also accuses her of being absent by not communicating, the other shoe literally drops out of the sky, and she takes the car keys and leaves. It is clear the hidden feelings all surfaced at the same time, and the shoe, the consequence, is that the love is all gone. The relationship is not there anymore.

Marvalyn

Marvalyn is the woman ironing in the basement of Ma Dudley's Boarding House (in act 1, scene 3, "This Hurts"). This is where she meets and talks to Steve as she irons her boyfriend Eric's shirts. She is obviously not happy in her relationship, because she and Eric fight a lot, and she is not happy ironing his shirts, for she wrinkles them up again in anger. She explains to Steve that she cannot be gone too long in the laundry room, for Eric is expecting her. He does not like it when she is gone. He is jealous and controlling. She meets and is attracted to Steve, who seems totally innocent and vulnerable. She takes the initiative with him, kissing him until he responds. She seems to be the therapy that Steve needs.

Paul

Paul is the brother of Steve in "This Hurts" (act 1, scene 3). Paul has tried to teach his brother Steve to be careful in life, helping him to make two lists, "Things That Can Hurt You," and "Things to Be Afraid Of." It turns out the most dangerous things are love and women. Paul is either overprotective or abusive, convincing Steve he is numb with "congenital analgesia." Steve is afraid of life.

Pete

Pete is the lover (in the prologue, interlogue, and epilogue) who is so clever with showing off his logic and knowledge of astronomy that he sends his lover away. There is a play on the concept and word *close*. In a paradox worthy of the metaphysical poetry of John Donne, Pete shows Ginette that if they consider the physics of sitting on a round globe, they are far apart when they are next to each other. If she sets off in the opposite direction, she will get "closer" and meet up with him eventually. Only when she goes away from him to circumnavigate the globe will she be moving closer to where he is. As she goes farther, he says they are getting closer. In the long run, he is right. She cannot get far away from him, as in Donne's famous metaphor of the compass in "A Valediction: Forbidding Mourning," for the spinning of the globe will bring her back to him. Meanwhile, he has confused her, for they do not seem to be speaking the same language. Everything he says sends her farther away.

Phil

Phil is the husband in "Where It Went" (act 2, scene 6). Phil seems a bit obtuse, not understanding his wife's grievances over the years, which by now have added up. He claims in his defense that she does not communicate them to him but smothers her feelings. He is so busy working, trying to support them, that he does not notice the things his family finds important. He cannot pay attention because of his work, he says. She proves that he does not see what is going on when he wishes on the planet Saturn instead of a shooting star, as she does. The weather station has been telling the position of Saturn all week, and he missed it just as he misses everything else.

Randy

Randy is one of the country boys in "They Fell" (act 2, scene 5). He tries to top Chad's story of a bad date by telling about his date with Yvonne, when he used too much muscle throwing her over his head in a dance and she smashed her face and had to go to the hospital. When Chad says he is in love with Randy, Randy is initially shocked and upset that Chad is ruining their perfect friendship, but then, when he begins to fall down, he understands he, too, is in love.

Rhonda

Rhonda is the tomboy (in act 2, scene 8, "Seeing the Thing") who thinks she is Dave's snowmobile buddy. She does not understand his romantic attentions, even when he makes a painting of a heart for her. She admits that she does not even know how to kiss, only arm wrestle. Once she gets the point, however, she is suddenly quite passionate and aggressive toward Dave, ripping off her snowsuit.

Sandrine

Sandrine is the former girlfriend of Jimmy at the Moose Paddy bar in "Sad and Glad" (act 1, scene 2). She is obviously embarrassed to be running into him, as she finally admits she will be married to someone else tomorrow and is out with the girls. She had apparently left Jimmy suddenly, with no explanation. When he tries to get her back, she resists his attempts. She lets him give her a little kiss, but she does not go to any length to explain or work through their past. She has already moved on, while he has not. Sandrine is the "glad" one in the "Sad and Glad" play.

Steve

Steve is the conflicted and frightened man in "This Hurts" (act 1, scene 3). His brother, Paul, has convinced him that he has a severe deficiency called congenital analgesia, meaning that he cannot feel pain. To compensate, Paul has helped him to compile lists of things that can hurt or things to be afraid of. When Marvalyn, whom he meets in the basement laundry room, burns her hand on the iron, he adds that to the list. When she smashes him in the head with the ironing board, she tells him it is supposed to hurt, so he writes it down but feels nothing. He believes only a discoloration or loss of blood shows an injury, but she mentions that things can hurt without that. Steve and Marvalyn are both being influenced by people who are not helpful to them. Steve is afraid to live for fear of being hurt. His analgesia seems to be a psychological numbness, for when Marvalyn kisses him, he feels that, and he begins to feel pain, cured of his ailment.

Suzzette

Suzzette is the surprise other woman who comes to the door to see what is keeping Daniel Harding in "The Story of Hope" (act 2, scene 7). Daniel answers the door to speak to Hope, who has come to say yes to his proposal of marriage years too late only to find another woman there.

THEMES

Romantic Love

These two-person scenes are all about falling in and out of romantic love. Love in all its shades of agony and ecstasy and surprise are suggested with the various couples and situations. Cariani, in his author's notes and instructions to the players, points out that the scenes could be played simply with a corny and shallow interpretation. Though they are brief, however, the scenes contain the deep emotions that surface when people open up to one another. Glory, in the first scene, has a broken heart and says she has never traveled so far before when she meets East. She is lonely and lost, appealing to him for help, apparently asking to camp out in his yard so she can see the northern lights. She is in grief over the death of her husband. Because she opens up to allow East to see something of her broken heart, he is able to respond to her and wants to fix it. She did not expect this.

All of the scenes contain some surprise about love. In "Sad and Glad," Jimmy explains his loneliness to Sandrine since they broke up. He tries to get back with her, only to find out she is getting married to someone else. She is glad, but he is sad, suffering from unrequited love. Just when he feels lost, he finds another woman, Villian, waiting in the wings. One of the funniest scenes is with Steve and Marvalyn in the laundry room of the boardinghouse. Steve is numb, unable to feel. He has to make a list of things that can hurt and to avoid because he claims he cannot feel pain. One of the things on his list to avoid is falling in love. Marvalyn kisses him, and suddenly he can feel pain when she whacks him with the ironing board. The two, pain and joy, go together—the vulnerability of feeling and falling in love brings with it the uncertainty of whether pain or happiness lies ahead.

All of these couples are stiff with each other in the beginning. Jimmy and Sandrine's meeting, as former lovers, is extremely painful, and their dialogue is reduced to repetitions of asking so, how are you? Some scenes are lovers' quarrels, as with Phil and Marci, the married couple who do not feel close anymore, and Lendell and Gayle, who seem to be breaking up over a misunderstanding. Love's loss is represented in Hope's story. Daniel proposed to her the night before she left for college, and she did not even wait to give him an answer. Many years later, she

TOPICS FOR FURTHER STUDY

- Cariani has said he likes the love and magic in Shakespeare's comedies. Pick one of the Shakespeare comedies and write a short critical paper about the love and magic there, comparing it to Cariani's use of these elements in *Almost, Maine*. Give concrete examples and quotes from both plays.

- Create a slide show on the geography, climate, and lifestyle of Maine, showing the difference between the eastern coast and northern Maine. Include Mt. Katahdin (visited by Henry David Thoreau) and other national parks, like Acadia National Park. Discuss in a group how Cariani capitalizes on Maine's landscape for his themes.

- Add a scene to *Almost, Maine* by writing a dialogue between two lovers. The scene should have a surprise, something unexpected. Use Cariani's technique of including pregnant pauses (beats) at meaningful emotional moments. Stage these scenes for the group.

- Robert Lowell and Elizabeth Bishop were two famous poets who spent summers in Maine, where they met and fell in love. They wrote to each other through poetry and letters for the next thirty years. Have one person give a brief biographical overview of their lives and relationship. Then read aloud their love for each other in their poems with a Maine landscape—Bishop's "North Haven," a eulogy to Robert Lowell, and Lowell's "Water." Read both poems aloud in a group and then perform parts of Sarah Ruhl's play *Dear Elizabeth* (2011), a two-person play consisting of a dialogue fashioned from parts of their letters. Write a short paper summarizing your impression of their fondness for Maine as a symbol of their love, using quotes from the poems.

- As a group, read the young-adult novel *If You Come Softly* (1998), by African American novelist Jacqueline Woodson, about a Jewish girl and an African American boy who fall in love in New York. The progress of their love is beautifully and lyrically described against the backdrop of New York urban life, and it is perhaps the urban stress that turns their story to tragedy. Discuss the special problems involved in love when there are issues of race. Make a website or wiki on famous loves that have crossed lines of race, class, nationality, or religion (for instance, the abdication of the British throne by Edward VIII for the American Mrs. Wallis Simpson).

---

returns, understanding that she loves Daniel and wants to say yes to him. He, however, is with another woman by now. This is a subtle scene, for Daniel never complains about how Hope treated him. He has changed in appearance so much that Hope does not recognize him. His aging and wasting away to a mere shell of his former athletic prowess suggest the toll that her folly took on him. Both have wasted their lives by missing the opportunity they had. The many moods of love, even one scene of gay love between Chad and Randy, are delicately and suspensefully shown, as the couples experience the moment of surprise when there is a revelation of the heart. It may be a moment of falling in love or out of love, but it takes them beyond business as usual. The comedy of Rhonda and Dave, for instance, the two snowmobilers who have been best friends for many years, and Rhonda's surprise when Dave shows her he does not want a buddy but a mate, ends in the defensive facades melting suddenly as Rhonda stops being dense and acting like a lumberjack.

Misunderstanding

Cariani says in his notes that he sees the play as a midwinter night's dream, both funny and sad. In this, he suggests that it plays off Shakespeare's

A Midsummer Night's Dream with the two couples—four young people, Lysander, Demetrius, Helena, and Hermia—getting mixed up and falling in and out of love with each other, because it is a night of fairy magic. Their illusions are played out before dawn, when they remember who they are really in love with. *Almost, Maine* has this type of confusion caused by love's emotions. The couples work through misunderstandings, having difficulty communicating their deepest feelings. In Lendall and Gayle's scene, for instance, Gayle returns Lendall's love to him in a big bag, because he has not taken the next step in their courtship of proposing marriage. She had asked him if they were going to get married some time, and he became quiet. Marvalyn told herself his silence meant that he did not love her. Gayle is angry that she has given so much love and that he will not reciprocate. When she asks for her love back, he gives her a tiny bag. Inside is an engagement ring. He tells her all the love she gave is concentrated in that. The two are reconciled.

On the other hand, the married couple, Marci and Phil, are together but lonely and apart, since they cannot communicate anymore. Marci accuses Phil of not paying attention, and he accuses her of lying. The name of this scene is "Where It Went," demonstrating that love can die over time, especially when two people grow apart. The worst example of miscommunication is in the story of Hope and Daniel. Her name indicates how hope gets lost in love. She did not have enough awareness to deal properly with Daniel's proposal. Not giving him the courtesy of an answer, she disappears, leaving him wondering. Years later, she tries to pick up the pieces, but he has moved on. Now she is the one left without hope.

Cariani uses a visible metaphor and joke to demonstrate how lovers misunderstand. In the prologue, Ginette and Pete are courting, sitting on a bench, in the middle of their first declaration of love. Ginette says she feels close to him, having said, "I love you." Pete immediately destroys this closeness by going into an intellectual explanation of how technically they are not close if you look at it in terms of the round earth. They may appear physically close together on the bench, but if you look at the earth's curvature and calculate their distance from each other in that way, they are far apart equatorially. He demonstrates with a snowball representing the

sphere of the world. There is a whole world between them. She ceases to feel close to him when he says this, not sure of his intent, and moves away. He tells her she is getting closer, when she moves away from him, demonstrating the paradox from physics but meanwhile screwing up the love scene. This paradox is only resolved in the epilogue when Ginette returns to Pete from the other side of the stage, having traversed the distance between them and come closer at last. This is love's journey.

Happiness
Cariani warns the actors not to play the scenes as if to show the triumph of love as two people getting together. He claims there are no resolutions to the scenes, but rather a sense of suspense: "The residents of Almost are *about* to experience joy. Great joy. But not just yet." The real joy happens after the curtain falls. The characters are surprised by a joy about to happen as they fall in love. It is not a certainty, however, because love is delicate and uncertain. The audience is looking forward to a positive resolution, but the suspense is held. He mentions that "Joy has to be earned," and only in the last scene with Rhonda and Dave is love's fulfillment finally suggested. In "Sad and Glad" Sandrine is happy because she is about to be married, while Jimmy is sad because he has lost her to another. In the first scene, "Her Heart," Glory is sad because she is mourning her husband, but East is happy in the anticipation of fixing her broken heart. In "This Hurts" Steve is finally happy to feel pain because it means he will also be able to feel love. Chad and Randy have a hard time with female dates, but they are happy at the sudden, difficult recognition that they prefer each other over anyone else. The possibility of happiness in love is symbolized by the aurora borealis, which suddenly appears at the end of scenes. Happiness may be emphasized, but as the author has commented, there is also ache and sadness in love, and the two are sometimes not that far apart.

Rural Life
Almost, Maine, is in the middle of nowhere as Cariani establishes through images of remoteness. First, it is midwinter dark, and the characters in the outdoor scenes are bundled up in parkas. They are in twos, rather than in crowds. Only "Sad and Glad," which takes place in the Moose Paddy Bar, suggests a lot of people. The first scene, "Her Heart," is located on a former

Many of the vignettes in Almost, Maine *are about love and heartbreak* (© *Rock and Wasp* /
Shutterstock.com)

potato farm where Glory is camping out to see the northern lights. Glory says that it is the farthest she has ever traveled, and she feels as if it is the end of the earth. Hope tells Daniel she took a taxi from Bangor, Maine, and it is 163 miles from Almost. Phil and Marci have been skating on Echo Pond alone under the night sky. Randy and Chad are outside in a potato field, drinking beer. Pete and Ginette are outside on a bench. Rhonda and Dave reach her house in snowmobiles.

In his notes, Cariani goes to some trouble to paint his mythical town of Almost, Maine, located exactly where Cariani's hometown of Presque Isle, Maine, is in northernmost Maine. He notes that Almost is sometimes lonely, and the cold and dark emphasize the characters' search for warmth, love, and companionship. In both the notes and the first scene, Cariani dissociates the characters of this town as stereotypes of down-easter or stupid Yankee farmers, a comic staple in movies and plays. All of

Cariani's characters are common laborers, repairmen, roofers, or local business people, like the owner of a business dealing in heating and air conditioning. They are not professionals, yet these people do not have the Yankee accents of fishermen and farmers on the coast of Maine. He wants the town to be seen as a special place, a rural town that seems bleak but where the people live "uncluttered lives." Using a winter landscape, he evokes a pastoral simplicity where life is seen in its essential character and emotions. This is not the sophisticated humor and witty dialogue of city life. He makes clear, however, that this does not mean the people are dull or uninteresting because they are rural: "They are extremely dignified. They are honest and true. They are not cynical. They are not sarcastic." They are full of wonder about life and speak from the heart, he concludes. This presents Almost as an idyllic place, untainted by urban woes. Cariani underlines this with minimal sets and props.

STYLE

Skits or Sketches

Cariani wrote these skits or sketches, two-person dialogues for audition or rehearsal pieces for actors. Later, at the suggestion of director Gabriel Barre, he strung them into a play. They are connected by the imaginary place Almost, Maine; through stand-alone dramas, the characters of each piece refer by name to the characters of other pieces to create the illusion that they are all townspeople or a community. These are short dramatic scenes in which actors can develop character and the skill of delivery of lines. Cariani's dramatic instructions teach beginning or seasoned actors how to perform to bring out the subtlety of the moments, for each is a magic moment, he says, in the discovery of love. In one note, he admonishes the actors to play the scenes as they are and not to make them sentimental, because the material itself is sweet. The characters should be portrayed as honest and straightforward in dealing with love, which is a very tricky business. The characters are open and vulnerable, not cynical or backward and dumb.

Setting

Almost, Maine, is an imaginary town based on Cariani's hometown of Presque Isle, in northern Maine. The name of Almost suggests that there is a lot of hope there and positive energy but that it is not complete fulfillment. East in scene 1 mentions that the town is not on any map because they never got organized. It is a place just manifesting, as it were, with life in its promise. The people there are discovering the laws of love. It is not a realistic environment. It has magical realism, with the aurora borealis going off in the sky when people fall in love. People carry love in bags or their broken hearts in bags. Almost suggests other imaginary towns like Brigadoon, remote from ordinary life, although it has contemporary artifacts like snowmobiles. People have names like Glory, East, or Hope. Cariani emphasizes the unreality of the place with sparse scenery and few props. As in Shakespearean theater, the place is imagined by the audience through character and dialogue. The lighting between scenes suggests the magic of the aurora borealis. All the dramas are happening under its auspices.

Visual Metaphors and Jokes

Cariani's comedy is delivered through visual jokes and metaphors. Randy and Chad, for instance, two male friends just hanging out having beers, discover the glimmer of a romantic attachment to each other. They keep falling down onstage, suggesting the helpless feeling of falling in love. This is physical slapstick comedy to suggest the unspeakable feelings they are having. Glory carries around her broken heart in a bag, like pieces of sharp slate, that East, a repairman, takes out and repairs. The unrecognized love between Rhonda and Dave is symbolized in a painting he made for her to get her to understand he loves her. It is a pointillistic painting, in which the dots could come together as anything. She is unable to interpret the visual clues; instead of the heart he has painted, she sees roadkill, or a dead raccoon. Steve has no feelings and cannot feel pain, a defense against love, for he has a list of dangerous things to avoid, including love. Not until Marvalyn kisses him can he feel the pain of the ironing board she keeps hitting him with, demonstrating the awakening of all feelings with love, both pleasant and unpleasant.

Interrupted Dialogue

Cariani's notes explain that the play uses overlapping dialogue. One character starts speaking before another has finished. This is effective for his theme of portraying the awkwardness of love. The characters are angry or ecstatic or unsure of themselves and speak sometimes simultaneously, as in real life. This method became very popular, for instance, in Woody Allen films, where the characters are trying to communicate in broken phrases or embarrassed starts and stops. It is poignant in "Glad and Sad" when Jimmy meets his former girlfriend Sandrine, who obviously is not happy to run into him. They repeat meaningless phrases about how they are, interrupting each other—their overlapping comments indicated by parallel lines placed between the text of their speech on the script page. Or else, to keep Sandrine's attention, Jimmy keeps talking his point until he is finished, which is indicated by an angle bracket on the script page, showing how he drives through his line over her speech. This hesitant and overlapping speech allows for more heartfelt delivery, full of emotion. Cariani also mentions in his notes that these directions show that the characters are not listening to each other. He admits that this style of delivery is difficult, but the symbols are specifically placed in the script to create a certain effect.

Suspended Time

The imaginary quality of Almost, Maine, is suggested by its suspension of time or, rather, simultaneous time. All the plays are magical moments at the same moment, 9:00 on a winter's Friday night in Almost. Relationships are formed or undone in that magic moment. If the play is a "midwinter's night dream" as Cariani says in his notes, then, like Shakespeare's *A Midsummer Night's Dream*, it is not set in ordinary time.

Beats or Silent Pauses

The playwright includes in the text a place where the actor should pause for a silent space so the words or reaction can be felt by the audience. The word *Beat* in parentheses after a line means that the actor must pause and wait, carrying the feeling into the silent space. Cariani says the silent moments should be "full and electric. . . . There's a buoyancy to the material. A lightness. And I think it's in the language." This putting in silent pauses or beats is a technique used by poetry through line breaks or other punctuation, to produce a little silence where meaning can build or resonate. Cariani uses such beats or pauses for moments of epiphany in each scene, where the characters suddenly recognize their feelings.

HISTORICAL CONTEXT

Maine History

The state of Maine has a romantic image in Cariani's play *Almost, Maine*. Almost, Maine, is a fictitious town based on Cariani's hometown of Presque Isle, the French for "almost an island," because it is on land that is a peninsula in the Aroostook River. It is a small town with a population of ten thousand, near the Canadian border, with French Canada on one side and British Canada on the other, reflecting the fight of the French and British over Maine territory. The Native American inhabitants of Maine when Europeans came included the Wabanaki peoples—the Abenaki, Passamaquoddy, and Penobscots. The Presque Isle region is home to the Micmac tribes. The Presque Isle Air Force Base was important for US fighter pilots leaving for Europe during World War II and was the location for a film about this period, *Island in the Sky* (1953), with John Wayne as a fighter pilot. Presque Isle was named an All-America City in 1966.

In order to impress the actors in his stage directions on the loneliness and wilderness quality of northern Maine, Cariani includes two pages of statistics in the script, including the sparse population and the fact that 90 percent of the state is woods. The average temperature in January is 9 degrees, and there are only nine hours of daylight. He recommends visiting the website www.crownofmaine.com for pictures of northern Maine.

The remote wild of Maine has always had a romantic association for travelers. Glory in scene 1 of *Almost, Maine* feels that she has come to the end of the world, looking for a sign of her dead husband in the aurora borealis, for everyone knows the newly dead are the torchbearers who make the northern lights, she says. She has with her a Maine tourism brochure bragging of the friendly nature of Mainers and their ideal life, suggested in the state motto "The Way Life Should Be." Early explorers were looking for the fabled city in Maine called Norumbega, a myth circulated in Europe about a land of milk and honey where the natives wore silver and gold and pearls. These stories were told in England by traveler David Ingram in the 1550s; he claimed to have found gold nuggets as big as his fist. These early legends of Maine as a rich and idyllic place helped to get funding for more expeditions. The first settlement on Saint Croix Island by the French occurred in 1604, and they named the area Acadia, after the idyllic land of Arcadia in Greece, synonymous with unspoiled nature. Today the name remains in Acadia National Park, located on Mount Desert Island. Captain John Smith, known as the father of New England, wrote a *Description of New England* after his 1614 voyage that also circulated fantastic stories of Maine's riches. If no gold was found, Europeans did find riches in the form of timber, fur, and fish. Whaling and fur trading were lucrative but more difficult in Maine's rougher environment than in Massachusetts.

A French trading post at Castine, Fort Penatgouet, in 1613 was one of the first permanent settlements in New England. Plymouth Colony, founded on Cape Cod Bay in 1620, sponsored their own trading post at Penobscot Bay in the 1620s. A land grant given to Sir Ferdinando Gorges and John Mason in 1622 between the Merrimack and Kennebec Rivers was called the Province of Maine. Many early attempts at settlement by both the English and French failed

COMPARE
&
CONTRAST

- **2004:** Winter sports such as snowmobiling are featured in *Almost, Maine*. Such staple winter Maine sports as bear hunting and snowmobiling have few legal restrictions at this time but are a source of concern for the bear population and because of rising snowmobile fatalities.

  Today: Because of the growing popularity of winter sports in Maine, there are more legal restrictions for bear hunting and snowmobiling on the state's thousands of miles of snow trail.

- **2004:** Though homosexuality is not as controversial as it once was, it is still a touchy issue for some high schools to stage *Almost, Maine* because there is a gay love scene in it. At this time, gay domestic partnerships are accepted in Maine, while gay marriage is legalized in Nova Scotia and Quebec, Canada, bordering Maine.

  Today: Gay marriage is legal in Maine since 2012. The gay scene is less of an issue, since *Almost, Maine* has played all over the world and, in the United States, President Barack Obama has officially designated Stonewall National Monument as an historic site to honor LGBT rights.

- **2004:** As East tells Glory, the aurora borealis hunter in scene 1, the phenomenon is unpredictable. Because of strong solar flares in 2004, some of the coronal mass ejections hit earth's magnetic field, and the northern lights can be seen this year as far south as North Carolina.

  Today: An eleven-year solar cycle is ending, and the aurora borealis may be dimmer until 2024. The year 2016 is the last big chance to see this phenomenon in northern spots like Canada, Alaska, and northern Maine.

because of the severity of the climate. Maine was colder then than it is today, immersed in a mini-ice age from 1300 to 1700, though it has the same latitude as England. The woods were thick, and a lack of roads kept settlements near the shores, rivers, and lakes. The summer growing season was short, and all activity was to prepare for winter. The French and English fought over Maine until the 1750s, when the English won out during the French and Indian War (1754–1763).

Maine was a strong Patriot colony during the American Revolution, with many Maine privateers attacking British ships. Maine became a state in 1820 as part of the Missouri Compromise. Missouri was admitted as a slave state in exchange for Maine as a free state, a compromise to keep northern and southern interests in balance. Presque Isle was in the middle of the dispute over Maine's boundary with Canada in 1839, called the Aroostook War. Four regiments of Maine militia left Bangor and marched to the border to stop lumbermen from taking Maine timber, but there was no fighting. The border was settled through diplomacy, and thus the idyllic and quiet nature of Almost, Maine, has some precedent in history.

Bangor became a lumber boomtown, and the rivers transported the logs to the mills. In the nineteenth century, logging, the railroad, shipbuilding, and cotton textiles were the main industries. Granite and slate quarrying, brick making and shoemaking, and pulp and paper mills were also important. The railroad made Portland, the largest city, an important center. Maine, however, always had a largely rural population, as pictured in *Almost, Maine*. There were many family farms and small towns far apart. Maine soil was rocky, and farms did not flourish, except for those growing potatoes. Starting in the nineteenth century Maine became known as Vacationland for people in cities on the East Coast, especially places

The vignettes take place on a winter night in the mythical town of Almost, Maine. (© Smit | Shutterstock.com)

like Bar Harbor, where the Rockefellers settled, and Kennebunkport, the Bush summer home.

Maine Lore

Maine has fostered stereotypes of the homespun and backward Yankee with a strong rural accent and frugal nature, in such famous characters as Major Jack Downing, created by Maine humorist Seba Smith in his *Way Down East; or, Portraitures of Yankee Life* (1854). Smith was the Will Rogers of Maine and his character, Downing, is a wise fool like Forrest Gump, who meets famous people to satirize the events of the day. Another figure, Artemus Ward, a Yankee showman created by Charles Farrar Browne (*Artemus Ward, His Book*, 1862) was a favorite of President Abraham Lincoln and inspired Mark Twain. The expression "down east" refers to the eastern coastal region of New England and Canada that once was Acadia. For Maine people, "down east" is colloquial for a mythical land east of wherever you are. Cariani goes to some lengths in his stage directions to tell actors to avoid these Yankee stereotypes. The northern Mainer does not have a Yankee accent or a

stupid, naive character. His rural people are dignified and simple but not ignorant, he points out. They are not fishermen on the coast. They live in a flat, sparsely populated land where snowmobiles are the way to get around. The outlet L. L. Bean, in Freeport, Maine, sells the kind of winter clothing that Cariani's characters wear.

Maine has attracted many famous artists. Harriet Beecher Stowe was writing *Uncle Tom's Cabin* in 1852 in Maine while her husband taught religion at Bowdoin College in Brunswick, Maine. Several Bowdoin alumni are well known, including Henry Wadsworth Longfellow, America's most widely read Victorian poet, who popularized local history. His poem *Evangeline: A Tale of Acadia* (1847) is about the history of the Acadians, French settlers in Maine who were expelled from their homes (1755–1764) by the victorious English after the French and Indian War. Nathaniel Hawthorne was also a graduate of Bowdoin, becoming one of the United States's most celebrated authors in his time. The wilderness of Maine was celebrated by Henry David Thoreau in *The Maine Woods* (1864), describing his explorations of the region. Painters Thomas

Cole (*Dream of Arcadia*, 1838) Winslow Homer (*High Cliff, Coast of Maine*, 1894), and Andrew Wyeth (*Christina's World*, 1948) have all made landscapes of Maine famous. Maine has been the birthplace or adopted country of Pulitzer Prize–winning authors such as Edna St. Vincent Millay, Robert Lowell, Jean Stafford, and Elizabeth Bishop. *Almost, Maine* represents Cariani's pride in the pastoral qualities of his hometown and home state, a contrast to stressed urban centers like New York and Boston.

CRITICAL OVERVIEW

Almost, Maine premiered at Portland Stage Company in 2004 and made a huge hit in regional theater reviews. In a review of the Portland production in *American Theatre* for October 2004, Peter Royston quotes Cariani as saying the big sky of northern Maine is important for understanding the characters. The big night sky makes a human feel small. Royston comments that the characters

> interact with unexpressed yearning, holding their emotions so tightly under layers of clothing that the sentiments spill out in an unexpected way: in a cascade of magic realism, where the lines between the literal and the figurative blur.

The play opened off Broadway in 2006 at the Daryl Roth Theatre to mostly positive reviews, but New Yorkers were not as charmed as regional theatergoers, and some critics dismissed it as a flop. Mark Steyn, for instance, in a review for *New Criterion* in February 2006, sees no coherence in the play and objects to it as too sweet. Charles Isherwood, in a review from the *New York Times* called "Down East, So Much Love, Exciting and New," mentions that people would love the play or hate it. He himself finds it as cloying as a Sno-Cone. In a review for *Variety* Marilyn Stasio speaks of the characters as being almost too cute but saved by the direction of Gabriel Barre, who keeps them real. She observes that a "cross-section of the love-starved inhabitants of this tiny township tentatively reach out for human warmth," but she has a problem with the surreal style in which Cariani treats them. She admits the play will do better in regional theaters than in "stonehearted New York." On the other hand, Ellis Nassour, in an online review for *TotalTheater.com*, mentions that the New York audiences themselves were

responsive. They did not seem to be responsive enough for the play to last; it closed after forty-seven performances.

The performance in Los Angeles in 2008 at the Hudson Mainstage was reviewed favorably by Charlotte Stoudt in "Love and Kisses in L.L. Bean Land" for the *L.A. Times*. She comments on the visual puns and finds the goofy humor appealing. In a 2010 review for the *New York Times*, "New York Flop Becomes Hit Everywhere Else," Cara Joy David wrote a little history of Cariani's luck with his play around the country. She notes that it was pronounced by some critics to be one of the worst shows in New York in 2006 but has since been a Cinderella story, being frequently performed in regional theater around the country as it caught on by word of mouth. The *L.A. Times* review for a 2014 production in Los Angeles found "the quirky little fables" pleasing. Margaret Gray observes that "whenever the cutesiness threatens to cloy, the script throws in a palate-cleansing taste of tart or bitter."

Almost, Maine did better when it returned to New York in the 2013/2014 seasons. Anita Gates of the *New York Times*, writing in "All Bundled Up, but with Hearts on the Wing," speaks of the play's being well structured, unsentimental, and witty as performed at TheaterWorks Hartford. Catherine Rampell, in a review for the *New York Times* ("When Love Hits, It Can Really Send You Reeling") of a production of the play in the West Village at the Gym at Judson, compares the play to the feel-good film *Love, Actually*, noting the awkward and funny dialogue. It may be a bit cheesy, but it is earnest. In an online review for *Fast Company* titled "How a Complete Flop Became the Most Popular Play in America," Chris Chafin gives the production history to date, including its now worldwide appeal. He mentions that it is the most produced play in American high schools because it is easy for drama teachers to stage, good for both beginning and experienced actors, and not offensive.

CRITICISM

Susan K. Andersen

Andersen is a writer and teacher with a PhD in English literature. In the following essay, she considers Cariani's play Almost, Maine *in light of Shakespeare's* A Midsummer Night's Dream *and the theme of love's transforming power.*

WHAT DO I READ NEXT?

- Love's surprises are found in *Two Suns in the Sky*, by Miriam Bat-Ami (1999), a young-adult tale involving two fifteen-year-olds: Christine Cook, a Catholic American, and Adam Bornstein, a Jewish Holocaust survivor from Yugoslavia, who fall in love at a refugee shelter in New York.

- Cariani's third play, *Last Gas*, was produced in Portland in 2010 and has been available in print since 2014. It is a more realistic look at northern Maine and the story of two people who are not brave enough to admit their love.

- John Crowley, a fantasy and fiction writer from Cariani's hometown, Presque Isle, Maine, the model for Almost, Maine, is best known for his novel *Little, Big; or, The Fairies Parliament* (1981), for which he won a World Fantasy Award in 1982. It concerns a house on the magical border of another world, a story of fantastic love and loss.

- Mexican author Laura Esquivel presents a love story with magical realism in *Like Water for Chocolate* (1989), showing the extraordinary lengths to which thwarted lovers go to be together.

- Sarah Orne Jewett's *The Country of Pointed Firs* (1896) contains short sketches of characters in the fictional Maine fishing village of Dunnet Landing in southern Maine. The place is seen by the narrator as idyllic for writing and contemplation.

- Edna St. Vincent Millay's famous poem "Renascence" (1912) was written when she was nineteen, standing on Mt. Battie in Camden, Maine, and contemplating the sky and landscape in a sense of wonder.

- William Saroyan's novel *The Human Comedy* (1943) tells a beautiful nostalgic story of love and loss among the soldiers of World War II in the fictional town of Ithaca, California, based on Saroyan's hometown of Fresno. Saroyan's characters are all wise, saturated with a Whitmanesque vision of America, a philosophy to buoy up American troops about what they were fighting for.

- Kate Douglas Wiggin's *Rebecca of Sunnybrook Farm* (1903) is a coming-of-age young-adult novel set in the fictional village of Riverboro, Maine, where Rebecca's cheerful imagination and resourcefulness presage her writing ability. Planning to be a teacher, she is saved by an inheritance and becomes an independent woman able to help her family.

- E. B. White escaped the noise of New York to buy a farm in Brooklin, Maine, where he lived with his family. He published the children's novel *Charlotte's Web* in 1952, about a friendship between a pig and a spider, one of the best-selling children's novels of all time. He based the story on a sick pig he had but could not save, and so he saved the pig in fiction.

- Thornton Wilder's *Our Town* (1938), which won a Pulitzer Prize for drama, is set in the fictional small town Grover's Corners, New Hampshire, and spans the years 1901–1913. Thornton treats his rural characters with respect and fondness, as Cariani does. Act I is "Daily Living"; Act II is "Love and Marriage"; Act III is "Death and Dying." Like Cariani's play, Wilder's is frequently performed in high schools and regional theaters.

- In Jungian analyst Robert A. Johnson's *We: Understanding the Psychology of Romantic Love* (1983), Johnson dissects the great love story of Tristan and Iseult to expose illusions and unconscious beliefs about love that are not helpful and redefines love in terms of its psychological dynamics.

CARIANI TAKES THE AUDIENCE IN A DIFFERENT

DIRECTION WITH THE MAGIC REALISM, THE

WONDER, THE SURREAL, THE JOKES, THE SURPRISES—

PLACES THE JADED INTELLECT CANNOT GO."

Cariani's *Almost, Maine* is a play about transformations, and love performs the delicate alchemy. In each play there is some moment of revelation or discovery as the characters fall in or out of love or discover something new. It is as much of a discovery for the audience as for the characters. In his production notes, Cariani says,

> [The audience] think they're watching a simple, realistic little comedy...and then, all of a sudden, they're not. They're watching something that isn't simple or real or comic at all. Nothing is what it seems....Make them laugh and gasp and utter. Make them desperately wonder if what seems to be unfolding before their very eyes...is actually unfolding.

The author gives an important clue to how he thinks of the play when he says it is "a midwinter night's dream." Like Shakespeare's comedy *A Midsummer Night's Dream*, the play has humor, lovers, confusion, and transformation. Instead of fairies, Cariani suggests supernatural magic afoot with the lights of the aurora borealis between scenes. He says it must be understood that the nine playlets are moments all happening at the same time, on a moonless winter Friday at 9:00 p.m. in the extraordinary magic and imaginary place Almost, Maine, a town that seems to be almost there but not actually there. In many ways, *A Midsummer Night's Dream* is an important inspiration for the play and explains certain themes and effects that have puzzled critics. Cara Joy David, writing about a production of *Almost, Maine* for the *New York Times*, includes an interview with Cariani, who said he was influenced in his playwriting by Shakespeare. His favorite play is *The Winter's Tale*. He noticed that people going to Shakespeare plays like them for the love story and the fantastic elements. Contemporary theater, on the other hand, has too many intellectual ideas, he notes. Cariani takes the audience in a different direction with the magic realism, the wonder, the surreal, the jokes, the surprises—places the jaded intellect cannot go.

A Midsummer Night's Dream happens at midsummer in the woods, where the lovers are directly affected by the magic of fairies and the forces of nature. It is important that many scenes in *Almost, Maine* are set outdoors too. In all ways, Cariani optimizes the cold, the vastness, the loneliness, and the big sky in northern Maine. Characters look up at the night sky, the stars, the aurora borealis. They are aware of being small in a vast expanse. This creates a sense of awe and reflection on the essentials of life. It is also the landscape for transformation, as Shakespeare's characters spend all night in the wilderness and come out changed and paired with someone else. Cariani has said that while some see the skits as sentimental, for him they are full of the ache of people longing for love. Somehow this seems even more poignant when people are bundled up in parkas than when they are dressed in Greek tunics.

In *A Midsummer Night's Dream*, there is confusion in the beginning, as the lovers do not seem to agree on who is their mate. Both Demetrius and Lysander love Hermia, and Helena is scorned, though she loves Demetrius. On the magic night, they switch partners many times before knowing their true loves by morning. In *Almost, Maine* lovers begin as confused or going in one direction, and suddenly they are going in an opposite direction. Glory thinks she is mourning her dead husband but instead finds a new mate, East, who is a repairman to fix her heart. Jimmy is trying to get Sandrine back on the eve of her wedding to someone else and suddenly discovers Villian. Steve believes his inability to feel pain means that he is a deficient human being and must avoid love. When Marvalyn whacks him with an ironing board after kissing him and then he feels pain, it could be slapstick, but it is also a tender reminder of how love destroys the numbness around us so the world can be felt in its paradoxical wonder. The scene of Gayle and Lendall's trading and comparing sacks that quantify the love they have given each other is an example of how we want to make sure we are not getting cheated by a lover. Gayle believes she is giving more than Lendall and thinks the bag he owes her should look bigger than the little one he hands her. However, it contains the engagement ring she has been waiting for. Randy and Chad are a complete surprise in terms of audience expectations. So far, all have been stories of men and women discovering each other. After Chad and Randy complain about how their girlfriends treat them, they finally turn to each other and realize they like each other best and are in love. On the other hand, Phil and Marci share a moment under the stars as they skate on Echo Pond, where they once fell in love, accepting that though they are married with a family, they no longer love each other. Rhonda and Dave are snowmobile buddies and drink beer together. She is a tomboy, and, in a very funny scene, she cannot register Dave's attempt to turn the relationship in a romantic direction. When she does get it, she begins to rip off her snowmobile suit in passion.

By far the most subtle and sad scene is "Story of Hope." Although it is a dialogue, the scene is told mostly from Hope's point of view, since she does most of the talking. She has come back to Almost looking for her high school sweetheart, Daniel, who asked her to marry him just before she went off to college. She did not give him an answer but just left. Now, many years later, after being disillusioned by the world, she goes back to give her answer of "yes." She is too late. Just as she is about to say the word, Daniel's wife calls him back into the house. It is the story of the one true love who got away. The woman's name is Hope. She seems to be the loser, but the skit suggests a Rod Serling *Twilight Zone* twist, with Daniel's sad and constant fantasy, or Hope, that his lost love would one day knock on his door. The production notes emphasize that Daniel is the example of Hope lost. He was once a big, strong athlete and is now short and shriveled, with glasses, as though he has wasted away. He goes meekly back into the house when his wife calls him. He is half the man he was, without Hope, another literal/metaphoric play on words.

The magic realism or surreal mood helps create the out-of-the-world feel of Almost as a place of unexpected reversals. On the other hand, some reviewers have not understood the slapstick comedy that Cariani uses with literal metaphors, such as when Randy and Chad fall down on the floor over and over as they "fall" in love or Glory's carrying her broken heart as pieces of slate in a bag. In this, perhaps Cariani also learned from Shakespeare. Peter Quince's play of *Pyramus and Thisbe*, put on for the Duke's nuptial in *A Midsummer Night's Dream*, is funny because the workmen of Athens do not

understand the difference between literal and metaphoric language. They explain to the audience the physical props that are Wall, Moonlight, and Lion so they will not make the metaphoric leap of faith. Afraid the ladies will take the dramatic lion as a real one, Snug explains that he is really Snug the joiner in a costume, playing a lion. Though the Duke, Theseus, and his audience laugh at the clumsiness of the workers, the Duke is genuinely pleased by the play, saying, "Never any thing can be amiss / When simpleness and duty tender it" (act 5, scene 1, lines 83–84) It was the simple workman, Bottom the Weaver, who after all was forever changed by his encounter with Titania, Queen of Fairies. Whatever else happens, he will always have "Bottom's Dream," "because it hath no bottom." (act 4, scene 1, lines 215–216). Love visits and transforms even the most common person.

In such a tender way does Cariani treat his characters. The rural Maine people are isolated in a cold and dark climate. They are attired for a Maine winter night with heavy parkas. They are innocent and wide-eyed and appreciate falling in love instead of carrying on a clever put-down contest with the opposite sex. Are they for real? Cariani responds affirmatively in his production notes. The people are "not hicks or rednecks. . . . They're very smart. They just take time to wonder about things." The reader or audience member, too, has to take time to wonder about things in order to get the most out of Almost. Cariani skillfully builds in pauses at the right moment (given by the stage direction "*Beat*"), where everything stops as the actors look at one another or realize what has happened. These beats are necessary for both the jokes and the drama, a space for the point to come home, such as Marci's leading up to the physical and metaphorical shoe that she drops out of the blue to tell Phil their marriage is over. The pauses are what create the piece as good drama when performed by a skilled actor. That is where the emotion or epiphany happens, as when Glory shows East her broken heart in a bag. It could be a corny pun, unless the actor holds the emotion in silence. If it comes off, the audience feels the physical heaviness of a broken heart.

Cariani claims there are no endings at the end of each play, only "*suspensions*" where the characters are about to experience joy, but there is uncertainty. The moments of all the plays build into

The first vignette centers on a woman with a broken heart. *(©Robsonphoto | Shutterstock.com)*

"the overall arc of the play" where the audience is waiting for catharsis or fulfillment. Only by the end of the last play is there a feeling of resolution as Rhonda and Dave seem to be moving toward the bedroom and removing their parkas. He comments, "The *almost*-happiness of Scenes One through Five and the . . . *bitterness* . . . of Scenes Six and Seven will make the end of Scene Eight wonderfully cathartic. . . . The joy there has been earned." Cariani shows his understanding of rhythm, pause, and climax to create transformation. Hippolyta mentions to Duke Theseus in *A Midsummer Night's Dream* that she believes in the stories the lovers told because "all their minds transfigur'd so together" (act 5, scene 1, line 24). The aurora borealis between scenes in *Almost, Maine* is to remind the audience that all the plays are happening at the same moment to transfigure the residents all together. All these individual moments of love add up to an enchanted climax where, it is hoped, the audience, too, has remembered the tender but paradoxical nature of love.

Source: Susan K. Andersen, Critical Essay on *Almost, Maine*, in *Drama for Students*, Gale, Cengage Learning, 2017.

Alex Rubin

In the following interview, Cariani discusses the success of Almost, Maine *as well as how Shakespeare influenced his writing and why he started writing.*

When John Cariani wrote *Almost, Maine* in 1996, he was in his early 20s. An actor in New York, he was wan to find audition monologues he connected to. So, he wrote his own. Those early works became *Almost, Maine*, his first of now four plays. Today, he stars in Broadway's *Something Rotten!* as playwright Nigel Bottom, who aspires to the writing prowess of William Shakespeare. In real life, the actor and playwright seems to have attained that goal. *Dramatics Magazine* reports Cariani's own play has edged out Shakespeare's *A Midsummer Night's Dream* as the most produced play in North American high schools. Eleven scenes of love and loss comprise the show set in the fictional town: Almost, Maine. Here, Cariani talks about *Almost, Maine's* success, what it feels like to outdo Shakespeare and why more actors should write plays.

In Something Rotten! *you play a writer competing with Shakespeare. In real life, your play is*

"MY PLAYS ARE ROMANTIC. ANY ACTOR IN ANY
OF MY PLAYS SHOULD BE A ROMANTIC BECAUSE THE
CHARACTERS IN *ALMOST, MAINE* ARE ROMANTICS."

*more widely produced in North American high
schools than any of his. Do you feel some satisfaction about beating your* Something Rotten! *rival?*

JC: YES! It's crazy! And kind of unimaginable. It's a surreal and excellent life-imitating-art
or art-imitating-life kind of thing. It's funny,
Horatio tells Hamlet, "There are more things in
heaven and earth than are dreamt of in your
philosophy." That's how I describe the trajectory of *Almost, Maine*. I never imagined this to
be its path. I was a kid when I wrote it, and it's
taken such a long time for it to catch on!

Why do you think that is?

JC: Many people have told me it's because
when it opened Off-Broadway in 2006, the kind of
humor that was in vogue was a bit snarky, ironic,
self-aware. Maybe the world is a little more ready
for open-hearted and earnest comedy now.

Why do you think Almost, Maine *appeals to
high school students?*

JC: A friend of mine, Dick Mullen, is a
wonderful theatre teacher at Cape Elizabeth
High School in Cape Elizabeth, ME, and he
directed the first high school production of
Almost, Maine in 2007. I thought he was crazy
to tackle the play with high school kids. In my
mind, it's a play for adults! But Dick reminded
me that high school kids are in that strange place
between adulthood and childhood. They're experiencing first love, first loss, first big pain. But,
they're still hopeful because they haven't been
beaten up by life yet. There's something about
where young adults are in their lives that syncs up
well with the un-cynical, sometimes guileless
characters in *Almost, Maine*.

*Does it also have to do with the "producibility"
of the play?*

JC: Sure, but I don't think a play gets done
as much as *Almost, Maine* gets done because it's
"producible." It has to be good. I think people do
Almost, Maine because they love the story

(or stories) it tells. And kids are a little nuts for
it. After almost every performance of *Something
Rotten!* kids ask me to sign their *Almost, Maine*
scripts. Some kids from Vancouver were at the
show last week and told me they had just done
the play and, "Jeezum Crow, they loved it," and
they loved how it's helped them think about life
and love. One young woman told me that I'm like
the Taylor Swift of playwrights. I'll take that!

In terms of producibility, every scene in
Almost, Maine is a two-hander. So each scene
can be rehearsed independent of the others. I'm
sure that's a plus for directors. And the cast size
is expandable. The play was written for four
actors, but can be performed by as many as 19
because there are 19 awesome roles, which is
great if you need a large cast.

*Have high school students told you about spe-
cific characters or scenes that resonated with them?*

JC: Kids often say, "You helped me through
a really rough time." And then they tell me a sad
or uplifting personal story. One girl told me she
had gone through a break up and understood
what breaking up is because of the scene "Getting It Back." Most kids say that the stories
about the outsiders speak to them because I
think every high school kid feels like an outsider.
Heck, we all feel like outsiders!

*When you were in high school, was there some-
thing missing for you in the shows you performed?*

JC: I grew up in a small remote town in
northern Maine where curse words still pack a
huge punch. I know that we could never do any
of the plays that were running on Broadway or
Off-Broadway because of language issues, first,
and content issues, second. And there aren't "junior" versions of Mamet or Shepard. So, it was
hard to find great contemporary material we
could sink our teeth into. Also, I couldn't understand why the books to musicals so rarely made
sense. I love plots that all make sense. I do think
that that's the art of play-writing: plot. Great
plots make magic. A plot that constantly moves
forward and constantly surprises: magic. And
action that keeps audiences wanting more: magic.

Last year, a production of Almost, Maine *at
a North Carolina school was canceled allegedly
because the scene "They Fell" features two men
falling in love. What can you tell us about this
incident?*

JC: I feel that the media was a bit quick to
attack the principal of Maiden High School.

Two small, fringe churches went to the principal at Maiden and pushed him to cancel the production supposedly on the grounds that there is alcohol, sexual innuendo and sexual situations in the play that might not be appropriate for high school students. If that's why the principal canceled the production, I can't blame him. However, if the production was canceled because of a completely chaste scene that depicted first love between two young men, well, that's another matter entirely. I wrote a statement that sums up how I feel.

But the students took the show off campus.

JC: They mounted the production off-site with the support of people like Keith Martin (who was the artistic director of The Charlotte Repertory Theatre back in the '90s and had go to court in order to proceed with their production of *Angels in America*). The kids did a beautiful job. After the show, several people came up to me and said, "We're Christians, we go to church and we believe that Jesus is love and this play is about love." It opened my mind. Yes, there were a couple of churches that called for the cancellation of the play, but there are a lot of churches that have no problem with the play.

A school in Baltimore originally cut "They Fell" from the play and then reinstated it after the American Civil Liberties Union of Maryland got involved. Would you have allowed a production of your show to go one with a scene cut?

JC: No. Because it's not *Almost, Maine* without "They Fell." Because it's a beautiful, gentle, sweet, chaste play about two young men discovering their love for each other. I wrote it to help people understand that we don't chose who we fall in love with. It just happens.

Has Shakespeare's work influenced your writing?

JC: Yes. Absolutely. *The Winter's Tale* is my favorite Shakespeare play and it's full of magic—and magical realism —and romance. And I think it had a huge influence on me as I made *Almost, Maine*. I was in a spectacular production of *The Winter's Tale* at The Hudson Valley Shakespeare Festival, and I realized that people love fairytales. Adult fairytales. Done well! I consider *Almost, Maine* to be a collection of adult fairytales. And adult fairytales are romantic. I learned from *The Winter's Tale* what a romance is. Shakespeare's romances are called "problem plays" because they have happy-*ish* endings. You're left wondering if the lovers are going to be okay. That happy-ish-ness—that's romance! Romance is all about imminent disaster.

F. Scott Fitzgerald wrote, "The sentimental person thinks things will last. The romantic person has a desperate confidence that they won't." I am romantic. My plays are romantic. Any actor in any of my plays should be a romantic because the characters in *Almost, Maine* are romantics. They are people who are on the verge of happiness—but they're terrified everything is going to go to hell at any second!

Why did you start writing?

JC: Most of the stories being told in plays [I saw] were city-stories—mostly about wealthy, worldly, powerful, well-educated people who live and worked in the closed quarters of the concrete and steel canyons. This was thrilling because the city and its stories and its people were new to me! But, I started to get sick of those stories. What about rural stories? What about stories about the people I grew up with? I always wanted to write stories that featured characters that could be played by people who aren't hot. I wanted to see regular people get the girl. Or guy. I also think more actors need to write plays. We live inside plays, and we know them better than anybody.

Source: Alex Rubin, " *Something Rotten!*'s John Cariani Talks Beating the Bard—But Not at the St. James Theatre," in Playbill, March 19, 2016.

Chris Chafin

In the following essay, Chafin details how Almost, Maine *went from flopping after opening in 2006 to becoming the most-produced high school play in America by 2010.*

When *Almost Maine* made its Off-Broadway premiere in 2006, it closed after a month due to poor ticket sales. Charles Isherwood, reviewing it for the *New York Times*, wrote that it "may leave the cloying aftertaste of an overly sweetened Sno-Cone."

But our second act contains surprises: The play survived a death-sentence review to become one of the biggest hits in contemporary global theater.

Almost, Maine is a series of loosely intertwined scenes about love and loss that take place over one night in a fictional Maine town. Today, it is massively popular with community

> IN FACT, *ALMOST, MAINE* HAS SOME UNIQUE STRUCTURAL ADVANTAGES THAT MAKE IT VERY APPEALING TO HIGH SCHOOLS. IT COMBINES TWO VERY DESIRABLE TRAITS NOT OFTEN FOUND TOGETHER: IT CAN ACCOMMODATE A LARGE CAST, BUT DOESN'T REQUIRE THAT CAST TO ALL APPEAR ONSTAGE TOGETHER AT ANY POINT."

theaters, regional repertory houses, and international performance groups. It has been performed in 20 countries, and translated into more than a dozen languages, including Spanish, French, German, Hungarian, Romanian, Russian, Finnish, Dutch, Flemish, Gujarati (India) and Korean. According to Dramatists Play Service, which owns the rights, there have been 2,777 productions in the United States and Canada alone since it began licensing the play in 2008—that's more than one production per day, every day, for seven years.

To put this in perspective, the most popular purely professional production of the 2014–2015 season, Christopher Durang's *Vanya and Sonia and Masha and Spike*, had only 27 productions. While Dramatists and the play's author, John Cariani, refuse to release financials for the play (and estimating its revenue is somewhat complicated), it is very likely that the piece has produced in excess of $1 million in revenue through licensing alone.

"I kind of thought it was a terrible play for a while," says Cariani. "After it started to get popular again, I was like, you know, this is not terrible! It's a good play! I believe in this play! I love this play!"

One place *Almost, Maine* is particularly popular is in American high schools, where it was the No. 1 most-produced play from 2010 until 2013, according to statistics compiled by *Dramatics* magazine. During the 2013–2014 school year, it was No. 2, edged out by a little number called *A Midsummer Night's Dream*, by a guy you may be familiar with (hint: William Shakespeare).

So how did this massive popularity happen? How did the play peel itself off the morgue slab to crack the boards so thunderously?

That's where the plot thickens.

"I think its popularity stems from a production at the annual festival that we do," says Don Corathers, the director of publications at *Dramatics* referring to Thespian Festival, an annual youth theater conference held at the University of Nebraska–Lincoln, which draws educators and performers from around the country. "It's a great showcase."

Cariani disagrees. "This is what's so cool," he tells me. "People read it and wanted to do it. We didn't do anything. The *New York Times* said something about how we gave out postcards, and I don't know where they got that information" (The *Times* in fact claimed that Dramatists handed out buttons at conferences.) He does credit a 2007 performance at the respected Florida Repertory Theatre, in Fort Myers, as helping rehabilitate and popularize the show.

At 44 years old, Cariani retains the youthful energy and enthusiasm that suffuse his play. He is thin and vaguely Muppet-like, with a long neck leading to a face that scrunches mightily when he smiles, which he is doing in almost every photograph of him I've seen. When startled, more than one of his characters wholesomely shouts "Jeezum Crow," which the script helpfully explains how to pronounce ("'JEE-zum CROW'–it's a euphemism"). More than once while I am speaking with him, Cariani fills a gap in the conversation by effusively complimenting me, at one point exclaiming, "These questions are so good! They're awesome, by the way. They really are! Really interesting!"

Cariani was born in rural Maine, and came to New York in the 1990s to try to find work as a writer and actor. In the latter part of that decade, he began writing and performing pieces for Performance Space NBC, a special theater the television network set up in the hopes of finding a replacement for its then-aging tentpole programs *Seinfeld* and *Friends*. Cariani, without much forethought, wrote several short scenes to showcase himself, all set in some version of his hometown.

"I didn't really know I was writing a play until some really great helpful artists who were directors and producers pointed out that I had a theme going," Cariani says. "They helped me pull from what I had the skeleton that became *Almost, Maine*."

The resulting play is 11 scenes of mostly independent action between couples or small groups. It can be played by as few as four actors or as many as 19.

Cariani cites *The Twilight Zone* as an influence, and virtually all the scenes in *Almost, Maine* have a less-than-subtle metaphorical twist or set piece. One character carries her broken heart in a paper bag, only to happen upon a repairman who quickly falls in love with her. A man is physically unable to feel pain until he begins to fall in love. In a scene that's recently caused some controversy, two longtime male friends literally fall in love with each other, repeatedly collapsing onstage at the scene's climax (typically to howls of laughter from high school audiences). One couple, recently broken up, has this exchange:

> GAYLE: (she's been in a bit of a state) I want it
> back.
> LENDALL: What?
> GAYLE: All the love I gave you? I want it back.
> LENDALL: What?
> GAYLE: Now.
> LENDALL: (Little beat.) I don't understand—
> GALE: Yours is in the car.

Soon, they begin hurling love at each other, described in the script as "an ENORMOUS bunch of HUGE red bags."

Almost, Maine's initial run in New York was not a success. "It's tough for me when people say it's a flop," says Cariani, "because we ran a month in previews and then for a month. That's the typical run of a show at a not-for-profit theater." That's all well and good, except the show was performed at a commercial for-profit theater. "We could only survive if we sold tickets," Cariani continues. "And unfortunately, we didn't sell enough tickets. And I was pretty sad. I had big dreams, you know?"

This was in 2006. By 2010, it was the most-produced high school play in America. Cariani was shocked, he said, when he first heard a high school was going to be mounting a production. "There's no way a high school can do this play," he thought at the time. "It's a play for adults."

In fact, *Almost, Maine* has some unique structural advantages that make it very appealing to high schools. It combines two very desirable traits not often found together: It can accommodate a large cast, but doesn't require that cast to all appear onstage together at any point. Drama teachers are often under pressure to showcase as many students as possible, but face challenges when trying to corral students to appear in a big musical number or courtroom scene. The scenes were written as acting exercises, so they're short and allow young actors to show a range of emotions. The dialogue is written naturally and is easy to comprehend.

Joe Crnich is the drama teacher at Juan Diego Catholic High School in Salt Lake City, Utah. He first heard of the play when a neighboring school put on a production. "I didn't know much about it, so I read it," he says. "I got through the first three scenes, and I was like, 'Eh, this is actually pretty campy and hokey.' And I read it again, and thought, you know, this is actually pretty cool. I kept picking it up and putting it down and eventually I fell in love with it." That's when he decided to mount his own production.

I spoke with Crnich before a dress rehearsal two days ahead of opening night. What had drawn him to the play? Some things were logistic. "They're all two-person scenes, which makes it really easy to work, schedule-wise, with kids," he says. "To tax a very busy student body, when they're going 50 different directions . . . It makes it pretty easy to schedule rehearsals . . . [also] the simplicity of the sets, because some schools have very little resources for sets and costumes. So you can get a winter coat anywhere, or you can go really crazy with things. It just kind of lends itself to a variety of different budgets that high schools have. But he also liked the script. "The fact that [actors] can deal with it on a very surface level, or go as deep as you want to go in terms of intimacy and immersion in the emotion of each scene," appealed to him, he notes. "You can play it for comedy, or you can be very straight about it. I've seen some YouTube clips that make it very campy. I don't really agree with that very much."

Cariani agrees. "If it's only funny, it's terrible, and if it's only cute, it's terrible, and if it's only sad and depressing, it's terrible," he said. "It's tough for me when people play it for broad comedy. That's not what I want it to be."

Still, this is a route many productions take. YouTube is full of clips of high school actors shouting the lines to each other, mugging, and self-consciously wriggling around on the stage.

These productions seem to get the biggest audience responses, with the sound of parents' digital cameras drowned out by the hysterical laughter of the crowd. The straight productions are more emotionally resonant, but leave the audience silent and the actors seemingly more uncomfortable.

Erica Tryon picked *Almost, Maine* for the all-girls boarding school where she teaches, Emma Willard, in Troy, New York. "I think it can be a challenge to find plays for a younger audience that are smart and funny and touching and relatable," she says, "and I felt like *Almost, Maine* is all of those. It has an innocence without being a naive play. . . . I think there are some shows where you can't understand it until you're 60, and there are some shows that are really only amusing while you're still 16. I think *Almost, Maine* kind of crosses all these different stages of life."

Charles Isherwood, the *New York Times* theater critic who wrote about the play's original run, points out that there's something else that makes the play so popular in schools. "There's nothing to offend in it," he says. "It doesn't bring up any religious or political themes. There's no overt sexuality. I think it can be done by virtually any theater company without offending anyone. It's an anodyne piece of writing, a sweet one."

Improbably, the play has found itself recently embroiled in scandal. A high school in North Carolina canceled its production over local protests over the scene "They Fell," which very lightly deals with homosexuality (though it must be said the scene seems to conflate love and friendship). Cariani, ever chipper, found nothing about which to be upset, even in the censorship of his own play. Except, perhaps, that "people from New York were lambasting that poor principal," who canceled the production, he says. "I felt bad for the guy."

"I can say actually it's probably a play better suited to regional theaters and places less cynical than New York," says Isherwood. "Because it has a certain sentimentality and whimsical quality to it. I think that probably plays better to the less hardened among us. And if you live in New York, you become hardened to a certain degree. I mean, you do if you survive."

Surviving as a New York playwright is exactly the thing at which Cariani is struggling. As an actor, he is doing well: nominated for a Tony for a 2004 revival of *Fiddler on the Roof* and currently starring on Broadway in the Shakespeare-aping comedy *Something Rotten!*. As a writer, though, he's still on the outside, despite his huge success.

"I'm not really considered a New York playwright, and that's the saddest thing to me," he says. Cariani still feels that the New York nonprofit theater establishment refuses to give his work a fair hearing. "I'm desperate for the not-for-profit circles to just take a look at my new work, because I feel like the popularity of this play—I think I'm entitled to a chance."

His biggest fans tend to be teenagers located far from New York. "One girl came up to me and said, 'I like you like I like Taylor Swift,'" Cariani said. "And that's one of the best things anybody's ever said to me. The plays are kind of Taylor Swifty, you know? She's so good at writing about romance and heartbreak and the pain of love, and that's kind of what *Almost, Maine* is about.

"Where I'm from is kind of like the Midwest," he continues. "It's rural, and a lot of the country is rural. There are a lot of us who live in places that aren't cities, and we have ideas and thoughts and opinions that matter. I do feel that life is really complex, but it can also be really simple. Living in a place like northern Maine—life is a bit simpler there. And that's valid, you know?"

Much of the world, it seems, does know.

Source: Chris Chafin, "How a Complete Flop Became the Most Popular Play in America," in *Fast Company*, March 16, 2015.

Zack Ford

In the following article, Ford covers the controversy over the production of the play, which alludes to a same-sex relationship, at Maiden High School in North Carolina.

In the romantic comedy play *Almost, Maine*, one of the nine vignettes features two men discussing their negative experiences with dating girls and realizing that they love each other by comically falling—literally physically falling—on the stage. Though the scene fades on the gag before the men can even reach each other, Maiden High School in North Carolina feels that the play is too controversial, canceling a pending production by the Main Street Players, the students' acclaimed theatre and performing arts troupe.

WSOC reports that according to students, "some parents and area churches complained" about the play's inclusion of a same-sex couple. Principal Rob Bliss released a statement describing the play as having "sexually-explicit overtones and multiple sexual innuendos that are not aligned with our mission and educational objectives."

Bliss also claimed that "no final decision has been made regarding whether and what drama performances are to be presented this fall," but the students tell a different story. An alumnus who posted about the controversy on *Reddit* connected *Think Progress* with Conner Baker, a junior at Maiden High School and the student director for the Main Street Players. According to Baker, not only had the club gotten approval for the play, but they'd already paid for it too.

Baker told *Think Progress* that the Players had sought approval for *Almost, Maine* earlier in the school year, receiving it from both Principal Bliss and Catawba County Schools Superintendent Dan Brigman. Brigman and Bliss stipulated, however, that every student wishing to audition or assist with the production must receive parental permission to do so. The club then spent over $300 to reserve the rights and rent the scripts for the show, and followed through on this requirement. Only one student was prevented from auditioning by the permission-slip process. Baker said that the show had already been cast and was beginning rehearsals when the production was canceled last Thursday. She did not personally know who in the community objected to the play's content.

Think Progress reached out to Bliss for clarification about this conflicting account of events, but did not receive a response. An online petition started by students and alumni to allow the show has already garnered over 1,000 signatures.

In 2010, *Almost, Maine* was listed as the most-produced play in North American high schools. In fact, numerous clips of the "They Fell" vignette as performed in high schools across the country can easily be found on YouTube.

... The controversy at Maiden High School is eerily similar to a story that played out this summer at South Williamsport High School in Pennsylvania. There, school officials canceled a production of *Monty Python's Spamalot*, claiming its inclusion of a same-sex wedding was inappropriate but explaining to the press that it had never actually been approved in the first place. Emails later revealed that not only had it been approved, but the principal had even signed the check reserving the rights for the production.

Incidentally, same-sex marriage became legal in North Carolina last week.

Source: Zack Ford, "High School Cancels Popular Play over Allusion to Same-Sex Relationship," in *Think Progress*, October 16, 2014.

Peter Royston

In the following review, Royston discusses the yearning and repression the characters' experience in the play.

It's become traditional for New England playwrights to write about the repressed lives of New Englanders, whether it's Eugene O'Neill setting *The Oresteia* in Massachusetts, or Thornton Wilder observing the dead wryly lamenting the blindness of the living in New Hampshire. But for John Cariani, whose romantic comedy *Almost, Maine* opens Oct. 26 at Portland Stage Company (then moves Off-Broadway in early 2005), New Englanders aren't repressed. They're just cold.

"I don't think that society is so puritanical up there," he says. "I just think it's the weather! It's so cold that you wear a lot of clothes, but people still have burning passions underneath. They still ache—and the ache is what really interests me."

That ache takes solid form in *Almost, Maine*. The play is set during a winter night, as the people in an isolated Maine town interact with unexpressed yearning, holding their emotions so tightly under layers of clothing that the sentiments spill out in an unexpected way: in a cascade of magic realism, where the lines between the literal and the figurative blur. Characters "fall" in love—literally fall to the ground, unable to stand—or watch as "the other shoe" drops out of the sky. The citizens of Almost, Maine, don't put their hearts on their sleeves—they carry them around in bags.

Cariani, who won acclaim this season playing Motel in the Broadway revival of *Fiddler on the Roof*, based *Almost, Maine* on his own childhood in "potato country," as Mainers call the state's northern tip. As Portland Stage's managing director Tamera Ramaker says, "All you have to do is look at a map to get a sense of it ... there's only one highway to get you there. There are places where there's no road accessibility at all. That's Maine."

"My friends always said they understood Chekhov, because we're from a place that's so cold and so hard to get out of," says Cariani. "Here in New York, you're busy all the time. When you're in a place with a big sky, you're more aware of how small you are as a human being. The sky is so much bigger than the world."

Source: Peter Royston, "Portland, Maine: Portland Exposure," in *American Theatre*, Vol. 21, No. 8, October 2004, p. 10.

SOURCES

Cariani, John, *Almost, Maine*, revised edition, 2007, 2008, Dramatists Play Service, pp. 7, 17, 71–73, 75.

Chafin, Chris, "How a Complete Flop Became the Most Popular Play in America," in *Fast Company*, March 16, 2015, www.fastcompany.com/3043584/my-creative-life/how-a-complete-flop-became-the-most-popular-play-in-america (accessed July 27, 2016).

David, Cara Joy, "New York Flop Becomes Hit Everywhere Else," in *New York Times*, December 17, 2010, www.nytimes.com/2010/12/18/theater/18almost.html?_r=O (accessed July 27, 2016).

Gates, Anita, "All Bundled Up, but with Hearts on the Wing," in *New York Times*, February 15, 2013, www.nytimes.com/2013/02/17/nyregion/a-review-of-almost-maine-at-theaterworks-hartford.html (accessed July 27, 2016).

Gray, Margaret, Review of *Almost, Maine*, in *L.A. Times,* December 11, 2014, http://www.latimes.com/entertainment/arts/la-et-cm-almost-maine-at-hudson-mainstage-20141209-story.html/ (accessed July 27, 2016).

Isherwood, Charles, "Down East, So Much Love, Exciting and New," in *New York Times*, January 16, 2006, http://www.nytimes.com/2006/01/16/theater/reviews/down-east-so-much-love-exciting-and-new.html/ (accessed July 27, 2016).

Judd, Richard W., Edwin A. Churchill, and Joel W. Eastman, eds., *Maine: The Pine Tree State from Prehistory to the Present*, University of Maine Press, 1995, pp. 31–49, 52–61, 76–82, 253–59, 480–504.

Nassour, Ellis, "Maine Man: Joseph [sic] Cariani Tells His Stories," in TotalTheater.com, http://www.totaltheater.com/?q=node/318/ (accessed July 27, 2016).

Rampell, Catherine, "When Love Hits, It Can Really Send You Reeling," in *New York Times*, February 6, 2014, Vol. 263, No. 56404, p. C5.

Royston, Peter, "Portland, Maine: Portland Exposure," in *American Theatre*, Vol. 21, No. 8, October 2004, p. 10.

Shakespeare, William, *A Midsummer Night's Dream*, Riverside Edition, edited by G. Blakemore Evans, Houghton Mifflin, 1975, pp. 241–42.

Stasio, Marilyn, Review of *Almost, Maine*, in *Variety*, January 16, 2006, Vol. 401, No. 9, p. 42.

Steyn, Mark, Review of *Almost, Maine*, in *New Criterion*, Vol. 24, No. 6, February 2006, pp. 40–44.

Stoudt, Charlotte, "Love and Loss in L.L. Bean Land," in *L.A. Times*, February 12, 2008, www.articles.latimes.com/2008/feb/12/entertainment/et-maine12 (accessed July 27, 2016).

Weaver, Neal, Review of *Almost, Maine*, in *Stage Raw*, December 12, 2014, http://stageraw.com/2014/12/11/almost-maine/ (accessed July 27, 2016).

FURTHER READING

Bantu, Maya, "Q & A with Actor and Playwright John Cariani," *Broadway World*, May 10, 2006, http://www.broadwayworld.com/article/QA-with-Actor-and-Playwright-John-Cariani-20060510 (accessed July 27, 2016).
    Cariani explains why his experience as an actor inspired him to become a playwright.

Bogan, Louise, *The Blue Estuaries: Poems, 1923–1968*, Farrar, Strauss and Giroux, 1995.
    Bogan was born to a lower-class Irish family in Livermore Falls, Maine, and, like Edna St. Vincent Millay, another rural Maine poet, escaped conventional life for the romantic wandering life of a poet, ending as the poetry editor for the *New Yorker*.

Flewelling, Lynn, *Luck in the Shadows*, Spectra, 1996.
    Maine seems to produce abundant writers of poetry and fantasy. Another writer from Presque Isle, Maine, Flewelling is a fantasy writer and a Buddhist, including LGBT themes in her fiction. This fantasy is being made into a film, about a thief and apprentice involved in politics, followed by magic forces.

Roberts, Kenneth, *Arundel*, Down East Books, 1995.
    Roberts was born in Kennebunk, Maine, and wrote historical fiction about Maine. *Arundel* is about the American Revolution. The characters, including Steven Nason, leave the town of Arundel, Maine, to march with Benedict Arnold to Quebec.

Thoreau, Henry David, *The Maine Woods*, Penguin Nature Library, 1988.
    Thoreau writes of his three trips over three years to the Maine woods, where he climbed mountains and paddled his canoe on lakes. His famous experience on Mt. Katahdin is included, where, contrary to his usual descriptions of nature, he found nature to be hostile.

Van Es, Bart, *Shakespeare's Comedies: A Very Short Introduction*, Oxford University Press, 2016.
    Van Es is Renaissance Lecturer at Oxford. He explains the historical context of the comedies and the techniques that make them successful.

Cariani's background includes acting in Shakespeare comedies; this experience, he admits, gave him hints about how to write successful comedy.

SUGGESTED SEARCH TERMS

John Cariani

Cariani AND *Almost, Maine*

aurora borealis

history AND Maine

Presque Isle, Maine

Something Rotten!

poetry AND Maine

reviews AND *Almost, Maine*

gay rights AND Maine

Amadeus

Amadeus is a fictionalized account of the historical figures Wolfgang Amadeus Mozart and Antonio Salieri. Both men were successful composers in the late eighteenth century, but although Mozart's work continued to be known and loved around the world, Salieri was largely forgotten. Speculations about Salieri's jealousy over Mozart's success, coupled with the fact of Mozart's early death, led the playwright Peter Shaffer to create *Amadeus*, in which a bitter, guilt-ridden Salieri confesses his plot to hire Mozart to write a magnificent requiem, murder Mozart, and then present the requiem as his own work, dedicated to the late Mozart.

Although Shaffer based the 1984 film on his play, the screenplay was almost a completely new creation. He and the director Milos Forman sequestered themselves in a Connecticut farmhouse to transform the play, which contained abstract elements and elevated language suitable for the theater, to a screenplay that was more realistic and appropriate to Forman's intention to film entirely on location. For example, in the play, Salieri directly addresses the audience, but the film introduces the character of a priest to whom Salieri tells his tale, turning a soliloquy into a conversation. While creating the final movie script, Forman and Shaffer argued constantly and included nothing that both did not approve. The result is an amazing study of genius and jealousy. Forman's direction and the locations and dazzling costumes—not to mention

Milos Forman (© *Vittorio Zunino Celotto / Getty Images*)

Mozart's iconic music—make the finished film a feast for both the eyes and the ears.

PLOT SUMMARY

As *Amadeus* begins, a valet tempts his master, Antonio Salieri, with sweets to coax him to open the door. When Salieri refuses, the valet breaks down the door down and discovers that Salieri has tried to kill himself by slitting his own throat. The old man is carried through the snowy streets to a mental asylum. The next morning, Salieri, with bandages wrapped around his throat, begins telling his story to a priest, Father Vogler. The rest of the film alternates between Salieri's conversation with the priest and flashbacks.

Salieri insists that he is responsible for the death of his fellow composer Wolfgang Amadeus Mozart. He explains how he has always idolized Mozart and envied the attentions Leopold Mozart paid to his son, in comparison

with Salieri's own father, who did not care for music. If his father had not died, Salieri would likely not have been allowed to pursue a career in music.

In a flashback, Salieri first sees Mozart, who acts like a silly boy, flirting with a woman—Constanze, who will soon become his wife—with crude jokes until he hears the orchestra has started the performance without him. Mozart's entire demeanor changes as he stands and leaves the room to join the other musicians. Salieri struggles to believe that the immature jokester is the Mozart he has admired by reputation since his boyhood. Archbishop Colloredo of Salzburg, who has sponsored the concert, scolds Mozart for his lateness.

Emperor Joseph II and his advisers are discussing Mozart as a newcomer to the Vienna music scene. Baron van Swieten raves about Mozart's work, but Count Orsini-Rosenberg finds it tiresome. Joseph decides to tempt Mozart away from the employ of the archbishop by the offer of an opera for the national theater. The men debate whether Mozart deserves such a commission and whether the work should be in Italian or German.

When Mozart is first presented to Joseph, Salieri writes a march in Mozart's honor. The emperor awkwardly plays the new piece on the pianoforte as Mozart enters and then offers him the opera commission. Mozart argues passionately for the work to be in German and proposes a story set in a harem, which many of the advisers believe is inappropriate. Joseph ignores his advisers and accepts all of Mozart's ideas. Mozart sits at the pianoforte and effortlessly improvises variations on Salieri's march.

Salieri's student, the beautiful soprano Katerina Cavalieri, comes for a lesson and asks about a possible role for herself in Mozart's new opera. Salieri advises her against it because of the shocking setting, but the next scene shows her onstage during the premier performance. The emperor applauds enthusiastically at the finish and congratulates the cast but tells Mozart the piece has too many notes. Mozart is insulted. Constanze and her mother, Frau Weber, arrive on the scene. Katerina is jealous when she realizes that Mozart is engaged to be married, and Salieri is jealous when he realizes that Katerina and Mozart likely had a brief affair.

Leopold Mozart speaks to the archbishop, entreating him to give his son another chance.

FILM
TECHNIQUE

- Forman decided to film the movie entirely on location in and around Prague, where many period buildings remained. This, coupled with filling the streets with countless extras in period costume, lends a realism to the film that would not have been possible on recreated sets. Vincent Canby of the *New York Times* writes, "The movie looks wonderfully authentic."

- The lighting used for the film also adds realism. The critic Brian Eggert, writing in *Deep Focus Review*, points out that rather than use bright electric lights, which were not available in the eighteenth century, "Cinematographer Miroslav Ondricek shoots night scenes by candlelight, but with an amazing clarity and atmosphere."

- The costumes and makeup in *Amadeus* were praised by critics and were awarded Oscars. Roger Ebert mentioned how the costume choices enhanced the characterization, particularly of Mozart. Ebert notes that "in a film where everybody wears wigs, Mozart's wigs...do not look like everybody else's. They have just the slightest suggestion of punk, just the smallest shading of pink." The apartment where the Mozarts live also adds to the viewer's impression of Mozart, Ebert believes, recalling the "pad of a newly-rich rock musician.... The furnishings are sparse and haphazard, work is scattered everywhere, housekeeping has been neglected, there are empty bottles in the corners." The contrast to Salieri's tidy, established household and his more conservative personal style is telling.

- In great contrast to the lavish sets and costumes of the flashback scenes are those featuring Salieri and the priest in the asylum. The color palette is subdued: mostly black, white, and brown. The lighting is sunlight coming through the window or a few candles. The camera work is also more static than usual: most of the shots frame the actors' heads and shoulders, although occasionally the camera zooms in to highlight a particularly intense emotional moment. The simplicity of the scene and the framing focuses the viewer's attention on what is being said. Salieri's words are more important than the physical action.

He writes to Mozart, begging him to delay his marriage, but Mozart's return letter informs Leopold that the wedding has already occurred.

The emperor hopes to hire Mozart as a music instructor for his niece. His advisers insist that a committee be formed to make a decision, to avoid any appearance of favoritism. Mozart angrily refuses to submit his music to the committee, but Constanze brings some of her husband's music to Salieri to ask for his help in securing the job. She admits that they need the steady money the teaching position would bring. After Constanze explains that she cannot leave the music, because the pages are the originals and there are no copies, Salieri marvels that the pages show no changes or corrections. He is overcome by the beauty of the music.

Salieri agrees to help but implies that Constanze will have to commit adultery with him to ensure Mozart will be appointed to the position. However, when she returns that evening, he sends her away. Stewing in anger and jealousy, Salieri declares to God, "From now on, we are enemies, You and I."

Mozart comes to Salieri for help. He admits that he needs money and asks for a loan. The position of tutor to the princess has been filled, but Salieri offers to recommend Mozart for another, less prestigious position teaching a wealthy man's daughter. The student's parents insist on staying in the room with their misbehaving dogs, who howl as Mozart plays the pianoforte. Mozart stalks out, humiliated.

Leopold arrives for a visit and openly disapproves of Constanze's housekeeping. Mozart lies about his finances, wanting to impress his father. Leopold comments on Constanze's obvious pregnancy, and to avoid awkward conversation, Mozart drags everyone out to a costume party, where Salieri watches from the sidelines. When Mozart loses a party game and must perform on the pianoforte for the crowd as a penalty, he imitates Salieri by playing an overly simplistic melody. Salieri is hurt and embarrassed.

A young woman named Lorl appears at the Mozart apartment offering her services as a maid. Her salary is to be paid by an anonymous admirer. Constanze is pleased to have the help, but Leopold objects, believing it is inappropriate to accept such a gift and to allow a servant into their home without the proper references. As Leopold and Constanze begin to argue, Mozart loses himself in his work. Lorl reports what she sees at the Mozart home to Salieri, who has sent her to spy for him. She also lets him into the apartment when no one else is at home, and he sees from Mozart's papers that he has begun work on a new opera.

Salieri tells Count Orsini-Rosenberg about Mozart's new project: an opera based on the play *The Marriage of Figaro*, which the emperor has banned because the story shows a servant outwitting his master—a dangerous idea in a time when revolution is brewing against monarchs around the world. When called before the emperor, Mozart is able to convince him that the opera will be charming—and harmless in political terms—and rehearsals for the opera begin.

Again Salieri tries to foil Mozart by reporting that a ballet is part of the opera—the emperor has also forbidden ballet to appear in his commissioned works. However, Salieri's plan backfires when the emperor steps in, accepting Mozart's explanation that the dancing is within the context of the story, at the celebration of Figaro's wedding.

At the first performance of *The Marriage of Figaro*, Salieri is deeply affected by the beauty of Mozart's music. His jealousy makes him happy to see the emperor yawn, dooming the opera to only a few performances, but he attends every one of those performances, helpless to resist the call of the music.

Both the emperor and Mozart attend a performance of Salieri's new opera. Joseph praises the work, presenting Salieri with the Civilian Medal, but Mozart makes neutral remarks, such as "I never knew that music like that was possible," that Salieri interprets as flattery.

Mozart arrives home with a group of friends, including the composer and performer Emanuel Schikaneder. Several unfamiliar gentlemen are at the apartment with Constanze, who breaks the news that Leopold has died. Salieri attends a performance of Mozart's *Don Giovanni* and sees in the "dreadful ghost" the fears and insecurities of a guilty son: "the horrifying apparition was Leopold, raised from the dead." Salieri begins to hatch a plan.

Schikaneder's theater troupe performs a parody of *Don Giovanni*. Mozart and his family are in the audience. Schikaneder comes out to speak with them, encouraging Mozart to write something for the common people instead of the court. The idea appeals to Mozart, but Constanze believes it is risky to rely on takings from the box office for payment. She would prefer he get work from patrons like the emperor who pay up front.

Mozart's financial situation deteriorates. He asks for loans and begs for students, but no one will help because of his heavy drinking. Van Swieten asks Salieri to help, and Salieri launches his plan. He appears at Mozart's door in the forbidding black mask Leopold has worn to the costume party and commissions a requiem mass. Constanze is thrilled with the money Salieri leaves.

When the flashback is over, Salieri explains his plan to the priest. Once Mozart has finished the requiem, Salieri will kill him and then present the mass at Mozart's funeral as his own work, dedicated to his devoted friend.

Mozart works on the requiem frantically. When there is a knock at the door, he tells Constanze not to answer, fearing it is the man in the mask. Instead it is Schikaneder, coming to check on Mozart's progress on a piece for him. Schikaneder becomes angry that Mozart has no sheet music to show him but is somewhat placated when Mozart explains the whole opera is in his head—he only needs to write it down.

When Salieri next visits in the mask, Constanze urges Mozart to finish the piece and earn the handsome payment promised. She also expresses concern that Mozart is making himself ill by working and frustration that he focuses on the opera for Schikaneder rather than the mass for the masked patron. Mozart admits his fear that writing the mass is killing him.

Constanze leaves Mozart, taking their young son, Karl. Mozart's condition declines further, and he collapses during a performance of *The Magic Flute* at Schikaneder's theater. Salieri, who has come surreptitiously to see the opera, has Mozart carried to his carriage to take him home. After Salieri gets Mozart settled in bed, he answers a knock at the door. It is Schikaneder with Mozart's share of the profits from the theater, but Salieri tells Mozart the money has come from the masked patron, which spurs Mozart to resume work on the requiem.

Salieri takes dictation because Mozart is too ill to complete the work himself. Before they can finish, however, Constanze returns. She takes the music from Salieri and locks it in a cabinet, refusing to let Mozart continue working on a project that has made him so sick. While Salieri and Constanze argue coldly, Mozart dies. His funeral is meager because Constanze cannot afford much. His body is thrown into a mass grave with other paupers.

Father Vogler attempts to dissuade old Salieri from the conviction that he has killed Mozart. Salieri does not listen: he knows that he has poisoned Mozart's life even if he has not directly murdered him. As Salieri is taken from the room in his wheelchair, he calls out blessings on the asylum's other inmates.

CHARACTERS

Kapellmeister Giuseppe Bonno
Bonno is a figure at Joseph's court—one of the emperor's musical advisers. His accent marks him as Italian, and he advises the emperor to commission an opera in his native tongue, believing German to be to "too *bruta* for singing, too rough." Rather than put his own opinions forward, Bonno seems to parrot the views of Orsini-Rosenberg.

Katerina Cavalieri
Katerina is an opera singer and Salieri's student. As an old man, Salieri tells the priest that he was in love with Katerina and admits that he was jealous of her suspected affair with Mozart.

Archbishop Colloredo
The archbishop is Leopold Mozart's patron. Leopold does his best to keep his son in the archbishop's good graces, but Mozart's vanity and impudence offend the archbishop.

Princess Elizabeth
Elizabeth is Joseph's niece. Mozart refuses to submit his work as an audition for the chance to become her music teacher, but Constanze brings the music to Salieri and asks for help.

Joseph II
Joseph II is Holy Roman Emperor. True to historical fact, the emperor is shown to have a great interest in music, believing that it will enrich the lives of his people and please him personally. Joseph commissions an opera from Mozart and is willing to listen to Mozart's explanation of why the story of *The Marriage of Figaro* does not contain dangerously revolutionary ideas, as some of Joseph's advisers fear.

Lorl
Lorl is the servant Salieri hires to work for Mozart. Constanze accepts the help happily, which sparks an argument between her and Leopold, who feels accepting such a gift from an unknown source is inappropriate. As she performs her duties, Lorl keeps her eyes open and reports what she learns to Salieri.

Constanze Mozart
Constanze is Mozart's wife. Leopold does not approve of Mozart's marriage, and he and Constanze never get along. However, just as Leopold does what he believes will most help his son's career, Constanze also works to make sure Mozart's temper and impetuous behavior do not ruin him. Without Mozart's knowledge, Constanze goes to Salieri to ask for help in finding pupils for Mozart and in landing commissions from the emperor.

Karl Mozart
In the film, Constanze and Wolfgang Mozart have one child, Karl, who is shown as a young boy. In reality, the Mozarts had six children, four of whom died in infancy. Karl had only one brother who survived to adulthood, Franz.

Leopold Mozart
Leopold is Mozart's father. The film's portrayal is accurate in terms of Leopold's ambition for his

son: Mozart toured the courts of Europe from a young age. In the film, Leopold is a stern man, frowning while his son laughs and smiles and arguing with his daughter-in-law.

Wolfgang Amadeus Mozart

The Mozart depicted in the movie is a vain, crude, and often silly man with a ridiculous laugh. He takes only his music seriously. Mozart is shown as a genius able to play musical improvisations the moment he sits down at his instrument. When Constanze shares pages of Mozart's work, Salieri marvels at the absence of corrections and changes. Although this point is exaggerated for effect in the film, musicologists do point out the surprisingly minimal revisions on Mozart's compositions.

Mozart's relationship with his father is fraught with insecurity. While he longs for his father's approval, he also has a natural desire to make his own way in the world. Rather than accept the security of a wealthy patron, as Leopold does with the archbishop, Mozart prefers the freedom of earning his living as he can. However, he exceeds his income through lavish living and is always in debt. Salieri is able to take advantage of both Mozart's desperate financial state and his complicated relationship with his father in furthering his diabolical plan.

Count Orsini-Rosenberg

As the director of the opera, Orsini-Rosenberg is an influential figure at Joseph's court. He is not impressed by Mozart, describing him as a "young man trying to impress beyond his abilities." When advising the emperor, Orsini-Rosenberg discourages the idea of hiring Mozart to write an opera.

Antonio Salieri

Salieri is the central character of the film. The framing story shows Salieri as an old man, explaining to a priest the plot to steal a bit of Mozart's glory for himself. He pretends to be a friend to Mozart while planning to murder him and present Mozart's last great work as his own. Salieri has a deep love of music but is bitter because he believes God has given him enough talent to recognize Mozart's genius but not enough to create brilliant work himself.

Emanuel Schikaneder

Schikaneder (1751–1812) is a historical figure. He wrote the libretto of *The Magic Flute*, in which he played the part of Papageno, as is shown in the film. In *Amadeus*, Mozart enjoys the fun and freedom of collaborating with Schikaneder, though Constanze would prefer that he take commissions from the emperor, believing that that work will bring more financial security and prestige.

Valet

Salieri's valet coaxes him to open the door. When that fails, he breaks down the door and finds Salieri covered in blood, having attempted to kill himself.

Baron van Swieten

Van Swieten is the imperial librarian of Joseph's court. He is an enthusiastic fan of Mozart's work—one of the few who speak well of him.

Father Vogler

Vogler is the priest in the asylum to whom Salieri confesses his plot against Mozart.

Count Johann Von Strack

Von Strack is Joseph's chamberlain. He insists that Mozart must apply for the honor of instructing the emperor's niece rather than simply being appointed without proving himself.

Frau Weber

Frau Weber is Constanze's mother and Mozart's mother-in-law. Her manners are not quite appropriate for the circles in which Mozart socializes, which illustrates that Constanze has come from a less elevated social level.

THEMES

Jealousy

The main conflict in *Amadeus* arises from Salieri's jealousy of Mozart. He is jealous that Mozart occupies so much of his father's attention, jealous of Mozart's talent and his success, and jealous of his seemingly effortless compositions. As the lives of Salieri and Mozart become more entwined, Salieri becomes jealous that Mozart has an affair with Katerina Cavalieri and navigates the intrigue at court by luck rather than plotting. Consumed by his jealousy, Salieri hatches the plan to anonymously hire Mozart to write a requiem, kill Mozart, and take credit for writing the mass himself.

The theme of jealousy is also reflected in many smaller threads throughout the film. Constanze

READ. WATCH. WRITE.

- Using print and online resources, research eighteenth-century fashion. Watch *Amadeus* to carefully analyze the wigs and costumes. Determine the accuracy of the clothing and hairstyles used in the film in terms of both the time period and the wealth and social standing of the characters. Share your findings with your class in a formal presentation. Be sure to include images in your presentation to illustrate your points.

- Joseph Haydn was already a famous composer when Mozart was a child, but there is strong historical evidence that the two men were friendly and greatly respected one another's work. Using print and online resources, research Haydn's life and work. Imagine how a movie about Mozart's life would be different if Haydn were the central character rather than Salieri. Examine whether Haydn acts as a true mentor to Mozart rather than working behind the scenes to thwart him. Think about whether he would side with Leopold Mozart in encouraging the young Mozart to align himself with a patron, ensuring financial security. Write a scene from this imagined movie that depicts the relationship between Haydn and Mozart. Ask a classmate to perform with you, presenting your scene to your class or recording it and posting it online.

- Working with a group, watch *Amadeus* again, paying particular attention to the character of Constanze Mozart. Note the measures she takes to ensure her husband's success and financial security for herself and her child. Research the social standing of women in the late eighteenth century. What would Constanze do without Mozart's support, either when he is ill or after he dies? Think about her decisions: to share her husband's compositions with Salieri without permission, to even consider committing adultery to land Mozart a lucrative position. Stage a debate with your classmates about whether you believe her behavior is justified.

- Using print and online resources, research Mozart's life and personality. Think about why you believe the portrayal of him in the film is or is not accurate. Write an essay to explain your opinion. Cite specific examples from the movie, comparing the fictionalized scenes with historical fact.

- Read Tara Kelly's 2011 young-adult novel *Amplified*, in which the protagonist, Jasmine, defies her father's instructions to go to college and instead runs off to Los Angeles to join a rock band. Think about how Kelly portrays parental expectations and how Jasmine acts against them. Compare Jasmine's situation with Mozart's relationship with his father as depicted in *Amadeus*. Think about whether the younger generation goes against their parents' wishes because they know they are choosing the right path for themselves or whether they are simply rebelling. Write an essay explaining the motivations of both parents and children. Use examples from the book and the film to support your opinions.

Mozart is jealous of her husband's flirtations and affairs with other women. The politics of the court stem from rivalry and jealousy: all of the court officials try to garner more of the emperor's favor to forward their own ends. Even the attention Leopold Mozart directs toward his son may be a result of jealousy. Leopold may drive his son relentlessly in part because he knows that Wolfgang has more talent, of which the father is jealous even though he does not recognize this feeling.

Parent-Child Relationships

The film sets up Mozart and Salieri as the two central characters and offers their relationships with their fathers as a major point of contrast

Milos Forman and Saul Zaentz, respectively director and producer of Amadeus (© *ROB BOREN | Getty Images*)

between them. Leopold Mozart takes an intense interest in his son's career and devotes much energy to his success. Leopold's attention, however, is a mixed blessing. Mozart begins touring at a very young age—clearly he did not have much of a childhood. His father pushes him to take on a patron, as Leopold himself worked for many years for the archbishop of Salzburg. He seems to think he has the right to direct his son's life. Leopold's controlling nature leads to arguments with his daughter-in-law, though Mozart himself never stands up to his father.

The relationship that Mozart has with his own son, Karl, is not explored at length, but in one scene, in which the family is watching the farcical production of *Don Giovanni* in Schikaneder's theater, Mozart is silly and playful when talking to his son, a marked contrast to his own stern father. This suggests that Mozart has no wish to become like Leopold.

In contrast, Salieri's father does not believe that a career in music is worthwhile or respectable. As a boy, Salieri knows that he will not be allowed to study music and become a composer. He is released from this restriction only when his father dies suddenly. Salieri takes a macabre joy in his father's death, seeing it as God's answer to his prayer that he be allowed to pursue his dream. When talking to the priest, Salieri is clearly jealous of Mozart's musical genius, but he seems almost equally envious of Leopold's encouragement and interest in his son.

Salieri takes advantage of Mozart's complicated relationship with his father: when arriving at Mozart's door to commission the requiem, Salieri dons the same costume Leopold wears at the masquerade ball. Mozart pales at the sight. For a moment he seems to fear that his father has come back from the dead. Thus Salieri takes advantage of the instinctive fear and respect Mozart feels for his father, ensuring his compliance with Salieri's plan.

STYLE

Music

It is no surprise that in a film centered on the musical world of the Viennese court of Joseph II, music is an important element. Perhaps the most obvious role music plays in the film is in the staged performances, from the grand operas commissioned by the emperor to the fun, sometimes crude productions intended for the common people at Schikaneder's theater. These musical performances are part of the story of the film but also draw particular attention to Mozart's work, allowing Forman to feature Mozart's compositions in a realistic way within the context of the film.

Music is also of central importance to the overall mood of the film. The soundtrack of *Amadeus* both reflects and enhances the tone of each scene. For example, the costume party scene is accompanied by light, playful music. By contrast, the forbidding music that plays whenever Leopold shows up clues in the audience to Mozart's fear of his father's disapproval. This music is echoed when Salieri appears in Leopold's mask dressed all in black. Mozart's *Requiem* plays in later scenes as the viewer sees Mozart's health failing and Salieri pushing forward with his murderous plans. Selections from the *Requiem* also play throughout the film's epilogue, during which the audience is shown Mozart's body dumped in a pauper's grave. The use of Mozart's music increases the drama and sense of tragedy at the film's close.

Flashbacks

The structure of *Amadeus* includes a framing story surrounding a series of flashbacks. The framing story shows Salieri as an old man. He attempts suicide and is taken to an asylum, where he explains to a patient priest his reasons for wanting to die. As Salieri confesses, his memories are portrayed in extended flashbacks that form the main action of the story.

The flashback structure of the film is effective for this story because the wisdom of Salieri as an old man gives him perspective on his actions when he was younger. His comments to the priest add depth to the viewer's understanding of the character and his motivations. Salieri's wry comments add a certain humor. F. Murray Abraham's performance was lauded by critics, and his skill is particularly evident in the asylum scenes. His expressions convey piercing emotion, such as when he closes his eyes, hearing Mozart's music in his head, and is transported anew by the mere memory.

CULTURAL CONTEXT

Joseph II and Musical Patronage

Joseph II (1741–1790) became Holy Roman Emperor after the death of his father, Francis I, in 1765. However, Joseph's mother, Maria Theresa, was still ruler of the Hapsburg empire and retained most of the power. Her worldview contrasted greatly to that of Joseph, who was influenced by the revolutionary ideas of the Enlightenment, a movement in the eighteenth century that put faith in knowledge, logic, and science rather than blind trust in religion and tradition. Therefore, Joseph's goals were very different from those of his mother. He fought to improve the lives of his people, even the poorest peasants, and this concern extended to their happiness in addition to their basic material needs. There are even tales of his traveling in disguise to witness firsthand how the common people lived.

Joseph II was a surprisingly progressive leader. He believed in religious tolerance, relaxed laws of censorship, instigated reforms that eventually put an end to the feudal system, and improved the public education system. As an ardent music lover, Joseph made sure that music was a part of the educational curriculum. Also, for his own enjoyment and for the common good, he invested money in the arts, evidenced throughout the film by the number of officials in Joseph's court concerned with the production of music and in the emperor's commissioning an opera from Mozart. The liberal atmosphere of Joseph's court drew musicians from all over Europe.

At this time in Europe, the easiest way for a composer to make a living was to secure a position with a patron: a wealthy noble who would pay a musician to write and perform pieces. This system had its advantages, as exemplified by the careers of Mozart (1756–1791) and Joseph Haydn (1732–1809). The two men were friendly and well acquainted with each other's music. Haydn, perhaps because he was older than Mozart, firmly established himself in the patronage system. He was supported by Prince Miklós József (Nikolaus) Esterházy of Hungary for almost thirty years.

Under Miklós József's patronage, Haydn's responsibilities included composing music, conducting performances, training other musicians in the prince's employ (including an orchestra of approximately two dozen), and maintaining the estate's instruments. In exchange, Haydn lived in a grand palace and had financial security.

F. Murray Abraham And Tom Hulce In Amadeus *(@copy;Archive Photos | Getty Images)*

Composers employed under the patronage system were treated as servants. They served at the pleasure of their patron and were sometimes required to wear a court uniform. Living in isolation on a county estate, they might be cut off from other musicians and developments in popular music. Some critics, however, believe that this isolation allowed Haydn to create his unique style.

Mozart, by contrast, did not enter into an arrangement with a long-term patron. His father worked for the archbishop of Salzburg, and *Amadeus* shows him attempting to push his son into a similar arrangement, thus ensuring a measure of financial security. Mozart resisted the creative restrictions of working for a patron and instead supported himself through concerts and giving lessons in piano and composition. Because of the lack of steady income and the mismanagement of what money he did earn, Mozart struggled financially for most of his life.

The differences between Haydn's career and Mozart's show the evolution of how musicians supported themselves. Haydn is a prime example of the patronage system, in which spaces for public performance were few. With Joseph II's cultural reforms, more venues opened for public concerts, and musicians no longer had to rely on the sponsorship of wealthy families. Public concerts became far more popular, and the patronage system began to fade.

CRITICAL OVERVIEW

Critical reception of *Amadeus* as a film was overwhelmingly positive. The legendary film reviewer Roger Ebert praised Forman's direction, pointing out that "the key precursor was *Hair*," which Forman directed in 1979. Ebert notes that Forman "sees Wolfgang Amadeus Mozart as a spiritual brother of the hippies who thumbed their noses at convention, muddled their senses with intoxicants, and delighted in lecturing their elders." Forman captures the decadence of Mozart's lifestyle, Ebert writes, by presenting the audience with "a visual feast of palaces, costumes, wigs, feasts, opening nights, champagne, and mountains of debt. " Other critics also rave about the production in terms of its visual effects. Vincent Canby of the *New York Times* draws attention to the film's setting:

> Having been shot entirely in and around Prague—which stands in for Emperor Joseph II's Vienna—the movie looks wonderfully authentic. A centerpiece of the musical sequence is Prague's jewel-like Tyl Theater, where Mozart actually conducted the first performance of *Don Giovanni*. Never for a minute does this *Amadeus* seem like a filmed play.

David Shariatmadari, writing for the *Guardian*, agrees that filming on location adds to the film's impact: "The streets of Vienna are meticulously recreated and filled with a seemingly limitless supply of costumed citizens. Parts of several operas are staged, lavish performances within a performance." The cumulative effect, according to Shariatmadari, is "a slightly hallucinatory interpretation of late 18th-century Austro-Hungarian splendour, complete with vertigo-inducing wigs, flaming candelabra and heaving bosoms."

In spite of the epic drama of the movie's costumes, sets, and recreated operas, the story captures the truth of human emotion. In *Empire*, Ian Nathan notes that the "film, so magnificent and ornate, is posing very human conflicts on a grand scale: self-aware mediocrity versus blind talent, liberated creativity versus the establishment." Nathan applauds Shaffer for "trimming the over-explanatory aspects of his play" and instead including "very modern preoccupations without ever breaking the spell: homoeroticism, ego, creative rivalry, the nature of identity and evil all bubbling and boiling to the surface." Brian Eggert writes in *Deep Focus Review*:

> Deeply cinematic flourishes in art design, magnificently ornamented sets and costumes, and the sheer dramatic profundity of what becomes a severe comic tragedy are marked by playful quirks in characters that live and breathe in spite of their sometimes ostentatious behavior.

Several critics believe that the film's emotional truth is due to the skill and subtlety of the individual performances. Although the entire cast is noted appreciatively time and time again, F. Murray Abraham in particular is singled out for praise. Ebert urges viewers to "watch Abraham's face as he internalizes envy, resentment and rage. What a smile he puts on the face of his misery!" Shariatmadari also waxes enthusiastic about Abraham's performance, which "you feel deserves not just the Oscar it won, but several more on top. It is a brilliant, humanistic portrait of jealousy, guilt and, in the end, a kind of redemption."

The most common criticism of the film is its willingness to stray from historical fact. According to Simon P. Keefe of *Musical Times*, "*Amadeus* has proved highly contentious in scholarly circles. Detractors focus on factual inaccuracies." Eggert admits that the production's "extravagant details" do not "equate to historical accuracy." However, he points out that the liberties were taken for a purpose: "Shaffer's script abandons strict detail to instead tell a compelling story with moments that may never have occurred but contain a pronounced drama." Eggert explains that

> pointing out these historical deviations is not to discredit Shaffer's screenplay or Forman's production, only enhance the viewer's appreciation of how cleverly both men have manipulated history into a compelling story about the artistic process and its consequences.

Furthermore, Keefe indicates that, in spite of its inaccuracies, the film "captures Mozart['s] reception from the last 200-or-so years in microcosm" by "foreshadowing scholarly concerns that have assumed particular prominence since the film's original release (such as the study of Mozart's music in relation to that of contemporaries, and the study of Mozart['s] reception)."

James Berardinelli, in *Reelviews Movie Reviews* describes *Amadeus* as "arguably the best motion picture ever made about the process of creation and the creator." He calls the film a fascinating character study and argues that "no movie before or since has so effectively woven music into the tapestry of the motion picture. Many films treat sound as an adjunct to the visual aspects; *Amadeus* views them as equals." All of these virtues led Berardinelli to summarize the film as a modern classic.

CRITICISM

Kristen Sarlin Greenberg

Greenberg is a freelance writer and editor with a background in literature and philosophy. In the following essay, she examines the significance of religion in the film Amadeus.

Shaffer's film adaptation of *Amadeus* is different in many ways from the original script of his play. However, one thing remains constant: Salieri's struggle with his faith is a central theme. On the surface, Salieri seems to be a deeply religious man, but a closer examination shows that his piety is conditional. He maintains his trust in God only as long as he believes God is giving him what he wants.

The earliest flashbacks in the film show Salieri as a young man. He acts superior when he notes to the priest that "my father prayed earnestly to God to protect commerce," but Salieri himself also prays selfishly: "Let me celebrate your glory through music." At first, his prayer sounds pious, but he continues, "and be celebrated myself. Make me famous through the world, dear God! . . . After I die let people speak my name forever with love for what I wrote!" More than wanting to celebrate God, he wants his music to make him famous.

There is an obstacle in Salieri's path to stardom: his father thinks that a career in music is impractical, risky, and inappropriate for his son. Salieri pledges his chastity to God if God will make it possible for him to study music. When his father dies suddenly, Salieri believes it is God's answer to his prayers: "I knew God had arranged it all; that was obvious." Salieri says to Father Vogler, "Tell me, if you had been me, wouldn't you have thought God had accepted your vow?" For all his scorn about his father's praying about commerce, Salieri seems to see his prayers and God's responses in terms of a commercial transaction: because God has granted Salieri's wish by removing his father's objections to a music career, Salieri is happy. He feels that God has earned his loyalty.

When he meets Mozart, however, Salieri can never be content again after experiencing the mastery of Mozart's compositions. Salieri first hears Mozart's music at the archbishop's palace and is completely overcome by its perfection. Salieri tells Father Vogler: "This was a music I'd never heard. Filled with such longing, such unfulfillable longing, it had me trembling. It seemed to me that

> SALIERI'S VANITY IS STRONGER THAN HIS PIETY: HE CANNOT ACCEPT THE IDEA THAT HE COULD KEEP HIS VOW AND MAKE MUSIC TO CELEBRATE GOD EVEN IF HE DOES NOT BELIEVE HIMSELF TO BE THE BEST."

I was hearing a voice of God." After seeing Mozart's crude, immature behavior, Salieri cannot believe such a man has composed a piece of such incomparable beauty. He demands of Father Vogler, "Why? Would God choose an obscene child to be His instrument?"

This experience casts the first shadow of doubt on Salieri's certainty that God will continue to give him what he wants. For the time being, he continues to work on his music. As he is composing at the pianoforte and creates a passage that particularly pleases him, he looks up to his crucifix and happily says, "Grazie, Signore," thanking God for his favor. Later, when his jealousy and anger over Mozart's talent get the better of him, Salieri repeats the same phrase of thanks, but the second time his voice drips with sarcasm. Salieri's vanity is stronger than his piety: he cannot accept the idea that he can keep his vow and make music to celebrate God even if he does not believe himself to be the best.

At first, Salieri's anger is directed at Mozart. He confesses to Father Vogler, "My heart was filling up with such hatred for that little man. For the first time in my life I began to know really violent thoughts." However, rather than pray for humility and the patience to withstand Mozart's presence, Salieri asks God to remove the problem: "Please! Please! Send him away, back to Salzburg. For his sake as well as mine." Soon after, Salieri directs his wrath to God himself.

Salieri's jealousy increases when Constanze brings him Mozart's original pages of sheet music. He explains to the priest how marvelous Mozart's work was:

> These were first and only drafts of music yet they showed no corrections of any kind. Not one. . . . He'd simply put down music already finished in his head. Page after page of it, as if he was just taking dictation.

WHAT DO I SEE NEXT?

- The British Broadcasting Company 2004 television miniseries *The Genius of Mozart* portrays Mozart's life in great detail, from his childhood as a traveling prodigy to the height of his creative genius to his premature death.

- Clint Eastwood directed the 1988 biopic *Bird*, which depicts scenes of the life of the legendary jazz saxophone player Charlie "Bird" Parker, played by Forest Whitaker. The film tells the story of Parker's childhood, his important relationships with other musicians, and his tragic death while still in his thirties. Because the film is rated R, it is more appropriate for older students.

- Ed Harris stars as Ludwig van Beethoven, and Diane Kruger plays his young assistant in *Copying Beethoven* (2006), directed by Agnieszka Holland. The film shows Beethoven in the last years of his life, when, because of his deafness and his ailing health, he needs help to transcribe his compositions. The film is rated PG-13.

- The heavy metal band X Japan is wildly popular in Japan and has been torn apart by tragedy. Stephen Kijak's documentary *We Are X* (2016) follows Yoshiki, the drummer and pianist for the band, who also writes most of the group's songs.

- Phil Grabsky wrote and directed the documentary *In Search of Mozart* (2007) in honor of the 250th anniversary of Mozart's birth. Grabsky uses a combination of examples of Mozart's music, actors reading his letters, and footage of his extensive travels to bring the great composer to life.

- Jamie Foxx stars as the renowned blues musician Ray Charles in Taylor Hackford's 2004 film *Ray* (PG-13). The movie follows Charles from his southern boyhood to his superstardom in the middle of the twentieth century.

- Like Mozart, many musicians take students out of financial necessity. In the film *Mr. Holland's Opus* (1995), which is suitable for young adults, a frustrated composer takes a job as a high school music teacher to make ends meet while he writes his masterpiece. He believes the position to be temporary, but he finds fulfillment, and the job turns into a decades-long career.

- Daniel Anker's unrated young-adult documentary *Music from the Inside Out* (2004) gives a detailed picture of the lives of professional musicians through interviews and concert footage of members of the Philadelphia Orchestra.

Again, Mozart's work echoes in Salieri's ear as "the very voice of God." Whereas Salieri struggles to capture a phrase of music and make it sound the way he wants it to, he sees Mozart's music as being handed to him, a direct gift from God. The title Shaffer has chosen is significant: *Amadeus* means "beloved by God." Salieri believes God is unfair, showing favor to Mozart while taunting Salieri. He feels he is "nothing to God" and insists, "There is no God of Mercy, Father. Just a God of torture." Because Salieri does not get what he wants—the highest personal glory in the music world—he believes that God is punishing him.

Salieri declares to God, "From now on, we are enemies, You and I." He places his crucifix on the fire. He is angry that God has given Mozart incredible musical talent but given him, Salieri, only enough "ability to recognize the Incarnation." When Salieri hears Mozart's grating laugh, he explains to Father Vogler: "That was not Mozart laughing, Father.... That was God! God laughing at me through that obscene giggle. Go on, Signore. Laugh.... Show my mediocrity for all to see." He believes God is mocking him, as if God would take pleasure in Salieri's failures. Salieri vows revenge: "You wait! I will laugh at You! Before I leave this earth, I will laugh at You!" He adds "Amen!" at the close of this angry speech, in a mockery of a true prayer.

Though he rejects God in his anger, Salieri does not completely lose his faith. When he speaks of Mozart's music, his vocabulary is filled with words referencing religion. As he sits in the audience watching *The Marriage of Figaro*, he hears "a perfect absolution" in the beauty of the music. Though Salieri's anger leads him to ensure that *Don Giovanni* closes after only five performances, he attends each show and spends every moment "worshipping sound I alone seemed to hear." Salieri can no longer trust in God's benevolence, but he still believes in God's punishment. When Mozart is on his deathbed and asks Salieri if he still believes in "a fire which never dies," Salieri immediately answers "Oh, yes."

Rather than feeling anger toward Mozart, Salieri comes to place Mozart in a class with himself: victim of God's vindictiveness. "Don't pity me. Pity yourself," Salieri says to Father Vogler and then continues:

> You serve a wicked God. He killed Mozart, not I. . . . He destroyed His beloved rather than let a mediocrity like me get the smallest share in his glory. He doesn't care. . . God cares nothing for the man He denies and nothing either for the man He uses. He broke Mozart in half when He'd finished with him. Like an old, worn out flute.

Throughout most of his life, Salieri believes himself to be a devout man. In truth, however, his piety is not faith at all. A man of faith is supposed to accept God's will, but Salieri wants to bend God's will to his own. Once things cease to go as he wishes, he acts like a spoiled child: if he does not get what he wants, he pouts and becomes angry, throwing his crucifix on the fire.

Salieri's telling his story to Father Vogler is like a religious confession: afterward, Salieri seems lighter. He is pushed down the hall in his wheelchair, calling out benedictions to the other inmates of the asylum. However, this does not mean that Salieri's faith in God has been restored. Instead, he declares firmly that he is the patron saint of mediocrities and that though God "may forgive me: I shall never forgive Him."

Source: Kristen Sarlin Greenberg, Critical Essay on *Amadeus*, in *Drama for Students*, Gale, Cengage Learning, 2017.

Charles P. Mitchell

In the following excerpt, Mitchell offers both fact and speculation about the circumstances surrounding Mozart's death and analyzes the film.

. . . *Amadeus* is the only composer's film to win an Academy Award for Best Motion Picture, an honor it fully deserves as a spellbinding work that rates with the best. Lavishly filmed in Prague, *Amadeus* recreates the late eighteenth century with meticulous detail, with magnificent costumes, brilliant cinematography and exceptional art direction. It is not, nor was it ever intended to be, an accurate biopic of Mozart. The author of the screenplay and the original 1979 play, Peter Shaffer, is the first to point this out, admitting that he blends actual events into his story with fantastic invention, taking his inspiration from the 1830 verse drama by Pushkin. It should also be pointed out that despite the title, the film is actually about Antonio Salieri.

Shaffer uses his artistic license masterfully in his script which is extraordinarily faithful to Mozart's music so that not a single note of his or Salieri's music is altered. The general outline of events is followed in broad strokes, although the details may be significantly changed. Mozart's son Karl appears in the story, for example, but his second son Franz Xaver (born July 1791) is eliminated. Shaffer had to alter part of the career of Salieri, who spent much of his time during the 1780s not in Vienna as court composer, but rather in Rome, Milan and Paris. Although he first became involved with the Viennese court in 1774, it wasn't until 1788 that he was named Kapellmeister, a position he then held for over thirty-five years. However, Shaffer had to show Salieri as the central music figure at the court when Mozart arrived in Vienna in 1781 for purposes of his story.

There are numerous other examples of Shaffer's sleight of hand with historical fact, but his storytelling is so compelling that further nitpicking is superfluous. Shaffer simply combines the *Requiem* and Salieri myths in brilliant fashion, making his drama a universal parable of talent, inspiration, genius, desire, jealousy and divine providence. Some have interpreted the plot as a disguised version of Cain and Able from the Bible. Shaffer is matched by the directorial genius of Milos Forman and the acting prowess of a superlative cast from stars F. Murray Abraham and Tom Hulce, brilliant character roles by Jeffrey Jones as the emperor and Simon

Callow as Emanuel Schikaneder to remarkable vignettes by Vincent Schiavelli as Salieri's valet, Kenny Baker as the parody Commendatore and Miroslav Sekera as Mozart at age seven. F. Murray Abraham won an Academy Award for his dazzling portrayal of Salieri.

Hulce's reading of Mozart is vibrant. A few had questioned the validity, but Mozart's earliest biographers had described his sometimes childlike nature. His infectious silly laugh (Hulce's trademark) was mentioned in contemporary documents, and his vulgarity and crude bathroom humor can be found in the composer's letters. Incidentally, Salieri is also provided with a distinctive laugh, patterned after Vincent Price's sinister chuckle in *The Abominable Dr. Phibes* (1971). Hulce brings the character of Mozart to life in an unforgettable way. Only the briefest synopsis is needed since the film is so well known. The elderly Salieri, after a suicide attempt in 1824, tells his confession to a priest. He describes his resentment of Mozart, whom he sees as a petulant and ignoble character inexplicably graced with divine and effortless talent. Salieri alone recognizes the voice of God in Mozart's music, a quality he desperately wants. Feeling cheated by God because of his own mediocre abilities, Salieri vows to destroy Mozart. When he notices that his rival is afraid of his father, Leopold, he decides to capitalize on this fear. After Leopold dies, Salieri rents a costume and mask identical to one worn by the elder Mozart at a masquerade party and commissions a *Requiem* from the composer. Initially, he plans to save the piece and pass it off as his own after he kills Mozart. However, as Salieri sees it, God steps in and kills Mozart Himself with a sudden illness, depriving Salieri of his grand design to pass off the *Requiem* as his own. (In real life, Salieri did compose a requiem in 1804, one of his last major works.) This confession apparently undermines the faith of the young priest. Salieri celebrates this "victory" by proclaiming himself the patron saint of mediocrity.

The music in the film is highlighted throughout in splendid fashion. Even the few Salieri opera excerpts have an unexpected allure. There are numerous examples of the unusual prominence of the music. Salieri's poetic analysis of the adagio movement from Mozart's *Serenade for Wind Instruments in E Flat Major* is incomparable. When Salieri reviews the manuscripts brought to him by Constanze, the soundtrack lets us hear the music Salieri is reading, including excerpts from Mozart's *Concerto for Flute and Harp in C Major*, his *Concerto for Two Pianos in E Flat Major*, his *Symphony No. 29* and the "Kyrie" from his *Mass in C Minor*.

The greatest use of the music, and perhaps the finest composing scene in all cinema, is when the dying Mozart dictates the "Confutatis Maledictis" from his *Requiem* to Salieri. This scene, partially improvised, has Mozart describing the various components of the music, and the soundtrack lets the audience hear each component part as it is narrated. The effect, when all the elements are heard together (chorus, horns, strings and kettledrums), is overwhelming in its intensity.

The operatic excerpts, choreographed by Twyla Tharp, are truly sublime. The climax of *Don Giovanni*, when the statue of the Commendatore comes to life to drag the Don to hell, is magnificent and even breathtaking. In addition, this scene was filmed on the stage of the National Theater in Prague, where Mozart himself had conducted the premiere performance of *Don Giovanni* in October 1787. Hulce and Abraham, moreover, are fully convincing in their scenes in which they conduct, appropriate to the style of the era. Even though the music was dubbed in later, Hulce's performances at the keyboard (while held upside down in one scene) are so impressive that it is surprising to learn that he never played the piano before he was cast in the role of Mozart.

The lengthier director's cut of *Amadeus* has appeared on video recently. Salieri appears even more villainous in this version. In one scene, he induces Constanze to strip and then has his servant toss her out. There are also some light-hearted scenes in the expanded version, such as when Mozart performs for a wealthy new pupil, but finds his playing disrupted by the rich patron's dogs. On the whole, the expanded version is interesting but does not improve on the original *Amadeus*, which is a virtually perfect film in its original version. *Amadeus* may be one of the most influential films of the 1980s, serving to introduce countless viewers to Mozart and his music and even influencing a fashion craze for paisley that appeared shortly after the film's release....

Source: Charles P. Mitchell, "Wolfgang Amadeus Mozart," in *The Great Composers Portrayed on Film, 1913 through 2002*, McFarland, 2004, pp. 141–44.

IN THE BEGINNING OF THE PLAY SALIERI HAS
SUMMONED UP THE AUDIENCE JUST AS IF HE WERE
INVOKING THE GODS. IN THE END, HE REVERSES THE
SITUATION AND TREATS THE AUDIENCE AS
MEDIOCRITIES. HE DIMINISHES THE WORLD
AROUND HIM AND PARTAKES OF THE GREATEST
ILLUSION OF ALL."

Paul Rosefeldt

*In the following excerpt, Rosefeldt discusses how
the search for absent fathers represents the search
for God in Shaffer's play.*

...Salieri's nemesis is Mozart, Amadeus
Mozart, God's beloved. Yet Mozart is more
than a foil for Salieri. Hinden believes that
"Mozart is Salieri's rival, not his double." But in
many ways both men are doomed by the search to
appease and reject the absent father. According to
Berman, "Both men display deep disappointment
toward their fathers. Salieri's rage toward God
parallels Mozart's aggression toward Leopold."
Both men also connect the father to a godlike
projection. Londre finds "Both Mozart and Salieri's attitudes toward God were apparently shaped
by their relationships with their fathers. As the
son of a merchant, Salieri tried to make a deal
with God. Mozart served as an instrument first of
his father and ultimately with God." Mozart, like
Salieri, is bound to the absent father. Sullivan
notes "Leopold Mozart, although he never
appears in propia persona in the play, exercises
from the distance of Salzburg, and from even
farther off after his physical death, an almost
complete control over Mozart's emotional and
psychological being."

Leopold is depicted as a "bad-tempered
Salzburg musician" who made Mozart "play
the keyboard blindfolded with one finger." He
has dominated Mozart, yet Leopold has spoiled
Mozart too. When Mozart's music is not ingenious, Salieri labels him "Leopold's swanky
son—nothing more." Moreover, the father still
controls Mozart who waits for Leopold's consent to marry. Constanze tells Mozart that he
would not marry without his father's consent:

"You're too scared of him." Repeating the
words of the absent father, Constanze pronoun-
ces the father's curse: "If you marry that dreadful girl, you'll end up lying on straw with beggars
for children." He marries without his father's
consent and carries out the father's prophecy.
Ailing and impoverished, he later tells Constanze, "Papa was right. We end exactly as he
said. Beggars." Thus, Mozart fulfills the father's
prophecy.

Like Salieri, Mozart, too, lives in a wasteland. He is told that his music has "too many
notes"; his operas are all given minimal performances; he cannot get enough pupils to support
himself. When he loses the position as tutor to
Princess Elizabeth, the voice of the father speaks
to him. "My father always writes I should be
more obedient. Know My Place." Yet Mozart
cannot accept his place among the mediocrities
of the court. Even when he is given a position, he
does not get enough money to support himself.
Eventually, Mozart, the darling of Europe, finds
himself dying in a slum.

Mozart ends up regressing more and more
into a childhood world from which he cannot
extricate himself. His wife Constanze says about
Leopold "He kept you a baby all your life." In the
end, Mozart and Constanze are reduced to playing nonsense games in which Mozart's endearments move from "pussy-wussy" to "Pappy" to
"Pappa-Pappa," echoing Papageno's lines in *The
Magic Flute*. Mozart's signs of affection become
the child's call to his absent father. Even as father
of a child, Mozart is "a baby himself."

Unlike Salieri, who could manipulate the substitute fathers, Mozart can only alienate them.
Like his father, Mozart is "a little stubborn." He
cannot control his mouth, calling Salieri a "musical
idiot" and labeling the Emperor "Kaiser Keepit"
for his stinginess. He knows that he should control
his mouth. He remarks "I shouldn't have said that,
should I...Forgive me. It was just a joke." Rebelling against his father, he is not able to hold to his
father's advice: "My father's right. He always tells
me I should padlock my mouth." He attacks the
Italian court musicians as "Foppy wops," which he
converts to "Foppy Poppy," seeing them as negative father figures.

Sullivan notes that the closest figure to
Mozart's father is Van Swieten who tries to
help and advise Mozart, getting him fugues to
arrange and supplying him with donations from
brother Masons. When Van Swieten chides

Mozart for writing vulgar farces, Mozart hears the voice of his father. Van Swieten says, "When I reproved him, he said I reminded him of his father." In the end, Mozart alienates Van Swieten by revealing the secrets of the Masons in *The Magic Flute*. Sullivan notes about Van Swieten that "the parallels with Leopold ... the provider, the restrainer, and the wounded progenitor, are clear." In the end "Leopold/Van Swieten is [Mozart's] 'candle-smoked' God." Mozart, like Salieri, is trapped in the world of the absent father. Salieri is driven mad because he cannot form "adequate relationships with authority figures (whether his middle class 'God of Bargains' or the Emperor Joseph II, whom he so obligingly serves) ... Mozart suffers a similar fate rebelling against the very authorities upon whom he most depends" (Morace).

The power of the absent father over both men is seen most distinctly in Salieri's self-destructive attempt to destroy Mozart. Salieri seeks revenge on the Father God by trying to eliminate God's creature. Obsessed with rage against the father, he wants to murder the father by killing the son. The Transcendent Father is absent, but his creature provides an adequate substitute. Salieri easily finds Mozart's weakness in his relationship with his father Leopold. When Mozart's father would not grant consent for his marriage, Salieri, the father surrogate says, "My advice to you is to marry and be happy." When Mozart believes that Salieri has gotten him a court post, he begs Salieri's forgiveness just as he would beg his father's forgiveness. He tells Salieri "Oh forgive me! You're a good man."

Mozart, the rebel son, accuses his father: "He's a bitter man, of course. After he finished showing me off around Europe, he never went anywhere himself. He just stayed in Salzburg ... kissing the ring of the fart bishop." Mozart confesses "He's jealous ... He'll never forgive me for being cleverer than he is ... Leopold Mozart is just a jealous dried up old turd." When Mozart describes his father to Salieri, he could just as well be speaking of Salieri, for it is Salieri who is a "bitter man," a man who plays up to the Emperor the way Leopold does to the bishop. It is Salieri who is "jealous" and who will "never forgive [Mozart] for being cleverer than he is." Salieri and Leopold are one. When Leopold dies, Mozart proclaims "There's no one else. No one who understands the wickedness around me. I can't see it." Salieri, of course, is the one who has been watching Mozart, and Salieri is the one who

sees the wickedness. Tormented by guilt at his betrayal of the father, Mozart yells in pain "Oh God," then Salieri says "Lean on me" and "opens his arms in a wide gesture of paternal benevolence." Mozart does not accept the embrace, but calls out "Papa." Salieri links Mozart's father to the Ghost Father in *Don Giovanni*. This absent father appears on the backdrop "a giant black figure in cloak and tricorn hat" who "extends its arms menacingly and engulfingly toward its begetter."

Salieri sees Mozart haunted by the grey figure of the angry father, but he also beholds the other side of the father in the High Priest in *The Magic Flute*: "I saw his father! No more an accusing figure but forgiving ... the highest priest of the Order ... his hand extended to the world in love." But Salieri tries to get beyond the forgiving father, and masked as the figure in grey, haunts Mozart. Mozart is writing a Requiem for the father, but in the father he sees God, the Father. He tells Salieri, who is masked as the Death Father, "God can't want it unfinished ... Here's the Kyrie ... Take that to Him ... He'll see it's not unworthy." Mozart even repudiates his former work and says "I've written nothing finally good!" The scene is overdetermined with the presence of the absent father. Salieri, who is battling with the absent Father God, is dressed like the Ghost Father in *Don Giovanni*, who is a representation of Mozart's father Leopold. Mozart sees Salieri as the avenging father figure representing God, the Father, who is a projection of Mozart's father. Because of his need for forgiveness, Mozart gives the Father God the Kyrie, a plea for mercy and absolution. Speaking for God, the Father. Salieri tells Mozart "God does not love you Amadeus ... He can only use. You are no use to him any more."

Both Salieri and Mozart are united under the power of the absent father. Moreover, Salieri eats Mozart's music in a mock communion and says "We are both poisoned, Amadeus. I with you: you with me." Mozart, however, regresses to a child and sees Salieri as his father: "Take me Papa. Take me. Put down your arms and I'll hop into them. Just as we used to do ... Hold me close to you Papa. Let's sing our kissing song together." Mozart, like many a lost son, wants to escape into a childhood paradise. He returns to the father as a child. Salieri destroys Mozart but cannot destroy Mozart's music. In one last desperate attempt, he tries to gain immortality by making people believe he is Mozart's murderer. But the people only see him as "a deluded old man." Just as Mozart grows infantile, Salieri becomes senile. Mozart escapes to a childhood world that is forever in the lost past while Salieri creates an illusory future that can never be.

In the beginning of the play Salieri has summoned up the audience just as if he were invoking the gods. In the end, he reverses the situation and treats the audience as mediocrities. He diminishes the world around him and partakes of the greatest illusion of all. Instead of being a servant of God, he becomes like God with the power to absolve the sins of mediocrities, not only in the present, but for all time. He proclaims "Mediocrities everywhere...now and to come...I absolve you all. Amen!" In the pastoral gesture "He extends his arms upward and outward to embrace the assembled audience in a wide gesture of benediction." The deluded Salieri, as he did with Mozart, extends the embrace of the father in an attempt to become the Father.

Amadeus is a play about the search for an absent father and the need to be his chosen son. Both Mozart and Salieri begin life in a protected world of the father. Mozart is a pampered and spoiled young man. In the world of harsh realities, Mozart cannot understand why the paternal paradise has vanished: "Once the world was so full, so happy...Everyone smiled at me once...the king of Schonbrunn; the princess at Versailles—they lit my way...my father bowing...with such joy! 'Chevalier Mozart, my miraculous son!'" Mozart asks, "Why has it all gone?...Why?...Was I so bad? So wicked?...Answer for Him and tell me." Mozart questions God and asks Him what sins he has committed to deserve the loss of paradise. His only hope is to regress into an infantile state and join the father.

Salieri also starts out in the protected world of the court, enjoys success, and achieves fame, but he knows he is not the chosen son and cannot achieve immortality. Like Mozart, he questions God, for he believes he has done everything he can do to appease God, the Father. Like Mozart, he too finds himself disillusioned and escapes to the father through an illusion. He becomes not only "the Patron Saint of Mediocrities" but assumes God's power to forgive and absolve the human race, once and for all time. In a last gesture he folds "his arms high across his own breast," a gesture of "self-sanctification." In the end, both men are destroyed by their obsession with an absent and elusive father.

Source: Paul Rosefeldt, "Battling with God, the Father: Peter Shaffer's *Amadeus*," in *The Absent Father in Modern Drama*, Peter Lang, 1995, pp. 102–105.

SOURCES

"After an Attempt: A Guide for Taking Care of Your Family Member after Treatment in the Emergency Department," http://www.suicidepreventionlifeline.org/app_files/media/pdf/lifeline_afteranattempt_forfamily-members.pdf (accessed July 6, 2016).

Altizer, Katherine Rebecca Carter, "From the Courts to the Marketplace: The Evolution of Viennese Musical Patronage c. 1740–c. 1831," master's thesis, West Virginia University, 2009, http://pqdtopen.proquest.com/doc/305032512.html?FMT = AI (accessed July 5, 2016).

Amadeus, directed by Milos Forman, Warner Home Video, 1984.

Berardinelli, James, Review of *Amadeus*, in *Reelviews Movie Reviews*, http://www.reelviews.net/reelviews/amadeus (accessed July 5, 2016).

Canby, Vincent, Review of *Amadeus*, in *New York Times*, September 19, 1984, http://www.nytimes.com/movie/review?res = 9901E1DE173BF93AA2575AC0A962948260? (accessed July 5, 2016).

Ebert, Roger, Review of *Amadeus*, RogerEbert.com, http://www.rogerebert.com/reviews/great-movie-amadeus-1984 (accessed July 5, 2016).

Eggert, Brian, Review of *Amadeus*, in *Deep Focus Review*, March 24, 2012, http://www.deepfocusreview.com/reviews/amadeus.asp (accessed July 5, 2016).

"Emanuel Schikaneder," in *Encyclopædia Britannica*, https://www.britannica.com/biography/Emanuel-Schikaneder (accessed July 7, 2016).

Hanning, Barbara Russano, "The Late Eighteenth Century: Haydn and Mozart," in *Concise History of Western Music*, 3rd ed., W. W. Norton, 2006.

"Joseph II," Biography.com, http://www.biography.com/people/joseph-ii-9358214 (accessed July 6, 2016).

Kakutani, Michiko, "How *Amadeus* Was Translated from Play to Film," in *New York Times*, September 16, 1984, http://www.nytimes.com/1984/09/16/movies/how-amadeus-wastranslated-from-play-to-film.html?pagewanted = all (accessed July 7, 2016).

Keefe, Simon P., "Beyond Fact and Fiction, Scholarly and Popular: Peter Shaffer and Milos Forman's *Amadeus* at 25," in *Musical Times*, Vol. 150, No. 1906, Spring 2009, pp. 45–53.

Nathan, Ian, Review of *Amadeus*, in *Empire*, http://www.empireonline.com/movies/amadeus/review (accessed July 5, 2016).

Shaffer, Peter, *Amadeus*, in Internet Movie Script Database (IMSDb), http://www.imsdb.com/scripts/Amadeus.html (accessed July 29, 2016).

Shariatmadari, David, "My Favourite Film: *Amadeus*," in *Guardian*, https://www.theguardian.com/film/2011/dec/20/my-favourite-film-amadeus (accessed July 5, 2016).

FURTHER READING

Abert, Hermann, *W. A. Mozart*, translated by Stewart Spencer, edited by Cliff Eisen, Yale University Press, 2007.

    Abert's astonishingly thorough biography was originally published in German in 1917 but was not translated into English until this 2007 edition. Abert provides a detailed look at Mozart's life, including his personality, his family, his views on religion, and much more. Abert also gives insightful analysis of the composer's work. Meticulous annotation by Eisen adds information discovered about Mozart since the original version of the work.

Braunbehrens, Volkmar, *Maligned Master: The Real Story of Antonio Salieri*, Fromm International Publishing Corporation, 1993.

    In this biography, Braunbehrens sets out to prove that theories of Salieri's envy of Mozart are ridiculous. Braunbehrens provides detailed historical evidence that Salieri's position in the Vienna court and the music world was well established. Salieri wrote more than forty operas, and his students included Beethoven, Liszt, and Schubert. Braunbehrens presents a strong case that Salieri would have had no reason to feel threatened by another composer, even one as talented as Mozart.

Mitchell, Charles P., *The Great Composers Portrayed on Film, 1913 through 2002*, McFarland, 2004.

    In addition to a comprehensive overview of both fictionalized films and documentaries about composers, Mitchell offers brief biographies.

Pushkin, Aleksandr, *Mozart and Salieri: The Little Tragedies*, 2nd ed., translated by A. Wood, Angel Books, 1987.

    Originally written in 1830 and published in 1832, this short play is written in verse. Some consider Pushkin's *Little Tragedies* to be the best example of blank verse in all of Russian literature. *Mozart and Salieri* is the only one of Pushkin's plays that was produced while he was alive.

SUGGESTED SEARCH TERMS

Wolfgang Amadeus Mozart AND Antonio Salieri

Peter Shaffer AND film adaptations

Amadeus AND historical accuracy

Amadeus AND Academy Awards

film techniques AND Amadeus

eighteenth-century composers

Milos Forman AND films

biographical films

BFE

JULIA CHO
2005

BFE is a comedic play by Julia Cho, who uses dark humor to address serious subjects. In this work, Cho blends humor with surrealism in a coming-of-age story in which the main character is surrounded by danger and murder. The play was first produced in 2005. Set in the Arizona desert, *BFE* is one of Cho's desert plays and is based on the author's adolescence. The title is a slang expression referring to the middle of nowhere or the boondocks. One of Cho's earlier works, the play examines the theme of isolation and the effects of an image-obsessed society on people who do not meet cultural standards of beauty. *BFE* was published by Dramatists Play Service in 2006.

AUTHOR BIOGRAPHY

Cho was born in 1975 in Los Angeles, California, the child of Korean immigrants. The family moved to Arizona when she was twelve and lived there until she was sixteen, according to her interview with Sung Rno in *American Theater*. The landscape of the Arizona desert became a setting for several of her early plays, including *BFE*, because these years were, she tells Rno, "*the* most impressionable period of adolescence."

Cho developed a love of theater as a teenager, but she did not immediately pursue a career in the theater. She graduated from Amherst

Julia Cho with actress Jayne Houdyshell.
(© WENN Ltd | Alamy Stock Photo)

College in 1996 with a bachelor of arts degree in English. She went on to earn a master's degree in English literature from the University of California, Berkeley and then completed a master of fine arts degree at New York University. She was a 2001–2002 Lila Acheson Wallace American Playwright fellow at the Juilliard School. During the fellowship, Cho wrote *99 Histories* and *BFE*. The New York Theater Workshop commissioned *BFE* in 2001, but the play was not produced until 2005, following the 2004 premiere of *The Architecture of Loss. Durango* followed in 2006. These three plays all take place in the Arizona desert.

Cho continued writing popular plays, including *The Piano Teacher* in 2007 and *The Language Archive* in 2010. *The Language Archive* won the Susan Smith Blackburn Prize. Along with full productions, Cho wrote one-act plays, such as *How to Be a Good Son* in 2004 and *First Tree in America* in 2007. Cho also wrote for television series, including *Big Love*, *Fringe*, and *Betrayal*.

After taking a break from playwriting for a few years, Cho returned to the theater with the completion of the plays *Aubergine* and *Office Hour* in 2016. As of 2010, Cho was living in Los Angeles with her husband.

PLOT SUMMARY

BFE is a one-act play composed of twenty-four scenes. It is set in Arizona in the 1990s.

Scene 1
Panny, a fourteen-year-old Korean American girl, begins a monologue. She explains that she lives in a small, boring town but that strange things do happen. For example, her friend sees a UFO. The friend's mother is looking the other way and misses seeing it. Also, someone is taking girls to the desert and killing them. Rumors spread about what has happened to Panny in the desert, but they depend on perspective. Panny takes the audience back one month. She has just started high school, and that day at school there was a moment of silence for a recently murdered student.

Scene 2
Panny is in Walgreens reading fashion magazines. Her friend Nancy is working at the store. Nancy is blonde and fifteen years old. She scolds Panny for creasing the magazines and reminds her that there is a curfew. Panny asks Nancy to go to Denny's with her after work, and she mentions that the restaurant will give her a free meal. Panny subtly hints that it is her birthday. Nancy, however, has plans with her boyfriend. Panny learns that Nancy is sexually active. When Nancy is not looking, Panny sees the Man steal a Walkman music player. She tries to tell Nancy, but Nancy is annoyed with her, and she stays silent.

Scene 3
Panny is at home when her uncle Lefty enters the house. She is surprised to see him, and he tells her that someone has asked him to trade work shifts. Having convinced her that he has forgotten her birthday, Lefty surprises Panny with a cake. Isabel, Panny's mother, enters and asks about the cake. Isabel has obviously forgotten about Panny's birthday, and she says the wrong age when she claims that she has a gift. Lefty

gives Panny a pair of earrings, and Isabel offers her plastic surgery.

Scene 4

Panny explains the term *unheimlich* in a monologue. The term suggests that something known becomes odd. Her mother had plastic surgery years earlier, and Panny thinks she looks beautiful but disturbing. Isabel has not left the house since undergoing the procedure.

Panny brings dinner to Isabel's room. Isabel is watching the news about the murdered girls. She says that there is no need to worry about Panny because the murdered girls were beautiful blondes. She asks Panny what surgery she wants and suggests doing her nose or her eyes. Isabel informs Panny that beauty is a choice that requires sacrifice.

Scene 5

Panny defines the term *doppelgänger* in a monologue. Hae-Yoon, Panny's Korean pen pal through school, gives a monologue, which is her letter to Panny. She loves the idea of America and asks Panny to call her Elizabeth. She loves Coke and asks Panny if her hair is blonde.

Panny is in the basement with Lefty, who is working on his Dungeons and Dragons figurines. Panny is considering her response to Hae-Yoon. She is unhappy about having an Asian pen pal. Lefty asks Panny why she does not wear the earrings he gave her, and she reminds him that she does not have pierced ears. Lefty is against Panny's having plastic surgery, calling it immature. Panny jokes about his hobby, and Lefty says that he wants her to be happy and that the teen years are the best.

Scene 6

Lefty goes to the jewelry counter in the mall where he works to return Panny's earrings. Evvie is reading a book and tells him to wait. As she makes the return, she talks about the self-help book she is reading, *How to Make the Most of Your Hidden Talent*. She tells him that her talent is the ability to see color. He decides that he is good with his hands.

Scene 7

Hae-Yoon responds to Panny's letter. She is disappointed that Panny is Asian American, and she does not understand the term that Panny has used to describe the middle of nowhere. She wants to teach English one day with American movies. Hae-Yoon has had surgery on her eyes, like many of her friends. She may have surgery done on her legs because her mother does not like their shape. She also sends Panny a packet of her favorite gum.

Scene 8

Panny dials the phone from her bed and asks for Nancy after Hugo picks up. He calls her back after she accidentally calls the wrong number again and hangs up on him. He persuades her to talk, and they begin a friendship. She learns that he is twenty years old, and she tells him that she is eighteen. Hugo is a Mormon, and his father died when he was young. Panny's father left before she was born. Hugo persuades her to share a secret. She says that she once saw her reflection and looked beautiful even though she knows that she is not. Hugo confesses that he likes her voice better than the voice of any other woman.

Scene 9

Panny brings Isabel food on a tray. Isabel says that keeping up with the news has made her hungry. Panny asks what Isabel is watching and discovers that it is a documentary about World War II. After Panny leaves, Isabel fantasizes about romance with General Douglas MacArthur, who confesses his love and calls her beautiful.

Scene 10

In the mall, Evvie reads a self-help book to Lefty. He gives her a miniature he made. She asks what the character is and if she can keep her. Lefty tells her that it is a healer and that he made it for her.

Scene 11

Panny and Hugo are talking on the phone. She describes her bedroom in detail and tells him she is in bed. They pretend to be in bed together, but Hugo gets in bed with her on stage. She tells him that she is afraid he will not like her once he sees her. He tells her that he genuinely cares about her, and she abruptly hangs up the phone.

Scene 12

Lefty and Evvie are eating at the food court in the mall. He is wearing a tie Evvie has borrowed from the store. He asks if they are on a date, and she says she has not been on a date in more than ten years. She is forty years old and has a grown daughter. Lefty tells her that the only thing in his life besides his home with his sister and her daughter is his role-playing game. He tells her that she is a unique African American woman. When she asks why, he responds that she likes him. They agree to go on a date after work.

Scene 13

Lefty comes home and orders a pizza. Isabel tells him that the murderer is still at large, but Lefty is not paying attention. He is eager to change and leave. Isabel is upset when Lefty gives her money for the pizza and says he is going out with friends. Isabel tells him to change his plans because she wants a family dinner. She reminds him that they have only each other. Lefty leaves, but Isabel cannot follow him past the front door. She finds the book *How to Start Living for Yourself* in his uniform pocket.

Scene 14

Panny is talking to Hugo on the phone. He keeps trying to persuade her to set up a time and a place to meet him. She is nervous and finds an excuse to avoid each suggestion. He ends the conversation by telling her that he will be at Walgreens in an hour if she wants to meet him.

Scene 15

Panny and Isabel share the stage, but neither one can see the other in the house. Panny is reading a magazine and following its instructions for applying makeup. Isabel recalls how she was determined not to be like her mother and how she created rules to make herself fascinating to men. Isabel recites her rules as Panny reads and follows the instructions. Panny runs into difficulty when she realizes that she does not have a crease in her eyelids. Panny finishes her makeup and decides to meet Hugo. Isabel fantasizes about General MacArthur again when the doorbell rings. Jack, played by the same actor who plays MacArthur, is standing in the doorway with the pizza.

Scene 16

Lefty is at Evvie's home and sees a picture of her daughter. Evvie tells him that she is divorced and that her daughter is in college. Lefty says that he has never married because he has been busy taking care of Isabel and Panny. He and Isabel were adopted, and their family was not sure what to do about them. The two have never felt that they fit in anywhere. Lefty tells Evvie that he feels as if he fits with her. She tries to teach him how to read her aura, and as he looks at her, he tells her that he loves her. He asks if he can stay, and she says yes.

Scene 17

Panny is at Walgreens. When Hugo enters, he does not pay any attention to her. She says his name, but he does not hear her. Nancy sees Panny and says that she is leaving work early. She informs Panny that she has broken up with her boyfriend, and then she sees Hugo. Nancy talks to Hugo and persuades him to give her a ride home. She introduces Panny as her friend, but he does not acknowledge her. Nancy calls Panny by name as they leave, and Hugo laughs at Panny, accusing her of playing a joke.

The Man talks to Panny about the price of water as he fills up a container. When she cries, he gives her a handkerchief and attempts to comfort her. He asks her to help him bring the water to his car. Panny tells the audience that she later remembers seeing him steal the Walkman, but she does not recall this when she goes to his car.

Scene 18

Isabel pretends that she cannot find the money for the pizza as Jack waits inside. She offers him a drink, and he sees the cash on the table. Isabel attempts to seduce him, but Jack thinks that it is a joke. He apologizes when he realizes she is sincere, and they share the pizza.

Scene 19

Panny is in the desert with the Man. He offers her his jacket, but she declines. He tells her that she has sneaked out of the house, and no one knows she is gone. Panny reminds him that she is not his type, and he admits that he was stalking Nancy. He has taken Panny only because she was convenient. He gives her a blonde wig and tells her to wear it. She begins crying.

Scene 20

Lefty and Evvie are thrilled that he is moving in with her. He plans to get his things and stay only long enough to tell Panny where he is going. He tells Evvie that she will love Panny and assumes that Panny will move in with them one day. Evvie, however, does not want to be a mother again. Lefty tells her that he wants a family of his own, and they realize that they are at an impasse.

Scene 21

Jack and Isabel are in her living room. He is afraid of losing his job and hurries to leave. Isabel wants him to stay and asks him when he will return. Jack says that he will get her number from work and call her later. He calls her

Mirabel as he leaves, and she follows him to the door asking how he can call if he does not know her name. After Jack leaves, the fantasy of General MacArthur also departs.

Scene 22

Panny and the Man are still in the desert. She is wearing the wig. He asks her if she has been kissed, and she tells him she has not. He kisses her. When he leans in to kiss her again, the action stops. She tells the audience that she has gouged his eyes and run away.

Hae-Yoon interrupts and tells her that she has not escaped, that Panny is saying what she wishes had happened. Hae-Yoon goes on to explain that it is safe to get into a stranger's car in Korea but that everyone knows it is dangerous in America. She brings up *The Silence of the Lambs* before reminding Panny that she has only made the Man angry.

The action continues, and the Man pushes Panny down before a fade. Panny tells the audience that the Man has beaten her but left her alive because she is not beautiful. She knows because he has carved the word *ugly* on her.

Scene 23

Panny reads her letter to Hae-Yoon, whom she addresses as Elizabeth. She tells her that she has had plastic surgery on her eyes. They are covered in gauze, and she is wearing dark glasses. She goes on to talk about a dream. There are round blue birds that resemble water balloons, and she pokes them.

Panny asks for water so she can take her pain medication, and Hugo knocks. He comes in and gives Panny flowers. Nancy figured out what happened to Panny, and told Hugo where to find her. He asks about her eyes, and she tells him that she chose the surgery. She goes on to say that she meant what she said, and he tells her that he knows. Hugo gives Panny her water and leaves without saying goodbye. She cries and tells Lefty not to look at her.

Scene 24

Hae-Yoon responds to Panny's letter, saying that it was gloomy. She has decided to cheer up Panny with pictures of her fat dog and music from her favorite Korean group. She also tells a joke about a cow falling down a hill, but she admits it is better in Korean. Hae-Yoon ends by

reminding Panny that she is in America, so life cannot be terrible.

Panny, Lefty, and Isabel are watching television together. The phone rings, and no one answers it.

CHARACTERS

Elizabeth

See Hae-Yoon.

Evvie

Evvie is a forty-year-old African American woman who works at the same mall as Lefty. She always reads self-help books, and she develops a relationship with Lefty. Evvie is divorced and has a daughter in college. She likes Lefty, but they want different things in a relationship.

Hae-Yoon

Hae-Yoon is Panny's pen pal in Korea, but she wants to be called Elizabeth. Like Panny, she is fourteen. She loves Coca-Cola and all things American. She embraces plastic surgery and hopes to teach English by using American movies.

Hugo

Hugo is a twenty-year-old Mormon college student who develops a relationship with Panny after she accidentally dials his number. He tells Panny that he cares about her, but he laughs when they meet.

Isabel

Isabel is Panny's mother and Lefty's sister. She is a Korean American and obsessed with beauty. Isabel has had plastic surgery to make herself beautiful, but she is unable to leave the house after her recovery. Isabel is not able to take care of Panny, and she offers her daughter plastic surgery as a birthday gift. Isabel fantasizes about General Douglas MacArthur and seduces the pizza delivery driver, Jack.

Jack

Jack delivers pizza to Isabel. She seduces him, and he calls her the wrong name when he leaves.

Lefty

Lefty is Isabel's older brother and Panny's uncle. He works as a security guard at the mall to take care of the family. His only hobby is playing

Dungeons and Dragons and making figurines for the game. He almost moves in with Evvie, but he wants a family, and she does not.

Man

The Man abducts and murders young blonde women. He stalks Nancy but takes Panny because she is convenient. He does not kill Panny, however, because she is not his type.

General Douglas McArthur

General Douglas MacArthur served in World War II and the Korean War. Isabel has a fantasy romance with him.

Nancy

Nancy is Panny's childhood friend. She is fifteen years old and blonde. Nancy is more interested in dating than in maintaining a friendship with Panny.

Panny

Panny is the fourteen-year-old main character in the play. She is Isabel's daughter and Lefty's niece. She does not know who her father is, and she does not have many friends. She develops a relationship with Hugo on the phone after accidentally calling him. Isabel offers Panny plastic surgery, but Panny does not immediately accept it. After Hugo rejects her and she is abducted, Panny has plastic surgery on her eyes.

THEMES

Beauty

The theme of beauty dominates *BFE*. For example, the girls found dead in the desert are considered beautiful. They are young, thin, and blonde, the symbols of Western beauty standards. Isabel tells Panny that they were pretty and says that she does not have to worry about Panny's being abducted. This statement indicates that Isabel does not consider Panny beautiful. She also offers Panny plastic surgery as a birthday gift and pressures her to have her nose or eyes operated on.

Isabel has undergone plastic surgery years before the action of the play. Panny says that she looks beautiful, but the change makes Panny want to run from her. Isabel considers the attainment of beauty both a sacrifice and a goal. She says, "True beauty is an act of will." Isabel does

not leave the house after she recovers from the plastic surgery.

Hae-Yoon also undergoes plastic surgery on her eyes, like many of the other girls she knows in Korea. It makes her happy that plastic surgery can help her be beautiful. Panny struggles with her own self-image throughout the play. She confesses that she has seen herself as beautiful just for one moment, but in the end she, too, chooses to undergo surgery on her eyes.

The pursuit of physical perfection dictated by society does not bring any character a sense of connection or authenticity. Isabel has agoraphobia, and Hae-Yoon must undergo more surgery to become acceptable to a mother who thinks she has fat legs. Being perceived as physically beautiful does not help anyone, particularly the girls found in the desert.

Isolation

The title *BFE* refers to the middle of nowhere. In the isolated landscape of the desert, Panny's family members face their isolation. Lefty and Isabel have a sense of isolation that spans their entire lives. They have been adopted as children, and Lefty hints that the people who adopted them were not Korean. Brother and sister depend on each other because no one else has understood them. Isabel tells Lefty, "It will always *be* just you and me." The siblings' separation from the world around them continues into their adult lives.

Isabel never leaves the house after undergoing plastic surgery, fully isolating herself. She does not even connect with her family. She forgets Panny's birthday and takes her meals in her room. Isabel desires a family meal only when Lefty makes plans for dinner. She lives alone with her fantasies of General Douglas MacArthur and her constant monitoring of the murderer loose in her community.

Lefty works to take care of his sister and niece. Although he does leave the house and enjoys a role-playing game, he rarely interacts with other people until he meets Evvie. They have a chance at happiness, but she also isolates herself. She has not dated in ten years, and she is certain that she no longer wants to be part of a family or social group.

Finally, Panny finds herself experiencing the normal feelings of loneliness that many teenagers do, but being a minority in a small town does not help. The only friend she reaches out to is Nancy, but the beautiful blonde has moved on

TOPICS FOR FURTHER STUDY

- Read *Speak*, by Laurie Halse Anderson. This young-adult novel tells the story of Melinda, who suffers in isolation after a traumatic event. Write a short story in which Melinda and Panny converse. How would they meet, and what would they say to each other? Using traditional tools or a computer, illustrate your story and share it with the class.

- Research Korean Americans and the impact they have had on American culture. Create a web page that provides an overview of the history and famous individuals. Be sure to include links to political, scientific, and artistic achievements.

- Read Judith Ortiz's young-adult novel *Call Me Maria*. The story follows the life of Maria as she struggles to find herself after moving from Puerto Rico to New York. Find a partner to work with you. One will create a blog for one of the characters from the novel, and another for a character from *BFE*. Have each character comment on the other's blog posts. Consider what your chosen character would post. How would the character comment and respond? What advice or information can the character provide?

- Research the history of Asian Americans and theater. Who are important figures, and what are some common themes? How have the ideas and themes changed over time? Examine a play by another Asian American playwright, and compare and contrast it with *BFE*. Write an essay that explains how the themes and styles are similar and how they are different.

- Consider consumerism and image in American society, and research the history. Use the information you find to write a report that explains the effects on people, cultures, and the economy. Discuss whether all people are affected and represented equally. Share your paper with the class and discuss your findings as a group. Use a web tool such as easel.ly to create graphics that organize your information and present your findings to the class.

---

since she started dating, leaving Panny alone with a socially awkward uncle and a mother incapable of caring for her. The only connection that Panny manages to make is with Hugo, but the relationship is based on lies.

Society

The play takes place in a small town, but the impact of larger American society is evident. As Korean Americans, Panny's family does not reflect the American ideal. Hae-Yoon, for example, asks if Panny is blonde, and she is disappointed to discover that her pen pal is "not full American." The pressure to fit in and be beautiful is based on Western standards and features, making it impossible for Panny to achieve the goal of fitting in without surgical change.

Hae-Yoon and Isabel have both embraced the idea of undergoing plastic surgery to become beautiful. Panny, however, hesitates when Isabel encourages her to have her eyes done for her birthday. Although she hesitates, Panny does desire to be attractive. In fact, she begins the action in scene 2 by reading fashion magazines and commenting on the models. When Panny attempts to follow a magazine's guides for applying makeup, she discovers that the rules do not apply to her because she has no crease in her eyelids. After her encounter with the Man, Panny chooses to change her eyes.

Judging women on the basis of appearance is prevalent throughout the play. Hugo, who gets to know Panny over the phone, develops feelings for her, but he laughs when he finally sees her. Although their age difference is extreme, he is

The story is set in an Arizona suburb *(© SoleilC | Shutterstock.com)*

comfortable talking to Nancy, who is only a year older than Panny. Clearly, Panny's appearance is less appealing to him than Nancy's.

Societal pressure to fit into a single standard of beauty is damaging for those who cannot achieve it, but it offers no guarantees for those who can. The pretty, blonde Nancy may have an active dating life, but she is being stalked by the Man. Had she left the store alone, he would have killed her as he has the other two girls. Nancy is objectified as any other woman is and is reduced to her appearance.

STYLE

Comedy

BFE is a comedy. It is specifically listed as a dark comedy, as Irene Backalenick pointed out in *New York–Connecticut Theater Scene*. The play has funny moments, such as Hae-Yoon's enthusiasm about Coke and her sarcastic comment to Panny that everyone knows better than to go near a strange car in America. The subject

matter of the comedy, however, is serious, which is what classifies it as a dark comedy.

When Hae-Yoon says, "I could have told you, stupid nut, do not get in guy's car. Haven't you seen *Silence of the Lambs*? . . . I am not even American and I know this. Sheeeesh," Cho uses dark or black humor. Dark humor is an essential part of dark comedy. In *A Handbook to Literature*, William Harmon defines black humor as "the use of the morbid and the absurd for darkly comic purposes." Although her statement is funny, Hae-Yoon makes it when Panny describes a moment of physical danger that she has faced.

Surrealism

Elements of surrealism appear throughout *BFE*. As M. H. Abrams explains in *A Glossary of Literary Terms*, surrealism is an "experiment with free association, a broken syntax, nonlogical and nonchronological order, dreamlike and nightmarish sequences, and the juxtaposition of bizarre, shocking, or seemingly unrelated images." Isabel's fantasies about General Douglas MacArthur are examples of surrealism because her dreams come to life for the audience. Additionally, Panny and Hae-Yoon's argument during Panny's attack is surreal. The conversation alters the chronology and cannot occur because the two girls never see each other.

Monologue

According to Harmon, a monologue gives "the discourse to one speaker." Panny begins with a monologue to the audience, and she has several other monologues throughout the play. Hae-Yoon's letters are also examples of monologues. They are one-sided conversations for the benefit of the audience.

HISTORICAL CONTEXT

Korean Americans and Immigration

In 1902, Korean laborers arrived in Hawaii to work on plantations. According to Marcus Noland in "The Impact of Korean Immigration on the US Economy," this was "the first organized migration to the United States." Noland noted that one hundred thousand people immigrated in 1903. With the growing population of Korean Americans and other minority groups, anti-immigration laws soon followed. Scott Ingram pointed out that California's Webb-Haney Act, also known as the Alien Land Law of 1913. Growing prejudice against Asian Americans led to stricter immigration laws, including the Oriental Exclusion Act, which was part of the Immigration Act of 1924, and brought an end to the first wave of Korean immigration.

The Korean War and its aftermath brought another wave of immigration to the United States. American soldiers brought home Korean spouses, and American families adopted Korean orphans. Arissa Oh points out in the *Journal of American Ethnic History*, "The Refugee Relief Act (RRA) of 1953 provided the first crucial opening for what would develop into large-scale, systematic adoption from Korea." The RRA was created for children of World War II, but it soon extended to children from Korea. When the RRA expired, it was replaced by the Refugee Escape Act of 1957 and subsequent laws that allowed the adoptions to continue. Many of the first adoptees were biracial children of American servicemen, but Americans soon embraced Korean orphans. Many children,

like Isabel and Lefty in *BFE*, were placed in white American homes, where they were separated from their cultural heritage. The adoption of Korean children continued long after the war ended. As Deann Borshay Liem writes in "Adoption History," "the largest number of children were sent overseas after the country had long recovered from war—the 1980s."

The third wave of Korean immigration came with the Immigration and Nationality Act of 1965, also known as the Hart-Celler Act, which "opened the door for greatly expanded immigration from non-European countries," according to Noland. Immigrants were typically educated, and they immigrated with their families. Many of these immigrants became entrepreneurs or worked in professional roles, contributing to the nation's economy.

America in the 1990s

The 1990s was a decade of change. It began with the Persian Gulf War, which was triggered by Iraq's invasion of Kuwait in August 1990 and lasted until early 1991. Also in 1991, the Cold War came to an end when the Soviet Union dissolved. Global changes affected domestic policies. There was a rise in anti-immigration legislative proposals, particularly after the 1993 bombing of the World Trade Center. Many of the lawmakers singled out Mexico in their regulations, but the legislation affected all immigrants. The Illegal Immigration Reform and Immigrant Responsibility Act of 1996 created stricter rules, such as deporting immigrants for misdemeanors. Many Korean Americans opposed the legislation. President Bill Clinton, however, signed it into law.

On a positive note, 1991 saw a weak American economy began to shift. There was a "sustained period of expansion that, as of mid-2000, was the third longest since World War II," according to the *Encyclopedia of the Nations*. Unemployment decreased to 4.5 percent by the end of the decade. President Clinton took office in 1992 and worked to increase the minimum wage from $4.25 to $5.15, according to Richard A. Schwartz in *The 1990s*. The economic boom was supported by advances in technology, which increased consumerism.

The consumer culture in the United States was well established before the 1990s. As Celia Lury points out in *Consumer Culture*, America already had more malls than high schools in the

COMPARE
&
CONTRAST

- **1990s:** The United States experiences an economic boom that improves the lives of many Americans. The improved economy, however, does not benefit everyone equally.

  2000s: The Great Recession of 2008 harms the global economy. Unemployment rises, and many Americans lose their savings in the financial disaster.

  Today: The US economy has improved, but it is not entirely recovered. Income inequality is growing and damaging the middle class. *CBS News* reports that the middle class is shrinking, and most Americans believe it is harder to maintain a livelihood than it was twenty-five years ago.

- **1990s:** The stronger economy provides more Americans with disposable income, which increases consumerism. New technology and a strong housing market increase consumer spending, and people use objects to define their self-image.

  2000s: The recession results in the loss of homes and possessions for many Americans. Still, the development of new products and technology maintains consumerism.

  Today: Younger Americans are less likely to make the same large purchases that previous generations did, but consumerism is alive and well. Luxury items such as the latest smart phones, tablets, and accessories are necessary for American society.

- **1990s:** Korean immigration to the United States continues but at a slower rate than in the past. There is a political push to tighten immigration laws and benefits, and Korean Americans are not immune to the effects of laws such as the Illegal Immigration Reform and Immigrant Responsibility Act of 1996.

  2000s: The effects of 9/11 and the Great Recession play a role in immigration policy and reform. Immigrants still face obstacles, but Asian Americans are often considered model minorities.

  Today: According to Pyong Gap in *Development and Society*, "The Korean population, including the multiracial, in the United States has grown to more than 1.7 million in 2010." Korean Americans have strong communities but also contribute to the larger American society. Immigration, however, is highly debated.

1980s. By 1992, however, Lury notes, "shopping is the second most popular leisure pursuit . . . after watching television." American consumerism and personal image became linked. Items were purchased because they were desired and also because they helped established status. American consumerism was not limited to the nation itself. International business deals brought products, movies, and fast-food chains to countries around the world. This view of consumerism is seen in *BFE* in the character Hae-Yoon. She equates America with movies and products. The consumer culture she sees equals happiness in her mind.

CRITICAL OVERVIEW

Like most playwrights, Cho has had her share of both positive and negative reviews. Early in her career, many critics saw her potential. Regarding the premiere of *The Architecture of Loss*, for example, Francine Russo writes that there were a few powerfully written scenes. That view of Cho's ability continued when *BFE* premiered a year later, in 2005. Terry Teachout calls it a flawed but interesting play. The *New York Times* reviewer, Anita Gates, is more complimentary, writing, "Ms. Cho has written an insightful, beautifully structured drama about

Panny believes herself to be ugly because she has fixated on a narrow standard of beauty (© Mygate /
Shutterstock.com)

the agonies and comforts of isolation." Other critics were less enthusiastic. Martin Denton calls *BFE* "a very sloppily and lazily written work." Despite some negative criticism, the play won the Arnold Weissberger Award and continued to be well respected.

Cho developed a reputation for her skillful scripts. *The Piano Teacher* met with acclaim in 2007. Hilton Als of the *New Yorker* writes that the play, "with its gothic mysteries, finds its triumph, finally, in dramatizing the unknown." The 2010 play *The Language Archive* was very successful, winning the Susan Smith Blackburn Prize. Critics, however, were not universally impressed. Teachout, for example, gives a mixed review, writing that the positive aspects of the play "all float in a sea of sentiment," blaming some of the perceived flaws on Cho's work in television.

Despite any negativity from critics, Cho's work has greatly influenced theater in the twenty-first century. Her plays have been produced by the New York Theater Workshop, the Silk Road Theater Project, and the East West Players. She was creating thoughtful pieces for both the stage and screen as of 2016.

CRITICISM

April Paris

Paris is a freelance writer with a degree in classical literature and a background in academic writing. In the following essay, she examines how responses to social influences isolate the characters in BFE.

A press release for *BFE*, quoted by Kenneth Jones in *Playbill*, points out that *BFE* is "A cautionary tale about the devastating effects of an image-obsessed society." All the main characters are trapped by the social world in which they live, leaving each one unable to connect with other people. This isolation persists despite efforts to develop close relationships. The inability to make close social ties leaves Isabel, Panny, Lefty, Hugo, and Evvie cut off from each other. The loneliness and isolation stem from the views the characters have of themselves and from the outside expectations placed on them by society.

The most isolated character in the play is Isabel. She separates herself from others both physically and emotionally. She is a strange blend of fear and determination. The compulsion to remain apart springs from her childhood. As a young girl, Isabel was adopted into a culture not her own after being rejected by her biological family. As Lefty explains, the only bond Isabel ever had was with him "because the family that raised us sure didn't know what to make of us." Rejected by both her biological and adoptive families, Isabel lives her life by attempting to control herself and those around her. This need to control prevents the character from developing genuine connections.

Isabel is a force of will, and she goes to great lengths to achieve her goals. Although she has grown up feeling that she is not entirely accepted into American society, she embraces the conventional standards of beauty found in American popular culture. Isabel is determined to be beautiful and believes that "true beauty is an act of will." With the strength of her belief, she takes action and undergoes plastic surgery to change her features so that she looks less Korean and more American. The physical transformation terrifies her daughter and does not fully satisfy Isabel. After Isabel attains the beauty that she desires, she finds herself unable to leave the house. The physical improvement leads to a mental deterioration, causing her to vacate her job and any contact with the world. As she tells Jack, "I never really liked going out in the first place. . . . But lately, I can't even bring myself to leave the house."

Despite her facade of strength and determination, Isabel lives her life in fear. She is afraid that despite all of her actions, other people will not see her as beautiful. In her fantasy, the general calls her beautiful because this is what she wants to hear from other people. Isabel's fear of being unattractive is apparent when Jack insults her and does not address her as Miss. She panics and cries until he compliments her appearance in scene 18. This scene is Isabel at her most vulnerable. She has lost control of her brother to romance, and she reaches out to the only person available, a person with whom she has no chance of developing a relationship, the pizza delivery man, Jack.

Isabel's only real connection is with Lefty and later Panny. They are, however, more like her caretakers than her family members. Panny serves Isabel's meals, and Lefty supports her financially, but they are not close. Having grown up in the same environment as Isabel, Lefty makes no effort to conform to standards or ideals of American society. He accepts his isolation, working as a security guard, playing Dungeons and Dragons, and creating figurines for the game. Lefty wants more in his life, but he does not seek out anything because he is convinced that he cannot have it. His entire world changes, however, when he meets Evvie.

As Anita Gates pointed outs in "Asian and Isolated in a Desert of Blondes and Coca-Cola," Lefty opens up to Evvie. The connection between the two is possible because she accepts Lefty for who he is and finds his socially awkward manner endearing. In fact, Evvie goes as far as to admire a Dungeons and Dragons figurine Lefty makes for her. Both Evvie and Lefty have lived lonely lives before meeting: she is divorced and has not had a date for ten years. In the same vein, Lefty appreciates the quirks that make up Evvie. For example, he enjoys the self-help books that she always reads, and he respects the changes that she has made in her life. He also likes her spirituality, and as she teaches him to read her aura, he tells her he loves her.

As a couple who connect on a deep and meaningful level, Lefty and Evvie are the only two in the play who have the chance to find happiness together. Their romance, however, is short-lived. As Gates notes, "Neither is willing to compromise on living arrangements." Once Lefty can have a life of his own, he is unwilling to bend. He refuses to sacrifice the desire to have a family of his own, even when he has the chance to share his life with someone he loves. Evvie, on the other hand, refuses even to consider having a family with Lefty because her desire is to live her

WHAT DO I READ NEXT?

- *Tales of the Lost Formicans*, by Constance Congdon, was first produced in 1989. The play combines comedy with social commentary. Congdon influenced Cho and her work.

- *The Korean Americans*, by Won Moo Hurh, was published in 1998. Hurh provides an overview of Korean Americans and their impact on the nation. This nonfiction book is a useful introduction for anyone who wants to understand the history of Korean Americans.

- *A Step from Heaven* (2001), by An Na, is a young-adult novel about Ju and her family as they immigrate to America. The story examines the themes of isolation and society.

- Published in 2000, *Mexican WhiteBoy*, by Matt de la Peña, is a young-adult novel that tells the story of Danny, a boy of mixed heritage. The isolation that Danny feels resembles the isolation in *BFE*.

- Published in 1998, the nonfiction book *A Cultural History of the United States through the Decades—1990s*, edited by Stuart A. Kallen, examines the decade in which *BFE* takes places. The text explores the history, politics, and culture of the decade.

- Cho's award-winning play *The Language Archive*, first performed in 2010, tells the story of a linguist who is unable to find a way to communicate in his marriage. The play is told from a male point of view and shows Cho's versatility.

own life. Both Lefty and Evvie choose to return to their previous lives rather than try to stay together.

Having been raised by Isabel and Lefty, Panny has poor role models to teach her self-confidence and how to connect with others. Isabel desires to fit in and be admired, whereas Lefty makes himself comfortable on the fringes. Panny handles the pressure of society by developing a hard shell. She uses sarcasm to protect herself from the cruelty of the world and family dysfunction.

Isabel pressures Panny to have plastic surgery so that she can live up to her potential. Panny, however, does not make up her mind immediately. Although she knows that Isabel is conventionally beautiful, the initial change disturbs Panny. Her mother no longer looks like herself. Like Isabel, Panny's pen pal, Hae-Yoon, tells Panny that she has had surgery on her eyes and is happy that she can be beautiful. Despite the external influences, Panny resists the idea.

Panny's relationships are mainly superficial. She does not share a close bond with Isabel, and although Lefty loves her, he is not capable of providing the support that she needs. Outside of her family, Panny is isolated: her childhood friend, Nancy, no longer has any time for her, and she is afraid of developing a reputation as a geek at school. The futility of Panny's social life is best seen in the first few scenes in which she tries to find someone to celebrate her birthday with her. The only person who remembers is Lefty.

In a chance moment, Panny encounters the only person she can connect with when she dials a wrong number. She develops an emotional bond with Hugo, but this relationship is based on a lie about her age. Beginning a relationship with deception dooms it from the beginning. Panny knows that Hugo will never accept her when he sees her, but she takes the risk after he tells her how much he cares. By lying, Panny sabotages her ability to connect genuinely with him. Her fears are realized when she meets Hugo, and he accuses her of playing a joke on him. This moment breaks her heart and their connection. Hugo finally does acknowledge that Panny's feelings are real, but he chooses to remain disconnected from her.

Like the other characters, Hugo is influenced by the pressures of image and society. He has romanticized Panny, confident that her exterior will match the personality he comes to know. Despite the large age difference between him and Panny, Hugo has no problem maintaining a friendship with the cute, blonde Nancy, who is only one year older than Panny. It is Nancy who gives Hugo Panny's address. As they do for everyone else, image and social expectations affect Hugo's ability to connect with other people.

Panny is rejected by two men in one night: Hugo and a serial killer, both of whom prefer

Nancy to Panny. After comforting a distraught Panny, the Man earns her trust and kidnaps her because she is convenient. The Man is unable to kill Panny, even when she fights back, because she is not blonde like his other victims. He does, however, leave his mark on her by carving the word *ugly* into her skin. The trauma of the night leaves Panny marked in more ways than one, and she takes drastic steps to take back control of her life. She undergoes plastic surgery on her eyes.

Cho explains in her *American Theater* interview with Eric Ting, "I think that people who have been through really traumatic experiences, in some way, claim back their own body." Of all the characters, Panny undergoes the greatest change. That she does not meet the social standards of beauty saves her life, but it also reminds her that she is different and has been rejected. Her future, like the future of the other characters, remains uncertain. Whether they move from their isolation depends on their point of view.

Source: April Paris, Critical Essay on *BFE*, in *Drama for Students*, Gale, Cengage Learning, 2017.

Misha Berson

In the following review, Berson describes Cho's writing as "deft."

Panny is a perceptive suburban teenager with eccentric relations and her own idiosyncratic view of the world.

But that is about where the similarities between the lead characters in the hit indie film *Juno* and in Julia Cho's admirable Off Broadway play *BFE* end.

Now in its West Coast debut at Richard Hugo House, *BFE* zeroes in on a 14-year-old, Korean-American misfit who is far more insecure than young Juno ever was.

Portrayed by Leah Cohen-Sapida, Panny is convinced of her ugliness, and unfavorably compares her Korean-American facial features with the WASP prettiness of her twinkie girlfriend, Nancy (Sydney Tucker).

To make matters worse, Panny has a narcissistic, agoraphobic single mother, Isabel (Roberta Furst) whose birthday present to her daughter is an offer of cosmetic facial surgery. She also has teenybopper pen pal in Korea (the very funny Maia Lee) who seems to be having a much happier adolescence than Panny is.

While wisecracking teen angst is nothing new, Cho's deft play could not be mistaken for a glib TV sitcom. Though it yields plenty of bone-wry witticisms and laughs, *BFE* offers a darker summary of modern American life from a nonconformist teen's vantage point.

Isolation and loneliness are communicable diseases in Panny's world, and nearly everyone close to her is infected. And neither she nor her peers can ever escape the specter of terrible sexual violence lurking in the shadows of this "typical" suburban landscape.

Furst's delusional mother is like a Korean-American Blanche du Bois as she wafts around in her lingerie and makes an amazed pizza delivery boy's day. (As the latter, Eric Riedmann is a hoot.)

Panny's phone buddy Hugo (Lincoln Grismer), a quirky college student, longs to connect with a girl as offbeat as he is. Panny's dutiful uncle Lefty (Sam Tsubota) hungers for a love connection too, as does Evvie (feisty Trina Griffin), a gregarious store clerk and self-help-book devotee Lefty hopes to hook up with.

Every character in *BFE* is ridiculous in one way or another. But a strength of Cho's writing is her empathy for those who stumble toward and slip away from intimacies they desperately covet—but aren't equipped to handle.

By choosing *BFE* as the first play of its new residency at Richard Hugo House, SiS Productions (best known for its serial comedy, *Sex in Seattle*) is bringing us a contemporary Asian-American play of merit, that we might otherwise not see.

Some actors *BFE* under Leticia Lopez's lucid direction, lack polish. But that absence of slickness tends to serve a tale that has so many moments of social awkwardness.

Tackling a tough role, Bellevue high-school student Cohen-Sapida seems touchingly genuine here. The show also benefits from a spare, eerie score by composer Byron Au Yong, and a low-key yet entirely creepy turn by Scott Plusquellec, as the boogeyman of every teenage girl's nightmares.

Source: Misha Berson, "*BFE* a Funny/Sad Portrait of Teenage Isolation," in *Seattle Times*, February 28, 2008.

John Lahr

In the following excerpt, Lahr admits Cho's talent but faults the ending of BFE *as somewhat trite.*

. . . Julia Cho's *BFE* (at Playwrights Horizons) is a tale of sound and fury told by a

Panny makes a lucky connection with Hugo after dialing a wrong number (© Skylines / Shutterstock.com)

fourteen-year-old, Panny (Olivia Oguma), and signifying less than meets the eye. The title stands for "Bum F– Egypt"—the narrator's sour little joke about the Southwestern suburban wasteland where she, her mother and her uncle are living out their aimless days. The story that Panny has to tell is of her abduction and assault by the town ne'er-do-well. "I wasn't his type," she says. "I was too ugly, even for him." (Her attacker carved the word "ugly" on her belly.) Panny can't get anyone to really look at her: not her narcissistic mother, who suggests plastic surgery; not her twenty-year-old telephone friend, Hugo (James McMenamin); not her Korean pen pal (the excellent Sue Jean Kim), who is excited about all things American—"I have long hair the color of Coca-Cola and I drink Coca-Cola every chance I can"—and who is Cho's most vivid portrait here.

Cho has talent, but she has not yet found a form with which to dramatize the particular punishing problems of Asian-American identity. Her litany of regret in *BFE* includes Panny's lonely uncle's fling and her agoraphobic mother's clumsily told and demented romantic fantasies (in a woefully misjudged performance by Kate Rigg, which the director, Gordon Edelstein, should have attended to). Cho leaves her heroine nestled comatose between mother and uncle—three lost souls—as the light of the television flickers across their bodies and the night sky twinkles behind them. The bleakness feels young; the vacancy, however, is as old as the American landscape.

Source: John Lahr, "Sweet and Sour," in *New Yorker*, Vol. 81, No. 17, June 13, 2005, p. 181.

Marilyn Stasio

In the following review, Stasio highlights Cho's potential as a young playwright.

Julia Cho is a talented young playwright who deserves better than indulgent workshop productions that fail to help her develop her voice, focus her vision and shape her material into a stageworthy theatrical style. After going through more than a half-dozen developmental workshops (at New York Theater Workshop, the Mark Taper Forum and Chi's Goodman, among others), this coming-of-age play emerges in rough and ragged form, its promise still unrealized.

It's hard to know exactly what Cho (*The Architecture of Loss*) wants to say in this diffuse play about an Asian teen who lives with her spacey mother and spineless uncle in a desert town somewhere in *BFE* (an acronym for "Butt-F— Egypt"—connoting "the back of beyond"). Fourteen-year-old Panny (Olivia Oguma) is clearly the centerpiece of the story. But she is an inconsistent narrator and is missing in action from so many scenes that her character development lacks a smooth arc.

Cho gives Panny the requisite teen angst about being too-fat-too-ugly-too-clumsy to make it through her freshman year of high school with her ego intact. To these adolescent agonies is added the extra anxiety of being too Asian to score the white boy with whom she's been carrying on a phone flirtation. At least the poor child doesn't have to worry about the serial killer (a Ted Bundyesque charmer in Scott Hudson's smart perf) prowling the desert landscape raping and killing pretty, popular girls with naturally blond hair and perfect complexions. Or does she?

Oguma plays Panny with a sweet awkwardness that gently exposes the ignorance of her youth while still respecting her intelligence. (In Jayde Chabot's girlish outfits, she even looks the part of a child who isn't quite ready to claim the rights—and fashion sense—of a woman in bud.) But despite her pivotal role, Panny is surprisingly inarticulate at times when she should be finding her voice.

In an exchange of correspondence with a Korean pen pal named Hae-Yoon, Panny is dismissive and evasive, while Hae-Yoon (in a sparkling comic perf from Sue Jean Kim) bubbles over with enthusiasm for all the cheap consumer trappings she takes for authentic Americana. Every letter not sent to Hae-Yoon is a missed opportunity for Panny to express her own thoughts on the national religion that worships beauty.

In the same way, every domestic scene without Panny is another lost chance for her to examine her adolescent confusions in a broader context. There are many such scenes in the play—between Panny's mother, Isabel (Kate Rigg), and uncle Leffy (James Saito); between Lefty and his girlfriend Evvie (Karen Kandel); between Isabel and the pizza delivery guy.

Not only do they not impact directly on Panny's developmental education, but in Gordon Edelstein's overly literal production, they are so drawn out and self-consciously performed that they slow down the momentum of the real action—which, however obliquely referenced in Cho's text, is Panny's journey to self-awareness.

If stripped down, cleaned up and refocused on a more articulate Panny, *BFE* might yet take this kid where she needs to go. On the other hand, one really hesitates to suggest yet another workshop.

Source: Marilyn Stasio, Review of *BFE*, in *Variety*, Vol. 399, No. 3, June 6, 2005, p. 35.

SOURCES

Abrams, M. H., "Surrealism," in *A Glossary of Literary Terms*, Harcourt Brace College Publishers, 1999, pp. 310–11.

Als, Hilton, "In Search of Lost Times," in *New Yorker*, Vol. 83, No. 38, December 3, 2007, http://www.newyorker.com/magazine/2007/12/03/in-search-of-lost-times (accessed July 7, 2016).

Backalenick, Irene, Review of *BFE*, in *New York–Connecticut Theater Scene*, http://www.nytheaterscene.com/RevCBFE.htm (accessed on July 5, 2016).

Cho, Julia, *BFE*, Dramatists Play Service, 2006.

Denton, Martin, Review of *BFE*, in *Indie Theater Now*, May 29, 2005, http://www.nytheatre.com/Review/martin-denton-2005-5-29-bfe (accessed July 5, 2016).

Gap, Pyong, "The Immigration of Koreans to the United States: A Review of 45 Year (1965–2009) Trends," in *Development and Society*, Vol. 40, No. 2, December 2011.

Gates, Anita, "Asian and Isolated in a Desert of Blondes and Coca-Cola," in *New York Times*, June 1, 2005, http://www.nytimes.com/2005/06/01/theater/reviews/asian-and-isolated-in-a-desert-of-blondes-and-cocacola.html?_r=0 (accessed July 3, 2016).

Harmon, William, "Black Humor," in *A Handbook to Literature*, Prentice Hall, 2003, p. 62.

———, "Monologue," in *A Handbook to Literature*, Prentice Hall, 2003, p. 320.

Ingram, Scott, *Korean Americans*, World Almanac Library, 2007, p. 25.

Jones, Kenneth, "Asian-American Family Struggles in Julia Cho's BFE, Getting NYC Premiere May 19–June 12," in *Playbill*, May 19, 2005, http://www.playbill.com/article/asian-american-family-struggles-in-julia-chos-bfe-getting-nyc-premiere-may-19-june-12-com-125981 (accessed July 6, 2016).

Kakkar, Mahira, "Julia Cho: A Playwright Drawn to the 'What Ifs'," in *Juilliard Journal*, December 2007–January 2008, http://www.juilliard.edu/journal/julia-cho-playwright-drawn-what-ifs (accessed July 6, 2016).

Lee, Esther Kim, ed., *Seven Contemporary Plays from the Korean Diaspora in the Americas*, Duke University Press, 2012, p. 21.

Liem, Deann Borshay, "Adoption History," in *First Person Plural*, PBS website, 2000, http://www.pbs.org/pov/firstpersonplural/history/4/#.V38txpMrKRs (accessed July 7, 2016).

Lury, Celia, *Consumer Culture*, 2nd ed. Polity Press, 2011, p. 2.

Noland, Marcus, "The Impact of Korean Immigration on the US Economy," in *The Korean Diaspora in the World Economy*, edited by C. Fred Bergsten and Inbom Choi, Institute for International Economics, 2003, pp. 62–63.

Oh, Arissa H., "From War Waif to Ideal Immigrant: The Cold War Transformation of the Korean Orphan," in *Journal of American Ethnic History*, Vol. 31, No. 4, Summer 2012, pp. 34–55.

Picchi, Aimee, "7 Signs You're Dropping Out of the Middle Class," in *Moneywatch*, December 2, 2015, http://www.cbsnews.com/media/7-signs-youre-dropping-out-of-the-middle-class (accessed July 5, 2016).

Rno, Sung, "Julia Cho: Desert Memories," in *American Theater*, April 2005, pp. 46–49.

Russo, Francine, Review of *The Architecture of Loss*, in *Village Voice*, January 21–27, 2004, p. C70.

Schwartz, Richard A., *The 1990s*, Facts on File, 2006, p. 266.

Teachout, Terry, "Theater: Too Cute for Words," in *Wall Street Journal*, October 18, 2010, p. A27.

Ting, Eric, "The Eyes Have It," in *American Theater*, Vol. 27, No. 7, September 2005, p. 46.

"United States—Economy," in *Encyclopedia of the Nations*, http://www.nationsencyclopedia.com/Americas/United-States-ECONOMY.html (accessed July 6, 2016).

Wada, Karen, "Julia Cho Is at Home at South Coast Repertory," in *Los Angeles Times*, April 2, 2010, http://articles.latimes.com/2010/apr/02/entertainment/la-et-julia-cho2-2010apr02 (accessed July 5, 2016).

FURTHER READING

Bryer, Jackson R., and Mary C. Hartig, *Encyclopedia of American Drama*, Infobase Learning, 2015.

This informative text examines the history and lives of American playwrights, including Cho. Any student interested in American theater will find this book a useful tool.

Gap Min, Pyong, and Thomas Chung, *Younger-Generation Korean Experiences in the United States: Personal Narratives on Ethnic and Racial Identities*, Lexington Books, 2014.

This nonfiction text is composed of personal narratives. It gives insight into understanding Korean American identity.

Nelson, Kim Park, *Invisible Asians: Korean American Adoptees, Asian American Experiences, and Racial Exceptionalism*, Rutgers University Press, 2016.

This nonfiction text examines the history of Korean adoption and the long-term effects. The inclusion life stories provide narratives that are easy to understand, making the material more accessible.

Ochoa, George, *America in the 1990s*, Facts on File, 2005.

Ochoa's young-adult text provides an overview of the decade. The nonfiction book is beneficial for anyone interested in learning about art, science, and history of the decade.

Xu, Wenying, *Historical Dictionary of Asian American Theater*, Scarecrow Press, 2012.

The collection examines the works and history of East Asian American authors. The work includes terminology, history, and genres over the years and is a useful text for anyone interested in learning more about Asian American theater.

SUGGESTED SEARCH TERMS

Julia Cho AND playwright

Julia Cho AND biography

Julia Cho AND BFE

Julia Cho AND criticism

Korean immigration AND America

Korean Americans AND history

United States AND 1990s

American history AND 1990s

American culture AND 1990s

Korea AND American adoption

Blues for Mister Charlie

Blues for Mister Charlie is a three-act tragedy by twentieth-century novelist, essayist, and dramatist James Baldwin. It was first produced at New York City's ANAT Theater in April 1964 and was published the same year. At the time, "Mister Charlie" was a term used by African Americans to refer to whites. The play is very loosely based on the case of Emmet Till, a fourteen-year-old African American boy who was murdered by two white men in Mississippi in 1955 after allegedly flirting with a white woman in a grocery store. The story centers on a young African American man named Richard who returns to his hometown in the South after living in the North for eight years. Richard is murdered by Lyle, a white man, following an incident in Lyle's grocery store. Set in 1964 during the height of the civil rights movement, the play is a fierce denunciation of the white racism and bigotry in the South that has resulted in the suppression and frequent killing of African Americans.

JAMES BALDWIN

1964

AUTHOR BIOGRAPHY

Baldwin was born on August 2, 1924, in Harlem, New York City, to Emma Jones, a single woman. When he was three, his mother married David Baldwin, a Baptist minister. The family was poor. Baldwin, however, received a good education, showing literary talent as early as

James Baldwin (© *Ulf Andersen | Getty Images*)

middle school. At DeWitt Clinton High School in the Bronx, he made numerous contributions in the school magazine, including poems, short stories, and plays. During this time, he became a youth minister and preached in some Harlem churches.

After graduating from high school in 1942, Baldwin took on various jobs to help financially support his family, which included seven younger siblings. In 1943, his stepfather died, and Baldwin moved to Greenwich Village in New York City, a well-known gathering place for writers. He worked odd jobs and pursued his writing projects. Within a few years, essays and reviews by Baldwin began to appear in journals such as the *Nation*. Baldwin was particularly concerned about the problem of racism, of which, as an African American, he had had much firsthand experience. It was in part because of the discrimination he suffered that he decided in 1948 to move to Paris, France. It was also around this time that he came to terms with the fact that he was gay, which had earlier troubled him.

In 1953, Baldwin published his first novel, an autobiographical account based on his early life, titled *Go Tell It on the Mountain*. Two years later, some of his articles and essays were collected in *Notes of a Native Son*. His next novel, *Giovanni's Room* (1956), is set in Paris and tells the story of an American man's relationship with an Italian man named David. The success of these three publications established Baldwin as a well-known literary figure.

After returning to Greenwich Village in 1957, Baldwin visited the South, where the civil rights movement was already under way. *Nobody Knows My Name*, a collection of essays on race, culture, and society, was published in 1961, followed in 1962 by the novel *Another Country*. *The Fire Next Time* (1963), about the legacy of racism and the need to overcome it, was a best seller that established Baldwin as a powerful voice in the civil rights movement. In 1964, Baldwin's play *Blues for Mister Charlie* was produced on Broadway. Later in the decade, he published the essay *Nothing Personal* (1965), the short-story collection *Going to Meet the Man* (1965), and the novel *Tell Me How Long the Train's Been Gone* (1968).

In the early 1970s, Baldwin lived in the south of France and spent about half his time there for the remainder of the decade and into the 1980s. An autobiographical essay, *No Name in the Street*, was published in 1972, followed by the novel *If Beale Street Could Talk* in 1974. *The Devil Finds Work*, which explores American movies and how they present issues of race came out in 1976. Baldwin's final novel was *Just above My Head* (1979).

In the 1980s, Baldwin was frequently in ill health, but he managed to publish *Evidence of Things Not Seen* (1985), which is about racism in the context of a number of child murders in Atlanta; *Jimmy's Blues* (1985), a collection of poetry; and *The Price of the Ticket* (1985), a collection of previously published essays. Baldwin died in Saint-Paul-de-Vence, France, of stomach cancer, on December 1, 1987.

PLOT SUMMARY

Act 1

The play begins with the sound of a gunshot. As the lights go up, Lyle Britten is seen picking up Richard Henry's body and dumping it upstage.

The Reverend Meridian Henry is at his church persuading some of his young African American parishioners to speak out loud the insulting way white people speak to them. Some more young people enter, having returned from a nonviolent civil rights demonstration. One of them, Lorenzo, complains that they have made only small progress after a year of effort. There is to be a funeral at the church the following night for the reverend's son, Richard, and Meridian hopes that the killer will be brought to trial. Lorenzo points out that the alleged killer, Lyle Britten, has killed an African American man before, and nothing was ever done about it. Parnell James, a white man considered a friend by the African American community, enters with the news that Lyle will be arrested and charged with murder.

The scene switches to Lyle and Jo Britten and their two-month-old son. Lyle explains his plans to expand the store he owns, even though the African Americans in the town are boycotting it. He does not expect the boycott to last long and wants to begin selling a line of ladies' clothing. Jo is worried about the possibility of Lyle's being arrested and points out to him that he was the last person to see Richard alive. She mentions the earlier case in which an African American man—named later in the play as Old Bill—was killed, but Lyle explains that he acted in self-defense.

Parnell enters and informs his longtime friend Lyle about his forthcoming arrest. Lyle says he will never be convicted. It transpires that the murdered man had lived in the North for some years, where he became a drug addict. Lyle claims he has nothing against African Americans; he just does not want to mix with them.

The scene shifts back to the church, where Juanita, Richard's former girlfriend, remembers Richard with Meridian and Mother Henry. They recall his love of singing, and then a flashback shows Richard in a dialogue with Mother Henry. Richard expresses his dissatisfaction with being in the South again after living in New York, even though he faced difficulties in the city. They talk about the death of his mother, who fell down some steps at a white-owned hotel. Richard believes she was pushed. He speaks of his hatred of the white man, and his grandmother rebukes him. Then he shows her a gun. He explains that he carries it to protect himself against the whites and boasts that he will not be afraid to use it when

necessary. Mother Henry asks him to give her the gun, but he refuses.

In the flashback, Mother Henry exits, and Juanita enters, followed by Pete. The three of them go to Papa D.'s bar, where music plays on the jukebox and couples are dancing. As they sit down, Pete and Juanita tell Richard about Lyle and how he shot an African American man who objected to Lyle's affair with his wife. Richard boasts about all the white women he has been with in New York. He shows them some photographs. When Papa D. sees the photos, he tells Richard to put them away; they could get him into serious trouble. After Pete goes off to dance, Richard tells Juanita that he became a drug addict in New York about five years ago.

Lyle enters. He and Papa D. are on friendly terms, even though the African American community is boycotting Lyle's store. Lyle wants some change for cigarettes. On his way out, he bumps into Juanita, who is dancing with Richard. Richard and Lyle exchange some words, with Richard feeling no apparent need to conceal his contempt for the man.

Back at home, Richard has a frank discussion with his father, who thinks he should get back together with Juanita. Richard hands over his gun, asking Meridian to keep it for him until he needs it.

Parnell returns to the church. He and Meridian talk about how bad the situation is in their town regarding violence against African Americans. Meridian speaks of his doubts about Christianity, wondering whether it is partly to blame for the subjugation of African Americans by the whites. He and Parnell talk about the upcoming trial. Meridian is convinced that Lyle is guilty, but Parnell says they must let the process of justice take its course. Lyle has not yet been proved guilty in a legal proceeding. He admits, however, that the jury will never convict Lyle, even if he is guilty.

Act 2

Early on Sunday morning, some friends—all white—have gathered at the Brittens' house to celebrate the couple's first wedding anniversary. One of the ladies, Lillian, has made a cake, and Hazel has just taken it out of the oven. Jo serves some drinks, and the group offers a toast to Lyle and Jo. The talk turns to race relations in the town; Jo says she is scared of African Americans now, although she never used to be. The

Reverend Phelps believes the African Americans have turned away from God, while Susan thinks that racially integrated schools will never work. The men agree that they must be vigilant in protecting their women against sexual assault by African American men.

Parnell arrives, and it is soon apparent that he is not on the best of terms with all the townspeople when the talk turns to race relations. Some of them think his newspaper espouses communist ideas, and they want to know whether he is with them or against them. They criticize him in personal terms, saying he expresses subversive ideas just to get attention. Parnell replies that he is simply dedicated to social justice, but the others are not interested in the arguments he puts forward.

Lyle, who has been sleeping late, enters. The Reverend Phelps tells him that all the white people in the town are on his side. Lyle says he is not worried about it. Ellis says there is going to be an attempt to put African Americans on the jury, which horrifies Hazel, but Parnell says he supports the idea.

Everyone leaves except Parnell. Lyle talks about how he plans to make his store flourish so he can leave something to his son. He also speaks proudly of his wife. After he exits to take a bath, Jo ask Parnell if it was true that Lyle was having an affair with Old Bill's wife and that was why Lyle shot Bill. Parnell says it would violate his friendship with Lyle if he answered her question. Jo then asks him whether he has ever had an affair with an African American. Parnell replies that when he was eighteen he loved a seventeen-year-old African American girl named Pearl. The affair ended when Pearl's mother found the two of them kissing. After that, Pearl was sent away. Parnell says he has never forgotten her. Jo reacts by saying that if Lyle loved Willa Mae, Old Bill's wife, he could have shot her husband to stop him from talking about it. If he had done that, he was also capable of killing Richard, and that, she acknowledges, would be murder. Lyle then returns, carrying the baby.

The scene shifts to Lyle's store in the early evening, where Lyle and Parnell are talking. Lyle recalls his relationship with Willa Mae and how Old Bill had come into his store looking as if he wanted to kill Lyle. Lyle also remembers the time he encountered Richard at Papa D.'s, claiming that Richard insulted his wife. He then recalls how Richard came to his store on a Monday afternoon.

After Parnell exits, that scene is then enacted in a flashback. Richard and Lorenzo approach the store, and Richard goes in and asks for a Coke, even though Lorenzo tells him that Lyle's store is being boycotted. Richard speaks insultingly to Jo. He offers a twenty-dollar bill in payment. Lyle enters carrying a hammer that he has been using and in answer to Jo's questions says he has no change. Richard mocks and taunts Lyle, angering him. Lyle tells him to leave the store. Richard continues to insult him, and a struggle ensues. Lorenzo enters the store. Richard knocks the hammer from Lyle's hand and then knocks him down. Richard mocks Lyle again, and then he and Lorenzo exit the store.

The scene returns to Lyle and Parnell in the store. Lyle refers to Richard's body lying face down in the weeds, and Parnell's reaction makes it clear that information regarding the position of the body was not reported in the newspapers, although Lyle insists that it was. Parnell leaves to attend Richard's funeral.

The scene changes to the church, where Meridian preaches at the funeral about the sufferings of African Americans.

Act 3

Two months have passed, and Lyle's trial is in progress. On the witness stand, Jo lies, saying that Richard tried to sexually assault her in the store. Under questioning, she says she did not report the assault because she did not want to create more trouble in the town. The Counsel for the Bereaved tries to cast doubt on her claim that Lyle, even though he supposedly knew that his wife had been assaulted, agreed to do nothing about it. Counsel for the Bereaved also brings attention to the fact that originally Jo had said Lyle spent the whole night of Richard's death at the store, but she has now altered her story, claiming that Lyle came home at one o'clock in the morning and went straight to bed.

Papa D. takes the stand. He says he and Lyle are longtime friends, but he also says Lyle is hard on African Americans. He recalls his meeting with Richard at his bar the night the young man died. While Papa D. was closing the bar, he saw Richard and Lyle leave together. He says he is certain Lyle killed him.

Lorenzo is next to take the stand. He testifies that Richard did not assault Jo; he did not even touch her. The prosecutor tries to get Lorenzo to say that Richard was either drunk or on drugs, but Lorenzo says that was not so. Under questioning from the Counsel for the Bereaved, Lorenzo says that Richard had overcome his former addiction to drugs.

Next on the stand is Juanita. The prosecutor tries to imply that she has had many boyfriends and that anything she says about Richard, with whom she had at one time been involved, will be unreliable. She testifies that before the fight between Lyle and Richard at the store, Richard was sober, and he was sober after the fight too. Juanita says that she tried to persuade him to leave town and take her with him, but Richard insisted that he was not going to run from white people anymore. She concludes her testimony by saying that Lyle killed Richard.

The court adjourns until the next morning, when Mother Henry takes the stand. She says she did not see Richard with a gun and that he was not under the influence of drugs. Next on the stand is Meridian, who says his son was not armed. The prosecutor criticizes him for his sermons, in which he preaches social equality and even implies that his inflammatory sermons contributed to his son's death. The prosecutor also accuses Meridian of being so full of race hatred that he is incapable of telling the truth.

Next on the stand is Parnell. Under questioning, he defends what he knows about Richard's character, refusing to say he was a dangerous influence in the town. He admits that Richard showed him pictures of white women but denies that the photos were obscene, as the prosecutor alleges. He says they were just pictures of people Richard had known in the North. When the prosecutor mentions the allegation of attempted rape by Richard, Parnell says it is the first time he has heard such a charge. However, when the prosecutor describes Jo's allegations, Parnell does not say they are false.

The jury finds Lyle not guilty. Afterwards, Parnell tells Lyle that he knows Jo was lying about the sexual assault and that Lyle put her up to it. Lyle responds angrily to him. Meridian and Lyle also exchange angry words, which leads into a flashback portraying the final confrontation between Lyle and Richard. Lyle demands an apology from Richard, which Richard refuses to give. Richard speaks to him in what Lyle regards as an insulting way, and Lyle shoots him. Then he says he had to kill him because he does not allow anyone to talk to him like that.

He dumps the body in the weeds. He says he is not sorry.

The play ends with many of the African American characters starting off on a civil rights march. Parnell joins them.

CHARACTERS

Arthur
Arthur is a young African American man who is being trained by Meridian to participate in the civil rights campaign in the local town.

Jo Britten
Jo Britten is Lyle's wife. They have been married for only a year and have an infant son. During the play, Jo becomes aware of the possibility that Lyle killed Richard. She changes her story to the police to make it appear that he could not have committed the crime, and she lies on the witness stand, claiming that Richard tried to sexually assault her in the store.

Lyle Britten
Lyle Britten is a white man who owns a grocery store. He is married to Jo and they have an infant son. Lyle's store is being boycotted by the town's African American community, although he has plans to expand it with the help of a bank loan. Lyle is the man who kills Richard Henry, although he denies doing so. He has killed an African American man before: Old Bill, after Bill heard that Lyle was carrying on an affair with his wife. No charges were brought against Lyle for that incident. Lyle gets along well with Papa D. and insists he is not against African Americans, saying merely that he prefers not to mix with them. Lyle shares the general condescending and superior attitude that many others in the town have towards African Americans. For example, Pete thinks that Lyle expects African Americans to step off the sidewalk to let him go by.

Lyle takes exception to Richard's manner when Richard comes into the store to buy a Coke; they also have an unfriendly encounter in Papa D.'s bar. Later, Lyle demands that Richard apologize, and when Richard refuses and makes what Lyle deems to be unacceptable remarks, Lyle shoots him dead and dumps his body in the weeds. Lyle is charged with murder, but he does not expect to get convicted; he turns out to be right. Lyle is friends with Parnell, who speaks up for him to Meridian, Richard's father, saying "He's hot-tempered and he's far from being the brightest man in the world—but he's not mean, he's not cruel."

Counsel for the Bereaved

At Lyle's trial, the Counsel for the Bereaved attempts to cast doubt on Jo's claim that Richard sexually assaulted her.

Ellis

Ellis is one of the white townspeople. He is an old friend of Lyle's, although he sees less of him now that Lyle is married and has a child. Ellis shares the racist views of his friends. He believes that African American men cannot control their sexual desires.

George

George is one of the white townspeople and a friend of the Brittens. He expresses racist views similar to those of most of the other whites.

Hazel

Hazel is an older woman who helps out in the Brittens' kitchen on Sunday morning as people gather in anticipation of celebrating the couple's wedding anniversary in the evening. She does not seem to be as racist as the others, recalling with affection an African American nanny who helped to raise her and her siblings.

Meridian Henry

Meridian Henry is the father of Richard Henry, a minister, and a widower. His wife died following a fall down the steps at the white-owned hotel where she worked. Meridian believes that she was pushed. During the play, Meridian expresses doubts about his Christian faith, wondering whether it is a contributing factor in white racism, and he becomes more radical in his support of civil rights for African Americans, speaking forcefully on the subject on the witness stand when he is called to testify in Lyle's trial.

Mother Henry

Mother Henry is Meridian Henry's mother and Richard's grandmother. Her parents were born into slavery, but she was born free. When Richard returns from the North to live with his family again, Mother Henry, who is a religious woman, does her best to keep him on the right track in life. She tells him she raised him to know right from wrong. She and Richard do not really

see eye to eye on important matters, but she trusts that he will be all right in life; she advises him not to give in to hatred.

Richard Henry

Richard Henry is Meridian Henry's son. He left the South eight years before the events presented in the play and went to live in New York City, where he became quite a successful musician and performer and had, according to his own account, great success with white woman. He also fell into drug addiction after three years in the North. On his return to the South, he claims to have overcome his drug habit. Richard is a spirited, talented, outspoken young man who is determined not to just sit back passively and accept the deep-rooted racism that exists in the town in which he grew up. He admits to his grandmother that he hates white people for the suffering they have inflicted on African Americans. To protect himself, Richard has a gun, although he allows his father to keep it for him. In the past, Richard dated Juanita, and there are signs that the couple might get together again, but any such development, which Richard's father encourages, is cut short when Richard is murdered.

Parnell James

Parnell James is the editor of the local newspaper. He comes from a wealthy background and had some of his schooling in Switzerland. His view of life is therefore much broader than that of most of the townspeople. He espouses liberal views and believes in the equality of the races. With a foot in both camps, he manages to be friends with both Lyle Britten and Meridian Henry, although many of the local white people are suspicious of him and wonder whose side he is on. It is Parnell who does everything he can to ensure that Lyle faces trial for the murder of Richard. Parnell is a bachelor, although he has a girlfriend, Loretta. He reveals to Jo that when he was eighteen, he was in love with an African American girl named Pearl, and he has never forgotten her.

Juanita

Juanita is a young African American woman who takes part in the civil rights demonstrations. She was Richard's girlfriend before he went north, and she loved him. When Richard returns, they reconnect. Juanita is an attractive woman, and Parnell and Meridian are both interested in her, as is Pete. Since Richard has returned, Pete complains to Juanita that she has been avoiding him. She has no desire to get married in the near future because she is attending college and considering going north to law school after graduation.

Ken

Ken is a young African American man being groomed by Meridian to participate in the civil rights campaign in the local town.

Lillian

Lillian is a friend of Lyle and Jo's. She bakes the cake that will be eaten at the couple's anniversary celebration. She does not care for Parnell and his newspaper, regarding it as a communist publication. The idea of the mixing of the races fills her with horror.

Lorenzo

Lorenzo is a young African American man who is taking part in the civil rights demonstrations in the local town. He is also friends with Richard Henry. Lorenzo is frustrated with nonviolent protest and wishes he could respond with guns to the violence that African Americans have long endured. He complains that the nonviolent protests have met with few gains. Lorenzo is with Richard when Richard decides to go into Lyle's store to buy a Coke. He waits outside but then rushes into the store when he hears a commotion. After Richard knocks Lyle down, Lorenzo takes Lyle's hammer with him as they leave the store.

Old Bill

Old Bill is the African American man Lyle shot because of an argument over his affair with Bill's wife.

Papa D.

Papa D. is the African American owner of a juke joint. He stays on good terms with Lyle and continues to trade with him, despite the boycott. Therefore the local African American community considers him to be something of an Uncle Tom. On the witness stand, however, Papa D. denounces Lyle.

Pearl

Pearl is the young African American girl sent away for kissing Parnell when the two were teenagers.

Pete

Pete is a young African American man participating in the civil rights demonstrations. He is friends with Juanita and tells her he loves her. He is disappointed that since Richard returned, Juanita has been avoiding him. He really wants to be with her, promising to be faithful to her.

Reverend Phelps

Reverend Phelps is a white minister. When he gathers with the townspeople in the home of Lyle and Jo, he offers the view that the African Americans have turned away from God and are listening to communists who want to promote racial integration.

Ralph

Ralph is one of the white townspeople present at the gathering at the Brittens' house on the day of their anniversary party. He tells his wife, Susan, that children are being taught atheism in the schools, which makes the United States little better than communist countries.

State

The State is the prosecuting attorney in Lyle's trial. The State tries unsuccessfully to establish that Richard was drunk or on drugs when he entered Lyle's store. The State is also hard on Juanita on the witness stand, implying that she has had many boyfriends.

Susan

Susan is one of the white townspeople. She is married to Ralph and attends the anniversary gathering at the Brittens' house. She is against ending racial segregation in schools.

Tom

Tom is a young African American man being trained by Meridian to participate in the civil rights campaign in the local town.

Willa Mae

Willa Mae is Old Bill's wife. Conflict over her affair with Lyle led to her husband's death at Lyle's hand.

THEMES

Racism

Racism, specifically here the belief of many white people in the South that African Americans are not their equals, is fundamental to the play. Racism is revealed in word and action. Lyle, a white man, kills Richard, an African American, because he thinks Richard overstepped his place by behaving insolently in his store. Racism is tellingly revealed when the white townspeople gather in the Brittens' house to celebrate the young couple's anniversary. When the talk turns to race and race relations, they all reveal their prejudice. They believe that African Americans are inferior; they fail to understand the grievances of African Americans, believing they are treated well. The white characters seem to have no idea why the African Americans are protesting and demonstrating and put it down to the infiltration of communist ideas. They do not believe the races should mix; they simply accept racial segregation as natural and proper, something that must be preserved for the good of the white race.

Racism is also apparent from the stories and remarks of the African American characters, who are on the receiving end of the insults, violence, and oppression to which such ingrained, stubborn racism inevitably leads. The situation has become even worse now that the African Americans have started their collective, nonviolent protests. When the young people come in from their demonstration in act 1, some are injured following attacks by whites, and it is clear that this is not the first time this has happened.

The play also brings to the fore the question of how best to combat racism. In 1964, when the play is set, the nonviolent civil rights movement was on the rise, and this is the approach that Reverend Henry and his followers have been taking—boycotting Lyle's store, for example, and going on marches. Historically, this approach was inspired and led by Dr. Martin Luther King Jr. and was supported by many African American Christian churches. However, in the play there is clearly an impatience building with this approach, which is yielding only slow gains. Lorenzo, for example, one of the young men who has been out demonstrating, comes out with a tirade that links the oppression of African Americans with Christianity and the church:

> ...that white man's God is *white*. It's that
> damn white God that's been lynching us and

TOPICS FOR FURTHER STUDY

- Research the Voting Rights Act of 1965. How did it help the cause of civil rights for African Americans? Also, research the 2013 Supreme Court decision in the case of *Shelby County v. Holder*, which overturned an important section of the Voting Rights Act. What was the court's reasoning in that case, and what effect has it had on voting rights, especially in the South? Give a class presentation in which you explain the issue.

- Learn one of the speeches in the play that you like best and deliver it as a performance to your class.

- In the mid-2010s, there have been a number of highly publicized incidents in American cities in which unarmed African Americans have been killed by police officers. The incidents have given rise to the organization Black Lives Matter. Give a class presentation in which you relate this development to the situation presented in the play from over fifty years ago. What are the parallels, and what are the differences? What progress has been made since that time and what further progress is still needed, given the present situation regarding civil rights and race relations, particularly in terms of law enforcement?

- Consult Sara Bullard's *Free at Last: A History of the Civil Rights Movement and Those Who Died in the Struggle* (1994), which is an illustrated history of the civil rights movement for young-adult readers. Write an essay in which you relate *Blues for Mister Charlie* to the wider civil rights struggle during the 1960s. What specific issues does Baldwin's play bring to life? Upload the essay to your blog and invite comment from classmates.

burning us and castrating us and raping our women and robbing us of everything that makes a man a man for all these hundreds of years.

Lyle is acquitted at his trial, but a flashback shows the audience that he is indeed guilty (© *Matt Benoit /
Shutterstock.com*)

The character who most embodies a new approach to tackling white racism is Richard. He is angry at the white man for disempowering African Americans and believes that "the only way the black man's going to *get* any power is to drive all the white men into the sea." Richard possesses a gun and says he is prepared to use it if he has to. (He does agree, however, to hand over the gun to his father for safekeeping.) Richard's approach is more militant than the one advocated by the mainstream civil rights movement in the mid-1960s and is associated historically with figures such as Stokely Carmichael and Malcolm X rather than with Dr. King.

Injustice

Racism implies injustice, and such is the case in the play. The discrimination and violence suffered by African Americans is institutionalized in the sense that neither the police nor the courts have any interest in addressing the problem. Indeed, the authorities seem to encourage such unfair treatment. The African American characters know this very well. In act 1, when the demonstrators return and gather in the church, having suffered assaults from brick-throwing whites, Lorenzo remarks, "The cops ain't going to protect us. They call up the people and tell them where we are and say 'Go get them!'"

When sometime in the past, before the action of the play begins, Lyle killed Old Bill, there appears to have been no official investigation of the death, and Lyle got away with it. The death of an African American man, it seems, even in such violent circumstances, is of little public interest. After Lyle murders Richard, almost nobody in the town, of either race, expects Lyle to be arrested. It appears to be only due to the efforts of Parnell James, in combination with the circumstances of this particular case—Lyle is obviously a prime suspect—that forces a reluctant chief of police to charge Lyle with murder.

In spite of this, the injustice of the judicial system becomes plain when Lyle is acquitted, as everyone knew he would be. On the witness stand, Richard's father, Meridian, gives powerful expression to the notion that the entire social system, rather than just one man, contributed to his death, which was caused by: "*your* guns, *your* hoses, *your* dogs, *your* judges, *your* law-makers, *your* folly, *your* pride, *your* cruelty, *your* cowardice, *your* money, *your* chain gangs, and *your* churches!"

STYLE

Flashbacks

The play does not present a linear sequence of events. Instead, the action weaves smoothly back and forth in time by means of flashbacks. In fact, the beginning of the play itself is a flashback, showing as it does Lyle's shooting of Richard. The dramatist shows this at the beginning so that the audience is absolutely clear that Lyle is guilty. Act 1 contains two flashbacks that show Richard interacting with his grandmother Juanita and his father. The beginning of each flashback is marked by Richard's singing or by the sound of his guitar. Another flashback occurs in act 2, which shows Richard's encounter with Lyle at the grocery store. Act 3, near the end, has a flashback that shows the final confrontation between Lyle and Richard, including Richard's death. Thus, although Richard is already dead when the main action of the play begins, his story unfolds through flashbacks as the play proceeds.

Set

The framework of the set in the first two acts is the African American church, and in the final act it is the courthouse. Church and courthouse are on opposite sides of a street. When the action is in the church, the audience is also aware of the dome of the courthouse and the American flag. In act 3, the steeple and the cross should be visible. This arrangement makes clear the connection between the local events enacted in the play and the wider connections to religion, the judicial system, and the nation as a whole.

The church is divided by an aisle, which serves to mark the separation between what are called Whitetown and Blacktown. When a scene takes place involving white characters, it is therefore confined to one side of the stage, and vice versa. This means that the audience is always kept visually aware of the system of racial segregation. It is also a reminder that in act 3 the action takes place in a segregated courtroom. Within this framework, details of other locations specified in the play, such as Richard's room, Papa D.'s juke joint, and Lyle's store, are left to the audience's imagination.

HISTORICAL CONTEXT

Civil Rights Movement

Baldwin based his play very loosely on the case of Emmett Till. Till was a fourteen-year-old African American boy from Chicago who in August 1955 was visiting relatives in the South. He allegedly tried to flirt with a young white woman in a grocery store. A few days later, Till was abducted and killed by the woman's husband and another man in Money, Mississippi. The killers were tried and acquitted but later confessed to the crime. The case received national publicity. During the 1950s and 1960s, such violence by whites against African Americans in the South was common, and more often than not it went unpunished. The fact that it forms the basis of *Blues for Mister Charlie* shows how relevant the themes of the play were to the situation in the South in the mid-1960s.

Just four months after the murder of Till, in December 1955, the spark that ignited the modern civil rights movement was lit in Montgomery, Alabama, when Rosa Parks refused to give up her seat on a bus to a white person, as custom dictated. The subsequent bus boycott by African Americans lasted for over one year, before the buses in Alabama were officially desegregated in December 1956. The civil rights movement had thus already been in progress for nine years when *Blues for Mister Charlie* was produced in 1964. Nonviolent protest across the South had led to a number of significant gains, including the landmark Civil Rights Act of 1964, which banned discrimination based on race, color, religion, gender, or national origin in employment, schools, or public places.

A frequent tactic employed by civil rights campaigners (which the African American characters in the play are using) was the boycotting of white businesses, with the aim of forcing them to treat African American customers the same as they did whites and also to hire African American employees. Demonstrations also called for an end to segregation in public facilities, such as parks, theaters, swimming pools, and libraries. In the play, Lorenzo discloses that as a result of their protests, they are now allowed to use the

COMPARE
&
CONTRAST

- **1964:** There is a voter registration drive in Mississippi. Three workers who participate in the registration drive—two of them, both white, are from New York, and the other is an African American man from Mississippi—are murdered by the Ku Klux Klan. This is not the only incident in the South during this year in which those who are working for racial integration are attacked and beaten or killed.

  Today: According to FBI data, African Americans are more likely to be the target of hate crimes than any other group in the United States. In 2012, more than fifty out of every one million African Americans is a victim of a race-based hate crime, which is twice as high as any other group.

- **1964:** Two plays about race relations by African American playwright Amiri Baraka are produced for the first time on Broadway. The plays are *Dutchman* and *The Slave*.

  Today: As part of its CS Digital Initiative, Center Stage in Baltimore produces a series of six short video plays collectively titled *My America Too,* set in places such as Sanford, Florida; Cleveland, Ohio; Ferguson, Missouri; Staten Island, New York; Baltimore, Maryland; and Charleston, South Carolina, all of which have recently witnessed highly publicized killings of African Americans.

- **1964:** The Civil Rights Act is passed and is followed one year later by another landmark achievement of the civil rights movement, the Voting Rights Act.

  Today: New voting restrictions exist in seventeen US states following the 2013 Supreme Court ruling in *Shelby County v. Holder,* which invalidated sections of the Voting Rights Act. Under that ruling, states with histories of voter discrimination against minorities no longer have to ask permission from the federal government before changing their voter laws.

---

public library, but they are still not allowed in the swimming pool.

In the play, Lorenzo also complains that "we still can't vote, we can't even get registered." Campaigning for the right to vote was another key element in the movement, and voter registration drives were held across the South by civil rights groups. Although in theory African Americans had the legal right to vote based on the Fifteenth Amendment of 1870, in practice, southern states had many discriminatory practices that prevented African Americans from voting. One such practice was a literacy test; many African Americans, having been denied educational opportunity, would fail.

Campaigning for voting rights was often dangerous during the 1960s. In March 1965, a peaceful march from Selma to Montgomery, Alabama, was disrupted by state troopers, who attacked the marchers, beating many of them.

Five months later, President Lyndon Johnson signed the Voting Rights Act into law. Literacy tests were banned, as were other measures such as poll taxes that had been used to prevent African Americans from voting.

CRITICAL OVERVIEW

When *Blues for Mister Charlie* was first produced in New York City, Howard Taubman gave it a respectful and appreciative, although not uncritical, review in the *New York Times*. It "is not a tidy play. Its structure is loose, and it makes valid points as if they were clichés. But it throbs with fierce energy and passion. It is like a thunderous battle cry," Taubman writes. He notes that Baldwin was not concerned about creating suspense, or, in act 3, in "the niceties of legal procedure." Instead, he was out to convey "the fundamental

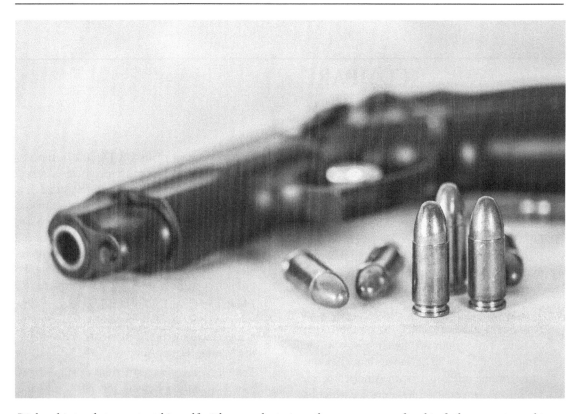

Richard intends to protect himself with a gun but gives the weapon up after his father convinces him a nonviolent path is best (© fotorawin | Shutterstock.com)

forces that lead to" the crime around which the play revolves, the murder of Richard Henry. Taubman concludes that "although Mr. Baldwin has not yet mastered all the problems and challenges of the theater, *Blues for Mister Charlie* brings eloquence and conviction to one of the momentous themes of our era." In a piece written just a few weeks later, in May 1964, the same critic offers the view that the play "is an angry sermon and a pain-wracked lament. It draws together the humiliation, degradation, frustration and resentment felt by millions relegated to second-class citizenship and transmutes the accumulated bitterness into a roar of fury."

Since the 1960s, the play has occasionally been revived. Reviewing a production at the Tri-cycle Theatre in June 2004, Elisabeth Mahoney writes in the *Guardian*:

> Uncompromising in his portrayal of both sides of the racial divide, Baldwin doesn't flinch from trying to understand the white murderer, and he shows the black community lost between turning the other cheek and violent revenge for oppression; its questions remain urgent and uncomfortable 40 years on.

Nearly fifty years after its first performance, the play was revived at the New Haarlem Arts Theatre in New York in June 2011. Joe Dziemia-nowicz writes in the *New York Daily News*, "The seldom-revived play still burns." However, he added that "after nearly a half-century, the play's retro earnestness and heavy-handedness has downgraded its blaze from four-alarm to something less explosive."

CRITICISM

Bryan Aubrey

Aubrey holds a PhD in English. In the following essay, he discusses Blues for Mister Charlie *in terms of what Baldwin might have meant when he wrote that the play was his attempt to bear witness to the "power of light."*

The year 1964, when Baldwin's *Blues for Mister Charlie* was first produced, was a landmark year for civil rights in the United States with the passage of the Civil Rights Act, one of

WHAT DO I READ NEXT?

- *The Fire Next Time* (1963) is Baldwin's examination of racial tensions and problems in the United States in the 1960s. Consisting of two essays, the book was well received by critics and became a best seller. It goes deeper into some of the issues raised in *Blues for Mister Charlie.*

- *The National Black Drama Anthology: Eleven Plays from America's Leading African-American Theaters* (2000), edited by Woodie King, is an anthology of plays by African American dramatists that have been produced by the New Federal Theatre in New York, which was founded by King in 1970. The collection features the work of minority dramatists.

- *Spinning into Butter* (2000), a play by Rebecca Gilman, is set on a mostly white college campus in Vermont. Sarah Daniels, a liberal dean of students, investigates racist incidents aimed at one of the college's African American students. As a result, she is compelled to examine her own feelings about racism. The play was first performed at the Goodman Theatre in Chicago in May 1999.

- *Clybourne Park* (2011), by Bruce Norris, is set in two very different eras. In 1959, an African American family moves into a white neighborhood, to the consternation of the existing residents. Fifty years later, in 2009, a young white couple is about to buy the property, raze it, and rebuild, but this time the largely African American neighborhood objects to what it sees as a spoiling of their gentrifying area. The play won the 2011 Pulitzer Prize for Drama and the 2012 Tony Award for Best Play.

- *Honky* (2014) is a satirical comedy by Greg Kalleres that explores racism. After a young African American is killed for his expensive basketball shoes, sales surge among white teenagers. A shoe designer, an advertising writer, and a shoe salesman are among the characters, white and African American, as the play explores in humorous fashion the relationship between race and commercialism.

- *Scenes for Teens: 50 Original Comedy and Drama Scenes for Teenage Actors*, by Mike Kimmel (2014), is a collection of drama scripts that can be performed by aspiring young actors. Each scene is for two actors, who can be either male or female.

---

the great achievements of the civil rights movement that began in the mid-1950s. However, the work of the movement was hardly done, and the brutal nature of the obstacles still faced by African Americans in their quest for equality and fair treatment continued to be brought home in that and subsequent years by the violent, endemic racism in the South. The deep-rooted racial prejudices of white people and the pain of the African Americans who have long had to endure it are well brought out in Baldwin's play, which throbs with raw emotion, pain, and also defiance.

However, in an era of hope, when the whole nation was inspired by the moving speeches of Dr. Martin Luther King Jr. and progress in civil rights was being made, it might appear at first that there is not a not a great deal of hope conveyed in *Blues for Mister Charlie*. It seems that hope is more often frustrated than fulfilled. African Americans are harassed and killed indiscriminately, and no one is brought to justice for the crimes. There are, in fact, three deaths in the play, two of which have already happened before the play begins—that of Meridian's wife under suspicious circumstances in a white-owned hotel and that of Old Bill, who dared to challenge Lyle for having an affair with his wife. Then, at the very beginning of the play, the death of Richard is shown—killed by Lyle after a pointless and trivial disagreement. In his notes to the published edition of the play, Baldwin acknowledged that in the United States "we are walking in terrible darkness here," and yet he added that the play was "one man's attempt to bear witness to the reality and the power of light."

The latter remark suggests that in spite of the dark deeds it records, Baldwin conceived his work in a spirit of hope and that the power of light might have the strength to overcome the power of darkness. The phrase he used puts in mind the words of the Gospel of John (chapter 1, verse 5): "The light shines in the darkness, and the darkness has not overcome it." Baldwin, however, as he revealed in many of his writings, was no friend of Christianity as it manifested in twentieth-century America, so it might seem unlikely that he meant "the power of light" in any traditional religious sense. Indeed, the play presents a negative picture of Christianity. The younger generation of the African American community, although they meet at the church, seem to have little patience with religion as they have experienced it. Lorenzo, for example, describes the church as "the house of this damn almighty God who don't care what happens to nobody, unless, of course, they're white."

Given this perspective, if Christianity is to be the vehicle of hope for African Americans or to embody in any way the "power of light," it is going to have to change. The most profound critique of the religious status quo is given in the play by one who has earned the right to do so—the Reverend Meridian Henry, father of the murdered Richard. In act 1, in conversation with Parnell, Meridian says that his family going back generations have been Christian, but then he utters a staggeringly radical thought regarding Christianity and matters of race. Before Christ lived, Meridian says,

> black people weren't raised to turn the other cheek, and in the hope of heaven. No, then they didn't have to take low. Before Christ. They walked around just as good as anybody else, and when they died, they didn't go to heaven, they went to join their ancestors.

In contrast, according to Christianity, Meridian says, his murdered son has not gone to join his ancestors but is in hell, as befits a sinner. "Is that such an improvement, such a mighty advance over B.C.?" he asks.

Not everyone has the ability to question the very foundations of the belief system that has sustained them for their entire lives, but Meridian shows such an ability here. He also remains aware of the appeal that Christianity has always had to oppressed people (the early Christians in the Roman Empire, for example): "Since I wasn't a man in men's eyes, then I could be a man in the eyes of God." However, Meridian now fears that such a belief is not enough, because it did not protect either his wife or his son, both of whom are now dead. He permits himself another radical, indeed heretical thought, especially for a preacher: "The eyes of God—maybe those eyes are blind."

Parnell picks up on what he hears as the rage and even hatred in Meridian's tone, and Meridian does not deny it. However, such feelings and attitudes seem in this context to be part of, or at least the precursor to, the "power of light" to which Baldwin refers. They are part of the awakening process for African Americans, although the older generation, as represented in the play by Mother Henry, Meridian's mother, will have no part of it. Mother Henry's traditional, deep, nonpolitical faith, her inability to conceive what her grandson Richard means by professing atheism, since she raised her children "in the fear of God," is presented as being out of touch with what the times need.

Meridian, however, is not prepared to let hatred take him over completely. In act 2, he delivers what is perhaps the most ringing, passionate, heartfelt speech in the entire play, as he preaches in the church at Richard's funeral. In a direct address to God, Meridian confesses that when young people come to him and ask him what direction they should take in trying to achieve racial justice, he is unsure of what advice to give them. Should he tell them just to go on enduring the miseries that are heaped upon them by the whites? He says that a great darkness is ruling both African American and white people, but he will not let it defeat him. Still asking for a message from God that will tell him what to advise his people, he concludes, "Let not our suffering endure forever. Teach us to trust the great gift of life and learn to love one another and dare to walk the earth like men. Amen."

The call for love is a moving one, but it is not the dominant note of his speech or of the play. The key phrase here is actually the last one, which refers to walking on the earth "like men." The civil rights movement as presented in the play is about African Americans asserting their full humanity even in the face of those who would deny it. This involves courage and a kind of liberation from deeply ingrained patterns of the past. It also involves confrontation, a refusal to accept the status quo. This, as the play bears witness to, is a highly dangerous stance when faced with the institutionalized, ruthless power of an entrenched oppressor. The best example of this is, of course, Richard Henry.

Richard is by no means a perfect standard bearer for this new, liberated consciousness. He is headstrong, reckless, and careless of his own safety, but having returned from living eight years in the North, he sees his hometown in the South through radically different eyes. He has broken through the subservient mindset that has for so long gripped the other African American townspeople—and there is no going back. In act 3, the trial scene, Juanita reports that Richard said he was never going to run away from white people again; he was "going to stay and be a man—a *man!* right here." In his final confrontation with Lyle, Richard says, "You a man and I'm a man," speaking to Lyle as an equal. Richard's father Meridian speaks in similar language from the witness stand in the trial: "I am a man. *A man!* I tried to help my son become a man. But manhood is a dangerous pursuit, here."

Blues for Mister Charlie bears vivid witness to Meridian's last words here, yet it is this pursuit of full humanity, in one's own eyes and those of others, both African American and white, that emerges as the brave, courageous, and absolutely necessary act that is demanded of the African Americans living in this time and place. It is this assertion of a birthright, which carries the hope and "the power of light," that can be

> " THE FINAL QUESTION THAT BALDWIN RAISES IN *BLUES* IS ONE OF ACCOUNTABILITY."

heard in this play as a stirring counterpoint to the other, darker reality that is given equally powerful expression—the terrible sadness, misery, and pain that the African American community has endured.

Source: Bryan Aubrey, Critical Essay on *Blues for Mister Charlie*, in *Drama for Students*, Gale, Cengage Learning, 2017.

Louis H. Pratt

In the following excerpt, Pratt looks at themes of race and accountability in Blues for Mister Charlie.

C. WHEN THE BATTLE LINES ARE DRAWN

... After Lyle has been tried and acquitted, he breaks down and admits his crime to his wife. His rationale is clearly reflective of the warped, twisted psyche from which he suffers: "I had to kill him. I'm a white man! Can't nobody talk that way to me!" Equally contemptible and indicative of this sickness is the totally indifferent response which Josephine makes to his admission of guilt: "Come on, Lyle. We got to get on home. We got to get the little one home. ... He's hungry. I got to feed him." Unmoved by Lyle's description of the wanton murder, Josephine has preoccupations far beyond those of the violation of black humanity.

For Lyle and Josephine, those actions that cannot be justified in the name of humanity must be rationalized in the light of racial superiority. George identifies with this concept when Parnell reminds him that he did not have to compete with blacks for his job as shoe salesman. He is forced to acknowledge that he has no other qualification for the job other than his race: "Well, goddammit, white men come before niggers! They *got* to!"

Pseudo-liberalism is symbolized in the play by Parnell James, the local newspaperman who tries to stake his claim in the best of all possible worlds: Full membership in the white race and complete acceptance among those in the

Lyle incriminates himself by mentioning that Richard's body was found face down in the weeds when Parnell never described the crime scene (© blphoto1 | Shutterstock.com)

community who are black. In befriending Meridian and Lyle, Parnell overextends himself, and we discover that he is regarded with suspicion and cynicism by both races. These misgivings eventually give rise to an open confrontation between Parnell and a group of whites in the kitchen of the Britten home. All whites, these people feel, should be united in their efforts to keep the black man in his place. But Parnell is the renegade, the "Communist," who preaches social justice for blacks. He is "*worse* than a nigger" because he cannot be trusted. As Reverend Phelps joins the conversation, he tells Parnell that the situation "has become much too serious for flippancy and cynicism." The battle lines have been drawn, and he must take a side; "Are you with us or against us?... We've put up with your irresponsibility long enough. We won't tolerate it any longer. Do I make myself clear?"

This same wariness is also shared by the blacks in the community. After Richard has been killed, Meridian begins to reexamine his own attitudes and values, and this serves to objectify the growing distrust of white "liberalism."

Believing, like Phelps, that blacks are a "simple people," Parnell cannot understand the bitterness that Meridian now feels toward whites. This failure, Meridian concludes, is symbolic of Parnell's own inability to perceive the black man as a human being with human emotions. This lack of sensitivity is discovered by Meridian as Parnell and the Police Chief discuss Richard's murder: "For both of you—I watched this, I never watched it before—it was just a black boy that was dead, and that was a problem. He saw the problem one way, you saw it another way. But it wasn't a *man* that was dead, not my *son*—you held yourselves away from *that*."

Parnell's real test, however, comes when he is called upon to testify at Lyle Britten's trial. At this crucial point in the drama, Parnell is in a position to help effect the "social justice" to which he gives lip service in his newspaper. He is now able to function as an agent for positive change in the black community. But he cannot contradict Josephine Britten's testimony because she is *white*. Unable to reject the concept of white supremacy and the cultural institutions of power which it symbolizes, he finds himself incapable of serving the ends of justice. Hence, for Baldwin, Parnell becomes typical of all "liberals" who "are operating in this part of the forest because this is where they find themselves, and it is easy for them—but it has nothing whatever to do with love or justice or any of the things they think it has to do with. And when the chips are down, it comes out. Their status in their own eyes is much more important than any real changes." Parnell's inability to rise to this challenge is not his own unique affliction; it is the plague of race which afflicts the entire community. It is the blind adherence to a creed which demands that justice and humanity be defined explicitly in terms of whiteness.

D. DARKNESS AND LIGHT

The two ministers—Reverend Phelps and Reverend Henry—both serve as vehicles for the development of Baldwin's views concerning the second aspect of the plague, our concept of religion: "...the principles governing the rites and customs of the churches in which I grew up did not differ from the principles governing the rites and customs of other churches, white. The principles were Blindness, Loneliness, and Terror, the first principle necessarily and actively cultivated in order to deny the two others." We take Reverend Phelps as tangible evidence of this blindness in the white community. When Lyle is arrested, he is among the whites who visit him in order to reassure him of their support: "We only came by to let you know that we're with you and every white person in this town is with you." Thus, Phelps is able, in good conscience, to console his parishioner who has yet to be brought to trial. The God that Phelps represents permits him the luxury of partiality: Innocent or guilty, he is with Lyle because they both are white. This attitude is similar to the perverse reaction that Lorenzo exhibits in his comments on Richard's death: "This damn almighty God...don't care what happens to nobody unless, of course, they're white...." In order to understand this attitude, we must recognize the fact that both Lorenzo and Phelps have been taught that "This world is white....White people hold the power, which means that they are superior to blacks (intrinsically, that is: God decreed it so), and the world has innumerable ways of making this difference known and felt and feared."

There is nothing mystifying, then, about Phelps' inability to understand black people and

to provide a true Christian perspective for the guidance of his parishioners. Phelps' religion is a spirituality of convenience which functions to reinforce the "superior worth" of the white man in our society. The purpose of the local civil rights demonstrations escapes him because he lacks the objectivity with which to view the black man's struggle for equality. Instead, he attributes the black reaction to injustice to outside influences: "They're a simple peoples—warm hearted and good-natured. But they are easily led, and now they are harkening to the counsel of these degenerate Communist race-mixers. And they don't know what terrible harm they can bring on themselves—and on us all." It is far easier to blame the problems of a society on forces that lie outside of that society than it is to recognize and embrace reality. And this is the road that Phelps has conveniently taken.

Reverend Meridian Henry, obviously enough, stands as the symbol of religion in the black community. Having been deprived of the dignity of manhood in the secular world, he seeks this respectability in the world of religion: "I've had to think—would I have *been* such a Christian if I hadn't been born black?" For him, dignity is defined in the simplest terms which any husband and father might require: the protection of his wife and his son. Why is it, then, that his concept of religion has resulted in the formulation of values that have been just as ineffectual as the religious convictions to which Phelps adheres? First of all, Meridian uses religion as an escape mechanism to protect himself from the stark realities of life. In strictly ostrich-like fashion, he has stuck his head into the sand of religion, using the Bible as a shield and a solution to the multiplicity of real problems in a real world ruled not by the word of God but by the written and unwritten laws of men. He seeks to deal with the secular world strictly in accordance with Biblical precept, and he finds that this course of action is insufficient: His son and his wife have been wantonly killed by the plague of hate.

Slowly, Meridian becomes aware that yesterday's ineffective solutions will not provide answers to the problems of today. Established values must be reexamined and new ones created in order to deal effectively with these issues. He acknowledges his role as a leader of his people: It is to him that generations yet unborn will turn for a sign, and he does not yet know what that sign must be:

Now, when the children come, my Lord, and ask which road to follow, my tongue stammers and my heart fails. . . . But can I ask the children forever to sustain the cruelty inflicted on them by those who have been their masters, and who are now, in very truth, their kinfolk, their brothers and their sisters and their parents? . . . I have set my face against the darkness, I will not let it conquer me, even though it will, I know, one day, destroy this body. But, my Lord, what of the children? What shall I tell the children?

Meridian begins to move toward these new values, and in Act III we see on the witness stand a man whose faith has begun to falter under the oppressive forces exerted by a society that has been blinded by the plague of race: ". . . both my son and I have profound reservations concerning the behavior of Christians. He wondered why they treated black people as they do. And I was unable to give him a satisfactory answer." Thus he has begun to come to grips with himself. He comes to the awareness that being a man in the sight of God is not enough. But he must, in fact, stake his claim to manhood in the world of men. He now feels compelled to stand before the court, a microcosm of the local power structure, and declare, "I am a man. A *man*! I tried to help my son become a man. But manhood is a dangerous pursuit, here. And that pursuit undid him because of your guns, *your* hoses, *your* dogs, *your* judges, *your* lawmakers, *your* folly, *your* pride, *your* cruelty, *your* cowardice, *your* money, *your* chain gangs, and *your* churches. . . ."

Finally Meridian discovers the answer that he must pass on to posterity. In the closing scene outside the courthouse, Mother Henry issues the call for a prayer march. Meridian, however, has learned that prayer is only half the answer which he must give: "You know, for us, it all began with the Bible and the gun. Maybe it will end with the Bible and the gun." We must not ask God to do for us that which we can do for ourselves. He has made us men biologically, but to us falls the responsibility of asserting our manhood within the social context. It is incumbent upon us to employ both the Bible and the gun—to use nonviolence as well as, violence in order to achieve this end.

The final question that Baldwin raises in *Blues* is one of accountability. Each of us, as members of the universal brotherhood of man, Baldwin contends, has a solemn moral obligation to understand the white racist and to attempt the liberation of his children because the

> *BLUES FOR MISTER CHARLIE* FLUCTUATES AMONG EIGHT DIFFERENT COMBINATIONS OF THESE SIX ELEMENTS: BLACK ATMOSPHERE, WHITE ATMOSPHERE, TIME PRESENT, TIME PAST, REPRESENTATIONAL STYLE, SOLILOQUY STYLE."

responsibility for this man's crimes falls squarely upon the shoulders of the American people: ". . . it is we who put the cattle-prodder in his hands. . . . It is we who have locked him in the prison of his color. It is we who have persuaded him that Negroes are worthless human beings, and that it is his sacred duty, as a white man, to protect the honor and purity of his tribe. . . . It is we who have made it mandatory—honorable— that white father should deny black son." Our only salvation, then, lies in our children—white and black. It is they who must help us to become "equal to ourselves." Only they can lead us "to become a people so free in ourselves that we will have no need to fear others and have no need to murder others." . . .

Source: Louis H. Pratt, "The Darkness Within," in *James Baldwin*, Twayne, 1978, pp. 93–97.

Carlton W. Molette

In the following excerpt, Molette discusses the difficulties in staging the play.

At first glance, the whole subject of Baldwin as a playwright seems destined to be rather uncomplicated. After all, he has had only two plays professionally produced, and subsequently published. But the depth of Baldwin's characters simply does not permit uncomplicated answers to questions of some substance. Baldwin's characters—those in his plays—have the same kind of depth and complexity with which the characters in his novels are endowed. After all, he is a novelist; and novelists—the good ones— are supposed to be able to do that: create characters of great depth and complexity. But novels provide ways of delving into character that plays do not have at their disposal. And the concern here is with plays.

I will leave it to the literary critics to examine Baldwin's literature—to examine Baldwin as a writer. I am a theater worker, and I will confine my concern to Baldwin as a playwright, and to the plays that he has wrought. I would further like to emphasize that plays are *wrought*, not written. This is an important concept to reckon with. Writers work wherever and whenever they will. Playwrights must work with and for the other theater workers, or theater-wrights. Plays are events that occur, not words that are written. So, to examine James Baldwin as a playwright is to examine something that only seldom, and quite inadvertently, has to do with things literary. My concerns with any script have largely to do with such questions as: Does it come alive on the stage? Does the action of the play flow smoothly and continuously? Will it hold the attention of the audience? Will it have meaning and worth for the audience? There have been many great writers throughout history who have not been able to *wright* a play that is successful, according to the above criteria.

... One of the most illuminating moments that I have spent in a theater was spent in watching a particular scene in *Blues for Mister Charlie*. This particular scene is a soliloquy. I am sure that, if I had read the scene prior to seeing it performed, I would have said, "It will not work on the stage. It is too long. And besides, soliloquies are no longer acceptable as a principal means of character revelation." Fortunately, I was privileged to witness a truly gifted actress, Miss Diana Sands, perform the soliloquy before I had an opportunity to say all of those incorrect things. But again the question arises, Is it the play? Or did Miss Sands make it work in spite of the script rather than because of it? After all Diana Sands could transform even *The Owl and the Pussycat* into an arresting evening of theater. I am afraid that, in the hands of a lesser artist than Miss Sands, that soliloquy could be transformed from the highpoint to the lowpoint of the play. On the other hand, this soliloquy does not stand out as a readily perceived flaw. The play is too complex, really, for anything to stand out as a readily perceived anything. Again Baldwin has wrought a play in which its worst theatrical characteristics are its best literary characteristics. As a piece of literature, the complexity of *Blues for Mister Charlie* is an admirable trait; as a theatrical event, that same complexity is its major flaw.

But, before we get into the details of the above assertion, let us look for a moment at both of these plays, and the times out of which they grew. *The Amen Corner* is a play of the 1950s. It tells a story of love and hope for a better tomorrow. The story is told in an uncomplicated, straightforward manner. It grew out of the years just before college students were marching, arm in arm, to the strains of "We Shall Overcome." On the other hand, *Blues for Mister Charlie* grew out of the years just before Watts, and the others, burned. *Blues for Mister Charlie* is a "protest" play. It is a complicated, angry play. It is a play that is self-consciously black. When blacks do protest plays, to whom do they protest? To whites, of course. So *Blues for Mister Charlie* is largely aimed at a white audience. This is not intended to imply that the play says nothing to blacks. On the other hand, *The Amen Corner* does not protest to whites; it informs, educates, illuminates blacks. The play was first staged on the campus of a black university. It is not self-consciously black. The play assumes that there are some elementary aspects of black culture that do not require explanation within the body of the play. It assumes, in effect, a black audience. It is not an anti-white play, it is an a-white play.

Blues for Mister Charlie tries to be all things to all people. It tries to explain whites to blacks and blacks to whites. That probably requires two different plays. That is certainly one major reason for the complexity of the play. And, since plays must be absorbed in the span of time it takes to perform them, complexity can be a liability. Conversations among average white audience members in the theater lobby during intermission and following *Blues for Mister Charlie* all seemed to resolve around the fact that there was content that the blacks understood that the whites did not. "What are they laughing at?"—meaning the blacks in the audience—the whites kept asking each other. But the reverse situation applied as well. The white characters were frequently not understood, or not accepted as valid, by the black audience members. Actually, blacks did not want to face an essential truth in the character of Lyle Britten. That truth is that Lyle is not some kind of a demonic redneck character. Lyle is *not* a bad guy—just ask Lyle, he'll tell you. Baldwin says, "No man is a villain in his own eyes." So most blacks in the audience were presented with a character that they either refused to admit was there, or refused to admit was true. What they

Blues for Mister Charlie

wanted was some kind of wild-eyed, nigger-hating, stereotyped redneck villain. Instead they got a real man who was backed into a corner, not by Richard Henry but by the system.

But that is only one of a number of paradoxes. Richard Henry thinks he must destroy "Mr. Charlie" in order to achieve his own salvation. On the other hand, he knows that the system is programmed to destroy him if he attempts to destroy the man. He knows that he cannot realistically expect to beat the whole system singlehandedly. So he knows that his act of destruction perpetrated against "Mr. Charlie" will inevitably result in his own destruction. Yet he wants to live. He is not suicidal. Still a third paradox. And this one clearly marks this as a statement of 1960s point of view. The leader of the white community and the leader of the black community get together to tell each other how much progress they are making within the system. But even they know that it is a lie.

In addition to these, and other, paradoxes, Blues for Mister Charlie is made even more complicated by a number of fluctuations. There are fluctuations in at least three major aspects of the production: time, locale, and acting style. Time fluctuates between time present and time past. The locale of the play also fluctuates between two distinctly different atmospheres. There are black locales and white locales. There is a fluctuation between two distinct acting styles. Most of the performance requires an illusionistic, representational style of acting—one in which the action of the play revolves around relationships between the actors. But there is some fluctuation into the realm of soliloquy that requires quite a different approach, or style, for the actors. When the play moves into the realm of soliloquy, a less illusionistic style is necessitated—one that requires the actor to relate more inwardly to his own character; and at the same time, more outwardly to the audience, but not to the other characters.

Blues for Mister Charlie fluctuates among eight different combinations of these six elements: black atmosphere, white atmosphere, time present, time past, representational style, soliloquy style. If the play is to have its optimum effect upon the audience, the audience must be able to keep up with these fluctuations. Further, the audience must manage this without devoting a great deal of concentration to the effort. After all, primary attention must be devoted to receiving the message, not to determining the where, the when, and the how of the transmission of the message. In spite of all these complexities, the play can work as a play. The inherent complexities do create production problems. Actually, the script would work better as a film than it does as a play. But Baldwin has achieved one very important requisite for *wrighting* a play. Further, this achievement is undoubtedly why the play works, despite its complexity. Baldwin has not attempted to provide complete verbal transitions for all of these fluctuations and paradoxes.

I am sure that such restraint must be difficult for a novelist to achieve. Such restraint must be particularly difficult for a novelist to achieve because it requires that one artist turn his creative efforts over to someone else before it can be completed. So the transitions are achieved through the use of music, lighting, scenery, costume, and, of course, acting. That requires from the playwright a trust of and a reliance upon many other artists. The ability to accomplish that collaborative working relationship may very well be the reason for Baldwin's success as a playwright where so many other novelists have failed.

Certainly, Baldwin would be an even better playwright if he would gain more experience in the theater. But who can blame him for not doing so? After all, his first obligation is the physical and artistic survival of James Baldwin. Given the present system of producing plays professionally in the United States, we are lucky indeed to get one play per decade from the likes of James Baldwin.

Source: Carlton W. Molette, "James Baldwin as a Playwright," in *James Baldwin: A Critical Evaluation*, edited by Therman B. O'Daniel, Howard University Press, 1977, pp. 183, 185–88.

SOURCES

Baldwin, James, *Blues for Mister Charlie*, Dial Press, 1964.

Berman, Ari, "The Gutting of the Voting Rights Act Could Decide the 2016 Election," in *Nation*, June 21, 2016, https://www.thenation.com/article/the-gutting-of-the-voting-rights-act-could-decide-the-2016-election/ (accessed June 24, 2016).

Dziemianowicz, Joe, "'Blues for Mister Charlie': Revival Far Less Explosive than 1964 Original," in *New York Daily News*, June 11, 2011, http://www.nydailynews.com/entertainment/

8 6

Drama for Students, Volume 34

music-arts/blues-mister-charlie-revival-explosive-1964-original-article-1.129518 (accessed June 25, 2016).

"FBI: Blacks Most Often Targeted in Hate Crimes," in *PBS Newshour*, June 20, 2015, http://www.pbs.org/newshour/bb/fbi-blacks-often-targeted-hate-crimes/ (accessed June 23, 2016).

"The Gospel According to St. John," in *The Holy Bible*, rev. standard version, Oxford University Press, 1952, p. 1118.

Mahoney, Elisabeth, Review of *Blues for Mister Charlie*, in *Guardian*, June 17, 2004, https://www.theguardian.com/stage/2004/jun/18/theatre (accessed June 28, 2016).

My America Too, Center Stage, CS Digital website, http://www.centerstage.org/ShowsandEvents/CSDigital.aspx (accessed June 23, 2016).

Taubman, Howard, "Common Burden: Baldwin Points Duty of Negro and White," in *New York Times*, May 3, 1964, https://www.nytimes.com/books/98/03/29/specials/baldwin-burden.html (accessed June 28, 2016).

———, "Theater: 'Blues for Mister Charlie,'" in *New York Times*, April 24, 1964, https://www.nytimes.com/books/98/03/29/specials/baldwin-charlie.html (accessed June 28, 2016).

"Voting Rights Act," History.com, http://www.history.com/topics/black-history/voting-rights-act (accessed June 17, 2016).

FURTHER READING

Elam, Michele, ed., *The Cambridge Companion to James Baldwin*, Cambridge University Press, 2015.
    This collection of essays explores Baldwin's work in novels, poetry, children's literature, and drama, as well as his nonfiction. Patrick

Johnson's essay, "Baldwin's Theater," includes discussion of *Blues for Mister Charlie*.

Leeming, David, *James Baldwin: A Biography*, Arcade, 1994.
    Leeming was Baldwin's personal secretary and friend over a twenty-five-year period, and this is a biography authorized by Baldwin in 1979. Leeming sees his subject as akin to an Old Testament prophet.

Malburne, Meredith M., "No Blues for Mister Henry: Locating Richard's Revolution," in *Reading Contemporary African American Drama: Fragments of History, Fragments of Self*, edited by Trudier Harris and Jennifer Larson, Peter Lang, 2007, pp. 9–57.
    Malburne offers a character study of Richard Henry in the play.

Standley, Fred R., and Louis H. Pratt, *Conversations with James Baldwin*, University Press of Mississippi, 1989.
    This is a collection of twenty-seven interviews with Baldwin that span the period 1961–1987.

SUGGESTED SEARCH TERMS

James Baldwin

Blues for Mister Charlie

Civil Rights Act

Voting Rights Act

James Baldwin AND Christianity

James Baldwin AND civil rights movement

civil rights AND time line AND 1964

civil rights movement AND business boycotts

Black Lives Matter

The Curious Savage

JOHN PATRICK

1950

The Curious Savage, by John Patrick, is a play about the elderly Ethel Savage, very young at heart, whose life has been revolutionized after the passing of her wealthy husband, who effectively left the estate in her hands. The play takes place in the Cloisters, a home for people whose life experiences have left them disconnected from the real world—"not an 'asylum,'" in Patrick's own phrasing in the foreword—which is where Mrs. Savage's three stepchildren have forcibly placed her. In their eyes, her recent behavior has been too erratic, and exactly what has become of the family fortune is an open question, one that becomes more pressing as the play proceeds.

Patrick earned recognition as a master craftsman for his prolific and ultimately profitable work as a playwright in several different media—radio, film, and the stage. *The Curious Savage*, the fifth of his dozens of stage plays, was first produced on Broadway in 1950 and published in 1951. Opening at the Martin Beck Theatre, the play had an initial run that lasted for only thirty-one performances—but with its loveable characters, nimble wit, and clever plotting, it went on to become one of the most popular modern-day selections for regional production in American history.

AUTHOR BIOGRAPHY

John Patrick Goggan was born on May 17, 1905, in Louisville, Kentucky, to parents who largely

Mrs. Savage is committed to the sanatorium by her greedy stepchildren (© Pressmaster / Shutterstock.com)

failed him: he was abandoned by both and left to be raised in successions of foster homes and boarding schools. In his recollection, the boarding schools were like prisons; he remembered only two specific schools, in Austin, Texas, and New Orleans, Louisiana. Resigning himself to homeless life as a teenager, he made his way through hobo camps and ended up in San Francisco at age nineteen, where he eventually managed to gain a post as an announcer with KPO Radio. It was when he first did enough writing to earn himself a byline that he legally dropped his last name. From 1929 on, Patrick wrote hundreds of scripts for *Cecil and Sally*, a skit show that he performed with a coworker. Patrick switched to NBC Radio in 1933 and continued writing radio plays until 1936.

Patrick's first Broadway production came in 1935 with *Hell Freezes Over*, about an airship crash in Antarctica; reviewers were unanimously unimpressed, and the show lasted only twenty-five performances. Ironically, with one critic of the play, as cited in Patrick's *Los Angeles Times* obituary, writing, "Back to the ashcan with this Hollywood writer"—though Patrick had never

been to Hollywood, that was where he ended up. Twentieth Century-Fox soon offered him a three-year contract as a team scriptwriter. Beginning in 1936, he helped craft some nineteen feature films. Patrick's life took a detour during World War II, when he served as an ambulance driver with the American Field Service, including in Egypt, Syria, and Southeast Asia. Returning to the states, Patrick met with success on both the New York and London stages with *The Hasty Heart*, set in a military field hospital in Burma based on one where he had been treated for malaria, with characters based on the real-life patients he had known, including two memorable Scotsmen. The proceeds from productions of *The Hasty Heart*, which ran for six months on Broadway, allowed Patrick to buy himself sixty-five rural acres in Rockland, New York, where he honed his skill at organic farming and raised prize-winning cattle, goats, and sheep.

While his earliest plays were rather serious (and he tended toward melodrama throughout his career) Patrick turned to gentle comedy with *The Curious Savage*. Despite its limited run on Broadway, beginning October 24, 1950, the play proved an instant classic once released to amateur groups, whose productions earned Patrick over eighty thousand dollars in royalties in the first year alone. The play also gained him international renown. New York critics were not entirely favorable in their assessments of the play, finding the subject of insanity to be a poor choice for the entertainment of theatergoing audiences. Nonetheless, the play remained a box-office hit in regional theaters for decades to come.

Patrick went on to write many more original plays for the stage as well as several adaptations of novels to film. His biggest stage hit was *The Teahouse of the August Moon* (1953), adapted from the Vern Sneider novel, which won both the Pulitzer Prize and the Tony Award for best play, along with several other honors. He continued writing plays for Broadway, producing successes and failures, through the early 1960s. By the late 1960s, he was writing plays expressly for regional theaters, including series at the Albuquerque Little Theatre in New Mexico, and at the Berea Summer Theatre in Ohio; there, Baldwin-Wallace College supplemented his earlier course work at Columbia and Harvard universities with an honorary doctorate. By the late 1970s, Patrick was living on Saint Thomas, in the Virgin Islands. He died on November 7, 1995, in an assisted care facility in Delray Beach, Florida. He committed suicide and left behind a poem, titled "A Suicide Note," indicating that his life had lost the rhyme and reason that once gave it meaning.

PLOT SUMMARY

Act 1

SCENE 1

The Curious Savage opens in the well-appointed living room of the Cloisters, where four people are present: Fairy May is watching out the window, apparently awaiting someone, while Jeffrey peruses the bookshelves, Florence plays a board game alone, and Hannibal tunes his violin. Florence asks Hannibal to play something, but first Fairy interrupts by telling a tall tale, and then Jeff suddenly needs a book he cannot reach. This inspires everyone to pitch in to help reach the book, with Fairy using Hannibal's bow. Suddenly, the lights are turned off—by Mrs. Paddy, who has surreptitiously entered the room—but Miss Willie enters, turns them

MEDIA ADAPTATIONS

A televised film version of "The Curious Savage" was produced for the British program *ITV Play of the Week*, airing on August 6, 1958. It was directed by Henry Kaplan and adapted by Gerald Savory, and it featured a young Maggie Smith as Fairy.

back on, and gently scolds Mrs. Paddy. By now it is fairly clear, from the characters' variously aberrant behaviors, that this is a rest home of sorts, and the people present are the residents (though they are called "guests" in the dramatis personae), being cared for by Miss Willie.

The phone rings, and Miss Willie takes a call from Dr. Emmett, who asks that the room be tidied up, apparently for the arrival of a new guest. When Fairy, looking through the keyhole, reports seeing three strangers emerge from the doctor's office, the guests assume that they are to be sent away, so they decide to hide in the hall to eavesdrop. In come the three adult Savage children, Titus, Lily Belle, and Samuel. The doctor reassures them about the suitability of the Cloisters for their mother. When their mother, Ethel Savage, is brought in—having thwarted the doctor trying to complete her file—the children beg the doctor to stay to mediate the parting conversation. Upon entering, Mrs. Savage speaks rudely and in childish rhymes, insulting and ignoring her children. Hoping to avoid further incident, they depart. Miss Willie tries to help the flustered yet self-assured Mrs. Savage feel at home. When Miss Willie leaves for the office, the five guests enter and make introductions. Mrs. Savage takes their idiosyncrasies in stride.

Soon the buzzer sounds for the guests to go to their separate rooms. As people leave, Mrs. Savage learns in more detail the nature of everyone's quirks. When Miss Willie enters with her suitcase, Mrs. Savage describes for her new companions the course of events that have led to this point in her life—a self-effacing role in marriage, her husband's death, the embrace of freedom. She laments the injustice of her situation.

SCENE 2

The next morning, Hannibal is playing a tune—two notes on one string monotonously repeated. After that, Mrs. Savage tells the guests about her exhilarating, if not successful, acting experiences. Mrs. Savage goes to read the newspaper but finds it to be yesterday's. She turns the radio on, but it fails to work; Mrs. Paddy has stolen the tubes. Mrs. Savage starts thinking about escaping. When the buzzer signals the gardening hour, Mrs. Savage lingers in order to privately offer Miss Willie an enormous bribe to help her escape. Miss Willie declines, however, and Mrs. Savage goes out. When Doctor Emmett enters, Miss Willie reports the bribe attempt. In turn, he shows her a newspaper story: somehow Mrs. Savage has dispensed with the balance of the family estate, to the tune of ten million dollars. She is summoned, and the doctor asks how she could have spent it so quickly. She says that she has hidden it. The doctor draws from Hannibal's statistical knowledge to impress on her the true value of such a vast sum—a sum not to be squandered or lost. Hannibal plays the same tune again and announces to be "The Flight of the Bumble Bee," to Mrs. Savage's great amusement.

Act 2

SCENE 1

That night, Mrs. Paddy is sitting at her canvas, Mrs. Savage is reading, and Fairy May is sauntering about while the other three guests play cards. As Fairy makes repeated inquiries, Mrs. Savage gives interesting advice about communicating love, doing mathematics, and being wicked. She also tells about the difficult upbringing of her stepchildren, who resented her but who are already visiting again. After showing everyone Lily Belle's picture in the newspaper, Mrs. Savage pins it up and throws darts at it.

Miss Willie enters and sends everyone but Mrs. Savage upstairs. Her three children are ushered in, and Miss Willie leaves them to talk. She confirms that she has sold all of the family's assets and buried the ten million dollars' worth of negotiable bonds. Resisting her children's attempts to bully the whereabouts out of her—and calling for Miss Willie when Lily Belle tries to take her teddy bear—Mrs. Savage ends the discussion by declaring she must have a particular headache medicine to continue. She then slyly communicates to each

child in turn that the bonds are buried in a certain place: to Samuel, she says that they are under the chimney at home; to Lily Belle, in a stuffed porpoise in the Natural History Museum; and to Titus, in the president's greenhouse. When the Savage children have left, the guests burst in and confess to eavesdropping. Mrs. Savage affirms that the fortune is in none of those spots—but her children will dig anyway.

SCENE 2

A few nights later, Mrs. Savage is sitting alone. Jeff enters and strikes a surprising chord; made suddenly aware of her presence, Jeff reverts to his abashed manner. Fairy rushes in shrieking about a rat, but when she is called out by Miss Willie, she admits that she was merely trying to liven things up for Mrs. Savage. Mrs. Savage seeks news from Miss Willie, who says she will ask the doctor. Meanwhile, Mrs. Savage teaches Hannibal to get exercise by scattering playing cards and picking them up.

The doctor enters and sends all the guests but Mrs. Savage upstairs. The newspapers are reporting, to Mrs. Savage's delight, that the senator and Lily Belle were detained by the police and that Samuel has had an accident. The children enter, outraged. They resume trying to bully their mother into revealing the location of the bonds, but she resists. Seeing a magazine cover, Lily Belle rushes out to talk to Dr. Emmett. Meanwhile the other two, convinced that getting their mother released from the Cloisters is the wisest course of action, write up and sign a release statement, but when Lily returns, she tears it up. She instead suggests using a truth serum, and they instruct Dr. Emmett to administer it. Miss Willie professionally objects, but he points out that even if he refuses, they could easily force her to submit to the drug elsewhere.

Finally Mrs. Savage relents and *shows* everyone the bonds' hiding place—inside her precious teddy bear. She tosses them on the table, but just as the Savage children move forward to secure them, Mrs. Paddy hits the lights, and commotion ensues. When the lights are finally turned back on by Dr. Emmett, the bonds have disappeared, as has Mrs. Paddy. He sends Miss Willie out to alert security, and the Savage children act alarmed and disturbed.

Act 3

The curtain opens on a scene only a few minutes later. Dr. Emmett is taking a call from Miss

Willie. Afterward, he confirms to the others that the grounds are secure. Although Mrs. Paddy is implicitly suspected by everyone, Mrs. Savage points out that someone else might have taken the bonds. Titus takes command of the situation to ensure that no one escapes and to try to deduce the thief's identity. Hannibal is suspected because he was closest to the table.

Just then, Mrs. Paddy unwittingly slides backward into the room everyone still occupies, to be at once confronted by Dr. Emmett. She answers his urgent questions by nodding both yes and no ambiguously. Despite advice to the contrary, Titus tries to bully the location of the bonds out of her. Miss Willie enters, having found the radio tubes. When the idea of searching Mrs. Paddy proves problematic, Titus insists that everyone else, at least, be searched. Fairy volunteers, and Miss Willie ushers her out. Jeff then confesses to throwing the bonds out the (closed) window, but Miss Willie, returning, gives him an alibi: he was wrapped in her arms in the darkness. Fairy, having returned, reports a fire in the bathtub, but no one believes her. Next, Florence confesses to the crime and leaves with Miss Willie to be searched. Hannibal indicates that a woman pushed him aside to take the bonds, and he can identify her by her perfume. When he starts sniffing Lily Belle, however, he smells only smoke. Miss Willie then enters with a basin of ashes, in which only a corner of one of the bonds can be identified.

The Savage children, in despair, depart. Dr. Emmett suggests that, under the circumstances, he can probably secure Mrs. Savage's release, needing only to call the state medical inspector. Miss Willie goes to pack Mrs. Savage's things, and the guests all leave to collect going-away presents: a napkin from Fairy, a silver salt shaker from Florence, a book from Jeff, and a button-eye for the teddy bear from Mrs. Paddy. Miss Willie also has a gift: the bonds. She had only burned some newspaper, along with that one corner of a document. Dr. Emmett enters and announces that the station wagon is ready to drive her away. Mrs. Savage voices a wish to stay after all, but the doctor declares that she does not belong in the fragile world that the others all need to inhabit. She relents, and he encourages her in her plan to establish a memorial fund, among other words of advice. Hannibal returns to finally offer a present: a song. It starts out the same as before, but Mrs. Paddy hits the lights, and in the dark the playing ceases, to resume

with a true rendition of Ravel's "Berceuse sur le nom [de Gabriel] Fauré."

In low light, a closing scene is pantomimed in spotlighting: Mrs. Savage picks up her gifts and the teddy bear, then turns to see Jeff and Hannibal playing the piano and violin, respectively, while Mrs. Paddy paints a beautiful seascape, Florence sits with her living son, and Fairy enters elegantly dressed. Mrs. Savage throws a kiss and departs, leaving the teddy bear sitting on the table.

CHARACTERS

Doctor Emmett

As director of the Cloisters, Dr. Emmett is responsible for most all official decisions and reports that take place during the play. He is not entirely unbiased with regard to Mrs. Savage's treatment, because her children are paying for her to be housed there; if he attempts to resist their directives in light of his own ideas about what is morally right, they can simply remove her from his care. Thus, he encourages her to reveal where she has hidden the bonds, and since he is obliged to assent to the plan to use a truth drug on Mrs. Savage, it is left to Miss Willie to offer resistance. Still, the doctor is a sympathetic figure; when all is said and done, and Mrs. Savage has proved herself of sound mind despite what appeared on the surface to be irrational antics (e.g., carrying the teddy bear around), he arranges to secure her full release on medical grounds.

Fairy May

Fairy May seems to have a problem with telling the truth, constantly fibbing, especially about things she has done, apparently only to liven up conversations and situations. She also has a sometimes desperate need to hear confirmation that she is loved. The audience may well deduce that Fairy May endured some form of abandonment as a child, leaving her socially and emotionally insecure and compulsively trying to ingratiate herself with or impress others through made-up stories—but the play does not confirm any of these notions. Fairy May declares that she and Hannibal are the only ones who are to free to leave the Cloisters if they wish, but of course it is hard to believe her. Despite having an appearance that lacks polish, Fairy lives beautifully, sharing her enthusiasm and consistently demonstrating compassion for those around her. She leads the charge, so to speak, in the guests' aggressive befriending and defense of the beleaguered Mrs. Savage.

Florence

Florence (who at one point says her last name is Williams) acts in every way elegantly, politely, and rationally—except when it comes to the doll whom she calls her son, John Thomas. She twice signals that her son is stricken with measles, indicating that Florence must have lost her mental balance when her true son was taken from her by that disease. Though generally sophisticated in nature, Florence is not averse to joining the others in benevolently pacing the untrodden edges of the carpet. Otherwise, she helps keep the group grounded.

Hannibal

Good-natured and somewhat self-deprecating—though not with regard to his extraordinary violin playing—Hannibal somewhat represents the morale of the group. He is generally buoyant, but he is conscious of his flaws to such a degree that, for example, he is open to new ideas about how to give himself exercise. Indeed, he so thoroughly takes to the trick of scattering a deck of cards to pick up that he enacts the exercise several times in efforts to help others get a grasp on their situation. Formerly a statistician, Hannibal is quick with figures and mathematical perspectives. With regard to his residency at the Cloisters, he seems to have responded poorly to losing his job to a machine; he sought to find a line of work that would earn money without needing costly resources, but his efforts at learning the violin—his apparent solution—have stalled.

Jeffrey

Jeff survived a crash in World War II that killed everyone else among his plane's crew. His survivor's guilt is so overwhelming that he believes his face to have been horrifically scarred by the fire—though he remains perfectly handsome, as Miss Willie tells him. He bristles stiffly, though politely, whenever she gives him extra attention, as it flusters him and makes him fear what his wife would think if she knew. He has the talent of a concert pianist but has been unable to play; in his current mental state, he is too bashful To help endorse the confusion after the bonds go missing, Jeff nobly tries to take the blame. But Miss Willie—who turns out to be his wife—produces an alibi to clear his name.

Lily Belle

Having presumably lost the Savage name somewhere along the line of her six marriages, Lily Belle is known by what appear to be her two given names alone. She was a terror to her stepmother, Ethel, reportedly biting her every day until she was ten. Mrs. Savage openly declares her dislike for Lily Belle and occasionally makes pointed reference to aspects of her romantic failings. Like her siblings, Lily Belle greedily swallows her mother's false report of the bonds' hiding place and thus makes a fool of herself, being arrested at the museum. When the bonds are swiped in the dark and apparently destroyed, Lily Belle depends upon her brothers for support.

Mrs. Paddy

The most cryptic of the guests at the Cloisters, Mrs. Paddy responded to an oppressive husband's command ten years ago to shut up by refusing to engage in conversation ever since. Never answering questions straightforwardly, she only ever reels off lists of things that she hates. Being inclined to give things up (like the gift of expression), she has sworn off electricity, apparently for Lent, and has a tendency to turn the lights out on everyone (which makes for an excellent plot device). With a close-cropped haircut perhaps meant to signal her sexuality, she bids Mrs. Savage good-bye by openly declaring her love for her—a sentiment that comes as no surprise to Jeffrey, for one. Mrs. Paddy was not the one who took the bonds.

Ethel Savage

The focal point and central protagonist of the play, Mrs. Savage earns every bit of attention she gets through her idiosyncratic, at times outlandish comments and behaviors. The seemingly erratic actions that spurred her children to have her committed included giving away money for whimsical reasons—a two-hundred-dollar tombstone for a peddler's horse, for example—becoming a laughingstock of an actress at an elderly age, and carrying around her teddy bear for no apparent reason other than to get attention. In conversation with the other guests at the Cloisters and with Miss Willie, Mrs. Savage reveals how things came to be as they are in her life. Her children try to depict her as an unbalanced and even greedy stepmother, but she does not want the money for herself—she only wants to fulfill people's otherwise impossible wishes in order to make them happy. She believes this goal is not at all inferior to her children's use of family money—for Lily Belle, paying millions to half a dozen ex-husbands, and for Titus and Samuel, gaining status and prestige that they do not deserve. Mrs. Savage is out to thwart the system—capitalism, patriarchy, and even science—and is willing to go out on multiple limbs to achieve what her conscience tells her is right.

Samuel Savage

A judge said to hold the distinction of having more decisions than any other overturned—indicating his poor readings of the laws in question—Samuel seems utterly lacking in self-assertion. He mostly lingers in the background while Titus manages their tricky family situations. He is motivated to action only when his mother secretly suggests he should dig under the chimney at home for the bonds—and he was put in danger when the chimney collapsed. Mrs. Savage reveals that Samuel used family money to underhandedly attain his judicial post.

Titus Savage

An apparently respectable senator, Titus is belittled by his mother as holding the post only because the state's voters want to keep him away in Washington, DC—and because, like Samuel, he used his wealth to unfairly gain influence and power. Titus seems to be accustomed to simply getting his way, such that when his mother stonewalls his attempts at extracting information from her, his intuitive response is to get angry and simply voice his demands more loudly. Nevertheless, he is open to compromise; when he realizes it may be the easiest way of getting the bonds back from their mother, he readily signs a statement releasing her from the Cloisters. And in the end, when he understands the bonds to have been destroyed through no fault of his mother's, he affirms that he has no intention of fulfilling his threat to have her put into a public institution for the (purportedly) insane.

Miss Wilhelmina

Miss Willie, as she is affectionately known, takes excellent care of all of the guests at the Cloisters, catering to their fantasies when appropriate, but otherwise ensuring that they remain in touch with the needs in the day-to-day lives of everyone there. She seems to have a special place in her heart for Jeff, as if simply because he is handsome and vulnerable, but it is revealed that despite his failure to recognize her, she is actually his wife and is working at the Cloisters in order to remain by his side. She sympathizes with Mrs. Savage, and though she cannot say just why she does it, she steals the bonds in the darkness, sets some newspapers on fire, and shows the ashes to everyone, leaving Titus and his siblings convinced that the bonds have been irreparably burned. She then returns the bonds to Mrs. Savage, seeking no reward, though Mrs. Savage suggests Miss Willie will get one.

THEMES

Madness

One of the play's most prominent and interesting themes is the blurry line between sanity and insanity and how appropriate it is to judge people based on the side of the line on which society has situated them. Patrick sets up this theme offstage, in the foreword, which is meant to be read not by audiences but by the director and actors staging the play. There, he asserts that a play must be produced in sympathy with the intents of the playwright, lest the message be undermined or even distorted. In *The Curious Savage*, the idiosyncrasies of the guests of the Cloisters could easily be overplayed for comic effect, turning the play from a straight comedy into a farce and taking away the dignity of the characters being depicted. In other words, their idiosyncrasies, even if judged to be marks of insanity by society at large, must ultimately be recognized as aspects of the greater human condition, possible mental fates of any individual under the right, or wrong, sorts of circumstances.

Most of the guests have undergone severe traumas—the sorts that would likely cause what in the modern day is called posttraumatic stress disorder at the least and, indeed, insanity at worst. Florence lost a child to disease, perhaps blaming herself—she indicates that her maternal instincts were called into question, saying, "My husband warned me I'd be a bad mother"—and cannot come to grips with the young child's death. Jeffrey lost his closest wartime companions in a terrible crash and cannot forgive himself for surviving. Mrs. Paddy, in her relationship with her husband, had her ability to speak for herself taken from her, and thenceforth committed to enacting that very

TOPICS FOR FURTHER STUDY

- Imagine that you have been randomly contacted by Dr. Emmett because he habitually seeks the opinion of the "woman or man on the street" with regard to the progress of his patients, since everyday intuition is sometimes more effective than medical science. Having learned of the five guests at the Cloisters—Florence, Hannibal, Fairy May, Jeffrey, and Mrs. Paddy—through *The Curious Savage*, write a report to Dr. Emmett with a thoughtful paragraph on each guest suggesting activities, exercises, and experiences that might bring about further improvements in their mental state.

- Compile a list of at least half a dozen other plays and half a dozen novels in which characters do foolish, stupid, or amazing things in hopes of gaining money, using your own store of knowledge as well as judicious Internet searching to fill out your list. (Note that simply committing a crime for the sake of money is not quite interesting enough.) Then write about the items on your list—at least twelve altogether—in the form of a blog post meant to be a resource for anyone looking to find quality literary works featuring this sort of dramatic action.

- Research the Make-a-Wish Foundation and write a report on its origins, mission, methods, organization, and any notable commendations or criticisms it has received. Close your report by comparing the foundation to Mrs. Savage's Memorial Foundation and discussing whether either casts the other in a different light.

- Read the young-adult novel *Counting Backwards* (2012), by Laura Lascarso, in which Taylor is arrested with a stolen car and ends up placed in a psychiatric correctional facility called Sunny Meadows. Write a paper in which you compare Taylor's experience at Sunny Meadows with Mrs. Savage's experience at the Cloisters, considering such topics as family conflict, the kindness of the staff, and friendship.

disempowerment as a means of protest. These reactions can hardly be called insane, and as Patrick insists in the foreword, these people cannot accurately be called "lunatics." They have reacted to extreme circumstances with extreme responses, almost unintentionally, and unfortunately seem to be trapped in—or perhaps simply devoted to—those responses. They have found ways in which they can be at peace, even if only to modest extents, in their daily lives, and though it may involve some delusion (the part that leaves others questioning their sanity), they have survived; they are survivors.

Money

While the play effectively casts fresh light on the idea of judging people like the guests at the Cloisters, it also paints people who would ordinarily be considered sane in a different light. The three Savage children have all achieved success by ordinary societal measures—they are a senator, a (former) wife of luminaries, and a judge, respectively—but Patrick indicates that this is no proof that they do not act irrationally. And this is especially the case where money is concerned. The sum of ten million dollars—in 1950, a huge fortune—is certainly large enough to potentially make anyone act irrationally in attempts to procure it. But the three Savage children act with such blatant greed-inspired foolishness that they end up being parodied as "savages" whose frenzied activities—digging in the president's garden (opposing the government), digging under a chimney (undermining infrastructure), and gutting a stuffed porpoise (being rapacious, or obstructing science)—are quite clearly *uncivilized*. When the motivation of money is introduced, the Savage children are shown to act in utterly irrational ways.

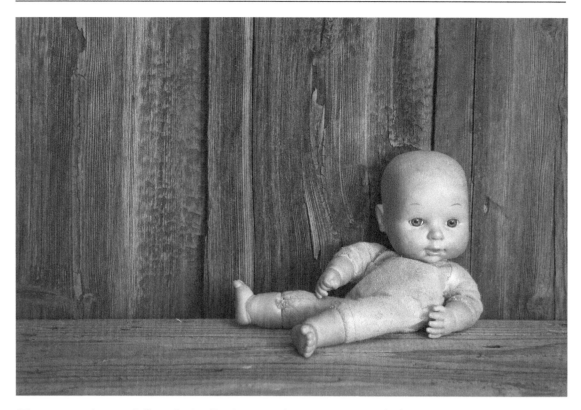

Florence speaks to a doll as if it is alive because she cannot cope with the death of her young son
(© Aksenova Natalya | Shutterstock.com)

It is worth observing here that Patrick's use of the term *savage* as the family's name is arguably insensitive, if it is seen to suggest qualities stereotypically, but wrongly, associated with "savages," which must be recognized as a derogatory term toward people with indigenous lifestyles. That is, indigenous peoples act with far more dignity and grace, under the influence of whatever motivators, than do the Savages under the influence of money. On the other hand, if Mrs. Savage is seen to better embody the name than her children, then this potentially casts her brand of wisdom in the light of ancient traditions, in which case the use of Savage as *her* name, at least, can be seen as meant as a compliment to the character.

Modern Life

The clash of the greed and practical insanity of the Savage children with the compassion and friendship of the guests at the Cloisters spurs several questions, as well as possible answers, with regard to modern life. Hannibal's particular problem seems to be that he cannot cope with

having been replaced by a machine in his line of work—a common issue for workers throughout the Industrial Revolution and the age of machines. Meanwhile, all the guests bristle at the Cloisters' use of a buzzer to indicate when they need to be going to their gardens or to bed. But this, of course, is modern life in a nutshell: lining up obligations, having to be certain places at certain times, and obeying the summons of the clock, regardless of one's state of mind at the time. The guests at the Cloisters do not need to work, of course, which gives them an advantage in coping with modern life. But it is especially people like them, people who have proved to be badly adapted for living independently, who highlight the problems that modern life itself can create. The problems of war and the senseless deaths it randomly causes; of the illusion that humankind can rely on medicine to thwart natural processes, including death by disease; of the deficit in emotional life caused when parents fail in their responsibilities and there is no community to take up the slack—such problems might be avoided in a village-level community. Without the technology of motor vehicles, there can be no death in a crash. Where death is recognized as an ever-present possibility, the death of a single child, however saddening, will be less likely to compromise the mother's mental state. And in a close-knit community, any abandoned or neglected child is likely to find surrogate parents who can ensure a loving upbringing. Modern civilization cannot be undone, but if people focus on connections, friendship, and mutual support instead of competition, money, and personal gain, they can live better, happier lives.

STYLE

Madhouse Comedy
Despite Patrick's assertion in the foreword that the Cloisters is no lunatic asylum, it is hard to dispute Titus's counter-assertion—with Mrs. Paddy having flicked the lights off and fled, Hannibal tossing a deck's worth of cards into the air, and Mrs. Savage leading Fairy and Florence in a procession around the unworn edges of the carpet—that "this is simply a *madhouse!*" Gathering several people with various quirks in personality and behavior in a single room certainly sets the stage for noteworthy dramatic action, and Patrick takes the opportunity to elicit a few laughs. This can be seen in Fairy's outrageous claims about her past, Mrs. Paddy's long and seemingly random—yet somehow poetic—lists of the things she hates, and Hannibal's failure to recognize his two-note screeching on the violin as unsatisfactory. While recurrences of these kinds of event motifs are bound to elicit laughs, Jeff's unjustified bashfulness is more endearing than funny, while Florence's attachment to a doll in lieu of her deceased son is too tragic to be fully amusing. Thus, Patrick ensures that the serious nature of these people's quirks—indeed the traumas underlying them—are not overlooked. In the end, it is likely the sweetness and compassion of the guests at the Cloisters, especially toward their newfound friend Mrs. Savage, that inspire the most smiles and laughs on the part of the audience. These characters are willing to do whatever seems appropriate to support and help each other, whether playing along with Florence's conception of her doll as a real boy, encouraging Hannibal in his excruciating performances, or lying about the theft of the bonds in order to throw the

Savage children off the scent. The guests' quirks may be what get the audience laughing at things for being different, but their fresh perspective on friendship and even on being alive are what leave the audience delighted to be looking at the world differently.

Drawing Room Mystery
Although technically the room in which *The Curious Savage* takes place is referred to as the "living room" of the Cloisters, it has all the characteristics of the sort of drawing room in which many a dramatic mystery is centrally located. (See the 1976 film *Murder by Death* for a send-up of the genre.) In such a room, an abundance of personalities, several of which naturally clash, are gathered in accord with some pretext that detains them, and sooner or later a criminal action by an unknown person takes place, leaving everyone to figure out who did it. In Patrick's play, the pretext for the assemblage is the Savage children's need to determine the whereabouts of the family fortune: their desire for the money keeps them at the Cloisters, while all the others either work or live there. The crime that takes place, facilitated by Mrs. Paddy's opposition to electricity, is the swiping of the bonds. Prior to that mysterious action, the audience is held in suspense through the uncertainty regarding the whereabouts of the enormous sum of ten million dollars in negotiable bonds, which are worthless if lost. Thus, the suspense of classic mystery is introduced by the end of the first act—the time of Mrs. Savage's revelation of her hiding the bonds—while before then the play is driven simply by the audience's desire to get to know and understand the setting, just as Mrs. Savage must, and by the slow contextualization of the reason for her being there in the first place. In the end, although *The Curious Savage* would not be described as a "mystery," it uses mystery conventions to give dramatic momentum to what is otherwise more of a social comedy.

HISTORICAL CONTEXT

"Solutions" to Mental Distress in Mid-Twentieth-Century America
The middle of the twentieth century was a dangerous time to be judged stricken with mental illness in the United States. In the 1930s, several controversial treatments for mental illness arose

COMPARE
&
CONTRAST

- **1950:** Mental health treatment is in the midst of one of its most precarious periods in history, with humans taking the enormous and generally disastrous step of physically assaulting the structure of the brain—through insulin shock, electroshock, and lobotomies—in attempts to rid people of madness, despite a total lack of knowledge or precision to justify such steps.

  Today: After the hasty dismantling of the influential theories of Sigmund Freud in the late twentieth and early twenty-first centuries, talk therapy is frequently bypassed in favor of the far simpler distribution of medications. Mood-altering drugs interact with brain chemistry in definite ways but fail to address the underlying life conditions that produce many mental difficulties in the first place.

- **1950:** The United States sees an estimated three to four million cases of measles annually, with some five hundred cases ending in death. More than 50 percent of the population contract measles by age six, while more than 90 percent contract it by age fifteen.

  Today: Following the development of a measles vaccine in 1963, the numbers of

cases decreased dramatically. Although the years 1989 to 1991 saw a resurgence, by the early 2000s, the disease was effectively eradicated domestically. Of the 220 cases of measles reported in the United States in 2011, most were brought into the country by unvaccinated people.

- **1950:** The sort of mental breakdown produced in some soldiers by the stress of war was called "shell shock" after World War I and combat stress reaction or "battle fatigue" after World War II. Not until 1952 does the first edition of the *Diagnostic and Statistical Manual of Mental Disorders* (DSM-I) describe something called "gross stress reaction" to capture what soldiers experience. However, in 1968, DSM-II reduces this to "adjustment reaction to adult life."

  Today: After posttraumatic stress disorder was first added to the DSM-III in 1980, based on research with Vietnam veterans, Holocaust survivors, sexual trauma victims, and others, returning soldiers began to receive more focused long-term care with regard to repairing their mental state after the inhumane trials of war.

---

in institutional settings. One of these was insulin shock therapy, developed beginning in 1933, whereby the patient was given alarming doses of insulin to bring about epileptic seizures or perhaps a coma, along with profuse perspiration. Basically amounting to a physiological assault on the human organism, the therapy was slowed little by death rates of between 2 and 5 percent. Similar in its approach to offering a "cure" was electroconvulsive therapy (ECT), developed in 1938, which even more reliably created seizures in patients receiving it. Both of these forms of therapy were justified by little more than anecdotal claims of reduced manic activity on the part of patients—but, of course,

reduced activity in general was to be expected, as Harvard neurologist and ECT detractor Stanley Cobb saw it. As reported by Andrew Scull in *Madness in Civilization*, Cobb recognized early on that through ECT and other shock therapies, brain cells were quite simply being destroyed, irretrievably. Proponents of such therapy either dismissed such criticisms or suggested, utterly without evidence, that only malignant brain cells were being destroyed.

Even more dramatic in method and effects was the procedure of lobotomy, the destruction of or severing of connections between brain tissue in the frontal lobe. The procedure was first developed in late 1935 in the context of a right-wing dictatorship in Portugal by neurologist Egas Moniz, who claimed a 70 percent rate of moderate to high success—a rate entirely disputed by Sobral Cid, the psychiatrist who had supplied him with patients. Cid saw only profound damage to his clients and ultimately stopped sending any to Moniz. Nonetheless, American doctors Walter Freeman and James Watts were inspired by Moniz's claims to introduce the practice in America, where they first operated in 1936. Lobotomy procedures variously involved indiscriminate alcohol injections, drilling into the skull, sweeps of knife blades, and even ice picks applied around the eye sockets. Freeman and Watts achieved dramatic increases in their implementation of the procedure over the next two decades. Between 1936 and 1948 the two performed some 625 operations together; as of 1957 Freeman alone had conducted some 2,400 more operations. Meanwhile, state hospitals nationwide began using the procedure in the late 1940s. Moniz won the Nobel Prize in Medicine in 1949, accounting for a fourfold increase in lobotomies in the United States over the course of the year. By 1953, total US procedures numbered in the tens of thousands.

These procedures, especially the lobotomy, were only gradually recognized by society as horrific and inhumane—as literal unending nightmares for the patients. Although the 1948 film *The Snake Pit* used electroshock therapy as a positive plot device, later books written by authors personally familiar with the therapies and their effects helped contribute to a turn in public opinion against them. Especially notable were Janet Frame's *Faces in the Water* (1961) and Ken Kesey's *One Flew over the Cuckoo's Nest* (1962). Ernest Hemingway and Sylvia Plath, who committed suicide in 1961 and 1963, respectively, both experienced electroshock therapy and left behind unqualified denouncements of its terrible effects. Finally the procedures were widely recognized, in Scull's words, "as symbols of psychiatric oppression." In *The Curious Savage*, Titus's threat to have his mother dispatched to a public institution if she fails to cooperate certainly seems unkind, but only with a fuller understanding of just what could happen in such institutions can the audience realize how lucky Mrs. Savage and all the guests are to find themselves at a well-meaning, humane place like the Cloisters.

The bonds are hidden inside the stuffed bear Mrs. Savage carries (© Leon Rafael | Shutterstock.com)

CRITICAL OVERVIEW

Patrick enjoyed an undeniably, if at times unevenly, successful career as an author of radio plays, screenplays, and stage plays, but his popular renown and financial windfalls did not always come with glowing critical assessments. John Marion, in *Twentieth-Century American Dramatists*, sums up the critical perspective on Patrick in the context of his aims and career:

As a playwright, Patrick has always considered himself a craftsman first, an artist second, and an entertainer always. His scripts are sentimental and relentless in their affirmation of man's better qualities. Unpretentious, often brilliantly and outrageously theatrical, they have had enormous appeal for audiences all over the world. Despite the often caustic criticism by New York reviewers that at times has been justified, Patrick's plays have successfully entertained popular audiences.

Marion affirms that *The Curious Savage* is "one of his best comedies." Unsurprisingly, for an initial run that lasted only a month, Marion vaguely signals that the play did not earn much critical favor: "Though the play's critical reception was not entirely negative, some critics felt the subject matter, insanity, to be in bad taste."

In response to more recent regional productions, reviewers have reflected on how well the play has aged. Reviewing a production of *The Curious Savage* in Washington State for the *Islands' Sounder* in 2011, Tom Welch called it "a funny, heartwarming play" that features a "hilarious struggle" between the characters and amounts to a "delightful parable." In the *Los Angeles Times*, Todd Everett gave modest kudos to the play as staged in Oxnard in 1995, commenting, "For all of its clichés, Patrick's unpretentious play is often amusing, and frequently radiates a pleasant warmth." He did call the play "dusty" and added that "there's nothing about it that will dazzle audiences, . . . but those who see the play are likely to have felt their money to be well-spent."

Other reviewers, apparently the more jaded generally speaking, have had harsher words for the play. A professedly amateur reviewer for the *Albuquerque Journal* suggested that with an otherwise admirable 2008 production in New Mexico, "the play selection . . . doomed the enterprise." The reviewer commented that "the play's pace is sluggish and the message saccharine." Writing for *Variety* about a 1996 Los Angeles production, Julio Martinez slighted the play in calling it a "quaint but lightweight 1950s comedy" in which the plot "is tidy and oh so predictable." He suggests that it would take unusual directorial insight "to raise this museum piece from the community theater environs in which it belongs." Regardless of how highly one happens to regard his plays, Patrick, in Marion's words, "will be remembered as a superb craftsman of popular comedies."

CRITICISM

Michael Allen Holmes

Holmes is a writer with existential interests. In the following essay, he evaluates what The Curious Savage *ultimately suggests about people with mental challenges by comparing the foreword with the dramatic close of the final scene.*

In the foreword to his long-loved 1950 comedy *The Curious Savage*, John Patrick takes a rather unusual step: declining to place full artistic trust in any director wishing to stage the play,

> THE WAY THE GUESTS REFUSE TO SAY GOOD-BYE IN THE CLOSING SCENE SEEMS TO SIGNIFY NOT AN ALTERNATIVE CULTURAL OR PHILOSOPHICAL PERSPECTIVE BUT SIMPLY AN EXTENSION OF THEIR DELUSIONS—AN INABILITY TO RECOGNIZE THE WORLD FOR WHAT IT REALLY IS."

Patrick applies ethical pressure to help ensure that any stagings will treat the guests at the Cloisters with the utmost respect as human beings. It is easy to see why Patrick might have feared condescending portrayals, in an era when racial minorities were played in the most appalling stereotypical ways in both film and television, while acts like the Marx Brothers and the Three Stooges made a point of lampooning foolishness and apparent stupidity of all kinds. The guests at the Cloisters could easily be tipped into absurdity with a little overacting—for Jeff, all-out melodramatic shame over his imaginary scars; for Florence, affection for her doll well beyond ordinary parental affection; for Fairy, stupefied confusion whenever people doubt her tall tales; for Hannibal, excessive grace and decorum in executing his performances; and for Mrs. Paddy, frumpiness to the point of slapstick. But Patrick explicitly pulls the plug on such notions: these are human beings, not lunatics, and should be portrayed accordingly. The reader of the play thus easily imagines the characters' delusions being played out in everyday senses—not as bombastic gags—showing how some people understand and interact with the world around them in atypical ways. Their dignity, without doubt, remains intact. And yet, when the end of the play is reached, it seems as if Patrick retracts his affirmation of the dignity of people dealing with mental delusions, feedback loops, and other issues.

Beyond the foreword, to which audiences are unlikely to be exposed (unless the producers have quoted the foreword in the playbill), Patrick internally frames the depiction of the guests at the Cloisters by having Dr. Emmett tell Titus, "The guests in this wing are in their final stage of

WHAT DO I READ NEXT?

- Readers and audiences who appreciate Patrick's clean brand of comedy might next turn to *Everybody Loves Opal* (1961), the beginning of his series about an idiosyncratic junk collector named Opal Kronkie who wins people over with her warmth.

- One of the earliest American dramas taking place in a house full of slightly off-center people was *You Can't Take It with You* (1936), focusing on a large and quirky New York family. The play won the Pulitzer Prize, and the 1938 film adaptation won the Oscar for Best Picture; modern filmgoers may be reminded of Wes Anderson's *The Royal Tenenbaums* (2001).

- Patrick uses the term *savage* to comment on civilized versus barbaric behavior. The ironies of Western civilization are elsewhere considered in the six plays collected in *Briefcase Warriors* (2001), by Ojibwa author E. Donald Two-Rivers, who was born in Canada but moved to Chicago as a teenager and went on to found the city's Red Path Theater in the mid-1990s.

- The Cloisters represents the most agreeable sort of institution for mental care. Ken Kesey offers the flip side of the coin, an enlightening (and at times joyous) but ultimately nightmarish experience of institutionalization, in *One Flew over the Cuckoo's Nest* (1962). The tale was adapted for the stage and ran on Broadway beginning in November 1963.

- Mary Chase's play *Harvey* (1944) centers on the question of how to treat someone with a mental illness and also involves inventive and psychologically tweaked comedy. A man has been living with an imaginary friend—a giant rabbit—and so his sister has him committed to an institution in the hope of ridding him of the delusion.

- *Lie, Cheat, and Genuflect* (1981), a play by Billy Van Zandt and Jane Milmore, involves a pair of brothers bumbling over how to secure a share of their grandfather's inheritance—and eventually attempting an unlikely disguise.

- Brad Schreiber exposes a different level of insanity in the theater—not within the plays but among the cast and crew creating them—in his informative and entertaining volume *Stop the Show! A History of Insane Incidents and Absurd Accidents in the Theater* (2006).

- In a semiautobiographical novel aimed at relatively mature young adults, *It's Kind of a Funny Story* (2006), Ned Vizzini portrays the struggles of a teen who is hospitalized for his depression and is helped by the people he meets there. The book was adapted to film in 2010.

---

treatment. They are extremely kind and cooperative. On the surface, most of them would seem quite as normal as, say, yourself, Senator." The implication with the reference to *stages* is that their mental conditions were once worse, they have been making progress, and they are expected to someday recover, or at least cross a threshold of sanity beyond which they can function in everyday society (if perhaps with a little support). And indeed, having the doctor affirm that they are "as normal as" the crooked Savage children accomplishes two things: it both advances the play's agenda, again as put forth in the foreword, that those at the Cloisters are perhaps more levelheaded than "the insane outside world," and it holds the director accountable for the depictions of the guests—if they are being overplayed, this line exposes the farce.

Mrs. Savage at first seems to fit right in with a crowd of people with mental challenges—in fact she seems the craziest of the lot, what with her speaking in disagreeable nursery rhymes, clutching her bear like a true friend, and making inappropriate comments about Lily Belle's mating habits. Yet as soon as her children disappear, she lifts the veil of foolishness for Miss Willie, who has called her out with regard to inflating the traditional number of "dirty Republi-kins" in a rhyme. Mrs. Savage forthrightly states, "It's a fault of mine—exaggeration. It's stupid of me to try to irritate them like this—I just irritate myself. Well, I suppose it has to be exasperating now to be funny later." These surely strike the audience as the fully self-aware thoughts of a fully sane person. Thus, in being introduced to the full-time guests at the Cloisters, the demonstrably sane Mrs. Savage must be on her guard not to offend her new daily companions. She humors Fairy's prevarications, treats Florence's doll as real, pretends to appreciate Hannibal's tunes, and regards Mrs. Paddy's long lists of things hated as perfectly explicable (except for the rhubarb). There may be an air of condescension to Mrs. Savage's manner with the other guests, but she is nonetheless sympathetic; she clearly wants to help them feel good about themselves and their place in the world, as nice people generally do.

The audience witnesses something of an evolution in Mrs. Savage's relations with the guests in the beginning of the second act, when Fairy reaches such a point of curiosity about Mrs. Savage's opinions and perspectives that she starts compulsively interrupting Mrs. Savage to ask her about this and that. It starts when Mrs. Savage helps address one of Fairy's persistent issues: feeling a recurring, perhaps constant, need to be told that she is loved. No matter how much we love someone, we can only tell them so many times before we both wish to be saying something else, as part of freedom of thought and expression, and feel that the sentiment starts to lose its value if repeated so often. Thus, an excessively insecure person can feel a need to be told more often that he or she is loved: the reassurance cannot be repeated often enough to satisfy that need. Mrs. Savage addresses what has presumably been a long-term issue for Fairy quite cleverly, by pointing out that any caring comment, any comment offered with a person's best interest in mind, is a way of revealing that one loves that person, in the sort of brotherly or sisterly (as opposed to romantic) way that Fairy has in mind. Thus does "Don't eat too fast" become a quite legitimate, if not explicit, profession of love. This is an important lesson for Fairy, one that cannot be overlooked.

Mrs. Savage's next lessons, however, are perhaps less graspable. It can certainly give one a feeling of renewed control to ignore the ordinary authoritarian rules of mathematics to reach whatever sums one pleases, but this will not help a person get out of a place like the Cloisters. As for the notion of being wicked, it might be possible to morally justify wickedness through some reference to the greater good of humanity, especially the greater good of the person to whom one would be wicked, but Mrs. Savage does not seem to get very far with the claim that "we have to be wicked once in a while to get God's attention." All this is to say that while Mrs. Savage may have something to teach the guests, she has only so much; she is not so elevated above them that she can come through like a whirlwind and completely revolutionize their lives. Hannibal does take to the card-scattering activity, while Fanny and Florence both seem to enjoy parading around the carpet—yet, while both of these ideas deserve merit for getting the body up and moving, again, they are hardly activities that will lead someone out of a so-called nuthouse; rather, they are the very activities that lead Titus to declare that the Cloisters *is* "a *madhouse.*"

All in all, Patrick has been playing his dramatic cards, so to speak, with an even hand, indeed keeping the guests somewhat on the level with the Savages. The audience can justifiably regard the peaceable, amicable, generally content guests as just as sane as the dishonest, self-absorbed, possessive Savages, if not more so. They have their quirks—their minds are a bit off-center in one or two respects—but their hearts are in the right place. Part of the play's message is that care must be taken in calling people with mental obstacles "insane" and in treating superficially respectable people as presumably "sane." The world itself is a little crazy, and everyone is just trying to live in it.

The tables turn, however, in the play's closing scene, even though it seems so heartwarming. Indeed, the scene must seem downright magical to audiences, as all the guests are transformed into the ideals they retain in their minds: Hannibal and Jeff playing beautiful music, Fanny with an exterior that better matches the integrity of her soul, Florence with a living boy appreciating her love, and Mrs. Paddy with a work of true artistic genius to her credit. It is one of those moments when the roof of the theater seems to come off, as the real-life ceilings in the characters' lives are lifted and an ethereal vision, as if of heaven on earth, is permitted to come to life. And yet, what does this vision suggest about these characters, especially in light of the dialogue between Mrs. Savage and Dr. Emmett that precedes it? Mrs. Savage, idealizing the peace and friendship of the Cloisters, expresses a desire to remain there, but Dr. Emmett second-guesses her. His character is given a perfect doctoral dignity by the script, and so there is not much room to question his disparaging characterization of the environs and the people under his care:

> The peace you find here is the moon reflected on a dark lake. Strike the surface and you destroy it. Is that the kind of peace you want?...They've found refuge in an egg-shell world where you don't belong. For you see yourself clearly, I'm sure.

All of a sudden, it seems, the outlook for the Cloisters' guests is grim. They are now framed not as recovering patients with one foot out the door on the way to reality, but as "lifers" who can expect no more than to cling to a precarious existence in a fragile, illusory world whose integrity depends on the indulgences of the doctor, the nurse, and each other. Mrs. Savage, to be sure, does not fit right in with them, as it seemed at first; nor is she someone who can offer genuine help on their way to recovery. Her lesson about loving communication certainly sank in, what with Fairy ("Take an umbrella—it's raining"), Hannibal ("Watch out—don't break your neck"), and Jeff ("You have a good seat") all using phrases she cited in order to bid a loving good-bye. But each of these usages has a comic edge, since it is not actually raining (perfect for Fanny); Mrs. Savage was sort of joking in suggesting that "even 'Watch out, you'll break your neck'" signifies love; and although *seat* can mean one's posture on a horse, since Mrs. Savage is not currently riding a horse, it may not be the most appropriate comment. In turn, there is certainly a beauty about not believing in saying "good-bye." That word signals a certain finality, in contrast to something like "see you later" (a common way of saying good-bye in several languages) even when no reunion is expected; it can never be known when two people will be swept back together again by fate, and even from afar people can retain spiritual connections. This lofty interpretation, though, is not always apt. The way the guests refuse to say good-bye in the closing scene seems to signify not an alternative cultural or philosophical perspective but simply an

extension of their delusions—an inability to recognize the world for what it really is. As Florence says in what seems a somewhat childish way, "Come, Fairy—let's pretend it's Garden Hour."

Whether it was Patrick's intention or not, the closing scene is arguably a pessimistic one as far as the guests at the Cloisters are concerned. They are not envisioned moving through and beyond the current stages of their mental states, overcoming the obstacles that stand between them and a true understanding of the world. Rather, they are further indulged, this time not by each other or their caretakers but by the playwright. Hannibal becomes a master violinist, though surely he will never do so, and would be better off moving on to a new phase in his life. Jeff is whisked off to a world where the war never happened and his identity as a concert pianist flourishes, when it would be much more satisfying for him to accept life for precisely what it is, sadness and all—and finally recognize his wife. Fairy, instead of simply donning a more flattering but still humble outfit and stepping out the door, appears in a ball gown that represents precisely the exaggerations she clings to, rather than a grounded reality, and seats herself squarely on the Cloisters' floor. Mrs. Paddy, not unlike Hannibal, is given a degree of fantasized talent, evidenced in the now masterful seascape—the beauty of which indicates that her one wavy line really was, as far as art goes, pathetic and nothing to be proud of, as opposed to beautiful in its simplicity. And most heart-rending of all, Florence, instead of for once picking up her inanimate doll and recognizing that it is not, after all, her living son—that her son is gone; she must mourn and go on without him—is dreamily situated alongside an imaginary boy she can never know. At the beginning of *The Curious Savage*, or rather even before the beginning, the guests are given the full dignity of human beings. By the end, it seems, they have been dismissed as beyond help, as fit only to persist in their egg-shell fantasies, permanently disconnected from life as sane people know it. The end of the play as written may feel inspiring when one sees or reads it; but some viewers and readers might prefer to believe that there remains hope for true, not illusory, contentedness, and indeed sanity, for everyone.

Source: Michael Allen Holmes, Critical Essay on *The Curious Savage*, in *Drama for Students*, Gale, Cengage Learning, 2017.

The final scene is a kind of idealized fantasy in which Hannibal can play the violin, Mrs. Paddy can paint, and Florence has a real child to take care of (© *Artem Furman / Shutterstock.com*)

Ronald Comer

In the following review, Comer describes the play as "heartwarming."

This is a feel-good play filled with heart in its contrasts of avarice with generosity. Ethel Savage, a new widow has been left with a substantial fortune for which her three grown children; a senator, a judge and a gold-digger of a daughter, are intent on keeping her from disposing any way she chooses. So they conspire to have her committed to a private sanatorium known as "The Cloisters." There Ethel is left to work out how she will deal with her spiteful offspring, while getting to know five colorful characters who are long-term patients in the same facility.

Susan Lonker, an Old Academy Players regular, offers a sympathetic and somewhat subdued portrayal of Ethel Savage. Paul Gordon and Cary Gottlieb as Ethel's senator and judge sons are appropriately obnoxious in their roles which call for them to be considerably bombastic in their relationship both with their put-upon mother as well as with their mother's well-intentioned fellow Cloisters inmates. Courtney Bambrick fills the stage with her booming voice and wonderful facial expressions as Ethel's vainglorious daughter, Lilly Belle, who demonstrates little patience for her mother's sentiments regarding alternative ways in which the fortune could be put to good use. Together Ethel's three offspring well represent the spirit of avarice against which Ethel must find the strength to resist.

As she gets to know the five other residents on her ward, Ethel discovers through their generosity of spirit her own inner conviction to do what she has to do to fend off her loathsome brood. Each of her fellow Cloister inmates is uniquely drawn and brings to the story special elements of charm and sensitivity. Kristin Foreman as Florence, the delusion-ridden mother, is a delight to watch as she portrays with tragic eloquence in both her voice and movement the inner sorrow of her character who struggles nonetheless to bestow only peace and happiness to all others. As the love-starved Fairy May, Rachel Brodeur conveys just the right mix of gregariousness and fragility in her energetic performance.

The three other residents who each in their own special way befriend Ethel are: Hannibal (Thomas Abraham), a former statistician who now thinks of himself as a violinist; Jeffrey (Carl Levie) a former fighter pilot who still carries an imaginary scar from his war experience; and Mrs Paddy (Michelle Moscicki) who can only recite lists of things she hates and who gave up any other form of talking one day when her husband told her to "shut up." Rounding out the list of characters in *The Curious Savage* is Dr. Emmett, played by T.J. DeLuca, who does an excellent job of making this difficult part believable. And, as the doctor's nurse assistant, Miss Willie, Marisa Block is also skillful in portraying her character's dual role in this unfolding comedy-drama.

Adding to fun of seeing this production is its location in a historic building upon whose stage Grace Kelly and Robert Prosky took their earliest steps as actors. It's a bit tricky to find, situated as it is in the East Falls neighborhood behind the former Women's Medical College of Pennsylvania. However, for historic community theater lovers, it's worth mapquesting. They also do a terrific job of displaying photos of nearly all of their past productions in an upstairs room in which intermission refreshments are served.

Source: Ronald Comer, Review of *The Curious Savage*, in *Stage*, May 1, 2011.

Tom Welch

In the following review, Welch praises a local production of the play.

Doug Bechtel has shown us once again what an accomplished director can do with a talented cast, showcasing a stunning array of local actors in a funny, heartwarming play that has more than a little topicality. *The Curious Savage*, John Patrick's delightful parable about greed, age, love, and a whole host of other important topics, is the perfect vehicle for a laugh-filled evening at the Grange. Set at The Cloisters, a genteel asylum for "guests" struggling to cope with some kind of problem, *The Curious Savage* centers on the hilarious struggle between an elderly lady and the grasping stepchildren out to get their hands on her fortune.

The "guests" at The Cloisters include Florence, struggling with the loss of her son, played beautifully be Luann Pamatian; Hannibal, a tone-deaf violin player nicely underplayed by Tom Gossett; and Miss Paddy, who hates everything, doesn't believe in electricity, and constantly paints a seashore she's never seen, wonderfully acted by Lin McNulty. Zach Knight gives his role as Jeff, a "guest" with deep emotional scars from the war, more than one dimension, while Regina Zwitling, stepping in for an ailing Maria Massey, was perfect as Nurse Willie.

Tony Lee, playing the kindly Dr. Emmett, has all the right moves in the smooth performance we've come to expect from him. Katie Zwilling, as Fairy May, the young "guest" who is convinced that she is stunningly beautiful despite all available evidence, and who needs to be constantly reassured that everyone loves her, was a sparkling, stunning delight in the first of what this reviewer hopes will be many, many performances on the local stage.

The evil stepchildren were played by three well-known local actors of more than passing ability, with John Mazzarella large in his role as Judge Samuel Savage, Maura O'Neill delightfully perfect as the grasping, much-married Lily Belle Savage, and Ron Herman the blustering image of a shopworn politician. As the worldly counterparts to the warm and gentle lifestyle of the "guests" at The Cloisters, Mazzarella, O'Neill and Herman are ideally cast. Quin Wildman-Gossett threw the flannel quilt over our hearts as Florence's young son John Thomas in the final scene of the play, as the audience drew in the artful imagery of each of the "guests" realizing their dream.

These strong performances by amazingly capable local actors were needed to offset the sheer PRESENCE of Leslie Liddle, who gave a beautiful, gentle, funny and touching performance as Ethel Savage, the wealthy widow. Liddle is an impressive performer, and this role suits her very, very well. Kate Hansen, Bill Westlake, Lynda Sanders and many others played important parts in bringing this wonderful production to the stage, but I have to say that Doug Bechtel takes the cake. His art and creativity in selecting, casting and staging a play like *The Curious Savage* is a gift to us all. Go to the Grange and see this play—it's delicious and delightful.

Source: Tom Welch, Review of *The Curious Savage*, in *Islands' Sounder*, February 18, 2011.

Abby Scalf

In the following excerpt, Scalf asserts that audiences enjoy The Curious Savage *because it is funny but also appreciate its message.*

The Kirk Players will bring an audience favorite back to the stage for the third time to conclude its 38th season.

The Mundelein troupe will present *Curious Savage*. . . .

The Kirk Players first performed the comedy as a road show in the mid-1980s for various organizations out of town, said John Lynn, founder and director. This year will be the third time *Curious Savage* is part of the subscription series. The comedy was first presented in 1968. It was performed as the group's 25th anniversary show in 1990.

Lynn said audiences love *Curious Savage* because it is a comedy with meaning.

"They like to laugh, but they don't mind if there is a message behind the laughter," he said.

Written by John Patrick, *Curious Savage* is about an elderly woman, Mrs. Savage (played by Bobbi Houser of Mundelein), who is spending her husband's inheritance on foolish things she gave up to make him happy. Her three stepchildren send her to an asylum hoping she will return to her senses and they will still get part of the inheritance.

Houser said Mrs. Savage is trying to teach her children not to be so spoiled. She wants them to see more important things in life.

"She's a loving woman from beginning to end," she said.

Her stepchildren are Titus, played by Jon Matousek of Mundelein, a sober, humorless and direct U.S. senator. Lily Belle, played by Wendi-Lynn Zimmermann of Grayslake, is an heiress who has settled more than $1 million on her six husbands. Samuel, played by John Kelly of Mundelein, is a judge who has had more decisions reversed than any other man in jurisprudence.

In the institution, Mrs. Savage discovers sweet, loving inmates who look out for each other and care for her, as well.

Among the inmates are Florence, played by Bev Johnson of Mundelein, who has her imaginary 5-year-old son constantly by her side. Hannibal, played by Gary Guenther of Mundelein, was once a statistician and believes he can play the violin, but in reality only knows two notes. Fairy May, played by Tania Lynn, thinks she is beautiful, but is rather plain.

There also is Mrs. Paddy, played by Fran Hanson of Buffalo Grove. She likes to paint the ocean even though she has never seen it. Jeffrey, played by Fred Vipond of Mundelein, was shot

PATRICK HIMSELF WAS ALREADY GETTING A REPUTATION FOR HIS TEMPERAMENT."

down during the war and was the only one of his crew to survive.

"He has scars much deeper than his face," Lynn said.

The 11-member cast features a family twist as Houser joins the stage with her daughter WendiLynn Zimmermann and granddaughter Tania Lynn. Tania also is John Lynn's granddaughter.

Houser, who performed with Zimmermann and Tania nine years ago in *Steel Magnolias*, said it is wonderful to join family on stage again. Their bond shows in a scene when Tania's character hugs her and says she loves her.

"I don't have to act. We just connect," Houser said.

Lynn said the audience once again will come away asking the question who really belongs in the institution, the sweet people who live there or the greedy stepchildren.

"The audience will not only be entertained, but will be left with a feeling that the neglected virtues of kindness and affection have not been entirely lost in a world that seems motivated much of the time by greed and dishonesty," he said.

Source: Abby Scalf, "Laughter and Tears: Kirk Players, Audience Falling for *Curious Savage* Again," in *Daily Herald*, June 9, 2004, p. 1.

Tom Vallance

In the following obituary, Vallance gives an overview of Patrick's career.

Winner of the Pulitzer Prize for his play *The Teahouse of the August Moon*, a world-wide success which was later filmed, John Patrick was a prolific writer for both stage and screen, and a volatile personality. His other plays included *The Hasty Heart*, which was also later filmed; while his scenarios included such box office hits as *Three Coins in the Fountain*, *High Society* and *Love is a Many Splendored Thing*. The bursts of temperament that accompanied rehearsals of his work were legendary, but his suicide last month shocked and surprised his friends.

Born John Patrick Goggan in Louisville, Kentucky, he attended Harvard and Columbia Universities before starting his writing career in radio as a script writer for NBC. His first play, *Hell Freezes Over* (1935), Joshua Logan's first directorial assignment on Broadway, was a gloomy tale of seven survivors of a dirigible crash in the South Pole who meet their fates through gangrene, suicide, exposure and murder. The curtain fell as the last survivor waited to die of starvation. It ran for 25 performances and prompted the critic George Jean Nathan to suggest that the author be "tossed into the Hollywood ashcan."

Patrick did go to Hollywood, where he co-wrote 24 scripts in two and a half years—most of them "B" movies for 20th Century Fox including vehicles for Jane Withers (*The Holy Terror*, 1937), Dolores Del Rio (*International Settlement*, 1938), the Dionne Quintuplets (*Five of a Kind*. 1939) and Peter Lorre (*Mr Moto Takes a Chance*, 1939). Convinced that he had now learnt his craft, he moved to Boston and wrote two more plays, one of which, *The Willow and I*, had a brief Broadway run in 1942. In the same year he joined the American Field Service, serving as an ambulance driver with the British in North Africa, Syria, India and Burma.

He wrote *The Hasty Heart* in 12 days while en route to the United States from Burma, and when produced on Broadway in 1946 it brought him his first success. Set in a military hospital camp, its tale of a fiercely proud and independent Scot who discovers he is dying and finally is able to make friends with other inmates was told with compassion, humour and sensitivity. The film version (scripted by Ronald MacDougal) was made in England in 1949, starred Ronald Reagan and Patricia Neal and brought fame to Richard Todd as the testy Scot.

Patrick himself was already getting a reputation for his temperament. With the profits from *The Hasty Heart* he bought a farm in Suffern, New York, and installed every modern convenience. When he applied to the local authorities for an extra power line to be supplied, their interminable unfulfilled promises to comply so angered him that he armed himself with a chainsaw and threatened to cut down an elm tree on the president of the power company's lawn. Such anger extended to rehearsals of his work, where Patrick referred to his outbursts as

"anger that I have to generate and use as a whip to drive myself."

His next two plays, one of which starred Dorothy Gish (*The Story of Mary Seurat*, 1947), were flops, but in 1953 came the biggest success of his career. The actor-producer Maurice Evans had long owned the rights to Vern Sneider's novel *The Teahouse of the August Moon*, which amusingly told of the relationship between the occupying American military in Japan and the outwardly unsophisticated people of Okinawa, with the "simple" islanders ultimately proving that they know more about how to live well than the figures of authority.

Evans himself planned to play the central character of the wily interpreter Sakini and, on the basis of Patrick's handling of the military background in *The Hasty Heart*, asked him to do the stage adaptation. The two men were soon battling over the show's conception, however, and when Evans insisted that a major character omitted from the adaptation be reinstated, communication between the two of them broke down and a co-producer, George Schaefer, was brought in as a means of liaison. (Evans later partly blamed himself, "I obviously lacked finesse in winning my point—it is one thing to have a conviction, but quite another to convey it to a sensitive writer.") Since public feuding between himself and the playwright would endanger possible backing, Evans forsook his ambition to play Sakini, and David Wayne was cast in the part of the lovable rogue who is constantly confiding with the "lovely ladies, kind gentlemen" of the audience, with John Forsythe as the American captain.

Patrick next feuded with the director, Robert Lewis, who wanted to change some dialogue, and hostilities did not end with the show's triumphant opening. When Evans arrived for the first-night party, he found a glass of champagne hurtling through the air to shatter the wall behind him. "Fortunately," he said later, "the attacker was not armed with a chainsaw." The play won not only the Pulitzer Prize, but the Tony Award and the New York Critics Circle Award. Eli Wallach played Sakini in the London production (where George Schaefer had to place guards at the stage door to deny Patrick admittance), and Burgess Meredith played the role for the long and successful tour. The film version, written by Patrick and starring Marlon Brando, lacked the play's lightness and cartoon-like simplicity (Peter Larkin's original sets had made

Okinawa an Oriental wonderland) but was successful.

In 1953 Patrick returned to Fox. Hollywood had nominated Patrick for an Oscar in 1946 for his original story *The Strange Love of Martha Ivers*, which was made into a superior film noir starring Barbara Stanwyck, and he wrote the story for *Framed* (1947), a typical 1940s thriller of a rover (Glenn Ford) duped by a beautiful blonde (Janis Carter). For Sam Goldwyn, he scripted *Enchantment*, a love story of two generations narrated, probably uniquely, by a house. This time he was working on big-budget movies: *The President's Lady* (1953), with Charlton Heston as Andrew Jackson and Susan Hayward as his wife, and two gigantic Cinemascope hits, *Three Coins in the Fountain* (1954), telling of three American office girls finding romance in Rome, and *Love is a Many Splendored Thing* (1955), from Han Suyin's autobiographical novel of a Eurasian girl's ill-fated affair with an American war correspondent. Both films benefited from enormously popular theme songs.

At MGM he adapted Philip Barry's *The Philadelphia Story* into a musical, *High Society* (1956), which due largely to its high-powered cast—Bing Crosby, Frank Sinatra and Grace Kelly—was another big success, and *Les Girls* (1957), which wittily used a Rashomon-like construction, as three showgirls tell a jury their own version of past events and their relationship with their male partner, played by Gene Kelly in his last screen musical. Chosen for the Royal Film Performance, the film was more successful in Europe (Truffaut was one of its champions in France) than in America, and won Patrick the Screen Guild Award.

He was less successful trying to gain cohesion from James Jones's sprawling novel *Some Came Running* (1958), or adapting Paul Osborne's synthetic play *The World of Suzie Wong* (1961). His final film credits were *Gigot* (1962) with Jackie Gleason as a deaf mute, *The Main Attraction* (1963), a musical drama produced by Patrick in England, and *The Shoes of the Fisherman* (1968), a lengthy and poorly received version of Morris L. West's novel about a Russian pope (played by Anthony Quinn).

He wrote over a dozen more plays (and an ill-fated musical version of *Teahouse of the August Moon*, entitled *Lovely Ladies, Kind Gentlemen*) but none successful, though some are popular with repertory companies, particularly *Everybody Loves Opal* (1962), a favourite of middle-aged actresses. In later years he often directed his own work in provincial theatres, and in 1972 was made an honorary Doctor of Fine Arts at Baldwin-Wallace College.

He had, more recently, for some years been living with a long-time companion at his farm, which he proclaimed maintained his sense of values. "If things go well, I go to work at the typewriter," he once said. "If not, I get out the tractor."

Source: Tom Vallance, "Obituary: John Patrick," in *Independent*, December 3, 1995.

SOURCES

"Epidemiology and Prevention of Vaccine-Preventable Diseases," Centers for Disease Control and Prevention website, http://www.cdc.gov/vaccines/pubs/pinkbook/meas.html (accessed July 3, 2016).

Everett, Todd, "Greed, Insanity Create Amusing Comedy," Review of *The Curious Savage*, in *Los Angeles Times*, July 27, 1995, http://articles.latimes.com/1995-07-27/news/vl-28261_1_curious-savage (accessed July 2, 2016).

Friedman, Matthew J., "History of PTSD in Veterans: Civil War to DSM-5," US Department of Veterans Affairs website, August 13, 2015, http://www.ptsd.va.gov/public/PTSD-overview/basics/history-of-ptsd-vets.asp (accessed July 3, 2016).

Marion, John, "John Patrick," in *Dictionary of Literary Biography*, Vol. 7, *Twentieth-Century American Dramatists*, edited by John MacNicholas, Gale Research, 1981.

Martinez, Julio, Review of *The Curious Savage*, Stella Adler Theatre, in *Variety*, December 3, 1996, http://variety.com/1996/legit/reviews/the-curious-savage-1200448169/ (accessed July 2, 2016).

Oliver, Myrna, "John Patrick; Playwright, Screenwriter Won Pulitzer," In *Los Angeles Times*, November 10, 1995, http://articles.latimes.com/1995-11-10/news/mn-1721_1_john-patrick (accessed July 1, 2016).

Patrick, John, *The Curious Savage*, Dramatists Play Service, 1979.

Review of *The Curious Savage*, Auxiliary Dog Theatre, in *Albuquerque Journal*, February 25, 2008, http://www.abqjournal.com/911/review-the-curious-savage-by-john-patrick-feb-25.html (accessed July 2, 2016).

Scull, Andrew, *Madness in Civilization: A Cultural History of Insanity from the Bible to Freud, from the Madhouse to Modern Medicine*, Princeton University Press, 2015, pp. 308–21.

Welch, Tom, Review of *The Curious Savage*, at the Grange, in *Islands' Sounder* (Eastsound, WA), February 18, 2011, http://www.islandssounder.com/entertainment/116486328.html (accessed July 2, 2016).

FURTHER READING

Brown, Elizabeth B., *Surviving the Loss of a Child: Support for Grieving Parents*, Revell, 2010.
 Among the many published books aimed at helping parents deal with the most devastating possible loss, Brown paces through stages of grief and ways to cope, including the beneficial role that spirituality can play.

Carter, Rosalynn, and Susan K. Golant, *Helping Someone with Mental Illness: A Compassionate Guide for Family, Friends, and Caregivers*, Times Books, 1998.
 One need not be a professional to interact with people with mental illness in ways that help them; in fact, it is crucial for family and friends to offer the kind of support that is needed. Carter and Golant aim to address the potential roles that relations and caregivers can play.

Doller, Trish, *Something like Normal*, Bloomsbury, 2012.
 In this young-adult novel, a modern-day protagonist returns from the war in Afghanistan and must adapt to ordinary life in the wake of his traumatic experiences, including the loss of his best friend.

Greed: A Dictionary for the Selfish, Adams Media, 2011.
 Although people such as the Savage children would theoretically make the ideal readership for this helpful—if generally ironic—primer on selfishness, anyone can learn the sorts of habits to *avoid* if they actually want to be upstanding individuals.

SUGGESTED SEARCH TERMS

John Patrick AND The Curious Savage

The Curious Savage AND reviews

John Patrick AND Pulitzer Prize

John Patrick AND stage plays OR screenplays

theater AND drawing room mystery

theater AND inheritance conflict

theater AND insane asylum OR madhouse comedy

play OR film OR novel AND insanity AND comedy

Deathtrap

IRA LEVIN

1978

Deathtrap is a two-act play from the pen of American playwright Ira Levin. The play, one of the longest-running comedy thrillers in Broadway history, opened at the Music Box Theatre on February 26, 1978. The final months of its four-year run, which ended on June 13, 1982, were at New York's Biltmore Theatre (now called the Samuel J. Friedman Theatre). At the same time, the play ran at London's Garrick Theatre from 1978 to 1981. In a footnote to theatrical history, Marian Seldes, who played the part of Myra Bruhl, did so for the play's entire New York run of 1,793 performances.

Deathtrap earned a nomination for a Tony Award for Best Play for 1978 (losing to *Da*, by Irish playwright Hugh Leonard) and won the Edgar Allan Poe ("Edgar") Award for best play in 1980. The source of the play's long-running appeal continues to be its fiendishly clever plot. The core of the play is the corrosive envy that appears to be felt by once-successful playwright Sidney Bruhl, whose career has hit the skids. Sidney, however, receives in the mail a manuscript copy of a play titled *Deathtrap*. According to Sidney, the play, written by a former student named Clifford Anderson, is a perfect example of a murder mystery/thriller, one that could become a smash hit and revive his, Sidney's, flagging career, if only he could knock off Clifford and purloin his play. What follows are a series of ingenious plot twists, subterfuges, and

Ira Levin (© *Matthew Peyton / Getty Images*)

feints that mislead the audience about the true nature of the events taking place.

A published edition of *Deathtrap: A Thriller in Two Acts* is available from Random House (1979). Also available is an edition from Dramatists Play Service, (1979), which includes not only the script but also production notes, including a set diagram, a prop inventory, set changes as the play proceeds, and an inventory of costumes for the play's five actors.

AUTHOR BIOGRAPHY

Levin was born in New York City on August 27, 1929, to Russian immigrants Charles Levin and Beatrice Schlansky. Expectations were that he would follow his father into the toy-importing business, but by age fifteen he had decided that he wanted to pursue a career as a writer, particularly after his parents took him to a New York performance of Agatha Christie's cunning mystery *Ten Little Indians* (a title changed to *And Then There Were None* in later publications of the novel on which the play was based). He was

educated at the Horace Mann School, an elite private prep school in the Bronx, before attending Drake University in Des Moines, Iowa, for two years (1946–1948). He transferred to New York University, where he earned bachelor's degrees in philosophy and English in 1950. During his senior year he entered a television-screenwriting contest; his entry, "The Old Woman," garnered second place, winning $200, and he was later able to sell it to NBC for the network's *Lights Out* series.

In 1953 Levin was drafted into the army and served two years in the Army Signal Corps. Returning to civilian life and drawing on his military experience, he adapted Mac Hyman's bestselling novel, *No Time for Sergeants* (1955), for the *United States Steel Hour* television series. He expanded his adaptation that year as a Broadway stage play, and a later film version of the play helped launch the careers of Andy Griffith and Don Knotts. Levin also wrote his first novel, *A Kiss before Dying* (1953), which in 1954 won the first of his two Edgar Awards.

In the years that followed, Levin's career sputtered. A 1958 play, *Interlock*, was not a success; a 1960 comedy, *Critic's Choice*, did somewhat better, but it soon closed. A 1965 musical, *Drat! That Cat!*, closed after only eight performances. *Veronica's Room* opened in 1973 and did not enjoy a long run, although in later years actors and directors came to admire the enticing intricacy of the plot and have mounted revivals of the play. *Break a Leg* (1979) closed after exactly one performance. In the 1960s and 1970s, Levin found more success as a novelist than as a playwright. Perhaps his best-known novel is *Rosemary's Baby* (1967), which in 1968 was turned into a highly regarded feature film directed by Roman Polanski and starring Mia Farrow. Moviegoers are also likely to be familiar with screen adaptations of two other popular novels by Levin, *The Stepford Wives* (1972), which starred Katharine Ross in a 1975 version and Nicole Kidman in a 2004 remake, and *The Boys from Brazil* (1976), which showcased Gregory Peck and Sir Laurence Olivier in 1978. Then, in 1978, Levin launched his most popular theatrical work, *Deathtrap*, which also was adapted for the silver screen in 1982, with Michael Caine and Christopher Reeve in starring roles. In 1991 Levin published *Sliver*, a psychological thriller that in 1993 was turned into a film starring Sharon Stone.

Levin was married twice. With his first wife, Gabrielle Aronsohn, he had three sons: Adam, Jared, and Nicholas. The two divorced in 1968. In 1979 he married Phyllis Finkel, to whom *Deathtrap* is dedicated, but the two divorced in 1981. On November 12, 2007, Levin died of a heart attack in his New York City apartment.

PLOT SUMMARY

Deathtrap is a two-act play with three scenes in each act.

Act 1

SCENE 1

Deathtrap is set in the cluttered study in playwright Sidney Bruhl's home in Westport, Connecticut; the study is a converted stable attached to a colonial house. Sidney used to be a successful playwright, but in recent years his plays have been flops, and he is in a creative rut, leaving him and his wife, Myra, in a bit of a financial bind. One afternoon in October he tells Myra that he has received in the mail a copy of a play titled *Deathtrap*, which was written by one of his former seminar students, Clifford Anderson; like Levin's play, Anderson's is in two acts with five characters. Sidney says that the play is sure to be a box office hit, and he appears to become intensely jealous that this virtually anonymous former student can write a hit when he cannot. As he describes the play to Myra, he kiddingly suggests that he might murder Clifford and steal the play for himself to resuscitate his career. He calls Clifford on the phone and invites him to his home to offer suggestions on ways to improve the play.

SCENE 2

That evening, Clifford arrives in Westport by train. Sidney picks him up at the station and brings him home. Clifford admires Sidney's collection of exotic weapons. Myra urges Sidney to put aside the play he is working on and collaborate with Clifford on improving his play. Sidney questions Clifford to learn whether there are other copies of the play besides those currently in his study. When Sidney is assured that no other copies exist, he horrifies Myra by attacking Clifford with a garrote. Although Myra is nearly overcome by grief and shock, she helps her husband drag Clifford's apparently lifeless body away.

MEDIA ADAPTATIONS

- In 1982, *Deathtrap* was made into a motion picture directed by Sidney Lumet. The film starred Michael Caine, Dyan Cannon, and Christopher Reeve. The film, available on DVD, was released by Warner Home Video in 1999. Running time is 116 minutes.

SCENE 3

Sidney returns to his study after disposing of Clifford's body. Helga ten Dorp, a neighbor with psychic powers, comes to the Bruhls' home and tells Sidney and Myra that she is having visions of pain emanating from the house. She wanders about, saying that she is having visions, but Sidney expresses relief that her visions seem to be only partly accurate and that she has not sensed that a murder has taken place. Myra confesses to Sidney that she secretly hoped that he would knock off Clifford in order to purloin the play. Just as the two are about to retire for the night, Clifford appears, covered in dirt. He seizes Sidney from behind and appears to pummel him to death with a piece of firewood. After Sidney collapses, Clifford menaces Myra, who becomes so terrified that she has a heart attack, collapses, and dies. After Clifford confirms that she is dead, Sidney rises, unharmed. Clifford remarks to Sidney that their plan to stage Clifford's murder and shock Myra to death has succeeded. The "firewood" is made of Styrofoam, and the two men had earlier rehearsed the "murder" scene in a motel. Clifford will move in with Sidney. Helga was correct that no murder had taken place.

Act 2

SCENE 1

Two weeks later, Clifford has moved in with Sidney and is working on a play in Sidney's study. Writer's block, however, continues to dog Sidney, who grows increasingly irritated at Clifford's effortless ability to write. Sidney's lawyer, Porter Milgrim, casts suspicion on Clifford when he tells Sidney that he happened to notice that Clifford locked up the manuscript of his play in his desk drawer. When Clifford is absent on a shopping errand, Sidney manages to break into the desk, furtively read the manuscript, and discover that the play Clifford is writing, titled *Deathtrap*, is based on the two men's plot to bump off Myra. After Sidney challenges Clifford, the latter threatens to move out and continue writing the play, despite any objections Sidney might have. Finally, Sidney agrees to help Clifford with his play.

SCENE 2

Helga cautions Sidney that Clifford intends to assault him. Sidney informs Clifford that he has finished working on the second act of the play but he has to conduct a test to determine whether what he has written is credible. His intention, however, is actually to bump off Clifford in order to prevent him from completing a play about the murder of Myra and subjecting him to suspicion of murder. To that end he wants to try out elements of the play to establish the belief that he will have killed Clifford in self-defense. Clifford, however, is on to Sidney. He puts blanks in Sidney's gun and, and armed himself with a gun with real bullets, compels Sidney to handcuff himself to a chair. Sidney's effort to murder Clifford has given the latter the plot elements required for him to finish his play. The handcuffs, however, turn out to be fake. Sidney escapes from them and shoots Clifford with a medieval crossbow, then throws the manuscript of Clifford's play into the fire. As Sidney telephones the police to claim that Clifford was coming at him with an ax and that he shot Clifford in self-defense, Clifford rallies, pulls the crossbow bolt from his body, and repeatedly stabs Clifford with it. Both men die.

SCENE 3

In Sidney's study with Porter, Helga has a psychic vision of what really happened. When she describes the scene to Porter, the two suddenly realize that the events would form the basis of a top-drawer thriller the two could produce and that *Deathtrap* would be the perfect title. However, the two begin to argue and issue threats about how they will split the profits from their version of *Deathtrap*. In particular, Helga threatens to inform the authorities that Porter is given to making obscene phone calls. As the curtain falls, Porter is menacing Helga,

who has grabbed a dagger, and the two circle the desk as Porter calls her vile names.

CHARACTERS

Clifford Anderson
Clifford Anderson is a man in his mid-twenties who seems to have sent to his mentor, Sidney, a copy of a manuscript of a play titled *Deathtrap*. He arrives at Sidney's home ostensibly to consult with the older, more experienced playwright about revisions and improvements he can make to the play. As events unfold, however, it becomes clear that Clifford is in league with Sidney in an elaborate scheme to scare Sidney's wife, Myra, to death. Later, to prevent Clifford from writing a play based on the scheme, Sidney shoots him with a crossbow. Clifford manages to pull the bolt out of his body and stab Sidney with it. It is generally believed that audiences are to understand that Clifford and Sidney have a same-sex relationship.

Myra Bruhl
Myra Bruhl is Sidney Bruhl's wife. She supports him in his career as a playwright and sympathizes with her husband as he laments the creative drought he has been experiencing. She believes that Clifford's play will help revitalize her husband's career. Meanwhile, she has experienced health problems that weaken her heart. What she does not know is that Sidney and Clifford are plotting her demise and that no such play exists. After Sidney apparently kills Clifford and Clifford reappears to apparently kill Sidney, Myra, in terror, collapses and dies of a heart attack.

Sidney Bruhl
Sidney Bruhl is an attractive man of about fifty years of age. He was formerly a successful playwright, but recently he has been in a rut and unable to produce another Broadway hit, so he limps along, trading on his fame to give seminars to would-be playwrights. He appears to have received in the mail a manuscript copy of a play written by a former seminar student, Clifford Anderson. In reality, he and Clifford have concocted a plan to eliminate Sidney's wife by literally scaring her to death. Later, when Sidney learns that Clifford is writing a play that mirrors their scheme, he becomes terrified that the authorities will catch on and that he will be

prosecuted. Audiences are to understand that Sidney and Clifford have a romantic relationship, although this relationship is tacit and only briefly referred to. In the end, Sidney kills Clifford with a crossbow but not before Clifford stabs him to death with the crossbow's bolt.

Porter Milgrim

Porter Milgrim, a man in his mid-fifties, is Sidney's attorney, who visits to discuss with Sidney the playwright's financial situation and his will. His chief role is to alert Sidney to the possibility that Clifford is writing a play that he is trying to keep away from Sidney's eyes. In the play's final scene, he and Helga ten Dorp recognize the dramatic possibilities of the events that have transpired in the Bruhl home, but they quarrel over how the rewards of such a production should be shared.

Helga ten Dorp

Helga ten Dorp, Sidney and Myra's neighbor, is a stocky Dutch woman with a pronounced accent who claims to have psychic powers. She arrives at the Bruhl home after the apparent murder of Clifford and claims to sense pain in the house. In the play's final scene, she accurately describes for Porter Milgrim the events that have taken place in the Bruhl home. The two agree that these events would form the basis of a thriller titled *Deathtrap*, but they argue over how the earnings would be shared.

THEMES

Murder

Throughout literary history, murder has been a common theme in literature. So-called murder ballads have been produced in broadsheet form since the seventeenth century. Usually, murder is likely to figure prominently in tragic literature—Shakespeare's play *Macbeth* is a noteworthy example—but murder can play a role in comic literature as well: numerous dinner theaters around the country stage comic murder mysteries with a heavy dose of audience interaction, various drama services provide comic murder mysteries for school and amateur theater groups, and Clue remains a popular board game ("Colonel Mustard in the study with the candlestick"). A stroll through a bookstore will reveal a large section of crime fiction, much of it having to do

with murder. In this sense, murder mysteries form a subgenre of crime fiction. Perhaps the appeal of murder as a theme in literature is that it is the ultimate crime. Property can be restored, money can be returned, people can recover from assaults, but murder is singular in its finality.

The typical murder mystery involves a closed setting; a group of characters who all have motive, means, and opportunity; a sleuth, whether a police detective, a private investigator, or a civilian, who assembles clues and uses his or her powers of deduction to identify the killer; and a final "reveal," when the sleuth triumphantly exposes the killer. In this regard, *Deathtrap* is not precisely a murder mystery. There is no sleuth, and the audience knows who is perpetrating the crimes. Nevertheless, the play's shock value depends heavily on the commission of the ultimate crime. Sidney and Clifford plot the death of Sidney's wife, Myra, and Sidney, out of fear and perhaps professional jealousy, murders Clifford. Indeed, the events of a play form a kind of "deathtrap," where the characters commit crimes because they are ensnared by their own passions: greed, jealousy, hatred, revenge, fear. Even in the final scene, as Porter and Helga argue, it seems as though one of the two will meet his or her end as events and their own greed entraps them.

Homosexuality

Sidney and Clifford have a gay relationship, although that relationship is not heavily emphasized. In the first scene of act 1, Porter comments to Sidney that Clifford is a good-looking man. Sidney then asks Porter whether he thinks Clifford is gay, adding the word *homosexual* by way of explanation. Porter responds that he knows what the meaning of *gay* is. He does not think so, but Sidney says that he has a "sneaking suspicion he might be." Additionally, Sidney at one point refers to himself as a "fag." It should be noted that in recent years the gay and lesbian community has come to object to the term *homosexual*, for the word historically was used in a clinical sense to refer to a psychological disorder.

The issue of whether homosexuality is a prominent theme in the play depends in large part on how it is staged and how the director and actors interpret the characters. In the 1982 film version the two male leads share a romantic kiss. In 2012, the L.A. Gay and Lesbian Center in Los Angeles planned a production of the play that would include a brief scene during which

TOPICS FOR FURTHER STUDY

- Investigate the process of mounting a Broadway production of a play. Pretend that you have in hand a play that you have written. What do you do next? Who decides what plays are produced? How is such a play financed? How are actors found and hired? Directors? Costume and set designers? A stage? Share what you learn with your classmates in an oral presentation.

- Imagine that your school is mounting a production of *Deathtrap*. Create a casting call or audition listing that describes the necessary attributes of the actors who will fill the roles. Post the casting call on a website you create and invite each of your classmates to indicate which role he or she might best fill.

- If you have artistic talent, design and execute a monthly wall calendar with a *Deathtrap* theme. Post the calendar in your classroom and invite classmates to comment.

- Ten years before starring in the 1982 film version of *Deathtrap*, veteran actor Michael Caine starred onstage in *Sleuth*, a mystery thriller by Anthony Shaffer that, in the view of many theatergoers, may have provided Levin with inspiration for his play. *Sleuth* originated as a Broadway play in 1970 and, in fact, premiered at the Music Box Theatre, where *Deathtrap* enjoyed most of its run. Either locate the script of the play or watch the film version. Develop a chart for your classmates in which you trace the similarities between the two works. (Note that in 2007 a film remake of *Sleuth* was released, with Michael Caine now starring as the older character in the story.)

- Imagine that you have been asked to write a one-act play in which you will star as a police detective investigating the death of Myra Bruhl. The investigation will require you to interrogate Sidney, Clifford, Helga, Porter, and perhaps others. With a group of willing classmates, brainstorm ideas for the play, then perform it for your classmates. As an alternative, using an Internet tool such as Flibbix, develop *Deathtrap* into a board game that can be played by members of your class.

- *Witch Dreams*, a young-adult novel by Vivian Vande Velde (Marshall Cavendish, 2005), like *Deathtrap*, relies on a character with paranormal abilities; her ability to read people's dreams allows sixteen-year-old Nyssa to solve the mystery surrounding the murder of her parents. Read the novel, then adapt a portion of it as a one-person stage presentation. Present your creation to your classmates.

- Francine Craft is the best-selling author of *Dying on the Edge* (published under her independent label, Craft's New America Press, in 2011 but also available from Amazon Digital Services). The novel, subtitled *A Multicultural Thriller*, features a film star who murders the wife of her lover, the owner of a film studio, so that she can have him all to herself. What follows is a series of entanglements that deepen the mystery. Read the novel, then write a review of it. Post your review on your social networking site and invite your classmates to comment.

Clifford is seen nude from the back. The production also planned to include some moments of physical affection between the two male leads. This planned staging, however, became controversial. Levin's literary estate, which is managed by his three sons, objected, revoked their permission for the center to stage the play, and issued a cease-and-desist order, indicating that the center could produce the play only under the condition that the staging would include no indication of a

At the start of the play, Sidney is struggling with writer's block *(© Nuk2013 | Shutterstock.com)*

physical relationship between the characters. Ultimately, each reader and viewer will have to decide whether to assume that the men are gay and in a relationship and whether that relationship is part of the motivation behind the murder of Myra and perhaps in some way behind the murder of Clifford. Given that *Deathtrap* is a stage play and that it exists principally on the stage rather than in a book, that decision is likely to be shaped in large part by the ways the actors interpret the roles.

STYLE

Plot

The essence of *Deathtrap* is the construction of the plot, which serves not only to advance the action but also, more important, to bamboozle the audience about what is transpiring. In 2004, Christopher Booker published a work of literary analysis titled *The Seven Basic Plots: Why We Tell Stories*. In addition to describing basic plot structures such as "the quest" and "the voyage

and return," Booker advances the notion of what he calls the meta-plot, a fundamental, underlying structure that all basic plots follow. *Deathtrap* embodies the elements of the meta-plot. The first element is the *anticipation* stage, when the hero (or antihero—in this case Sidney) is summoned to an adventure (in this case, by his relationship with Clifford and their wish to be together and dispose of Myra). In the *dream* stage, the work's adventure begins, and the hero, experiencing some success, has an illusion of invulnerability; Sidney, with Clifford's help, carries out the initial stages of their conspiracy, so all seems to be proceeding according to plan. In the *frustration* stage, the hero experiences defeat and loses his sense of invulnerability; this moment comes in *Deathtrap* when Sidney discovers that Clifford is writing a play about their murder of Myra, therefore turning into his adversary. In the *nightmare* stage, hope is lost as Clifford rallies from having been shot with a bow and stabs Sidney to death. A work with a *resolution* stage allows the hero to overcome his challenges, but there is no resolution for Sidney, although there is for Helga and Porter, who rise phoenix-like from the ashes of the chaos surrounding them to succumb to the enticements of the "deathtrap."

Comedy

Deathtrap owed a great deal of its popularity to the comedy that pervades the play. Numerous instances of witty remarks, most of them from Sidney, could be cited. One involves the psychic Helga ten Dorp, who arrives at the Bruhl home and informs Sidney and Myra that she senses pain in the house. She says that she envisions two people, one named Smith and the other named Colonna, and she asks whether the play Sidney is writing contains a small black character. The comic reference is to the small, black Smith-Corona typewriter that is part of the stage set, as well as possibly to the Smith & Wesson firearm that is part of Sidney's collection of weapons. After Helga leaves, Myra grows fretful that the police will arrive to investigate the "murder" of Clifford and that if Helga tells the police what she believes, they will be arrested. Sidney replies:

> I don't see how. If the police *do* come by, and *do* bring her into it—which hardly seems likely—well, what of it? She'll have them combing the tri-state area for a small black boy with two spools of ribbon. One here, one here, going through his mouth.

Much of the comedy of the play comes from Helga, who, she tells the Bruhls, could never play hide-and-seek when she was a child because her psychic powers made the game way too easy and whose parents did not wrap her Christmas presents because doing so was a waste of paper. This kind of comic banter and wordplay introduces a farcical element that counterbalances the seriousness of the crimes being depicted.

HISTORICAL CONTEXT

Deathtrap is in many respects a reflection of American popular culture during the 1970s. Accordingly, it makes a number of topical references that could be unfamiliar to playgoers in the twenty-first century, references that root the play in a particular historical and cultural milieu—and to a time when manual typewriters, carbon copies, and slow, bulky, and sometimes moody Xerox machines were the best that technology had to offer to writers. The lawyer Porter Milgrim, for example, who represents other writers, comments to Sidney that he tried to write a

play of his own one time. The play was to be about the US Supreme Court justice he most admired. The title, though, would be a problem, for the justice was Frankfurter. The reference is to Felix Frankfurter, who served on the Supreme Court from 1939 to 1962 (and who frequently clashed on a personal level with other justices). Of course, the reference is an easy joke, given that the word *frankfurter* is a common synonym for *hot dog*. Other examples are provided by Sidney's references to David Merrick and Hal Prince. Merrick (1911–2000) was a major Tony Award–winning theatrical producer (*Oliver!*, *Hello, Dolly!*), as was Prince (b. 1928), who won twenty-one Tony Awards and whose stage credits as producer and/or director include *West Side Story*, *Fiddler on the Roof*, *Cabaret*, and *Sweeney Todd*. Sidney says that his play *The Murder Game* was revised by George S. Kaufman. Kaufman (1889–1961) was a real-life playwright, director, and producer and the winner of two Pulitzer Prizes for Drama and one Tony Award. Thus, *Deathtrap* is steeped in the mid-twentieth-century entertainment business.

Reference is also made to Merv Griffin. Griffin (1925–2007) was a major figure in American entertainment in the years surrounding the debut of *Deathtrap*. He was the host of the *Merv Griffin Show*, a popular talk show that ran on broadcast television and in syndication at various times throughout the 1960s and 1970s and beyond. He was also the creator of the popular TV game shows *Jeopardy!* and *Wheel of Fortune*. Helga ten Dorp indicates that she is slated to appear with Peter Hurkos on Griffin's talk show and urges Sidney and Myra to watch. Hurkos (1911–1988) was a historical figure who appeared on such programs as the *Phil Donahue Show* and *The Tonight Show Starring Johnny Carson*, where he entertained viewers by performing what he claimed were psychic feats. Hurkos gained a reputation for claims that he helped the police on a number of high-profile investigations, including those surrounding the Manson family murders and the Boston Strangler. During the 1970s, the New Age movement boosted the popularity of a host of alternative beliefs and practices, among them extrasensory perception (ESP), channeling, reincarnation, clairvoyance, occult beliefs, and various other forms of psychic phenomena. Levin himself rode this wave of interest in the otherworldly with such novels as *Rosemary's Baby*.

COMPARE & CONTRAST

- **1978:** Authors typically write their works on a typewriter; although electric typewriters are in common use, many writers continue to prefer manual typewriters such as the Smith-Corona referred to in *Deathtrap*. Typescripts often include carbon copies, and works are further copied on Xerox machines.

  Today: While some authors continue to use typewriters, most are likely to write and store their works on a computer using a word-processing program. The work can then be reproduced on a printer attached to the computer, although production of multiple copies remains easier with a photocopier. The carbon copy is a thing of the past.

- **1978:** By the 1970s, the use of the word *gay* to refer to men in same-sex relationships has become well established; the term *homosexual* is growing objectionable for being outdated and derogatory, at best overly clinical.

  Today: Women attracted to members of the same sex have successfully fostered the more inclusive usage of *gays and lesbians*, while the bisexual and transgender community has fostered inclusion through the common use of the acronym LGBT to refer to all people with nonheterosexual orientations.

- **1978:** During the decade, the New Age movement brought interest in psychic powers, clairvoyance, extrasensory perception, and similar phenomena into the mainstream of Western culture; the American military and the CIA try to develop paranormal programs.

  Today: While some people claim to be "psychic detectives" able to solve crimes using paranormal abilities, US law enforcement agencies, including the FBI and police departments, remain highly skeptical and treat tips from psychics as they treat any other contacts from the public regarding a crime.

It should also be noted that the early 1970s witnessed the emergence of the Gay Liberation Movement, a movement given a boost when the American Psychological Association removed "homosexuality" from its *Diagnostic and Statistical Manual of Mental Disorders*. During the 1970s and beyond, greater acceptance of bisexuals and transgenders was promoted by the LGBT movement. While some theatergoers may have been offended by the gay sexuality implicit in *Deathtrap*, a growing number of people were coming to think differently in the wake of the civil rights struggles—and advances—of the 1960s.

CRITICAL OVERVIEW

The critical response to any play is complicated by the fact that stage dramas are a form of performance art, so the success of the play can be as much a function of the skill of the director and actors as it is that of the playwright. Nonetheless, numerous critics, in reviewing productions of *Deathtrap*, commented on the play as a play as well as on the quality of the performance. April Forreron, in a review for the *MD Theater Guide* (Baltimore, MD), noted that

> Ira Levin wrote *Deathtrap* with only one set and five characters. It opened on Broadway in February of 1978 to rave reviews and closed four years later with the record for the longest running comedy-thriller on Broadway.

Forreron praised the play as one "with so many twists and turns it is sure to make anyone dizzy."

Aileen Jacobson, in a review for the *New York Times*, pointed out:

> When *Deathtrap* opened on Broadway in 1978, Richard Eder, the *New York Times* theater critic, disliked its twists and turns, saying it "pretty well

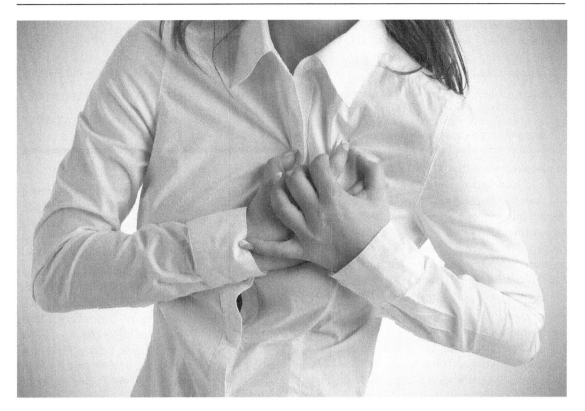

Myra, shocked at Clifford's return, has a heart attack and dies (© ruigsantos / Shutterstock.com)

consumes itself before it ends." However, Walter Kerr, the Sunday reviewer, weighing in a few days later, called the work...."an absolute knockout of a suspense melodrama." Audiences sided with Mr. Kerr, and the play ran for four years.

Critics generally have high praise for *Deathtrap*, although Charles Spencer, in a review for the London *Telegraph*, remarked that "the contrivances of the plot are pretty clunky, and...the piece is stronger on style and jokes than dramatic substance." Nevertheless, Spencer praised the play for its "serpentine plot," "humour," and "sudden thrills." Writing for the London *Times*, John Higgins commented:

> Ira Levin has written one of those plays off which a part of the theatre once fed and grew fat. The audience is enticed along, hoodwinked into believing that it knows a little more than the characters on stage, and then fooled, to its humiliated delight, about every five minutes.

Higgins went on to employ a play on words to remark that Levin has given the thriller genre "a new lease of death."

Irving Wardle, who reviewed a different staging of the play for the London *Times*, was of two minds. On one hand, he suggested that *Deathtrap* can be seen as "ghastly evidence of Broadway's debasement of the drama to an artificial ritual whose only contact with life is the size of the weekly gross." At the same time, Wardle conceded that the author "has turned the crippling commercial restrictions into the material of a piece that fully earns the flattering epithets he bestows on it in his opening lines."

Other critics have agreed with the latter assessment by Spencer. Colin Douglas, writing for the *Chicago Theatre Review*, commented: "Violence, plot twists and unexpected character developments provide continual surprises for the audience as the story gathers momentum and frantically drives to its final, startling conclusion." Douglas went on to call the play a "masterwork" and "one of theatre's finest comedy-mysteries." Douglas concluded by noting that *Deathtrap* is "filled with unpredictable turns of events, surprising character reversals and unexpected humor juxtaposed against brutal violence."

Jeffrey Walker, reviewing the play for *Broadway World*, called it "an old fashioned, twisty thrill ride" and a "venerable potboiler." Walker continued:

> Sure it's a little old fashioned, but once in a while, the theatre is a great place for an escape into a neglected dramatic form that used to fill Broadway houses every season but is now relegated to regional and community theatres.

Walker noted that Levin "took many tropes of the [thriller] genre and wrapped them around into a comic puzzler that kept a tongue in the cheek while delivering chilling moments of murderous intent." Walker's only objection was to the play's final scene: "The very last scene, when there are only a few characters left, just made me want to cry out 'Foul!' like a testy referee."

Keith Loria, writing for *DC Theatre Scene*, found *Deathtrap* a "diabolically clever thriller that combines acerbic wit, mysterious anticipation and plenty of mayhem." Calling the play "ingeniously crafted," Loria concluded: "The dark comedy combines wit and suspense in a way that's rarely seen on stage." Finally, Jason Blake, in a review for the *Sydney Morning Herald*, observed:

> The dramatic principle known as Chekhov's Gun has it that if a weapon appears on stage, even if it's hanging on a wall as an ornament, it must be used. Novelist and playwright Ira Levin took that maxim to absurd lengths in his smash hit 1978 comedy thriller *Deathtrap*, which presents its audience with a pick 'n' mix of clubs, swords, knives, battle axes, pistols and a medieval crossbow.

While feeling that "*Deathtrap* has the faint whiff of museum piece to it," Blake conceded that "they don't make 'em like this anymore."

CRITICISM

Michael J. O'Neal

O'Neal holds a PhD in English. In the following essay, he examines Deathtrap *as a play about the theater and thus about illusion.*

Throughout the history of theater—at least most of it—the pretense that has been maintained is that a "fourth wall" has been removed from the stage and that the audience is allowed to watch and eavesdrop on neighbors who are going about their lives as they interact with each other. "Going about their lives" might include the

> *DEATHTRAP*, HOWEVER, BEING A PLAY ABOUT PLAYS AND THE ILLUSIONS THEY CREATE, SHAMELESSLY EXPOSES ITS OWN ARTIFICIALITY."

murderous intentions of Shakespeare's Macbeth or the comic misadventures of the love-struck central characters in the Bard's *A Midsummer Night's Dream*. In the modern era, audience members delight in eavesdropping on such characters as Candida and her husband in George Bernard Shaw's play of the same name, and theaters regularly stage revivals of the plays of such realist dramatists as August Strindberg (*Miss Julie*), Henrik Ibsen (*A Doll's House, Hedda Gabler*), Anton Chekov (*Uncle Vanya, Three Sisters, The Cherry Orchard*), and Eugene O'Neill (*Long Day's Journey into Night, Desire under the Elms, Strange Interlude, Mourning Becomes Electra*). These and numerous other playwrights established a set of theatrical conventions that continue to hold sway with actors, directors, and audiences in the twenty-first century.

But not always. During the twentieth century, a growing number of dramatists worked to subvert the traditional conventions of the theater. They came to favor plays that invert or defy conventions, challenge the audience's core beliefs and values, and otherwise puzzle, bewilder, provoke, disorient, and possibly even anger the theatergoer. Audiences were no longer allowed to be passive spectators, peering through the fourth wall. They were required to engage in the construction of the meaning of the play or to be in on a complex, cosmic joke that they share with the playwright. This is the bedrock effect of *Deathtrap*. The audience does not leave the theater shaken by the ominous events of a Shakespearean tragedy, or edified by the social commentary of a nineteenth-century realist play, or humming tunes from an uplifting musical. Audience members leave the theater having "gotten" the comic self-referential nature of the play, allowing them to laugh with Levin not only at the absurdity of human venality and greed but also at the futility of plans that go terribly awry.

Put simply, *Deathtrap* is a play about the theater—about actors and producers and sets

WHAT DO I READ NEXT?

- Levin's first novel, *A Kiss before Dying* (Pegasus Crime, 2011), was published in 1953 and won the first of the author's Edgar Allan Poe Awards. It tells the story of an ambitious man who will stop at nothing to get what he wants. The book is regarded as a classic of psychological suspense.

- *The Mousetrap* (Samuel French, 2014) is a comic mystery from the pen of Agatha Christie. The play, based on an earlier radio play titled "Three Blind Mice," opened in the West End of London (London's theater district) in 1952, and, with more than twenty-six thousand performances, it stands (as of 2016) as by far the longest continuously running play in history.

- *Wolf Rider*, by popular award-winning young-adult novelist Avi (Simon and Schuster, 2008), was first published in 1986. The novel is a psychological thriller about a fifteen-year-old boy who receives a mysterious phone call that appears to be the confession of a murderer.

- John Russell Brown is the editor of *The Oxford Illustrated History of the Theatre* (Oxford University Press, 2001), a compendium of entries examining thousands of years of theatrical history.

- Readers interested in the culture, politics, and personalities of the 1970s, the decade in which *Deathtrap* first appeared, will enjoy *The Times of the Seventies* (Black Dog & Leventhal, 2013), produced by the *New York Times* and Clyde Haberman.

- The New Age movement of the 1970s and beyond is examined in Hugh B. Urban's *New Age, Neopagan, and New Religious Movements: Alternative Spirituality in Contemporary America* (University of California Press, 2015).

- A prolific and best-selling author of crime fiction is Walter Mosley. *Charcoal Joe* (Doubleday, 2016) continues his series of novels featuring hard-bitten private detective Easy Rawlins. In this novel he contends with racism and discrimination in the 1960s as he tries to prove the innocence of a friend's son charged with murder.

and footlights and titles and audiences and all the other trappings and paraphernalia of a slick, highly popular Broadway production. As a play about plays, it is then fundamentally a play about illusion and about the creation of illusion. Sidney is a playwright who has run out of gas. In the play's opening scene he cracks a number of in-jokes about the theatrical world; he tells Myra, for instance, that he is devious and underhanded enough to be a murderer but not enough so to be a theatrical producer. The scene is laced with theatrical references: plays that Sidney has written, drafts of plays, the theater marketplace, royalties, revenue-sharing arrangements, play production, and the like. The audience is immediately immersed in the culture of theatrical illusion.

Even the set is self-referential, for it is dominated by the various weapons—maces, garrotes, pistols, handcuffs, swords, battle-axes, a crossbow—that each served a purpose in the plays Sidney wrote during his productive years—plays that are preserved on the stage in the form of wall posters. Sidney makes reference to key figures in Broadway history—David Merrick, Hal Prince, Stanley Kaufman—and to major thrillers that earned for their writers immense sums of money. One of these was *Sleuth*, a mystery thriller set in an English manor house and featuring a lead character who is obsessed with the inventions of fiction. Another is *Dial "M" for Murder*, about a man who plans the (not-so-perfect) "perfect" murder of his wife to gain control of her money. Both of these plays suggest parallels with *Deathtrap*—both Levin's real-life play and the play within the play being written by Clifford. Later, after the arrival of Clifford, Sidney makes reference to the play *Angel Street*, the American title of a 1938 play by Patrick Hamilton called *Gas Light* in England. The play is an atmospheric psychological thriller about a domineering man who tries to drive his wife insane to cover his attempt to steal the jewels of a woman who lived in an upstairs apartment by murdering her. The play enjoyed a run of 1,295 performances in London in the 1940s and was revived on Broadway in the late 1940s and the mid-1970s, making it a fixture in the Broadway community. These kinds of knowing references and in-jokes contribute to the self-referential nature of the play.

The sense of self-referential theatrical illusion is maintained after Clifford arrives at the Bruhl home. Sidney remarks that the fascination with thrillers is a disease, which he terms *"thrill-eritis malignis*, the fevered pursuit of the one-set five-character moneymaker"* (which is exactly what *Deathtrap* is). Clifford responds:

It's *not* a disease, it's a tradition: a superbly challenging theatrical framework in which every possible variation seems to have been played. Can I conjure up a few new ones? Can I startle an audience that's *been* on Angel Street, that's dialed 'M' for murder, that's witnessed the prosecution, that's played the murder game—

(Note that "witnessed the prosecution" is a glancing reference to an Agatha Christie short story, "The Witness for the Prosecution," which was turned into a highly successful film in 1957.) Clifford appears at this point to be simply offering some notions he has about the theater and playwriting, but as the events of the play unfold, it becomes clear that in reality he is describing the "play" that he and Sidney are enacting that will lead to Myra's death—a play, we are told, that the two of them had rehearsed in a hotel room. Reality for the two men is a staged series of events, and in this sense the word *plot* takes on a double meaning.

The theme of theatrical illusion is sustained in the first scene of act 2. Sidney is nonplussed by his discovery that Clifford is writing "Death-trap." Clifford, in response, circles around to the scheme that he and Sidney concocted.

Stop and think for a minute, will you? Think. About that night. Try to see it all from an audience's viewpoint. *Everything we did to*

convince Myra that she was seeing a real murder—would have exactly the same effect on them. Weren't *we* giving a play? Didn't we write it, rehearse it? Wasn't *she* our audience?

Sidney later responds:

I can see the little box in *New York Magazine* now: "Tongues are wagging about interesting similarities between events in the new play *Deathtrap* and the private lives of its author Clifford Anderson and his employer Sidney Bruhl, who committed suicide on opening night."

The notion of *Deathtrap* as a self-referential play about illusion reaches its apogee in the climactic scene of act 2. As Clifford and Sidney act out the stage action of Clifford's "Deathtrap," various of the stage properties are called into play. Then, Clifford, armed with a gun, says:

Good-by, Sidney. (*Sidney hesitates an instant, then shoots; the blast is louder than the thunder. Clifford stands for a moment and scratches himself.*) ... Sit down—dum-dum. (*Sidney stands staring at him.*) Sit *down*. Peripeteia? Reversal? You talked about it the first day of the seminar. Important element of all drama.

Peripeteia is a Greek word that means "reversal" or "sudden change." In drama, the term is used to refer to a sudden or unexpected reversal of circumstances, usually representing a turning point in the fortunes of the hero. The concept was discussed by Aristotle in his *Poetics* as part of his discussion of the elements of a tragedy. Peripeteia has been a staple of drama for centuries, and *Deathtrap* is replete with instances of it, from the "resurrection" of Clifford from the dead in act 1 through to the demise of the two men in act 2. Plays, however, seldom rely on the vocabulary of dramatic construction: Playwrights *incorporate* peripeteia, but they do not typically call attention to it by naming it. *Deathtrap*, however, being a play about plays and the illusions they create, shamelessly exposes its own artificiality.

Clifford sums up this notion when he says to Sidney in the climactic scene: "*Deathtrap* is over. We're now into theater *vérité*." In the end, the appeal of *Deathtrap* is that it parries every effort of the audience to seize hold of the truth, and the theater *vérité*, or theater of the real, takes over as the characters of the play within the play step out of their roles into the play that Levin wrote.

Source: Michael J. O'Neal, Critical Essay on *Deathtrap*, in *Drama for Students*, Gale, Cengage Learning, 2017.

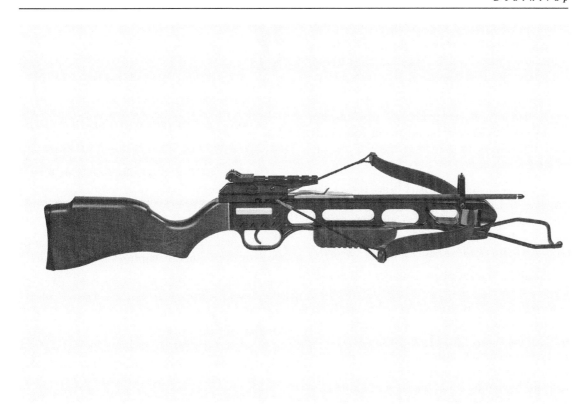

The plot twists at the end of the play including fake handcuffs and a crossbow keep the audience guessing (© Maffi | Shutterstock.com)

Keith Loria

In the following review, Loria praises the balance between humor and suspense in Deathtrap.

It's sometimes hard to properly merge comedy with suspense on the stage, but at NextStop Theatre, *Deathtrap* is a diabolically clever thriller that combines acerbic wit, mysterious anticipation and plenty of mayhem.

Ira Levin's ingeniously crafted play brings the scares and surprises coming until the final curtain, and director Evan Hoffmann manages plenty of gasps from the audience thanks to slight-of-hand stage direction and a perfectly paced production.

Even those familiar with the show's plot—whether through the original Tony-nominated Broadway production that ran from 1978–1982, or from the popular film starring Michael Caine and Christopher Reeve or its numerous stagings since—will not foresee everything the play has in store.

NextStop Theatre's intimate space provides the perfect setting for the thriller, as the audience is up front and close to the action, creating an almost immersive experience. At several points during the show, audience members literally jumped in their seats.

Peter Holdway, a prominent actor in the UK, makes his DC-area debut as Sidney Bruhl, a fading mystery playwright who hasn't seen a hit for nearly two decades. Forced to peddle his fame conducting seminars for wannabe writers, his life seems somewhat desperate and sad. When one of those aspiring writers sends him a script that knocks his socks off, Bruhl "jokes" with his wife about possible claiming it for his own and "taking care" of the student.

Holdway captures the desperation of a fading celebrity to a tee, and is an acid-tongued delight with a sarcastic wit that never quite lets you know if his murderous thoughts are genuine. Would he really kill for another shot at fame and fortune?

James Finley plays the gifted student in question, Clifford Anderson, and his marvelous script is entitled, *Deathtrap*, presenting a wink-wink, nudge-nudge to the audience that what we're watching is really a play within a play. It's a format that provides some nice laughs, without ever letting the dark comedy spill over to farce.

Just as in the play itself, the in-play *Deathtrap* is also a thriller in two parts, with one set and five characters. Without giving too much away, the fun is in watching the two scripts collide and intersect.

Finley is for the most part believable as the innocent student, but he telegraphs some of the action at a pivotal point in the production, and he might be better off taking a more laid back approach in his dealings with Holdway's Sidney.

Susan D. Garvey plays Sidney's loving wife Myra, who doesn't actually believe that her husband would ever do the evil deeds he distills on her. But once Clifford arrives and Sidney seems to be taking a dark turn, you can see the fear in her eyes at what her husband might be about to do. It's Garvey who keeps the play—and her husband—grounded and she is a delight. Her chemistry with Holdway is spot-on and you believe their years of marriage together.

Lorraine Magee is a hoot as the world-renowned psychic, Helga ten Dorp, who is vacationing next door in order to refresh her visions. She comes barging in early on and somewhat accurately predicts what will happen—both scaring and delighting Bruhl. It's another sign of deviousness that Holdway showcases well. Magee is meant to add a bout of comedy to the darkness setting in, and her cantering around the room and playing with the ancient weaponry as she "recreates" the future, does just that.

Frank Britton is also solid as Porter Milgrim, Sidney's agent, who has a surprising role to play in the action, as well.

The action takes place in Bruhl's personal study situated in a picturesque country house in Westport, Conn. Scenic designer JD Madsen presents a marvelous look into the mind of a man who could be contemplating such deviousness with ominously displayed weapons (including guns, handcuffs, maces, broadswords, and battle-axes), some having been used in past productions of his work, plus framed theatrical window cards reminding him of his past glory.

If you're looking for a frightfully fun time at the theater, *Deathtrap* is the perfect way to spend an evening. The dark comedy combines wit and

> EVEN THOUGH MYRA IS REACTING TO SIDNEY AND CLIFFORD'S FABRICATED SCENARIO SHE HITS UPON A CRUCIAL TRUTH: THAT HER HUSBAND IS CAPABLE OF MURDER. SHE SIMPLY HAS NOT REALIZED THAT HE IS CAPABLE OF *HER* MURDER."

suspense in a way that's rarely seen on stage, and NextStop's production captures it wonderfully.

Source: Keith Loria, "*Deathtrap*, Frightfully Fun, at Next-Stop Theatre," in *DC Theatre Scene*, November 3, 2015.

Jordan Schildcrout
In the following excerpt, Schildcrout equates the desperate need to hide a murder plot with the desperate need to hide one's sexuality in a prejudiced society.

... After successful tryouts in Boston and a brief preview in New York, *Deathtrap* opened on Broadway at the Music Box Theatre on 26 February 1978. Directed by Robert Moore (who also staged the landmark gay play *The Boys in the Band*), the cast included John Wood as Sidney Bruhl, Marian Seldes as his wife Myra, and Victor Garber as his student Clifford. *Deathtrap* opened to mixed reviews, with an especially bad notice from *New York Times* critic Richard Eder. In the Sunday *New York Times*, however, Walter Kerr raved about *Deathtrap*, as did other critics, who praised the play's clever plotting and mixture of witty comedy, thrilling suspense, and knowing satire of the theatre world. In general, critics who liked the play usually kept its secrets, making little or no mention of the queer "surprise"; critics who did not like the play, however, felt less of an obligation to be discrete [sic]. Eder led the pack by boldly stating: "Mr. Wood and the student are revealed to be homosexual lovers." Erika Munk in the *Village Voice* made the same revelation, adding that "the use of homosexuality as a plot device is pure exploitation."

While these critics should not, perhaps, have let the queer cat out of the bag, they did not ruin *Deathtrap* for audiences, since homosexuality is not just a shocking surprise at the end of act 1; indeed, the entire play can be read as a dark exploration of the sinister yet exciting duplicity involved in constructing and maintaining the queer closet. *Deathtrap* is remarkable because the characters, particularly Sidney as the masterful author of stage thrillers, are amazingly skillful and clever (and therefore entertaining to watch) as they manipulate the truth and one another to achieve their goals. For Sidney, the big deception, the one that masks the darkest truth and the one that is worth killing for, is the pretense of heterosexuality. By killing Myra, he avoids a messy divorce that could expose his homosexual affair. By killing Clifford, he prevents the younger man from writing a play about their relationship. Sidney is motivated by the desire for wealth, fame, artistic success, and romantic happiness, but all of these can be sacrificed if the appearance of heterosexuality is in danger. The closet must be maintained at all costs, even murder.

Sidney spends much of act 1 constructing his closet. One of the key techniques he uses is to accuse other people of queerness. Sometimes the comments are off-handed and comical, such as when Myra reprimands him for not knowing about their new neighbor, Helga ten Dorp:

> Myra: Sidney, what were you smoking Friday night when the rest of us were smoking grass? She's taken the McBain cottage for six months. Paul Wyman is doing a book with her. He was impersonating her for fifteen minutes.

> Sidney: Oh. I thought he was finally coming out of the closet.

Sidney's bitchy, gratuitous comment is for the benefit of Myra *and* the audience. Already, in the very first scene, he has commented derisively on someone else's closet, thereby deflecting any suspicions about his own. This first scene also establishes Sidney as a habitual liar on matters both large and small, causing Myra (and the audience) to second guess his motives and intentions. When friends call to invite them out, Sidney conceals their reason for staying home: to meet with a young playwright. Worried that Sidney is seriously planning a murder, Myra asks him why he lied—to which he responds: "Is it their business? I don't know why I lied; I'm just a liar."

In act 2, after Clifford has moved in with Sidney and is even sharing a symbolically loaded partners' desk with him, Sidney goes out of his way to maintain his closet. To divert any suspicions that his friend and lawyer Porter Milgrim may entertain about his relationship with

Clifford, Sidney uses the technique of preemptive accusation against his lover. Sidney exposes and then defuses the issue by asking Porter if he thinks Clifford is gay. Sidney says: "I have a sneaking suspicion he might be.... But, as long as he does his job well I suppose it's none of my business, is it?... Besides, people would talk if I took in a female secretary, wouldn't they?" Through savvy manipulation, Sidney convinces Porter (who represents Sidney's privileged access to legal, financial, and social networks) that the very fact of hiring a handsome young male secretary, even one who "might be" gay, is proof of his own heterosexuality. For the audience, however, which already knows that Sidney and Clifford are lovers, this exchange is loaded with dramatic irony. Sidney must continue to hide his relationship with Clifford, because that relationship is based on two crimes: murder and queer sexuality—exposure of either will also expose the other. Another important element of Sidney's exchange with Porter is the revelation of his readiness to betray his lover in the interests of preserving his own closet.

Sidney's wife, the first victim of his duplicity, becomes another member of Levin's doomed wives' club. At the beginning of the play, Sidney's announcement that he has received a "perfect play" from a former student clues the audience into Myra's impending demise:

> Myra: I should think you'd be proud that one of your students has written a salable play.

> Sidney: For the first time in eleven years of marriage, darling—drop dead.

Dropping dead is precisely what Myra will do at the end of the first act. In contrast, however, to the heroines of *Rosemary's Baby* and *The Stepford Wives*, Myra is not a wholly sympathetic victim. As a character, she is often unpleasant—both agitated and agitating with her fears and demands. She is also ethically challenged: after Clifford's murder, she does not turn her husband over to the police and she admits: "Part of me was hoping you would do it."

Genre conventions, however, dictate that Myra will not be an accessory, but a victim. For a brief moment after Clifford's staged murder, Myra has a glimmer of insight into Sidney's duplicity. Telling him that his action is incomprehensible, she says: "You're—alien to me, Sidney, and it can't be only since five o'clock this afternoon. You must always have been very different from the person I thought you were." Myra seems to be tapping into the core of the duplicitous-spouse drama: in the final analysis, other people, even our most intimate and trusted companions, are unknowable and potentially dangerous. Even though Myra is reacting to Sidney and Clifford's fabricated scenario she hits upon a crucial truth: that her husband is capable of murder. She simply has not realized that he is capable of *her* murder. Sidney wants to keep Myra's wealth, but he does not want to keep her. More importantly, he wants—perhaps needs—to maintain silence about his reasons for rejecting Myra, a secret better contained through murder than divorce. Myra is not the victim of Sidney's queer sexuality, but of his need to conceal his queer identity.

The representation of queerness is oddly coded in *Deathtrap*. Both Sidney and Clifford exhibit attributes that might be read as stereotypically gay: Sidney "prowl[s] the antique shops" and Clifford "work[s] out with weights every morning." Even their mutual love of thrillers sounds vaguely like an obsolete idea of homosexuality: each was exposed to and "got hooked" on thrillers as adolescents, causing Myra to comment: "It sounds like a disease, being passed from generation to generation." Furthermore, Clifford attaches a note to the manuscript he sends to Sidney, which says: "I couldn't stand the thought of waiting a few days to send my firstborn child off to its spiritual father." Thrillers are both the carriers of a disease between men *and* the product of male-male intercourse.

A full revelation of queer sexuality comes at the end of act 1, shortly after Sidney and Clifford are exposed as accomplices in Myra's murder. Eschewing a sensational, shocking revelation of queerness, Levin instead lets it creep out through an exchange of smiles between the two men, with Sidney suggestively instructing Clifford to "get into bed and stay there." Queerness becomes more explicit in the second act as Sidney and Clifford live and work—and fight—together as a couple. When Clifford threatens to move out because he suspects that Sidney might harm him, Sidney makes a protestation of love:

> Sidney: Don't be silly. I—I love you; I wouldn't think of—trying to harm you. Besides, you'd break my neck.
>
> Clifford: Goddamn right I would.

This moment, the most forthrightly "gay" in the play, is couched in threats and fears of physical violence, which is consistent with the representation of same-sex desire throughout the play. Sidney and Clifford speak to each other without the usual endearments, and physical contact only happens in moments of violent physical attack. Since the play does not depict homoerotic sexuality, homoerotic violence stands in its place. The play's only other moment of affection occurs as Sidney prepares to kill Clifford: he points a gun at the young man and sighs, "Oh God, I shall miss you very much"—not, however, enough to stay his hand.

Ultimately, the real conflict between Sidney and Clifford, the one that leads to the second murder, is sparked by the closet. Sidney is terrified of being known as the "fag who knocked off his wife": his concern about being exposed as queer equals his concern about being exposed as a killer, especially since the two crimes are intertwined and collectively accomplished with the same man. That man, however, does not share Sidney's concerns about "public humiliation." Trying to convince Sidney to collaborate on *Deathtrap*, Clifford argues, "Everybody's opening up about everything these days, aren't they?" and accuses Sidney of being old-fashioned and uptight. It is hard to understand someone being "old-fashioned and uptight" about being accused, tried, and convicted of murder. Clifford's argument makes sense only insofar as it applies to coming out of the closet. In this, Clifford displays something of a gay liberation-era freedom from shame, while the older Sidney is still firmly rooted in embarrassment, secrecy, and lies. As Clifford notes: "Sidney uses three kinds of deodorant and four kinds of mouthwash; not for him the whiff of scandal." But if Clifford "comes out" by writing *Deathtrap*, he will drag Sidney out of the closet with him; therefore to stop Clifford from betraying the mutual secrecy that binds collaborators, conspirators, and secret lovers, Sidney chooses to eliminate him. The closet must be maintained.

Many critics consider the coda to *Deathtrap* odd and unnecessary, but it presents yet another view of the closet and the desire to kill. With the three main characters dead by the final scene, psychic Helga ten Dorp is left to explain to lawyer Porter Milgrim exactly what has happened. Both have the same idea: that the events would make a sure-fire hit play. But they begin to argue over the rights to this theatrical goldmine. Helga threatens to expose Porter's dirty secret (he makes obscene telephone calls to friends) if he refuses to give her half the profits, and Porter retorts by hurling slurs at Helga—as she advances threateningly on him with a dagger. Although both characters are motivated primarily by greed in this comic scene, is it coincidence that Levin raises the specter of "perversion" once more before the final curtain descends? Apparently everyone has some sexual secret, some closet, or some queerness that can be exposed or exploited, and the need to prevent exposure leads inevitably to violence. . . .

Source: Jordan Schildcrout, "The Closet Is a Deathtrap: Bisexuality, Duplicity, and the Dangers of the Closet in the Postmodern Thriller," in *Theatre Journal*, Vol. 63, 2011, pp. 51–54.

Pauline Kael

In the following review, Kael pans the film version of the play.

. . . Ira Levin's wisecracking whodunit, which is in its fifth year on Broadway, is a pastiche of murder mystery tricks. It's the sort of cumbersomely ingenious entertainment that's meant to be played by slick, easy actors; it has to be done frivolously and artificially to compensate for the fact that it's just a machine for making money, cranking its way across the stage. But the director, Sidney Lumet, and the screenwriter, Jay Presson Allen (she's also the executive producer), have decided to make the movie version as realistic as possible. What this comes down to is a very broad, obvious movie that looks like an ugly play and appears to be a vile vision of life. When the central character (Michael Caine), a playwright who had a series of hit thrillers but, more recently, has been having one flop after another, is in his luxurious East Hampton home (a large converted windmill structure), he talks on the telephone to a former student (Christopher Reeve) whose flawless play *Deathtrap* he means to steal, and, to create movement, Lumet has the camera go with him as he keeps walking in a circle with the phone, while in the background his rich wife (Dyan Cannon) dutifully registers reactions to her husband's wickedness. It has already been planted that she has a bad heart, so we wait for her to keel over. The basic plot twist is out of *Diabolique*, and Ira Levin provides the playwright with a vast collection of medieval murder weapons and instruments of torture and such later devices as Harry Houdini's handcuffs. (This movie is for people who dream of seeing *Sleuth* again—there must be at least one or two of them.) In another scene, Caine, on the porch of the manse, talks with poor Cannon, who must busy herself among the outdoor plants—misting them, or something, with a tiny spray bottle. The movie clanks and klunks. Irene Worth comes running in, as a Dutch psychic who's living in the house next door (which, from the look of this one, must be quite a distance away). And bewilderingly, though the master bedroom is in the tower and the creaking windmill makes quite a ruckus, it has no plot function at all. There's also a bizarre early sequence, before the action settles down in the house: Caine, returning from Manhattan by train, sleeps past the East Hampton station, gets off at Montauk, and takes a taxi home. Maybe Lumet and Mrs. Allen thought we needed an excursion?

This movie grows worse and worse, with each twist and reversal destroying whatever involvement we had before, and at the end the staging and editing are so fast and muddled that you can't be sure what's happening. Except for the shouting, which has become *de rigueur* in a Lumet film, the actors don't disgrace themselves. Caine is a virtuoso at letting us know what his character is thinking. Reeve seems less beefy these days and can look craggy and sinister, though at times his pecs compete with Dyan Cannon's. She's cruelly treated by the camera and doesn't do anything she hasn't done before and better, such as her startled shriek from *Heaven Can Wait*; still, she's in there trying and gets a couple of laughs. And initially Irene Worth is certainly more welcome than she was in *Eyewitness*. But what we should never see in a movie of this type is actors working hard; yet that's all we see, and their acting gave me no pleasure. It's not a kick when the characters who are meant to be homosexual are mincingly vicious and effete. And it's not a kick, at the very start, before Caine gets on the commuter train home, when he's in the theatre where his latest play is collapsing, and the producer (Joe Silver) turns to him and, in full-screen, large-nosed profile, yells, "Putz!" That's the Lumet touch.

Source: Pauline Kael, "Comedians: *Deathtrap*," in *Taking It All In*, Holt, Rinehart and Winston, 1984, pp. 326–27.

SOURCES

"Angel Street," Internet Broadway Database, https://www.ibdb.com/Production/View/1145 (accessed May 30, 2016).

Blake, Jason, "*Deathtrap* Review: Ira Levin's House of Horrors Still Twists and Thrills," in *Sydney Morning Herald*, April 15, 2015, http://www.smh.com.au/entertainment/theatre/deathtrap-review-ira-levins-house-of-horrors-still-twists-and-thrills-20150415-1mlea6.html (accessed May 26, 2016).

Booker, Christopher, *The Seven Basic Plots: Why We Tell Stories*, Continuum Press, 2004.

"Deathtrap," Internet Broadway Database, https://www.ibdb.com/Production/View/4042 (accessed May 20, 2016).

Douglas, Colin, "Playwriting Can Be Murder," in *Chicago Theatre Review*, September 6, 2014, http://www.chicagotheatrereview.com/2014/09/playwrighting-can-be-murder/ (accessed May 26, 2016).

Forreron, April, Review of *Deathtrap*, in *MD Theater Guide*, December 15, 2014, http://mdtheatreguide.com/2014/12/theatre-review-deathtrap-at-everyman-theatre/ (accessed May 26, 2016).

Fox, John, "The Supreme Court: Biographies of the Robes: Felix Frankfurter," PBS website, 2006, http://www.pbs.org/wnet/supremecourt/rights/robes_frankfurter.html (accessed May 25, 2016).

"George S. Kaufman," Internet Broadway Database, https://www.ibdb.com/Person/View/5827 (accessed May 28, 2016).

GLAAD Media Reference Guide, Gay and Lesbian Alliance against Defamation website, 2010, http://www.glaad.org/files/MediaReferenceGuide2010.pdf (accessed May 22, 2016).

Guttridge, Peter, "Ira Levin" (obituary), in *Independent* (London, England), November 14, 2007, www.independent.co.uk/news/obituaries/ira-levin-400405/html (accessed May 23, 2016).

Hawtree, Christopher, "Ira Levin" (obituary), in *Guardian* (London, England), November 15, 2007, http://www.theguardian.com/news/2007/nov/15/guardianobituaries.booksobituaries (accessed May 20, 2016).

Higgins, John, "Ira Levin's New Lease of Death," in *Times* (London, England), March 22, 1978, p. 11.

"Ira Levin," NNDB website, 2014, http://www.nndb.com/people/424/000044292/ (accessed May 20, 2016).

Jacobson, Aileen, "One Might Kill for a Play like That," Review of *Deathtrap*, in *New York Times*, August 15, 2014, http://www.nytimes.com/2014/08/17/nyregion/a-review-of-deathtrap-in-northport.html?_r=0 (accessed May 26, 2016).

Levin, Ira, *Deathtrap: A Thriller in Two Acts*, Dramatists Play Service, 1979.

———, *Deathtrap: A Thriller in Two Acts*, Random House, 1979.

Loria, Keith, Review of *Deathtrap*, in *DC Theatre Scene*, November 3, 2015, http://dctheatrescene.com/2015/11/03/deathtrap-frightfully-fun-at-nextstop-theatre-review/ (accessed May 26, 2016).

McGraw, Carol, "Peter Hurkos: Detective Who Used Psychic Powers" (obituary), in *Los Angeles Times*, June 2, 1988, http://articles.latimes.com/1988-06-02/news/mn-5822_1_peter-hurkos (accessed May 25, 2016).

"Merv Griffin," NNDB website, 2014, http://www.nndb.com/people/418/000022352/ (accessed May 25, 2016).

Ng, David, "*Deathtrap* Canceled after Objections to Nudity and Gay Content," in *Los Angeles Times*, August 27, 2012, http://articles.latimes.com/2012/aug/27/entertainment/la-et-cm-deathtrap-ira-levin-canceled-nudity-20120827 (accessed May 21, 2016).

Spencer, Charles, Review of *Deathtrap*, in *Telegraph* (London, England), September 8, 2010, http://www.telegraph.co.uk/culture/theatre/theatre-reviews/7988972/Deathtrap-Noel-Coward-Theatre-review.html (accessed May 27, 2016).

Van Zandt, Cliff, "Shoe Leather, not Sixth Sense, Breaks Cases Open," in *The Abrams Report*, August 17, 2005, http://www.nbcnews.com/id/7320305/#.V0MM3eRoCJE (accessed May 23, 2016)

Walker, Jeffrey, "*Deathtrap* Ensnares with Wit and Style," in *Broadway World*, November 4, 2015, http://www.broadwayworld.com/washington-dc/article/BWW-Review-DEATHTRAP-Ensnares-with-Wit-and-Style-at-NextStop-Theatre-Company-20151104# (accessed May 26, 2016).

Wardle, Irving, Review of *Deathtrap*, in *Times* (London, England), October 27, 1978, p. 12.

FURTHER READING

Fisher, James, *Historical Dictionary of Contemporary American Theater: 1930–2010*, Scarecrow Press, 2011.
    Readers interested in contemporary theater will find in this volume discussion of the plays, people, movements, and institutions that shaped the American stage. The book includes a chronology, an introductory essay, an extensive bibliography, and more than fifteen hundred cross-referenced dictionary entries.

Lachman, Marvin, *The Villainous Stage: Crime Plays on Broadway and in the West End*, McFarland, 2014.
    Readers interested in crime dramas on stage will find this volume useful. It examines productions of crime dramas from the eighteenth century to the 2013–2014 theater season. Among the twenty-plus categories and nearly nine hundred plays discussed are whodunits, comic mysteries, courtroom dramas, musicals, crook plays, and important names such as Sherlock Holmes and Agatha Christie. Included are responses to the plays from critics and audiences.

Polsky, Milton E., *You Can Write a Play*, Applause Books, 2002.
    Polsky is a teacher of the art of playwriting. This highly respected book offers insights into

ways to shape a dramatic vision into a play, with exercises, suggestions, and examples from established playwrights. The book has often served as a textbook or classroom supplement.

Tepper, Jennifer Ashley, *The Untold Stories of Broadway: Tales from the World's Most Famous Theaters*, Dress Circle Publishing, 2013–2014.

Tepper's work is a two-volume set that takes an insider's view of the "Great White Way." It includes the history of Broadway's most famous theaters and anecdotes from Broadway producers, directors, writers, musicians, company managers, dressers, set designers, and even stagehands, ushers, and doormen.

SUGGESTED SEARCH TERMS

Broadway theater history

Edgar Awards

Gay Liberation Movement

Ira Levin

Ira Levin AND A Kiss before Dying

Ira Levin AND Deathtrap

Ira Levin AND Rosemary's Baby

mystery thrillers and plays

New Age movement

psychics

A Free Man of Color

JOHN GUARE

2010

A Free Man of Color, by the American dramatist John Guare, was first produced by Lincoln Center Theater at the Vivian Beaumont Theater, New York City, in December 2010, directed by George C. Wolfe. The play was published in 2014. With lavish costumes and sets, *A Free Man of Color* presents a witty, fast-moving look at life in the thriving city of New Orleans between 1801 and 1806 and in other locations in Europe and America. The large cast of characters includes many historical figures, such as Napoleon Bonaparte, Thomas Jefferson, Meriwether Lewis, Toussaint Louverture, and many others. The period depicted was an important one for New Orleans, since in those years it was controlled at different times by Spain, France, and the United States. The play, which is by turns comic and serious, explores issues of freedom and slavery, relations between the races, the nature of identity, and the interplay of money and political power, all set against the background of world events that alter the future of the city.

AUTHOR BIOGRAPHY

Guare was born on February 5, 1938, in New York City. Even as a child he was interested in the theater, and he wrote his first play at the age of eleven. He graduated with a BA from Georgetown University in 1960 and then attended Yale School of Drama,

(1979). He received an Oscar nomination for the screenplay of *Atlantic City* (1980), directed by Louis Malle. In the 1980s, Guare wrote a series of plays set in the United States in the nineteenth century that explored various attempts to build utopian societies. These were *Gardenia* (1982), *Lydie Breeze* (1982), and *Women and Water* (1985). *Moon over Miami* followed in 1987. Guare had his greatest success with *Six Degrees of Separation* (1990), and it is the play for which he is best known. It received the Drama Critics Circle Award for Best Play in 1990–1991 and in 1993 was made into a film starring Stockard Channing, Donald Sutherland, and Will Smith. *Four Baboons Adoring the Sun* (1992) was nominated for the Tony Award for Best Play in 1992. Three other plays followed around the turn of the twenty-first century: *Lake Hollywood* (2001), *Chaucer in Rome* (2001), and *A Few Stout Individuals* (2002).

Guare resumed his output of plays during the 2010s. In 2010, *A Free Man of Color* was produced at the Vivian Beaumont Theater in New York City. This was followed by *Erased/Elzbieta* (2011), *Are You There, McPhee?* (2012), and *3 Kinds of Exile* (2013). Guare, who is married to Adele Chatfield Taylor, an arts administrator, received the Dramatists Guild Lifetime Achievement Award from the Dramatists Guild in 2014.

John Guare *(© lev radin / Shutterstock.com)*

receiving an MA in playwriting in 1963. Many of his plays during the 1960s were one-act comedies. These included *To Wally Pantoni, We Leave a Credenza* (1965), *Muzeeka* (1968), and *Cop-Out* (1969). In 1971, one of his most successful plays, the dark comedy *The House of Blue Leaves*, was produced. Set in Queens, New York City, in 1965, on the day that Pope Paul VI visited New York City, the play won the Drama Critics Circle Award and the Obie Award for Best American Play, 1970–1971. By this time, Guare was establishing a reputation for writing nonrealistic plays that defied traditional categories of genre and also sought to probe beneath surface appearances to reveal a more profound truth. Also in 1971, Guare ventured into musical theater. With Mel Shapiro, he wrote the libretto for the musical *Two Gentlemen of Verona*, and the two writers shared the 1972 Drama Desk Award for Outstanding Book of a musical. (Guare also wrote the book for the musical *Sweet Smell of Success* in 2002.)

Later in the 1970s, Guare wrote *Marco Polo Sings a Solo* (1977) and *Bosoms and Neglect*

PLOT SUMMARY

Act 1

It is 1801 in the thriving city of New Orleans. The main character, Jacques Cornet, enters, dressed, as is his custom, in magnificent style. Jacques is a former slave who has purchased his freedom and is now rich because he has inherited the wealth of his white father. His slave, Murmur, is with him. Jacques announces that he is writing a play (which is the play the audience is witnessing).

A shipment of silk cloth arrives from Shanghai. It has taken three years to arrive in New Orleans. Jacques demands to see his maps, which he collects. He is anxious to find a western route across the American continent that will enable shipments from Asia to arrive faster. He hopes there is a river from California that meets the Mississippi.

Dr. Toubib, who is of African descent, enters and announces that this is Jacques's home, where every Tuesday he meets with men such as

Harcourt and Sparks, who sell him maps of America created by Indians. (Jacques also makes a habit of seducing their wives.) There is a card game in process in which money is gambled. Toubib says it is the festival of Mardi Gras, during which all social barriers come down in what is already, according to him, the freest city in the world, where the races mingle.

More characters unveil themselves, including Mme. Mandragola, who keeps a brothel. Jacques is a valued client, and Mme. Mandragola's girls all seem to like him. This is the first of many references to Jacques's prowess as a lover.

Two more characters enter. Juan Ventura Morales is the Spanish *intendante* of New Orleans. He is impatient because Jacques is keeping all the girls to himself. While Jacques is engaged in his amorous exploits, Zeus-Marie Pincepousse, Jacques' white half-brother, enters. He complains that the house, which Jacques has inherited, is rightfully his.

Historical characters then appear. Toussaint Louverture, who led a slave rebellion in Saint-Domingue (called Sante Domingue in the play), appeals to the French for support. (Saint-Domingue was the name of the French colony on the western third of Hispaniola, and Santo Domingo was the Spanish colony on the eastern two-thirds. The two became Haiti and the Dominican Republic.) Napoleon Bonaparte is shown lying in a bathtub plotting how to outmaneuver the British in the struggle for empire. Talleyrand, Napoleon's foreign minister, delivers Toussaint's letter to Napoleon and tells Napoleon that a foothold in the West Indies would allow France entry to America. Napoleon, however, is interested only in defeating the British.

Thomas Jefferson and Meriwether Lewis appear, discussing American affairs. Meriwether wants to explore what he calls the white spaces of the continent. Like Jacques, he wants to find the river that connects east and west, but Jefferson is not interested in giving him any money to do so. He is willing, however, to support Toussaint because America needs to ensure the supply of the sugar that Sante Domingue produces.

Back in New Orleans, a top secret, coded message arrives from Spain. Pincepousse, who is accompanied by his wife, Margery Jolicoeur, conveys it to Morales. Margery falls for Jacques as soon as she sees him. Jacques, however, is terrified when he hears his half-brother wonder whether the coded message is an instruction to restore *le code noir* (French for black code), a repressive code enacted in 1685 that instituted severe measures regarding black people in Louisiana, affording them no rights whatsoever. Jacques fears that if the code is reinstated, he may lose his freedom.

While Jacques tries hard to stay out of the clutches of his wife, Doña Athene, Morales's wife, Doña Smeralda, appears with Count Achille Creux, Morales's cousin, and his scientist wife, Doña Polissena. They have escaped from the rebellion in Sante Domingue, leaving all their belongings behind. Creux holds a very negative view of blacks.

Meanwhile, in Paris, Talleyrand arranges for France to purchase Louisiana from the Spanish. The treaty is to be kept secret until Napoleon is within sight of New Orleans (which means that most of the characters in the play do not know of it).

While Jacques seduces Doña Smeralda, under the nose of her husband, Creux talks about the necessity of restoring *le code noir*. Jacques, addressing the audience, says that New Orleans, thanks to the American Revolution and the French Revolution, has entered the Age of Enlightenment and can never turn the clock back and readopt the repressive code.

While Morales tries to decode the letter, so does Jefferson, who has received the same message in Washington, DC. Finally, it is revealed: Spain has given Louisiana to France. Both Jefferson and Morales are angered by the message. Morales, Pincepousse, and Creux plan to foment a revolution and get Jacques unwittingly to finance it. Morales plans to become ruler of a united North and South America with Pincepousse as his deputy.

Jacques knows something is afoot and goes about his business of seducing wives in order to gain information about the activities of their husbands. Mrs. Sparks, for example, says that her husband relays information to the US State Department. Lady Harcourt tells him her husband is a British spy. Harcourt, however, appears to know nothing about France's buying Louisiana. Frustrated at not being able to get information, Jacques devises a plan. He gets Murmur to stage a fake shooting. It is to appear as if Jacques has been shot in the groin (appropriately enough for a renowned lover and seducer). Then he will spread the news that he is near death and has left a will. He wants to make all his male acquaintances believe they are his sole heirs.

Meanwhile, the French make plans to take New Orleans, Jefferson sends a diplomat, Robert Livingston, to France, authorizing him to buy Louisiana from France for the United States.

Act 2

At a ball in New Orleans, Dr. Toubib brings the news that Jacques has been shot. The women receive the news with distress. Toubib distributes copies of the will separately to four men: Morales, Remy Dorilante, Sparks, and Harcourt, each of whom then thinks that he is Jacques's sole heir. They are delighted and hypocritically express their affection for him. Jacques pretends to be at death's door as his half-brother Pincepousse visits him, saying he has a map that shows the passage to the west, but it will cost Jacques a lot of money. Jacques is not interested, however; whatever information he needs from Pincepousse he thinks he can get from Pincepousse's wife, Margery. After Pincepousse leaves, Margery jumps into bed with Jacques, but he is disappointed to find that she knows nothing.

Meanwhile, France sends troops to Sante Domingue to put down Toussaint's rebellion. Jefferson has promised to send US supplies to help Toussaint in the adjoining colony of Santo Domingo (formerly belonging to Spain but at this point belonging to France), after Toussaint invades it in order to end slavery and unite the entire island. But now Jefferson orders that the supplies be stopped, since he does not want to offend France, given that he wants New Orleans.

It is Easter Sunday, and Jacques, fed up with his forty-day isolation, goes to visits Doña Polissena, who peers into her microscope, examining a mosquito. She is trying to discern the cause of yellow fever, which is devastating the population of Santo Domingo. Jacques wastes no time in getting her into bed.

As the French fight in Santo Domingo, their troops die of yellow fever. General Leclerc, Napoleon's brother-in-law, orders that shiploads of infected black people should be sent to New Orleans to inflict the plague on that city. Morales and Creux get wind of this plan and are desperate to block the entry of the ships into the harbor. They enlist the help of Jacques, hoping they can buy off the French using Jacques's money. At that point, Leclerc dies of the fever. Jacques insists on seeing the ship with Morales. He looks down into the hold to see the suffering people there and falls in. Murmur pulls him back up, and they all escape

in a rowboat as the ship turns away into the gulf. Jacques is deeply moved by the suffering he has witnessed, and he weeps.

Back in New Orleans, a changed Jacques, identifying strongly with the suffering slaves, decides to free Murmur. Margery reveals that she is pregnant by Jacques, and soon all the other women he has seduced become aware that Jacques is not mortally wounded. Still enamored of him, they advance in his direction, wanting to claim him. Meanwhile the men who thought they were about to inherit his property realize they have been tricked.

Morales shuts down the port, on which the citizens depend for food. The Mississippi River is closed. When people protest, Morales tells them that Jacques is to blame. Jacques, Murmur, and Dr. Toubib manage to escape to the bayou. Pincepousse, angry that Jacques has stolen his wife, finds Jacques, and they fight a duel. Pincepousse is killed.

As Jacques flees with his maps into the white spaces, the unknown interior of the continent, some of the townspeople discover Pincepousse's body and angrily organize a search for Jacques.

Napoleon orders the sale of the Louisiana territory in its entirety to the United States for fifteen million dollars. He plans to triumph in the wars against Britain and then attack the United States and reclaim Louisiana. Jefferson sends Meriwether with William Clark to explore the new territory.

In the Indian territory in November 1803, Meriwether encounters a man covered in bearskins whom he believes to be an Indian. It is in fact a disheveled-looking Jacques. Meriwether informs him that the United States now owns all of Louisiana and tells him that as a result, slavery will end because the nation is committed to the notion that all men are created equal.

Convinced that he will be safe, Jacques returns to New Orleans, where he encounters Murmur. Murmur tells him that Dr. Toubib, as a former slave in Boston, has been reclaimed by his owner and taken away. Jacques's wife, Lady Harcourt, Mme. Dorilante, and Mrs. Sparks, abandoned by their husbands, have become nuns.

Jacques is seized and put in shackles by Sparks, Harcourt, and Dorilante. Murmur has betrayed him and has purchased his own freedom with the reward money. Jacques's property has been seized by the US government, and he is to be auctioned. Jacques protests, and Jefferson appears. Jacques insists to Jefferson that he is a free man and identifies himself. It turns out that Jefferson knew his father. Jacques demands his rights to be treated equally, since the equality of men is stated in the Declaration of Independence. Jefferson replies that those words are not in the Constitution, in which the laws are enshrined. Jefferson says he hates slavery but that it is necessary for the nation to flourish. Jacques accuses Jefferson of hypocrisy, but his arguments do not sway the president.

Meriwether appears and says that he has failed to find a direct water route across the land. He is shattered by this failure, feeling that he has let Jefferson down. He shoots himself dead.

Sparks sells Jacques to a new owner. Margery, who has been claimed by Sparks, declares her love for Jacques. Creux gives a speech saying that blacks are dangerous and must be kept down. Jacques has a vision of the future in which he sees how Hurricane Katrina will devastate New Orleans. After a brief flashback to happier days in 1801, the play ends with Dr. Toubib addressing the audience, telling them the title of Jacques's play, *A Free Man of Color or How One Man Became an American.*

CHARACTERS

Achille Alciabiade
Achille Alciabiade has moved to New Orleans to become a furniture trader. He claims to be from Norway, and he speaks with a Norwegian accent, although he is actually from Barbados. He says he is white. He visits Jacques's home and plays cards there. Like many other visitors, he tries to sell Jacques a map of the American interior. He says it was given to him by an Indian on his deathbed.

Doña Athene
Doña Athene is Jacques's wife, whom he professes to detest. She loves him to begin with but soon falls out of love when she discovers his infidelity. She lets all the women and the cuckolded husbands know that she knows what has been going on. She is hoping to incite their hostility toward him.

Napoleon Bonaparte
At the time the play is set, Napoleon Bonaparte (1769–1821) is first consul of France. Later he proclaims himself emperor. In the play, he is presented as having a lust for power. He is intent on building up the French overseas possessions and getting the better of the British, who are competing with France for global empire. After having acquired Louisiana from Spain, Napoleon quickly sells it to the United States, since at this point he has no interest in the New World. In doing so, he goes against the advice of Talleyrand. Napoleon plans to recapture North America later, after he has defeated Britain, but historically, this does not occur.

Calliope
Calliope is one of the prostitutes employed by Mme. Mandragola. Like the other girls, she adores Jacques.

Jacques Cornet
Jacques Cornet is the main character in the play. He is the son of a wealthy white man and a slave woman. He has inherited his father's wealth and become a rich man and a prominent figure in the life of New Orleans. He loves expensive clothes and is known as a fine dresser. He also collects maps of America because his desire is to find a water route from the Mississippi River to the West Coast, which will enable him to have goods shipped to New Orleans from locations in Asia, such as China, much faster. Jacques is also a womanizer and the favorite customer of the prostitutes at Mme. Mandragola's brothel. He makes a habit of seducing other men's wives, who seem to find him irresistible. Jacques later undergoes a transformation and becomes much more serious in his attitudes, feeling compassion for the slaves and freeing Murmur.

Count Achille Creux
Count Achille Creux is a cousin of Morales. He and his wife have recently escaped the rebellion in Sante Domingue, where they had to leave all their property behind. He dislikes all black people and seems to have an irrational fear of them too. He hates the very idea of revolution, including the American and French revolutions, because they have given people too much freedom. He hopes that *le code noir* will be restored.

King Carlos Cuarto

Carlos Cuarto, as he is named in the play, is King Carlos IV of Spain (1748–1819). He sees no point in retaining control of Louisiana, regarding it as a mere nuisance. He gives it to France in exchange for Etrutia (Tuscany) in Italy, which he wants because it will enable him to provide a kingdom for his daughter, the Infanta, to rule.

Mme. Dorilante

Mme. Dorilante is the wife of Remy Dorilante. She is one of Jacques's many lovers.

Remy Dorilante

Remy Dorilante gambles in card games at Jacques's home. He appears also to be a painter, since he tells Jacques he has painted his portrait. He also tries to sell maps to Jacques. Like others, he is duped into believing that a mortally wounded Jacques has made him his sole heir.

Euterpe

Euterpe is one of the prostitute's in Mme. Mandragola's brothel.

Georges Feydeau

Georges Feydeau (1862–1921) was a French playwright renowned for his farces. He appears just once in the play, giving his advice about how to write a play.

Lady Harcourt

Lady Harcourt is the wife of Lord Harcourt. She is seduced by Jacques.

Lord Sidney Harcourt

Lord Sidney Harcourt is a fur trader. He ingratiates himself with Jacques because of his wealth and turns a blind eye to the fact that Jacques has seduced his wife. Harcourt is also a spy for the British. He is duped into believing that a mortally wounded Jacques has made him his sole heir.

Infanta

The Infanta (1782–1824) is Maria Luisa, the daughter of King Carlos Cuarto. She has only one eye and behaves strangely, gorging herself with grapes and choking on them. She wants to become queen of Tuscany mostly so her husband can be the king. She is spoiled and manipulative.

Thomas Jefferson

Thomas Jefferson (1743–1826) is one of the founding fathers of the United States. He wrote the Declaration of Independence and served as the nation's third president, from 1801 to 1809. The play brings out the contradiction involved in Jefferson's professed love of freedom and the fact that he keeps slaves and sees no need for slavery to end. Jefferson makes the Louisiana Purchase from France in 1803 and sends Meriwether Lewis and William Clark out to explore the newly acquired territory.

Margery Jolicoeur

Margery Jolicoeur is Pincepousse's black wife, but she has no love for him. She loves New Orleans, though, and she falls in love with Jacques and bears him a child. After Pincepousse's death, Sparks sells Margery's child but keeps Margery, claiming her as his. Margery, however, continues to profess her love for Jacques.

Josephine

Josephine (1763–1814) is the wife of Napoleon Bonaparte. In the play, she is presented as small-minded and petty, concerned mostly about her clothes. She has no interest in politics or Napoleon's grand enterprises.

General Leclerc

General Charles Leclerc (1772–1802) is Napoleon's brother-in-law. He leads French forces that put down the slave rebellion in Sante Domingue but dies of yellow fever.

Leclerc's Captain

Leclerc's Captain announces that Leclerc is dead.

Leda

Leda is the slave of the Moraleses. They believe she is happy being a slave, but she tells the audience she would chop their heads off if she could.

Meriwether Lewis

Meriwether Lewis (1774–1809), along with William Clark, was sent out by Jefferson to chart the newly acquired Louisiana Territory. In the play, he encounters Jacques in Indian territory and explains that New Orleans is now under American control and that since the new nation believes in equality, it would be safe for the former slave Jacques to return there. Near the end of the play, Meriwether reappears. He is a bitterly disappointed man, having failed to find a direct waterway across the continent. Believing that he has let Jefferson down, he commits suicide.

Robert Livingston

Robert Livingston (1746–1813) is sent by Jefferson to negotiate with the French diplomat Talleyrand the purchase of New Orleans. He ends up returning with the whole of the Louisiana Territory.

Mme. Mandragola

Mme. Mandragola is in charge of a brothel to which Jacques is a frequent visitor. She likes Jacques but dislikes Morales, who also seeks out her girls.

Melpomene

Melpomene is a prostitute in Mme. Mandragola's brothel. She likes Jacques and cannot stand Morales.

Mercure

Mercure is a newcomer to Jacques's home. He tries to sell Jacques a map that he claims shows an underground connection between the East and West Coasts that runs through caves. Jacques buys it.

James Monroe

James Monroe (1758–1831) was one of the founding fathers of the United States. He was sent by Jefferson to join Robert Livingston in negotiating the purchase of New Orleans from France. Later, he became the fifth US president, serving from 1817 to 1825.

Juan Ventura Morales

At the time of the play, Juan Ventura Morales (1756–1819) is the *supreme intendante* of New Orleans. He controls access to the Mississippi, including the port of New Orleans and can shut it down if he wishes. He is presented in the play as rather conceited and arrogant with an inflated idea of his own importance. He plans to foment a revolution that he hopes will lead to his becoming the leader of a united North and South America.

Cupidon Murmur

Cupidon Murmur is Jacques's slave, although his manner toward his owner is not at all subservient. Murmur later betrays Jacques, buying his own freedom in the process.

Orphee

Orphee is a slave of the Moraleses. Creux shoots at him.

Zeus-Marie Pincepousse

Zeus-Marie Pincepousse is Jacques' white half-brother. He hates Jacques because Jacques has inherited their father's property, which Pincepousse thinks is rightfully his. Pincepousse is angry at Jacques's seduction of his wife, Margery, and attacks Jacques. They fight a duel in which Pincepousse is killed.

Doña Polissena

Doña Polissena is Creux's wife. She is a scientist and is dedicated to finding the cause of yellow fever, which she correctly believes is spread by mosquitoes. Jacques seduces her. She eventually dies of the disease.

Pythagore

Pythagore plays cards at Jacques's home. He also tries to sell Jacques a map.

Major Walter Reed

Major Walter Reed (1851–1902) is the US Army physician who proved that yellow fever is transmitted by mosquitoes.

Doña Smeralda

Doña Smeralda is Morales's wife. She is also one of Jacques's conquests. She is eventually killed by her husband.

Jonathan Sparks

Jonathan Sparks is one of the visitors to Jacques's house who tries to sell Jacques maps. He is later duped into believing that a mortally wounded Jacques has made him his sole heir.

Mrs. Sparks

Mrs. Sparks is Jonathan Sparks's wife. She willingly becomes one of Jacques's conquests.

Talleyrand

Talleyrand, whose full name (not used in the play), was Charles Maurice de Talleyrand-Perigord (1754–1838) was a French diplomat who urged Napoleon to acquire territory in the New World, because of the wealth it could bring to France. But Napoleon does not listen to him. Eventually, Talleyrand negotiates with Livingston and Monroe for the sale of Louisiana to the United States.

Terpsichore

Terpsichore is one of the prostitutes in Mme. Mandragola's brothel. Her favorite client is Jacques, and she refuses Morales.

Dr. Toubib

Dr. Toubib is a doctor who informs the audience of some of the background of the play, describing the life of the city in 1801, for example, and narrating some of the historical events that are relevant to the action of the play. After the purchase of Louisiana by the United States, Dr. Toubib is recaptured as an escaped slave and returned to Boston.

Toussaint Louverture

Toussaint's full name was François-Dominique Toussaint Louverture (1743–1803). He led a slave rebellion on the French colony of Saint-Domingue and established it as an independent nation. He asked for French support, but Napoleon instead sent an army to defeat the rebellion and restore slavery. Toussaint also invaded the former Spanish colony of Santo Domingo (at that time under French control) and appealed for American support, but Jefferson reneged on a promise and did not deliver it. In the play, Toussaint tells the audience that he died in a French prison around the time of the Louisiana Purchase.

THEMES

Freedom

Freedom takes a variety of forms in the play. Freedom is contrasted to slavery, for example. The play that Jacques, a former slave, is writing (which is also the play the audience happens to be watching) is called *A Free Man of Color*. By the end of the play, however, Jacques has lost his cherished freedom and is to be sold as a slave. In terms of the theme of freedom and slavery, the play references three eras: a former era, dating from the late seventeenth century, in which the repressive and cruel *le code noir* was applied; the era of freedom in which Jacques lives in 1801; and the new repression that begins in 1803 after New Orleans is incorporated into the United States as a result of the Louisiana Purchase. The irony (and hypocrisy) of the return of New Orleans to a previous dark era of slavery while being a part of a nation that is supposedly

TOPICS FOR FURTHER STUDY

- With Jacques Cornet's confrontation with Thomas Jefferson in mind, select another character from history and write a scene in which you (or someone else) confront the character about a controversial issue in which the character played a major part. With a classmate, act out the scene in your class.

- Examine Jefferson's explanation in the play for the beginning of slavery and the reasons he gives for its continued existence. Discuss your opinion of whether his explanation is historically accurate. Research the origins of slavery in America both before and after the Declaration of Independence, and write an essay in which you explain its origins and continuance in the American South up to the period covered by the play.

- *A Free Man of Color* has a large cast of both fictional and historical characters. Go to the Pinterest page https://www.pinterest.com/pin/188517934379172665 and read about character maps. Create a character map for the play that shows all the characters and their relationships.

- Read *My Mother the Cheerleader* (2007), a young-adult novel set in New Orleans in the 1960s. As it was in the early 1800s, change is in the air. New Orleans is still largely segregated by race, but desegregation is on the way. In the course of the novel, the characters express various attitudes and views regarding race. Write an essay in which you describe the range of views presented. Where appropriate, compare these to the prevailing ideas in the same city over 150 years earlier, as presented in *A Free Man of Color*. What has changed since then? What has remained the same?

founded on the principle that all men are created equal is brought out near the end in the dialogue between Jacques and Jefferson.

When the play begins, New Orleans is not quite as free as its advocates proclaim it to be. Dr. Toubib may refer to it as the "free-est city in the world," but it does still permit slavery. Murmur, for example, is Jacques's slave. Margery, however, a newcomer to the city, does not think this much of a barrier to the freedom that is embodied in the city: "Oh, there are slaves but if you're a slave you can work to buy your freedom because the more people that are free, the better we all will be."

Margery immediately takes a liking to the city because there are so many different races and nationalities, and people mingle freely regardless of race. She says, "No city on this planet can be more varied, more motley, more multifarious. Is there another place where no barriers exist between people? A world where people join, meet, all equals." In New Orleans in 1801, the fetters of race barely exist because so many people are of mixed race, and no one makes an issue of it. This is the freedom to which Dr. Toubib refers. He also comments, "Imagine the unimaginable. Race is a celebration! See the lush palette of skin tones in New Orleans." Harcourt points out that although he is truly white, it affords him "no privilege. Here's it's just another color." A note that appears in the published version of the play points out that at the time there were more than one hundred terms for people of mixed race. Those who were a mixture of "'pure' white and 'pure' black = mulatto; mulatto and black = sambo; mulatto and white = quadroon (*quarteron*); a *meamelouc* was '113 of 120 parts white,' etc." In addition, the play begins during the festival of Mardi Gras, during which the barriers between people are even lower than they normally were in the city. A spirit of freedom and gaiety is in the air.

New Orleans is also free in the sense that people can reinvent themselves and become who they want to be. Dr. Toubib points out that few people come to the New World of their own volition. Many have shady backgrounds; they may have been deported or disinherited or "escaped the police. They spy, steal, smuggle, sometimes even work honestly, until the day their fortune will surely appear." The New World as it manifests itself in New Orleans is thus a world of opportunity and transformation for those who are willing to make such things happen. Achille Alciabiade, for example, claims to be from Norway and speaks with a Norwegian accent, although actually he is from Barbados. The discrepancy

does not seem to matter to anyone. Jacques is a former slave who because of an inheritance is now a dandy and a playboy who has a slave of his own and an envied position in society.

Compassion

The theme of compassion emerges in act 2, in the person of Jacques. This represents a remarkable change and transformation from the conceited, superficial character who struts around the stage in act 1. In act 1, Jacques appears to care for nothing other than his fancy clothes. The only reason he collects maps is so that he can discover a cross-continental water route that will allow his shipments of exotic clothing from Asia to arrive much more quickly. He says to Murmur that the play he is writing is about "the sanctity of surfaces, the value of veneer." There seems to be no depth at all to the man. His favorite occupation is seducing women, preferably married ones, although he aspires to be a political power broker in the city.

All Jacques's superficiality changes in act 2, although at first Jacques acts as usual from merely selfish motives. New Orleans is threatened by yellow fever, and Morales convinces Jacques that only he can save the city—by buying off the French so that the ships carrying black people from Santo Domingo who have the disease do not enter the harbor. Jacques wants to play the hero, but he ends up being affected quite differently from what he had imagined. He goes to see the ship himself, and as he looks down into the hold, where the sick people are, he immediately becomes conscious of the fact that he shares the racial heritage of the victims: "I see people the color of my mother reaching up." Then he falls into the hold, an act that symbolically suggests that he is completely identifying with the victims and their fate. The full horror of their experience impresses itself on him as the stricken people clutch at him.

After Murmur pulls him up, Jacques exclaims, "O miserable mankind, to what fall degraded, to what wretched state reserved!" He feels their suffering so keenly that he cannot stop himself from weeping. After this, he is a changed man, and he frees Murmur. The change in Jacques marks a change in the nature of the play, which veers from comedy to near tragedy as Jacques is eventually reenslaved. As he earnestly debates Thomas Jefferson regarding the existence of slavery in a new nation dedicated to

Most of the story takes place in New Orleans *(© Frontpage | Shutterstock.com)*

the notion of the equality of all men, Jacques is an utterly different man from the amoral fop who when the play began cared only for the showy exteriors of life and the gratification of personal desire.

STYLE

Restoration Comedy

The play cannot be classified in a single genre, but much of it, especially act 1, is a comedy of manners, with particular reference to English Restoration comedy. Restoration comedy first appeared in 1660, when the monarchy was restored after Puritan rule, and the theaters were reopened. Such comedies present relationships between men and women in the upper levels of society that defy social conventions. The dialogue is clever, featuring short, sharp exchanges often known as repartee, which as M. H. Abrams notes in *A Glossary of Literary Terms*, is "a witty conversational give-and-take which constitutes a kind of verbal fencing match."

The situations presented in Restoration comedy are often immoral and somewhat indecent, and a cynical attitude toward marriage is common. One of the best writers of Restoration comedy was William Congreve. In his play *The Way of the World* (first produced in 1700), one character, Mirabell, says to another, Mrs. Fainall, "You should have just so much disgust for your husband as may be sufficient to make you relish your lover."

Guare follows these conventions in *A Free Man of Color*. The dialogue is witty and fast-moving and has frequent double entendres (double meanings) that refer to sexual activity. Jacques subverts social norms by constantly seducing other mens' wives, and marriage is denigrated in a comic manner throughout. Jacques, for example, cannot stand his wife and tries to avoid her at all costs. "I didn't buy myself out of one slavery to move into another," he tells Murmur. There is not a single happily married couple in the play. The women Jacques seduces are either indifferent to or actively dislike their husbands (thus following Mirabell's advice to Mrs. Fainall in *The Way of the World*). Even the historical characters get in on the long-running marriage joke. Meriwether Lewis tells Jefferson that he would like to be out exploring the continent: "I want to decipher what is unknown," he says, to which Jefferson replies, "If you want the unknowable, get a wife." Meriwether responds, "I'd rather climb in bed with my maps."

Nonrealistic Drama

The play does not follow the conventions of realistic drama, in which a play attempts to be as true as possible to real life. The characters sometimes step outside the frame of the play to deliver information or make an observation directly to the audience, thus breaking the fourth wall, the separation traditionally observed between audience and performers. (This has a parallel in Restoration comedy in the form of the aside, a comment made by one of the characters that is heard by the audience but by convention not by the other characters on stage.) These moments include observations, opinions, and information that would not have been available to either fictional or historical characters, since they refer to later times. For example, Napoleon, in explaining his dislike of the British, goes on a comic, historical-time-defying rant in which he says, "When the future comes, I will hate Big Ben. Queen Victoria. James Bond. Charles Dickens. Florence Nightingale. British Air. Julie Andrews. Mick Jagger. No, I will like him." Jacques announces the date, 1801, at the beginning of the play and adds that "this is the last time men will dress like this" (referring to his elaborate garb), which reveals knowledge that the character, if presented realistically, would not have. Another nonrealistic element is to present Jacques as the author of the play the audience is watching. At the end, the play is renamed, with an added subtitle "*or How One Man Became an American,*" as Dr. Toubib tells the audience. Yet another example is when Dr. Toubib announces, in the context of Doña Polissena's belief that yellow fever is caused by the mosquito, that this will not be confirmed until 1900, when Major Walter Reed will announce it.

HISTORICAL CONTEXT

New Orleans under Spain and France

The original inhabitants of the area now known as New Orleans were Native Americans, who were likely there some three thousand years before the first Europeans arrived. In 1682, France claimed the area, naming it Louisiana in honor of King Louis XIV. In 1718, a Frenchman, Jean Baptiste Le Moyne, Sieur de Bienville, built a city, La Nouvelle-Orléans, which became the capital of Louisiana in 1723. Nearly half a century later, in 1763, France's King Louis XV ceded Louisiana to his ally and Spanish cousin, King Charles III, under the Treaty of Paris, which ended the Seven Years' War. That war had begun in 1756 and involved France, Britain, Spain, and a number of other European nations. Under this treaty, France lost its colonial possessions in North America to Britain.

Under Spanish rule, people of color in New Orleans were able to flourish because they were allowed to be free. (Hence, Jacques in the play can become a prominent free citizen of the city.) Spanish rule, however, continued only until 1801 (the year in which *A Free Man of Color* begins), when Spain returned it to France. This was a result of the Third Treaty of Ildefonso, signed in 1800, between France and Spain. For a while, the treaty was kept secret, so in the play the citizens of New Orleans and its Spanish ruler, Juan Ventura Morales, still think that Spain controls the city. Spain was ready to cede Louisiana to France because it was going through a period of economic uncertainty and was not able to support its colony or profit from it.

Louisiana Purchase

The transfer of Louisiana to France was not well received in the United States. The US president Thomas Jefferson feared that if France controlled New Orleans, it would also control the Gulf of Mexico and the Atlantic Ocean. For a while, he considered forming an alliance with Great Britain to counter the perceived threat. Jefferson also sent negotiators to Paris to try to buy from the French a relatively small amount of territory consisting of New Orleans and West Florida. Napoleon surprised Jefferson by offering the entirety of Louisiana, and Jefferson was at first doubtful that he had the constitutional authority to make the deal. But he went ahead anyway and made the Louisiana Purchase for the sum of fifteen million dollars. Napoleon may have had a variety of reasons for selling the territory. France was distracted by a slave rebellion in Haiti and was also about to embark on another war with Great Britain. The Treaty of Amiens, a peace treaty between the three global powers, Britain, France, and Spain, had

COMPARE
&
CONTRAST

- **1801–1806:** On Sundays in New Orleans, Congo Square is a meeting place for slaves, where they play music and dance. In act 1 of the play, Dona Smeralda refers to it, saying she goes there to learn the dances.

  Today: Congo Square is located in New Orleans in an open area of Louis Armstrong Memorial Park. It is an important symbol, especially for African Americans, because of its historical links to black music, including jazz.

- **1801–1806:** The annual festival of Mardi Gras is already a well-established tradition in the thriving city of New Orleans. The population is rapidly growing. In a period of thirteen years, from 1797 to 1810, the population grows from eight thousand to over seventeen thousand. Most of the population speaks French.

  Today: The annual celebration of Mardi Gras in February or March continues to be a highlight of life in New Orleans. The population of the city as of 2015 is 389,617. It is a multiracial city, whites accounting for about 33 percent of the population, blacks 60 percent, and Hispanics just over 5 percent.

- **1801–1806:** In 1801, Toussaint Louverture, a former black slave, assumes power in Haiti after leading a revolution against French colonial power. Controlling the entire island of Hispaniola, he abolishes slavery. A year later, French forces under Charles Leclerc fail to retake the country. Toussaint Louverture, however, dies in a French prison in 1803.

  Today: Haiti is the poorest country in the Western Hemisphere. It is recovering from a massive earthquake that took place in January 2010. Four people out of every five live below the poverty line.

---

been signed in 1802 but would last for only a little over one year before hostilities resumed. Napoleon may also simply have been short of money.

The Louisiana Purchase, consisting of eight hundred thousand square miles, vastly expanded the size of the United States. It has since been considered one of the best real estate bargains of all time. Out of the territory acquired, six new US states would eventually be formed. The first of these was Louisiana, which in 1812 became the eighteenth state.

CRITICAL OVERVIEW

The play met with mixed reviews when it began its run at the Vivian Beaumont Theater, Lincoln Center, New York City, in November 2010. Ben Brantley, in the *New York Times* calls it a "big, untidy historical comedy" that never manages to pull all its disparate elements into a coherent whole. Brantley faults not only the plot but also the dialogue: "whether it takes the form of surreal political satire or world-weary epigrams, nearly all the dialogue feels ersatz." Suggesting that Guare was unsuccessfully attempting to capture the "the epic, time-bending sweep and political philosophizing of Tony Kushner's *Angels in America*," Brantley concludes that "perhaps the kindest way to look upon it is as an extravagant costume party, like the bal masqué that begins the second act." Joe Dziemianowicz, in the New York *Daily News*, acknowledged the ambitious nature of the play and the glamour of the costumes and set, but like Brantley he did not regard it as a success. He writes that the play

> suffers from a schizophrenic tone that jerks from light to dark and back again, cartoonlike characterizations and a confusing plot that skitters between the U.S., Spain, France and colonial Haiti. History buffs may have an edge.

Haitian Leader Toussaint L'Ouverture asks the US government to help Haiti fight France

(© Everett Historical / Shutterstock.com)

William W. Demastes, in *Theatre Journal*, took a more positive view. He writes that the play

> celebrates self-invention and sensual indulgence as the characters embrace mutability, chance, and materiality, but also undermines the life-limiting constrictions of order, civilization, and law. Imbued with life-embracing vitality, this brilliant production created a sort of three-ring circus of continuous action.

Scott Brown in *Vulture* also appreciated the energy and zest of the production, although like Brantley and Dziemianowicz, he thought the play as a whole was not a success. He writes that it does, however, have elements that work well, along with some failures:

> by turns, uproarious, cornball, breathtaking, incoherent, deeply moving, and often just unaccountably silly. *Free Man*'s bones never quite knit, and its history as a commissioned epic, crazy-quilted out of lavish, loving research, can be detected at every bumpy seam.

CRITICISM

Bryan Aubrey

Aubrey holds a PhD in English. In the following essay, Aubrey examines the irony A Free Man of Color *reveals whereby black people in New Orleans were better off under the rule of Spain than under the ostensibly freedom-loving United States after the Louisiana Purchase.*

A Free Man of Color is a *tour de force*, a dazzling, bawdy, comic romp that recreates the boisterous life of New Orleans in the earliest years of the nineteenth century. Change is in the air, and events elsewhere on the globe involving the great powers of the day eventually impinge in a catastrophic manner on life in this important port city, in particular on the main character, Jacques Cornet. In this sense, the play veers from the playful to the serious, from comedy to tragedy, and as it does so, it makes a profound impact on the audience, who are left to contemplate the somewhat awkward truth that as far as matters of race and freedom are concerned, people in New Orleans appear to have been better off under the rule of Spain—one of the autocratic powers of the Old World—than they were under the deceptively bright promise of the new power in the New World, ostensibly established on the principle that all men are created equal.

When the play begins, Jacques is doing well. He is in his element, a former slave who earns his freedom and finds New Orleans to his liking. Later, he twice refers to New Orleans as a paradise, the second reference comes at the end of the play as, reenslaved, Jacques looks nostalgically at former times. The key to this paradise, as far as Jacques is concerned, is that in New Orleans, unlike under the dreaded *code noir*, social status and political power are based not on race but mostly on money. This makes Jacques happy because he is wealthy, thanks to his inheritance from his white father. Somewhat ironically, at the beginning of the play, in contrast to his blunt exchange with Thomas Jefferson in act 2, he is not at all interested in the concept of the equality of all men. In the eyes of Jacques, "Clothes tell the ranks," in which case there is no doubt that he is of the first order, since as the stage directions state, his appearance is spectacular: "His coat is made of purple satin and embroidered and laced with gold. His shoes have diamond buckles. His bewigged hair, powdered."

WHAT DO I READ NEXT?

- *Six Degrees of Separation* (produced in 1990) is Guare's best-known play. Based on the idea that anyone in the world can be connected to anyone else by pursuing a chain of introductions through no more than six friends or acquaintances, this comedy shows a young African American man gaining access to wealthy New Yorkers by pretending to be the son of a famous actor. The play exposes hypocrisy in matters of race. It was published by Dramatists Play Service in 1992.

- Guare's comedy *The House of Blue Leaves* (1971; available in a 2011 edition), which won an Obie award, is set in New York City on the day the pope visits. Unhappy in his marriage, the songwriter Artie Shaughnessy hopes to elope with another woman and write a hit song.

- The plays in *The Fire This Time: African-American Plays for the 21st Century* (2002), edited by Harry J. Elam Jr. and Robert Alexander, take place in a variety of settings, from the Harlem Renaissance to the Nat Turner slave rebellion, and cover many themes

and topics, including homelessness, civil rights, gangsta lifestyle, and coming of age.

- *Beautiful Crescent: A History of New Orleans* (2013, originally published in 1982), by Joan Garvey and Mary Lou Widmer, is a concise history of New Orleans from its founding to the early twenty-first century. It provides useful information about the city under the rule of Spain and France that will enrich a reader's understanding of *A Free Man of Color*.

- *New Found Land: Lewis and Clark's Voyage of Discovery* (2004), by Allan Wolf, is a poetic novel that tells the story of the journey of Lewis and Clark from a number of perspectives. The novel was an American Library Association Best Book for Young Adults and a School Library Journal Best Book of the Year.

- *A Wilderness So Immense: The Louisiana Purchase and the Destiny of America* (2003), by Jon Kukia, is a very readable account of the Louisiana Purchase that covers the roles played by all the historical characters who appear in *A Free Man of Color*.

To Jacques, appearances are everything; there are no deeper truths to be unearthed or examined. A quick-witted, scheming rogue who cheats at cards and who possesses great ingenuity and boundless self-confidence—not to mention an effortless ability to seduce other mens' wives—Jacques makes a fine comic figure. In the end, however, he becomes much more than this as he is forced to confront uncomfortable truths about race and power and to come face to face with human suffering in a way that demands his compassionate understanding.

The problem for Jacques is that he is in charge of his world only to a point, and not even as much as he thinks. He wants to use his

money to become a power broker in the city, but New Orleans, it turns out—in spite of being proclaimed by Dr. Toubib as the freest city in the world—is little more than a pawn or bargaining chip in a game played by the global powers Spain, France, and Great Britain, as they jockey for advantage on the world stage. It is an irony of the play, and of history, that although in 1803 the United States, through the Louisiana Purchase, becomes the great beneficiary of these maneuverings, for people of color in New Orleans, like Jacques, it is hardly a change for the better. Jacques, who struts around so confidently at first, eventually becomes a victim of historical forces that are far beyond his control.

> IT IS AN IRONY OF THE PLAY, AND OF HISTORY,
> THAT ALTHOUGH IN 1803 THE UNITED STATES,
> THROUGH THE LOUISIANA PURCHASE, BECOMES
> THE GREAT BENEFICIARY OF THESE MANEUVERINGS,
> FOR PEOPLE OF COLOR IN NEW ORLEANS,
> LIKE JACQUES, IT IS HARDLY A CHANGE FOR
> THE BETTER."

First, the play must show those forces at work, and it does so by creating many vignettes of historical characters as they play out their roles in the global drama. Once introduced, these vignettes come thick and fast, and the audience must be alert to all the historical allusions contained in them. Some of the portraits are satirical or otherwise comic. Napoleon, who has not yet crowned himself emperor but holds the title of first consul, is first seen lying in a bathtub examining a terry cloth map of the world. He is presented as being obsessed with defeating Great Britain, but he is short of cash and has to put up with a nagging wife, Josephine, and her petty, self-centered concerns about her clothes. Josephine is shown dealing tarot cards, and to her annoyance, they always show up referring to the need for money. (Later, she is still nagging poor Napoleon, but all he wants is a bit of peace and quiet so he can finish his bath.) The French foreign minister, Talleyrand, is presented as an obnoxious toady, praising Napoleon to the skies and seeking personal advantage while trying to persuade him to concentrate on the New World. Like Napoleon, Carlos Cuarto, the king of Spain, is short of money, but this does nothing to dent his belief in his own greatness.

If the representatives of Old World power are presented in a somewhat mocking, satirical manner, such does not apply to the fiery, heroic Toussaint Louverture, who has led a slave rebellion and is creating a new democracy in Saint-Domingue (called Sante Domingue in the play), soon to be named Haiti, against all the odds. "Victory or death for freedom" is his cry. As for the Americans, Thomas Jefferson's personal assistant Meriwether Lewis, eager, young, and visionary, is shown trying to persuade a reluctant,

diffident Jefferson to let him explore the great unknown continent, the white spaces. (This is two years before the Louisiana Purchase.) Jefferson says no because, first, the alien whiteness belongs to another country, Spain, and, second, the government has no money to fund such an expedition. Jefferson in the play is much more interested in planning a dinner party than in listening to the ideas of his young assistant.

As the great powers begin to carry out their plans, the first whiff of radical uncertainty enters Jacques's otherwise happy, self-absorbed life. He gets wind of a secret coded message sent by the king of Spain to Juan Ventura Morales, Spain's *supreme intendante* in New Orleans. The speculation is that Spain might be planning to restore the infamous *code noir*, a highly repressive law first passed by the French that stripped black people of all their rights, making them no more than pieces of property. In fact, Spain has no such plans, and, indeed, under Spanish control black people in New Orleans did better than they did under French rule. This is shown clearly when Pincepousse, Jacques's white half-brother, reveals that he has married a black woman, Margery Jolicoeur, by making use of a local law known as *plaçage*, which according to Dr. Toubib, is "a local law allowing white men to enter into an official arrangement with a woman of color—It protects her—It protects him." Just moments later, however, Morales's cousin, Count Achille Creux, arrives with his wife as refugees from Sante Domingue. Creux is a classic white racist if ever there was one, and he rages against what he calls the black beasts who have taken over the island. Later, after the United States has taken control of New Orleans, Creux stokes white fears, warning the nation, "Be vigilant or your Negroes will riot and rape your women. Hordes of crazed Othellos will debase our unwilling Desdemonas and then dance on your corpses."

Creux's appearance is a clue for the audience that such racist feelings do exist among those newly entering New Orleans and that the threat to Jacques (and presumably to other freed slaves) is real and dire, although it will not, in the end, come from Spain or from the likes of Creux. Nor will it find Jacques unchanged. The change in him occurs quite unexpectedly, when he falls into the hold of the ship carrying the victims of yellow fever. For the first time he starts to identify with black people, the race to which his mother belonged. He feels empathy for the suffering people and is deeply moved by their tragic fate. This is a clever touch on the part of the dramatist, since nothing has prepared the audience for it. Jacques seems to be the last person who would be able to experience empathy. Yet perhaps the incident reveals a truth about human life: under extreme circumstances, a person may reveal some sterling personal qualities that up to that point no one, least of all he himself, would have guessed that he might possess. And so it is with Jacques. The profound change Jacques undergoes also gives the dramatist the opportunity to turn his play toward the serious rather than the comic as it nears its climax (although he never entirely abandons the comic element).

The climax is marked by a difficult encounter between Jacques and Thomas Jefferson. Having been counseled by the optimistic but naive Meriwether, Jacques has returned to New Orleans with high hopes, believing that a golden age is about to dawn now that the freedom-loving United States has taken control of New Orleans. He has a touching faith that the fine and famous words enshrined in the Declaration of Independence are going to be put into practice. Instead, as he is immediately re-enslaved, he finds that he has stumbled upon what might be called the shadow side of the new nation—founded on high ideals but with those ideals very selectively applied. Bewildered and angry, Jacques summons up Jefferson, the author of the Declaration of Independence. The dramatic scene that follows makes for fine theater, and most readers or audience members will likely conclude that the revered but slave-owning Jefferson does not come out of it very well. He in effect has no answer to Jacques's insistence on his rights and his attack on Jefferson's hypocrisy. Defensive and evasive, Jefferson ducks and weaves (like a modern-day politician, one is tempted to say). "Slavery is a terrible thing," he admits, but it just grew up because of economic market forces, those market forces became ever more insistent, and now the nation finds itself dependent on slavery and there is nothing that can be done about it. Jacques knows that it is a feeble argument, the audience knows it, and Jefferson may know it too.

Jacques's rhetorical skill in besting Jefferson does not help him in any practical sense. As the play ends, the audience realizes that, comedy of manners notwithstanding, ultimately the play is serious in intent and subversive of America's

Historical figures like Thomas Jefferson and Napoleon appear as characters in the play

(© Everett Historical / Shutterstock.com)

carefully cultivated self-image—its view of itself and the principles on which it was founded. It is for this reason that the final line of the play, delivered to the audience by Dr. Toubib while Jacques stands in his chains, reverberates with a horrible irony that many African Americans may still keenly feel today: *"A Free Man of Color or How One Man Became an American."*

Source: Bryan Aubrey, Critical Essay on *A Free Man of Color*, in *Drama for Students*, Gale, Cengage Learning, 2017.

Marilyn Stasio

In the following review, Stasio criticizes Guare's characterization of the protagonist as "buffoonish."

Let the weeping and wailing (and public floggings) begin. *A Free Man of Color*, John Guare's epic play about the fortunes of a wealthy free man of color in New Orleans during that revolutionary era when the 1803 Louisiana Purchase made an empire of our small nation, is not the glorious work it might have been. Through some misguided impulse to play its high comic elements as low sex farce, both scribe and helmer George C. Wolfe have undermined the play's grand historical sweep. Despite some dazzling writing, spectacular stage effects, a cast of thousands, and a lavish production budget, much of Guare's ambitious work is reduced to a busy bore.

Lincoln Center's vast Beaumont stage was built for epic theater and Wolfe is the kind of visionary director who isn't afraid to use it, so this lavish production does not lack for spectacle.

The ornate proscenium stage that frames the action in David Rockwell's expansive set design boldly establishes the show's inherent theatricality. Through the magic of theater (and the professional savvy of an inspired design team), the great stage here accommodates such wonders as a full-dress Mardi Gras ball, the vast unexplored wilderness of the Louisiana territory, and flying trips to France, Spain, and the West Indies. Collectively, the scenes present the rich historical panorama of a young nation emerging from its 18th-century birth and groping for political purchase in modern times. Individually, they capture deciding moments in history, wittily re-told from Guare's irreverent modern perspective.

Here's Napoleon (Triney Sandoval) immersed in his bath and brooding over his territorial losses to England: "I hate the British. I hate Shakespeare. I hate Chaucer. I hate Richard the Lion-Hearted. And when the future comes, I will hate Queen Victoria, James Bond, Charles Dickens."

But while Guare's jaunty deconstructions of these complex historical events—part of a cheeky trend currently represented on Broadway by *Bloody Bloody Andrew Jackson* and *Colin Quinn: Long Story Short*—are staged with wonderful crispness and clarity, they are shouted down by the buffoonish character in the drama at the heart of the piece. This is the story of Jacques Cornet (Jeffrey Wright), a mulatto born into slavery who used his inheritance from his white father to buy his freedom and become the wealthiest man in New Orleans. For a libertine with Cornet's rich endowments—as a man of great wealth, extravagant tastes, and insatiable sexual appetite—the sexually permissive and racially progressive city of New Orleans is paradise on earth.

But while sexual licentiousness satisfies Cornet's manhood, it's fashion that feeds his narcissistic ego—and brings him to grief.

This Beau Brummel is so enamored of the luxurious fabrics he buys from Persia and China (on gorgeous display in Ann Hould-Ward's elaborate costumes) that he becomes obsessed

with finding a quicker route to transport these goods to the Port of New Orleans. To this end, he collects maps of the wilderness west of the Mississippi, where a great inland river is rumored to exist. It is Guare's most amusing conceit that America's acquisition of Louisiana hinges on Cornet's love of high fashion.

In concept, Cornet is a fabulous character of infinite charm. In Wright's bombastic pert, he's a vulgar fool who doesn't seduce women as much as devour them. Guare may have concocted his clever plot from some of the greatest farces in the English language (and lifted some good stuff from Moliere), but his broad treatment of his sources ignores the elegance of the form. And unlike his smooth handling of the historical scenes of political satire, Wolfe's coarse approach to sex comedy kills what remains of the humor.

Some members of the ensemble manage to make it to high ground. Mos brings as much dignity to Cornet's browbeaten slave, Murmur, as he does to the noble revolutionary Toussaint Louverture. Another of Cornet's slaves, Dr. Toubib, is indeed the voice of reason in Joseph Marcell's unmannered perf. And Veanne Cox is such a comic perfectionist that she survives one of Cornet's most ridiculous seductions.

Performers cast in multiple roles invariably do their best work when they're satirizing historical figures. But it takes a strong-willed thesp—someone like young Nicole Beharie, who is quite cute as Margery Jolicoeur, the naughty "country wife" who innocently delivers Cornet to his enemies—to keep from being swept up in Cornet's clownish games.

Source: Marilyn Stasio, Review of *A Free Man of Color*, in *Variety*, November 18, 2010.

Gene A. Plunka
In the following excerpt, Plunka offers an overview of the playwright's work.

. . . Guare writes about a crazed, chaotic society of bewildered people out of touch with their individuality yet mesmerized by a media and pop culture hype of fame and fortune. His characters are confused by their insurmountable dilemma, always wondering why they cannot make the most of their lives and why certain people can achieve celebrity status while others, no matter how hard they strive, will never be able to do so. This "invisibility of Anono-Mass," as Ruth Goetz calls it, causes loneliness, bitterness, frustration, and resentment. Louis Malle, who directed

> TO GUARE, THE THEATER IS A VENUE TO
> LIBERATE OUR IMAGINATIONS AND RETURN US TO A
> PLACE OF POETRY, AS IN THE CLASSICAL GREEK
> DRAMA, WHERE LANGUAGE REIGNED."

Guare's *Atlantic City* and *Lydie Breeze*, writes in his foreword to three of Guare's dramas, "In Guare's plays, characters are forever whirling about, always trying to find out about themselves. They go all the way, exposing their fears, their contradictions, their false identities." James Houghton, the artistic director of the Signature Theatre who staged three of Guare's plays during the 1998–1999 season, noted, "John reveals a wildly vivid imagination and insight in to the struggle each of us has to make a difference and feel we belong. All his plays deal with the need for us to matter." Usually, the search for worth and recognition in modern society is often futile or fleeting. The resulting sense of alienation and angoisse often leads Guare's protagonists into violence as a means of expressing their frustrations. Life in Guare's world, much of it expressed in New York City as a microcosm for the craziness of contemporary urban life, is synonymous with violence and teeming hostilities. When Guare's characters ultimately realize their unfulfilled dreams, the consequences are often brutal. Guare reminds us through the violence that our wounds never disappear and that this modern neurosis is never pleasant.

Although much of Guare's focus is on individuals who are mesmerized by the cult of celebrity fame and fortune, Guare is also critical of those who cannot learn from the past. In addition, Guare refuses to empathize with those who feel paralyzed by history, trapped in their past. Instead, he believes that we can assimilate something positive from America's heritage. Guare, whose roots are in the Nantucket society of nineteenth-century New England, understands the importance of the strong moral sensibility that once was the backbone behind U.S. culture. However, instead of learning from what has been the moral fiber of our historical heritage, we tend to fictionalize our pasts. Guare realizes "We see it differently from what it really was. That difference can create neuroses and insecurity. To understand ourselves we must reinterpret that past. And each human connection that we can trust helps us." The promise of the future of America, as expressed by the moral optimism of our Founding Fathers and further demonstrated by the rise of utopian communities in the nineteenth century, has degenerated in to the pop-art fantasies of frustrated and bewildered little people who find their dreams vanishing. As John Lahr astutely notes, "Guare evokes the central sadness of modern America—a culture groping for a destiny it betrayed: violent and ruthless in its old age."

Despite the overtly pessimistic attitude prevailing in many of Guare's plays, he demonstrates a belief in the natural goodness of humanity. Guare prefers to confront the moral decay and corruption of modern society rather than ignoring our neuroses. He states, "The obligation of plays is to say, 'Oh, that is the worst thing that happened to me, and I want to keep it alive, I don't want to become dead to the great emotional moments in life.' Mental health is not analogous to amnesia." Guare is interested in exploring how we can remain true to the ideals on which American society was originally established. He is convinced that the individual can make a difference in his or her own life and subsequently in the lives of others. The little person can have value. Guare revels in the pioneer spirit of colonial America: "What's important is to honor that revolutionary spirit: 'I can change. I will make a difference.'" The fragmented life of modern urban society may corrupt us and channel us in to disingenuous behavior, but the utopian spirit and our personal dreams can still exist. The neuroticism of the modern age must be subsumed by our personal desires, drives, and instincts that will help us create our own unique mythologies free from pop art and commercialized media icons. Our fraudulent way of life must be replaced by a community of lives that touch each other. We must gain the self-understanding and spiritual self-awareness that once defined our greatness and created high culture. Guare thus often allows his protagonists to dream, even if their utopian desires are ultimately dashed by the brutalities of the real world.

As a result of the bizarre, absurd world that Guare depicts onstage, critics have accused him of creating cartoonish characters whose eccentricities bear little resemblance to reality. He admitted, "People ask, 'Where do you get those bizarre ideas, Mr. Guare?' And I want to say, 'Bizarre? That's every day life.'" In Guare's theater, art imitates life, and as we all know, truth can be stranger than fiction. One may even find the seeds of Guare's "cartoonish eccentricities" on the pages of the *New York Times* or *New York Post*. Guare finds the sources for his "bizarre" material in everyday life. He acknowledged, "I always think that strange things happen in ordinary places. I think everybody's life is strange. If anybody had a dramatist or a hidden movie camera in their apartment recording the event, we would say, God, this is astonishing." Thus, what we find in a Guare play is never far removed from our own very real neuroses that are painful to recognize but easy to dismiss as someone else's distorted nightmarish vision. Guare explained his need to present images onstage that correspond to the reality of modern society:

> Henry James once said you can soar as high as you can, but you've always got to hang onto a string—the string which holds onto that balloon— and that's a very demanding image. I love to anchor things in reality. My current play, *Six Degrees of Separation*, was inspired in part by an actual event reported in the *Times*. *Bosoms and Neglect* is based on a terribly real event that happened to me. I believe that any reality is there to use and explore. We have nothing else but that.

Guare is constantly on the alert for life's amusing, yet terrifying, anecdotes, which he carefully constructs into his bizarre comedy. He revealed, "Mainly, what I do is like listening through a wall. One night in a New Orleans hotel room, I heard someone scratching on a wall next door and crying, 'Help me!' I'm always trying to find out what that is."

Guare believes that much of theater's potential to enrich people's lives is due to its ability to penetrate their unconscious states, the deepest part of their psyches. Guare has taught his playwriting students at Yale University that nightmares are the origins of comedy Theater is not merely an imitation of reality; it is also a means of shaping and defining our innermost drives, impulses, and desires. Guare has learned "that theater has to get into the deepest part of your dreams, has to show you a mirror you might recoil from, but also show you reality so you might know what to do with it." In short, Guare has also realized that the knowledge he has gained from the theater has prepared him for the greatest experiences in his life.

Depicting how our innermost dreams conflict with the neuroses of modern life, Guare finds comedy to be the most suitable medium to present such

ideas onstage. To represent the violence and zany madness of contemporary American life, he uses farce, black humor, and tragicomedy. He writes both to gain insight into the individual's dilemma in a society that worships celebrity and to determine our raison d'etres in this absurd lifestyle. Guare asserts, "Comedies are traditionally resolved in marriage—that new beginning. I think that, finally, the plays are about how we wed ourselves to life." Guare also finds comedy to be a more suitable medium than serious philosophical drama because "laughter allows you to relax so more doors inside you can open up."

Although Guare is a great innovator of the modern theater, he is not interested in consciously exploring new forms of drama per se. He works with what he knows best—comedy—and while he is interested in extending the limits of that genre, he is not engaged in a theoretical exploration of dramatic structure. Comedy simply allows the audience to participate more fully in the play onstage. The comic characters onstage concomitantly need the laughter of the audience. Guare likes comedy because it has the capacity to liberate the audience from the fourth wall. Guare states, "I think that a play is about making the audience *crazy*. You want to get people off the streets into this dark room and give them that feeling of delight or laughter that makes them crazy. Farce is always being pushed toward hysteria."

Guare is a highly adventurous playwright who tries to push comedy to its limits. In doing so, he has influenced several contemporary American playwrights. Keith Reddin, one of Guare's playwriting students at Yale University, commented, "John didn't set down blueprints for plays. He showed us how you could stop the action, or digress, or take wild turns. He encouraged us to free our imaginations." To Guare, the theater is a venue to liberate our imaginations and return us to a place of poetry, as in the classical Greek drama, where language reigned. Guare prefers the zany antics of farce, in which the audience is enthralled and surprised at what may happen next onstage while at the same time being awed at the wit and verbal virtuosity of the dramatist. Guare expressed the importance of the playwright as a poet-vaudevillian:

> But the theater remains a place for language, a place to be *talked* to. It's as though we lived in a dark room. It's the playwright's job to illuminate and transform that room with all the means at his disposal, and finally to open the door—not to a dead-end, but to yet another room.

Thus, Guare expects a highly educated, sophisticated audience who will be able to appreciate his witty dialogue, his satirical jabs at pop culture, and his ability to keep the action moving at all times. One cannot and will not doze when watching a John Guare play.

Guare sees comedy as a means of opening the door to all of the possibilities of the stage, whereas naturalism, or "kitchen-sink" drama, limits what the playwright can do. Guare learned the fundamentals of playwriting when he took a class from venerable theater critic John Gassner at Yale University. Guare recalls, "Gassner emphasized the word 'wright' in 'playwright,' speaking of it as a craft." Gassner praised Ibsen's realist dramas for adhering to strict formulaic rules of playwriting. Ibsen, he noted, constructed dramas out of iron, whereas Chekhov, much the inferior playwright in Gassner's mind, built plays out of molasses. Although Ibsen is one of his favorite playwrights, Guare nevertheless objected to Gassner's confining definitions of what a play should be. As a child, Guare saw a performance of *Raisin in the Sun*, which became a model for his ideal type of theater and a reaction to Gassner's limited perspective: "The play burst out of its four-walled naturalism. Poetry breathed on that stage. . . . I swore that when I became a playwright I would never settle for a single brief moment of lightning. My plays would live in that lightning. The violent fabric of my dream life would not be forced into any pre-existing mold." Another such model was the theater of Thornton Wilder, which was never constrained by the logic of naturalism. Guare remarked, "Naturalism kills; it's deadly to the theater. I remember the revelation when, as a boy, I read Thornton Wilder's *Our Town*. The Stage Manager says: 'See that boy. He will be killed in the war.' And there's no boy onstage, of course. So I realized you are not bound by four walls." . . .

Source: Gene A. Plunka, "Introduction," in *The Black Comedy of John Guare*, University of Delaware Press, 2002, pp. 16–20.

nytimes.com/2010/11/19/theater/reviews/19free.html?_r=0 (accessed July 5, 2016).

Brown, Scott, "Review: John Guare's Wildly Ambitious *A Free Man of Color*," in *Vulture*, November 18, 2010, http://www.vulture.com/2010/11/review_john_guares_wildly_ambi.html (accessed July 9, 2016).

"Congo Square, the Soul of New Orleans," African American Registry website, http://www.aaregistry.org/historic_events/view/congo-square-soul-new-orleans (accessed July 8, 2016).

Congreve, William, *The Way of the World*, edited by Kathleen M. Lynch, University of Nebraska, 1965, p. 41.

Crabb, William J., "John Guare," TheatreHistory.com, April 25, 2002, http://www.theatrehistory.com/american/guare001.html (accessed July 14, 2016).

Demastes, William W., Review of *A Free Man of Color*, in *Theatre Journal*, Vol. 63. No. 3, October 2011, pp. 451–53.

Dziemianowicz, Joe, "*A Free Man of Color* Review: John Guare's New Play Is Beautiful to Look at, but Unsatisfying," in *Daily News*, November 19, 2010, http://www.nydailynews.com/entertainment/music-arts/free-man-color-review-john-guare-new-play-beautiful-unsatisfying-article-1.452220 (accessed July 8, 2016).

Guare, John, *A Free Man of Color*, Dramatists Play Service, 2014.

"Haiti," in *CIA: World Factbook*, https://www.cia.gov/library/publications/the-world-factbook/geos/ha.html (accessed July 12, 2016).

"Haiti Profile—Timelines," BBC News website, http://www.bbc.com/news/world-latin-america-19548814 (accessed July 12, 2016).

Ketelby, C. D. M., *A History of Modern Times, from 1789*, 4th ed., George G. Harrap, 1966, pp. 618–19.

"Louisiana Purchase," History.com, http://www.history.com/topics/louisiana-purchase (accessed July 8, 2016).

Plunka, Gene, "John Guare," in *Dictionary of Literary Biography*, Vol. 249, *Twentieth-Century American Dramatists: Third Series*, edited by Christopher J. Wheatley, The Gale Group, 2002.

"Quick Facts, New Orleans City, Louisiana," US Department of Commerce, Bureau of the Census, https://www.census.gov/quickfacts/table/PST045215/2255000 (accessed July 9, 2016).

SOURCES

Abrams, M. H., *A Glossary of Literary Terms*, 4th ed., Holt, Rinehart and Winston, 1981, p. 26.

Brantley, Ben, "A Gaudy Swashbuckle through History," in *New York Times*, November 18, 2010, http://www.

FURTHER READING

Fenster, Julie M., *Jefferson's America: The President, the Purchase, and the Explorers Who Transformed a Nation*, Crown, 2016.

Fenster tells the story of Jefferson's presidency, including the Louisiana Purchase and the

Lewis and Clark expedition. Her vivid account has won extensive praise from reviewers.

James, C. L. R., *The Black Jacobins: Toussaint L'Ouverture and the San Domingo Revolution*, Vintage, 1989.
This is a vivid account of the revolution in Haiti that took place between 1794 and 1803.

Plunka, Gene A., *The Black Comedy of John Guare*, University of Delaware Press, 2002.
This first book written about Guare is a thorough examination of his work up to the earliest years of the twenty-first century.

Sauer, David K., *American Drama and the Postmodern: Fracturing the Realistic Stage*, Cambria Press, 2011.
Sauer suggests that contemporary American drama has taken a new form that is neither realism nor expressionism. He analyzes a range of plays and playwrights, including Guare.

SUGGESTED SEARCH TERMS

John Guare

Guare AND A Free Man of Color

New Orleans AND history

Louisiana Purchase

Thomas Jefferson

Napoleon AND Louisiana Purchase

Talleyrand

King Carlos IV of Spain

Toussaint Louverture OR Toussaint-L'Ouverture

Meriwether Lewis

Glengarry Glen Ross

Glengarry Glen Ross is a 1992 film combining elements of drama, realism, crime caper, and dark comedy, directed by James Foley and adapted for the screen by David Mamet from his 1983 stage play of the same name. The film was a commercial failure whose earnings at the box office fell short of its budget. Nevertheless, this tale of four desperate, temperamental real estate salesmen struggling to survive in a company devoid of morals won praise from many critics for its dialogue, mood, tone, and ensemble cast.

The play on which the film is based opened in 1983 in London; its US premiere the following year in Chicago, followed by a production on Broadway, earned Mamet a Pulitzer Prize, among others. His previous work for the stage had been produced off Broadway and, while receiving positive attention from critics, did not approach the success of *Glengarry Glen Ross*, which, along with many subsequent stage plays and screenplays, has won Mamet a reputation as a master of American drama.

Over the course of two days the story's four salesmen use every trick at their disposal (fraud, conspiracy, burglary, etc.) to maintain their unstable positions in the merciless company that employs them. They themselves are an unstable mix of pride and bravado, fear, envy, ruthlessness, and often uncontrolled rage. The tale is bleak and the settings claustrophobic, but it transcends its base material with dark humor

1992

James Foley *(© Helga Esteb / Shutterstock.com)*

and an ear for ultrarealistic dialogue. Readers should be aware that both the play and the film are notorious for their copious profanity and controversial for two passages involving racism toward Indian Americans. Mamet dropped these two passages for the play's 2005 revival.

PLOT SUMMARY

The film opens in a phone booth, glowing red in a darkened hallway, at a Chinese restaurant as Shelley Levene, an older, careworn real estate agent, talks reassuringly to his daughter, who is in a hospital with a serious but unnamed condition. A younger fellow agent, Dave Moss, takes over the booth next to Levene's and makes a phone call to a prospective buyer, becoming briefly belligerent as the camera tracks back and forth between the two men.

(This scene and the remaining scenes in the restaurant are a significant rewrite by Mamet of

the original scene in his play, which opened with Levene and the office manager, John Williamson, arguing about leads. The opening moments, in which Levene talks to his daughter, emphasize her position in his life; they raise the stakes for his success, since her care depends on his ability to pay for it and make him a much more sympathetic character.)

In the restroom, Moss confronts the office manager, John Williamson, about the poor quality of the leads he is giving the agents. Levene approaches Williamson after Moss leaves, attempting to initiate a private conversation about those same leads, but Williamson rebuffs him and leaves the restaurant to prepare for a mysterious sales meeting just as a third agent, Ricky Roma, arrives. Roma and Levene sit at the bar, where Roma notices a man drinking by himself and begins talking, ostensibly to Levene, about the weather; his real goal is to capture the attention of the lone drinker, James Lingk, whom he will treat as a potential buyer.

Levene exits the restaurant, and the camera pans to follow him across the street in the nighttime rain to an office building where Premier Properties is located. The firm's fourth agent, George Aaronow, laments the difficulty he is having making a sale; Moss arrives, and the three men get settled in for the sales meeting.

The meeting, which Roma misses, consists of a lecture given by a man who does not offer his name (though he is identified as Blake in the film's credits). He proceeds, after a bluntly offensive introduction, to announce the terms of a weeklong sales contest in which only the top two salesmen will keep their jobs, the best to be given a Cadillac into the bargain and the second best a set of steak knives. At one point he brandishes a stack of excellent leads that will be given only to the winning agents. In the face of the agents' incredulity and outrage, he assures them that he is there at the request of Mitch and Murray, the owners of the firm. The rest of the meeting consists of the man's insulting, hectoring, and threatening the agents in a variety of ways and in the coarsest of terms before he leaves. (This scene is a famous change to the script for the original play, which lacked the sales meeting and the character of Blake altogether. It exaggerates the cruelly oppressive environment in which these men work, giving them extra motivation for their anger and bitterness.)

FILM TECHNIQUE

- Foley's direction dispenses with more blatantly "cinematic" effects; there are no fades to black, no dissolves or wipes. Instead, there are multiple abrupt cuts, both within scenes and from one scene to another. The effect is one of displacement or interruption, rarely subtle. The camera is frequently in motion as well, restlessly tracking or panning along with the salesmen as they hurry from place to place. Many reviewers referred (both admiringly and critically) to a sense of claustrophobia created by the film. One way in which camera work accomplishes this sense is to frame the characters rather tightly together. There are frequent close-ups, a few of them extreme. Long shots are more rare. One such shot is of the office manager, Williamson, locking the premium leads away in a file cabinet, seemingly from Levene's point of view. There are also several of Levene, or Moss and Aaronow, hurrying across the street between car or office and the restaurant in the rain; the deserted streets relieve the claustrophobic feel but, in turn, create a sense of isolation. One striking shot occurs as Levene is regaling Roma with the tale of his seemingly successful sale to the Nyborgs. As the older agent describes the transaction in excited terms, the camera slowly dollies back, from a medium-range shot to a long shot of the two men isolated in the center of the drab office, adding some corrective context to Levene's happiness.

- *Glengarry Glen Ross* varies between bright and dark lighting, with little in the midrange. The entire first half of the film is shot at night, in the rain for exterior shots or in cars and restaurants. The colors are garish primary ones—a hallway illuminated with a dark, almost midnight blue, for example, in the opening scene at the Chinese restaurant, with the phone booths saturated in red. The office, by contrast, is a grimy-looking off-white, with little to relieve the generally harsh light. The second half of the film takes place the following day, but natural light is abandoned almost immediately for the artificial light of Premier Properties, where the action takes place.

As Moss and Aaronow discuss the meeting, Levene calls the hospital again. Then, after he and the others complain once more about the quality of the leads he has given them, the camera focuses on Williamson locking the leads away in a file cabinet. In several close-ups, the film focuses first on Aaronow's sales pitch, an awkward and fumbling mess, and then Levene's, which is soothing and expertly delivered to one Mrs. Nyborg. Aaronow joins Moss for a ride in which the two men commiserate about the impossibility of working with their leads, Moss especially strong in his denunciations of the system, Aaronow dutifully agreeing with him.

The camera cuts to a black wall across which it tracks to the interior of Premier Properties, where Levene is making an unsuccessful sales attempt over the phone. When Williamson emerges from the back office to leave for home, Levene accosts him about the leads; the two men argue about Levene's performance and abilities as a salesman, but Williamson refuses to give Levene any of the premium leads displayed during the sales meeting earlier. Levene pursues him to his car in the rain, finally offering to bribe him; Williamson names a figure too high for the impoverished agent to afford, and the agent exits the car into the rain. The camera cuts to Moss and Aaronow leaving a house in the same downpour, also having failed to make a sale. At a late-night diner the two men resume their discussion of the right and wrong way to run a business, Aaronow continuing to obligingly repeat everything Moss says.

In the next scene, a homeowner, Larry Spannel, opens the door to find Levene standing in the rain. Levene manages to enter Spannel's house and tries to interest the man in an "investment," but Spannel is adamant that he has no interest and ushers Levene out, closing the door in his face. In a long shot Levene is filmed disconsolately facing the rainy street outside Spannel's beautiful home. (This scene is another addition to the original script.)

Moss and Aaronow, meanwhile, drive to the Chinese restaurant across the street from Premier Properties; Moss suggests to Aaronow that someone should take revenge on Mitch and Murray. Inside the restaurant, Roma's sales pitch to Lingk is gathering steam. His method is to challenge any and all commonly held wisdom, including any notions of morality. Lingk is impressed as Roma moves into a hushed but heartfelt monologue about fear and how it constrains people from acting. Sitting at the bar, Moss finally reveals to Aaronow his intention to have the office broken into and the leads stolen; Moss will then sell the leads to a rival agency and the two agents will split the profits.

There follows a brief scene in which Levene, in another red-lit phone booth, this one on a drenched street corner, calls the hospital to find that his daughter's care has been jeopardized by his failure to pay bills. He promises to bring the money the next day. Back in the restaurant, Moss takes advantage of Aaronow's weak will to gradually lead him into complicity with the idea of a break-in, coercing Aaronow to rob the office himself and suggesting his guilt whether or not he actually does it, simply because he has been listening to the plan. As Levene talks on the phone with his next sales target, the Nyborgs, Roma continues seducing Lingk into buying land, finally showing him a brochure about a development called Glengarry Highlands in Florida.

This scene, ending at the fifty-minute mark, concludes the first part of the movie, which is divided into two precise halves for a total of one hour and forty minutes. The camera cuts from a close-up of Roma and Lingk to the elevated train rumbling past and then to the exterior of Premier Properties, where Roma pulls up to find patrol cars and police officers outside and a crew cleaning broken glass. An officer informs him that the office was broken into the night before. Roma barges into Williamson's office, interrupting Williamson and a detective who is interviewing Moss about the break-in; when Williamson assures him that his contract with Lingk from the previous evening was successfully filed, Roma triumphantly demands the Cadillac and brushes off the detective.

Roma talks with Aaronow, reassuring the weaker agent about his talents and discussing their upcoming interviews with the detective. Roma says that the authorities will never catch the thief because of their stupidity and that Aaronow has nothing to worry about, since his nervousness around the police is a sign of innocence. Williamson parcels out two more leads to Roma, whose lesser contracts were stolen, but Roma goes on a tirade about the wretched quality of the leads, particularly one involving Indian Americans, who (he insists) never buy. Levene arrives, excited about his successful sale to the Nyborgs, only to discover the office in disarray from the burglary. Immediately afterward Moss exits the office in which the detective is interviewing the agents, and Aaronow is summoned in.

The next scene involves a complex three-way interaction between Roma, Moss, and Levene. Shaken by his experience at the hands of the detective, Moss wants to hear nothing of the sale that has so excited Levene and which Roma is interested in. Moss starts to demand more leads and then decides to go home instead; when he is informed that the leads have been stolen anyway, he asks if any contracts are missing; Roma asks him why he cares about the theft of contracts, since he has made no sales lately. At this point Aaronow opens the door and asks if someone could get him a cup of coffee. This prompts Moss to ask him, in a quiet aside, how he's doing. Aaronow simply repeats his request for coffee and closes the door. Moss returns to his spat with Roma, who he feels has disrespected him; during their bitter back-and-forth Levene keeps trying to describe his sales experience, but a sudden outburst from Moss quells the older agent's enthusiasm. Roma and Moss proceed to belittle each other, but Roma keeps his cool while Moss completely loses his temper, finally condemning the entire office and its denizens and storming out with a vow to leave for Wisconsin.

Roma persuades Levene to pick up the thread of his story. As Levene describes his tactics, the long moments of uncertainty as the Nyborgs dither, and their final capitulation, the camera pans back from a tight shot of the two men to a broad view of the office in which Roma and Levene are nearly lost in an environment of desks, filing cabinets, dry-erase boards, and other dreary office paraphernalia. When Williamson emerges from the room where Aaronow is being interviewed, Levene jubilantly mocks him for his lack of faith, growing increasingly insulting over the course of their exchange. Williamson no sooner returns to the detective's interview with Aaronow than Roma spots Lingk approaching the office door. Instantly he turns to Levene, telling him to adopt the persona of a client to whom Roma has just sold a parcel in Glengarry. As Lingk enters, the two agents playact a discussion about the sale, Roma pretending not to notice the distraught Lingk. When Roma does finally notice him, he introduces Levene as D. Ray Morton, director of sales and services for American Express in Europe.

Roma has almost managed to escape from the office with Levene when Lingk says his wife has balked and wants to cancel the contract; she has already been in touch with a consumer protection agency. As Roma reassures him that the check has not been cashed yet and that there is still time to stop it from going through, Aaronow emerges from the back room uncharacteristically outraged by his interview with the detective, angrily and shakily denouncing the whole process. Williamson finally comes out as well and demands that Aaronow leave, since he is creating a disturbance. Lingk asks what is going on and is told that the office has been burglarized. Williamson misreads the man's agitation and assures him that his check has, in fact, been deposited. At this, Lingk, completely flustered, backs out of the office, muttering apologies to Roma; it is clear that he and his wife are going to take legal action to stop the sales process and cancel the contract. Roma turns on Williamson in fury. He is interrupted in his tirade by the detective, who summons him into the back room.

Levene picks up the thread, castigating the manager mercilessly for the ineptitude that cost Roma his contract with Lingk. In the course of his sneering attack, he tells Williamson that, if he is going to lie, the lie should help the agents, not hurt them; he is, evidently, referring to Williamson's statement about Lingk's contract and check already being in the bank. Williamson demands to know how Levene knew it was a lie, since as a rule he always files contracts and checks before the end of the night, but last night

was the one night out of the year he had not gotten to it—it was still lying on his desk when the break-in occurred, a fact only the thief would know. Levene dodges the manager's increasingly direct questions but finally admits that it was, in fact, he himself who broke in and stole the contracts. He further admits that he did it at Moss's behest and that the two men split the profits after selling the leads to a rival real estate agency.

Levene desperately cajoles Williamson not to go to the detective with this information, promising him 50 percent of all his future commissions as well as the $2,500 he earned from the break-in, but Williamson refuses to go along. When Levene, broken, asks why, Williamson says he simply does not like him. Levene's final, most desperate gambit, in which he brings up his daughter, leaves Williamson totally unmoved.

As the full extent of his ruin (imminent arrest and imprisonment as well as the end of his ability to support his daughter's care) dawns on him, Levene sinks into the chair at his desk. Roma, meanwhile, unaware of the older agent's catastrophe, casually tells him they will go out for lunch later. The detective opens the door of the back room, calling Levene's name. Levene attempts to get Roma's attention, but the successful agent is on the phone, in the middle of a sale, and Levene is left to meet his doom by himself.

Aaronow, now calm, reenters the office and, after some small talk with Roma, sits at his desk, moaning about how much he dislikes his job. The camera tracks Roma as he strides out the door on his way to the restaurant across the street, then returns to Aaronow as he picks up the phone and begins another sales pitch. The scene cuts abruptly to the elevated train rushing past as Irving Berlin's famously optimistic song "Blue Skies," performed at a swift and nervous tempo by Al Jarreau, begins to play. The credits roll.

CHARACTERS

George Aaronow

Aaronow, played by Alan Arkin, is the most ineffectual individual in the firm. While his fellow agents rage, manipulate, and engage in various illegal activities to protect themselves and their positions, he simply plods on, unable to admit defeat and unwilling to challenge his fate. The economy of the office operates using "leads" (the names of potential buyers) as a sort of currency; all of the agents are desperate to acquire decent ones. The leads Aaronow is given by the office manager, Williamson, are no good, as the people involved are unlikely to be able or willing to buy; he complains about this, but his complaints lack any real vigor.

When Moss, a better salesman, corners him and attempts to verbally manipulate him into breaking into the office to steal better leads, he reacts only with confusion and weak protests and nothing in the way of a firm refusal. The break-in a day later suggests that Moss has succeeded in convincing Aaronow. But Aaronow's fundamentally passive nature has, in fact, saved him; at the film's end the viewer learns that he is innocent of the break-in and that Moss's belligerent psychological tactics were no match for Aaronow's passivity.

Blake

Blake, played by Alec Baldwin, is not identified by name in the film, only in the credits; in the film, when asked who he is, he identifies himself with an expletive. He is a mysterious and threatening figure who appears at the office to declare, at the outset of a venomous and profane monologue, that everyone there is in imminent danger of losing his job and that each agent has a limited amount of time to make a decent sale and restore himself to the firm's good graces. The best salesman wins a Cadillac and the next best a set of steak knives; the rest will be fired.

His preferred oratorical method is the blistering attack. In the course of the meeting, he proceeds to diminish each and every one of the firm's employees in a variety of ways, calling them names, cursing at them, and assailing their manhood, their intelligence, and their basic role in the world. When Moss protests, Blake increases the level of his attack to such a degree that Moss, typically a bully himself, is stunned into quiet submission.

He claims that he is himself enormously successful in real estate and that he has appeared at the office as a favor to the firm's owners, Mitch and Murray. His brutal, vulgar demeanor and the heartless way in which he initiates the contest for survival are emblematic of the firm's ruthlessness and amorality, qualities that have affected each of the employees to varying degrees. This character was developed by Mamet for the film adaptation and does not appear in the play.

Detective

The detective, played by Jude Ciccolella, is an overbearing man in charge of interrogating the firm's employees as part of his investigation into the break-in. For the most part his nature is revealed to the viewer indirectly, by the effect it has on those who come into contact with him. He appears for moments at a time, coming out of a back room to summon one agent after another by name; each of them emerges deeply offended and complaining of their treatment at his hands. Even the mild-mannered Aaronow is moved by the detective's manner to mount an unusually angry protest to the office at large.

Shelley Levene

Levene, played by Jack Lemmon, is a careworn salesman in his sixties, once a successful agent in the firm, now failing miserably at his job and desperate to make a sale or get fired. His daughter is in the hospital with a serious but unnamed medical condition, and this weighs on him throughout the film. He is reduced to attempting to bribe Williamson for decent leads.

As the film progresses, he struggles without success to sell worthless land to unwilling buyers. He finally succeeds in persuading one of his targets to make an expensive purchase, which will redeem his position in the company and safeguard his daughter's future, but he brings disaster on himself with an accidental admission that he burglarized the office the night before to steal better leads and sell them to a rival real estate firm. The disaster is made complete when Williamson tells him that the clients Levene thought he had made a sale to are bankrupt and simply enjoy talking to salesmen. Williamson refuses to let Levene off the hook and directs him into a back room to admit his crime to a detective, thereby destroying his hopes and dreams.

Despite his willingness to lie, cheat, and steal to earn a living, Levene is the film's only truly sympathetic character. His genuine concern for his daughter, coupled with his age and desperation, make his fall at the film's end a genuine tragedy. In fact, Mamet develops Levene's role as anxious father much further in the film than he does in the play. Jack Lemmon was voted Best Actor by the National Board of Review for his work as Levene.

James Lingk

Lingk, played by Jonathan Pryce, is first seen in the bar where the salesmen congregate for drinks. Roma, the firm's top agent, sits down with him and begins a lengthy sales pitch marked by slick-sounding insider's tips about the way the world works, and Lingk is clearly flattered to be welcomed into Roma's confidences.

Later in the film he enters the office in a panic, desperate to cancel the deal he has made with Roma; his wife, to whom he typically defers, has told him to retrieve the check he wrote and have nothing further to do with Roma. Roma enlists Levene's help in an elaborate ruse to mollify Lingk's concerns, and their deceit almost works until Williamson, the manager, accidentally exposes the deceit. Lingk, horrified, departs to notify his wife, who will deprive Roma of the sale he so badly needed.

Dave Moss

Moss, played by Ed Harris, is a younger salesman and a good one. He resents the company just as much as the others, but his aggressive nature inclines him to strike back, rather than merely suffer and muddle through, as Levene and Aaronow do, or hone his sales abilities to their sharpest edge, as Roma does.

The film opens with his angry denunciations of the company and his heavy-handed efforts to make a sale. He is number two on the company's contest board, meaning that he will be able keep his job there. Nevertheless, he uses his aggressive, manipulative sales technique to try to persuade his fellow salesman Aaronow to burglarize the office and steal better leads, which they will sell to a rival firm.

At the film's conclusion it is revealed that Aaronow backed out of the plan but that Moss was able to persuade the more desperate Levene to commit the theft. Levene incriminates himself, ruining his hopes for a better life for himself and his daughter, and admits to the manager, Williamson, that he split the profits from the theft with Moss to the tune of $2,500 apiece. Moss, however, has already left the building in a fury; following his interrogation at the hands of the detective investigating the office break-in, he lashes out at everyone there before declaring his intention to quit the company and go to Wisconsin.

Ricky Roma

Roma, played by Al Pacino, is the firm's top employee. Vainglorious and manipulative, he cultivates an air of worldliness, and his sales pitches combine an acknowledgement of the world's basic flaws with an insider's scoop about the way it all works. No one else at the firm comes close to matching his sales prowess.

Near the opening of the film he targets a man in a bar, James Lingk, attracting his attention with a comment on the hot weather, then discoursing on a variety of contrarian philosophies. His eventual sale to Lingk is jeopardized by Lingk's wife's reluctance to go through with it; when Lingk shows up at the office to try to stop the check from being deposited, Roma enlists Levene's help to pacify Lingk. The two agents engage in an elaborate deceit in which Levene improvises a role as another buyer, satisfied with his real estate purchases, immensely wealthy, and in a hurry to catch a plane. Lingk is nearly mollified when Williamson, the office manager, accidentally ruins everything by assuring the nerve-wracked man that his check has been deposited.

Roma turns on Williamson; Williamson, fed up with the abuse continually directed at him by the office's agents, in turn destroys Levene. Roma is unaware of Levene's downfall and casually tells him to meet him later for a smoke at the nearby Chinese restaurant. Al Pacino was nominated for a Golden Globe for Best Supporting Actor in *Glengarry Glen Ross*, as well as for an Academy Award for Best Actor in a Supporting Role.

Larry Spannel

Spannel, played by Bruce Altman, is one of the leads given to Levene by Williamson, the office manager. Levene visits him in person, unannounced, and uses all of his skill as a salesman, but to no avail: Spannel is unwilling to discuss real estate and closes the door in his face.

John Williamson

Williamson, played by Kevin Spacey, is the firm's office manager, a proxy for the sadistic owners Mitch and Murray and therefore despised by everyone employed there. He is in charge of handing out the leads. These are a source of tremendous angst for everyone involved, since the good ones are given only to those agents already successful at selling real estate, while the lesser ones, essentially worthless, go to everyone else.

Williamson is willing to accept Levene's offer of a bribe for the better leads, even demanding more from the cash-strapped agent than he can afford; nevertheless, at the film's end, on learning of Levene's theft of the office, he callously gives him up to the investigating detective and adds insult to injury by revealing that the sale Levene thought would save his job is, in fact, doomed to fall through. He is, then, emblematic of the amoral principles used in the administration of the firm, the same ones that govern the professional and personal lives of the employees.

In addition to his function as the public face of the unseen but detested owners, Williamson spoils the precarious efforts of the firm's best salesman, Ricky Roma, to make a difficult sale, resulting in a series of personal verbal attacks against him by several agents. It is a mark of his role as the film's chief antagonist that despite these and other attacks, he remains a fundamentally unsympathetic character.

THEMES

Ambition
The agents of *Glengarry Glen Ross* depend on their salesmanship to survive and succeed; the more skilled they are, the more financial success they can expect. For Levene, in particular, whose daughter is lying in a hospital, success is critical because her life depends on the money he generates, but each of the agents is more or less desperate to succeed.

The real estate company for which they work, however, has created an environment in which mere individual success is not enough. Only the top two salesmen will be able to keep their jobs; the rest will be fired in a sadistic contest, and throughout the film the men are driven to use every means at their disposal to win. Only one man, Aaronow, seems to lack ambition to match his desperation. The others endure a grueling twenty-four hours, conniving, backbiting, lying, and thieving to claw their way toward the top.

Their motivation is piqued by Blake, the man who announces the terms of the contest to them and proceeds to belittle them to the limits of their endurance. He himself drives a BMW and wears a gold watch; he is the very symbol of the success these men are striving for, and yet he takes pains to tell them that they are doomed to failure. Indeed, in the end, despite the sales frenzy, their ambitions come to nothing.

Despair
Linked to the theme of ambition is that of despair. Levene exemplifies this theme; time and again, despite the successes of his past years in real estate, his efforts fall flat, and because of the sick daughter whose care he is nearly unable to provide for, the prospect of failure is unendurable. Jack Lemmon's award-winning performance succeeds by expertly capturing the brittle poise of a man teetering on the edge of ruin. At the film's conclusion, despair has utterly consumed Levene: not only is his own life destroyed by the extreme lengths he has been driven to, but his daughter's is as well.

Aaronow is another exemplar of this theme, but the film suggests that he yielded to despair long ago. He spends much of the film either in miserable silence or unable to complete a single sentence, and the ones he does complete are litanies of powerlessness. Oddly, in his case, an acceptance of defeat as a way of life saves him from the trap laid for him by the much more forceful Moss: despite the other man's best efforts to get him to rob the office, which at first seem successful because of Aaronow's helplessness, he backs out of the plan. Robbery requires too much self-confidence for a man like him.

Moss and Roma at first glance seem untouched by despair. They rage, they cajole, they lie, but they never seem to give up hope. But the circumstances under which they work are just as threatening as for Levene and Aaronow, and their vigor seems as much a response to the specter of despair as an innate characteristic.

Language
The power of language plays a crucial role in *Glengarry Glen Ross*. The film's roots in the stage are evident: it derives virtually all of its force from its dialogue. There are very few scenes without dialogue, and those last only moments (for example, exterior shots of a restaurant, the real estate office, and so on). Words alone propel the film forward from one moment to the next. For all the rage and despair these men feel, for all

READ.
WATCH.
WRITE.

- Mamet wrote both the stage play and the screenplay. Study both and make note of the differences: scenes, dialogue, characters, and so on added or deleted in the film adaptation. Using a computer program, create a graph in which you chart these differences. Add a written section in which you describe whether or not the film has a different message, or overall mood, from the play as a result. Focus on Levene, for whose portrayal Jack Lemmon won Best Actor from the National Board of Review. How exactly do his added lines, as well as Lemmon's performance, change the character as written in the play?

- *Glengarry Glen Ross* is famously character- and dialogue-driven: there are virtually no quiet, reflective moments. It can be easy for a viewer to focus exclusively on the characters themselves and their dynamics and lose sight of the larger environment in which they are working. Write an essay about this environment. What is the movie's broader take on office life, and corporate culture? How exactly do these environments shape the men who are a part of them? In what ways might they be changed for the better? From a broader perspective, what might the film be suggesting about life more broadly?

- Mamet added several scenes to the film. Try writing a *Glengarry Glen Ross* scene of your own, taking place after the action depicted in the movie but centering on the same agents: a visit from Roma while Levene is in prison, Moss working at another job while in hiding in Wisconsin, for example. Focus on how this character may have changed in the intervening period and on how he may have remained the same. Has the character had any epiphanies about himself, or is he still mired in the same old attitudes? How might his experiences with the real estate firm have shaped his future? Has he found success at last or perhaps survived financial disaster?

- Mamet's play included several racist tirades against Indian Americans and the difficulty in selling them real estate; he dropped these passages for the play's 2005 revival and made several significant alterations to them for the film while maintaining the agents' fundamental take on "Patels." Conduct personal interviews with people from different ethnic backgrounds in which you ask them for their responses to the offensive lines. Transcribe these interviews and add an overview of the ways in which these lines were received by different populations (critics, Indian American communities, and so on). Are the original passages an example of racial insensitivity on the part of the author, or are they strictly a commentary on the attitudes of the salesmen? Do Mamet's changes right a wrong, go too far, or fail to go far enough?

- *Matchstick Men* (2003, PG-13) concerns a con artist who discovers that he has a teen-aged daughter. When she enters his life, he proceeds, against his better judgment, to teach her the art of the con. Like *Glengarry Glen Ross*, it concerns (among other things) father-daughter relationships and confidence games; in both films, a man's shady business dealings have major implications for his fatherhood. In an essay, explore the ways in which the two films depict these jeopardized relationships, the role that dishonesty plays in their dynamics, and the differences in the film's resolutions.

the furious denunciations of the business owners, the office manager, the detective, and one another, there is not a single instance of violence; their inner turbulence is explored solely through dialogue, often coercive, sometimes nakedly aggressive.

The sales pitch is one way in which the persuasive power of language is showcased here. The film's ensemble cast does a remarkable job of switching into sales mode, and each character has a very specific style. Levene is almost oily, employing smooth, reassuring monologues like anti-anxiety drugs, in which he effortlessly lies about his role in the company and the value of the land he is selling. Roma takes his potential buyers into his confidences, imparting bits of faux wisdom one after the other so that there is little time to weigh their actual worth, until he senses that he has gained his audience's trust. Moss prefers to use brute force, bearing down on his would-be clients and berating them for any hesitancy until they finally cave. Aaronow alone has little actual skill: he forgets his clients' names and muddles through with no taste for the manipulation his job requires.

Moss's pitch to Aaronow, in which he tries to persuade the meek and mild-mannered agent to break into the office and steal the decent leads, is an excellent example of the coercive power of language. Moss brings the prospect up as an amusing hypothetical question, slowly but surely guiding Aaronow toward an actual consideration of the robbery, then accusing him of being an accessory to the still-unrealized robbery simply by having listened to his spiel; Moss's overbearing nature and Aaronow's submissive one result in a peculiar back-and-forth in which Aaronow mechanically repeats Moss's statements, following him from point to point until he finds himself nearly committed, against his will, to a course of action that he finds personally appalling.

Finally, Blake's famous lecture to the agents demonstrates the power of language to intimidate. Unlike the others, he never loses his temper; he delivers his outrageous insults with expertly controlled force, conveying an air of absolute conviction. It is a remarkable scene, much commented upon by critics for its relentless profanity and the manner in which Blake verbally whittles the men away to their most vulnerable cores.

Deception

Related to the theme of language in the film is that of deception. Much of the dialogue involves the characters' baring their souls (usually in anger), but there are ample scenes in which they employ deceit, almost instinctively, when making a sales pitch. These deceits serve

Playwright David Mamet also wrote the screenplay for the film adaptation (© Helga Esteb / Shutterstock.com)

two purposes: they lure potential buyers toward a sale, and they exaggerate the social rank of the agents. Typically the agents take on the identity of a vice president, on his way to the airport, who is interrupting his busy schedule to give the object of the sales pitch an "investment opportunity."

The film illustrates this tendency most clearly in the scene in which Roma spots Lingk, his extremely nervous client, approaching the office. In a single line of dialogue he bestows a false identity on Levene, enlisting the older agent to help him pacify Lingk with a show of worldliness and wealth. The two men proceed to work out the details of a nonexistent land deal and a nonexistent persona with Lingk standing in front of them; so practiced are they in the art of deception that, despite the seat-of-the-pants nature of their improvisation, Lingk remains unaware of it.

STYLE

Mood

Foley, the director of *Glengarry Glen Ross*, establishes a seedy noir atmosphere with the opening credits: surrounded by a neon glow, they flicker out one after another to the sound of an elevated train rushing past and a jazz number featuring a mournful saxophone. The first section of the movie maintains this tone. Shot at night, its sets alternate between dark, rain-soaked streets and the interiors of cheap offices, restaurants, and bars.

Mamet's original screenplay established much the same tone purely through dialogue. The dialogue is marked by extreme profanity, naturalistic pauses, frequent interruptions, and clumsy grammar, all features that capture the atmosphere of the streets of a major city.

Camera Work

The film has been described by many critics as "claustrophobic," and this is largely owing to Foley's use of confined spaces and tightly framed shots of actors, as befits the mental environment of the men the story revolves around: their lives are heavily constricted by their work, and the sales contest is only constricting them further.

On the other hand, the film is in no way static. The camera is often on the move, tracking restlessly side to side and dollying in and out; when filming dialogue, Foley often cuts back and forth from one speaker to the other. Again, the style fits the characters, who are never given a moment to stop and reflect; they are constantly on the move, both mentally and physically, to keep their jobs. The stage setting of the original play lends itself to that same sense of claustrophobia, as does the dialogue, which focuses exclusively, even obsessively, on sales or features furious arguments and one-upmanship and covers virtually no other topics (at least overtly).

Music

Glengarry Glen Ross features a score dominated by jazz, some composed for the movie by James Newton Howard and the rest consisting of jazz standards. Most of it ranges in tone from pensive to mildly agitated. Quick light drum work sometimes complements the hunched scuttling between one place and another by the agents when they are on the move; elsewhere, saxophone and piano move from melancholy notes to ominous ones.

It ends with Irving Berlin's "Blue Skies," performed in an almost aggressively bright and energetic style by Al Jarreau: its famous optimism is jarringly out of step with the movie's tone, just as the agents' sales pitches, so full of promise, stand in stark contrast to the desperation of their lives.

CULTURAL CONTEXT

When *Glengarry Glen Ross* was first produced in 1983, the United States was just recovering from a recession characterized by rising oil prices, inflation, and unemployment. The specter of financial ruin that haunts the film's salesmen is rooted in the very real events of the era, particularly as credit for home mortgages, at the time the play is set, is hard to come by, so that the substandard leads parceled out by the office manager cannot possibly yield successful sales. No one in the film, not even the best agent on the team, manages to finally close a deal with a buyer; the Nyborgs are bankrupt and insane, and Lingk is in mortal terror that the check he drunkenly wrote the night before will be cashed.

The city shown in the film, though it was produced well after the recession's end, reflects these hardships: neon signs display unlit letters, the streets are grimy and semideserted, and the restaurants and luncheonettes frequented by the agents look as if they are struggling to survive. Both the play and the film exacerbate this context with a few displays of conspicuous consumption, which pique the salesmen's envy, intentionally or not. Blake, whose announcement of a contest for their survival as employees galvanizes a night of frantic action, makes an arrogant display of his gold watch, which, he assures Moss, cost more than Moss's car. He drives a BMW; he is well groomed and wearing an expensively tailored suit. Roma, the firm's most successful agent, misses the meeting, but he, too, has a tanned, fit, and well-dressed look, in contrast to the threadbare appearance of his fellow agents, who speak of his success with jealous exasperation.

Many commentators have noted the exclusively male environment of both the play and the film. The film offers a brief glimpse of a coat-check girl at a Chinese restaurant, but except for references to women (Levene's daughter, Spannel's and Lingk's wives), this is a world defined by the men in it. In fact, the numbers of women

Kevin Spacey plays John Williamson, and Jack Lemmon plays Shelley Levene (© AF archive / Alamy Stock Photo)

in the workplace had been growing for several decades by the time the play was written, despite the various obstacles they faced compared with men; those numbers, as well as increased upward mobility for women, had swelled further by the time the film was made in 1992. But Mamet deliberately creates an almost archaic atmosphere in which traditionally male qualities of independence and assertiveness, confined in tight spaces and limited to a very small number of men, give way to their darker versions of isolation and aggressiveness.

Both the film and the play also feature two passages involving critiques of Indian Americans as potential buyers. No one with the last name of Patel, several agents assure one another, can be expected to buy anything, ever. The play, in particular, features a salesman using extremely vulgar language to dismiss this community. Racism, always an issue in the American cultural landscape to one degree or another, was present in the 1980s, and some saw it as a systemic problem: affirmative action had come under attack in Washington, for example, and black farmers

were being denied loans by the Department of Agriculture on the basis of race. Mamet's salesmen live and work in this environment and obviously share its racial outlook, but Mamet deleted the most offensive lines from his adaptation for the screen and eliminated the passages altogether from the 2005 revival of the play.

CRITICAL OVERVIEW

Glengarry Glen Ross was generally well received by critics. Its ensemble cast, in particular, won widespread praise, and Jack Lemmon's portrayal of Shelley Levene was singled out by many as a standout performance. Rita Kempley, for example, in a review for the *Washington Post*, wrote that "all the performances are exceptional. Lemmon's role is the most precarious, [displaying] a wide range of emotions from the visceral high of the close to the despondency of realizing his own ruin." Roger Ebert, writing in the *Chicago Sun-Times*, called one scene "the best work [Lemmon] has ever done.... There is a fine line in this scene between deception and breakdown, between Lemmon's false jollity and the possibility that he may collapse . . . surrendering all hope."

Reviewers also called attention to the unique challenges in adapting a stage play to the screen, and more than a few took issue with Foley's direction. Todd McCarthy, writing for *Variety*, wrote that "the theatrical roots show rather clearly." He added:

> Foley's attempts to keep the visuals lively and moving create their own sense of distraction. While Juan-Ruiz Anchia's lighting is enormously inventive and colorful, there are a few too many camera moves, unnecessarily elaborate setups and attention-getting cutting tricks.

Desson Howe, writing (like Kempley) for the *Washington Post*, wrote in the same vein: "Foley's attempts to 'open up' the play to the outside world are dismal. . . . If his intention is to create a sense of claustrophobia, he also creates the (presumably) unwanted effect of a soundstage." A line from Peter Travers's review for Rolling Stone sums up the film's overall reception:

> Now Mamet and director James Foley (*After Dark, My Sweet*) want to get the urgency of those verbal pyrotechnics onscreen. They don't always make it. But when they do, this brilliant black comedy doesn't just dazzle; it stings.

CRITICISM

William Rosencrans

Rosencrans is a writer and copy editor. In the following essay, he examines Glengarry Glen Ross *as a self-referential work about the nature of performance.*

Mamet's work has been called self-referential by a number of critics—that is, his plays often seem to call attention to themselves as plays; there is a degree of self-awareness about them. *Glengarry Glen Ross*, both as a play and as a film, very much calls attention to itself as a performance piece. In fact, the work is at least as much about the nature of acting as it is about masculinity, capitalism, the workplace, or any other variously explored themes; it is a study of both performance and, similarly, the art of misdirection.

This is most evident in the sales pitches made throughout the film. When a pitch fails, it is owing only to the salesman's too-naked approach. Aaronow, for example, is clearly reading from a jumbled script when the film records him calling

> **" THEN THE CAMERA GLIDES TO THE DESK OF SHELLEY LEVENE, WHO IS ALL SOOTHING, OILY PERFECTION; THERE IS NO HESITATION IN HIS DELIVERY, JUST THE REASSURING TONES, PRECISE DICTION, AND CASUALLY CALIBRATED MESSAGE OF A MAN OF WEALTH READY TO PARCEL OUT A REWARD—IN SHORT, EVERYTHING LEVENE IS NOT."**

one of his leads: he addresses the prospective buyer by the wrong name and embarks on a fumbling, unanimated effort. Then the camera glides to the desk of Shelley Levene, who is all soothing, oily perfection; there is no hesitation in his delivery, just the reassuring tones, precise diction, and casually calibrated message of a man of wealth ready to parcel out a reward—in short, everything Levene is not. The pitch is apparently successful, at least until it is revealed that Levene himself has been the victim of a performance by the prospective buyers, who are bankrupt and simply enjoy talking to salesmen.

Roma's pitches are even more subtly misdirecting. In his slow but sure seducing of Lingk, a stranger he meets at a bar, the pitch opens with an apparent address to Levene about the weather, then a contrary-sounding statement about the folly of drinking alcohol on hot days. Once Lingk, who has overheard these statements, is hooked, Roma focuses his attention on the lonely man, and the pitch turns into a series of personal observations about the nature of the world, all aimed at creating a sense of spontaneous intimacy. It is a great example of Mamet's writing abilities and an excellent illustration of the acting skills that make a successful salesman. (In writing *Glengarry Glen Ross*, Mamet drew on his experiences working in a similar real estate company years before. The film's depictions of successful and unsuccessful sales techniques are used by many actual sales firms as a teaching aid.) With a final soliloquy about the nature of loss and fear, Roma opens a sales brochure, but by this time the sale is a seamless part of his performance.

The most overt display of acting ability occurs in the second half of the film, when Roma and

WHAT DO I SEE NEXT?

- *99 Homes* (2014, Hyde Park Entertainment) is a drama about the effects of foreclosure on average residents. The film follows a construction worker who, when he, his mother, and his son are evicted from their home by a crooked real estate operator, winds up working for that same developer as a professional evictor in order to keep his home, in time earning enough money to put together his own shady real estate deals. The movie (rated R), has been widely praised for its acting and nuanced characters.

- *The Bling Ring* (2013, American Zoetrope), based on a true story, concerns a group of young criminals who break into the homes of wealthy celebrities, using the proceeds to live the glamorous lifestyles they read about in magazines. When they are finally apprehended, they turn on each other. The film (rated R), explores their amorality and is generally well reviewed, though some critics fault it for failing to commit itself to a moral stance on the subject matter.

- *Boiler Room* (2000, New Line Cinema), like *Glengarry Glen Ross*, explores the inner workings and dynamics of a shady company, in this case a brokerage firm that plies investors with stock whose value has been artificially inflated—a "pump and dump" operation. The brokers, unlike Premier Properties' agents, accrue tremendous wealth, but when the FBI becomes interested, relationships quickly sour. The film (rated R) has been praised for its incisive writing and pace.

- *Death of a Salesman* (1985, Robert F. Colesberry) is a film adaptation of the play by Arthur Miller, focusing on the last tormented days in the life of Willy Lomax, a salesman, as he argues with his sons, loses his job, and begins seeing and speaking to figures from his past. The play is one of the most famous American works for the stage and won a Pulitzer and a Tony; it has been adapted to the screen several times, and this adaptation (rated PG) is one of the most highly regarded.

- *Margin Call* (2011, Before the Door Pictures) follows the lives of several employees at a large Wall Street investment bank who realize that many of the bank's assets are toxic and must be sold off if the firm is to survive, even if this means severing relationships with their clients. In meetings with ever more highly positioned superiors, the employees learn that their bosses have known about this for some time. The next day, these employees attempt to dump as many of the assets as they can, whatever the consequences. The film (rated R) won widespread praise for its cast and intelligent script.

- *Nine Queens* (2000, Cecilia and Pablo Bossi) is an Argentinian crime drama about two con artists, Juan and Marco, who meet during a botched scam at a small shop and join forces, working their way up to a scheme involving the forging of rare stamps; the film then embarks on a merry-go-round of mutual suspicion, double- and triple-crossing, and so on. The film (rated R) won accolades for its inventive twists and turns, kinetic energy, and solid acting.

- *Office Space* (1999, Judgmental Films) is a social satire of the office environment, exploring a group of workers at an information technology firm who are fed up with their jobs and the petty tyranny of the office's manager; their efforts to strike back and reclaim some autonomy have made *Office Space* a cult film (rated R).

Levene combine their talents to dupe Lingk, frantic to cancel the check he wrote the night before. It is performance at its most challenging: the improvisation. Roma has only seconds to describe Levene's role to the older agent, but Levene, a past master, takes it on without a hitch, acting the part of the director of sales and services for American Express overseas. The two men build the character as they go, with Roma whispering to Lingk about the fabulous wealth, the extravagant house, the parties, and the fundamentally warm and generous nature of his supposed client.

The performance is spoiled by Williamson, the only man in the office who does not act, perhaps because he cannot. (Earlier, in a moment of overt cinematic self-reference, Levene urges Williamson not to "jump out of your 'manager' bag," that is, not to act the part of a manager but simply to interact with Levene as a human being. Williamson, unfortunately for Levene, is not acting. He is a heartless manager to the core. His inability to perform earns him the salesmen's fury and scorn; he does, however, have an eye for performance, and when Levene makes a very subtle slip exposing his guilt in the robbery, the manager catches it instantly, spelling the agent's doom.

Performance serves another purpose here, too. These men distract themselves from the misery of their own lives with a variety of performances, most especially Levene's as he narrates the tale of his successful morning to Roma. The tale begins in close-up, as Levene reenacts the various roles for Roma's benefit: himself holding a pen to the couple he is pitching to; his certainty as the seconds and minutes tick by that he has them in the palm of his hand; his mimicking of the manner in which they suddenly surrender to him. As the camera moves slowly away from the two men, Levene's victory is put into painful perspective: the performance loses its power the further the camera moves away until it reveals an old broken man doing his best to playact a victory in a sterile, oppressive environment.

It is worth remarking at this point on the most appropriate way to view these men who act for a living. The salesman is an iconic figure in American culture, and Mamet reduces this figure to a tiny handful of characteristics, mostly negative: a mixture of deceit, wounded pride, fear, and anger. Indeed, the salesmen are contemptible in many ways, but they are not themselves portrayed with contempt. Both their constant, reflexive performances and their apparent character flaws mask a certain decency. The intelligent viewer must see past their performances to perceive their basic inventiveness, their drive and work ethic, their occasional compassion and shows of mutual support. Aaronow, for example, despairing of his

abilities, is comforted by both Roma and Moss. While these moments may be performances as well, they are in the service of fundamentally decent impulses.

From this same broader perspective of the men as characters in a play or film, the plot itself looks occasionally like an exercise in misdirection. The most obvious example is Moss's effort to manipulate Aaronow to break into the office and steal the leads and that effort's aftermath. When Roma learns that the office has been robbed the following morning, the audience can only assume that Moss was successful and that Aaronow is guilty of the crime. The assumption is strengthened when Aaronow emerges briefly from his interview with the detective to ask the office at large if someone would bring him a cup of coffee. His expression is wooden, and the normally temperamental Moss, who was about to begin arguing with Roma, stops short and quietly asks if Aaronow is all right. He seems concerned about the salesman's ability to withstand the heavy-handed interrogation—another suggestion that Aaronow is the guilty party. Moss's subsequent abrupt departure from the office, after screaming at the other salesmen and claiming that he is going to Wisconsin, suggests fear of imminent betrayal. But Levene, not Moss, is the guilty party.

At the end of the film, Levene's days as a performer are over. The roles he has been playing for many years are finished. There are to be no more sales, no more efforts to ingratiate himself with anyone, no more displays of outrage or contempt for his office manager, and no more false reassurances to his daughter; he can only, finally, begin the process of living as he really is. The film culminates with a lesser actor, Aaronow, groaning about his job before getting on the phone and beginning another sales pitch while Levene reckons with his fate in another room. It is a bleak ending, but an oddly uplifting one as well: the performances will continue, the remaining actors working to the best of their abilities; the show must, after all, go on.

Source: William Rosencrans, Critical Essay on *Glengarry Glen Ross*, in *Drama for Students*, Gale, Cengage Learning, 2017.

Edward W. Younkins

In the following essay, Younkins ties together salesmanship and language in Glengarry Glen Ross.

Al Pacino won the Oscar for Best Supporting Actor as Ricky Roma (© ScreenProd | Photononstop | Alamy Stock Photo)

David Mamet's 1984 Pulitzer Prize winning play, *Glengarry Glen Ross*, is about the struggles of four shady small-time salesmen in a small branch of a larger real estate company located in Chicago. Taking place over two business days, the play portrays the dog-eat-dog world of real estate and the ends ruthless salesmen will go to in order to sell overpriced and undesirable land to uninterested and reluctant potential buyers. The cutthroat conniving salesmen resort to trickery, bribery, deceit, lying, and theft. This dark play successfully illustrates the social Darwinistic nature of the shady world of real estate in a big city and the Darwinian rules of the desperate salesmen's game. The title of the play refers to two unattractive and overvalued parcels of Florida land—Glengarry Heights and Glen Ross Farms. Mamet's play was also made into a fine 1992 film which incorporated two additional scenes.

The author, Mainet, had worked for a year in a Chicago real estate office where he observed salesmen's noble but often pathetic efforts to sell unwanted real estate. There he heard the coarse and vulgar language that depicted the high pressure felt by the agents. Mamet had first-hand experience of both the desperation and exhilaration of the salesmen's calling. He knew how they talked and incorporated much obscene and unprofessional language into the play's dialogue. Abrasive and pungent language is shown to constitute the jargon of the salesmen's trade. Such language also measures and connotes the intensity of the salesmen's quests.

Mamet shows how hucksters use language to con customers and each other. He employs sporadic conversations and erratic speech patterns to convey their thoughts and personalities. Mamet illustrates that language is a con man's tool and that conversation can be used to persuade, convince, and lie. His characters use language and storytelling in order to survive in their dismal and dreary situations and to exalt that survival. Mamet's characters define themselves through their language and discourse. Each character's ability or inability to sell is essential to his identity and relationships to the others.

The original play is set in two locations—a rundown Chinese restaurant across the street from the shabby real estate office, and the dingy office itself. The appearance of both the restaurant and the office sets us up for the darkness, gloom, and sense of despair of the salesmen themselves. The three scenes of Act I take place in the restaurant, and Act II entirely takes place the following day in the office. The film version is fairly true to the play with two scenes added. One scene shows one of the salesmen making an unsuccessful sales call at someone's home. The other scene effectively adds a new character who threatens the salesmen at the beginning of the screenplay version. Blake (played by Alec Baldwin), a slick troubleshooter from downtown, is sent to shake up the salesmen.

The very first scene of the film version is valuable by making explicit much of what is subsequently illustrated, explained, or implied in the succeeding events of the play. The film begins with an emergency meeting in the shabby real estate office. Blake, a tough emissary sent by downtown bosses Mitch and Murray, delivers a "pep talk" to the salesmen. He tells the salesmen that they are all fired and that the only way to get their jobs back is close enough deals in the sales contest he is instituting. Blake is arrogant,

> **PLAYING ROLES AND LIVING BY THEIR WITS SEEM TO COME NATURALLY FOR THESE SALESMEN. WE COULD SAY THAT THE CHARACTERS THEMSELVES ARE, IN FACT, ACTORS."**

pompous, and takes pleasure in demeaning the salesmen. He delivers his talk in unprofessional, negative, and vulgar language. He cracks the whip by pitting the salesmen against each other in a sales contest. They will be fired unless they get "on the board." There is an ever-present chalkboard in the front of the office that consistently reminds them of the contest at all times—it is literally in their faces.

Blake informs them that the winner will get a Cadillac, the second place finisher will receive a set of steak knives, and the rest of them will be fired. He says that each of them will be given two leads by Williamson, the office manager, and that they had until the next morning to turn them into sales. The salesmen know that the leads are old and worthless and two of them, Dave Moss and Shelly Levene, complain that they are old leads. Blake's attempts to "teach" the salesmen how to sell merely amount to repeating acronyms—ABC (Always Be Closing) and AIDA (Attention, Interest, Decision, and Action).

The first scene in Act I of the play shows Shelly "the Machine" Levene attempting to persuade John Williamson, the sales manager, to give him some of the premium leads locked up in the office. Williamson has 500 good Glengarry leads that are only to be distributed to "closers." The desperate and despairing Levene pleads, brags, flatters, bullies, and attempts to bribe the office manager in order to obtain the leads. Levene tries to bribe Williamson by offering him fifty dollars for every lead plus twenty percent of the profit made. The unsympathetic, heartless, and impassive office manager says he wants his money up front.

Levene, a great salesman in the past, needs money to pay for his sick daughter's medical bills. As a tragic figure who boasts about his past accomplishments, Levene brings to mind the character Willy Loman in Arthur Miller's 1949

play *Death of a Salesman*. Viewed by Williamson as expendable, Shelly, the worn-out sagging old timer, has been on a losing streak not having made a sale in months. Levene attributes his misfortunes on the economy and the lack of quality leads that Williamson gives him. He views Williamson as a naïve, incompetent, sadistic, and bureaucratic young man with no sales experience.

Williamson takes orders from Mitch and Murray, the downtown sales bosses. The uncharismatic and ruthless sales manager resorts to fear and intimidation and is not respected by the salesmen. They despise both Williamson and the system under which they work. Lacking in leadership skills, the spineless Williamson is a stooge for the main office downtown who has never had to live by his wits as a salesman on the front line.

In scene two of Act I, Dave Moss and George Aaronow are at the Chinese restaurant engaging in a conversation about the unfairness of the distribution of the leads. They are offended by the company's disrespect for its employees. In order to get the good leads one had to make sales and in order to make sales one needed to have the good leads. The angry and ruthless Moss shares his idea of stealing the leads and selling them to a former colleague and current competitor, Jerry Graff, who is in business for himself. The bitter, intimidating, and aggressive Moss wants the timid, reserved, and soft-spoken Aaronow to break into the office and steal the leads. Moss informs Aaronow that even if he did not participate in the robbery he would still be an accessory before the fact because he had talked to Moss about the robbery plot—for the salesmen it appears that talking implies action. He tells Aaronow that if he breaks in himself he will name Aaronow as an accomplice.

Ricky Roma, the star of the sales force, is also at the Chinese restaurant, Roma is a subtle, smooth, instinctual, and informal salesman who does not need a list of hot prospects to make sales—for him every person is a potential customer, even bar strangers. Roma is able to improvise according to his sense of each occasion. He works magic on potential customers by avoiding the hard sell and by getting the potential clients to trust him. Roma has the knack of persuading customers to purchase what they neither need nor want. He knows how to use language (often vulgar) to sell his point. He expertly employs language to engage prospective buyers in small talk, thereby placing them at ease. The charming Roma thinks out of the box and uses his finesse to manipulate his target. Roma's sales acumen embodies the art of selling. He knows how to get the potential customer to trust him. Of course, he does not really care about the customer but he has the ability to make the customer believe that he cares.

At the bar in the Chinese restaurant, Roma spots James Lingk and identifies him as a great target. Observing Roma in action permits us to experience vicariously the salesman's thrill of the chase. He shows us how talk can transfer needs from the salesman to the potential customer and power from the potential customer to the salesman. Realizing that Lingk does not believe he enjoys or is in control of his life, Roma engages in a philosophical monologue in which he talks about the meaning of life, risk-taking, and seizing the moment. Roma plays to Lingk's insecurities.

Approaching Lingk as a friend. Roma talks about opportunities and questions the idea of morality. Creating a comfortable setting for Lingk. Ricky uses vulgar language to proclaim the absence of absolute morality in the world and the responsibility of each person to be the master of his own fate. Roma never stops talking, suggests outrageous and extravagant opportunities, and gets Lingk to actually believe that he is his own man. The ace huckster gets Lingk to buy land that he can't afford. Roma does not even consider if he is doing anything wrong—he just does his job the best way that he knows how to do it.

Act II takes place the following morning at the shabby real estate office which consists of four desks, a coffee pot, the chalkboard, and a couple of windows. The office is disheveled and the leads, telephones, and some contracts had been stolen.

Williamson and Aaronow are in the outer office and Moss is being interrogated by a police detective named Baylen. When they arrive, both Roma and Levene believe that they have closed deals from the night before but their deals have not really been closed. Moss emerges from the inner office and is outraged by the way that the detective has treated him. The hot-headed Moss hears Levene raving about his successful deal and storms out. Moss's anger appears to be a charade to make him look to be uninvolved in the office break-in.

Shelly is heartened by his successful sale. When he enters the office he thinks that he is the new leader in the competition. Levene boasts about the $80,000 plus sale he made the previous night to Bruce and Harriett Nyborg. The self-secure Ricky Roma congratulates the sagging old-timer on the sale. When he hears about the robbery, Ricky is concerned about whether or not his deal from the night before has been processed.

James Lingk enters the office to renege on the deal he made with Roma. His wife does not approve of it. Knowing that he has three business days to change his mind, he wants to make certain that the contract has not yet been filed and that his check has not been cashed. Roma informs Lingk that neither event has occurred and that there is plenty of time to back out of the deal if he really wants to do so. Roma suggests that he and Lingk meet on Monday to discuss the situation knowing that by then it will be too late to cancel the deal.

Roma teams up with Levene to make it appear that Roma has an important satisfied client, a senior vice-president of American Express, who has bought property from Roma and who has to be rushed immediately to the airport. Roma and Levene improvise to mislead and manipulate the tearful, pathetic customer who came to the office to demand a refund. Ricky admires Shelly for his spontaneous ability to cleverly play their con game. He only had to give Levene a few cues regarding how to proceed.

Williamson emerges from his office to ruin Roma and Levene's team effort. The inexperienced office manager misreads the situation. He mistakenly thinks that Lingk is upset by the disorder of the office and reassures Lingk that the deal has gone through despite the robbery and that the contract has been processed and the check has been deposited the night before. At that point, Lingk realizes that he is being scammed. He leaves upset proclaiming that he is going to report Roma to the Attorney General.

Roma blows up and is furious with Williamson for sabotaging the deal. Levene joins Roma in berating and vilifying the office manager. After Roma goes in for questioning by Officer Baylen, Levene gets himself into serious trouble by telling Williamson that he should not have lied about having processed the deal and having cashed the check. Everyone knows that it was the office manager's policy to nightly take the checks to the bank and to file the contracts. As luck would have it, the previous night Williamson failed to do so. The only way Shelly could have known that was if he had been in the office the night before. Williamson is thereby tipped off that Levene was the guilty party who had robbed the office.

The office manager knows that Levene is guilty. Levene attempts to deny the crime but eventually folds, admits his guilt (and that of Moss), begs for mercy, and attempts to bribe Williamson. He admits to selling the leads to Graff. To add to Levene's woes, Williamson tells Levine that the Nyborgs's check is no good and that they are a crazy old couple who simply like to talk to salesmen. He had purposely given Shelly the worst possible leads. Levene asks Williamson why he is reporting him to the police and the office manager responds, "Because I don't like you." Levene had begun the day with pride believing that he had made a major sale but he certainly did not end the day that way.

Roma exits the interrogation, praises Levene, and attempts to convince Levene into being his partner so that he can share in the commission. Williamson has revealed Levene and Moss as the thieves to the detective. Shelly goes in to confess to Baylen just as Ricky is telling Levene how much he admires him. There is no closure at the end of the play. The selling goes on as we observe Ricky heading back to the Chinese restaurant

Mamet's character-centered play portrays a passionate, dismal, brutal world in which all of the characters are tragic figures. One moment a salesman praises a colleague and the next moment he betrays him. Teamwork is only evident among the salesmen when they conspire to bamboozle a customer or to steal from the company. The salesmen attempt to sound confident when they are on the phone but they are actually haunted by despair and desperation. They talk to make a living and most of the time they try to hide the truth. They appear to be addicted to what they do and exhibit the desire to manipulate. The main purpose of their talking is to claim power over others to withhold power from them. They lie that they are in town for only a few hours, that there are only a few lots left, and so on. Playing roles and living by their wits seem to come naturally for these salesmen. We could say that the characters themselves are, in fact, actors.

The reader might wonder if these salesmen are naturally deceitful scam-artists who are attracted to their profession or if their organizational climate requires them to act the way they do. There is no loyalty or trust by or to the organization. The salesmen are driven by the bosses to participate in the dog-eat-dog cutthroat competition. Leadership, if any, is boss-centered and Theory X oriented. The salesmen are not mentored. There is no goal clarification or participation and the employees are in no way empowered. They fear punishment and the only motivation provided is negation—the chance to keep their jobs. A leader should be able to motivate his subordinates through the joint formulation of goals and the facilitation of the attainment of their goals. The organization has no people-centered practices or policies. There is no talk about providing value to the customers.

This play can be looked at as a description of a new kind of American salesmanship, a detective story with a surprise ending, and as a dog-fight for power, domination, and survival. The excellent film adaptation includes a fine ensemble cast: Ricky (Al Pacino), Shelly (Jack Lemmon), Blake (Alec Baldwin), Dave (Ed Harris), George (Alan Arkin), John (Kevin Spacey), and James (Jonathan Pryce).

Source: Edward W. Younkins, "*Glengarry Glen Ross*: A David Mamet Word Play," in *Exploring Capitalist Fiction: Business through Literature and Film*, Lexington Books, 2014, pp. 217–22.

Carla J. McDonough

In the following excerpt, McDonough explains how the search for identity is complicated by preconceptions about masculinity in Glengarry Glen Ross.

. . . The overriding need of Mamet's male characters is for affirmation of their identity, for comfort, friendship, love, and understanding, yet this need is denied because of the fear that it is weak and unmanly to need anything or not to be secure in one's identity. The only two options, it would seem, are to be brash and cover up the emptiness or to be painfully honest and reveal it, but there is little offered in Mamet's stage world that will convert the emptiness these men feel into meaning. This fear is created by a distrust of the world in which the characters live. Fear of betrayal in sexual relationships, business transactions, and friendships leads to distrust in everyone, and this fear and distrust has its roots in the lack of confidence within the self. In support of this "catch-22" reading of male identity, Stephen Shapiro argues in his study of masculinity that

> THE PRESSURE TO PERFORM AT WORK IN ORDER TO MAINTAIN AN IDENTITY IS SO GREAT THAT THE CHARACTERS IN *GLENGARRY GLEN ROSS* CONTINUE TO SUBMIT TO THAT PRESSURE EVEN WHEN THEY MOST DESIRE TO ESCAPE IT."

male self-mistrust is caused by narcissism and reinforced by male silence, emotional inhibition, and puerile attitudes and behavior. The division inside men, in the male psyche, has the drastic social consequence of weakening trust in all other relationships.... The weakening of the bonds of trust in these relationships causes still further decay in male self-trust. We have only to regard our social world to see a mirror image of this growing mistrust, a tragic reflection of the inner world of men.

Reflecting Shapiro's view, Bernie and Edmond, and later characters such as Levene and Fox, are driven by a near hysterical insecurity about their manhood, a sense of powerlessness that they seek to over-compensate for, a need to establish their manhood in the face of real or imagined challenges to it. These challenges are often personal, internal insecurities, and they are regularly projected onto the outside world—often onto women, or else onto fellow businessmen, workers, or friends. More than anything, Mamet's men believe they have something to prove about themselves through competition with others and are therefore locked in a destructive sense of competition that they cannot escape.

Within Mamet's plays, ideals of masculinity are sought through competition and prove to be limiting even when attained. The competition takes place mainly with words—with storytelling—as characters seek to assert some image of themselves and of their actions through their dialogue. Action in Mamet's plays is almost always implied action; it usually occurs offstage and is merely recounted by the characters. Reality, action, the very worlds of these characters are linguistically signified, and since we are sometimes given conflicting information (the stories of the cook in *Lakeboat*) or stories that are too extreme to believe (such as Bernie's

sexual exploits), we find it difficult to accept the reality these characters are trying to create for themselves and for their listeners.

Mamet himself recognizes the competition that is at the heart of his plays. In an interview conducted by Matthew Roudané, Mamet explains that "one can only succeed at the cost of, the failure of another, which is what a lot of my plays—*American Buffalo* and *Glengarry Glen Ross*—are about." Although Mamet's comment does not overtly connect this competition with masculine identity, that connection is certainly apparent in his male-cast plays, reflecting what Ray Raphael emphasizes is part of the making of male identity:

> Whether purposely or inadvertently, we create a polarized tension between winning and losing in which the success of some is dependent upon the failure of others. Our male rites of passage therefore tend to become dysfunctional and counter-productive [Raphael].

Glengarry Glen Ross is practically a case study of the conflicts that Raphael describes, particularly because the language throughout the play is gender-coded to set up clearly limited and antagonistic definitions of masculinity. Success of one salesman depends upon the failure of the others—it is the Cadillac, the steak knives, or nothing—and only the top salesman's position is the truly masculine one. While some (one?) of Mamet's salesmen will win and thereby prove their manhood, the others (the losers) are left to wonder, am I really a man? The competition thus ensures failure for the majority, and this failure is not simply a failure to win, but to achieve an identity that is defined as masculine. Ultimately, then, *Glengarry Glen Ross* is less about the need to succeed in business than the need for men to establish and maintain a masculine identity through or within the system of business. In accord with this view, Hersh Zeifman has argued that the portrait of the business world in both *Glengarry* and *American Buffalo* presents "the debased values of an all-male business ethic in which the phallus reigns supreme," a world "in which men *define* themselves as 'men'"

The opening scenes of *Glengarry Glen Ross* establish the dangerous, ego-threatening world that its salesmen inhabit. Levene and Williamson, Moss and Aaronow, and Roma and Lingk play out the humiliating extremes necessary for them to hold onto their jobs. Levene, an older salesman who is not bringing in the revenues he used to, cajoles, bullies, pleads, and finally bribes his boss to give him better leads (names of prospective buyers). Moss, a disgruntled salesman, plans to rob the sales office and steal the leads by manipulating the less aggressive Aaronow into doing the actual break-in. And finally, top salesman Roma dazzles and manipulates the gullible Lingk into purchasing properties in return for Roma's supposed friendship. With these three scenes, act 1 sets up the tensions brewing among the salesmen who have relied on the tentative positions of their jobs for their sense of identity. Act 2 begins to develop more clearly exactly where the lines of identification are drawn and how narrow the space is between them.

Once again, the most often evoked image against which these men seek to define themselves is that of women. Shelley Levene tells Williamson at one point, "a man's his job." The obvious point is that doing a job is what makes a man, what gives a man identity. Levene goes on to say that if "you don't have the balls" to do the job then "you're a secretary," a job traditionally held by women. Or, as Roma exclaims to Williamson when the latter messes up a deal:

> Where did you learn your trade. You stupid.... You *idiot*. Whoever told you you could work with men?

If being a man relies on performing well at work, then failure to do so defines a worker as not-man, as woman. It is precisely the differentiation of these two narrowly prescriptive positions that offers any sense of identity for these characters. As in previous plays, the feminine is allotted a negative position; it is set up as the failure and lack that a man must overcome in order to establish and maintain his identity as a man. But, this construct of male identity remains extremely tenuous and is constantly threatened by the same competition that is supposed to create it.

The pressure to perform at work in order to maintain an identity is so great that the characters in *Glengarry Glen Ross* continue to submit to that pressure even when they most desire to escape it. While a character such as Edmond journeyed to a greater awareness of himself by embracing his fears and the supposedly negative sides of himself, the characters in *Glengarry Glen Ross* cannot break away from the system that defines them long enough to seek new identity. When Levene is at last revealed as the culprit of the robbery, an act that sought to break down the structure of the business that defines him, he explains his thought at the time of the break-in:

"I'm halfway hoping to get caught. To put me out of my ...." The desire to be put out of his misery, to escape the pressure, is great enough to drive him to act, yet Levene cannot actually give voice to this desire to escape precisely because this desire is also his greatest fear. If Levene's identity is based upon his job, then escaping the job means negating the self. Levene immediately follows the confession of his desire to escape with a rejection of that desire. He explains:

> But it *taught* me something. What it taught me, that you've got to get *out* there. Big deal. So I wasn't cut out to be a thief. I was cut out to be a salesman.

This assertion, of course, is belied by Levene's position at the end of the play.

Glengarry Glen Ross has been said to evoke *Death of a Salesman* in its exploration of the failure of the success myth. Interestingly enough, the main concern of Willy Loman was to be "well liked" or accepted in masculine society—given the recognition from other men that Raphael, Shapiro, and even Mamet in his essays describe as being vital to a man's sense of self-worth. But in *Glengarry*, the well-liked motif is rejected for a ruthlessness that Ricki Roma, the top salesman, epitomizes. Roma gains other characters' confidence or liking only so that he can use them for business ends. Although he knows how to act like an interested and sympathetic friend to both customers and fellow salesmen, ultimately he does not care about their opinions of him except as they serve his purpose of getting "on the board." His only desire is to be top salesman, because it is the *position* that gives him power and identity, rather than the admiration of others that Willy Loman desired.

Raphael has argued that "in our culture the practical effect of many of our so-called initiations is to separate the men from the men." *Glengarry Glen Ross* clearly develops this separation and isolation of the male characters. Any comfort they might take from each other, any support or friendship, is constantly undercut by the competition they are locked into. For example, the camaraderie of man-to-man talk developed so vividly in scene 3 between Roma and Lingk is undercut by the realization that all of Roma's shared confidence has been simply a lead-in to a sales pitch aimed at the unsuspecting Lingk. Lingk's desire to believe in Roma's friendship, in their understanding and acceptance of each other as men, continues even as

Roma's congame is revealed. Lingk shows up the next day to reclaim his check, but he makes it clear that he has been sent by his wife, that she is what has come between Roma and Lingk. He tells Roma "It's not me, it's my wife" who has driven him to ask for his money back, and this wife has taken away from him "the power to negotiate." Lingk, who evidently feels himself to be powerless, is perhaps drawn to Roma precisely because Roma has power, because his identity as a man is seemingly secure. Even when Lingk discovers that his check has already been cashed, that Roma has evidently been lying to him, he still feels that he, not Roma, has failed in some way. He apologizes to Roma in lines reminiscent of Bobby's at the end of *American Buffalo*: "I know I've let you down. I'm sorry."

Not only is any friendship between customer and salesman made impossible by the exploitative nature of the business, but so is any real respect or friendship between salesmen. In conning Lingk, Levene and Roma fall smoothly into a partnership of lies, but ultimately these men are separated by competition as well. Roma, the more successful, and younger, salesman realizes this while Levene, the failing older salesman, is still trying to operate on an older set of rules, those more along the lines of a Willy Loman. Levene insists that "a man who's your 'partner' *depends* on you...you have to go *with* him and *for* him...or you're shit, you're *shit*, you can't exist alone." Roma, the partner to whom Levene refers in this speech, is already setting up to betray Levene. Roma tells Williamson in the closing moments of the play, "I GET HIS [Levene's] ACTION. My stuff is *mine*, whatever *he* gets for himself, I'm taking half. You put me in with him." The "partnership" that Roma is setting up is completely exploitative because Roma realizes that his success is predicated on the failure of other salesmen. Subsequently, Levene has become another mark for Roma, just as Lingk had been, and the men in this play remain separated from each other by a competition that binds them into isolation. No wonder Aaronow, who voices despair throughout the play, has as his closing line, "God, I hate this job." Yet, however much they may hate their jobs, it is clear that these men cannot envision life for themselves beyond the office and its system of identification. As a result, they find themselves clinging to the very system that seeks to destroy them....

Source: Carla J. McDonough, "Competition for Identity: *Glengarry Glen Ross*," in *Staging Masculinity: Male Identity in Contemporary American Drama*, McFarland, 1997, pp. 85–89.

Owen Gleiberman

In the following review, Gleiberman praises the ensemble cast of the film.

Most movies about con artists let us revel in the vicarious thrill of the scam. It's a double-edged pleasure: Even as we share the hustler's amoral cleverness, we take a sadistic delight in laughing at the putz he has just conned, knowing full well it could have been us. *Glengarry Glen Ross*, the corrosively funny film version of David Mamet's Pulitzer Prize-winning play, is about a Chicago real estate office full of shabby, desperate swindlers—low-life "businessmen" who pass off swampland as the buy of a lifetime. Mamet's ingenious comic premise is that these bogus salesmen are the con men and the putzes. Braggarts and chiselers all, they're hooked on the high of selling; they're like gambling addicts who tell themselves that this time the dice are going to come up right. Yet their scams aren't getting them anywhere. They work harder executing hustles than they would if they made an honest living. The ones they're really conning are themselves.

On stage, *Glengarry Glen Ross* was explosive yet compact. Powered by the live-wire naturalism of Mamet's dialogue, it had the combustible force of a six-pack of dynamite. The movie version, directed with unobtrusive precision by James Foley, stays amazingly true to the play's feisty spirit. In *Glengarry*, Mamet orchestrates his usual blowhard patter—the herky-jerky repetitions, the profanity, the atmosphere of rapid-fire Scorsesean grittiness. This may be the one case, however, in which he has found a subject fully worthy of his characters' macho bluster. The salesmen in *Glengarry* are pathetic, but they're also quick, defiant, and hilarious—moral dwarfs with the verbal gifts of snake-oil salesmen. Mamet gazes at them with a kind of heartless clarity; his view is almost cathartically unsentimental. At the same time, he admires their crude, never-say-die energy. What makes these scuzzy losers appealing and resonant rather than depressing is the almost lunatic sense of dedication they bring to their disreputable calling.

In the early scenes, as they babble on about their eternal quest for "leads," we're not sure, exactly, what they're talking about, and that's part of the joke: We're witnessing a camaraderie as cultish and squalid as that of the gangsters in *GoodFellas*. The leads, it turns out, are what every salesman depends on: the names of potential suckers. Everyone wants leads, the fresher the better. But some need them more than others. Take Shelley Levene (Jack Lemmon). Sweaty and compulsive, edging past middle age. he's on a losing streak that's starting to look permanent. Then there's the short- tempered Dave (Ed Harris), who's just desperate enough to try and coerce his buddy George (Alan Arkin) into helping him execute what sounds like a perfect crime: breaking into their own office, stealing a list of 500 fresh leads, and selling them to a rival company.

Only one of the characters doesn't need to meditate on such schemes. Ricky Roma (Al Pacino) is the unofficial king of the salesmen, the sort of guy who could sell swampland to his grandmother (and, more to the point, who would). When we first meet him, he's seated at the bar of a tacky Chinese restaurant, working his magic on an eager-eyed mark (Jonathan Pryce). Ricky's whole trick is to avoid the hard sell. He flatters his customers, plies them with liquor, wins their trust. In his serpentine way, he turns duplicity into an art form.

Glengarry doesn't have—or need—much of a plot. It takes place during a single 24-hour period, during which the office is broken into (but by whom, it's not clear). In the morning the police show up to question everyone there. Yet for most of the salesmen, this isn't a major cause for concern. The real dilemma is that the deals they've made the night before are blowing up in their faces.

The performers achieve a true ensemble rhythm; at times, the entire office seems like a single, shouting organism. Yet a couple of the actors outdo themselves. As Ricky, Pacino demonstrates his peerless gift for comic volatility. When his mark from the night before shows up in the office, meekly requesting to be let out of the deal, Pacino feints, jabs, cajoles, and squirms—his performance becomes a small aria of sleaze. And Jack Lemmon, an actor I've seldom been able to watch without squirming myself, is a revelation. Lemmon hasn't abandoned his familiar mannerisms—the hammy, ingratiating whine, the tugging-at-the-collar nervousness. This time, though, he trots out his stale actor's gimmicks

knowingly, making them a satirical extension of the character's own weariness. Shelley's folly isn't just that he's a failed salesman. It's that he's nothing but a salesman, a walking compendium of cheap tricks that stopped working years ago. As Lemmon plays him, he's the weaselly soul of *Glengarry Glen Ross*—Willy Loman turned into a one-liner.

Source: Owen Gleiberman, Review of *Glengarry Glen Ross*, in *Entertainment Weekly*, October 9, 1992.

SOURCES

Bigsby, C. W. E., "*Glengarry, Glen Ross*," in *David Mamet*, Methuen, 1985, pp. 111–26.

Ebert, Roger, Review of *Glengarry Glen Ross*, in *Chicago Sun-Times*, October 2, 1992, http://www.rogerebert.com/reviews/glengarry-glen-ross-1992 (accessed June 8, 2016).

Howe, Desson, Review of *Glengarry Glen Ross*, in *Washington Post*, October 2, 1992, http://www.washingtonpost.com/wp-srv/style/longterm/movies/videos/glengarryglenrossrhowe_a0af12.htm (accessed June 8, 2016).

Kane, Leslie, "Caught in the American Machine," in *Weasels and Wisemen: Ethics and Ethnicity in the Work of David Mamet*, St. Martin's Press, 1999, pp. 57–102.

Kempley, Rita, Review of *Glengarry Glen Ross*, in *Washington Post*, October 2, 1992, http://www.washingtonpost.com/wp-srv/style/longterm/movies/videos/glengarryglenrosskempley_a0a32b.htm (accessed June 9, 2016).

Mamet, David, *Glengarry Glen Ross*, Grove Press, 1984.

Manish, "Mamet's Stain on Broadway," in *Sepia Mutiny*, April 3, 2005, http://sepiamutiny.com/blog/2005/04/03/mamets_racist_s/ (accessed May 31, 2016)

McCarthy, Todd, "Review: *Glengarry Glen Ross*," in *Variety*, August 31, 1992, http://variety.com/1992/film/reviews/glengarry-glen-ross-2-1200430456/ (accessed June 8, 2016).

Nightingale, Benedict, "*Glengarry Glen Ross*," in *The Cambridge Companion to David Mamet*, edited by Christopher Bigsby, Cambridge University Press, 2004, pp. 89–102.

Piette, Alan, "The 1980s," in *The Cambridge Companion to David Mamet*, edited by Christopher Bigsby, Cambridge University Press, 2004, pp. 76–80.

Sauer, David K., and Sauer, Janice, *David Mamet: A Research and Production Sourcebook*, Praeger Publishers, 2003, pp. 143–79.

Travers, Peter, Review of *Glengarry Glen Ross*, in *Rolling Stone*, October 2, 1992, http://www.rollingstone.com/movies/reviews/glengarry-glen-ross-19921002 (accessed June 9, 2016).

Tuttle, John, "'Be What You Are': Identity and Morality in *Edmond* and *Glengarry Glen Ross*," in *David Mamet's "Glengarry Glen Ross": Text and Performance*, edited by Leslie Kane, Garland Press, 1996, pp. 157–69.

FURTHER READING

Kane, Leslie, ed., *David Mamet: A Casebook*, Garland Press, 1992.

> Kane's book, a collection of critical essays about Mamet, was the first such collection to be published. The essays cover a broad range, from the literary and cultural heritage Mamet draws on to studies of his work and influence; it is essential reading for anyone making an in-depth study of the famous playwright, screenwriter, and director.

Day, Kathleen, *S&L Hell: How Politics Created a Trillion Dollar Debacle*, W. W. Norton, 1993.

> Mamet wrote *Glengarry Glen Ross* in the middle of the recession of the early 1980s. Day's book explores a major aftereffect of the recession: the savings-and-loan crisis, in which over a thousand S&L groups collapsed, at tremendous cost to taxpayers. Day's book highlights some of the fascinating, larger-than-life personalities behind the crisis, illustrating a blatantly unethical system akin to Mamet's real estate environment.

Saval, Nikil, *Cubed: A Secret History of the Workplace*, Doubleday, 2014.

> There are many studies of the American workplace. Critics lauded Saval's exploration of the history of the workplace and the dynamics within it for the book's thoroughness, engaging writing style, and surprising revelations about the nature and development of office space.

Kimmel, Michael, *Manhood in America: A Cultural History*, Free Press, 1996.

> *Glengarry Glen Ross* takes place in a world composed solely of men, at war with one another or working together; women are never seen, though they have an effect on the actions and motivations of the salesmen and their targets. Kimmel's book is an in-depth study of the transformation of the concept of masculinity and "manhood" over several centuries in America and is worth reading particularly for its take on that transformation in the 1980s and 1990s, when the play was written and the film was produced.

SUGGESTED SEARCH TERMS

Glengarry Glen Ross

Glengarry Glen Ross adaptation

David Mamet

Mamet AND Glengarry Glen Ross

James Foley

sales techniques

office culture

real estate scams

workplace AND stress

masculinity AND twentieth-century America

The God of Carnage

YASMINA REZA

2006

In Yasmina Reza's *The God of Carnage*, first produced in 2006, two couples meet to make peace after a playground fight between their sons leaves one boy with two broken teeth. Though the afternoon begins with espresso, small talk, and a spirit of compromise, the Reilles and the Vallons are soon consumed by the same animal rage that set their sons against each other. Within an hour, there are tears, vomit, tantrums, name calling, and violence, as the conventions of polite society break down to reveal the brutality beneath the polished middle-class exteriors of Alain, Annette, Véronique, and Michel. Winner of the Molière Award, the Laurence Olivier Award, and three Tony Awards, including Best Play, Best Director, and Best Leading Actress, *The God of Carnage* takes delight in the collapse of civilization.

AUTHOR BIOGRAPHY

Reza was born May 1, 1959, in Paris, France. She attended the University of Paris X in Nanterre, where she studied sociology and theater. After enrolling in the Jacques Lecocq International Drama School in Paris, she began a short-lived acting career. Struggling to find work as an actress, she began to write plays instead.

In 1987 her first play, *Conversations after a Burial* (*Conversations après un enterrement*) was

Yasmina Reza (© Everett Collection Inc | Alamy Stock Photo)

produced and won the coveted Molière Award. Her second play, *The Winter Crossing* (*La traversée de l'hiver*), was produced in 1989, for which Reza won a second Molière Award. International success and recognition came with the production of her third play, '*Art*,' which debuted in Paris in 1994 before opening in London's West End in 1996 and on Broadway in New York City in 1998. '*Art*' won the Molière Award in 1994, the Tony Award for Best Play in 1998, and the Laurence Olivier Award for Best Comedy that same year. She followed this success with *The Unexpected Man* (*L'homme du hasard*) in 1995, *Life x 3* (*Trois versions de la vie*) in 2000, and *A Spanish Play* (*Une pièce espagnole*) in 2004 and embarked upon a career as a novelist. She spent a year with French president Nicolas Sarkozy following his 2007 election campaign. Her book on the experience, *Dawn, Dusk, or Night* (*L'aube, le soir ou le nuit*), published in 2007, was wildly popular in France.

The God of Carnage (*Le dieu du carnage*) premiered in Zurich, Switzerland, in 2006. It then showed in Paris in 2007, London in 2008, and New York City in 2009. Reza became the first female playwright to win two Laurence Olivier Awards when *The God of Carnage* won for Best Comedy in 2009. That same year she became the first female playwright to win two Tony Awards for Best Play. In addition, Marcia Gay Harden won the Tony Award for Best Leading Actress in a Play for her portrayal of Véronique (changed to Veronica in the American production), and Matthew Warchus won the Tony Award for Best Director of a Play.

Reza is reticent toward the media, and little is known of her life outside her writing career. In *The Plays of Yasmina Reza on the English and American Stage*, Amanda Giguere writes of the mystery surrounding Reza's personal life: "Although Reza does occasionally give interviews, she has been known to avoid the press, and has even admitted to warping the truth when speaking to reporters."

PLOT SUMMARY

The God of Carnage begins as two couples in their forties—the Vallons and the Reilles—meet for the first time to discuss a violent incident between their sons. They sit facing each other in the Vallons's living room, which features a coffee table stacked with art books and a vase of tulips. Véronique Vallon reads a statement about the incident aloud for the group: following an argument at the Aspirant Dunant Gardens, eleven-year-old Ferdinand Reille, armed with a stick, struck Bruno Vallon in the face. The blow caused Bruno to lose two teeth and sustain nerve damage in his gums.

Alain Reille objects to the phrase "armed." Véronique suggests, "furnished" instead. They agree on this terminology, and Véronique corrects the statement. The couples thank each other for their willingness to settle the matter among themselves like adults. As Véronique says: "Fortunately, there is still such a thing as the art of co-existence, is there not?"

Annette Reille asks after Bruno's affected nerve, and the Vallons explain that the recovery will be complicated as his teeth are still growing, making permanent implants impossible until he is at least eighteen years old. After Annette compliments the tulips, Véronique tells her that Bruno refused to identify Ferdinand as his attacker at

MEDIA ADAPTATIONS

- *The God of Carnage*, adapted in a film titled *Carnage* by Roman Polanski and starring Jodie Foster, Kate Winslet, Christoph Waltz, and John C. Reilly, was produced by SBS Productions and distributed by Sony Picture Classics in 2011.

first. Michel Vallon, her husband, corrects her assessment that this is not necessarily admirable, as he did not want to be known as a snitch to his friends. Annette asks how they found out Ferdinand's name. The couple explains that they told Bruno that Ferdinand must be held accountable or else he might strike again and that surely his parents would want to know.

Alain's phone vibrates. He takes the call. He tells the man on the line, Maurice, that a report was published in *Le Monde* claiming that a pharmaceutical drug, Antril, has been discovered to cause a range of serious side effects. Alain tells Maurice in sharp tones that this discovery is extremely inconvenient to them and to find out where else this report has been published. He hangs up, apologizing to the room. He tells the Vallons that he is a lawyer. Michel is a wholesaler of household goods. Véronique is a writer who works part-time at a bookshop. A specialist in African studies, her book on the tragedy in Darfur will soon be published.

Annette asks if Bruno is their only child. Véronique tells her that Bruno has a nine-year-old sister, Camille, who is angry with her father for letting her hamster out. Michel explains that he hated the hamster, which made incessant noise throughout the night in its cage. Bruno could not get his needed rest and recovery with the hamster carrying on, and since Michel had always despised it, he decided finally to act. He left it outside in the gutter, thinking it would run free. Instead it sat paralyzed. In the morning it had vanished.

Véronique asks what Annette does for a living. Annette is in wealth management. Véronique

suggests that Ferdinand apologize to Bruno. Annette agrees, but Alain claims that Ferdinand does not understand the gravity of the situation: he is still a child. Véronique says he is not a baby, but Michel counters that he is not an adult either.

Michel offers the couple something to drink and insists the Reilles try the *clafoutis* his wife made. Alain asks Michel about his job selling household hardware, and Michel admits there is not much money in the business but it offers some stability. Annette cuts in suddenly to ask why Michel left the hamster in the gutter once he realized it was frozen with fear. Michel explains that he absolutely will not touch rodents. He had tipped it out of its cage onto the street and could not bring himself to pick it up with his bare hands. Véronique returns from the kitchen with the *clafoutis*, espresso, and water. When Annette asks what is in the *clafoutis*, she is taken aback when Véronique answers that there are apples and pears. The dessert is traditionally made with cherries, but this variation is Michel's mother's recipe. They try it and express delight at the taste. The secret ingredient is gingerbread crumbs.

Alain says that at least something good has come of the incident: a new recipe for *clafoutis*. Véronique takes offense, saying: "I'd have preferred it if it hadn't cost my son two teeth." Alain's phone rings, saving him from the awkward moment. Speaking to Maurice once more, he asks how long the company knew about the side effects and why they did not recall the product. He hangs up, dialing another number. As he speaks, he wolfs down *clafoutis*. He explains to a man named Serge that Maurice and the company have known about the dangerous side effects for two years. He says rather than reply immediately, they will acknowledge the report only if the story spreads. He hangs up, rejoining the conversation.

Speaking of the *clafoutis* recipe, Véronique mentions that Michel's mother must have an operation on her knee. The Reilles compliment the Vallons on their openness toward reconciliation. Annette brushes this aside: "Not at all. How many parents standing up for their children become infantile themselves?" Then, they immediately begin to argue over whether Ferdinand has disfigured Bruno. Véronique says yes. Annette says no. Michel says he has been disfigured temporarily. He wants to arrange a meeting for the boys, where Ferdinand can apologize. The couples wonder if they should be present or not.

When the Vallons ask if Ferdinand feels like apologizing, the Reilles are firm that his emotions toward the situation do not matter. Alain says: "Madame, our son is a savage. To hope for any kind of spontaneous repentance would be fanciful." The Reilles prepare to leave. They ask the Vallons to bring Bruno to their home around seven-thirty. Michel objects. He thinks Ferdinand should come to them, as Bruno is the victim. Véronique insists both parents be present. In that case, Alain says as his phone vibrates again, the reconciliation cannot take place tonight. He answers, telling the person on the other end that there is no evidence of wrongdoing, then hangs up. When Véronique expresses doubt that the apology will be effective, since the Reilles seem convinced of their son's savagery, Alain tells the Vallons that obviously they are better parents than he and his wife but that they cannot expect them to rise to their level immediately. Michel tries to urge everyone to calm down. Annette agrees, and the couple accepts Michel's offer to stay for another coffee while they try to work things out.

While they wait on coffee, Annette peruses the art books on the table. When Michel returns with the coffee, they try to understand the nature of the boys' argument. Bruno would not let Ferdinand join his gang. Michel did not know that Bruno had a gang. He thinks this is great news. He had a gang when he was young. Alain says he had a gang of his own as well. Michel is overcome with a memory of fighting and beating another boy who was bigger than he. When he describes the altercation, Véronique scolds him. She wants to personally speak to Ferdinand. Alain says she can if she wants, but he doubts it will have any effect. They get into a spat over each other's phrasing, which Annette tries to break up by agreeing to bring Ferdinand over that night. Alain's phone rings.

He tells the person on the other end not to take the drug off the market, or else the company will be admitting liability for the side effects. He says they will think of the victims later. He urges them not to make any statements and then phones a colleague. He tells him to write a press release denying all accusations. When he gets off the phone, Michel tells him pharmaceutical companies have no morals, only an eye for profit. The men argue, with Alain belittling Michel's career selling doorknobs and toilet fittings.

Véronique cuts in to their sarcastic exchange to ask if the Reilles plan on punishing Ferdinand.

Annette complains that she feels sick. As the Vallons try to help Annette, Alain calls his office but cannot find Serge. Annette says they will punish their son in a way they see fit. Michel agrees. Véronique disagrees—she thinks it is their business as well. Alain answers a call. Annette shouts at him to hang up the phone and join the conversation.

Alain says how dare she shout; Serge heard everything she said, and he is only here as a favor to her. Annette says she is about to vomit and begins to panic. Alain tries to talk her down, calling her Woof-woof, his pet name for her. She tells him to get away from her, sick of his disinterest in their domestic life. She vomits everywhere: on Alain, on the art books, all over the table. Chaos ensues. Alain shouts at her for not going to the bathroom to vomit. Véronique grabs a bowl for her in case it happens again. Michel swears it cannot be the *clafoutis*; it is nerves—a panic attack over her responsibilities as a mother. Annette half-listens to him, vomiting weakly into the bowl.

One of the art books ruined is out of print, and Michel works to salvage what he can of his wife's precious possession. Annette and Alain go to the bathroom to clean themselves up while Michel and Véronique clean the living room, spraying perfume and attempting to clean the table. They agree that the Reilles are awful, but Véronique scolds Michel for continually siding with them. They make fun of Annette's pet name, Woof-woof, until Alain interrupts them—having entered the room unseen—to defend the pet name. He hands them the hair dryer to help save the art books. They reconcile, the Vallons explaining that they call each other "darjeeling," which is just as silly. When Annette returns to the living room, Véronique apologizes for caring more about her book than about Annette's health.

The couples return to discussing their sons. Annette suggests that name calling, which Bruno engaged in before the attack, is another form of violence. If attacked, people naturally defend themselves. Michel tells her that she seems to have more energy now that she has vomited. He is admonished for being crude, but he argues that he will not allow the children to pull him down to their level. Alain and Annette say they must leave, and Véronique tells them to go, because she gives up.

Michel's mother calls. The doctors have given her Antril—the same medication Alain has been discussing—for her blood pressure. He tells her to stop taking it immediately. Michel stops the couple on the way out to tell them that it is clear from their behavior where Ferdinand gets his attitude. Annette fires back that at least they did not murder an innocent hamster, leaving it shivering with fear in the gutter.

Véronique agrees wholeheartedly, to Michel's shock. She thinks the hamster must have met a terrible fate. Michel defends himself. He thought the hamster would be happy to be free. Besides, he is terrified of rodents, snakes, and anything close to the ground. Alain asks why Véronique did not go looking for the hamster. She says Michel kept what he had done a secret. It had disappeared by the time she went searching. Annette asks if he feels guilty. Michel says no, that he is thrilled that it is gone. Annette counters that if Michel feels no guilt for murdering a hamster, why do the Vallons expect Ferdinand to feel guilt over beating Bruno?

Michel says he has had enough of these inane philosophical discussions. The truth is that he does not care: he is as uninterested as Alain. The meeting was Véronique's idea. Véronique says she is standing up for civilization. She begins to cry. Michel tries to comfort her unsuccessfully, before suggesting everyone take a drink of rum. Alain accepts the offer, forgetting his haste to leave. The Reilles take over comforting Véronique, and Alain admits that—like Michel—he had to be dragged to this meeting by his wife. Annette accepts a glass of rum, too. Véronique demands a drink, but Michel says no. They fight over the bottle until Michel relents. Michel tells them all that marriage and children ruin lives. Annette does not believe he means it, but Véronique assures her that he does. Alain pours himself another glass and takes a call. Annette complains loudly to the Vallons about Alain's excessive cell phone use. She says she will be sick again. Véronique hands her the basin in case she needs it. When he hangs up and sees Annette with the basin, he tells her that just because the Vallons have a miserable marriage does not mean they need to compete. Véronique starts to argue, but Alain's phone rings again. When he gets off the phone, he explains his philosophy toward the attack:

> They're young, they're kids, kids have always given each other a good drubbing during break. It's a law of life. . . . I believe in the god of carnage. He has ruled, uninterruptedly, since the dawn of time.

Annette dry-heaves but says that she is fine. Alain lectures Véronique on the state of affairs in the Congo, which he recently visited. When he brings up Darfur, Michel tells Alain not to get her started. Véronique throws herself, kicking and punching, at her husband, until Alain pulls her off. He says he is starting to like Véronique. Véronique tells him she does not like him. After dry-heaving again, Annette continues to drink rum. Véronique joins her and declares: "We're living in France according to the principles of Western society. What goes on in Aspirant Dunant Gardens reflects the values of Western society!"

Michel asks if spousal abuse is one of those principles. Alain says Michel should be flattered by her attention. Annette and Véronique mock their husbands for their boyhood gangs and the warrior urges that keep them from being any practical help at all around the house or with the children. Alain's phone rings again. Annette grabs the phone from him and drops it into the vase of tulips.

Annette and Véronique celebrate while Michel and Alain panic. Michel grabs the phone and uses the hair dryer to attempt to dry it. Alain tells Annette she should be locked away: his whole life was on that phone. Annette repeats this phrase, mocking him. The men scramble to save the phone while the women laugh cruelly and drink more rum. After a long minute of Michel's careful blow-drying, Alain tells him it is ruined. After a silence, Annette declares that she feels great. She believes a man who relies so heavily on an accessory appears weak. A man should wear his solitude proudly. Véronique says she has never been unhappier than she is at this moment. Alain slumps on the couch, defeated. The house phone rings.

Michel's mother has called back, asking about the medication. Michel hands the phone to Alain, demanding that he tell his mother everything. They talk, with Michel's mother mistakenly believing he is a doctor and Alain recommending she stop taking the medication at once. Michel takes the phone back and says good-bye. Annette asks if she should bring Ferdinand over tonight or not, though she personally believes there are wrongs on both sides. Véronique says she has had enough of Annette. She grabs Annette's handbag and throws it at the door. Annette cries for Alain to do something in a high-pitched voice, as if she were a little girl. Véronique mocks her. Alain gathers the pieces of his cell phone while Michel scolds Véronique for acting as if she has the high moral ground above them all. Annette tries to keep drinking, but Alain stops her. Véronique calls her a phony. Alain agrees, saying that Véronique is the only person involved who actually cares about the issue at hand and that her desire to make the world a fair, balanced place makes her less attractive to men and makes Michel depressed.

Véronique asks who cares what Alain likes in a woman, especially considering the way he conducts himself. Alain observes in the same tone that now she is yelling. Véronique asks if Annette yelled when she found out her son is a violent brute. The women start to taunt each other—calling their sons the same names their sons called each other before the fight. Annette pulls out the tulips from the vase and shreds them, making a great mess. She calls the flowers pathetic and declares this the worst day of her life as well.

After a stunned pause, Michel picks up Annette's glasses case from the floor and hands it to her. Alain starts to pick up flowers, but Michel tells him to stop. The phone rings. Véronique answers. Their daughter is on the phone asking about the hamster. Véronique assures her that they searched everywhere but that the hamster will survive on any number of things: leaves, acorns, worms, snails, even food from the trash. When she hangs up, Michel says that the hamster must be having a feast. Véronique says, flatly, no. After a silence, Michel asks, "What do we know?"

CHARACTERS

Didier Leglu

Didier was a boy whom Michel fought in single combat when he was the leader of his childhood gang. Michel remembers beating Didier with pride, as Didier was bigger than Michel.

Maurice

Maurice is Alain's client, who is panicking in light of a recent report that Antril, a drug that his company sells, causes ataxia and death. Alain has a very low opinion of Maurice.

Alain Reille

Alain is Ferdinand's father, Annette's husband, and a lawyer. While the couples talk, he takes calls from his client and colleagues over a recently published report that the client's pharmaceutical company produces a pill, Antril, which causes physically debilitating side effects. From the start, Alain urges his client not to admit any

knowledge of the side effects, though the company has known of them for over two years. Alain tries to leave the Vallons's home several times, telling them that Annette can handle this problem as he is utterly incapable of helping in these domestic affairs. Alain admits that he believes in the god of carnage, and his attitude toward his son's attack on Bruno reflects this belief. While he and Michel see eye to eye about matters of boyhood aggression and adult masculinity, Alain and Véronique do not mix well. He calls her insistence on pursuing what is morally right and fair to be an inherently unattractive trait in a woman. He attempts to explain the Darfur situation to her—though she is an expert in the situation, with a book coming out on the subject. He approves of her only when she physically assaults her husband. Alain is an insensitive but authoritative presence in the argument, arguing in favor of the brutal nature of existence. He admits that he has no real interest in the outcome of the discussion, as he considers his son a savage incapable of understanding the consequences of his actions.

Annette Reille

Annette is Ferdinand's mother, Alain's second wife, and works in wealth management. She finds aspects of her husband's behavior, especially his views on domestic roles and his phone use, literally sickening: she vomits after arguing with him over their roles in the home as well as the calls he insists on taking throughout their conversation with the Vallons. After vomiting, she goes on the offensive—accusing Bruno of provoking Ferdinand into his violent outburst. At different times throughout the protracted argument, Annette is aligned with Alain, Michel, and Véronique against the others. Ultimately, the room turns on her, with all three parents agreeing that she is a phony who does not actually care about the situation. She gets very drunk on rum with Véronique, though she retches several times into the bowl the Vallons have provided her each time her husband rants about gender roles or takes a phone call. She and Véronique mock their husbands for their delusions of masculinity until Véronique throws Annette's purse at the door and teases her cruelly for crying for Alain to help. Though Annette offers several times to bring her son over to apologize, this never provides an end to the debate.

Ferdinand Reille

Ferdinand is Alain and Annette's eleven-year-old son. After Bruno Vallon tells him he cannot be a member of Bruno's gang, Ferdinand strikes Bruno with a stick, knocking out two of his teeth. Though Annette is willing to bring Ferdinand to the Vallons's home so that he may apologize to Bruno, Alain maintains that Ferdinand is a savage who has no remorse for or understanding of his violent actions.

Serge

Serge is Alain's colleague, for whom he has a great deal of respect. Alain passes on the information Maurice provides him about the medication Antril to Serge throughout the play. He scolds his wife for shouting about Alain's incessant cell phone use when Serge can hear her.

Bruno Vallon

Bruno is the son of Michel and Véronique. The leader of a gang of boys, he insulted Ferdinand while the boys were playing at Aspirant Dunant Gardens. He called Ferdinand names and told him he could not join Bruno's gang. Ferdinand struck Bruno with a stick, causing significant facial swelling and breaking two of his teeth, one of which suffers nerve damage. Bruno will not give up the name of his attacker at first, unwilling to be seen as a snitch by his peers. It is only after Michel and Véronique convince him that it is the right thing to do that he admits that Ferdinand is the culprit.

Camille Vallon

Camille is the nine-year-old daughter of Véronique and Michel. After Michel leaves her hamster in the street, he attempts to convince Camille that it ran away. Camille does not believe her father, and during the play's events she is so angry with him that she will not speak to him. At the end of the play she calls her mother from her friend's house, asking if they have found her hamster. Véronique assures her that the hamster is happy to live in the wild and more than capable of taking care of itself.

Michel Vallon

Michel is Véronique's husband and Bruno's father. He is a wholesaler of home fixtures. Though he seems at first to be mild and companionable, he is, in fact, as disinterested in the proceedings of the meeting as Alain. He has a phobia of rodents that led him to release his daughter's hamster in the street, an unforgivable act of cruelty in the eyes of the gathered group as well as his daughter, who is not speaking to him. Like his

son, he was the leader of a gang when he was a boy, and he recognizes Bruno's reluctance to identify Ferdinand as his attacker as concern over being considered a snitch, not because of any righteous sense of honor, as Véronique believes. Michel switches sides constantly throughout the conversation. His wife scolds him over his flip-flopping when they get a moment alone. When Annette dunks her husband's phone in the vase, he works desperately to save it—using the hair dryer on the individual pieces long after Alain has given up hope for its survival. Michel puts on a liberal act to match his wife's, which soon crumbles to reveal his true self. He finds Véronique's concern for doing what is right exhausting and believes that schoolyard fights are a fact of life. The wives tease him for speaking as if he is a warrior when he is really so scared of the hamster that he cannot pick it up from the street once it is obvious the animal is paralyzed with fear.

Michel Vallon's Mother

Michel's mother is preparing for an operation on her knee. Véronique serves her recipe for *clafoutis* with apples and pears to the group. When Michel discovers that her doctors have given her Antril to lower her blood pressure prior to the surgery, he tells her to stop taking it immediately, fearing the side effects. When she calls again, Michel puts Alain on the phone to tell her to stop taking her medication. She mistakes him for a doctor.

Véronique Vallon

Véronique is Michel's wife and Bruno's mother. She is a writer with a book on the Darfur tragedy coming out in January. She is a moral crusader, whose insistence that the apology between the boys be meaningful stalls the proceedings between the two couples and leads directly to their chaotic fight. Véronique is acknowledged by the end of the play as the only decent parent in the room, but no one especially likes her for her zealousness. Even Michel is desperate to avoid talk of Darfur—the area of her expertise—so that he will not have to hear her go on about the injustices there. This leads to Véronique's physically attacking her husband, revealing her to be the most violent of the group. Véronique believes in civility and Western society, though she is more concerned about her rare art books than she is over Annette's health after Annette is suddenly sick. It is important to her that

Ferdinand apologize sincerely, and she cannot accept Alain's belief that his son is a savage who is sorry for nothing. She forms a brief bond with Annette over their husbands' ridiculous pretensions at masculinity, which is shattered after she throws Annette's handbag at the door and mocks her crying to her husband for help. When Alain condescends to Véronique about the political landscape of Darfur as well as how an attractive woman should behave, she tells him she could not care less what he thinks, as he is addicted to his phone and a terrible father. At the end of the play, Véronique reassures her daughter so effectively that even Michel believes her lie that the hamster will thrive in the wild.

THEMES

Childhood

A main concern of *The God of Carnage* is the question of childhood. At eleven years old, can Ferdinand be held responsible for his actions, be expected to apologize sincerely, or even comprehend what he has done? Is Ferdinand's attack symptomatic of a maladjusted personality? Or is this violence, like Bruno's gang, a part of childhood? While the parents attempt to answer these questions, they reveal themselves to be as violent, unapologetic, and capable of spontaneous brutality as their sons. They argue, mutter sarcastic slights against one another, interrupt, shout, and cry. They show no self-discipline, gulping down cake, rum, and cigars—indulging in vices like kids in a candy store. They tease, betray, and show no pity for their partners while treating the other couple with contempt and condescension. Their capacity for cruelty seems endless, and when they finally do collapse, it seems more from physical exhaustion than the exhaustion of their ability to find fault with one another. Annette vomits and cries out for protection in a little girl's voice. Véronique bullies those weaker than she is with physical violence, beating her husband and throwing Annette's purse. After Annette breaks Alain's favorite toy (his phone), he pouts, refusing to interact with the others anymore, while Michel tries to placate everyone at once, as if she were an anxious child of combative parents. Yet Michel, too, has shown a child's heartlessness in his selfish disposal of the hamster. The adults are too immature themselves to solve the issue of their sons' immaturity, but their

TOPICS FOR FURTHER STUDY

- Read Nancy Werlin's young-adult novel *The Rules of Survival* (2006). How does Alain's theory of the god of carnage apply to Werlin's novel? How do Matt's rules of survival differ from Alain's? What similarities and differences can you find between Matt, Ferdinand, and Bruno? Organize your answers into an essay.

- In small groups, act out an excerpt from the play. One member of your group should act as the director, giving the actor's notes on their performances and filming the scene for presentation to the class. Free video editing software is available at EDpuzzle.com.

- Choose one of the four main characters to examine more closely. Create a blog dedicated to this character in which you make a minimum of five posts exploring their beliefs, behavior, career, patterns of speech, and relationship to the other characters. Include photos of actors or actresses who have played the character you choose. Free blog space is available at blogspot.com.

- Reza's stage directions call for the action of *The God of Carnage* to take place in "A living room. No realism. Nothing superfluous." Design a set for the play. You may sketch, draw, paint, build a three-dimensional model of, or create a collage of your ideal set. Along with your design, write a brief explanation of how you feel your set design is appropriate for the play and Reza's instructions.

childishness raises more troubling questions. At forty, are these adults responsible for their own behavior? Can they say sorry and mean it? Do they understand what they have done?

Social Values

The meeting between the Vallons and Reilles takes place beneath the flag of upholding social values. Rather than squabble in court, the parents have decided that their reasonableness as adults will be enough to find a satisfying compromise. Determined to act civil, they make small talk over espresso and cake, congratulating themselves on their politesse. Véronique is especially firm in her belief that the values of Western society hinge on peacekeeping and personal growth. Michel demonstrates these values in action by pretending to care as much as his wife does about the meeting, avoiding conflict through playacting agreement. Annette, too, is willing to make a show of refined manners, but Alain breaks the rules immediately by taking calls on his cell phone. This rude behavior suggests that the meeting is not important to him, and he quickly admits that, in fact, it is not. He is the most honest about his disinterest because, as a rich, white male, he is allowed more leeway in society to break the rules.

His dismissal of the meeting's importance infuriates Véronique, who is a social crusader and enforcer of civility, but Véronique, too, steps over the line of polite society when she demands to know how Ferdinand will be punished, essentially telling the Reilles how to raise their child correctly. As the two dominant spouses, Alain and Véronique represent opposite philosophies of civilization. Véronique believes in fairness, equality, and compassion, while Alain believes in the god of carnage: the instincts to kill, steal, and exploit for personal gain. As pettiness and egotism gradually replace the couples' desire to uphold a façade of pleasantness, the god of carnage is set loose in the room. Each character spirals out of control, emerging from their disguises as good, reasonable, and respectful adults to reveal their grotesque true forms: childish, rampaging monsters with no concern for anyone but themselves.

Violence

Violence is the ultimate force in the play. The couples gather to settle the aftermath of violence between their sons only to be consumed by violence themselves. Véronique's insistence that people are good and that society brings individuals closer in a positive way is drowned out by the beating of war drums in her own living room. In fact, she is the most physically violent of the group, attacking her husband in a blind rage that makes Alain—high priest of carnage—laugh and declare after an hour of bitter argument that he likes her. Violence comes in all forms in the play: an attack with a stick, single combat, the presumed death of a hamster, the horrific

The play is set in a comfortable living room
(© Rodenberg Photography | Shutterstock.com)

reality of Darfur, shredded tulips, a destroyed phone, vomiting, verbal abuse, a scuffle over a bottle of rum, a purse hurled against the door, and the list goes on. Violence, not peace, is the characters' true nature, for when the trappings of polite society fall away, the violent tendencies of each character are unleashed full force. Véronique's goal of finding a compromise between families is revealed as a self-serving interest in stroking her own ego as a peacekeeper. Alain and Michel glory in the memory of their own schoolyard gangs, revealing their bias. Annette is too exhausted from the solitude of her child rearing, left alone while Alain ignores their family in favor of an affair with his telephone. She simply agrees to Véronique's requests, trying to speed the process up. The peace process is hopeless in such a gathering of greed, disillusionment, cowardice, and narcissism.

STYLE

In Medias Res

To start a work of literature in medias res means to start in the middle of the situation rather than from the beginning. *The God of Carnage* begins in medias res as Véronique is reading a statement describing the attack aloud to the Reilles. Rather than begin the play with the attack itself (the true origin of the drama) or at the beginning of the meeting, the in medias res introduction has all four parents seated in the Vallons's living room discussing the incident. Reza uses this technique to obscure the details of the attack, so that aspects of the incident (for example, "armed" versus "furnished") are up for debate. Like the parents, the audience is not present for the attack, learning only by word of mouth what happened. Without any witnesses to the event present, either in the characters or the audience, the only descriptions given of the attack are subjective—told through the eyes of the parents who are searching for blame.

Monologue

A monologue is a speech given by a single character in a drama. For example, Annette gives a lengthy, uninterrupted monologue on the subject of masculinity after the men give up their effort to save Alain's phone. After announcing that everyone feels better now that the phone is dead, she tells an anecdote about seeing an attractive man carrying a shoulder bag and finding him instantly undesirable. She believes a man should have an air of solitude, not be attached to an accessory like a phone or shoulder bag. Another example of a monologue is Véronique's reassurance of her daughter at the end of the play. Her long list of what the hamster will eat in the wild strikes a positive, healing note after so much destruction, though she reveals after hanging up that she does not believe a word of what she has just said. Monologues highlight a character's state of mind, personality, and patterns of speech, as they become the temporary focal point of the audience and other characters.

HISTORICAL CONTEXT

Darfur Tragedy

Considered by the United Nations to be the world's worst humanitarian crisis, the situation in Darfur is the result of the combination of several factors. After Sudan gained independence from British and Anglo-Egyptian rule in 1956, political chaos and civil war ravaged the country. In addition to endemic political instability, a devastating drought in the 1980s caused desertification of previously farmable land and resulted in ongoing famine. In 2002, before the outbreak of war, the population of the Darfur region of Sudan was estimated at six million, the majority of whom were farmers organized into groups on tracts of land called Dar. Traditionally the farmers of a Dar share the land with one another as well as with nomads who travel seasonally with their livestock. However, following the drought, tensions between farmers and nomads rose, as competition for fertile land grew heated. This discontent, fostered by the neglect of the Darfur region by the Sudanese government and the exploitation of Darfur's resources and its people by neighboring Libya, began to fester. Darfurians felt the Sudanese government in Khartoum ignored their increasingly desperate situation. Rebel groups began to form.

In February of 2003, the escalating tensions between the government and two rebel groups in particular—the Sudan Liberation Army (SLA) and the Justice and Equality Movement (JEM)—finally snapped as rebel forces attacked the al-Fashir airport. In response, the Sudanese government created the Janjawid, a militia recruited for the purpose of destroying the rebellion by any means necessary. The result has been the death of three hundred thousand Darfurians and the displacement of two million refugees. The international community was outraged by the atrocities committed by the Sudanese army and Janjawid, but Sudan has resisted much of the peacekeeping efforts. The United Nations International Criminal Court issued a warrant for Sudanese president Omer al-Bashir's arrest in March 2009, on charges of genocide and crimes against humanity.

The Bourgeoisie

In France, the middle class is also known as the bourgeoisie, making up more than half the population. First rising to prominence in the early to mid-1800s as the result of the advances of the Industrial Revolution, the bourgeoisie drive consumerist culture, seeking out material pleasures such as home furnishings, technology, and fashion. With a better education than the lower class, the bourgeoisie value participation in and knowledge of politics. Members of the bourgeoisie have time and energy to devote to changing the world around them for the better through activism, rather than spending their time in the act of daily survival, as is a necessity for those in the lower class, who cannot make ends meet. Concerning the early development of the strong social values of the bourgeoisie, Peter Stearns writes in "The Rise of the Middle Classes" in *European Society in Upheaval*: "They agreed that the family was the proper basis for society and the goal of economic effort. They agreed that sons should be give a good start in life, through...education and a solid inheritance."

Alan is a workaholic lawyer, always on the phone *(© TATSIANAMA | Shutterstock.com)*

The bourgeoisie are culturally and politically engaged and often take an active part in shaping their society and upholding its values.

CRITICAL OVERVIEW

The God of Carnage debuted to positive reviews, winning the 2009 Tony Award for Best Play as well as the 2009 Laurence Olivier Award for Best Comedy. Susannah Clapp writes in "Are You Sitting Uncomfortably?" for the London *Guardian* in praise of Reza's "singular theatrical shocks, shrewd circumstantial detail and soliloquies that give [actors] a moment in the sun with a big central subject."

Many critics note that while the play's text may at times seem dark, the stage brings the eccentricities and inherent humor in the couples' irreconcilable differences to light. Elysa Gardner calls the play "scabrously funny," in her review for *USA Today*, going on to say: "It's just a matter of time before the meeting devolves into an orgy of verbal and physical brawling—and a

showcase for first-rate ensemble acting." As a critique of middle-class values, the critics agree unanimously that *The God of Carnage* delivers a gut punch. In her review of the play for the London *Independent*, Alice Jones writes: "Reza has proved that she can skewer the middle classes like no other, revelling in the grotesque prejudices not only of her characters but also of the audience."

The combination of dark humor and subject matter that touches on the common fears of its audience results in new heights of hilarity as social nightmares (vomiting, crying, name calling, and tantrums) come to life. Terry Teachout writes in "Beating Up the Bourgeoisie" for the *Wall Street Journal*: "Reza is back on Broadway with another of her slightly pretentious, consummately effective comedies of middle-class manners. . . . By the play's end . . . the audience has laughed itself well past silly." As the couples' attempts at civility are shredded like Véronique's tulips, the audience sees what lies beneath the characters's adult identities: children just as brutal and unapologetic as their sons. Lucy Komisar writes in her review for the *Komisar Scoop*: "Reza's *God of Carnage* smartly shows the disintegration of the thin veneer of civilization that keeps people civil." *The God of Carnage* delights in the slow descent of the Reilles and Vallons from respectable, worldly citizens to violent beasts. Ben Brantley writes in "Rumble in the Living Room" for the *New York Times*: "A study in the tension between civilized surface and savage instinct, this play . . . is itself a satisfyingly primitive entertainment with an intellectual veneer."

CRITICISM

Amy L. Miller

Miller is a graduate of the University of Cincinnati. In the following essay, she examines the incongruity between Alain, Annette, Michel, and Véronique's language and their actions in Reza's The God of Carnage.

In Reza's *The God of Carnage*, four adults meet to find a solution to the animosity between their young sons, only to find that they, too, despise one another. The peacekeeping summit of the Vallons and Reilles deteriorates gradually: first devolving from four adults attempting a polite discussion to two couples trading insults, before collapsing into chaos as the coalition of each set of spouses fails, leaving every man and woman to fend for themselves. The play, which is performed without intermission in a single setting, examines the widening gap between the characters's words and actions as civilized language fails, replaced by outbursts of expressive violence. Annette, Alain, Michel, and Véronique arrive at the meeting disguised as adults—the concerned mother, successful businessman, supportive father, and rational peacekeeper—but soon drive each other, through taunting, teasing, bullying, and cruelty, to shed this false identity and reveal their true selves. Véronique declares: "What goes on in Aspirant Dunant Gardens reflects the values of Western society!" She means that actions in the public space of the garden are an expression of cultural identity, but what happens in the privacy of her living room is no different. The collapse of civilization takes place in small scale, from the betrayal of alliances as husband and wife turn on each other to the degradation of personal behavior as they abandon politeness in favor of brutality to the destruction of the environment as the living room is trashed. Alain may be correct in his belief in the god of carnage, but the embrace of such a deity

> ANNETTE, ALAIN, MICHEL, AND VÉRONIQUE ARRIVE AT THE MEETING DISGUISED AS ADULTS—THE CONCERNED MOTHER, SUCCESSFUL BUSINESSMAN, SUPPORTIVE FATHER, AND RATIONAL PEACEKEEPER— BUT SOON DRIVE EACH OTHER, THROUGH TAUNTING, TEASING, BULLYING, AND CRUELTY, TO SHED THIS FALSE IDENTITY AND REVEAL THEIR TRUE SELVES."

leaves the group with nothing to show for themselves but hurt feelings and broken connections.

Komisar writes: "Reza . . . has a habit of locating her dramas in living rooms. These tête-à-têtes ought to show the height of culture. Instead, they display the dark sides of polite society." The living room seems less a place for greeting guests and sitting down for a comfortable, intelligent discussion in the play than a cage no different from the hamster's—a place the four inhabitants are desperate to escape but cannot find a way out of either through discussion or simply walking out the door. Ironically, though it is the inanity and unpleasantness of the conversation that drive the Reilles to stand up to leave on multiple occasions, it is also the ongoing, frustrated discourse that lures them back into their seats, whether in the form of a plea to try again to find a solution or a parting shot fired just as they turn their backs to go. They cannot escape, and neither can the audience, as the play proceeds uninterrupted from start to finish. Like unhappy hamsters in a cage, the characters eventually tire themselves out, collapsing in their seats in emotional and physical exhaustion. Yet even then the Reilles do not leave. When the curtain goes down, the Vallons and Reilles are exactly where they started: the living room. The only difference is that they have both literally and figuratively destroyed the space they share.

The corrosion of the social fabric holding the group together can be blamed on the hypocrisies of the Reilles and Vallons. The disastrous results of the meeting represent four disingenuous people attempting to make believe that they are invested in finding a meaningful solution, with Véronique the driving force behind their

WHAT DO I READ NEXT?

- In Elizabeth Ross's young-adult novel *Belle Epoque* (2013), a desperate runaway in Paris answers an ad to serve as a plain friend to make the daughter of a countess seem more beautiful by comparison. Yet as Maude learns the secrets of Parisian society and the family she serves, keeping her secret becomes an impossible challenge.

- In Reza's first play, *Conversations after a Burial* (2000), six mourners gather after the burial of a man to discuss his life and death. Each has a unique perspective on Simon Weinberg's life, whether siblings, spouses, friends, or lovers, and each is allowed in their grief to recall the Simon they knew and loved best.

- A dinner party between two couples turns disastrous in Ayad Akhtar's Pulitzer Prize–winning play *Disgraced* (2012). The four successful friends—Amir, an ex-Muslim lawyer battling with internalized Islamophobia following the September 11 terrorist attacks; his wife, Emily; his colleague Jory; and Jory's husband, Isaac—quickly become embattled across lines of race, class, religion, and politics, as opinions are taken personally and lead to devastating revelations of betrayal.

- Timothy Murray's *Mimesis, Masochism, and Mime: The Politics of Theatricality in Contemporary French Thought* (1997) collects essays by leading voices in literature and philosophy of the effects of theater on French culture.

- In *Who's Afraid of Virginia Woolf?*, by Edward Albee (1962), George and Martha invite a young couple into their home for a night of mind games and cruel manipulations that blur the line between fantasy and reality.

- *Lord of the Flies*, by William Golding (1954), portrays the collapse of the values of Western society through the adventures of a small band of boys who are stranded on a remote island following a plane crash. The spirit of cooperation and optimism soon gives way to fear and violence as the boys turn to increasingly brutal means of survival.

- Two men wait by a tree in *Waiting for Godot*, by Samuel Beckett (1953). Bored, they speak in circles, carrying on surreal conversations that seem at once senseless and somehow profound. Those who pass by say that Godot is coming, and the characters believe that Godot will make things better, but Godot never comes. This masterpiece of the Theater of the Absurd showcases the genre's emphasis on minimalism and the gaps in communication—what is lost, misunderstood, and altered when two people attempt to connect through language.

- In *Topdog/Underdog*, by Suzan-Lori Parks (2001), two brothers, ironically named Lincoln and Booth, are pitted against each other in a decades-long sibling rivalry felt all the more acutely in the fact that they are each other's only family. After their parents abandoned them as children, they grew up reliant on each other. As adults, they must navigate the influence of outside forces alongside their own expectations of how they should carry themselves in the world.

- *No Exit*, by Jean-Paul Sartre (1944), features three characters trapped together in a room in Hell as punishment following their deaths. Expecting to be tortured by demons for their sins, the characters soon realize that they will be each other's torturers, their opinions and desires forever at odds in a room without escape.

---

quest. In another group of four parents, the meeting may have been settled in five minutes, taken to court, or not taken place at all. The Reilles have agreed already to pay for the dental procedures Bruno must endure for his broken teeth. The point of contention is not economic but philosophical: the abstract concept of an apology and the insistence that the apology be genuine. Annette offers several times to bring Ferdinand to the Vallons's home to make amends with Bruno, but this solution—and it is, in fact, the most rational solution available—is not good enough for Véronique. She insists Ferdinand understand his responsibilities, that he feel remorse and sympathy for Bruno, and that he be punished by the Reilles in a manner she sees as appropriate: "I'm only thinking of him," she says, defensively, "I'm only thinking of Ferdinand." Except that she is not. Véronique believes that she has the moral high ground, a belief supported by the revelation that the other parents are simply not as invested as she. The problem, however, is that her insistence on viewing the boys' fight as a microcosm of society as a whole leads her to attempt to solve the situation as she would solve the crisis in Darfur rather than as an isolated incident between two boys on the playground. The Reilles admit, early in the discussion, that they would not react as calmly as the Vallons had the boys' positions been reversed. But Bruno's victimization is an opportunity for Véronique —a crusader for victims—to merge her passion for equality, human rights, and the social contract with her passion for parenting. The combination is dangerous. Véronique's insistence that the solution be perfect alienates the Reilles, who take offense at the implication that they do not know how to raise their own child. Her attempt to reach an ideal solution and unwillingness to settle for less than exactly what she wants backfires utterly. In her attempt to summon peace and unity, the god of carnage arrives instead. Clapp writes: "The clafoutis-baking mother who goes on about Darfur...dismantles her peaceful, understanding profile when she hurls her guest's handbag across the room." When Véronique does not get what she wants, she throws a violent tantrum, revealing herself as a self-identified victim's advocate who bullies others to get her way.

Alain stands at the opposite philosophical extreme of Véronique, and, as the meeting turns from (in his eyes) distasteful liberal coddling to blunt honesty and viciousness, he becomes more interested in the proceedings. Positioned as he is at the top of the food chain—a perfect embodiment of white, male hegemony—Alain believes in the culture of violence: "You have to go through a kind of apprenticeship before violence gives way to what's right. Originally, let me remind you,

might was right." When Véronique objects that this law of brutality does not apply to Western society, Alain objects in turn to the idea that any society is different from any other, from antiquity to the present day. He and Michel bond over their childhood gangs, showing their complacency with the boys' fight. Alain's strong opinions, however powerfully delivered, are undermined by his reliance on his cell phone and uselessness as a father. Annette cannot stand to hear him go on about child rearing when he never even pushed the stroller. Her panic attacks and vomiting are linked directly to Alain's boasting, until at last she snaps. Brantley writes: "The play begins with the characters regarding their spouses as guaranteed confederates, and it ends with all of them realizing that they're on their own." When Annette drops Alain's cell phone—for her a symbol of his weakness, for him a symbol of his strength—into the vase of tulips, she does what Véronique could not do with words: she defeats him. His voice is all but silenced for the remainder of the play.

Just as Annette defeats Alain, Véronique is defeated by Michel. The passive partner in their marriage, Michel more than anyone else is pretending to be someone he is not for the sake of the meeting. A natural follower, Michel feels empowered by Alain's aggressive presence to stand up against his wife. But Michel makes an unconvincing hero following his cowardly and selfish destruction of his daughter's pet. Clapp writes:

> The central image of [Reza's] play is a tinkling irony: a pet hamster...proves as unable to cope with life outside as it was with life in a cage: the creature is neither wild nor tame.

The men, though they posture as wild, both panic at the loss of a cell phone. The women, though they feel they represent positive social values, reveal themselves to be violent and cruel. Those who appear passive strike their partners most viciously—for example, Annette's attack on the cell phone and Michel's dismissal of Véronique's interest in Darfur. Meanwhile those who dominate crumple easily, as seen in Alain's withdrawal after losing his phone and Véronique's weeping when she does not get her way. Those kept under heel by society at large relish in its destruction. This is why, for all his boasting, Alain falls hardest from his position at the top when the god of carnage arrives. Brantley writes: "Reza links the spouses' degeneration to a larger picture of a feral dog-eat-dog world." From the tragedy in Darfur to the heartlessness of Alain's

Though the characters' interactions are at first civil, emotions run high and communication breaks down (© Piotr Marcinski | Shutterstock.com)

response to the Antril scandal to the almost certain death of a hamster, the violence inside the living room is connected to the violence outside. Having pushed each other beyond all reasonable limits, having abandoned reason in favor of brutality, the couples must now slink away to lick their wounds, grateful the day's violence went only as far as it did and no further.

Source: Amy L. Miller, Critical Essay on *The God of Carnage*, in *Drama for Students*, Gale, Cengage Learning, 2017.

Amanda Giguere

In the following excerpt, Giguere highlights how the breakdown of language illustrates the fragility of civilization in The God of Carnage.

... *The God of Carnage* is about two sets of parents—Véronique and Michel Vallon, and Annette and Alain Reille—who meet to resolve an issue between their two 11-year-old sons. The boys have gotten into a fight on the playground, and the parents have gathered to make peace. Their meeting, which is initially laced

with politeness, quickly spirals out of control. The playground fight between the boys becomes a catalyst for both sets of parents to reveal their own inherent cruelty, savagery, and selfishness. The play brings up themes of savagery versus civilization, personal responsibility, parenting and global relations as Reza peels away the layers of these four characters to reveal their atrocious cores. With this play, Reza exposes the fragility and hollowness of civilization. The systems through which humans achieve political and social progress (the most crucial of which is language) are depicted as mere façades, and in the play, Reza illustrates that beneath humanity's civilized trappings, all people are savages. The four milestone productions in *Carnage*'s history (Zurich, Paris, London and New York) alternately emphasized, overlooked, and embellished upon the themes provided by Reza's text. This chapter considers the play from a three-pronged approach in order to unfold how it defines and expands upon Reza's theatrical poetics by exploring the plot, themes, and production choices.

> JUST AS WORLD LEADERS COME TOGETHER TO
> DISCUSS THE RELATIONSHIP BETWEEN COUNTRIES,
> SO THE CHARACTERS IN *CARNAGE* CONVERGE TO
> MAKE PEACE BETWEEN THEIR CHILDREN."

The plot of *The God of Carnage* employs familiar patterns and techniques in Reza's work, yet contains new innovations in her theatrical poetics. The basic downward-spiral structure of *Carnage* is not new for Reza's audiences, and she seems to have recycled elements from her previous plays in this seventh play. In *Life x 3*, two married couples gather for what they assume will be a polite dinner party, but they soon find themselves in a disastrous evening. Truths emerge, and the onstage relationships begin to disintegrate. Although *Carnage* follows this basic pattern, it lacks Reza's clever manipulation of the repeated evening. Even the characters in *Carnage* could be mapped onto the cast of *Life x 3*. Michel has traces of the emasculated Henry, Véronique is as dominating as Sonia, Alain is a lawyerly version of Hubert, and Annette matches Inez in timidity. As in *Conversations After a Burial*, *La Traversée de l'hiver*, *The Unexpected Man* and *Life x 3*, *The God of Carnage* has an equal division of male and female characters. *"Art"* follows a similar structure, in which characters begin the play as friends but gradually destroy each other. Like *"Art,"* *Carnage* also takes place entirely indoors. As in *Life x 3*, the children are referred to, but absent. The parallels between *Carnage* and her earlier works are abundant, suggesting that Reza has calculated a formula for commercial theater—position recognizable types onstage and let them attack each other until the hollowness of their relationships becomes evident—and she employs these plot devices in *Carnage*.

The God of Carnage is not entirely old material, however, and Reza's innovations with the play are noteworthy. Whereas Reza's earlier plays are about domestic themes, such as the family arguments in *Conversations* and Yvan's pre-marital woes in *"Art,"* this is her first play to deal directly with parenting. In *Carnage*, the inciting incident stems from a parenting issue,

and the characters interact primarily as parents of young children. They are all roughly the same age, and they seem more youthful than those in her earlier works. *Carnage* is also the first play to focus on an uninterrupted event with no scene breaks or asides. It is as if Reza wanted to see what would happen to her characters (traces of whom had appeared in earlier plays) if she left them alone in an onstage crucible. She allowed moments of respite in earlier plays. *Life x 3* escaped to the sidewalk for a scene with Inez and Hubert, *"Art"* moved between different apartments, and *A Spanish Play* and *The Unexpected Man* broke the action by allowing the audience to hear the characters' thoughts in asides. *Carnage*, however, never lets up on the audience; the action is persistent, and the audience members (and the characters) are given no release. Reza abandons the multi-generational thread that appears in her plays for a more targeted age, and she narrows the arena in which they play out their arguments. The play is much tighter, more focused and more persistent than any earlier Reza work.

There are several terms that must be defined in order to understand how Reza has structured the play. *The God of Carnage* is constructed as a collapse of *civilization*. Albert Schweitzer writes that civilization "consists in our giving ourselves, as human beings, to the effort to attain the perfecting of the human race and the actualization of progress of every sort in the circumstances of humanity and of the objective world." The key element in Schweitzer's definition is the notion of progress—moving in a positive direction toward the betterment of society. Civilization is the complex system(s) through which humans achieve positive change. It is composed of several systems (agriculture, art, and money, for example), but the most crucial aspect of civilization is *language*. Language, a system of verbal communication, is a fixed set of rules through which humans make knowledge claims, and eventually, make political progress. Language ultimately leads to this progress. When language breaks down, as it does in *Carnage*, the path toward social and political progress is blocked, which likewise leads to the breakdown of civilization. In contrast, *savagery* appears throughout *Carnage* in opposition to civilization. A savage, in the context of Reza's play, is one who does not participate in a complex system of progress, but one who acts alone, and in his or her best interest. A savage, likewise, does not use language to achieve positive change, but as a weapon, and in self-defense. When civilization crumbles, savagery is revealed as the natural state, and Reza argues that this state is within her characters all along—civilization simply masks it. This chapter also is predicated on the *failure* of language in *The God of Carnage*. Failure implies an incompletion of a linear journey toward success. In other words, failure is the inability to make progress or to move forward. Language fails in many ways in this play: vocabulary deteriorates as the characters resort to less refined, cruder words; they begin to use words as weapons rather than as tools that lead toward positive change; finally, words are replaced with silences. All of these small breakdowns contribute toward the overarching failure of language, which might leave Reza's audience members wondering whether communication, coexistence and civilization arc possible, or if these things are simply chimerical.

Structurally, the play begins at a point of imbalance, and some audience members might immediately sense an impending collapse. The characters attempt to be polite, but like a leaking water pipe, small comments drip out, followed by larger bursts, until the characters' facades explode to reveal their inner savagery. Reza situates her point of attack in the aftermath of the playground fight between the children. The boys have publicly battled, and one has been wounded, and the parents have gathered to make peace. The significance of the playground fight in the context of the collapse of civilization that follows is immense: a violent, nonverbal, savage act takes place, and the parents attempt to heal the physical act with language. As the play begins, the four characters believe that the worst has passed, and that language will repair the damage. Reza structures the play as a series of returns to the key issue; the characters incessantly revisit the inciting incident, the playground fight. The fight (which occurs offstage, before the play's start) serves as a touchstone for each character. Because each character has a savage within, the violent act that begins the story is more powerful than the words they use to describe it, and cannot be forgotten. With each return to the key issue, more truths are revealed—everything comes out, including bile from one character in a daring onstage vomit scene. As the play progresses, and the characters continue to skirt around, avoid, and eventually return to the idea of their sons' fight, they shed their layers of civilization; proper clothing, polite words, and marital solidarity are all quickly dropped. With each cycle, their language becomes cruder, their actions grow more violent, and they reveal that they truly are the playground bullies they purport to condemn. By the play's end, all four characters are stripped of their social niceties, and they are left in a crumpled heap onstage. The very last moment of the play, however, signals a reconstruction of language, and the possibility of progress. In a phone conversation (implying a link with the world outside the play) Véronique comforts her nine-year-old daughter with soothing words. Reza structures the play as a gradual collapse of civilization, as symbolized by the collapse of these four characters and the failure of their language, but the phone call suggests that the world might be rebuilt, despite the hollowness of the structure. This plot, which tracks the decline of civilization, invites larger questions about Reza's thematic underpinnings.

A close reading of the text suggests that *The God of Carnage* is largely about the clash between civilization and savagery, but the play also examines the arbitrariness of those distinctions. The play raises questions about domesticated versus wild animals, adults versus children, humans versus animals, and culture versus vulgarity. Reza seems to suggest that, despite the gulf that often separates civilization from savagery, they are closer than they appear, and the audience witnesses the collision of these two worlds in *Carnage*. Furthermore, *The God of Carnage* ruminates on the urge to compartmentalize. Michel demonstrates excessive cruelty toward a household pet, yet he fails to see the connection between that violence and the violence enacted on the playground. Véronique is an advocate for peace in Darfur, yet she physically attacks her houseguest with brute force. How do we divide ourselves? Does one action necessarily affect another action? Can we judge another person based on a single action? To what extent are we all guilty of the crimes we condemn? By mingling the savage world with the civilized world, Reza asks her audience to blur these lines, and to see that the self cannot be compartmentalized. We are savage and civil, domesticated and wild, grown up and childish. Though we try to divide ourselves and set ourselves apart, these categories are arbitrary, and they quickly bleed together, making one brilliantly messy picture.

In addition to these central themes, the play is also about parenthood. To what extent do a child's actions reflect the worldview of the parents? Are parents meant to apologize for their children, or to defend them at all costs? Are parents necessarily better if they are deeply involved in their children's lives, or do children learn best when left to figure things out on their own? And what happens when a parent tries to offer parenting advice to another parent? Parenting can also be seen on a larger scale as a metaphor for global relations. Parents try to make the best possible decisions for their children's future, and a nation's leader aims to look after its county's interests. What happens when two countries come into conflict? Just as world leaders come together to discuss the relationship between countries, so the characters in *Carnage* converge to make peace between their children. If this play is, however, a metaphor for global relations, as the references of Darfur, violence, and peace talks suggest, the conclusion is rather grim. One may only hope that peace negotiations—both domestic and global—have a more productive outcome than the one found in *Carnage*.

The production choices made by the directors involved in the Zurich, Paris, London and New York productions have largely influenced the extent to which the breach appeared on the stage. When Reza directed the Paris production, was this necessarily a truer version of the play because of the playwright's hand in the direction? When Matthew Warchus directed the London and New York productions, how did the play change with different casts? By analyzing the productions of *Carnage* in these four major cities, with a particular focus on the English and American versions, the possibilities in performance emerge, and it becomes clear how each production emphasized, discarded and enhanced various themes.

With this seventh play, the breach seems to have evolved into something very different from the rupture of Reza's earlier plays. In *The God of Carnage*, the breach is no longer an addendum to the play, as it was in *Conversations After a Burial* and *La Traversée de l'hiver*, nor is it the formalistic narrative breach rooted in asides, as employed in *"Art"* and *The Unexpected Man*. *The God of Carnage* likewise abandons the overly visible meta-theatrical breach that appeared in *Life x 3* and *A Spanish Play*. Instead, Reza has turned on her very building blocks—the words she uses to construct her plays—and what appears in *Carnage* is a breach of language. The characters exist in a world where language fails. They struggle to apply words to their actions, to ask difficult questions, to

express their thoughts, but language repeatedly breaks down. This breach begins early in the play—from the first moment Alain questions Véronique's word choice—and it continually interrupts the flow of *Carnage*. This idea of conveying the broken quality of language is not new to theater, and one can find examples of a similar failure of language in the plays of Absurdist writers like Ionesco, Pinter and Beckett. In *The God of Carnage*, however, the broken quality of the language is far less overt than its Absurdist counterparts. On the contrary, it is almost impossible to discern, unless the audience members step back from the events as they unfold to realize that the characters' words are working against them. Throughout the play, sentences go unfinished, questions are left unanswered, and language is devalued by the violent actions that dominate the action. Although Reza did not invent the playwright's ability to manipulate language, the failure of language found in *The God of Carnage* represents a significant turning point in her career. It suggests that Reza was searching for a far subtler way to challenge her audience. Throughout Reza's career, the breach has become more fully integrated into each play, and slightly less visible with each play. In *Carnage*, the breach is almost impossible to discern, but a close examination suggests that Reza has built a world in which words are inadequate, sentences are slippery, and language fails to achieve progress. There might be no sudden moment of recognition for Reza's audience, in which they are asked to see the events of the play in a new way. There are no moments of direct address in which the characters break through the fourth wall. There is no structural rupture, in which time is repeated, or a layered reality is revealed. Instead, the focus is simply on these four characters and their broken words. An audience member at *The God of Carnage* might never recognize the failure of language within the play, because Reza keeps the representational reality intact, and offers her audience little reason to violate the theatrical illusion. This is the most invisible breach of her career, and its imperceptibility may be one reason for its mainstream success. The purpose of this chapter is to unfold a working definition of the breach in *Carnage* on the page and on the stage, to relate it to the use of the breach throughout Reza's plays to date, and to move the reader toward an understanding of Reza's poetics in her plays written between 1987 and 2006....

Source: Amanda Giguere, *"The God of Carnage* and the Failure of Language, 2006–2009," in *The Plays of*

Yasmina Reza on the English and American Stage, McFarland, 2010, pp. 117—21.

Charles McNulty

In the following review, McNulty describes the play as a "puncturing of bourgeois self-regard."

Reporting from New York—Civilization's thin veneer gets mercilessly stripped in *God of Carnage*, French playwright Yasmina Reza's savage comedy about two urban couples attempting to maturely resolve an altercation that occurred between their 11-year-old sons in a neighborhood park. This quartet fits the demographic that European writers and filmmakers love to defile—affluent, well-educated and liberal (sort of like their audience). In other words, don't count on the characters setting a sterling example for the kids.

The play, which opened Sunday at the Bernard B. Jacobs Theatre on Broadway in a translation by Christopher Hampton, might be even more puncturing of bourgeois self-regard than *"Art,"* Reza's international blockbuster that won the 1998 Tony for best play. It's also just as sleekly schematic, the action efficiently distilled to make a big cynical point about those most pompously self-deluding creatures known as Homo sapiens. (You know who you are.)

Fortunately, the presence of four of the more theatrically talented members of the species—Jeff Daniels, Hope Davis, James Gandolfini and a truly hilarious Marcia Gay Harden—adds diverse personality to a work that is très-très-français in its marriage of mechanical boulevard comedy and abstract drama of ideas. These sacred traditions in French theater don't square easily with our own less intellectual, more character-based sensibilities, but the actors find ways of fluffing out the play's chicly flat demonstration with their full-blooded individuality.

Directed by Matthew Warchus, a frequent collaborator with Reza, the production is set in a high-end Brooklyn loft, the kind that creative types love but only those in business can typically afford. The furniture is spare and contemporary, art books abound, and decorative touches include two glass vases stuffed to the brim with white tulips—floral arrangements that turn out to be almost as consequential as pistols that appear in the first acts of old-fashioned melodramas.

Mark Thompson's scenic design includes a red-wall backdrop, which along with the sound of jungle drums at the top of the show,

foreshadows Reza's central theme of a primitive aggression that's untameable by society. But the ambiance also ties in with the obsession Veronica (Harden) has for all things African, from the continent's art and artifacts to its genocides (she has a book coming out on Darfur).

Veronica prides herself on her enlightened consciousness, which is why she has eagerly enlisted her husband, Michael (Gandolfini), a wholesale supplier of domestic hardware, to host a U.N.-style diplomatic effort with Alan (Daniels) and Annette (Davis), the parents of the boy who knocked two teeth out of their son's mouth with a stick. Here's an opportunity for her to showcase her progressive chops and her inspired baking at the same time.

Alan, a lawyer who keeps taking calls on his cell phone about a pharmaceutical company he's defending, doesn't have patience for all this designer-parent negotiation. He'd rather just write a check to cover what the insurance company won't and get back to his ethically dubious machinations.

His self-effacing wife, Annette (Davis), however, is more concerned with neighborly appearances. She cringes at her husband's rude remarks and the way he hacks away at Veronica's home-made clafouti with specially prepared apples and pears.

Alan's behavior literally makes Annette sick. She vomits all over control-freak Veronica's precious art books, in a scene that is staged in more graphic detail than usual. It's gross. Reza clearly wants to unsettle audience members, to deny them the customary middle-class evasions and niceties.

She has also painted herself into a corner, confining the drama to one room and fueling it through increasingly acrimonious talk. The static nature of the situation provokes extreme gestures. Reza has given her grown-ups nothing to do but reveal their barely suppressed adolescent frustrations and rage, which Warchus coaxes into a free-form wrestling match with slapstick flourishes.

The amusement of the piece comes from watching masks fall. Self-engrossed and morally lax, Daniels' Alan may be the most immediately dislikable of the group, but he's also the most honest about his degenerate character. Ordering an espresso when Annette is barely able to ask for water, he's shamelessly unconcerned with what others think of him. Alan saves his double-talk for his job, not caring to put on a false face unless he's going to be amply paid for it.

Gandolfini's Michael doesn't want to disappoint his wife, who has a lot invested in sorting out this incident involving the children ("I'm standing up for civilization," she unironically announces after things start to go awry.) But once Michael breaks out a bottle of expensive rum, his behavior becomes debauched. The anecdote about what he did the previous night with his kid's poor hamster takes on a starker reality as his jaded nature cracks through.

Davis' Annette is in "wealth management," which fits into the play's grand scheme, but her mousy demeanor doesn't suggest such a professional identity anymore than Alan's slobby self-ishness makes it easy to believe that he's flying to the Hague tomorrow to prosecute a case in the International Criminal Court. (Hampton doesn't always nail the cultural nuances in this Americanized version).

Still, it's an enormous treat to watch self-contained Annette succumb to her pent-up rage at her husband. Davis, whose exquisite, slightly somber looks lend the impression of a fragile sang-froid, lucidly lays out Annette's journey from dutiful wife retching into a bucket to domestic terrorist targeting Alan's incessantly ringing cell phone.

But the theatrical pièce de résistance is in the hollering manner in which Harden's Veronica descends from her high-and-mighty perch into the muck of human relations. This concerned mom goes from earthy perfectionist to foul-mouth termagant, all the while defending the righteousness of her various causes.

God of Carnage may have the feel of a play in which characters have no choice but to fall in line with their playwright's nihilistic manipulations, but with actors this ferociously robust, human nature seems to have its own incorrigible agenda.

Source: Charles McNulty, Review of *God of Carnage*, in *Los Angeles Times*, March 22, 2009.

Amanda Beth Holden

In the following review, Holden discusses the trademark "breach" in Reza's plays.

Yasmina Reza's plays consistently have ninety-minute run-times, small casts, and abstract settings, but her most significant trademark is what I term the "breach": a moment of rupture, in which time or space shifts to reveal an unstable

foundation. In *Life X 3*, the same evening begins again, for the second, and then third time. *"Art"* violates the fourth wall with soliloquies, but restores it when characters share a scene. *Conversations After a Burial*'s out-of-body scene is a surprising end to a play that has hitherto obeyed the unity of place. *The God of Carnage* signals Reza's boldest breach yet by destabilizing her building blocks; in this production, scenic and sound design, gestures, noises, even silences all "voice" the playwright's theme of the failure of language.

The God of Carnage features two couples discussing a playground brawl between their sons. In the West End production, lawyer Alain Reille (Ralph Fiennes) and his poised wife Annette (Tamsin Greig) visited Véronique Vallon (Janet McTeer), a peace-loving Darfur advocate, and her cheerful husband Michel (Ken Stott). This polite attempt to compose a report of the playground scuffle became a savage blame-game—masks fell, characters exploded, and beneath the desire for peace surged the primal motto: every man, woman, and child for themselves. Although the characters began with the civilized task of drafting a statement of the playground incident, hoping to stabilize the event through language, they found it impossible to agree on a simple word. Was the Reille boy *armed* with a stick, or was he *furnished* with it? From here, language slipped from the characters' hands and repeatedly failed to contain any decipherable meaning.

The production's scenic and sound design contributed to the failure of language from the start. A pre-show white drop featured a child's red-ink drawing of a boy and his parents. The seasoned Reza fan could see this as childish vandalism on the controversial canvas from *"Art,"* but this drawing highlighted the disconnect between the primitive family portrait and the live actors who would emerge onstage moments later. Just as the child's messy drawing depicted actual people inaccurately, so too, the words in *The God of Carnage* disappointed the characters who employed them. Gary Yershon's music furthered this notion of failed language, when thumping jungle sounds filled the dark theatre, thrusting the audience into a savage environment. When the lights came up, however, the characters onstage spoke politely; their language failed to cooperate with Yershon's pounding jungle music. Mark Thompson's set design diverged equally from the language: his towering blood-red walls, matching red floor, and tables of natural, unfinished wood prepared the audience for a rough world, but the civil opening words of the play contradicted the more savage visual (and aural) clues.

Director Matthew Warchus emphasized language's unreliability with gestures that competed with words. After Véronique emasculated Michel by telling their guests of his motherly instincts, he stiffened, and his face fell from a cheerful grin to a blank stare. As his wife and the guests carried on their conversation, Michel seemed betrayed, but couldn't speak. The other characters continued talking and Michel stared fiercely at Véronique, eyes bulging, hands flailing. He tried to tell her something, but his language failed; he communicated through glares and hand gestures that battled with the language of the scene. Alain's gestures likewise competed with the dialogue. He quickly jerked his head to his wife in the midst of a conversation, signaling that they must leave. As language continued its decline, the characters found alternative means of communication. In a rare moment of marital solidarity, Michel and Véronique used their time alone to mock their guests' nickname, Woof Woof. Their inside joke turned into a barking game, as they growled hysterically, unable to express their thoughts in anything but bestial noises.

Beyond the gestures and noises that served where language failed, the characters often found themselves completely unable to communicate, and Warchus effectively manipulated these onstage silences to articulate the loss of language. Alain exploded at Véronique and headed to leave, wife in arm. Michel suggested more coffee; reluctantly, Alain agreed. The following silence was lengthy and deadly. Michel exited to prepare coffee, Alain plopped into a chair, and the women cautiously shared the couch. They stole slow glances at each other, wondering who would speak first. Annette, gesturing to the art books scattered across the coffee table, broke the silence by asking about Véronique's artistic interest. The silence returned. Picking up a book of Bacon paintings, Annette turned the pages, feigning engrossment. The silence stretched painfully. then, as if learning a language for the first time, the women resorted to one-word descriptions of the art:

> Annette: Cruelty. Majesty.
> Véronique: Chaos. Balance.

As language repeatedly broke down, the characters struggled for stability, often in silence.

The devaluation of language revealed truths about each character through actions: Annette vomited on the art books; Véronique assaulted Michel; Alain collapsed in defeat after Annette dunked his cell phone in the flower vase; Annette flung tulips through the air like a wild animal tearing through the jungle. The failure of language became a self-referential joke toward the play's end. After Michel dried the waterlogged phone with a hairdryer, he said, "I have to say ..., " and Annette interrupted, laughing hysterically, with "Yes, what is it you *have* to say, Michel?." Apparently she realized the futility of speaking when their actions had already revealed so much.

After the characters had torn one another apart and littered the stage with the evening's wreckage, the cell phone rang, and a tear-stained Véronique soothed her distraught child. The lights dimmed as music-box tones underscored Véronique's calming words. Annette cried against the red wail, Alain lay crumpled on the floor with the shredded tulips, and Michel sat upstage, puffing a cigar. The words of hope for the child sharply contrasted with the onstage debris, and once again, language was in conflict with the performed reality. This was Reza's latest breach: a playwright, whose profession relies on words to construct meaning, built a play in which language was empty, speech was meaningless, and nothing—not even a mother comforting her child—could be trusted.

Source: Amanda Beth Holden, Review of *The God of Carnage*, in *Theatre Journal*, June 13, 2008, pp. 126–28.

SOURCES

Brantley, Ben, "Rumble in the Living Room," in *New York Times*, June 6, 2010, http://www.nytimes.com/2009/03/23/theater/reviews/23carn.html?_r=0 (accessed June 15, 2016).

"Carnage (2011)," imbd.com, http://www.imdb.com/title/tt1692486/ (accessed June 15, 2016).

Clapp, Susannah, "Are You Sitting Uncomfortably?," in *Guardian* (London, England), March 30, 2008, https://www.theguardian.com/stage/2008/mar/30/theatre3 (accessed June 15, 2016).

Corder, Mike, "Omar al-Bashir Charged by Hague for Orchestrating Darfur Genocide," in *Christian Science Monitor*, July 12, 2010, http://www.csmonitor.com/From-the-news-wires/2010/0712/Omar-al-Bashir-charged-by-Hague-for-orchestrating-Darfur-genocide (accessed June 20, 2016).

Fukuyama, Francis, "The Middle-Class Revolution," in *Wall Street Journal*, June 28, 2013, http://www.wsj.com/articles/SB10001424127887323873904578571472700348086 (accessed June 20, 2016).

Gardner, Elysa, "God of Carnage, Blithe Spirit Lifting Spirits on Broadway," in *USA Today*, March 23, 2016, http://usatoday30.usatoday.com/life/theater/reviews/2009-03-22-carnage-blithe_N.htm (accessed June 15, 2016).

Giguere, Amanda, *The Plays of Yasmina Reza on the English and American Stage*, MacFarland, 2010, pp. 5–11, 116–49.

Jones, Alice, "God of Carnage, Gielgud Theatre, London," in *Independent* (London, England), March 26, 2008, http://www.independent.co.uk/arts-entertainment/theatre-dance/reviews/god-of-carnage-gielgud-theatre-london-801139.html (accessed June 15, 2016).

Komisar, Lucy, "The God of Carnage Watches Polite Society Disintegrate," in *The Komisar Scoop*, October 2009, http://www.thekomisarscoop.com/2009/10/the-god-of-carnage-watches-polite-society-disintegrate/ (accessed June 15, 2016).

Reza, Yasmina, *God of Carnage*, translated by Christopher Hampton, Faber and Faber, 2008.

Sikainga, Ahmad, "'The World's Worst Humanitarian Crisis': Understanding the Darfur Conflict," in *Origins*, Vol. 2, No. 5, February 2009, http://origins.osu.edu/article/worlds-worst-humanitarian-crisis-understanding-darfur-conflict (accessed June 20, 2016).

Spencer, Charles, "God of Carnage: Electrifying, Despite Lights Failing," in *Telegraph* (London, England), March 26, 2008, http://www.telegraph.co.uk/culture/theatre/drama/3672098/God-of-Carnage-Electrifying-despite-lights-failing.html (accessed June 15, 2016).

Stearns, Peter, "The Rise of the Middle Classes," in *European Society in Upheaval*, 1967, pp. 117–133, http://history.tamu.edu/faculty/resch/Stearns,%20Early%20Industrial%20Society%20(2).pdf (accessed June 20, 2016).

Teachout, Terry, "Beating Up the Bourgeoisie," in *Wall Street Journal*, March 27, 2009, http://www.wsj.com/articles/SB123810250214351659 (accessed June 15, 2016).

Venturi, Richard, "Up against the Wall: The French and American Middle Classes," in *France Stratégie*, February 2016, http://www.strategie.gouv.fr/sites/strategie.gouv.fr/files/atoms/files/the_middle_class_web.pdf (accessed June 20, 2016).

Waal, Alex de, "Tragedy in Darfur," in *Boston Review*, October 5, 2004, http://www.bostonreview.net/de-waal-tragedy-in-darfur (accessed June 20, 2016).

FURTHER READING

Bradby, David, *Modern French Drama: 1940–1990*, Cambridge University Press, 1991.

This volume traces the history of the theater from World War II to 1990, touching not only on influential literary superstars of the time, such as Samuel Beckett and Arthur Adamov, but also on the work of talented but lesser-known playwrights. A bibliography and black-and-white photos are included.

Finburgh, C., and C. Lavery, *Contemporary French Theatre and Performance*, Palgrave Macmillan, 2011.

This collection of essays explores the relationship of French theater to the nation's culture and history, covering both traditional and experimental performances as well as the specific influence of individual playwrights. Topics include the translation of text to stage, the effect of economy and politics on the theater, feminism, the role of dance and poetry, and amateur and street performances.

Reza, Yasmina, *'Art,'* Farrar, Straus, and Giroux, 1997.

In Reza's Tony Award–winning play, a man buys a pure white painting for a ludicrous sum of money, to the utter disbelief of his closest friends. A dark comedy that skewers modern conceptions of art and its value, the play also exposes the fault lines often present but overlooked within friendships, to disastrous, hilarious results.

Turk, Edward Baron, *French Theatre Today: The View from New York, Paris, and Avignon*, University of Iowa Press, 2011.

This study of French theater uses the author's attendance of over 150 performances over the course of a single year to draw conclusions about the state of twenty-first-century French theater: its relationship to the audience, its innovations and traditions, as well as the ways in which it reflects and distorts the society that surrounds it.

SUGGESTED SEARCH TERMS

Yasmina Reza

The God of Carnage

Yasmina Reza AND The God of Carnage

The God of Carnage AND drama

Yasmina Reza AND Tony Award

Yamina Reza AND Christopher Hampton

The God of Carnage AND violence

middle-class manners AND plays

Darfur, Sudan

The Hitch-Hiker

LUCILLE FLETCHER

1941

A product of the so-called Golden Age of Radio, Lucille Fletcher's radio play *The Hitch-Hiker* was aired by CBS on November 17, 1941, on the famed *Orson Welles Show*, a contemporary extension of the acclaimed *Mercury Theatre on the Air* program. Introduced by Welles himself, the presentation was set to a musical score and sound effects devised by Bernard Herrmann, Fletcher's husband and a famed composer in his own right. The radio play was well received by contemporary audiences and presented by Welles on numerous other occasions and for various networks and programs. *The Hitch-Hiker* is better remembered today not as a radio play but as a 1960 television episode of the *Twilight Zone*, adapted from Fletcher's play by famed producer and series creator Rod Sterling.

Counted as one of the early classics of suspense and psychological horror, Fletcher's radio play continues to appeal to humanity's most primal fears decades after its initial air date. *The Hitch-Hiker*, and pioneering thrillers like it, helped shape an entire modern genre premised on ambiguity, the unhinged mind, and terror of the unknown.

AUTHOR BIOGRAPHY

A native of Brooklyn, New York, Violet Lucille Fletcher was born on March 28, 1912, to working-class parents. She excelled at both local

Ronald Adams leaves New York on a rainy morning (© inigocia / Shutterstock.com)

public and technical schools and demonstrated an early aptitude and love for the expression afforded by words. As a high school student, Fletcher headed a chapter of the National Honors Society, served as editor of a school-run literary publication, and distinguished herself as a finalist in a national competition for oratory sponsored by the *New York Times* and judged by representatives of the US government. Fletcher continued to engage in contests of academic merit while pursuing a bachelor of arts in English at New York's Vassar College, from which she graduated with distinction in 1933.

Upon her graduation from university, Fletcher engaged in freelance writing for several notable publications, including the *New Yorker*, and acquired a job within the musical department of major broadcasting corporation CBS. It was there that she made the acquaintance of accomplished composer and music arranger Bernard Herrmann, whom she married five years later despite the anti-Semitic protests of her own family. The creator of over twenty acclaimed radio dramas for various broadcasting programs, Fletcher derived inspiration for her 1941 classic, *The Hitch-Hiker*, from an unsettling encounter she experienced while on a cross-country road trip with her husband. Afterward, Herrmann encouraged her writing and set the play to music for its initial airing on *The Orson Welles Show*. Along with the tremendous success of *The Hitch-Hiker*, Fletcher's best-known script, *Sorry, Wrong Number*, received an Edgar Allan Poe Award in 1960 for best radio drama.

The couple divorced in 1948 after raising two daughters but maintained contact as lifelong friends and literary associates. Fletcher married her second husband, novelist Douglass Wallop, the following year. Fletcher's second marriage coincided with her collaboration in the crafting of her own first full-length novel, *Night Man*, with established writer and publishing executive Allan Ullman. This joint endeavor proved successful and inspired the writing of six more successful novels of the mystery genre, many adapted to the stage and silver screen. Ever the Renaissance woman, Fletcher went on to author two of her own plays, advise on various movies and television series, and even craft a libretto to accompany the music of her first husband, Herrmann.

In her declining years, Fletcher moved from her native New York to Virginia and then to Maryland after Wallop's death in 1985. An enduring relic of the Golden Age of Radio,

Fletcher succumbed to a stroke in 2000 at the advanced age of eighty-eight.

PLOT SUMMARY

Introduction

Orson Welles, the radio announcer and show host, introduces himself to the listening audience and expounds on the virtues of a good ghost story. He goes on to praise the narrative advantages of subtlety and intrigue over sensational plot developments intended to shock and appall. Welles assures listeners that the story at hand is a psychological thriller of the highest order, undiminished by the cheap and ghoulish effects so often associated with the clichéd horror genre. The announcer makes a distinction between stories that appeal to the emotions, symbolized by the heart, and those that tap directly into the more primal and paranoid senses, represented by the spine. *The Hitch-Hiker*, Welles affirms to his audience, belongs wholly in this latter category.

Radio Play

A man identified as Ronald Adams appeals directly to the listening audience regarding the matter of his sanity. He identifies his present location as an auto camp in New Mexico and describes his age, appearance, marital status, and place of birth in distant Brooklyn. Adams expresses a sense of great urgency and seems afraid for his very life. He seizes this moment of mental clarity and relative composure to relate his chilling tale.

Six days earlier, Adams explains to the audience, he embarked on a cross-country road trip from his native Brooklyn to California, where he plans to stay for a period of three months. On the day of the journey, his doting mother insisted on seeing him off, expressing great concern for her son's safety and warning him against picking up hitchhikers. Adams was politely dismissive of his mother's worries and began his journey with pronounced high spirits and a growing feeling of liberation.

When Adams crossed the Brooklyn Bridge he was startled somewhat by the apparition of a thin, otherwise unremarkable hitchhiker who stepped into the road directly in front of the oncoming car. The driver was able to avoid a collision and forgot the incident entirely until he viewed the very same hitchhiker several hours

MEDIA ADAPTATIONS

- Although it originally aired as a 1941 radio play on an extension of *Mercury Theatre on the Air*, hosted by Orson Welles, *The Hitch-Hiker* inspired a 1960 episode of same name on the long-running television series *The Twilight Zone*. Despite a few notable differences, including the age and gender of the protagonist, Fletcher's plot was loyally adapted to the screen by series originator Rod Sterling and remains one of the show's most celebrated episodes.

later off a road in New Jersey. Adams was somewhat rattled by the reappearance of this strange figure but explained the incident away and continued driving to his ultimate destination. It was not until much later that night, this time on a lonely stretch of road between Harrisburg and Pittsburgh, that Adams encountered the hitchhiker a third time and was greatly alarmed by the uncanny coincidence and the man's unchanged appearance, right down to the spattering of rain on his shirt. This time, the hitchhiker hailed Adams directly, causing the driver to accelerate with a sudden rush of foreboding.

He stopped briefly at a roadside gas station to fill his tank and engage in a conversation with a friendly attendant. The mechanic revealed that the local weather had been unseasonably dry for quite some time, deepening the mystery of the apparition's rain-spattered shirt. He added that the inhospitable nature of the road turned away most hitchhikers. Deeply troubled by these revelations and their implications, Adams continued on his way and found lodgings for the night in Pittsburgh. His anxieties were lessened by a good night's sleep, and Adams was able to forget about the hitchhiker until their fourth meeting later that day, this time outside Zanesville, Ohio.

Adams withdraws from the narrative for a moment to describe the rural, idyllic setting for the sinister encounter and the unassuming, almost shabby appearance of the persistent hitchhiker. Because Adams was stopped and searching in vain for a detour, the hitchhiker misinterpreted his intentions and approached the car, inquiring of Adams's final destination. Beset by a sudden panic, the driver lied in response to this question and quickly pulled back on to the road. He began to feel very alone and almost reconsidered his initial, knee-jerk reaction to the hitchhiker's continued entreaties.

Adams drove on under a sense of inevitability and foreboding and braced himself for the next meeting with the hitchhiker. He eventually stopped at a roadside store, closed for the night, and woke the owner in search of a cup of black coffee. Although his request was denied, Adam used the pretense of the coffee to interact with another flesh-and-blood being and ease his acute pangs of loneliness. He related his nightmarish encounters with the hitchhiker and claimed to have seen him again just outside the owner's abode. Somewhat unnerved by the strange tenor of the conversation and suspecting an attempted ruse, the storekeeper accused Adams of being intoxicated and threatened to alert the local sheriff. Rather than be detained, the traveler left the premises and once again took to the road. He became aware of his growing fatigue and lamented the absence of inns in the towns along his route.

At a railroad crossing in Oklahoma Adams next encountered the hitchhiker, his shoulders still wet with rain despite the intense sun and famously dry climate of the area. Without thinking, the driver accelerated across the tracks and turned his wheel to strike the man, but his vehicle stalled right in the path of an oncoming train. The hitchhiker's face remained free of emotion but he beckoned to Adams, inviting him to his death.

Adams was able to reverse off the tracks an instant before a fatal collision with the train, but the near-miss brought him little satisfaction or comfort. When the train finally passed in its entirety, the hitchhiker was nowhere to be seen. The driver resolved to not be alone for the continued duration of the journey and picked up a hitchhiker, a young woman traveling to Texas. She asked for permission to get comfortable and slip off her shoes and flirtatiously praised Adams for his character, good looks, and the sportiness of his car.

Emboldened by these compliments, the driver began to ask increasingly obsessive questions of his passenger regarding the etiquette and mechanics governing hitchhiking. The girl interrupted this line of questioning by shouting for Adams to watch the road and avoid a direct collision with some cows and a barbed wire fence. Heedless of her warning, Adams continued to accelerate with the stated purpose of running down a hitchhiker visible only to him. Although both driver and passenger were unhurt in the resulting collision, the girl was seriously shaken by Adams's apparent volatility and insisted on being let out of the vehicle. Adams pled for her continued companionship on the road to California but to no avail.

Deep in the Texas prairies, Adams was overcome by fatigue and felt unable to continue driving without rest. He pulled over, arranged a makeshift bed in the car, and, just as he was about to lie down, caught sight of the phantom hitchhiker emerging from a herd of cows. Terror overcame exhaustion, and Adams drove off in a panic. He began to regret missing this final opportunity to confront the hitchhiker and, in his narrative, remarks on the growing frequency and incidental nature of their encounters from this point onward. Adams caught sight of his pursuer at every rest stop, roadside store, Indian reservation, and, eventually, at the start of each fresh mile of the journey.

The road took on a surreal, dreamlike quality as Adam succumbed to exhaustion and his rational mind began to drift. He eventually stopped at a New Mexico auto camp, determined to hear a familiar voice and thereby reclaim his sanity. Using a pay phone, Adams spoke to the operator and requested connection to his mother's house in far-off Brooklyn. While waiting for the call to be connected, he began to relish the prospect of speaking to his mother and deriving strength and comfort from the force of her maternal love. Adams was somewhat startled, then, to have the phone answered by the unfamiliar voice of a woman who identified herself as Mrs. Whitney. The woman claimed to be overseeing the house while its owner, a Mrs. Adams, remained hospitalized, recovering from the shock of her son's death in an auto collision on the Brooklyn Bridge six days earlier. Adams was dumbstruck by the horror of her words and the conversation was terminated by the operator before he could find the language to respond.

The narrative falls away and leaves Adams staring at a cloudless night sky, his lonely thoughts wandering among the cold and distant flicker of stars. No longer sure of his sanity or even his sense of self, he steels himself for a final confrontation with the hitchhiker and his discovery of the unutterable truth.

CHARACTERS

Ronald Adams
Described as tall and darkly handsome, Ronald Adams is a Brooklynite in search of adventure on the open road. Although he is approaching middle age, Adams is unmarried and deeply devoted to his doting mother, who frets over her son's safety on his long journey to the West Coast. Readers are afforded intimate knowledge of this character's thoughts, emotional fluctuations, and fraying state of sanity as the horror of his situation intensifies.

Girl
The unnamed young woman picked up by Adams as a hitchhiker possesses a bubbly and flirtatious demeanor and is quick to praise the driver's good looks and the sportiness of his vehicle. Her admiration turns to wariness, however, with the increasingly bizarre nature of Adams's inquiries and his allusion to a persistent phantom hitchhiker. When Adam swerves into a grouping of cows and a barbed wire fence with the avowed purpose of mowing down his invisible tormentor, the girl is deaf to his entreaties to stay and insists on being let out of the vehicle.

Henry
The owner of a roadside establishment in the American Midwest, Henry is immediately on guard against the seemingly crazed man who disturbs his late-night rest for a cup of black coffee. He is helpful but unyielding in his refusal of the visitor and believes Adams to be helplessly drunk and possibly dangerous. Henry seems poised to alert the local sheriff at the first sign of trouble.

Hitchhiker
The ordinary, somewhat shabby exterior of the unnamed hitchhiker seems at odds with the profound sense of terror and mental instability embodied by his character. The man's appearance remains eerily unchanged over the weeklong duration of the narrative, right down to his articles of clothing and the dotting of rain along the shoulders of his jacket. A dearth of dialogue characterizes the hitchhiker, and his persistent, unexplained presence comes to dominate Adams's thoughts and drive him closer to the brink of insanity.

Mechanic
The pleasant, easygoing mechanic overseeing a gas station in rural Pennsylvania is the first character Adams speaks to since beginning his long journey from Brooklyn. The mechanic assures his customer that the local weather has been uncharacteristically dry and that hitchhikers are scarce to nonexistent along the road, two revelations that serve to unsettle Adams as he continues his drive.

Mother
A consummate mother, Mrs. Adams is consumed by worries of her son's cross-country road trip and is unable to contain her emotions at their parting. Mrs. Whitney informs Adams of his mother's complete mental breakdown and subsequent hospitalization, upon hearing the report of her son's demise on the Brooklyn Bridge.

Operator
The soulless, disembodied drone of the operator interrupts Adams's one remaining link to sanity in his call home to his mother.

Orson Welles
The iconic radio host, thespian, and director Orson Welles introduces Fletcher's radio play and praises its merit as a masterpiece of suspense and subtlety.

Mrs. Whitney
Adams does not recognize the voice of the woman who delivers the terrible news of his mother's breakdown over the phone. Beyond identifying herself by name, Mrs. Whitney provides no further introduction or explanation of her presence in the Adams household.

Henry's Wife
Henry's wife assists her husband in the running of the inn and prepares all the food for the guests of the establishment. Concerned for her husband's safety and somewhat alarmed by the late night visitation, she calls out to Henry as he turns Adams away from the doorstep.

THEMES

Loneliness

On his car ride across the country, Adams complains of a persistent loneliness that plagues him from the journey's inception to its end. The vastness of the open road and dearth of available companionship begins as a source of exhilaration for Adams but later contributes to his deepening sense of horror with each sighting of the mysterious hitchhiker. Eventually, Adams's all-consuming need for companionship manifests itself in his late night confrontation with the innkeeper, Henry, and his unhinged encounter with the young woman traveling to Texas. The more desperately he seeks out interaction with others, the further he finds himself from the possibility of human connection. Ironically, the one passenger Adams repeatedly refuses to take on comes to represent the only source of familiarity in an increasingly unsure and alienated existence.

Even outside of the context of his cross-country road trip, Adams is something of a self-described loner. Although fast approaching middle age, he is unmarried and childless and seems to have no close friends or family beyond his aging and overprotective mother. When she suffers a nervous breakdown and is hospitalized at the end of the radio play, the loneliness of her son becomes absolute.

Murder

Although he is introduced as respectable, well mannered, and devoted to his mother, Adams heart turns toward the prospect of murder at several points during the narrative. He attempts to end the life of the mysterious hitchhiker not once but twice during his journey, the first time at a railroad crossing in Oklahoma and the second approaching the border of Texas. This violent instinct is awakened by panic rather than cold-blooded intent, but it seems to cause Adam no pangs of remorse or self-doubt. This somewhat unexpected facet of his character becomes increasingly unapologetic and obsessive as the narrative progresses, marking Adams as a psychopathic monster in the eyes of the young woman he takes on as a hitchhiker. Adams is understandably dismayed but also perplexed by his passenger's reaction, his confusion hinting at an increased disconnect from societal expectations and codes of human conduct. In fearing for his life, Adams sheds his veneer of civilization for an untapped savagery.

The main character's newfound murderousness also makes him reckless. When he confronts his elusive nemesis across the train tracks, for instance, Adams expresses little anxiety at the prospect of another man's death or even his own. Stalled on the tracks and in the direct path of an oncoming train, his most pronounced emotions remain fury and frustration rather than fear. He interprets the beckoning of the hitchhiker as a challenge and rushes into confrontation without any concern for personal safety or for morality. By the end of the radio play, the violent changes wrought in Adam make him unrecognizable even to himself.

Sanity

The persistent reappearance of the hitchhiker combines with startling plot developments and the exhaustion of the main character to shed doubt on Adams's perception of reality. As his initial dependence on rationality gives way to the dictates of instinct and paranoia, listeners become caught up in the inherent ambiguities of Fletcher's tale. The audience is forced to compare their personal interpretation of the narrative unfolding with the terrible revelation afforded Adam in his conversation with Mrs. Whitney, questioning the truth of their previous observations and judgments. In this way, the madness of Adams becomes contagious and slips the bounds of the story to infect those he addresses.

Adams begins his account by relating dry, biographical details of his life as if to ground the narrative in indisputable fact. The balance between known and unknown is irretrievably upset, however, when hidden facets of the narrator's personality come to light and his encounters with the hitchhiker become increasingly frequent and improbable. The unchanging appearance of the apparition despite variations in climate, location, or time of day affords a sharp contrast to the narrator's destabilized sense of self. In this way, the enduring emblem of Adams's insanity is transformed into his sole source of certainty. The gradual transition from rationality to insanity becomes complete.

Travel

Adams expresses a considerable degree of wanderlust in his desire to traverse the country from coast to coast in his car. The immense exhilaration of the open road and the alignment of travel with freedom from the expectations of

TOPICS FOR FURTHER STUDY

- Fletcher's radio play takes the form of a deranged travelogue recounted by Adams in his drive across country. Using such online resources as Google Maps or MapQuest, plan and design your own itinerary, real or imagined, to share with your classmates. In addition to making note of such details as mileage, approximate time, and potential gas use, conduct research on sources of lodging and refreshment along your route. Draw upon all these details to pitch your travel plans to your peers, as Adams does to his mother in the beginning of the radio play. Welcome their comments and criticisms.

- In introducing Fletcher's haunting tale, Welles praises the qualities of psychological intrigue and suspense over traditional horror clichés. In this same spirit and with a partner, compose your own storyboard with these qualities in mind. In crafting your own tale of terror, attempt to eliminate shocking imagery and rely entirely upon subtlety to hammer your core idea home. Have fun with this and do your best to straddle the line between the possible and the impossible, relatable experience and unsettling implication.

- In analyzing *The Hitch-Hiker*, several online and educational resources lead students to consider the tenuous connection between sight and conviction. Is seeing believing? With the aid of a partner, brainstorm an array of personal experiences and potential circumstances that either bolster or undermine this controversial assertion. Create a PowerPoint or Prezi display to showcase your argument and present your joint analysis to the class.

- Despite the advanced age of her son, the doting Mrs. Adams expresses great concern for him on his perilous road trip across country. Drawing upon your own experience as a dependent, compile a list of the many rules and concerns that govern your own household and impede your personal

sense of adventure and fulfillment. Select one of these rules to analyze and group its implications in a chart according to pro and con categories. Write a brief evaluation of your final judgment on the rule and its potential validity within your life.

- Read Ellen Conford's young-adult classic *To All My Fans with Love, from Sylvie* (1982) side by side with *The Hitch-Hiker* and consider possible points of intersection between the two tales. With the help of a Venn diagram, compare and contrast the motivations of Adams and Sylvie for wanting to leave the familiar behind. Finally, write a paragraph detailing your own plans for the future, including places you would like to visit, and maybe someday even live, to be shared with a partner.

- Although Fletcher's narrative is sparsely populated with characters to reinforce the loneliness of her central protagonist, Adams experiences three upsetting encounters with Henry, the unnamed girl, and, of course, the dreaded hitchhiker himself. As his self-image begins to warp and dissolve, Adams obsesses over how he is perceived by these outside characters and the implications for his personal sense of identity. Assume the persona of one of these three characters and, from his or her perspective, rewrite the description of their encounter with the increasingly unhinged Adams.

- The ordinary and the terrifying combine in *The Hitch-Hiker* to warp the expectations of the audience and immerse them in Adams's growing sense of unease. With a partner, research the Shakespearean sonnet form and compose the first fourteen lines about an everyday activity in your lives. For the last two lines of the poetic form, known as the volta and intended to signal a reversal of tone or sentiment, incorporate a dark turn to your otherwise mundane subject matter.

When Adams gives a young woman a ride, she is at first flirtatious, but she becomes frightened by his obsession with the hitchhiker (© pathdoc | Shutterstock.com)

family and society, imbues the opening of *The Hitch-Hiker* with a sense of optimism and limitless possibility. The initial allure of travel experienced by Adams is soon tempered, and eventually utterly transformed, however, by the terror of the unfamiliar. The vast openness and variety of terrain he encounters on his trip devolves from a symbol of freedom to a source of confinement. Adams comes to exchange his exhilaration for a nightmarish exhaustion, the majestic scenery of each passing mile blurring into an unchanging expanse of desolation.

Adams initially embraces the prospect of travel in part to escape the predictable routine of his life in Brooklyn. Significantly, his first encounter with the hitchhiker occurs on the Brooklyn Bridge, which spans the East River and connects to Manhattan and the world beyond. If the report of Mrs. Whitney is to be believed, Adams meets his fate on the border of his native borough, never escaping the narrow confines of his childhood

home. The hitchhiker doubles as a reminder of the main character's unrequited destiny and his inability to slip the limitations of his past and experience adventure in the wider world. In this way, *The Hitch-Hiker* is a work obsessed both with liberation and imprisonment, the allure of travel and the impossibility of escape.

STYLE

Flash-forward

As opposed to flashbacks, which recall a previous memory or incident providing context for an unfolding narrative, flash-forwards reveal future developments yet to be realized by the plot. Although comparatively rare, this device can be used to great effect to excite the curiosity of readers and provide instant immersion in a story's intrigue. By opening her tale with a deranged narrator in fear for his very life, for instance,

Fletcher wastes no time in commanding the full attention of her listeners. Because the outcome of Adams's story is known before its details, the excitement of the tale is sustained throughout its gradual unfolding and results in the air of suspense so praised by Welles.

Foreshadowing

The striking inclusion of foreshadowing in Fletcher's radio play, the suggestion of upcoming themes and plot developments, further contributes to *The Hitch-Hiker's* unmistakable air of suspense and foreboding. The seemingly disproportionate concern of Mrs. Adams for her adult son's safety on the road and her ominous warning not to entertain hitchhikers, combine to establish a framework of horror that persists throughout the narrative. Increasing in scope and frequency, the many encounters between driver and would-be passenger also serve to heighten suspense and point toward an unavoidable outcome of confrontation. Additionally, the increasing wariness with which characters like Henry and the girl regard Adams foreshadows the gradual distortion of identity suffered by the main character with each sighting of the hitchhiker. By the end of the radio play, Adams is unrecognizable even to himself and struggles against an all-consuming loneliness and looming insanity.

Pathetic Fallacy

In her description of Adams's gradual descent into madness, Fletcher uses the literary device known as pathetic fallacy, or the melding of human sentiment with aspects of the natural world, to powerful and poignant effect. In particular, the diverse landscapes that confront Adams as he drives from coast to coast come to increasingly mirror his fleeting moods and fraying emotional state. A desolate stretch of road in Pennsylvania heightens the driver's sense of isolation, for instance, while the oppressive heat and surreal landscape of the Texas prairies contributes to the exhaustion of his mental faculties. The angry red clay of Oklahoma corresponds with Adams's attempted murder of the hitchhiker and his growing distaste for the journey with an unchanging expanse of woodlands. Most strikingly, the narrative ends with Adams gazing into a cloudless desert sky, losing himself among the myriad constellations and in the lightless depths between.

Fletcher makes use of pathetic fallacy not only to complement but also to contrast with her main character's state of mind. This is most evident in the juxtaposition of the pastoral tranquility of a field in Ohio, where Adams stops to consult a map, and the traumatic reappearance of the hitchhiker, which begins his nightmare anew. The contrast between setting and sentiment is so sudden and so jarring as to extinguish any hope for a happy ending.

Prologue

Although not part of the narrative itself, the prologue provided by Orson Welles serves to set the stage for the unique brand of terror distinguishing Fletcher's script from a stereotypical ghost story. Welles accomplishes this by discounting the timeworn clichés of cheap scares, restless spirits, and murders most foul and elevating in their place the virtues of psychological intrigue and carefully crafted thriller. Additionally, the prologue suggests the timeless allure of the supernatural and its perseverance even in an age of optimism and rationality. He attributes this appreciation of the unsettling and the unworldly to the spine, hinting at its supremacy over the more traditionally recognized seat of emotion, the heart. Through the few lines of the prologue, Welles both promotes Fletcher's piece and provides the audience with insight into the darker recesses of their own psyches.

HISTORICAL CONTEXT

Until gradually being replaced by television in the latter half of the twentieth century, the radio reigned supreme in American households for three decades between 1920 and 1950 and constituted a primary source of personal communication, news, sports coverage, and entertainment. Initially conceived as an extension of the telegraph and later the telephone, radio first came into its own after several prominent studies demonstrating the existence and potential application of radio waves between 1870 and 1890. Despite widespread dismissal of the radio as a discovery of great intrigue but limited practical value, Italian-born inventor Guglielmo Marconi pioneered an apparatus to harness radio waves and, in 1901, achieved the first transatlantic radio transmission. This singular triumph signaled the start of renewed interest in the technology by

COMPARE
&
CONTRAST

- **1940s:** After returning from his command in Europe during World War II, future president Dwight D. Eisenhower is inspired by the nascent Autobahn system he observed in Germany to advance a comparable highway system in the United States.

  Today: Named for the man who first envisioned its construction, the Dwight D. Eisenhower System of Interstate and Defense Highways connects the forty-eight mainland states and encompasses roughly fifty thousand miles of regularly maintained road.

- **1940s:** Although the vast majority of calls are still connected by trained operators tending to vast circuit boards, pioneering telecommunications companies begin assigning personalized telephone numbers to paying individuals in the United States and Canada. Over the intervening decade, this initiative gains in momentum and becomes known as the North American Numbering Plan.

- **Today:** Personal, completely portable cell phones become increasingly in vogue among the American public as well as "smartphones" equipped with instant messaging features, advanced photographic and picture-sending capabilities, and unlimited Internet connectivity.

- **1940s:** Before World War II or the association of hitchhiking with counterculture youth and vagrancy, it is considered socially responsible and even patriotic to take on passengers and provide free transportation to those in need.

  Today: Uber becomes a popular form of transportation and taxi alternative across the United States. As the service evolves, company executives begin working on plans to establish a comparable car-pooling service, often compared to hitch-hiking, to economize and reduce traffic congestion in cities like New York.

---

governments worldwide and an enduring love affair between the medium and an ever-expanding listening audience.

In the decade and a half following this breakthrough, pioneering Americans performed broadcasts and experimented and improved upon the original transmission apparatus. These unregulated amateurs made great strides in advancing radio technologies but were shut down in 1917 with the entrance of the United States into World War I. In spite of a dearth of technological material and an increased emphasis on airwave regulation, radio grew in prominence and profitability following the war and through the 1920s in the United States. Like-minded corporations came together to construct radio stations in key cities and established regulated, nationwide broadcasting, which directly contributed to the rise of major networks.

One of these networks, CBS, began broadcasting the *Mercury Theatre on the Air* in 1938, which originated as the shared vision of Orson Welles and famed producer John Houseman and quickly gained acclaim as one of the finest radio dramas of the age. It was initially without funding, but Campbell's Soup adopted the endeavor within its first year and changed the name of the program to the *Campbell Playhouse* to reflect the change of sponsorship. From its initial broadcasts in 1938 to its dissolution in 1941, the program became famed for bringing classics of world literature as well as contemporary and Shakespearean plays to millions of enraptured American listeners. As a corollary endeavor, Welles began *The Orson Welles Show* in 1941, dedicated to experimental radio dramas and thrillers like *The War of the Worlds*, by H. G. Wells, and *The Hitch-Hiker*, by Lucille Fletcher.

Adams is maddened by his frequent sightings of the hitchhiker and resolves to run him down (© Mr.Exen / Shutterstock.com)

CRITICAL OVERVIEW

Although contemporary reviews of the original radio play authored by Fletcher and famously broadcast by Welles are scarce, the vignette has since been recognized not only for its creative merit but also for its stylistic contribution to later developments, on and off radio, within the suspense genre. Bruce Pilbeam of the *Old Time Radio Review* remarks on *The Hitch-Hiker's* continued popularity on various radio broadcasts and eventual adaptation to the silver screen as evidence of its classic status. While acknowledging the theatrical restraint of Welles and the musical genius of Bernard Herrmann in augmenting the original production, he takes care to praise the skillful writing at the heart of the radio play's success. In particular, Pilbeam credits Fletcher for her narrative's elusive, teasing quality and her use of scenic description to alert the listeners to impending calamity. Pilbeam writes,

> The feeling of slowly unfolding unease and foreboding is expertly built up and the periodic sightings of the hitchhiker leave the listener

keen to discover who—or what—he is. Yet as much as it is the figure of the hitchhiker that helps create the episode's unnerving atmosphere, so too do the descriptions of the barren, deserted landscapes the protagonist passes through.

Pilbeam goes on to explain that the relative familiarity of modern audiences with plot twists of the kind introduced by *The Hitch-Hiker* is further testament to the play's influence on subsequent television broadcasts. In a similar vein, media scholar Amy Lawrence credits such radio plays and, in particular, Fletcher's other great success, *Sorry, Wrong Number*, with anticipating the gradual shift from radio to television. She explains how the author balanced cinematic visuals and the cherished peculiarities of radio address to render her scripts so adaptable to the big screen. The dramatic telephone conversations contained in both of Fletcher's famous radio plays, for instance, revel in sound effects and dialogue but avoid awkward direct address in favor of the overheard quality so central to the emerging medium of film.

In constructing his larger case for the alignment of sound with signal in American wartime radio, scholar Neil Verma at once places *The Hitch-Hiker* at the heart of the emerging thriller and suspense genre and distinguishes it from other classic broadcasts of the era. Verma praises Fletcher's novel approach to the writing of radio plays and her reimagining and outright rejection of "the task of conveying exterior space" obsessing so many of her contemporaries. Rather than paint the world without, he contends, Fletcher pursued the opposite course and focused on the character within, fully immersing listeners in the psyche and perceptions of the narrator. In turn, this buffers listeners from larger concerns of the outside world and reduces social ramifications to the realm of the personal. Verma explains in his article "Honeymoon Shocker: Lucille Fletcher's 'Psychological' Sound Effects and Wartime Radio Drama,"

> In this way, Fletcher builds a world only to tell us that it is not there, using a theater that creates landscapes to develop a theater that imagines the psyche as itself a landscape. . . . In Fletcher's play, with the exception of the narrator, we do not get to know anyone very well, which gives the play a solipsism that prevents us from using the protagonist as a proxy to access scenes.

Dennis Wepman of *American National Biography* echoes this viewpoint and praises the unique brand of suspense that Fletcher helped to spawn as premised not so much on the uncertainty of the outside world as on the still more terrifying uncertainty within.

CRITICISM

Jeffrey Palmer

Palmer is a scholar, freelance writer, and teacher of high school English. In the following essay, he examines the unique role of Ruskin's "pathetic fallacy" in the scenic depictions of Fletcher's The Hitch-Hiker.

Writing almost a century before Fletcher and long before the advent of the first radio broadcasts, famed critic John Ruskin coined the term *pathetic fallacy* to help describe the artistic relationship between the human and the environment and to distinguish among different orders of creative genius. In his 1856 essay "Of the Pathetic Fallacy," Ruskin describes the seduction of this particular literary device to

> WHEN ADAMS GAZES INTO THE INFINITE, STAR-SPANGLED SKY OF THE AMERICAN SOUTHWEST, HE, TOO, FINDS HIMSELF UNDER THE INFLUENCES OF LARGER AND EVEN MORE UNFATHOMABLE POWERS THAN EMOTION."

authors of an inferior talent, likening it to a form of delusion and emotional hysteria. "All violent feelings have the same effect," he writes. "They produce in us a falseness in all our impressions of external things which I would generally characterize as the '*Pathetic Fallacy*'." His oft-cited conclusion, namely, that resistance to this brand of obscuring emotion signals true sight and artistic merit, is most often examined within the context of poetry but finds equal resonance in Lucille Fletcher's *The Hitch-Hiker*, crafted for a medium relying on evocative imagery and the immersion of the listening audience in an alien perspective.

Fletcher engages with Ruskin's argument, albeit unknowingly, in a manner consistent with the subtle complexity of her narrative and its avowed aim to undermine expectations. On the face of it, her main character, Adams, is a textbook offender of the charges levied against pathetic fallacy, allowing the scenery outside his car window to become a mirror to his changing moods and emotions. The narrator speaks of sleepy towns, dreaming fields, lonely country, and wild woods, matching scenic descriptions to his alternating states of exhaustion, paranoia, and intermittent fits of rage.

What begins as a clear-cut reliance on pathetic fallacy, however, soon manifests itself as a creeping inconsistency in the perfect alignment of landscape and emotion. Tranquil scenery becomes a trigger for unexpected trauma, as evidenced by the bucolic meadow where Adams takes on a passenger and suffers violent hallucinations, and open expanse, traditionally a symbol of freedom and limitless possibility, itself becomes a source of confinement and crushing loneliness. In this way, and with her characteristic subtlety, Fletcher begins to sow the seeds of doubt in the minds of her listeners.

WHAT DO I READ NEXT?

- Published in 1957 as one of the defining classics of the Beat Generation, Jack Kerouac's *On the Road* remains an enduring testament to American wanderlust and the freedom of the open road.

- *Journey to an 800 Number*, by E. L. Konigsburg, was first published in 1982 as a young-adult tale of unexpected adventure and self-discovery revolving around a pampered boy who sheds his wealthy expectations to travel the country with his father, an itinerant camel keeper involved in show business.

- Coauthored by Allan Ullman and encouraged by Fletcher's husband Douglass Wallop, *Night Man* is a 1951 adaptation of Fletcher's screenplay and her debut into the world of the novel.

- The 1897 science fiction classic of open war between humanity and extraterrestrial invaders, *The War of the Worlds* was authored by H. G. Wells and adapted to a famous Orson Welles radio broadcast in 1938. So enthralling and believable was its presentation that the broadcast caused widespread panic among listeners and garnered Welles considerable funding and praise.

- Written and compiled by series creator Rod Serling in 1960, *Stories from the Twilight Zone* showcases the most famous episodes of the television program, including "The Hitch-Hiker," adapted from Fletcher's original radio play.

- A beautifully written saga of an engineering marvel in a bygone America, David McCullough's 1972 *The Great Bridge* relates the compelling true story of the construction of Brooklyn's most famous landmark, the ill-fated bridge where Adams first encounters the hitchhiker.

- *A Heart at Fire's Center: The Life and Music of Bernard Herrmann* is a 1991 biography by Steven C. Smith written about Fletcher's first husband and his challenges as a family man.

- *The Year the Yankees Lost the Pennant* is a cherished American classic, written in 1954 by Fletcher's second husband, the novelist Douglass Wallop, and grafting elements of the fantastic on the turbulent, real-world baseball scene of the 1950s.

- One of the lesser-known works of famous wanderer, novelist, and chronicler of the American people John Steinbeck, *Travels with Charley in Search of America* was published in 1962 as the author's final attempt to regain a sense of connection with the country he so loved. Accompanied by his canine companion, Charley, the aging author leaves his home in New York to travel across the vast expanse of America in search of adventure and fresh inspiration.

- Brought together in a comprehensive and carefully edited volume in 1995, *Franz Kafka: The Complete Stories* showcases the collected works of Czech-Jewish author Franz Kafka, a celebrated master of the bizarre and the uncanny.

Not only do the natural and emotional distortions allowed by pathetic fallacy become increasingly unreliable within the narrative, they also become utterly untrustworthy. In attempting to demonstrate what he views as the ironclad divide between immutable quality and shifting perception, fanciful overlay and unyielding truth, Ruskin turns to a description of color in the natural world.

> Now, to get rid of all these ambiguities and troublesome words at once, be it observed that the word "Blue" does *not* mean the *sensation* caused by a gentian on the human eye; but it means the *power* of producing that sensation;

and this power is always there, in the thing, whether we are there to experience it or not, and would remain there though there were not left a man on the face of the earth.

This black-and-white understanding of inherent reality finds an opponent in Fletcher's radio play in a small but crucial detail of the hitchhiker's dress. The persistent dotting of rain on the shoulders of his coat confounds Adams's attempts at rational explanation and remains unchanging despite conditions of intense sun, dry heat, and even utter drought. Adams is denied even the comfort of being deceived by his senses, while this inherent quality of the jacket remains as immutable as it does impossible in the story. In this way, the "false appearances" that Ruskin believes undermine reality instead become its foundation. Adams does not betray the truth of the world through his emotional interpretation; rather, the truth of the world betrays him.

Radio critic and scholar Neil Verma believes that Fletcher's shocking inversion of internal and external realities is no accident. In his essay "Honeymoon Shocker: Lucille Fletcher's 'Psychological' Sound Effects and Wartime Radio Drama," Verma contends that this is an intentional, brilliant attempt on the part of the author to rewire the expectations of the audience and introduce an altogether novel form of broadcast. Fletcher's innovation elevates the importance of psychological nuance over more obvious physicality in the emerging suspense genre, altogether altering, but not dismissing, the import of Ruskin's examination. The hidden terrain of the mind, Fletcher suggests in her radio play, is infinitely more intriguing than the visible scenery without. Verma elaborates on this quality of Fletcher's work and links it to an isolation and self-reliance bordering on solipsism.

> In this way, Fletcher builds a world only to tell us that it is not there, using a theater that creates landscapes to develop a theater that imagines the psyche as itself a landscape.... In Fletcher's play, with the exception of the narrator, we do not get to know anyone very well, which gives the play a solipsism that prevents us from using the protagonist as a proxy to access scenes.

The sense of alienation resulting from this marked shift from exterior to interior impressions conveyed by Fletcher contributes to another possible point of intersection between *The Hitch-Hiker* and Ruskin's "Of the Pathetic Fallacy." The character of Adams, in the tenor of his emotions, in his deeply felt apartness from the greater tide of humanity, and in the magnitude of the forces arrayed against him, unveils and perhaps exemplifies an enigmatic inconsistency in the work of the famed critic. As the narrator and by extension the implied writer, Adams's heightened sensitivity and adherence to aspects of pathetic fallacy would seem to condemn him to the one of the lowest rungs of Ruskin's hierarchy, namely, the poetic temperament belonging to men who "feel strongly, think weakly, and see untruly." The simplicity of this categorization is potentially undermined, however, by two caveats contained in the critic's argument, inconsistencies, bordering on hypocrisy, noted by scholar Vernon Young in his article "Landscapes in Prose: The Pathetic Fallacy in the Southwest." These correspond roughly to the magnitude and nature of the influence exerted on the poet and justify, if not altogether excuse, otherwise impassioned and imprecise observations. Young writes, "Ruskin was not precisely consistent in his objections since he admitted and demonstrated that the practice was acceptable when controlled by a special kind of talent, or a unique condition of temperament."

The first of the inconsistencies alluded to by Young corresponds to Ruskin's assertion that literary personification falls short of true pathetic fallacy when "put into the mouth of the wrong passion." As a specific example of this exception, the critic cites curiosity and, by extension, states of confusion and unsureness as being altogether distinct from distortions resulting from pure emotion. He argues that characters seeking after truth, or unconvinced of the true nature of their surroundings, graft human qualities to inanimate objects not to express an unseemly overflow of sentiment, but merely to assist in the process of understanding. Introduced by his shattered sense of personal identity and utter loss of faith in reality, Adams falls neatly into this category. His "agonized curiosity," in the language of Ruskin, excuses his reliance on pathetic fallacy to help remap the world around him.

The second and by far the more intriguing loophole in Ruskin's rant against practitioners of pathetic fallacy can be explored through his categorization of the four classes of poetic temperament. While the first three of these classes resist or fall prey to the distortions of violent emotion, the fourth is subjected to an altogether different sort of influence. Ruskin does not exempt this final class from the charge of false-hood, but he praises this quality in such individuals and elevates it to the level of divine, albeit deluded inspiration. He likens these creative minds not to poets but to prophets, their rare glimpses of the world beyond intruding on and subsequently obscuring the readily discernible truth of this material one. Ruskin describes these rare beings as

> the men who, strong as human creatures can be, are yet submitted to influences stronger than they, and see in a sort untruly, because what they see is inconceivably above them. This last is the usual condition of prophetic inspiration.

When Adams gazes into the infinite, star-spangled sky of the American Southwest, he, too, finds himself under the influences of larger and even more unfathomable powers than emotion. The sheer force of revelation and of truth that assails Adams shakes him loose from the cozy convictions he previously enjoyed and threatens to altogether obliterate his sense of being. The elemental majesty and sublime terror of his environment play no small role in conveying this impression, dwarfing Adams and placing him, both liter-ally and figuratively, under the indisputable authority of the heavens.

The solipsistic isolation of Adams's charac-ter noted by critics like Verma combines with the unsettling conclusion of the narrative and Rus-kin's assertions to mark Fletcher's protagonist as a man not only apart from his fellows but also above them. Subjected to the grim wisdom of the grave and driven by an all-consuming hunger for understanding, Adams's brand of pathetic fal-lacy takes the form of vital necessity rather than poetic crutch. Neither asked for nor desired, his descriptive distortions are the pained and uncer-tain utterances of a prophet. Quite literally, his is a voice in the wilderness, calling us, the audience, to acceptance of a terrible and inescapable truth.

Source: Jeffrey Eugene Palmer, Critical Essay on *The Hitch-Hiker*, in *Drama for Students*, Gale, Cengage Learning, 2017.

Sarah Montague

In the following essay, Fletcher's legacy in the history of radio is described.

If the much-quoted tag line from *The Shadow* "Who knows what evil lurks in the heart of men? The Shadow knows!" (followed by sinister chuckle) is your idea of Golden Age radio, you don't know Lucille Fletcher, who was born 100 [years] ago today. A demure Vassar graduate from a working class family, Brook-lyn-born Fletcher was the author of two of the most famous radio dramas of all time—*The Hitchhiker* and *Sorry, Wrong Number*. Radio drama in the 1930s and 1940s was male domi-nated, and Fletcher initially got an entry-level job at CBS as a typist, but eventually began submitting work of her own. Once accepted into the ranks of radio dramatists, she helped to transformed the medium.

Orson Welles is associated primarily with Golden Age radio's most notorious broadcast, *The War of the Worlds*, but he was a presence in a number of other seminal works. He voiced the early *Shadow* dramas (and the network kept that trademark laugh), and was the lead in Archibald MacLeish's anti-totalitarian drama *The Fall of the City*. He also starred in Fletcher's *The Hitch-hiker*, which first aired in 1941. Welles later reprised the broadcast as part of his own Mercury Theatre, beginning with this tribute to Fletcher:

> We of the Mercury reckon that a story doesn't have to appeal to the heart, it can also appeal to the spine. Sometimes you want your heart to be warm, sometimes you want your spine to tin-gle. Well the tingling we hope will be quite audible as you listen tonight to [a] classic among radio thrillers. Its author is one of the most gifted writers who ever worked for this medium.

He went on to refer to *The Hitchhiker* as "a terrifying little tale of grue."

There was plenty of "grue" in radio, which was the country's dominant entertainment medium. Millions of people tuned into gritty crime dramas, and spooky series like *Suspense*, and Arch Obler's *Lights Out*, as well as to antic comedies and heart-warming family fare.

But Fletcher took the form to a whole new level. She knew instinctively that sound drama wasn't simply sound effects, but a psychic space in the brain, a landscape of the unknown. As she said in an interview with entertainment critic Leonard Maltin (cited in his book *The Great American Broadcast*), "The audience provided a good part of it; if you could excite their own imagination, they filled in the rest."

From the opening lines of *The Hitchhiker*, you know that, even though the narrator describes

Desperate, Adams finds a payphone and calls home, hoping that hearing a familiar voice will ground him (© Pumtek / Shutterstock.com)

his location, you are actually in *terra incognita*: "I'm in an auto camp on Route 66 just west of Gallup, New Mexico. If I tell it, maybe it will help me. It will keep me from going crazy."

And then, Fletcher pulls back the weird, and gives us the quotidian, because she knows that radio is the place where the membrane between the two is very thin, and the slow build from the known to the unknown is where the frisson lies.

The premise of *The Hitchhiker* is simple: Ronald Adams, a nice boy from Brooklyn, takes leave of his anxious mother to embark on a cross country drive. Early on in the journey, he is hailed by a hitchhiker, who thereafter appears to him over and over again: "I saw a man leaning against the cables. He seemed to be waiting for a lift. There were spots of fresh rain on his shoulders. He was carrying a cheap overnight bag in one hand. He was thin, nondescript, with a cap pulled down over his eyes."

As Adams' initial bemusement—how did the guy beat him to the next location?—gives way to

panic and dread, Fletcher deftly turns an innocuous journey into an existential nightmare.

She writes so that a tableau opens in your mind. She was helped by Welles' nuanced delivery—a boy from Wisconsin who nevertheless had what he called "a king voice" so that even the most ordinary remarks compelled, and the dramatic ones thrummed and haunted us.

The mood of the piece was also enhanced by the musical elements created by Fletcher's then boyfriend, Bernard Hermann, whom she subsequently married. Hermann, later to terrify us in *Psycho*, was the CBS network's resident conductor-composer, and for *Hitchhiker* he offered an eerie unresolved score that mirrors Ronald's sense of displacement and isolation.

Another thing that Fletcher knew instinctively was that drama is often most powerful when the audience is a step ahead of the characters—in *Hitchhiker*, Ronald is clinging to normality by trying to rationalize the figure's presence. But we know, before he does, that something ultimate is happening here.

When Fletcher does deliver the blow, it is through a mind-jangling device. At the time, coin-operated pay phones were everywhere, and Ronald's painful insertion of coins into the slot, so that he can call his mother and be reassured about the world, leaves us tense with expectation.

And when he does get through, it is only to be plunged—irrevocably this time—back into the nightmare. Ronald Adams, he is informed by the stranger who picks up the phone, died six days ago crossing the Brooklyn Bridge: "The vast, soulless night of New Mexico. A million stars are in the sky. Ahead of me stretch a thousand miles of empty mesa and mountains, prairies, desert. Somewhere among them, he is waiting for me—somewhere. Somewhere I shall know who he is. And who I am."

Oh, those last lines. Camus could not have done better.

Fletcher used a phone to even more terrifying effect two years later, in what Welles called the "greatest radio play ever written," *Sorry, Wrong Number*. Since it's original broadcast, on *Suspense*, which starred Agnes Moorehead, it has been performed all over the world, in at least fifteen languages including Zulu.

In that interview with Maltin, Fletcher said that part of radio's power was in its "spareness." If *Hitchhiker* is a horrible dream being played out all across the American continent, *Wrong Number* is the opposite—a triumph of the ordinary turned macabre, its only landscape the bedroom of a peevish invalid who slowly realizes that she is the intended victim of a murder.

Both *The Hitchhiker* and *Sorry, Wrong Number* were adapted—the former for a *Twilight Zone* episode, the latter into a film, starring Barbara Stanwyck, with a much more elaborate plot. But the plays lost some of their power once images took the place of our own agonized imaginings.

Fletcher is largely forgotten except by old-time radio buffs, but her legacy remains—in the works of sound artists such as Joe Frank and Jad Abumrad, who conjure up place with voice and sound, and in all of us who know that radio's whisper can be more powerful than a shout.

Source: Sarah Montague, "The Woman Who Taught Us to Listen: A Centenary Tribute to Lucille Fletcher," in *WNYC*, March 28, 2012.

Economist

In the following obituary, Fletcher's prominence in a genre dominated by male writers is highlighted.

A play called *Sorry, Wrong Number* written by Lucille Fletcher, was first broadcast on a New York radio station in 1943, and, in one form or another, in some part of the world, has been running almost continuously ever since. It has been translated into 15 languages, among them Zulu. It was made into two films, one a much praised Hollywood production and another for television. Two operas have been based on its story.

There are perhaps two interesting things to say about this history. One is that the play, which in its original form lasted only 22 minutes, brought Miss Fletcher a lot of money for not a great deal of work. The other is that, every now and again, a writer hits on an idea, perhaps randomly, which unexpectedly takes off. . . .

LEAVING IT TO THE IMAGINATION

Lucille Fletcher was one of the women writers who have come to dominate the mystery genre in the United States and Europe; some say she was the best. Women writers have been enthusiastically deploying their murderous imaginations for well over a century. This was an occupation without a sex bar. All the publisher wanted was a good story. . . .

When Miss Fletcher started writing in the 1930s the biggest audiences were provided by radio. "I grew up in an era when the radio was a wonderful medium for the imagination," she said. When the sound-effects man sank a knife into a cabbage the listener saw an axe crunching into the victim's head. One of the strengths of radio drama was, and is, that it could have more impact on the imagination of the audience than film or television.

The big test for the writer was to keep the suspense going though the breaks for advertisements for beer or cereal or whatever: eight minutes of them in a 30-minute programme. Miss Fletcher's strategy was to keep the plot simple: perhaps deploying just one idea with a central character caught in a "baffling and haunting situation, endlessly in doubt, tortured by circumstance, and then see what happens."

Fine performers were happy to speak her lines, among them Agnes Moorehead, Ida Lupino and Orson Welles. The plays were as precisely excellent, in their own way, as miniature paintings. Expanded into films, they lost some of their tension.

Later Lucille Fletcher wrote novels, all of them with dark themes, but more complex than her radio plays. "You bury the secret, lead the reader down the path, put in false leads and throughout the story remain completely logical," she said. A daughter recalls watching her mother writing at her typewriter as if she was "in a trance." The child would say, "Can I have $10,000?" and her mother would reply, absently, "It's in my purse." She wrote her last novel at the age of 75. It was a blood-curdling story called *Mirror Image. . . .*

Source: "Lucille Fletcher," in *Economist*, September 14, 2000.

SOURCES

Eder, Bruce, "Lucille Fletcher Biography," Fandango website, http://www.fandango.com/lucillefletcher/biography/p183399 (accessed July 1, 2016.)

Fletcher, Lucille, "The Hitchhiker Radio Play by Lucille Fletcher," D47 website, http://home.d47.org/jmludwig/files/2015/05/the-hitch-hiker-full-text.pdf (accessed July 1, 2016).

Gelder, Lawrence Van, "Lucille Fletcher, 88, Author Of 'Sorry, Wrong Number,'" in *New York Times*, http://www.nytimes.com/2000/09/06/arts/lucille-fletcher-88-author-of-sorry-wrong-number.html1 (accessed July 1, 2016).

"Highways Timeline," Greatest Engineering Achievements of the Twentieth Century, http://www.greatachievements.org/?id = 3786 (accessed July 1, 2016).

Lawrence, Amy, "'Sorry, Wrong Number': The Organizing Ear," in *Film Quarterly*, Vol. 40, No. 2, 1986, pp. 20–27.

Pierce, Art, "Orson Welles, the Mercury Theatre, and the Campbell Playhouse," Mercury Theatre on the Air, http://www.mercurytheatre.info/history (accessed July 1, 2016)

Pilbeam, Bruce, "The Hitchhiker," in *Old Time Radio Review: Suspense*, http://www.oldtimeradioreview.com/suspense—h.html (accessed July 1, 2016).

"Pioneering U.S. Radio Activities," United States Early Radio History, http://earlyradiohistory.us/ (accessed July 1, 2016).

Ruskin, John, "Of the Pathetic Fallacy," Our Civilisation website, http://www.ourcivilisation.com/smartboard/shop/ruskinj/ (accessed July 1, 2016).

Strand, Ginger, "Hitchhiking's Time Has Come Again," in *New York Times*, http://www.nytimes.com/2012/11/11/opinion/sunday/hitchhikings-time-has-come-again.html (accessed July 1, 2016).

"Telephone Timeline," Greatest Engineering Achievements of the Twentieth Century, http://www.greatachievements.org/?id = 3625 (accessed July 1, 2016).

Verma, Neil, "Honeymoon Shocker: Lucille Fletcher's 'Psychological' Sound Effects and Wartime Radio Drama," in *Journal of American Studies*, Vol. 44, No. 1, 2010, pp. 137–53.

Wepman, Dennis, "Fletcher, Lucille," in *American National Biography Online*, http://www.anb.org/articles/16/16-03528.html (accessed July 1, 2016).

Young, Vernon, "Landscapes in Prose: The Pathetic Fallacy in the Southwest," in *Southwest Review*, Vol. 34, No. 1, 1949, pp. 55–65.

FURTHER READING

Fletcher, Lucille, *Sorry, Wrong Number and The Hitch-Hiker*, Dramatists Play Service, 1998.
> The 1998 dual-edition of *Sorry, Wrong Number and The Hitch-Hiker* brings together two of Lucille Fletcher's most profound contributions to the glory of Old Time Radio and the emerging suspense genre

Maltin, Leonard, *The Great American Broadcast: A Celebration of Radio's Golden Age*, Dutton Adult, 1997.
> In his landmark work released in 1997, *The Great American Broadcast*, Leonard Maltin brings to life the incredible careers and personal stories of giants of the Golden Age of Radio, including many of Fletcher's most intimate creative contemporaries.

Heyer, Paul, *The Medium and the Magician: Orson Welles, the Radio Years*, Rowman and Littlefield Publishers, 2005.
> Paul Heyer's 2005 *The Medium and the Magician: Orson Welles, the Radio Years* is a comprehensive examination of the man's unparalleled impact upon an American listening audience wedded to their radios and beset by war and the tides of social change.

McCarthy, Mary, *The Group*, Harvest Books, 1991.
> A celebrated novelist who engaged in friendly competition with Lucille Fletcher throughout their shared years at Vassar, Mary McCarthy released her memoir *The Group* in 1963 as a classic of emerging womanhood, rebellion, and creative brilliance in a progressive college setting.

Weinman, Sarah, *Women Crime Writers: Eight Suspense Novels of the 1940s and 50s*, Library of America, 2015.

A compilation of some of the most influential thrillers and crime literature of the day, *Women Crime Writers: Eight Suspense Novels of the 1940s and 50s* is a Library of America box set released by editor Sarah Weinman in 2015.

Strand, Ginger, *Killer on the Road: Violence and the American Interstate*, Texas University Press, 2015.

Ginger Strand's 2012 *Killer on the Road: Violence and the American Interstate* relates real life anecdotes of murder and mayhem on the open road, incidents giving birth to the eternally ominous figure of "the hitch-hiker" capitalized on by Fletcher.

SUGGESTED SEARCH TERMS

The Hitch-Hiker AND radio play

Lucille Fletcher

The Hitch-Hiker AND Lucille Fletcher

Orson Welles AND The Hitch-Hiker

suspense AND The Hitch-Hiker

Mercury Theatre on the Air

old time radio broadcasts

Golden Age of Radio

The Hitch-Hiker AND the Twilight Zone

Lucille Fletcher AND Bernard Herrmann

Stop Kiss

DIANA SON

1998

Diana Son's *Stop Kiss*, first produced in 1998, tells the story of two women in New York City who fall unexpectedly in love. Callie, a traffic reporter without much direction in life, meets Sara, a bright-eyed newcomer to the city, through a friend of a friend when she agrees to watch Sara's cat. In the months that follow, the women find themselves enamored of each other—though they do their best to fight the current of attraction that pulls them closer. The scenes of this developing romance are interspersed with the aftermath, months later, of their first kiss, which was interrupted by a vicious attack from a homophobic stranger. As Sara lies in a coma, Callie is left alone to deal with the interference of Sara's disapproving family and her own confused emotions. *Stop Kiss* explores love and violence in New York City, as Callie chooses between a safe but listless life and the danger of giving her heart away for good.

AUTHOR BIOGRAPHY

Son was born in Philadelphia, Pennsylvania, in 1965. A first-generation Korean American, she grew up in Dover, Delaware. She developed an interest in writing in the fourth grade, encouraged by the recognition of her work by her teachers. After a high school field trip to see *Hamlet* at the Public Theater in New York City, Son became interested in a career as a playwright. She attended

Diana Son *(© Bruce Glikas / FilmMagic / Getty Images)*

New York University from 1983 to 1987, earning a bachelor's degree in dramatic literature.

Her plays include *R.A.W. (Because I'm a Woman)* (1996), *Boy* (1996), *Fishes* (1998), and *Satellites* (2006). *Stop Kiss* premiered at the Public Theater on December 8, 1998, to widespread critical acclaim. Son was awarded the GLAAD Media Award for Outstanding New York Production and the Berilla Kerr Award for Playwriting for *Stop Kiss*, which has been produced in more than a hundred theaters throughout the world.

A member of the Dramatists Guild of America and New Dramatists, Son served as the NEA/TCG playwright-in-residence at the Mark Taper Forum from 2000 to 2001. She taught play writing at the Yale School of Drama as a visiting lecturer. In addition to her work for the stage, Son is a successful television writer and producer. She has worked on *Blue Bloods, American Crime, Law & Order: Criminal Intent, Law & Order:*

Criminal Mind, Southland, The West Wing, Do No Harm, 13 Reasons Why, Love Is a Four-Letter Word, Jo, and *NYC 22*. She lives with her husband in New York City.

PLOT SUMMARY

Scene 1

Stop Kiss alternates between two time lines. The first begins inside the cluttered New York City apartment of Callie, a young, single woman. Her phone rings. Her friend George wonders why she is late, and Callie explains she is waiting for a friend of a friend to arrive at the apartment. The newcomer, Sara, buzzes the door to the apartment. Callie hangs up with George, scanning the apartment as if to clean up. However, judging it a lost cause, she goes to the door to let in Sara, who is holding a cat carrier. Sara introduces herself and her cat, Caesar, thanking Callie profusely for watching her cat (because she does not have room for him at her shared apartment) and admiring the size of her apartment. Callie inherited the apartment from an ex-boyfriend, who left New York City to move to Los Angeles with Callie's sister.

Sara is a new arrival in New York City from St. Louis, Missouri, where she lived close to her parents and taught third grade at a Quaker school. She tells Callie that life was easy and she is ready for the challenge of New York, but Callie is concerned about the school where Sara will be teaching: a student recently killed a teacher there. Callie is a traffic reporter for a news station, flying around the city in a helicopter—a job that impresses Sara, though Callie finds it repetitive. Sara finds Callie's Magic Eight Ball and shakes it, asking if moving to New York was a good idea, but it gets stuck between two sides. Callie tells Sara to feel free to come over to visit Caesar and offers to give her a tour of the neighborhood that weekend. Sara enthusiastically agrees.

Scene 2

The second time line of the story begins in a hospital examination room months later, with Callie sitting on the table while Detective Cole asks her questions about an attack. He asks if the attacker was coming on to her, but she says he was just saying "guy stuff." Callie reports that she wanted to leave, but Sara talked back to him.

When the detective calls Sara Callie's girlfriend, she is quick to correct him, saying they are just friends. She describes how the attacker beat Sara, making her lose consciousness.

The detective asks why Sara and Callie were in the park at four in the morning. Callie tells him they had just left a bar, but she cannot say who the bartender there was. The detective summarizes Callie's story: a man saw two women walking in a park, approached them with a pickup line, was rejected, and proceeded to beat one of the women into a coma. Callie confirms the summary. When the detective asks her to come to the police station to look at pictures of possible suspects, Callie says she cannot leave the hospital; she wants to be present in case Sara wakes up.

Scene 3

In the earlier time line, Sara is at Callie's apartment. She describes a man in the park who harasses her as she walks by every day. Sara says she should stand up for herself, but Callie advises her to keep her head down instead. George calls to invite Callie out to the bar, leaving a message that both women hear. Sara offers to leave, but Callie asks her to stay. When Sara asks whether George is Callie's boyfriend, Callie explains that the relationship is less serious than that, but they will probably end up married. Sara says she left her boyfriend of seven years, Peter, behind in St. Louis when she moved to New York. She remembers that Peter said he would call her at six—he is planning on visiting—but decides she can miss his call in order to stay at Callie's. A loud stomping sound comes from the apartment above. Sara is shocked, but Callie says it happens every Thursday and Saturday at six. Sara wants to go upstairs to complain, but Callie says no—she has adjusted to the stomping schedule.

Scene 4

Detective Cole interviews a smartly dressed businesswoman named Mrs. Winsley at the police station. She tells him the attacker directed a homophobic slur to Sara and Callie. He asks why, and Mrs. Winsley explains that this area, the West Village, has a high concentration of gay and lesbian bars, clubs, and residences—the chances are high, in her opinion, that the women were lesbians. She did not see what set the attacker off but heard the screams and looked out the window to witness the beating.

She called 911 and threw flowerpots at the attacker until he fled.

Scene 5

At home, Callie puts a fresh bouquet of flowers in a vase on the table and then begins to fuss over what to wear in front of a mirror. The door buzzes, and Callie accidentally knocks over the vase as she buzzes the guest into the building. When George walks through the front door, she is shocked. While George makes himself comfortable, Callie tells him she has plans to meet Sara for dinner.

When Sara arrives outside, Callie tells George it is time for him to leave. Callie opens the door, accepting a bouquet of small roses from Sara. They kiss each other awkwardly on the cheek. When George speaks, he startles Sara, who had not noticed him. George tries to invite himself along (they are planning on going to an elegant restaurant and a movie), but Callie refuses. George then asks what occasion they are celebrating, but neither woman has an answer. Sara invites George to accompany them for part of their evening, but after glancing at Callie, George declines.

Scene 6

At the police station, Detective Cole interviews Callie. He tells her about a discrepancy in their story: the bartender who had served them earlier that night was a woman, not a man. Callie says Sara was the one getting the drinks. He asks what they were doing in the park and whether the attacker called Sara a name; Callie denies it. He continues to press her, and she finally shouts that the attacker did use the homophobic slur that Mrs. Winsley overheard. When the detective asks why, Callie, defeated, admits that they were kissing. The man had interrupted them, and when Sara shouted at him, he beat her into a coma as Callie tried to rescue her.

Scene 7

Callie and Sara drink wine in Callie's apartment, talking about how they would react in different scenarios: swerve to avoid a pothole or an animal in the road or react some other way? Sara thinks Callie would swerve every time, and she imitates Sara swerving through life with her hands on the steering wheel. She invites a reluctant Callie to come to her school to meet her students.

Callie complains about her job; Sara urges her to quit, but Callie says she cannot. She offers Sara her sofa for the night. She says maybe Caesar, the cat, will finally come out of hiding to sleep with Sara, as he now sleeps with Callie each night. Sara calls the cat lucky. They pull out the sofa bed together and say goodnight. Sara calls in vain for Caesar. Sara asks Callie lie down with her until Caesar comes out of hiding. They steal glances at each other while pretending to be asleep.

Scene 8

George, wearing a bartender's uniform, bangs on Callie's door. When she answers in her pajamas, he loudly demands to know how long she has been home and why she did not tell him about the attack or ask him for a ride home from the hospital. Callie describes the scene at the hospital: Sara lying unresponsive with her bruised and swollen face. She asks George whether he remembers their first kiss. Neither of them does. But each night, saying good-bye to Sara, standing in the doorway watching her go, all Callie wanted to do was kiss her: "Sara is always asking me 'What do you *want*, Callie?' And finally, I let her know. I answered."

Scene 9

Callie struggles to hide the disastrous result of her attempt to roast a chicken as Sara waits outside the apartment. After disposing of the roasting pan, she opens the door for Sara. Sara complains about the smell but tells Callie that she made a fantastic impression on Sara's students when she came to visit the class earlier that day. Callie tells Sara the kids clearly adore her, and Sara preens as if no one has ever told her this before. The two leave for dinner just as the upstairs neighbors begin their six o'clock stomping.

Scene 10

Callie stands helpless in Sara's hospital room, thinking of what she can do to help. Finally, remembering the night they shared Callie's pull-out bed, she uncovers Sara's feet from the sheets so that she will not feel too hot.

Scene 11

Wearing nice clothes, Callie paces impatiently in her apartment. Sara arrives with a newspaper held over her head against the rain outside. Callie scolds Sara for being late and then because

her outfit is not suitable. Callie feels obligated to attend an event at work; she wants to take Sara but is afraid what people will think if they see Sara in Callie's borrowed clothes. They argue, and Callie tells Sara to leave and slams the door behind her.

Scene 12

Callie walks into the hospital waiting room where Peter, Sara's old boyfriend from St. Louis, is seated. Sara's parents, he tells Callie, are also with her. They never wanted Sara to move to New York to begin with, and once she regains consciousness they plan on moving her back to St. Louis. Callie points out that Sara loves her teaching job in New York, but Peter says her old school in St. Louis will take her back, if she can still teach. Peter admits he still cares for Sara and asks Callie to tell him what happened. Callie refuses, saying that the story is everywhere: on television as well as in the newspapers. Peter says the facts of the story still do not explain why Sara was out with Callie. They argue over which of them could or should have protected Sara, and why Sara had been protecting Callie from the attacker. Callie—though she looks Peter in the eyes—does not answer.

Scene 13

In her apartment, Callie's phone rings. When she answers, the person hangs up. She dials a number, regrets it, and hangs up. She begs Caesar to come out from hiding to talk to Sara on the phone for her, to apologize for her behavior. She calls George to invite him to dinner.

Scene 14

In Sara's hospital room, Callie talks to an unresponsive Sara. She says: "Your parents look at me...like I'm some dirty old man...and the newspapers, the TV, the radio—my station, my own station, when they ran the news about the attack, they identified me." Callie tells her that everyone thinks they are lovers. Sara opens her eyes.

Scene 15

Sara arrives at the apartment to apologize for the fight. Callie admits that she sometimes swerves, as Sara says. She won an award for traffic reporting at the event. Sara takes Callie's hand, proud of her, and they both say they wish Sara had been there.

Scene 16

Callie visits Sara's hospital room. The nurse is there, examining her chart. She offers to teach Callie how to bathe Sara. Callie panics and leaves in a hurry.

Scene 17

Sara and Callie walk into Callie's apartment holding shopping bags. Peter is coming to visit Sara. The women hesitantly discuss the subject of lesbian bars and their attraction to other women. Sara needs to be home by six, but Callie begs her to stay just a minute longer. When she does leave, they hug good-bye; the hug lasts longer than usual. They awkwardly untangle and say good-bye in a rush. After the door closes behind Sara, Callie screams into a pillow on the couch.

Scene 18

At a coffee shop, Callie thanks Mrs. Winsley for calling the police and stopping the attack. Mrs. Winsley assumes Callie and Sara had been together for some time before the attack and is shocked to realize that they are not an item. Her surprise only hurts Callie more, as she is reminded of how tenuous a connection she has to Sara.

Scene 19

At her apartment, George teases Callie for being nervous about meeting Peter, as she stresses over what to wear to the restaurant for their double date. Sara arrives alone. She had asked Peter to leave after he spent the day criticizing everything about her life in New York: "I've started something here and I—that's what—because it's . . . I love . . . New York!" Though Callie and George say they can cancel, Sara wants to go out anyway, to get to know George better. Callie lets them leave before her, running to her Magic Eight Ball to ask it a question. She shouts happily when it gives her the answer she wants.

Scene 20

Inside her hospital room, Sara sits in a wheelchair as Peter reads to her. She is weak, but her eyes are open. He puts the book away and hands her a homemade card from her old students in St. Louis. Callie steps into the room unnoticed, before withdrawing to a safe distance to watch. Sara grips the card in her hand with effort. Peter tells Sara how much he looks forward to bringing her home to St. Louis. Sara begins to cry.

Callie approaches the nurse at her station to ask whether she has time to teach Callie how to bathe Sara now.

Scene 21

Callie and Sara return to their apartment after dinner. Callie collapses on the sofa, but Sara remains standing, full of nervous energy. She wants to take Callie to a bar called Henrietta's, and they agree that it will be fun. They dance around the subject for a moment until Callie says out loud that it is a lesbian bar. They share a long look, but neither can think of what else to say.

Scene 22

At the hospital, Sara sits in a wheelchair, and Callie enters with a bag. Sara responds to her name when Callie tells her she brought her clothes to change into. Sara and Callie work together, though it is difficult, to get Sara out of her gown and into the clothes. Callie tells Sara: "I can do this, you see . . . . Choose me." Sara smiles at her.

Scene 23

The women walk together through the park after leaving Henrietta's. It is four in the morning, but they do not want to go home. Suddenly Callie kisses Sara. Sara cannot believe it. They kiss again, but bump noses. The third time they try, the kiss is just right.

CHARACTERS

Anita

Anita is Sara's mother. Sara is her only child. She disapproves of Sara's move to New York City and, after the attack, wants to move her back to St. Louis.

Attacker

The women's attacker approaches them while they are kissing and makes homophobic and sexist comments about them. Sara shouts at him to leave them alone. He attacks her, slamming her head against a wall while Callie tries to pull him off of Sara from behind. He runs away after Mrs. Winsley throws flowerpots at him from above and shouts that the police are coming.

Caesar

Caesar is Sara's cat, whom Callie agrees to watch for her. Because the apartment Sara shares is too small, Caesar lives with Callie—who wants to see if she is capable of taking care of a cat before she gets one of her own. Caesar never comes out to see Sara, and she believes he is holding a grudge against her. He sleeps with Callie at night, and the women use this habit as an excuse to share a bed one night when Sara sleeps over at Callie's apartment.

Detective Cole

Detective Cole investigates the attack that leaves Sara in a coma. Though he gets very little information out of Callie at first, his interview with Mrs. Winsley leads to his discovery of the motive behind the attacker's brutality. Callie admits the truth after he interviews her a second time, using Mrs. Winsley's information to draw out the fact that Callie and Sara were kissing.

George

George is Callie's friend from college. They have a casual, unofficial intimate relationship, though both get jealous of the other's romantic interests. George works as a bartender in a restaurant where he frequently dates the waitresses. He cares deeply for Callie, and—before she meets Sara—is the center of her social world. After Callie meets Sara, George is at first resentful of the attention Callie is paying her, until he meets Sara and is won over by her straightforward and enthusiastic personality. George is furious at Callie for letting him find out about the attack through a television report rather than directly from her.

Joe

Joe is Sara's father. After Sara is attacked, he wants to move Sara back home to St. Louis for her recovery. He disapproves of his only daughter's living in New York City.

Malik

Malik is one of Sara's students, an eight-year-old who one day waits for Sara after school in order to walk her home. When a man begins to harass Sara, Malik stands up for her, telling the man that Sara is his teacher. When Sara tells this story to Callie, she is upset that she did not stand up for herself, hiding behind Malik instead.

Man in the Park

The man in the park harasses Sara every day on her way home from work. Malik tells the man not to speak so rudely to his teacher.

Nurse

The nurse works at the hospital where Sara is treated following the attack. She offers to teach Callie how to give Sara a bath. Callie at first refuses and later accepts this help.

Peter

Peter is Sara's boyfriend of seven years whom she left behind in St. Louis when she moved to New York City. Sara moved out of their shared apartment and into her parents' home about a month before she left for New York. When Peter comes to visit, Sara asks him to leave almost immediately—he finds fault with everything about New York, from Sara's job to her neighborhood, and Sara does not want to hear what he has to say about Callie, with whom they were supposed to have a double date. After the attack, Peter returns to New York along with Sara's parents; they all intend to take her back to St. Louis. He still has feelings for her and would like her to move into his apartment. He gets angry with Callie for not sharing the story of the attack with him. He demands to know if the attacker was bigger than he, believing that he could have protected Sara and asking why Sara was the one protecting Callie. When Sara wakes up, Peter reads to Sara, but when he talks about bringing Sara to St. Louis, she cries.

Callie Pax

Callie attended college in New York, where she has lived for eleven years when she first meets Sara. She has an apartment she inherited from her ex-boyfriend and a job as a traffic reporter. Though Sara is impressed both by Callie's apartment and her job (she gets to fly in a helicopter), Callie finds her life underwhelming. Through a friend of a friend, she agrees to watch Sara's cat. The two women form a fast connection that soon overpowers Callie's other friendships, including her casual romantic relationship with George, an old friend from college whom Callie is resigned to marrying some day. Callie avoids strong emotion, conflict, and commitment. After finally facing her growing feelings toward Sara, Callie kisses her in the park. A man interrupts them, harassing them. Though Callie wants to avoid further conflict, Sara tells him to leave. When the man attacks Sara, Callie tries unsuccessfully to fight him off, suffering a cracked rib in the fight. After the news breaks that Callie was involved in the gay-bashing incident, her own news station identifies her as one of the women involved. Callie must confront her own overwhelming worry, fear, and love for Sara alongside the misconception that she and Sara were together long before the attack. She begs Sara to choose to stay with her in New York instead of going home to St. Louis with Peter and her parents. Sara seems to agree.

Callie's Ex-Boyfriend

Callie's ex-boyfriend ran off with Callie's sister, leaving her the apartment.

Callie's Sister

Callie's sister and her boyfriend—formerly Callie's boyfriend—now live together in Los Angeles.

Sara

Sara is new in New York City, having moved from her parents' home in St. Louis to an apartment she shares with two other people. She cannot keep her cat, Caesar, there, leading her to arrange for Caesar to stay with a friend of a friend, Callie. Sara won a fellowship to teach third grade at a school in the Bronx. Though New York is dangerous and challenging, Sara continually defends her choices to speak up for herself and take on the unknown. This attitude wins over Callie, as well as George, as Sara grows closer to Callie through visits to Callie's apartment. Sara begins to have feelings for Callie, and when her ex-boyfriend, Peter, comes to visit, she tells him to leave after he insults New York. That night, she asks if Callie will come out to a lesbian bar with her. Later, Callie kisses Sara in a park. When a man begins to harass them, Sara tells him to leave them alone. The man attacks Sara, beating her head against a wall until she falls unconscious. While Sara lies in a coma, her family and Peter arrive in town, making plans to take her home to St. Louis. After she wakes up, however, Callie begins to advocate for Sara to stay in New York with her. Sara smiles at this suggestion.

Mr. Winsley

Mr. Winsley is out late the night that Mrs. Winsley witnesses the attack on Sara and Callie. Though Mrs. Winsley will not admit it to Detective Cole, their marriage may be rocky. Mrs. Winsley maintains that she was up late because she has always had trouble sleeping, not because she was waiting for her husband to return.

Mrs. Winsley

Mrs. Winsley is a witness to the attack on Sara and Callie. She throws flowerpots from her balcony, shouting that she has called the police. Callie later thanks her for stopping the attack. Mrs. Winsley, like everyone else, assumed that Callie and Sara were an established couple at the time of the attack. She and her husband have lived in the West Village for eight years. After learning that Sara is new to the city, Mrs. Winsley tells Callie how, as a newcomer to New York, she used to smile at strangers and gave money to beggars.

THEMES

Love

Stop Kiss is the story of two women falling in love. Starting as strangers, they become friends. From their friendship, love grows. Remarkably, neither woman has acknowledged her attraction to women before. Yet both are able to overcome their uncertainty in order to embrace the directions of their heart. Love in *Stop Kiss* takes the form of nights in drinking wine, nights out at restaurants and clubs, and bedside vigils at the hospital. Love is the women's willingness to let each other further into their lives: from Callie's visit to Sara's class to Sara's insistence that Callie's award for traffic reporting be displayed. Though at first Sara comes to Callie's apartment to visit her cat, she returns again and again because she adores spending time with Callie. Likewise, Callie neglects her group of old college friends while making dates with Sara.

Each woman has an attachment to a man that she must overcome for them to be together. Callie must give up her easy intimacy with George to win a love that she must fight for, a love that requires her to be honest and take risks. For Sara, Callie does all this and more, making her intentions clear that she wants to have Sara by her side in New York City. Sara's love of the city is tangled up in her love for Callie. The two are one in her mind, which makes Peter's disapproval all the more hurtful. By rejecting the city, Peter rejects Sara's new identity. By threatening to take her home, he tries to stand in the way of

TOPICS FOR FURTHER STUDY

- Create a time line of significant moments in the LGBTQ (lesbian, gay, bisexual, transgender, and queer or questioning) rights movement from 1998 to the present day. Choose at least seven important events to highlight the progress made toward equality since the publication of *Stop Kiss*. Free infographics are available at https://www.easel.ly.

- Read Nina LaCour's young-adult novel *Everything Leads to You* (2014). What role does the setting of Los Angeles play in the budding relationship between Emi and Ava? How would you compare this role to the role of New York City in *Stop Kiss*? Organize your answers into an essay.

- What is the definition of a hate crime? What are the laws against hate crimes in your state? What groups of people are protected under the laws currently in place? When and how were these laws last modified? Search for these answers online from a reputable source. Take notes from your sources and use them to help lead a class discussion.

- Choose a scene from the play to write from the first-person perspective of either Callie or Sara. While incorporating the dialogue and action provided by the play, add their inner thoughts, hidden emotions, and sensory details to illustrate their subjective experience of the events depicted in scene.

---

her love. Sara is helpless due to the attack, unable to speak her mind, to ask for help, or to beg Callie to save her. But love prevails as Callie begs Sara instead to stay in the city and be Callie's, finally.

Paralysis

Paralysis appears throughout the play as a symptom of fear and violence. When the women first begin to feel their mutual attraction acutely, they each approach haltingly. Callie invites Sara to the awards ceremony, but she becomes frozen with fear at the thought of her coworkers sensing her romantic feelings toward Sara. Sara attempts to introduce the topic of girlfriends, lesbian bars, and her feelings toward Callie, but she cannot say what she means, too worried to lose what they have by taking the next step. Instead, Callie swerves through life to avoid direct confrontation while Sara drops hints rather than risk triggering Callie's instinct to swerve. So far, Callie's swerving has led to a job she finds unsatisfying and repetitive, a social life that has remained stagnant since college, and a relationship with George that keeps their feelings at arm's length. Callie has settled for less in life in favor of safety, standing in the shallows rather than swimming out into unknown waters.

The play's first time line tells the story of Callie's overcoming her paralysis to take a chance by kissing Sara—thus admitting that she cannot swerve, ignore, or settle for less when it comes to her love—and the second time line is the story of Sara's recovery from paralysis. She begins these scenes just as she stabilizes from critical condition following the beating, then languishes in a coma completely immobile, and finally wakes up but cannot yet speak. She sits in a wheelchair, forced to listen to Peter's plans to take her home without the power to tell him her wishes. As she recovers, she learns how to turn her head and grip a card between pinched fingers. When Callie comes to ask her to stay, Sara shows how she, too, can overcome paralysis and make her thoughts known by responding to Callie's plea with a smile.

Violence

The violent attack on Sara, motivated by homophobia, offers a grim counterpoint to the innocent scenes of their blossoming love. Foreshadowed by many of the characters' concern for Sara, including Callie, Sara's parents, Peter, and George, the violence that strikes Sara overpowers her, nearly kills her, and strips away her independence. Sara's job in the Bronx and her openness to confrontation make her especially vulnerable in the eyes of her friends and family. What Callie finds most appealing in Sara—her willingness to look conflict, commitment, and uncertainty right in the eye and assert herself—is also what leads to the attack. While Callie prefers to keep her head down and flee, Sara stands up for herself. Of course, she is right: why should a woman be expected to take harassment silently? The brutal beating steals her strong

Sara and Callie's first kiss is interrupted by an angry passerby, and Sara is seriously hurt (© Sebastian Gauert / Shutterstock.com)

voice from her, leaving Callie—who by comparison navigates life with a troubling ambivalence—to come to terms with her feelings alone. Violence steals away not only the women's first, deliriously happy moments together but also what should have been their first days as a couple and their sense of safety in the future. While Sara loses her ability to make herself heard, Callie loses the option of swerving to avoid her responsibilities. She must act for them both to repair the damage of their traumatic separation so that they can be together again.

Nonlinear Narrative

A nonlinear narrative is a story that is told out of chronological order. In *Stop Kiss*, the scenes alternate between two time lines: the first is the story of how Callie and Sara met and fell in love, the second is the story of the attack and its consequences. If told linearly, Callie and Sara would meet, fall in love, kiss, get attacked, Sara would be in a coma, the detective would question Callie, and Sara would wake up after the news broke that they were involved in a homophobic attack. By alternating back and forth between the two time lines, Son creates a structure in which the traumatic event, which is the turning point of the play, both has already happened and has not happened yet. The nonlinear narrative adds a sense of foreboding by placing hospital rooms and police stations, on one hand, next to the happy scenes at Callie's apartment, on the other hand.

Rising Action

The rising action of a narrative is the series of events that build up to the climax. In *Stop Kiss*, the rising action consists of the scenes that take place at Callie's apartment in the first time line of the play, as Sara and Callie become infatuated with each other. The women's growing bond, their arguments, their affection and attempts to deny it all lead to the climax: their first kiss and the attack that follows. The rising action of a narrative creates tensions that snap during the climax. For example, the tension between Callie

COMPARE
&
CONTRAST

- **1998:** Throughout the United States, marriage between same-sex couples is illegal and unrecognized.

  Today: Same-sex marriage is legal in all fifty states following the Supreme Court ruling *Obergefell v. Hodges* on June 26, 2015.

- **1998:** On October 6, twenty-one-year-old Matthew Shepard is pistol-whipped, tied to a fence, set on fire, and abandoned in freezing temperatures by Russell Henderson and Aaron McKinney. Matthew Shepard's gruesome murder leads national protests, as members of the LGBTQ community and their allies pressure government at the local, state, and national levels for equal rights and protection.

  Today: On June 12, 2016, Omar Mateen murders forty-nine people and injures fifty-three more when he opens fire at Latin Night at Pulse, a gay nightclub in Orlando, Florida, before police gun him down. The event is the single most deadly attack on the

LGBTQ community in US history and the largest terrorist attack on American soil since September 11, 2001.

- **1998:** In New York City, eighty-two anti-LGBTQ hate crimes are reported between January and October, a seventy-eight percent increase from the year before. New York, along with eighteen other states, has no legislation in place to deal specifically with hate crimes against members of the LGBTQ community.

  Today: Hate crimes against members of the New York City LGBTQ community have risen slightly each year between 2010 and 2013, with sixty-eight incidents reported by August of 2013, doubling the previous year's reports. In 2009, President Barack Obama signs the Matthew Shepard and James Byrd Jr. Hate Crimes Prevention Act, extending federal hate crime law protection to include crimes motivated by sexual orientation, gender identity, or disability.

---

and Sara as they try to understand their feeling toward each other results in a sudden kiss that shocks both women. Because of the nonlinear narrative, the effect of the rising action is doubled by a second time line describing the aftermath of the attack. The tension created by this time line is felt by the viewer, who knows throughout the innocent rising action of the first time line that the attack is coming, even though the characters do not.

HISTORICAL CONTEXT

Stonewall Riots

On June 28, 1969, the police raided a gay bar in Greenwich Village named the Stonewall Inn. The practice of raiding bars catering to the

LGBTQ community was a common one in New York City at the time, and police, staff, and patrons were familiar with the routine of raids. Because LGBTQ establishments were not permitted to have liquor licenses, these bars operated illegally. Homosexuality was considered a mental illness, and people could be evicted from their apartments, fired from their jobs, or arrested on the street for homosexual behavior. The raid on Stonewall was the last in a string of raids on gay bars in Greenwich Village, but when the police announced their presence to the crowded bar and began to arrest patrons, the crowd fought back. They threw pennies, bottles, and bricks. They taunted and teased officers and freed those who had been arrested from the patrol cars. Word spread around the neighborhood that the crowd at Stonewall was fighting the police, and soon a full-scale rebellion was

Callie and Sara are strolling through the West Village in Manhattan (© Ryan DeBerardinis | Shutterstock.com)

under way. The Tactical Patrol Force, specifically trained to quell riots, was called in, but the crowd did not disperse. Elaine Quijano and Kim Kennedy write in "Remembering the Stonewall Riot and the Start of a Movement" for CBS News: "For the first time, the gay community, so secretive until now, felt the force of its numbers. A movement was born." Pushed beyond their limit by police harassment, thousands of members of the previously invisible community protested for five days.

After the riots, members of the community began to discuss their lack of civil rights. Three newspapers and several gay rights advocacy groups formed in New York City, and the first pride parade was held the following year. The name *Stonewall* became synonymous around the country with the LGBTQ rights movement. As a tribute to the Stonewall Inn's historic significance to the cause of gay rights, the bar—still in operation in Greenwich Village—was chosen as the center of the celebrations in New York City after the legalization of same-sex marriage in the United States in June 2015.

Matthew Shepard

On October 6, 1998, Matthew Shepard, an openly gay student at the University of Wyoming in Laramie, Wyoming, was pistol-whipped, tied to a fence, set on fire, and left in the freezing cold to die by Aaron McKinney and Russell Henderson. A passerby discovered Shepard over twelve hours later, mistaking him for a scarecrow. He died in the hospital on October 12 at the age of twenty-one. McKinney and Henderson received two life sentences for Shepard's murder, but they could not be charged with a hate crime, as the legislation did not exist at the time in Wyoming.

Shepard's horrific death, widely covered by the national media, caused outrage and sparked heated discussion concerning the protection of the nation's LGBTQ community from harassment and assault, as well as against the culture of homophobia still prevalent in the United States. Shepard became a household name: his funeral was attended by more than a thousand mourners, Elton John sent flowers, Barbra Streisand and Madonna called officials in Laramie to ask what could be done, Ellen Degeneres presided over a vigil at the US Capitol building, and President Bill Clinton spoke to the press about the tragic loss. Candlelight vigils and protests were held globally in response to the attack. Shepard's family founded the Matthew Shepard Foundation to serve as a resource for struggling gay youth, as well as a center of education and advocacy for equal rights.

CRITICAL OVERVIEW

Stop Kiss debuted to positive reviews, and it was awarded the GLAAD Media Award for Outstanding New York Production. Critics praised the play's balance between lighthearted and serious subject matter. Elyse Sommer writes in her review of the play for *CurtainUp*: "This play is the breeze we've all awaited—bouncing from laughter to pathos without missing a beat and engaging your interest and emotions unflaggingly."

Critics adored the depiction of New York City in the play as a place of limitless potential, whether for positive or negative. Ben Brantley writes in "*Stop Kiss*: Comic in Spirit, Serious at Heart," for the *New York Times*: "In this delicately balanced comic drama, falling in love with New York or in New York is risky. Only the brave need apply."

Callie and Sara's love story struck critics and audiences alike as equal parts heartwarming and heartbreaking, as they are torn apart just as they admit their feelings for each other. Charles McNulty writes in "Moving Power of Love in *Stop Kiss* Confronts Brutality," for the *Los Angeles Times*: "To love is to declare oneself, and *Stop Kiss* should speak to anyone who has had to search deep within to find the strength and conviction to join hands with another."

In "*Stop Kiss*: The Harsh Realities of Romance," for the *Washington Post*, Peter Marks finds the developing romance between two women who had not previously dated other women to be handled effectively and believably: "The tale of the furtive lesbian romance that unfolds...before and after...a brutal hate crime, the piece sensitively chronicles the sexual awakening of two appealing young women as they tiptoe around mutual desire."

While the romance is ultimately between two women, and the attack motivated by homophobic hatred, Charles Isherwood believes the play holds an important reminder to people of all orientations to not let love slip away. He writes in his review of the play for *Variety* in praise of "the painful, beautiful spell cast by this winningly performed play and its whispered message: that we must hurry to embrace the possibilities in our hearts, for our lives and loves always hang by a thread."

CRITICISM

Amy L. Miller

Miller is a graduate of the University of Cincinnati. In the following essay, she examines how Son merges comedy, tragedy, hate, and love in her exploration of Callie and Sara's hesitant relationship in Stop Kiss.

In Son's *Stop Kiss*, Callie and Sara must come to terms with the revelation of their attraction to women before they can bring themselves to admit their feelings for each other. Both women have a history of dating men, and both carry the emotional baggage of their latest unsuccessful relationships. While this struggle over sexual identity could be a painful, protracted process, Son creates instead a light, often comedic mood as the women dance clumsily around their feelings. Son saves the pain for the moment of Callie and Sara's first kiss when a homophobic stranger beats Sara into a coma and the aftermath of the attack as Callie must come to terms with the trauma on her own. The play's nonlinear narrative presents two realities—one bright and full of nervous, excited energy, the other dark and frightening—side by side, juxtaposing comedy and tragedy to create a powerful double vision of the fragility of human connection. Through this plot structure, Son tells two stories at once: how Sara saved Callie from her bad habit of swerving through life and how Callie saved Sara from losing her true love: New York City.

As their friendship begins to deepen in significance, Sara knowingly teases Callie for her tendency to swerve through life, a trait that Sara is especially keen to notice, given that this is the exact reason Callie struggles to admit her feelings for Sara. To admit that she is in love would be to give up her life of easy drifting, just as to quit the job that she hates would require effort. McNulty writes: "Callie...is a radio traffic reporter surveying the city from a helicopter in

> THE PLAY'S NONLINEAR NARRATIVE PRESENTS TWO REALITIES—ONE BRIGHT AND FULL OF NERVOUS, EXCITED ENERGY, THE OTHER DARK AND FRIGHTENING—SIDE BY SIDE, JUXTAPOSING COMEDY AND TRAGEDY TO CREATE A POWERFUL DOUBLE VISION OF THE FRAGILITY OF HUMAN CONNECTION."

much the same way she floats above her uncommitted life as a detached observer." Life in New York City is hard, but Callie copes through practiced avoidance: keeping her head down, avoiding conflicts, and staying between the borders she has set for herself. The rut she has worn into the city runs so deep that even her job circling New York in a helicopter has become a subject she finds embarrassing to discuss, as if mortified that a good portion of the general public—Sara included—find helicopters inherently exciting. Callie will not stand for this kind of talk, but she also refuses to discuss quitting. She would rather stay at a job she does not enjoy, refusing either to attempt to find more joy in it or to attempt to change careers. McNulty writes: "She doesn't know what she wants because she's keeping a crucial part of her identity a secret from even herself." Callie's relationship with George is not without love, but the love they feel for each other is more platonic than romantic, despite their occasional flings. Still, Callie announces with resignation to Sara that she will probably marry him anyway, a statement Sara—always more firm in her beliefs—counters by saying she has no vision of herself at the head of a nuclear family. In Callie's mind, though, it would be more difficult later in life to stay single than to marry George. Like water, she rolls downhill, finding the path of least resistance. For this reason, Callie works a job she hates because it is the job she has, sees George because he is the man she is closest to, lets the neighbors stomp twice a week at six, and lets the clutter in her house build up past reason, until she hardly has a place to sit on the couch. Callie stopped trying long ago.

Sara saves Callie from her languid life by simply pointing out her habits of avoidance one night over a card game. Suddenly, Callie is hyperaware of her swerving nature, of the walls she has built in the name of self-preservation, and—worst of all—of the depth of her feelings for Sara. Isherwood writes: "A running gag is the invisibility of the cat that brought them together.... But the phantom feline also symbolizes something else lurking along the edges of the women's relationship: a growing, unspoken sexual attraction." When Callie takes in Sara's cat as an experiment to see if she is ready for a pet of her own, she unintentionally embarks on a second experiment: whether she is ready for a girlfriend. Sara feels the pull toward Callie just the same. Like Caesar, Sara too finds a home in the city with Callie. To Sara, New York is Callie, and Callie is New York embodied. She observes the city's daily movements from on high, like a goddess looking down at her people. She helps New Yorkers find their way, though she would deny it. She helps Sara find her way as well, though Callie herself is somewhat charmingly lost.

For all her self-confidence as an independent woman in the big city, Sara balks when it comes time to confess her feelings. Always so bold and quick with an opinion, she suddenly stammers: "Callie, I know that neither you nor I have ever—well at least I know that I haven't. I've never really asked—." Callie, sensing danger, interrupts her here, and Sara is quick to drop the train of thought. Later, after sending Peter away, Sara tries once more to express her desires, unsuccessfully: "I've started something here and I—that's what—because it's...I love...New York!" Loving New York is safer, for the moment, than loving Callie. But soon Sara's complicated love for both will collide when she is brutally attacked after their first kiss. In a nonlinear narrative in which the traumatic moment has both arrived already and lurks ominously in the future, Sara's defensiveness of her decision to live a challenging life in New York City is darkly foreboding. Viewed from hindsight following the attack, the happy, carefree scenes in Callie's apartment are cruel in their sweetness. Isherwood writes: "The scenes of their growing friendship are in fact fragments of a shattered past." As Sara slowly regains movement, the clock ticks on Callie's hesitation. If she swerves this challenge, she will lose Sara to Peter, her parents, and St. Louis, yet she cannot reconcile the widespread perception of their lesbian relationship with the reality: their first

WHAT DO I READ NEXT?

- David Levithan and Billy Merrell's collection for young adults, *The Full Spectrum: A New Generation of Writing about Gay, Lesbian, Bisexual, Transgender, Questioning, and Other Identities* (2006) gathers poems, short stories, and personal essays by young LGBTQ authors on the subject of coming out, activism, friendships, relationships, religion, and more.

- *Outlaw Marriages: The Hidden Histories of Fifteen Extraordinary Same-Sex Couples*, by Rodger Streitmatter (2012), tells the secret stories of highly influential American couples who lived and loved before same-sex marriage was legal, including Gertrude Stein and Alice B. Toklas, James Baldwin and Lucian Happersberger, Walt Whitman and Peter Doyle, and others.

- In Son's *Satellites* (2006), a young couple, Nina and Miles, move to Brooklyn with their daughter. As they struggle to find their footing in the big city, the stage itself shifts and moves beneath their feet.

- Anchee Min's memoir *Red Azalea* (1994) recounts her coming-of-age in China during Chairman Mao's Cultural Revolution. After distinguishing herself early as a loyal member of the Red Guard through the betrayal of her teacher, Min is sent to a work farm to learn the ways of peasant life, where amid the grueling and lonely days of labor she falls in love with a woman named Yan. She escapes her peasant life after winning a role in a propaganda film, but she must leave Yan behind for her new career as an actress.

- *M. Butterfly*, by David Henry Hwang (1988), received the Tony Award for Best Play and remains a classic of American literature. Based on a true story, *M. Butterfly* recounts the life of Rene Gallimard, who discovers that his mistress and love—a Chinese opera star named Shi Pei Pu—is in fact a man as well as a Communist spy.

- *The Laramie Project*, by Moisés Kaufman (2000), portrays the aftermath of the murder of Matthew Shepard, based on hundreds of interviews conducted in Laramie. The play takes the form of dramatic monologues that gradually illuminate the divided consciousness of a small town in the center of a national media spotlight.

- Tennessee Williams's Pulitzer Prize–winning play *A Streetcar Named Desire* (1947) tells the story of fallen southern belle Blanche Dubois, who moves in with her sister, Stella, and brother-in-law, Stanley, following the loss of their plantation home. In the sultry New Orleans heat, Stanley and Blanche circle each other like snarling dogs before a fight. When the blows finally come, the outcome is as shocking as it is unforgettable.

- In *Take Me Out*, by Richard Greenberg (2002), winner of the 2003 Tony Award for Best Play, Darren Lemming is a major league baseball star so outrageously beloved by his fans and teammates that when he announces he is gay he confidently expects nothing in his life to change. Instead, he finds himself facing reactions of his friends, family, colleagues, and supporters that range from supportive to dismayed to violent.

- Sixteen-year-old neighbors Jaime and Ste struggle with poverty and abuse in *Beautiful Thing* by Jonathan Harvey (1993). When Jaime realizes he has feelings for Ste that Ste returns, the two boys find a haven from the difficulty of their home lives and a cure for the loneliness that has shaped their teenage years.

- Winner of the Pulitzer Prize and the Tony Award for Best Play, *Angels in America: A Gay Fantasia on National Themes*, by Tony Kushner (1993), explores life as a gay man in the AIDS epidemic of the 1980s, using a large cast of characters—some alive, some dead, some supernatural—to portray life, death, fear, and love during a dark period in the history of the United States.

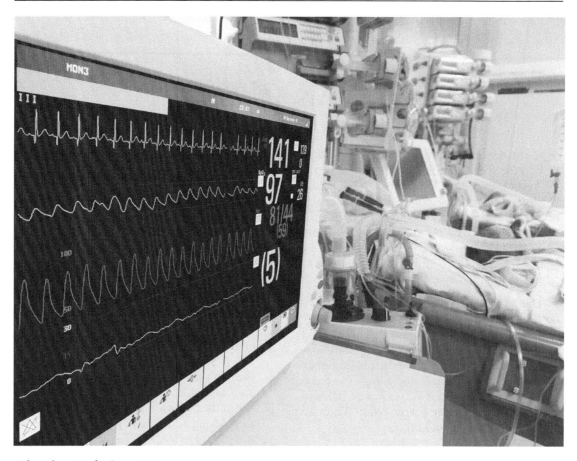

After the attack, Sara is in a coma *(© beerkoff / Shutterstock.com)*

tentative steps in that direction were destroyed before Callie's eyes. Now she sees Sara lying in the hospital unconscious while her family looks at Callie in silent rebuke.

To Sara's parents, Callie represents New York City as well: dangerous, unknown, and unable to shield their daughter from harm. Brantley writes: "Sirens, the horns, the tattoos beat by unknown hands and feet on doors and floors: the sounds of the city are edged in threats, signs of violence that has happened or is waiting to happen." Sara is not afraid, letting others worry for her. She is determined to make it, to keep her head up instead of down as Callie suggests, to insult those who insult her, and to refuse to let fear keep her from her favorite students. Peter's anticipation of bringing her home to St. Louis drives her to try harder than ever to break the paralysis that has settled over her body. "Best of luck," Callie says, the first time she meets Sara, "And . . . if it gets too rough—go home." Sara cannot speak to tell her friends,

Peter, or Sara what she wants, but in the play's final scenes it becomes obvious that Sara, in her infinite drive to succeed, wants to prove that even the horrific beating she endures will not drive her away from the place or the woman that she loves. When Callie offers to take care of Sara, in a glorious moment of neither swerving nor stalling but making surefooted forward progress, she saves Sara's future and her dream of a life in New York. Because she cannot ask, she depends on Callie to offer, having no one else to rely on. Though Callie could not save her from the attack, she saves her now.

Stop Kiss explores the extremes of violence, cowardice, hatred, and tragedy alongside comedy, bravery, friendship, and love. As a victim of a hate crime—her attacker aggravated by the sight of two women kissing—the attack on Sara brings to mind the dark legacy of homophobia in the United States and the many innocent people who have suffered and died simply for embracing their identity. Yet the message of

Stop Kiss reaches out further, past the category of sexual orientation, as Brantley writes: "What Son does ... is slyly place the occurrence in the context of a larger consideration of the perils of living life fully. Making choices and commitments is scary business ... but what is the alternative?" Callie and Sara awaken in each other a desire to make risks in order to chase their happiness. Callie, who has drifted all her life, suddenly feels the desire to fight and win. Sara, who left her home to move so far away, is struck with a fierce need to stay exactly where she is, no matter what. Together, they make each other better versions of themselves. Such a love cannot be easily stopped.

Source: Amy L. Miller, Critical Essay on *Stop Kiss*, in *Drama for Students*, Gale, Cengage Learning, 2017.

Charles McNulty

In the following review, McNulty admits he was deeply moved by the play.

At the center of Diana Son's drama *Stop Kiss* is a brutal attack on two women locked in an embrace. The scene is reported rather than graphically dramatized, but the violence clarifies so much about the tentative trajectory of this tenderly observed love story.

Produced at New York's Public Theater in 1998 in a memorable premiere starring Jessica Hecht and Sandra Oh, the play is clearly set in New York in the late 1990s. But though there are many markers of the period (at one point a Tower Records bag makes a ghostly appearance), the essential storyline doesn't feel dated in the least.

Making a winning directorial debut at Pasadena Playhouse, associate artistic director Seema Sueko beautifully traces the hesitant path toward intimacy of two characters who are redefining themselves in the face of hostile societal forces that don't require a horrific physical attack to be felt.

Callie (a superb Angela Lin), who moved to New York for college and hasn't left, is a radio traffic reporter surveying the city from a helicopter in much the same way she floats above her uncommitted life as a detached observer. She has a romantic friend (a terrific John Sloan) and an enviable Manhattan apartment, but she's more or less drifting her way into the future. She doesn't know what she wants because she's keeping a crucial part of her identity a secret from even herself.

Sara (a stunning Sharon Leal) has just arrived from St. Louis on a fellowship that has her teaching at a public school in the Bronx. Through a friend of friend, she meets Callie, who agrees to watch her cat while she settles into the big city.

These women are very different—Sara has ideals she wants to fight harder for, while Callie prefers to conveniently coast—but there's a strong attraction. They seem to unconsciously understand that they need each other to grow, which is to say they are falling, profoundly if unwittingly, in love.

Since writing *Stop Kiss*, Son has gone on to have a successful career as a TV writer and producer. (Her credits include *Blue Bloods*, *Southland* and *Law & Order: Criminal Intent*) She has a gift for capturing the textures and details of daily existence that the small screen thrives on.

But what has kept *Stop Kiss* fresh is its inventive dramatic structure. The chronology of events is fractured in such a manner that the play isn't simply leading up to a horrific gay-bashing incident. It's about the subtler effects of living in a society in which intolerance is an unspoken fact. Through the architecture of the drama, connections are forged between oppressive messages and inhibited souls.

Lin marvelously individualizes Callie's vagueness. She captures the comfortable yet exceedingly narrow band within which her character resides. But she also registers the tremors of longing that Callie has repressed but cannot shake.

Leal's beauty is exceptional, but her portrayal of Sara doesn't trade on it at all. (The sexual heat between Callie and Sara could if anything be turned up a notch.) Her Sara has a majestic integrity, and when she gazes at Callie you can tell that she's found home.

The attractive urban set by David F. Weiner isn't meant to be strictly realistic, though there are moments when Sueko's navigation seems a bit too casual. But strong performances throughout (the excellent supporting cast includes, in addition to Sloan, Jeff de Serrano, Amanda Carlin and Brandon Scott) override any superficial quibbles.

To love is to declare oneself, and *Stop Kiss* should speak to anyone who has had to search deep within to find the strength and conviction to join hands with another. I can't remember when a love story has moved me more.

Source: Charles McNulty, "Moving Power of Love in *Stop Kiss* Confronts Brutality," in *Los Angeles Times*, November 11, 2014.

Peter Marks

In the following review, Marks describes the play as "an absorbing public-service announcement."

Diana Son's *Stop Kiss* plays like an absorbing public-service announcement. The tale of the furtive lesbian romance that unfolds in the months before and after the commission of a brutal hate crime, the piece sensitively chronicles the sexual awakening of two appealing young women as they tiptoe around mutual desire.

The work radiated more urgency at its New York unveiling in 1998, when the recounting of the crime and the incremental tracking of the attraction between schoolteacher Sara and traffic reporter Callie seemed novel departures for a New York City story of love and self-acceptance....

Son's play intersperses the details of an evening during which Sara is beaten into a coma by a stranger with the backstory evolution of her affection for Callie. At the outset, both are in stages of disentangling themselves from heterosexual relationships. Sara, it seems, has fled St. Louis for a teaching job in the Bronx partly to escape the smothering attention of boyfriend Peter (Jonathan Lee Taylor). And Callie's attachment to restaurateur George (Bo Roddie) is propelled principally by George's willingness to be a mere back-seat passenger in Callie's life.

One of the more satisfying aspects of *Stop Kiss* is the slightly off-putting portrait of a whiny Callie, a woman not at all happy with her lot. In Zampelli's perceptive handling, there is a sadness to Callie, who's trapped in a job and sexual identity that don't fulfill her. That her work entails helping others navigate the city is ironic.

The piece, too, treats the graduated nature of Sara and Callie's halting romance with an affectionate wisdom, even when it's on the rocks. Increasingly skittish around each other as they sense their relationship moving toward a physical one, they find, as people do, the most picayune pretext for throwing cold water on their ever-harder-to-control feelings. On an important occasion for Callie, those sure-fire fighting words—"Is that what you're wearing?"—send them into a ridiculous argument, funny in its vehemence.

One could wish that a more contrasting rhythm might be set for the starker scenes involving the police investigation by Detective Cole (Howard Wahlberg). The idea that Son seems to be pursuing is how, even when a conventionally minded cop tries not to be insensitive to a coupling he doesn't quite understand, he still ends up asking questions that smack of judgment. You have to believe that Cole's interrogation of Callie could be more hackles-raising than the uncertainly paced proceedings evoked on this occasion.

On the other hand, Taylor injects just the right amount of clueless possessiveness in a strong scene with Zampelli's Callie outside Sara's convalescent room. It affirms Callie's observation that Sara's family blames her for the attack on Sara late one night, after they've emerged from a lesbian bar. The family looks at Callie, she says, "like I'm a dirty old man."...

Source: Peter Marks, "*Stop Kiss*: The Harsh Realities of Romance," in *Washington Post*, September 16, 2011.

SOURCES

"Anti-Gay Hate Crimes Set to Double in 2013," RT News website, August 19, 2013, https://www.rt.com/usa/anti-gay-crimes-double-691/ (accessed June 16, 2016).

Bindel, Julie, "The Truth Behind America's Most Famous Gay-Hate Murder," in *Guardian*, October 26, 2014, https://www.theguardian.com/world/2014/oct/26/the-truth-behind-americas-most-famous-gay-hate-murder-matthew-shepard (accessed June 16, 2016).

Brantley, Ben, "*Stop Kiss*: Comic in Spirit, Serious at Heart," in *New York Times*, December 7, 1998, http://partners.nytimes.com/library/theater/120798stopkiss-theater-review.html (accessed June 15, 2016).

Cooper, Michael, "Killing Shakes Complacency of the Gay Rights Movement," in *New York Times*, October 21, 1998, http://www.nytimes.com/1998/10/21/nyregion/killing-shakes-complacency-of-the-gay-rights-movement.html?rref=collection%2Ftimestopic%2FShepard%2C%20Matthew&action=click&contentCollection=timestopics&region=stream&module=stream_unit&version=latest&contentPlacement=9&pgtype=collection (accessed June 16, 2016).

"Diana Son," in *American Theatre Wing*, February 2006, https://web.archive.org/web/20060616114413/http://www.americantheatrewing.org/biography/detail/diana_son (accessed June 17, 2016).

"Diana Son," IMDb website, http://www.imdb.com/name/nm1788547/ (accessed June 17, 2016).

Franke-Ruta, Garance, "An Amazing 1969 Account of the Stonewall Uprising," in *Atlantic*, January 24, 2013, http://www.theatlantic.com/politics/archive/2013/01/an-amazing-1969-account-of-the-stonewall-uprising/272467/ (accessed June 16, 2016).

Hurt, Alyson, and Zambelich, Ariel, "Three Hours in Orlando: Piecing Together an Attack and Its Aftermath," NPR website, June 26, 2016, http://www.npr.org/2016/06/16/482322488/orlando-shooting-what-happened-update (accessed July 1, 2016).

Isherwood, Charles, Review of *Stop Kiss*, in *Variety*, December 7, 1998, http://variety.com/1998/legit/reviews/stop-kiss-1200456274/ (accessed June 15, 2016).

Kennedy, Kim, and Quijano, Elaine, "Remembering the Stonewall Riot and the Start of a Movement," CBS News website, June 28, 2015, http://www.cbsnews.com/news/lgbt-activists-remember-stonewall-riots-gay-rights-movement/ (accessed June 16, 2016).

Kim, Esther S., "Diana Son," in *Asian American Playwrights: a Bio-Bibliographical Critical Sourcebook*, edited by Miles Xian Liu, Greenwood Press, 2002, pp. 321–27.

Lower, Jenny, "A Play about Two Women Attacked for Kissing in Public," in *LA Weekly*, November 11, 2014, http://www.laweekly.com/arts/a-play-about-two-women-attacked-for-kissing-in-public-go-5204816 (accessed June 15, 2016).

Marks, Peter, "*Stop Kiss*: The Harsh Realities of Romance," in *Washington Post*, September 16, 2011, https://www.washingtonpost.com/lifestyle/style/stop-kiss-the-harsh-realities-of-romance/2011/09/15/gIQAUnBDYK_story.html (accessed June 15, 2016).

McNulty, Charles, "Moving Power of Love in *Stop Kiss* Confronts Brutality," in *Los Angeles Times*, November 11, 2014, http://www.latimes.com/entertainment/arts/la-et-stop-kiss-review-20141112-column.html (accessed June 15, 2016).

Sommer, Elyse, Review of *Stop Kiss*, in *CurtainUp*, December 5, 1998, http://www.curtainup.com/stop-kiss.html (accessed June 15, 2016).

Son, Diana, *Stop Kiss*, Dramatists Play Service, 2000.

"Stonewall Riots: The Beginning of the LGBT Movement," CivilRights.org, June 22, 2009, http://www.civilrights.org/archives/2009/06/449-stonewall.html (accessed June 16, 2016).

Vigil, Melanie, "Matthew Shepard Was Brutally Murdered in Laramie, Wyoming, in 1998. Last Night, the City Passed the First LGBT Nondiscrimination Ordinance in the State," ACLU website, 2015, https://www.aclu.org/blog/speak-freely/matthew-shepard-was-brutally-murdered-laramie-wyoming-1998-last-night-city-passed (accessed June 16, 2016).

Wright, Lionel, "The Stonewall Riots—1969: A Turning Point in the Struggle for Gay and Lesbian Liberation," in *Socialism Today*, No. 40, July 1999, http://www.socialistalternative.org/stonewall-riots-1969/ (accessed June 16, 2016).

Yurgaitis, Daniel, "Director's Notes on the NSU Theatre Presentation of *Stop Kiss*," December 11, 2006, http://www3.northern.edu/wild/0607Season/StopKiss/NTS_StopKiss.htm (accessed June 16, 2016).

FURTHER READING

Hodges, Ben, *The Play That Changed My Life: America's Foremost Playwrights on the Plays That Influenced Them*, Applause Theatre & Cinema Books, 2009.

This collection of essays by American playwrights on the works that inspired their careers includes "I Will Follow," a personal essay by Son, as well as essays by Suzan-Lori Parks, David Auburn, Tina Howe, Sarah Ruhl, and many more.

Lane, Eric, and Shengold, Nina, *The Actor's Book of Gay and Lesbian Plays*, Penguin Books, 1995.

Seventeen one-act plays by seventeen playwrights cover a range of topics relevant to LGBTQ life in *The Actor's Book of Gay and Lesbian Plays*.

Minwalla, Framji, and Solomon, Alisa, *The Queerest Art: Essays on Lesbian and Gay Theater*, NYU Press, 2002.

Minwalla and Solomon present evidence from diverse times and cultures around the world to support their argument that theater has consistently created a safe space for the expression of queer identity. The collection gathers interviews and essays from prominent members of the theatrical and LGBTQ communities, including David Savran, Stacy Wolf, Tim Miller, Lola Pashalinkski, Everett Quinton, Carmelita Tropicana, and more.

Sinfield, Alan, *Out on Stage: Lesbian and Gay Theater in the Twentieth Century*, Yale University Press, 1999.

Sinfield traces the history of LGBTQ theater from Oscar Wilde to the end of the millennium, with a particular focus on how Western society's prejudice, censorship, and oppression of homosexuality in the twentieth century fed the fires of LGBTQ theater rather than extinguishing the movement.

SUGGESTED SEARCH TERMS

Stop Kiss AND play

Diana Son

Diana Son AND Stop Kiss

Stop Kiss AND drama

Stop Kiss AND 1998

Stop Kiss AND LGBTQ literature

Stop Kiss AND lesbian literature

Stop Kiss AND homophobia

New York City AND LGBTQ literature

homosexuality AND violence

The Theory of Everything

PRINCE GOMOLVILAS

2002

Thai American playwright Prince Gomolvilas's two-act play *The Theory of Everything* (2002) is both tightly focused—taking place in a single static setting over just a couple of days with an entirely Asian American cast—and impressively expansive, encompassing a wide range of personalities and situations in its seven characters while hinging on the possibility, however remote, of extraterrestrial visitors to Earth. Billed as a comedy/drama, the play derives much of its narrative edge from the unique situation Gomolvilas has conceived: a weekly gathering of folks watching for UFOs on the roof of a Las Vegas wedding chapel. The gathering is infused with energy when one of them reports seeing something, inspiring a twenty-four-hour vigil for a possible return. However, the narrative is driven above all by the characters' attempts to work out the problems in their various life situations, testing ties of family, friendship, and love.

AUTHOR BIOGRAPHY

Khamolpat Gomolvilas was born on August 28, 1972, in Indianapolis, Indiana, to parents who immigrated from Thailand. The name "Prince" was arbitrarily bestowed on him by his kindergarten teacher, who could not pronounce his real first name and balked at his nickname, "Bin." The family moved to Southern California when

A group of Asian Americans meet each week on the roof of a Las Vegas wedding chapel to watch for signs of alien life in the skies (© Alina Zamogilnykh / Shutterstock.com)

Gomolvilas was seven, and he grew up mostly in the small city of Monrovia. He has also lived in Bangkok, Thailand.

After high school, he earned a bachelor's degree in film at San Francisco State University, which was where he saw his first play, David Mamet's *Oleanna*. He stayed on at San Francisco State and earned a master of fine arts degree in playwriting, with his creations being "mostly about werewolves," as he told *American Theatre* writer Jean Schiffman. In his personal life, Gomolvilas came out as gay when he was twenty-four years old.

Gomolvilas kicked off his career by earning the Lawrence and Lee Playwriting Award in 1994 for *All Men Are Liars*. His 1998 play *Donut Holes in Orbit* was published in *Ensemble Studio Theatre Marathon 1998: One-Act Plays*, edited by Marisa Smith. His plays often feature some sort of supernatural element or magic realism. *Big Hunk o' Burnin' Love* (1998) revolves around a Thai American man's need to marry by age thirty to avoid spontaneously combusting, as per a family curse, whereas in *Bee* (2001), a young Korean American man is invisible to everyone but a middle-aged African American woman. *The Theory of Everything* was first staged in 2000 and was honored thrice over, winning the Julie Harris Playwright Award, the International Herald Tribune/Singapore Repertory Theatre Playwriting Award, and the PEN Center USA West Literary Award for Drama.

Among the noteworthy companies that have staged Gomolvilas's plays are the Asian Stories in America (ASIA) Theatre, the Lorraine Hansberry Theatre, the Smithsonian Institution, and the New Conservatory Theatre Center in San Francisco, where he served as the first local playwright in residence. As of the mid-2010s, he had penned sixteen plays altogether, eight longer and eight shorter, and also cowrote with Brandon Patton a series of original theatrical shows featuring storytelling, songs, and bingo, titled *Jukebox Stories* and produced at the Impact Theatre in Berkeley in 2006, 2008, and 2013. He has also tried his hand at screenplays and has worked as associate editor of *Callboard* (now *Theatre Bay Area*) magazine and as a creative-advertising consultant. Most recently, he has been serving as the associate director of the master of professional writing program at the University of Southern California. As of the early 2010s, he was working on a play titled *The Brothers Paranormal*, a work of comedy/horror about Thai American ghost hunters. Gomolvilas has been living in the Glendale area of Los Angeles since 2002 and has a cat named Pork Chop.

PLOT SUMMARY

Act 1

SCENE 1

The Theory of Everything opens with a monologue on an otherwise unlit set. (Each character will have one throughout the play.) *Patty's monologue*: Patty tells the audience of her interest in aliens—not immigrants but the kind in UFOs. Hoping to get abducted, she has been studying up on Roswell, *The X-Files*, and so on.

SCENE 2

On a Las Vegas wedding chapel roof fitted out with lawn furniture, May sits preoccupied while Gilbert and Lana stand chatting. Overcoming Lana's repeated and increasingly belligerent rebukes to his attempts to speak—she was just dumped by her boyfriend—Gilbert succeeds in announcing that he henceforth wishes to be known as "Ibuprofen." He then shares his sudden idea that they should get married, which she ridicules. Instead, she intends to kill herself by jumping off the (one-story) roof; she was also just kicked out of law school for failing grades. She also considers merely contemplating suicide while playing keno. Gilbert suggests she join him working at a casino, but she scoffs at the idea. Patty enters the scene, acting the hostess. She is surprised to see Lana and asks if she will stay for the Saturday-night viewing party. Instead, Gilbert and Lana leave, for now, via the stairwell door. Patty's husband, Hiro, emerges. Patty opens a birthday present from her sister in Thailand—a 3-D picture book.

Shimmy comes out, wine bottle in hand, and tries to cater to Patty's UFO-watching hopes. Hiro goes down to get glasses. Patty relates her suspicion that Gilbert (Shimmy's son) and Lana are interested in each other. Shimmy points out that Lana has a boyfriend and then recounts her workday screening people at the airport.

When Gilbert and Lana return, Lana immediately reports Gilbert's proposal to his mother, despite his protests. Offering marriage advice, Patty points out the perfect success rate for marriages conducted at the wedding chapel she owns with Hiro. She reveals their secret: screening couples with the question of whether they would take a bullet for each other. She poses the question to Gilbert, who hedges and then admits that he would not. Patty declares the case closed.

Hiro pours wine. Lana's brother, Nef, arrives after the end of his class. He announces his Theory of Everything, an apparent improvement on Einstein's, centered on the concept of entropy—the inevitable breaking down of matter and energy. Hiro hails the theory with a word, and they all sip wine and watch the sky.

SCENE 3

Hiro's monologue: Hiro tells the audience about how he drives with his wife to California every Friday to play the lotto, because winning is his most cherished dream. He clings to it despite people's assurances that he will never win, since his other dream, to become martial arts film star Jackie Chan, is even less likely to come true.

SCENE 4

May calls out in hysterics from the darkness, and all six of the others emerge to hear her report having seen a UFO, complete with flashing lights, a blue beam, and the sensation of being pulled upward. Gilbert tries to suggest the sober truth—it was probably a helicopter or something—but Patty insists that the aliens are likely to return within twenty-four hours, and so they must keep a constant vigil. Eventually all of the others commit to the effort, even Gilbert, if the least willingly.

SCENE 5

Nef's monologue: Nef reveals his severe distaste for his parents' proclivity for chicken's feet, which cover their table at the dim sum restaurant on Sundays. His friend tells him this signifies a psychological revolt against his family's culture, but Nef asserts he simply finds them gross.

SCENE 6

While May keeps watching for UFOs, Hiro asks Shimmy whether she misses the Philippines—whether America simply does not feel like home. He also asks about her husband, who had an untimely death, and she reports dreaming about him every year. Hiro would like to go back to Japan. He is not attached to the Chapel of Love the way Patty is, in view of what she once found out (the reference, as revealed later, is to her being barren). Hiro has never told anyone these things.

Patty appears to tell Hiro that a couple seeking to marry has arrived, and Hiro goes down with her. Shimmy tries to interrogate May about the sighting, but her answers are cryptic. Gilbert and Nef enter, with Nef probing Gilbert about what he wants out of life; Shimmy departs. Gilbert resumes imploring Nef to influence Lana: now she has accepted the proposal, but he wants to retract it.

Nef bristles at Gilbert's expectations; he has had his own romantic difficulties recently, as his longtime girlfriend laughed off his very serious marriage proposal. Her parents think he is not Chinese enough. They talk about college—Nef is finishing, Gilbert may want to go—and Gilbert confides in Nef that the proposal may have come about out of sheer loneliness and insecurity. He tells Nef he *likes* him and then kisses his startled friend—but when he tries to touch Nef's face,

Nef slaps Gilbert's hand away, and in the commotion a cat statue is knocked over. Nef leaves. Then Gilbert leaves.

Patty returns and throws the now-broken statue in the garbage. With May as a sounding board, Patty meditates on the sociology of UFO sightings, the sun, and the identity of God. The sun rises.

Act 2

SCENE 1

Gilbert's monologue: Gilbert confesses to having always felt lost and to wanting to get out of his life, at least for a little while.

SCENE 2

As May sits, Patty tells Gilbert that the recently arrived couple passed the bullet test. Gilbert explains why he has chosen "Ibuprofen" as a new name. He feels like his mother's refusal to push him toward achievement and success has left him aimless. Patty relates that Shimmy's attitude is a result of how her husband died: her spurring gradually turned him from a waiter into an assistant to a bank president—and one day he was shot in a holdup. Gilbert tells Patty that she would be a good mother, but she says she is not interested in having children. Gilbert leaves for his casino shift.

Hiro and Shimmy return with strawberry daiquiri mix. Shimmy leaves again to go home and rest. Hiro gets around to telling Patty that he is leaving her, to go back to Japan; she has been physically and emotionally unreachable ever since she found out she was barren. Only in his home of Japan will Hiro feel alive again.

SCENE 3

Lana's monologue: Once mimicking an African tradition, Lana decided she should have her own song, and chose "I Am Woman." She has always been an achiever, fulfilling expectations, but now she feels like a failure.

SCENE 4

May is still onstage as Shimmy enters to find Hiro and tells him about her dream; for once, her pursuing husband caught up with her, but, under a pair of masks, he proved to look like Shimmy herself. Hiro reveals his plan to return to Japan and asks Shimmy to join him. She says she feels compelled to stay near her son. Lana returns from playing keno, accompanied by Nef, and Shimmy departs. Hiro follows her. Lana tells

Nef she went home and left a note to their parents about being kicked out of law school. She admits having felt pressured to go to law school, which was supposed to be a natural fit for a talkative girl. However, she was never self-motivated. Nef confesses to feeling existentially trapped himself. He exits.

SCENE 5

Shimmy's monologue: Having long ago taken a community English class where the teacher made the students write a page every week, Shimmy has continued the habit ever since. She reads the most recent of her many essays, titled "Why I Like Madonna." Madonna is framed as an inspiringly confident and self-assured woman. Shimmy always throws the essays away afterward, because her life is ever changing.

SCENE 6

Lana tries to tell May about her insecurity and personal crises, and May responds with a lesson in self-deprecating humor. Gilbert enters, and Lana asks whether he wants to get married. He explains why he does not want to marry, leaving her to point out the additional reason that she is a woman; Nef told her about Gilbert's revelation of his sexuality. Nef enters, and Lana starts to leave, but the two men tell her to stay. Gilbert then announces that he is leaving soon, for Pasadena, to start over. (Shimmy quietly appears at the door for long enough to hear this.) Nef tells Lana that their parents found the note and are very angry. As Nef and Lana head for home, Gilbert agrees to stick around until sunup on Monday morning, which is Patty's fortieth birthday.

Shimmy enters, teary eyed, and admits to Gilbert that she has also thought about leaving but decided against it. They hug. Patty laments the aliens' failure to appear again. Before leaving, Gilbert and Shimmy persuade Patty to hold out until sunrise. Patty tells May she wishes God would reward her motherly thoughts with the ability to bear children. She asks May point-blank whether she really saw a UFO, and May admits she did not.

SCENE 7

May's monologue: May starts to tell "The Story of Molly McButter" but is interrupted from offstage. She obligingly tells a quick anecdote about broken bones becoming stronger, then returns to McButter's story—but is interrupted again.

SCENE 8

As May sits gazing upward, Patty enters and also gazes, and then May fetches the ceramic cat from the trash and begins gluing it. As she does so, the others enter one by one—Gilbert, Lana, Hiro, Shimmy, and Nef—and look up at the sky, until May finishes gluing and looks up herself.

CHARACTERS

Gilbert

Gilbert, the young Filipino American son of Shimmy, comes across as the most psychologically conflicted of the group. His spur-of-the-moment proposal to Lana is defended with ironic indifference—when she points out that they do not love each other, he asks, "So?"—but is grounded in a real sense of isolation that threatens his mental life. This isolation is explained when his identity as a closeted homosexual is indicated; the fact that Lana, a close friend from early childhood, did not know suggests that no one knew. Furthermore, he grew up without a father and without understanding the impact his father's untimely death had on his mother. By the end of the play, having revealed his sexuality and come to terms with his mother's apparently laid-back involvement in his life, he is ready to start over in a new place.

Hiro

The Japanese American husband of Patty, Hiro is, through the early scenes, little more than laconic comic relief, offering sound bites suggestive of the classically detached and/or overwhelmed spouse of a woman with a strong personality. However, there are hints that this really is a dysfunctional relationship, such as in Shimmy's recognition that the two seem never to talk, only to fight. When his wife discovered she could not have children, Hiro stood by her in every facet of life, deferring to Patty's wishes with regard to their family (not adopting), livelihood (the wedding chapel), and locality (America), but this failed to lessen the emotional and physical distance that Patty left squarely between them. After a decade of this distance, Hiro is ready to give up on his marriage and leave the land where will never feel at home. He would like to start over with Shimmy, who now appeals to him far more than Patty.

Lana

Lana, Nef's sister, makes her capacity for self-assertiveness clear from the opening scene, in which she assumes a sardonically playful but nonetheless domineering demeanor when speaking with Gilbert. However, this self-assertiveness has perhaps long been hidden, because her logical genius, demonstrated through her chess championships, and general argumentative nature led those around her to push her to attend law school in a way that deceived her into thinking this was what she herself wanted. Time and failing grades proved otherwise, and now she is teetering on the edge of a dangerously self-destructive precipice. It is not entirely clear whether she is sharing suicidal thoughts more to dramatize and accentuate her extreme emotions or because she is truly experiencing an urge to kill herself. Either way, she must be taken seriously, which Gilbert does. His emotional support, along with Nef's, helps Lana begin to confront and resolve her difficult reality—the tens of thousands of dollars in debt, the angry parents—rather than try to escape it.

May

From the opening scene, May, Patty's mother, seems out of it, or, as the stage direction opening the second scene has it, "*she is apparently in her own world.*" Throughout the play, dialogue is carried on as if May were not there, as if she is too old, too concerned with UFOs, or too unfamiliar with English—or all of the above—for anyone to mind what she overhears. Sometimes May's responses to others' comments suggest confusion or misunderstanding on her part, but her perfectly functioning intellect is suggested when she gets deeper into conversation with Patty, especially in act 2, scene 6, when her intentional deception of Patty is made clear. Altogether, there is a sense that May is capable of offering universal acceptance of people for who they are in a way that is not found in society at large. She is family not just to Patty, it seems, but to everyone, as Lana suggests in calling her "Grandma May."

Nef

More than anyone else, Nef, Lana's brother, seems in control of his life in the present. His status as a student experiencing a degree of academic success rankles his flunked-out sister, and Gilbert clearly admires the sense of personal stability to which Nef's time in the navy perhaps contributed. However, even Nef is having difficulties, especially in his most recent romantic relationship, which is ending apparently because Nef is not Chinese enough for his girlfriend's family. His connection to Chinese culture seems to go little beyond his work delivering food for his parents' restaurant, as his diatribe against chicken feet suggests. Eventually Nef reveals feeling, much like everyone else, a sense of uncertainty about his identity that he is unsure how to resolve.

Patty

A Thai American woman approaching middle age, Patty is in several ways the center of the play. The chapel where the play is set is Patty's far more than her husband's, as reflected by her investment in the screening process, and generally her directive behavior befits a hostess. Moreover, as made clear in her opening monologue, Patty's interest in UFOs is the engine behind the Saturday-night rooftop gatherings that attract even Gilbert, a perfect skeptic, and it is for Patty's sake—not May's—that everyone commits to the group effort of a round-the-clock vigil for returning aliens. Patty's desires to host the regular community gathering, to promote lifelong love, and to believe that anything is possible all connect back to the biological reality that has shaped her life: her inability to bear children. The audience can only lament, along with Hiro, that Patty was not open to adopting children, which might have offered her precisely the maternal outlet she seems to be seeking in the other aspects of her life.

Shimmy

An immigrant from the Philippines, Shimmy acts as the carefree foil to the somewhat high-strung Patty. A good friend, Shimmy does what she can to make the watching parties as optimistic and enjoyable as possible. That Shimmy is very different from Patty in temperament makes her appealing to Hiro, who believes that he would be able to share in Shimmy's capacity to enjoy the present moment. Where Patty is content to live a life rendered permanent and unchanging in every sense, Shimmy shows through her weekly writings both her ongoing reflection on the world that surrounds her and her refusal to let her perspectives become permanent: each essay is not filed away but read once or twice and then thrown away. Shimmy considers accepting Hiro's proposal but indicates to her son, who she seems to sense still needs her maternal affection, that she has decided to stay in America.

THEMES

Human-Alien Encounters

Patty likely catches the reader off guard when she opens the play by declaring, "I want to talk about aliens. Not people from other countries. I want to talk about space creatures. Those types of aliens." Some people take UFO watching seriously, but not typically the liberal playgoers likely to inhabit Gomolvilas's audiences. Thus, one might imagine the playwright to be condescending to his humbly believing characters. However, the play never invites the audience to simply laugh at Patty or any of her family or friends for believing they might one day spot a UFO or aliens or perhaps even get abducted. There is indeed something *pathetic* about it, but in the sense of inspiring compassion: clearly something about Patty's life has led her to this juncture where belief in aliens— or perhaps more accurately, belief in the possibility of aliens—provides her with some sort of structure or stability.

This proves to be true when the audience at last learns the full extent of Patty's station in life: desolate over her inability to bear children and holding out hope, on some level, that a miracle might make motherhood happen for her. Indeed, by the play's end, Patty explicitly states this role of the idea of aliens: "If they exist, if they're real, then maybe anything is possible." This readily explains why May would fake a sighting—to stoke her daughter's faith in the universe.

This comes on top of Patty's earlier sociological explanation, drawn from Carl Jung, for why people in general invest faith in UFOs: "Such visions are experienced in times of collective distress or danger." This seems to better account for why not just Patty but all of the play's characters join in the Saturday-night sky-watching parties: they are all enduring the stress, to different degrees, of living in a land very different from their ancestral homeland. Even those characters either born in the United States or raised there since beyond memory—Nef, Lana, and Gilbert— as Asian Americans, remain outsiders in the eyes of many of their fellow citizens.

Immigrant Life

Each of the play's characters has struggled, to some degree, with life in an immigrant family, whether of the first or the second generation. The character who seems to have had the least trouble adapting is Patty; this might seem ironic,

TOPICS FOR FURTHER STUDY

- When reading her piece on Madonna, Shimmy provides a sample of the sort of essay she writes every week. Write one such brief and simple essay on behalf of each of the seven characters in the play, in their respective voices, discussing something that has come up in the course of their conversations.

- *The Theory of Everything* features very few stage directions with regard to the feelings invested in characters' movements. Actions are described only in the barest terms, never dictating the mood in which the part should be played. Pick a scene of at least several pages with some action of significance. Act the scene out for a video recording. Then rewrite that scene of the script with additional stage directions accounting for the moods and gestures that you use to bring out the characters' emotions. (If working alone instead of in a group, lend your acting skills to at least two different monologues.) It is up to you whether to first add the supplementary stage directions or act the scene(s) out.

- Gomolvilas has been featured in a TED^X talk titled "Mind the Gap," dealing with the importance of artistic integrity. Watch his thirteen-minute presentation, found on the TED^X website, and then write a paper in which you first recapitulate the main points and reconstruct the argument of his lecture and then identify and discuss an episode in your own life that his story relates to. If there are no obvious connections, try to think of an unconventional one—but be sure to find a significant, not merely trivial, relationship.

- Read *The Night the Heads Came* (1996), by William Sleator, a young-adult novel in which protagonist Leo and his friend Tim are abducted by aliens. Then write an essay in which you offer an independent assessment of this text—discussing characters, themes, and style—and then elaborate an argument for why this book or *The Theory of Everything*, with its mere gestures toward UFOs, makes for a better tale and why.

given the lack of balance suggested by her obsession with aliens, but it makes sense that, in light of her inability to bear children, she has been content to retreat into a sort of existential pigeonhole, serving a relatively minimal societal function—the people who come to her Chapel of Love could easily marry elsewhere—with a limited circle of fellow-immigrant friends and family.

Patty's excellent grasp of the English language, which she has been speaking since age sixteen, and evident studiousness might well have opened other doors in life for her, but such is less the case with Hiro and Shimmy. Hiro—who met Patty while working in a casino kitchen—cannot speak English as well as his wife and shows, through his own hesitant and limited speech, that language is a barrier he has had to deal with, deferring to Patty in most

matters of communication. That possibilities are limited for people like him is suggested by the fact that the dream he depends on to sustain himself is the idea of winning the lotto, while his second most significant dream is to become an international sensation like Jackie Chan. Outside of numerical luck and superstardom, both of which are extremely improbable, Hiro's only dream is to go back home to Japan.

Shimmy, meanwhile, finds in her job as an airport screener that passengers too often look at her as if she is "the mother of Satan." Such looks may or may not stem from racism, but the implied point is that Shimmy, working a position so easily despised, is left guessing. May, being older, shows even less of a grasp of English and appears even more isolated from ordinary American society; she has little to invest herself in other than her daughter and the idea of UFOs.

As they contemplate the stars, the characters confront their troubles (© *Roxana Bashyrova | Shutterstock.com*)

Things are not much easier for the youngest generation onstage, for various reasons. Many immigrants come to America precisely for the opportunity their children will have, but Lana ends up trapped by this sense of opportunity: given her high intelligence and other qualities, becoming a lawyer is a distinct potential future, one that she seems obliged to pursue as if to justify her parents' (or perhaps grandparents') having come to America in the first place. Nef, as opposed to not being American enough, is rather too American—that is, he is not Chinese enough for his longtime girlfriend. As for Gilbert, life in the in-between state that immigrants occupy has left him the least anchored to his own recognizable self, disconnected not only from broader heteronormative society but even from his own name.

Marriage

Through his spur-of-the-moment proposal to Lana, Gilbert posits marriage as one means of escaping the immigrant's isolation. It stands to reason that uniting with another person, ideally someone with common interests and goals,

would represent the surest bulwark against both loneliness and the depression and even suicidal thoughts it can bring about. However, the idea of marriage, indeed of coupling at all, is stymied at every turn in the play.

After Lana rejects Gilbert, bristling at the idea of a marriage enacted not out of love but out of rationality—much like the arranged marriages shared by many Asian immigrants—the tables gradually turn, and Gilbert ends up rejecting Lana. It turns out Gilbert would rather be linked to Nef, but the latter is not gay, leaving Gilbert isolated. Meanwhile Nef is having his own difficulties, because the different degrees of Chinese identity between him and his girlfriend thwart the notion of a permanent union. Hiro and Patty once had a happy marriage, but as their circumstances changed, they grew in different ways. Hiro now has a mind to unite with Shimmy, who lost her husband so long ago, but unlike him, she thinks of America as home, especially because her son is there. The answer to the immigrant outsider's uncertainty, Gomolvilas seems to be saying, lies not in escape from one's problems—and indeed in a sense from oneself—through marriage, but in the determined focus on and resolution of one's issues of identity.

Identity

Love for others can be helpful along the way, but love for and understanding of oneself is the key for the characters in this play. Gilbert has finally come around to making his true self not something kept hidden but something affirmed. Having gone through the phase of wanting to be called "Ibuprofen"—signaling the healing role he envisions himself playing in social relations—Gilbert is ready to find a new place to live, one not burdened by the years of hiding, one where he "can just gallop into town and say: 'Hello. Here I am. My name is Gilbert'"—a place where he can own his true name again.

The idea of masks is suggested by Shimmy's curious dream, where her husband removes one mask, then another, and proves to look like Shimmy herself. The audience must wonder, has she invested herself too much in her deceased husband? Has she failed to move beyond that coupled identity only out of fear? Nef and Lana both feel as if they are not who other people want them to be, which is who they became convinced they themselves wanted to be. Hiro finally discovers he needs to go home, and Shimmy finally realizes that her son, not her departed husband, is the most important person in her life.

As for May, she is perhaps the wisest among them. For all her non sequiturs and evasions, May is so comfortable in her identity that she can prove as much by making a joke about it— "At least I'm not some sixty-five-year-old lady sitting in lawn chair on top of roof in Las Vegas waiting for UFOs"—and herself be the one to laugh. She is who she is and can be happy.

STYLE

Comic Relief

The Theory of Everything's status as a comedy is apparent from the opening monologue, in which Patty immediately dispels the notion that this Asian American's play with an all Asian American cast will be a dry rehearsal of progressive sound bites. As soon as the lights come on and the setting of a rooftop UFO-watching party on a Las Vegas chapel becomes clear, the audience expects to enjoy its share of laughs. The tone is

further set by the opening dialogue between Gilbert and Lana, a collision of unique personalities under duress, both moderately unhinged at the moment and having known each other for so long that they can vent their most urgent feelings. Throughout the play, the comments are often wryly sardonic, the dialogue is crisp, and the wit is pinpoint sharp.

Threads like Gilbert's insistence that he be called "Ibuprofen," which naturally gets a laugh every time, culminate in rejoinders like Nef's joking that Gilbert now wants to be known as Keyser Söze—a character in the cult hit *The Usual Suspects* who pulls off one of the greatest identity deceptions in film history. Many of the comic moments depend on recognition of pop-culture references, which may not elicit laughs from every audience member, but even in-jokes that draw lesser responses keep the mood light throughout the theater.

All of these laughs not only add to the play's entertainment value but also keep the mood from growing dour in light of the characters' emotional difficulties, which extend as far as contemplation of suicide. Perhaps unsurprisingly, it is May who shows the angst-ridden Lana, as well as the audience, precisely why it is so important to be able to laugh, especially at oneself: it shows an ability to step back from a situation, emotionally disengage, and appreciate life for the smiles and laughs it can offer.

Adaptive English

One facet of the comedy that also has more profound undertones is the characters' use of adaptive English—that is, grammatically imperfect, sometimes vague phrasings that, in terms of communication, get the job done. It is worth recognizing that Gomolvilas prescribes particular levels of accents in his characters—thicker for May, Hiro, and Shimmy, minor for Patty, and none for the others—but has not written the accents into the dialogue. He has, however, written adaptive usages into the dialogue.

Regarding Lana and Gilbert's potential romance, Shimmy asks Patty, "You mean kissy-kissy, hug-hug?" May frequently speaks in ways that sidestep, and sometimes subvert, conventional usage, such as when she explains the fate of the cat statue with "The boys broke"—which, in leaving out the expected pronoun *it*, allows for multiple meanings, such as hinting at the boys' broken friendship (i.e., taking the verb as intransitive instead of transitive). Hiro, whose lines are littered with the verbal hesitation "uh," is liable to spout apparently fully formed adages—"All questions ... at their core ... are in actuality ... an inquiry into ... the meaning of life"—without having the slightest idea what they mean, as if empty rehearsed phrases might be preferable to any attempt at original expression. May, to the contrary, dismisses a quote Patty reads from Carl Jung as "too many fancy words."

Shimmy brings a language concern to the fore when she meditates on the seemingly nonsensical phrase "selling like hotcakes," which, practically speaking, might be improved by revision to "selling like bacon and eggs." Hiro signals his alliance with Shimmy when he uses her newly coined phrase to refer to how well daiquiri mix was selling. This likely gets a laugh and, as with many of Gomolvilas's comic lines, makes a sociological point at the same time: many an audience member with a native grasp of English will indeed laugh at Hiro for using this incorrect phrase: because the hotcakes, not the bacon and eggs, are part of the cultural lexicon, people generally would be uncertain about Hiro's point in using the phrase (even if the audience is able to understand it), making it "wrong." However, as he and Shimmy determine, from their perspective at least, the adapted phrasing makes more sense.

Thus is English figured as a privileged lexicon that immigrants must grasp as it is, regardless of whether it makes complete sense or not; Hiro and Shimmy can use their revised phrase, but at the cost of remaining outsiders from a broader standpoint. Yet again, this is one of the beauties of English, especially in America: in being open to so many linguistic influences, from Spanish in the South to French in the Northeast to Italian in New York City and Chinese in San Francisco, regional revisions and adaptations are inevitable, and any given adaptive usage, if apt, might catch on and become recognized usage.

HISTORICAL CONTEXT

Turn of the Twenty-First Century
Appropriately for a play titled *The Theory of Everything*, Gomolvilas offers a smorgasbord of characters, themes, and relationships as well as an abundance of cultural references befitting the time period of the turn of the twenty-first century. From *The X-Files* to the 3-D picture book to Jackie Chan to Madonna, not to mention the Beatles, Jim Brown, and the Berlin Wall, understanding of contemporary events goes a long way toward a full understanding of what is transpiring in the play. Lana's monologue hinges on the importance of Helen Reddy's 1971 song "I Am Woman," source of the classic line "I am woman, hear me roar." The song was adopted by the United Nations for its designation of 1975 as the Year of the Woman. Far less inspiring, naturally, are the songs cited from Beck and AC/DC, although the reader need not be familiar with them to know that "Loser" and "Highway to Hell" are anything but bastions of joy and optimism.

Two particular events mentioned in the play hold somewhat greater relevance than the scattered pop-culture references. One occurred at the Brookfield Zoo, in Chicago, in 1996, when a three-year-old boy fell into a pit inhabited by gorillas and lay unconscious for several minutes. Eventually one gorilla, Binti Jua, picked him up, cradled him in her arms, and carried him to the zookeepers. Gilbert tells this story in an attempt to express how he wants to be caring and helpful, but Shimmy slightly misreads his intent and asks, "Oh, Gilbert, what are you talking about? You want to be a monkey?" Again, Gomolvilas gets a laugh while also making a serious point, in this case a nod to the fact that people of nonwhite races are sometimes suggested by racists to resemble primate species; such a suggestion is as absurd as Shimmy's misreading of the point of the story. Moreover, Gilbert may precisely be acknowledging that, owing to the treatment he receives as an Asian American, not to mention his closeted sexual identity, he feels like so much of an outsider that he may as well be an animal.

Another highly relevant event, one with no comic undertones attached, is the tragedy that occurred in Stockton, California, on January 16, 1989, when a gunman opened fire at an elementary school, killing five children and wounding thirty other students and teachers. Four of the five killed were children of Cambodian refugees, and the unbalanced assailant had racist leanings. Patty draws on this event and the emotional response it evoked from her when she thinks about how much she still wishes she could be a mother. Once again, Gomolvilas shows how, in media-soaked American culture, events made familiar even only through television (or nowadays, the Internet) can have a profound impact

COMPARE & CONTRAST

- **ca. 2002:** While few Asian American stories have reached mainstream theatrical audiences, 2002 sees a Broadway revival of the 1958 Rodgers and Hammerstein musical *Flower Drum Song*, based on the novel by Chinese American author C. Y. Lee, which features mostly Asian characters.

  Today: In 2015 and beyond, revivals of *The King and I*, another Rodgers and Hammerstein production, and *Miss Saigon* likewise bring Asian stories back to the stage. Meanwhile, *Here Lies Love*, about the Philippines' first lady Imelda Marcos, enjoys a strong off-Broadway run, and Asian American actors are increasingly being cast in traditionally white roles such as Bill Sikes (in *Oliver!*) and Romeo.

- **ca. 2002:** Marriage licenses in Cook County, Nevada, which includes Las Vegas, having quintupled from just over 20,000 in 1954 to just over 100,000 in 1995, hover at a peak of around 120,000 through the early years of the twenty-first century.

- **Today:** The number of licenses issued in Cook County dropped sharply around the economic downturn of 2008, presumably owing to fewer romantic jaunts to Las Vegas, leaving the figure around 90,000 as of 2010.

- **ca. 2002:** When a child fell into a primate pit in a Chicago zoo in 1996, gorilla Binti Jua makes headlines for maternally cradling the boy and bringing him to the zookeepers, potentially saving his life from the zoo's more aggressive gorillas. The event remains fresh in some people's minds for years.

  Today: In 2016, a child falls into the gorilla pit at the Cincinnati Zoo. Although seventeen-year-old silverback Harambe at first appears to be helping him out of the water, once he starts dragging the boy by the foot, he is fatally shot by security. A public outcry blames the parents for the endangered gorilla's death, while some believe the zoo could have tranquilized the animal instead of killing him.

on one's psychological state—they are some of the various elements that go into not just American culture but the melting pot of each individual's life.

CRITICAL OVERVIEW

Allowing for the differences between actors and actresses and the approaches taken by various theater companies, critical assessments of productions of Gomolvilas's play have been mixed. The one keynote struck most frequently by reviewers is recognition of Gomolvilas's ambition—but this is typically couched in disapproving terms. Writing for *Gay Vancouver*, Mark Robins suggests, "While ethnic identity is the main theme here, . . . Gomolvilas crams so many other issues into his two hour

play that it seems at times to be as unwieldy as the alien-holding cosmos itself." Robins suggests, "Gomolvilas is so ambitious that he allows for few emotional connections to be made and in the end *The Theory of Everything* becomes a show about everything and nothing."

Nancy Worssam, writing for the *Seattle Times*, was equally frank in her criticism: "'Everything' is too much! Especially when it's stuffed into an hour and 45 minutes." She asserts that the play "has an overly ambitious agenda" and that the Seattle production "hasn't quite tamed it." Then Worssam disparagingly concludes, "What we have here are lots of ideas, good background sound, a sprinkling of humor and some fine acting. Sadly it's just not enough."

In her review of the play's premiere at the David Henry Hwang Theater in Los Angeles for

Hiro does not feel he belongs in America and wishes to return home to Japan *(© deeepblue | Shutterstock.com)*

Variety, Terri Roberts perhaps unintentionally points to several problems with critics' expectations and assessments. She writes:

> Aliens and outer space become easy metaphors for feeling like an outsider in a hostile world, and Gomolvilas becomes a bit overambitious in his effort to explore this topic. Not only does he delve into the culture-clash terrain, but he examines the resultant sense of alienation when people don't fit the norm in terms of sexuality, careers, family or marriage.... It's a lot to cram into one play.

To begin with, Roberts is content to reduce the motif of UFOs to a one-dimensional "easy metaphor"—a term of undisguised condescension—for the experiences of cultural aliens. However, Gomolvilas makes clear in the play that the motif is multidimensional, encompassing not only racial difference but also both collective distress and a psychologically complex desire to retain belief in possibilities. The metaphor is only "easy" if one fails to consider it closely enough.

Furthermore, Roberts speaks as if a nonwhite American playwright such as Gomolvilas, delving into "culture-clash terrain," should be doing so

exclusively, without adding messy details about sexuality, work, and relationships. This amounts to the absurd suggestion that a play featuring Asian Americans should be addressing only issues of Asian American identity, as if this can be done in isolation from all the other facets of people's lives. Part of Gomolvilas's point is precisely that Asian Americans should not and indeed cannot be reduced simply to their racial identity. If one merely reads the script of a play, it is difficult to imagine the impression one would get from a live production. Generally speaking, the suggestions that the play is overambitious seem sullied by an undercurrent of unconscious racism, reflecting critics' inability to absorb in one sitting such a diverse assortment of Asian American experiences.

CRITICISM

Michael Allen Holmes

Holmes is a writer with existential interests. In the following essay, he considers May's conversational contributions in The Theory of Everything *as equivalent to the digressive, recentering remarks*

WHAT DO I READ NEXT?

- David Henry Hwang, a Chinese American born in Los Angeles, is a patriarch among Asian American playwrights. He is best known for his 1988 play *M. Butterfly*, which won the Tony Award for Best Play and multiple other awards. Using Giacomo Puccini's opera *Madam Butterfly* as a point of departure, Hwang's play treats the relationship between a French diplomat and a male Chinese opera singer who passed as female throughout a twenty-year relationship between the two.

- Philip Kan Gotanda is another elder statesman among Asian American playwrights. He is of Japanese heritage and was born in Stockton, California. His 1985 play *The Wash* centers on a Japanese American couple's marriage and what happens when the husband and wife cope with traumatic realities in different ways.

- Wakako Yamauchi's 1974 play *And the Soul Shall Dance*, first staged by the East West Players, concerns a woman whose personal life and isolation lead to behaviors, especially heavy drinking, considered atypical by her Asian American neighbors.

- Gomolvilas has cited Craig Lucas as one of his favorite playwrights. Lucas's 1988 stage success *Prelude to a Kiss* concerns a couple whose perceptions and preconceived notions about love and gender are tested by a supernatural identity exchange.

- The young-adult novel *My Most Excellent Year* (2008), by Steve Kluger, depicts the life of athletic and dramatic Augie Hwong, who comes to a realization about his sexual identity.

- A treatment of the recent evolution of stage performance in Gomolvilas's ancestral homeland can be found in *Dance, Drama, and Theatre in Thailand: The Process of Development and Modernization* (1996), an informative work by Mattani Mojdara Rutnin.

by Zen monks that constitute enlightenment-oriented koans.

In Prince Gomolvilas's play *The Theory of Everything*, the character of May is construed as quite likely the most cracked out of all the currently unbalanced characters. One, most seriously, is talking about suicide, one wants to be abducted by UFOs, and one has changed his name to that of an over-the-counter medicine, but it is May who actually (at least apparently) *sees* a UFO. The report of flashing lights may be explained by, for example, Gilbert's suggestion that it was just a helicopter, but the blue beam and the pulling sensation are less easy to reconcile with reality. The audience—not learning until the play's end, of course, that May consciously fakes the sighting—likely imagines her to be so elderly that her mind no longer functions as well as it ought to, perhaps leaving her confused about where she is and how to draw the line between reality and imagination.

May sits through the first twenty pages of this seventy-page play without uttering a word, suggesting a mute insensibility to the world. That her capacity for expression in the English language is limited may give the impression, albeit false, that her intelligence, too, is limited. Throughout the play, May's comments ring like comic one-liners, as if unintentional on her part, so deft that in the later scenes the audience may only need to see May starting to speak in order to start laughing. Yet a closer look at the nature of her comments, especially in light of the idea of the Zen koan, suggests that she is accomplishing far more in her conversational contributions than meets the eye and ear.

The popular conception of the Zen koan is that of a pithy question or saying that has the potential to bring one's mind to a state of peak awareness or clarity. For example, although it is not a genuine koan, the question "If a tree falls in the forest and no one is around, does it make a sound?" is often put forth as one that cannot be answered—or at least, no matter what one might answer, an argument can be made for the opposite tack (e.g., the tree does produce vibrations in the molecules of the air, and yet perhaps these become a "sound" only when someone's ear registers those vibrations). Thinking about that question, one might find one's mind settling peaceably in the middle of the possibilities.

In Zen literature, koans are more often presented as a question in tandem with an answer.

> ONE MIGHT NOTICE HERE THE WAY IN WHICH THE NAME *MAY* IS A WORD THAT ALLOWS FOR ALL POSSIBILITIES."

For example, Heinrich Dumoulin, in *Zen Enlightenment: Origins and Meaning*, notes that in response to newcomers to a monastery asking a question such as "Can you show me the way to enlightenment?" the Zen master Chao-chou would respond, "Have you finished eating your rice gruel?... Then go wash your bowl!" Such a spontaneous comment can become the basis for a koan used in the deliberate instruction of novice monks. In this exchange, it seems as if Chao-chou has failed to answer the question posed, but his point is that in order to attain enlightenment, one must concentrate on and consciously perform one's everyday actions, fostering the immersion in the present moment that opens the door to enlightenment. His answer may hit the questioner sideways, so to speak, but precisely the unexpected angle is a key component of the koan's power (and actually, Zen masters are known to physically strike their students with a stick or a hand as a means of disrupting conventional thought).

With this perspective on the koan in mind, we can turn to May's lines in *The Theory of Everything* with a new sense of their possible significance. May's verbal introduction in act 1, scene 4, sets the stage for a singular pattern of communication. Her dramatic announcement about seeing the aliens is perhaps cued as false by the stage directions. At the scene's opening, they say *"The stage is black."* May then repeats several different cries in her native tongue, and given that the English-speaking audience likely cannot understand, the repetitiveness emphasizes a certain circuitousness of thought in May's mind. The stage directions then read, *"Lights up on the roof."* This leaves room for individual directors to choreograph the lighting as they see fit, but there is no suggestion that this should be any different from the stage lighting used throughout the play. Already, then, depending on the production, the audience may have the sense that May has not seen a thing—that she is wilier than one might expect.

Indeed, only in a very roundabout way does she come out and tell what she supposedly witnessed. She does declare, "I saw them," but pressed by Patty to explain whom she means, she replies, "Who you think?" This allows the questioner's expectations to dictate her listeners' perception of the event. Twice more she responds ambiguously or digressively. Next asked what she is saying, she notes, "I'm saying what I'm saying"—a convenient escape from many a request for further explanation, but one that is nonetheless true and somewhat Zen in character: people often want to read into other people's remarks, naturally seeking to understand as much as possible based on what someone has said. May takes a step back from this logic-oriented desire by temporarily stonewalling attempts to force her to deliberate on subtexts: the words that she used in and of themselves, and no more, are what she has uttered, and, in a sense, to insist on knowing more represents a refusal to accept the present for what it is.

In her next noteworthy comment in this exchange, when specifically asked what she saw, May declines to answer directly, saying only *where* she saw whatever she saw: "In the air. In the sky." By now her listeners are growing impatient, which allows for the (feigned) existential import of the event to build itself up on its own, through their increasingly anxious questions, perfectly framing the false account she finally gives. Yet before that, she still accomplishes one present-minded digression: in between two remarks communicating her displeasure with being left alone, Hiro reports that everyone was watching the California Lotto draw on TV, and so she points out, "We're not in California." It is almost surprising that May would think of such a detail at such a time, but it reflects her own perhaps legitimate surprise that, in the middle of their UFO-watching party, everyone is doubly removing their minds from the present, first in being absorbed in the artificial/virtual world represented by the television and second in caring about something not there in Nevada but in the next state over.

May's next koan-like comment comes at the end of a brief exchange with Shimmy, who is something of a daughter figure to May. Shimmy first asks May about the purported aliens and what they might want, leading May to once again take a detached point of view: "It's none of my business." It would be her business, of course, if they tried to abduct her, but May suggests regardless that attempting to rationally deduce others' inner thoughts is an interpersonal red herring: one is better off simply approaching the present, as well as other people, as precisely what they are, without always needing to logically dig deeper—they are what they are. May's dismissal also indicates a nonjudgmental viewpoint: she does not intend to try to determine whether any given aliens, or people, or anybody, are good or bad based on a superficial understanding of their actions. As the conversation moves on, May affirms the physical strength she gained and proved through accomplishing arduous chores in her younger days, recalling the Zen focus on conscious action in the present—the novice monk washing his bowl on the way toward enlightenment.

Shimmy then brings up the matter of May's prayers. Once again, May responds circuitously, never quite affirming that she does pray but only implying as much when she says, "What about it?" Shimmy quite reasonably asks, "When you pray, what do you pray for?" May perfectly sidesteps the question by once again responding with her own interrogation: "Is that trick question?" The sense of May's response is not immediately apparent, and indeed it would be hard to argue that any definitive meaning can be assigned to it. Several senses might be conjectured. Perhaps she is suggesting that if one asks such a question, one is likely looking for a certain response, as if to fulfill preconceived notions about what the other person's existential standpoint is, and this is not fair to the person being questioned. Or she might be suggesting that when one prays, one does not, or should not, be praying for anything in particular, because no one person is so important that the gods should be shifting the fated universe on his or her behalf. Or May might be evading the question, without concern for whether Shimmy realizes this or not, because she does not want to answer it, for any reason or no reason at all. Maybe—and one might notice here the way in which the name *May* is a word that allows for all possibilities, just as Patty desires—May is trying to avoid admitting that she is not actually praying, that she does not believe in any God in a conventional sense. Or May might think of prayers the way some people think of birthday wishes—if you share them, they never come true.

May next makes striking remarks after Gilbert and Nef have a small physical altercation, leaving the ceramic cat in pieces. In explaining to Patty, "The boys broke," May apparently speaks of the cat but also deftly alludes to the sense in which the friendship between them has been disrupted. When Patty shifts the conversation to Jung's assessment of the sociology of UFO sightings, May's antirational stance, part of the Zen outlook—that is, it is better to *do* things than to overthink them—is suggested when she calls Jung's thoughts "too many fancy words." She once again second-guesses ideas about God when she responds to Patty's conception that the sun might actually be God looking down on the world by pointing out that on cloudy days God would have to be "stupid" to have such a poor point of view, like sitting behind a pillar at a baseball game. This remark, like others of hers, seems silly, but it demonstrates that trying to conceive of God in definitive ways—locating him in the sun, or on a throne in the sky—inevitably leads in conceptually problematic directions.

From here, May's comments continue to construe things in koan-esque phrasings that represent diversion from existential roadblocks. When Lana and Nef's conversation about how stuck they are in their lives leads Nef to give up and declare he needs a burrito, May finally interjects a comment—not to offer Nef any ego-massaging consolation for his issues but simply to demand, "Bring me chips and salsa!" She is helping Nef focus not on his problems but simply on what he is doing in the present.

Likewise, when Lana gets wrapped up in a monologic commentary about all her "small problems" and "big crises" alike, May refuses to feed this egotistic fire and instead offers some pointed criticism: "You talk too much." May effectively tells Lana that she is overthinking things instead of just *being*, just existing in the world. Nor is May sorry for a comment that might seem insensitive; rather, she reinforces the goal of letting go of egotistic concerns to simply be whoever one happens to be and be able to laugh at oneself along the way.

Not much later, when Nef and Gilbert have a new exchange that comes to an awkward pause, May interjects again not to focus on any problems but to deflate them by indirectly suggesting that these problems are being blown out of proportion:

GILBERT. . . . I'm sorry.

NEF. For what?

GILBERT. For making you feel uncomfortable.

MAY *(pause)*. Where my chips and salsa?

This effectively relieves any building tension between Nef and Gilbert by turning the conversation elsewhere, toward why Nef has not brought any food back, a strictly practical concern.

May perhaps seems the most sensible when she finally gets around—again circuitously—to admitting to Patty that she never saw any UFOs. She pretended she did, naturally, because she understands her daughter perhaps better than Patty understands herself and because she loves her. As far as koan-like expressions go, it is May's showstopping monologue, the last of the seven, that seals the sense of the entire play. All six of the other characters have revealed a great deal about themselves through their respective monologues, and so the audience justifiably expects that May will do likewise, perhaps shedding more light on her past than her cleaning abilities alone provide. But what does May propose to spend her precious monologue time on? "The Story of Molly McButter." For all the play's inundation in Asian American issues, the last thing the audience can expect is a story about an Irish woman (with a patently funny name, no less—the story surely involves a slippery situation or two). Whoever is cued to be speaking to May from backstage surely interrupts because this really is not right, as if it is not in the script. As usual, May is taking things in subversive directions.

However, once again, a point can be gleaned from May's monologue, despite the fact that she never even begins the story. Irish immigrants, too, went through some turbulent and discriminatory times in their earliest collective years in the United States, so why should an Irish woman's story *not* bear relevance to those of a different set of immigrants? May once more figuratively hits the audience upside the head, to ensure that they avoid the trap of imagining that this play of Gomolvilas's is *only* about Asian Americans. Without a doubt, *The Theory of Everything* speaks truths about everyone, about people of all races.

May does squeeze a few lines of more obvious contextual import into her monologue, telling about how a broken bone heals back stronger. All things considered, the audience cannot be surprised that May is assigned the key action bringing the play to a close: gluing the Maneki Neko cat back together. All of the play's characters have been or are experiencing breaks in their lives, quite in accord with Nef's Theory of Everything, which sees everything ultimately breaking down into chaos. However, May demonstrates that people do not fit neatly into such a theory: breaks *are* repaired, people do heal, both alone and together, and if they focus on the right things—not superficial differences, not ego-related problems, but primarily the life at hand, the life before their eyes—anything truly will be possible.

Source: Michael Allen Holmes, Critical Essay on *The Theory of Everything*, in *Drama for Students*, Gale, Cengage Learning, 2017.

Ada Tseng

In the following essay, Gomolvilas describes his interest in the paranormal.

While researching *The Brothers Paranormal*, his latest comedy-horror play, about Thai-American brothers who launch a ghost-hunting business, Prince Gomolvilas was invited to go on a ghost hunt with the Los Angeles Paranormal Association.

The owner of a private residence in Santa Clarita had reported overwhelming paranormal activity: objects flying off shelves, a pinball machine that turned on even when unplugged, children talking to their invisible friends.

Gomolvilas, 40, who says he's "always on the lookout for proof of the paranormal," accompanied three investigators (including Layla Halfhill, a half-Thai American who was on Gomolvilas' favorite ghost-hunting show, Travel Channel's *Ghost Adventures*) to check it out.

Not only was the woman's house near the epicenter of 1928's St. Francis Dam disaster but the previous owners' daughter had died after falling down a well, and there was a cemetery in the backyard.

"When [the owner] mentioned that we were [also] near an Indian burial ground, I started laughing hysterically," Gomolvilas says. "It's like those stupid movies that overdo it. I could buy the dam, the girl and the cemetery. But the Indian burial ground? Come on, really?"

Five hours later—and one door opening by itself during the night—the results were inconclusive, and Gomolvilas still can't quite believe in the ghosts he writes about.

Born in Indianapolis and raised in Monrovia, Gomolvilas' career started while he was a college student in San Francisco. In the next decade, he became known for his plays, including *Big Hunk o' Burnin' Love* and *The Theory of Everything* (winner of the PEN Center USA

When May believes she sees a UFO, they decide to hold a two-day watch for other ships
(© Rawpixel.com / Shutterstock.com)

West Literary Award for Drama), which have been performed everywhere from L.A.'s East West Players to Singapore Repertory. He eventually made his way back to Los Angeles in 2002, and lives in Glendale.

Recently named the associate director of the Master of Professional Writing program at USC, founded in 1971 as the country's first multigenre creative writing program, Gomolvilas is an appropriate symbol of its multidimensional spirit. He is a rare Thai American playwright—he jokingly challenges you to find another, as he tried and failed while organizing a panel for Thai American writers at USC in 2010.

He also performs his own storytelling show, *Jukebox Stories*, with singer-songwriter Brandon Patton. For its third incarnation, which runs in Berkeley's Impact Theatre this month, Gomolvilas will be telling personal stories about tarot cards and fortunetelling.

As a "double minority," Gomolvilas explores his Asian-American and gay identities in his writing, but often through plots involving aliens, secret powers and fantasy worlds. Sometimes a curse that's befallen Thai-American bachelors who haven't married before they were 30 results in spontaneous combustion; other times, a high school nerd bitten by a radioactive ladybug becomes superhero Captain Queer.

While Gomolvilas didn't start exploring his Thai culture until college and didn't come out till he was 24, he has been obsessed with the supernatural since he was a child watching *The Twilight Zone* and reading Stephen King novels.

"If you want to pathologize it, it could be me growing up as the only Asian kid in Indiana, trying to escape," says Gomolvilas, whose kindergarten teacher arbitrarily crowned him "Prince" because she couldn't pronounce his Thai name, Khamolpat.

"The extreme of that is to escape into things that are outside of my realm of reality," he says. "I've always been interested in the tension between what is real and what is not. Not only in terms of the laws of the physical universe but also through the world as we know it: how we perceive things and how other people perceive us."

Source: Ada Tseng, "Prince Gomolvilas: The Only Gay, Thai, Science-Fiction Playwright," in *LA Weekly*, May 15, 2013.

Craig Hepworth

In the following interview, Gomolvilas talks about why he wanted to become a writer and lists other playwrights he admires.

Prince Gomolvilas is a Thai American playwright. He has written many plays which have been produced around the world and won several distinctive awards. His stage adaptation of *Mysterious Skin* based on the novel by Scott Heim has played to great acclaim and now the controversial drama is set to open in Manchester UK this May at the Three Minute Theatre, Manchester produced by Vertigo Theatre Productions and directed by award-nominated Craig Hepworth and Adele Stanhope.

Now co-director Hepworth interviews the playwright about the play, his other work and his favourite shows.

Hi Prince, can you tell us when you knew you wanted to be a playwright and what was the first theatre piece you ever wrote?

I didn't grow up going to the theatre, and I didn't even take drama in high school, so I didn't really "discover" playwriting until college. My early plays were just bad imitations of David Mamet. It wasn't until graduate school that I started connecting with my voice and began thinking about a life in the theatre.

Your background seems to be mostly comedy; what draws you to comedy writing?

I write a lot about social issues—in play form and otherwise—and I feel that comedy is the best way to communicate challenging or heavy subject matter without being didactic. Also, I like the instant gratification/feedback that comes from laughter.

What playwrights to do you look up to?

Annie Baker, Julia Cho, Craig Lucas, David Mamet, Paul Rudnick, Chay Yew. Oh, and Anton Chekhov. Chekhov should be on every playwright's list.

What was the last play you got to see that left a huge impression on you?

It's only every few years that I see something that absolutely blows me away. The last three that did that were *August: Osage County* by Tracy Letts, *Circle Mirror Transformation* by Annie Baker, and the recent revival of *West Side Story*, which incorporated a lot of the original choreography, book, and lyrics.

Jukebox Stories has enjoyed critical success and you have a new one opening, tell us about the premise.

Jukebox Stories is a two-man show that stars me and a musician named Brandon Patton. We tell stories and sing songs that are chosen at random by audience members, who also have an opportunity to win prizes because we integrate some kind of game into each show. *Jukebox Stories: The Secrets of Forking*, which will premiere at a literally underground theater in Berkeley, California, will have tarot cards and fortunetelling thrown into the mix.

You are working on a feature film called Straight Face, *what can you tell us about that?*

I'm working with director PJ Raval, whose feature documentary, *Before You Know It*, is making a big splash on the festival circuit. Our project is a narrative film based on a rather provocative magazine article that I can't really talk about yet, alas.

As a writer mainly known for comedy what drew you to adapting Mysterious Skin *to the stage?*

The novel is my favourite novel of all time. It affected me deeply, and I read it around the time that New Conservatory Theatre Center in San Francisco was asking me to pitch them ideas, as I had just closed a show with them.

How did you find adapting the piece for the stage?

It was great having a kind of template to work from, instead of having to start from scratch. My biggest concern was writing something that wouldn't disappoint Scott Heim, the novelist, particularly since I had to make a lot of changes to accommodate the stage and my vision of the story in a new form. Fortunately, he loves the play, and we've become friends.

Mysterious Skin has enjoyed some great critical acclaim; do you think the show will ever get a commercial run, say Off-Broadway?

I don't know. A rather edgy New York theatre some years ago told me it was much too graphic for them. And I don't think they were referring to the violence in the play, but, rather, some of the frank monologues.

What advice do you have for the cast and me and Adele as the directors of Mysterious Skin?

While there are many scenes of rapid-fire dialogue, don't be afraid to let the play "breathe." That is, look for opportunities to find comfort (and discomfort) in the quieter moments, in the silences, particularly in Act Two. Navigating fast pace and slow pace and figuring what each section needs will be one of the biggest challenges, but hopefully I've communicated a great deal of that on the page.

Source: Craig Hepworth, "Playwright Prince Gomolvilas," in *Broadway World*, March 27, 2013.

Terri Roberts

In the following review, Roberts praises the comedy in the play.

On the dilapidated rooftop of Las Vegas quickie wedding house the Chapel of Love, seven Asian-Americans gather to search the skies for roving bands of E.T.s. Most of them are struggling with issues of identity, love and which world is truly their home. Suspended above them, like flat alien spaceships, are several enormous playing cards. Most are hearts.

If the symbolism seems a little obvious, then it's an easy match for what's to be found in Prince Gomolvilas' *The Theory of Everything*, an amusing, albeit overly eager to please, comedy about belonging (or not), loving (or not) and the willingness (or not) to gamble on getting your heart's desire. This world-premiere play is receiving an international co-production between the L.A.-based East West Players and the Singapore Repertory Theatre, where it premiered earlier this fall.

Aliens and outer space become easy metaphors for feeling like an outsider in a hostile world, and Gomolvilas becomes a bit overambitious in his effort to explore this topic. Not only does he delve into the culture-clash terrain, but he examines the resultant sense of alienation when people don't fit the norm in terms of sexuality, careers, family or marriage.

Patty (Emily Kuroda) is the true believer in aliens; she wants to be abducted. Her mother, May (Marilyn Tokuda), wants to make her sad daughter happy. Patty's husband, Hiro (Ken Narasaki), longs to return to Japan. Her friend, Shimmy (Melody Butiu), has a frightening reoccurring dream about her dead husband. Shimmy's son, Gilbert (the delightful Kennedy Kabasares), wants to change his name to an over-the-counter medicine. His best friends are Lana (Michelle Chong), kicked out of school and dumped by her boyfriend on the same day, and Nef (stiff Brendon Marc Fernandez), a philosophy student who differs from Einstein on the physicist's theory of everything.

For Einstein, it was a unifying formula that would reveal how the universe works. For Nef, it's the concept of entropy. From the moment of creation, all living things are advancing toward death and nonexistence.

It's a lot to cram into one play. Director Tim Dang keeps the focus on the comic aspects, so some dramatic moments that call out for more thoughtful treatment get brushed over. Jose Lopez's lights offer an occasional sense of magic but fail to establish the nighttime-sunrise scenario. Victoria Petrovich's playing cards-rooftop set design admirably reflects the hope these people look for in the skies, and the disrepair of where they really are

Source: Terri Roberts, Review of *The Theory of Everything*, in *Variety*, November 13, 2000.

SOURCES

Dumoulin, Heinrich, *Zen Enlightenment: Origins and Meaning*, Shambhala, 2007, p. 71.

"15 Years Ago Today: Gorilla Rescues Boy Who Fell in Ape Pit," CBS Chicago website, August 16, 2011, http://chicago.cbslocal.com/2011/08/16/15-years-ago-today-gorilla-rescues-boy-who-fell-in-ape-pit/ (accessed June 17, 2016).

Gomolvilas, Prince, *The Theory of Everything*, Dramatic Publishing, 2002.

Healy, Patrick, "Here Lies Progress: Asian Actors Fill the Playbill," in *New York Times*, June 22, 2014, http://www.nytimes.com/2014/06/23/theater/here-lies-progress-asian-actors-fill-the-playbill.html?_r=0 (accessed June 17, 2016).

"Helen Reddy—'I Am Woman' (Live) 1975," https://www.youtube.com/watch?v=MUBnxqEVKlk (accessed June 15, 2016).

"Marriage License Application Statistics 1909 to Date," Insider Viewpoint of Las Vegas, http://www.insidervlv.com/marriagelicensestatistics.html (accessed June 17, 2016).

Park, Madison, Emanuella Grinberg, and Tiffany Ap, "'We'd Make the Same Decision,' Zoo Director Says of Gorilla Shooting," CNN website, May 31, 2016, http://www.cnn.com/2016/05/30/us/gorilla-shot-harambe/ (accessed June 17, 2016).

"Prince Gomolvilas," in *World Heritage Encyclopedia*, World Public Library, http://www.worldlibrary.org/articles/prince_gomolvilas (accessed June 14, 2016).

Richman, Josh, and Mark Evans, "Stockton Shooting: 25 Years Later, City Can't Forget Its Worst Day," *San Jose Mercury News* online, January 16, 2014, http://www.mercurynews.com/ci_24928327/stockton-shooting-25-years-later-city-cant-forget (accessed June 17, 2016).

Roberts, Terri, Review of *The Theory of Everything*, in *Variety*, November 13, 2000, http://variety.com/2000/legit/reviews/the-theory-of-everything-1200465425/ (accessed June 16, 2016).

Robins, Mark, "Theatre Review: *The Theory of Everything*—What Happens in Vegas Doesn't Always Stay," in *Gay Vancouver*, January 12, 2013, http://gayvancouver.net/theatre-2013/theatre-review-the-theory-of-everything-what-happens-in-vegas-doesnt-always-stay/ (accessed June 16, 2016).

Schiffman, Jean, "Prince Gomolvilas: No Limits," in *American Theatre*, Vol. 18, No. 7, September 2001, pp. 79–81.

Tseng, Ada, "Prince Gomolvilas: The Only Gay, Thai, Science-Fiction Playwright," in *LA Weekly* online, May 15, 2013, http://www.laweekly.com/arts/prince-gomolvilas-the-only-gay-thai-science-fiction-playwright-4184875 (accessed June 12, 2016).

Worssam, Nancy, "'The Theory of Everything': Vegas, Aliens and Identity Crises," in *Seattle Times* online, February 24, 2009, http://www.seattletimes.com/entertainment/the-theory-of-everything-vegas-aliens-and-identity-crises/ (accessed June 12, 2016).

FURTHER READING

Cowles, David W., *Complete Guide to Winning Keno: The Smart Player's Guide to Winning*, 2nd ed., Simon & Schuster, 2003.
  Offering everything from a brief history of the game to an explanation of the rules to detailed elaborations of strategies for winning, Cowles's book provides just what the title promises.

Hall, Richard, *Uninvited Guests: A Documented History of UFO Sightings, Alien Encounters & Coverups*, Aurora Press, 1988.
  Hall gives credence to the idea that many people—if not all who claim to have seen UFOs—have been witnessing phenomena that cannot be explained as anything other than extraterrestrial visitations. He explores the possibilities as to what such visits signify about alien interests and intents.

Peebles, Curtis, *Watch the Skies!: A Chronicle of the Flying Saucer Myth*, Berkley Books, 1995.
  In a book that serves as a counterpoint to Hall's, Peebles specifically approaches the idea of UFOs as a myth and aims to debunk notions that UFO sightings are anything more than human-built aircraft, hallucinations, or something in between.

Uno, Roberta, *Unbroken Thread: An Anthology of Plays by Asian American Women*, University of Massachusetts Press, 1993.
  This collection presents a number of relatively early plays largely concerning Asian American identity, featuring authors Jeannie Barroga, Velina Hasu Houston, Momoko Iko, Genny Lim, Elizabeth Wong, and Wakako Yamauchi.

SUGGESTED SEARCH TERMS

Prince Gomolvilas

Prince Gomolvilas AND interview

The Theory of Everything

Einstein AND theory of everything

Asian American theater

Asian American identity

Las Vegas AND wedding chapels

Las Vegas AND keno

Las Vegas AND UFOs

UFO sightings AND video

Glossary of Literary Terms

A

Abstract: Used as a noun, the term refers to a short summary or outline of a longer work. As an adjective applied to writing or literary works, abstract refers to words or phrases that name things not knowable through the five senses. Examples of abstracts include the *Cliffs Notes* summaries of major literary works. Examples of abstract terms or concepts include "idea," "guilt" "honesty," and "loyalty."

Absurd, Theater of the: See *Theater of the Absurd*

Absurdism: See *Theater of the Absurd*

Act: A major section of a play. Acts are divided into varying numbers of shorter scenes. From ancient times to the nineteenth century plays were generally constructed of five acts, but modern works typically consist of one, two, or three acts. Examples of five-act plays include the works of Sophocles and Shakespeare, while the plays of Arthur Miller commonly have a three-act structure.

Acto: A one-act Chicano theater piece developed out of collective improvisation. *Actos* were performed by members of Luis Valdez's Teatro Campesino in California during the mid-1960s.

Aestheticism: A literary and artistic movement of the nineteenth century. Followers of the movement believed that art should not be mixed with social, political, or moral teaching. The statement "art for art's sake" is a good summary of aestheticism. The movement had its roots in France, but it gained widespread importance in England in the last half of the nineteenth century, where it helped change the Victorian practice of including moral lessons in literature. Oscar Wilde is one of the best-known "aesthetes" of the late nineteenth century.

Age of Johnson: The period in English literature between 1750 and 1798, named after the most prominent literary figure of the age, Samuel Johnson. Works written during this time are noted for their emphasis on "sensibility," or emotional quality. These works formed a transition between the rational works of the Age of Reason, or Neoclassical period, and the emphasis on individual feelings and responses of the Romantic period. Significant writers during the Age of Johnson included the novelists Ann Radcliffe and Henry Mackenzie, dramatists Richard Sheridan and Oliver Goldsmith, and poets William Collins and Thomas Gray. Also known as Age of Sensibility

Age of Reason: See *Neoclassicism*

Age of Sensibility: See *Age of Johnson*

Alexandrine Meter: See *Meter*

Allegory: A narrative technique in which characters representing things or abstract ideas are used to convey a message or teach a lesson.

Allegory is typically used to teach moral, ethical, or religious lessons but is sometimes used for satiric or political purposes. Examples of allegorical works include Edmund Spenser's *The Faerie Queene* and John Bunyan's *The Pilgrim's Progress.*

Allusion: A reference to a familiar literary or historical person or event, used to make an idea more easily understood. For example, describing someone as a "Romeo" makes an allusion to William Shakespeare's famous young lover in *Romeo and Juliet.*

Amerind Literature: The writing and oral traditions of Native Americans. Native American literature was originally passed on by word of mouth, so it consisted largely of stories and events that were easily memorized. Amerind prose is often rhythmic like poetry because it was recited to the beat of a ceremonial drum. Examples of Amerind literature include the autobiographical *Black Elk Speaks,* the works of N. Scott Momaday, James Welch, and Craig Lee Strete, and the poetry of Luci Tapahonso.

Analogy: A comparison of two things made to explain something unfamiliar through its similarities to something familiar, or to prove one point based on the acceptedness of another. Similes and metaphors are types of analogies. Analogies often take the form of an extended simile, as in William Blake's aphorism: "As the caterpillar chooses the fairest leaves to lay her eggs on, so the priest lays his curse on the fairest joys."

Angry Young Men: A group of British writers of the 1950s whose work expressed bitterness and disillusionment with society. Common to their work is an anti-hero who rebels against a corrupt social order and strives for personal integrity. The term has been used to describe Kingsley Amis, John Osborne, Colin Wilson, John Wain, and others.

Antagonist: The major character in a narrative or drama who works against the hero or protagonist. An example of an evil antagonist is Richard Lovelace in Samuel Richardson's *Clarissa,* while a virtuous antagonist is Macduff in William Shakespeare's *Macbeth.*

Anthropomorphism: The presentation of animals or objects in human shape or with human characteristics. The term is derived from the Greek word for "human form." The fables of Aesop, the animated films of Walt Disney, and Richard Adams's *Watership Down* feature anthropomorphic characters.

Anti-hero: A central character in a work of literature who lacks traditional heroic qualities such as courage, physical prowess, and fortitude. Anti-heros typically distrust conventional values and are unable to commit themselves to any ideals. They generally feel helpless in a world over which they have no control. Anti-heroes usually accept, and often celebrate, their positions as social outcasts. A well-known anti-hero is Yossarian in Joseph Heller's novel *Catch-22.*

Antimasque: See *Masque*

Antithesis: The antithesis of something is its direct opposite. In literature, the use of antithesis as a figure of speech results in two statements that show a contrast through the balancing of two opposite ideas. Technically, it is the second portion of the statement that is defined as the "antithesis"; the first portion is the "thesis." An example of antithesis is found in the following portion of Abraham Lincoln's "Gettysburg Address"; notice the opposition between the verbs "remember" and "forget" and the phrases "what we say" and "what they did": "The world will little note nor long remember what we say here, but it can never forget what they did here."

Apocrypha: Writings tentatively attributed to an author but not proven or universally accepted to be their works. The term was originally applied to certain books of the Bible that were not considered inspired and so were not included in the "sacred canon." Geoffrey Chaucer, William Shakespeare, Thomas Kyd, Thomas Middleton, and John Marston all have apocrypha. Apocryphal books of the Bible include the Old Testament's Book of Enoch and New Testament's Gospel of Peter.

Apollonian and Dionysian: The two impulses believed to guide authors of dramatic tragedy. The Apollonian impulse is named after Apollo, the Greek god of light and beauty and the symbol of intellectual order. The Dionysian impulse is named after Dionysus, the Greek god of wine and the symbol of the unrestrained forces of nature. The Apollonian impulse is to create a rational, harmonious world, while the Dionysian is to express the irrational forces of personality. Friedrich Nietzche uses these terms in *The*

Birth of Tragedy to designate contrasting elements in Greek tragedy.

Apostrophe: A statement, question, or request addressed to an inanimate object or concept or to a nonexistent or absent person. Requests for inspiration from the muses in poetry are examples of apostrophe, as is Marc Antony's address to Caesar's corpse in William Shakespeare's *Julius Caesar*: "O, pardon me, thou bleeding piece of earth, That I am meek and gentle with these butchers!... Woe to the hand that shed this costly blood!..."

Archetype: The word archetype is commonly used to describe an original pattern or model from which all other things of the same kind are made. This term was introduced to literary criticism from the psychology of Carl Jung. It expresses Jung's theory that behind every person's "unconscious," or repressed memories of the past, lies the "collective unconscious" of the human race: memories of the countless typical experiences of our ancestors. These memories are said to prompt illogical associations that trigger powerful emotions in the reader. Often, the emotional process is primitive, even primordial. Archetypes are the literary images that grow out of the "collective unconscious." They appear in literature as incidents and plots that repeat basic patterns of life. They may also appear as stereotyped characters. Examples of literary archetypes include themes such as birth and death and characters such as the Earth Mother.

Argument: The argument of a work is the author's subject matter or principal idea. Examples of defined "argument" portions of works include John Milton's *Arguments* to each of the books of *Paradise Lost* and the "Argument" to Robert Herrick's *Hesperides*.

Aristotelian Criticism: Specifically, the method of evaluating and analyzing tragedy formulated by the Greek philosopher Aristotle in his *Poetics*. More generally, the term indicates any form of criticism that follows Aristotle's views. Aristotelian criticism focuses on the form and logical structure of a work, apart from its historical or social context, in contrast to "Platonic Criticism," which stresses the usefulness of art. Adherents of New Criticism including John Crowe Ransom and Cleanth Brooks utilize and value the basic ideas of Aristotelian criticism for textual analysis.

Art for Art's Sake: See *Aestheticism*

Aside: A comment made by a stage performer that is intended to be heard by the audience but supposedly not by other characters. Eugene O'Neill's *Strange Interlude* is an extended use of the aside in modern theater.

Audience: The people for whom a piece of literature is written. Authors usually write with a certain audience in mind, for example, children, members of a religious or ethnic group, or colleagues in a professional field. The term "audience" also applies to the people who gather to see or hear any performance, including plays, poetry readings, speeches, and concerts. Jane Austen's parody of the gothic novel, *Northanger Abbey,* was originally intended for (and also pokes fun at) an audience of young and avid female gothic novel readers.

Avant-garde: A French term meaning "vanguard." It is used in literary criticism to describe new writing that rejects traditional approaches to literature in favor of innovations in style or content. Twentieth-century examples of the literary *avant-garde* include the Black Mountain School of poets, the Bloomsbury Group, and the Beat Movement.

B

Ballad: A short poem that tells a simple story and has a repeated refrain. Ballads were originally intended to be sung. Early ballads, known as folk ballads, were passed down through generations, so their authors are often unknown. Later ballads composed by known authors are called literary ballads. An example of an anonymous folk ballad is "Edward," which dates from the Middle Ages. Samuel Taylor Coleridge's "The Rime of the Ancient Mariner" and John Keats's "La Belle Dame sans Merci" are examples of literary ballads.

Baroque: A term used in literary criticism to describe literature that is complex or ornate in style or diction. Baroque works typically express tension, anxiety, and violent emotion. The term "Baroque Age" designates a period in Western European literature beginning in the late sixteenth century and ending about one hundred years later. Works of this period often mirror the qualities of works more generally associated with the label "baroque" and sometimes feature elaborate conceits. Examples of Baroque works include John Lyly's *Euphues: The Anatomy of Wit,* Luis de Gongora's *Soledads,* and William Shakespeare's *As You Like It.*

Baroque Age: See *Baroque*

Baroque Period: See *Baroque*

Beat Generation: See *Beat Movement*

Beat Movement: A period featuring a group of American poets and novelists of the 1950s and 1960s—including Jack Kerouac, Allen Ginsberg, Gregory Corso, William S. Burroughs, and Lawrence Ferlinghetti—who rejected established social and literary values. Using such techniques as stream of consciousness writing and jazz-influenced free verse and focusing on unusual or abnormal states of mind—generated by religious ecstasy or the use of drugs—the Beat writers aimed to create works that were unconventional in both form and subject matter. Kerouac's *On the Road* is perhaps the best-known example of a Beat Generation novel, and Ginsberg's *Howl* is a famous collection of Beat poetry.

Black Aesthetic Movement: A period of artistic and literary development among African Americans in the 1960s and early 1970s. This was the first major African-American artistic movement since the Harlem Renaissance and was closely paralleled by the civil rights and black power movements. The black aesthetic writers attempted to produce works of art that would be meaningful to the black masses. Key figures in black aesthetics included one of its founders, poet and playwright Amiri Baraka, formerly known as LeRoi Jones; poet and essayist Haki R. Madhubuti, formerly Don L. Lee; poet and playwright Sonia Sanchez; and dramatist Ed Bullins. Works representative of the Black Aesthetic Movement include Amiri Baraka's play *Dutchman,* a 1964 Obie award-winner; *Black Fire: An Anthology of Afro-American Writing,* edited by Baraka and playwright Larry Neal and published in 1968; and Sonia Sanchez's poetry collection *We a BaddDDD People,* published in 1970. Also known as Black Arts Movement.

Black Arts Movement: See *Black Aesthetic Movement*

Black Comedy: See *Black Humor*

Black Humor: Writing that places grotesque elements side by side with humorous ones in an attempt to shock the reader, forcing him or her to laugh at the horrifying reality of a disordered world. Joseph Heller's novel *Catch-22* is considered a superb example of the use of black humor. Other well-known authors who use black humor include Kurt Vonnegut, Edward Albee, Eugene Ionesco, and Harold Pinter. Also known as Black Comedy.

Blank Verse: Loosely, any unrhymed poetry, but more generally, unrhymed iambic pentameter verse (composed of lines of five two-syllable feet with the first syllable accented, the second unaccented). Blank verse has been used by poets since the Renaissance for its flexibility and its graceful, dignified tone. John Milton's *Paradise Lost* is in blank verse, as are most of William Shakespeare's plays.

Bloomsbury Group: A group of English writers, artists, and intellectuals who held informal artistic and philosophical discussions in Bloomsbury, a district of London, from around 1907 to the early 1930s. The Bloomsbury Group held no uniform philosophical beliefs but did commonly express an aversion to moral prudery and a desire for greater social tolerance. At various times the circle included Virginia Woolf, E. M. Forster, Clive Bell, Lytton Strachey, and John Maynard Keynes.

Bon Mot: A French term meaning "good word." A *bon mot* is a witty remark or clever observation. Charles Lamb and Oscar Wilde are celebrated for their witty *bon mots.* Two examples by Oscar Wilde stand out: (1) "All women become their mothers. That is their tragedy. No man does. That's his." (2) "A man cannot be too careful in the choice of his enemies."

Breath Verse: See *Projective Verse*

Burlesque: Any literary work that uses exaggeration to make its subject appear ridiculous, either by treating a trivial subject with profound seriousness or by treating a dignified subject frivolously. The word "burlesque" may also be used as an adjective, as in "burlesque show," to mean "striptease act." Examples of literary burlesque include the comedies of Aristophanes, Miguel de Cervantes's *Don*

Quixote, Samuel Butler's poem "Hudibras," and John Gay's play *The Beggar's Opera.*

C

Cadence: The natural rhythm of language caused by the alternation of accented and unaccented syllables. Much modern poetry—notably free verse—deliberately manipulates cadence to create complex rhythmic effects. James Macpherson's "Ossian poems" are richly cadenced, as is the poetry of the Symbolists, Walt Whitman, and Amy Lowell.

Caesura: A pause in a line of poetry, usually occurring near the middle. It typically corresponds to a break in the natural rhythm or sense of the line but is sometimes shifted to create special meanings or rhythmic effects. The opening line of Edgar Allan Poe's "The Raven" contains a caesura following "dreary": "Once upon a midnight dreary, while I pondered weak and weary...."

Canzone: A short Italian or Provencal lyric poem, commonly about love and often set to music. The *canzone* has no set form but typically contains five or six stanzas made up of seven to twenty lines of eleven syllables each. A shorter, five- to ten-line "envoy," or concluding stanza, completes the poem. Masters of the *canzone* form include Petrarch, Dante Alighieri, Torquato Tasso, and Guido Cavalcanti.

Carpe Diem: A Latin term meaning "seize the day." This is a traditional theme of poetry, especially lyrics. A *carpe diem* poem advises the reader or the person it addresses to live for today and enjoy the pleasures of the moment. Two celebrated *carpe diem* poems are Andrew Marvell's "To His Coy Mistress" and Robert Herrick's poem beginning "Gather ye rosebuds while ye may...."

Catharsis: The release or purging of unwanted emotions—specifically fear and pity—brought about by exposure to art. The term was first used by the Greek philosopher Aristotle in his *Poetics* to refer to the desired effect of tragedy on spectators. A famous example of catharsis is realized in Sophocles's *Oedipus Rex,* when Oedipus discovers that his wife, Jacosta, is his own mother and that the stranger he killed on the road was his own father.

Celtic Renaissance: A period of Irish literary and cultural history at the end of the nineteenth century. Followers of the movement aimed to create a romantic vision of Celtic myth and legend. The most significant works of the Celtic Renaissance typically present a dreamy, unreal world, usually in reaction against the reality of contemporary problems. William Butler Yeats's *The Wanderings of Oisin* is among the most significant works of the Celtic Renaissance. Also known as Celtic Twilight.

Celtic Twilight: See *Celtic Renaissance*

Character: Broadly speaking, a person in a literary work. The actions of characters are what constitute the plot of a story, novel, or poem. There are numerous types of characters, ranging from simple, stereotypical figures to intricate, multifaceted ones. In the techniques of anthropomorphism and personification, animals—and even places or things—can assume aspects of character. "Characterization" is the process by which an author creates vivid, believable characters in a work of art. This may be done in a variety of ways, including (1) direct description of the character by the narrator; (2) the direct presentation of the speech, thoughts, or actions of the character; and (3) the responses of other characters to the character. The term "character" also refers to a form originated by the ancient Greek writer Theophrastus that later became popular in the seventeenth and eighteenth centuries. It is a short essay or sketch of a person who prominently displays a specific attribute or quality, such as miserliness or ambition. Notable characters in literature include Oedipus Rex, Don Quixote de la Mancha, Macbeth, Candide, Hester Prynne, Ebenezer Scrooge, Huckleberry Finn, Jay Gatsby, Scarlett O'Hara, James Bond, and Kunta Kinte.

Characterization: See *Character*

Chorus: In ancient Greek drama, a group of actors who commented on and interpreted the unfolding action on the stage. Initially the chorus was a major component of the presentation, but over time it became less significant, with its numbers reduced and its role eventually limited to commentary between acts. By the sixteenth century the chorus—if employed at all—was typically a single person who provided a prologue and an epilogue and occasionally appeared between acts to introduce or underscore an important event. The chorus in William Shakespeare's *Henry V* functions in this way. Modern dramas rarely feature a chorus, but T. S. Eliot's *Murder in the Cathedral* and Arthur Miller's *A View from the Bridge* are notable exceptions. The Stage Manager in Thornton Wilder's *Our Town* performs a role similar to that of the chorus.

Chronicle: A record of events presented in chronological order. Although the scope and level of detail provided varies greatly among the chronicles surviving from ancient times, some, such as the *Anglo-Saxon Chronicle,* feature vivid descriptions and a lively recounting of events. During the Elizabethan Age, many dramas—appropriately called "chronicle plays"—were based on material from chronicles. Many of William Shakespeare's dramas of English history as well as Christopher Marlowe's *Edward II* are based in part on Raphael Holinshead's *Chronicles of England, Scotland, and Ireland.*

Classical: In its strictest definition in literary criticism, classicism refers to works of ancient Greek or Roman literature. The term may also be used to describe a literary work of recognized importance (a "classic") from any time period or literature that exhibits the traits of classicism. Classical authors from ancient Greek and Roman times include Juvenal and Homer. Examples of later works and authors now described as classical include French literature of the seventeenth century, Western novels of the nineteenth century, and American fiction of the mid-nineteenth century such as that written by James Fenimore Cooper and Mark Twain.

Classicism: A term used in literary criticism to describe critical doctrines that have their roots in ancient Greek and Roman literature, philosophy, and art. Works associated with classicism typically exhibit restraint on the part of the author, unity of design and purpose, clarity, simplicity, logical organization, and respect for tradition. Examples of literary classicism include Cicero's prose, the dramas of Pierre Corneille and Jean Racine, the poetry of John Dryden and Alexander Pope, and the writings of J. W. von Goethe, G. E. Lessing, and T. S. Eliot.

Climax: The turning point in a narrative, the moment when the conflict is at its most intense. Typically, the structure of stories, novels, and plays is one of rising action, in which tension builds to the climax, followed by falling action, in which tension lessens as the story moves to its conclusion. The climax in James Fenimore Cooper's *The Last of the Mohicans* occurs when Magua and his captive Cora are pursued to the edge of a cliff by Uncas. Magua kills Uncas but is subsequently killed by Hawkeye.

Colloquialism: A word, phrase, or form of pronunciation that is acceptable in casual conversation but not in formal, written communication. It is considered more acceptable than slang. An example of colloquialism can be found in Rudyard Kipling's *Barrack-room Ballads:* When 'Omer smote 'is bloomin' lyre He'd 'eard men sing by land and sea; An' what he thought 'e might require 'E went an' took— the same as me!

Comedy: One of two major types of drama, the other being tragedy. Its aim is to amuse, and it typically ends happily. Comedy assumes many forms, such as farce and burlesque, and uses a variety of techniques, from parody to satire. In a restricted sense the term comedy refers only to dramatic presentations, but in general usage it is commonly applied to nondramatic works as well. Examples of comedies range from the plays of Aristophanes, Terrence, and Plautus, Dante Alighieri's *The Divine Comedy,* Francois Rabelais's *Pantagruel* and *Gargantua,* and some of Geoffrey Chaucer's tales and William Shakespeare's plays to Noel Coward's play *Private Lives* and James Thurber's short story "The Secret Life of Walter Mitty."

Comedy of Manners: A play about the manners and conventions of an aristocratic, highly sophisticated society. The characters are usually types rather than individualized personalities, and plot is less important than atmosphere. Such plays were an important aspect of late seventeenth-century English comedy. The comedy of manners was revived in the eighteenth century by Oliver Goldsmith and Richard Brinsley Sheridan, enjoyed a second revival in the late nineteenth century, and has endured into the twentieth century. Examples of comedies of manners include William Congreve's *The Way of the World* in the late seventeenth century, Oliver Goldsmith's *She Stoops to Conquer* and Richard Brinsley Sheridan's *The School for Scandal* in the eighteenth century, Oscar Wilde's *The Importance of Being Earnest* in the nineteenth century, and W. Somerset Maugham's *The Circle* in the twentieth century.

Comic Relief: The use of humor to lighten the mood of a serious or tragic story, especially in plays. The technique is very common in Elizabethan works, and can be an integral part of the plot or simply a brief event designed to break the tension of the scene. The Gravediggers' scene in William Shakespeare's *Hamlet* is a frequently cited example of comic relief.

Commedia dell'arte: An Italian term meaning "the comedy of guilds" or "the comedy of professional actors." This form of dramatic comedy was popular in Italy during the sixteenth century. Actors were assigned stock roles (such as Pulcinella, the stupid servant, or Pantalone, the old merchant) and given a basic plot to follow, but all dialogue was improvised. The roles were rigidly typed and the plots were formulaic, usually revolving around young lovers who thwarted their elders and attained wealth and happiness. A rigid convention of the *commedia dell'arte* is the periodic intrusion of Harlequin, who interrupts the play with low buffoonery. Peppino de Filippo's *Metamorphoses of a Wandering Minstrel* gave modern audiences an idea of what *commedia dell'arte* may have been like. Various scenarios for *commedia dell'arte* were compiled in Petraccone's *La commedia dell'arte, storia, technica, scenari,* published in 1927.

Complaint: A lyric poem, popular in the Renaissance, in which the speaker expresses sorrow about his or her condition. Typically, the speaker's sadness is caused by an unresponsive lover, but some complaints cite other sources of unhappiness, such as poverty or fate. A commonly cited example is "A Complaint by Night of the Lover Not Beloved" by Henry Howard, Earl of Surrey. Thomas Sackville's "Complaint of Henry, Duke of Buckingham" traces the duke's unhappiness to his ruthless ambition.

Conceit: A clever and fanciful metaphor, usually expressed through elaborate and extended comparison, that presents a striking parallel between two seemingly dissimilar things—for example, elaborately comparing a beautiful woman to an object like a garden or the sun. The conceit was a popular device throughout the Elizabethan Age and Baroque Age and was the principal technique of the seventeenth-century English metaphysical poets. This usage of the word conceit is unrelated to the best-known definition of conceit as an arrogant attitude or behavior. The conceit figures prominently in the works of John Donne, Emily Dickinson, and T. S. Eliot.

Concrete: Concrete is the opposite of abstract, and refers to a thing that actually exists or a description that allows the reader to experience an object or concept with the senses. Henry David Thoreau's *Walden* contains much concrete description of nature and wildlife.

Concrete Poetry: Poetry in which visual elements play a large part in the poetic effect. Punctuation marks, letters, or words are arranged on a page to form a visual design: a cross, for example, or a bumblebee. Max Bill and Eugene Gomringer were among the early practitioners of concrete poetry; Haroldo de Campos and Augusto de Campos are among contemporary authors of concrete poetry.

Confessional Poetry: A form of poetry in which the poet reveals very personal, intimate, sometimes shocking information about himself or herself. Anne Sexton, Sylvia Plath, Robert Lowell, and John Berryman wrote poetry in the confessional vein.

Conflict: The conflict in a work of fiction is the issue to be resolved in the story. It usually occurs between two characters, the protagonist and the antagonist, or between the protagonist and society or the protagonist and himself or herself. Conflict in Theodore Dreiser's novel *Sister Carrie* comes as a result of urban society, while Jack London's short story "To Build a Fire" concerns the protagonist's battle against the cold and himself.

Connotation: The impression that a word gives beyond its defined meaning. Connotations may be universally understood or may be significant only to a certain group. Both "horse" and "steed" denote the same animal, but "steed" has a different connotation, deriving from the chivalrous or romantic narratives in which the word was once often used.

Consonance: Consonance occurs in poetry when words appearing at the ends of two or more verses have similar final consonant sounds but have final vowel sounds that differ, as with "stuff" and "off." Consonance is found in "The curfew tolls the knells of parting day" from Thomas Grey's "An Elegy Written in a Country Church Yard." Also known as Half Rhyme or Slant Rhyme.

Convention: Any widely accepted literary device, style, or form. A soliloquy, in which a character reveals to the audience his or her private thoughts, is an example of a dramatic convention.

Corrido: A Mexican ballad. Examples of *corridos* include "Muerte del afamado Bilito," "La voz de mi conciencia," "Lucio Perez," "La juida," and "Los presos."

Couplet: Two lines of poetry with the same rhyme and meter, often expressing a complete and self-contained thought. The following couplet is from Alexander Pope's "Elegy to the Memory of an Unfortunate Lady": 'Tis Use alone that sanctifies Expense, And Splendour borrows all her rays from Sense.

Criticism: The systematic study and evaluation of literary works, usually based on a specific method or set of principles. An important part of literary studies since ancient times, the practice of criticism has given rise to numerous theories, methods, and "schools," sometimes producing conflicting, even contradictory, interpretations of literature in general as well as of individual works. Even such basic issues as what constitutes a poem or a novel have been the subject of much criticism over the centuries. Seminal texts of literary criticism include Plato's *Republic,* Aristotle's *Poetics,* Sir Philip Sidney's *The Defence of Poesie,* John Dryden's *Of Dramatic Poesie,* and William Wordsworth's "Preface" to the second edition of his *Lyrical Ballads.* Contemporary schools of criticism include deconstruction, feminist, psychoanalytic, poststructuralist, new historicist, post-colonialist, and reader- response.

D

Dactyl: See *Foot*

Dadaism: A protest movement in art and literature founded by Tristan Tzara in 1916. Followers of the movement expressed their outrage at the destruction brought about by World War I by revolting against numerous forms of social convention. The Dadaists presented works marked by calculated madness and flamboyant nonsense. They stressed total freedom of expression, commonly through primitive displays of emotion and illogical, often senseless, poetry. The movement ended shortly after the war, when it was replaced by surrealism. Proponents of Dadaism include Andre Breton, Louis Aragon, Philippe Soupault, and Paul Eluard.

Decadent: See *Decadents*

Decadents: The followers of a nineteenth-century literary movement that had its beginnings in French aestheticism. Decadent literature displays a fascination with perverse and morbid states; a search for novelty and sensation—the "new thrill"; a preoccupation with mysticism; and a belief in the senselessness of human existence. The movement is closely associated with the doctrine Art for Art's Sake. The term "decadence" is sometimes used to denote a decline in the quality of art or literature following a period of greatness. Major French decadents are Charles Baudelaire and Arthur Rimbaud. English decadents include Oscar Wilde, Ernest Dowson, and Frank Harris.

Deconstruction: A method of literary criticism developed by Jacques Derrida and characterized by multiple conflicting interpretations of a given work. Deconstructionists consider the impact of the language of a work and suggest that the true meaning of the work is not necessarily the meaning that the author intended. Jacques Derrida's *De la grammatologie* is the seminal text on deconstructive strategies; among American practitioners of this method of criticism are Paul de Man and J. Hillis Miller.

Deduction: The process of reaching a conclusion through reasoning from general premises to a specific premise. An example of deduction is present in the following syllogism: Premise: All mammals are animals. Premise: All whales are mammals. Conclusion: Therefore, all whales are animals.

Denotation: The definition of a word, apart from the impressions or feelings it creates in the reader. The word "apartheid" denotes a political and economic policy of segregation by race, but its connotations—oppression, slavery, inequality—are numerous.

Denouement: A French word meaning "the unknotting." In literary criticism, it denotes the resolution of conflict in fiction or drama. The *denouement* follows the climax and provides an outcome to the primary plot situation as well as an explanation of secondary plot complications. The *denouement* often involves a character's recognition of his or her state of mind or moral condition. A well-known example of *denouement* is the last scene of the play *As You Like It* by William Shakespeare, in which couples are married, an evildoer repents, the identities of two disguised characters are revealed, and a ruler is restored to power. Also known as Falling Action.

Description: Descriptive writing is intended to allow a reader to picture the scene or setting in which the action of a story takes place. The form this description takes often evokes an intended emotional response—a dark, spooky graveyard will evoke fear, and a peaceful, sunny meadow will evoke calmness. An example of a descriptive story is Edgar Allan Poe's *Landor's Cottage,* which offers a detailed depiction of a New York country estate.

Detective Story: A narrative about the solution of a mystery or the identification of a criminal. The conventions of the detective story include the detective's scrupulous use of logic in solving the mystery; incompetent or ineffectual police; a suspect who appears guilty at first but is later proved innocent; and the detective's friend or confidant—often the narrator—whose slowness in interpreting clues emphasizes by contrast the detective's brilliance. Edgar Allan Poe's "Murders in the Rue Morgue" is commonly regarded as the earliest example of this type of story. With this work, Poe established many of the conventions of the detective story genre, which are still in practice. Other practitioners of this vast and extremely popular genre include Arthur Conan Doyle, Dashiell Hammett, and Agatha Christie.

Deus ex machina: A Latin term meaning "god out of a machine." In Greek drama, a god was often lowered onto the stage by a mechanism of some kind to rescue the hero or untangle the plot. By extension, the term refers to any artificial device or coincidence used to bring about a convenient and simple solution to a plot. This is a common device in melodramas and includes such fortunate circumstances as the sudden receipt of a legacy to save the family farm or a last-minute stay of execution. The *deus ex machina* invariably rewards the virtuous and punishes evildoers. Examples of *deus ex machina* include King Louis XIV in Jean-Baptiste Moliere's *Tartuffe* and Queen Victoria in *The Pirates of Penzance* by William Gilbert and Arthur Sullivan. Bertolt Brecht parodies the abuse of such devices in the conclusion of his *Threepenny Opera.*

Dialogue: In its widest sense, dialogue is simply conversation between people in a literary work; in its most restricted sense, it refers specifically to the speech of characters in a drama. As a specific literary genre, a "dialogue" is a composition in which characters debate an issue or idea. The Greek philosopher Plato frequently expounded his theories in the form of dialogues.

Diction: The selection and arrangement of words in a literary work. Either or both may vary depending on the desired effect. There are four general types of diction: "formal," used in scholarly or lofty writing; "informal," used in relaxed but educated conversation; "colloquial," used in everyday speech; and "slang," containing newly coined words and other terms not accepted in formal usage.

Didactic: A term used to describe works of literature that aim to teach some moral, religious, political, or practical lesson. Although didactic elements are often found in artistically pleasing works, the term "didactic" usually refers to literature in which the message is more important than the form. The term may also be used to criticize a work that the critic finds "overly didactic," that is, heavy-handed in its delivery of a lesson. Examples of didactic literature include John Bunyan's *Pilgrim's Progress,* Alexander Pope's *Essay on Criticism,* Jean-Jacques Rousseau's *Emile,* and Elizabeth Inchbald's *Simple Story.*

Dimeter: See *Meter*

Dionysian: See *Apollonian and Dionysian*

Discordia concours: A Latin phrase meaning "discord in harmony." The term was coined by the eighteenth-century English writer Samuel

Johnson to describe "a combination of dissimilar images or discovery of occult resemblances in things apparently unlike." Johnson created the expression by reversing a phrase by the Latin poet Horace. The metaphysical poetry of John Donne, Richard Crashaw, Abraham Cowley, George Herbert, and Edward Taylor among others, contains many examples of *discordia concours*. In Donne's "A Valediction: Forbidding Mourning," the poet compares the union of himself with his lover to a draftsman's compass: If they be two, they are two so, As stiff twin compasses are two: Thy soul, the fixed foot, makes no show To move, but doth, if the other do; And though it in the center sit, Yet when the other far doth roam, It leans, and hearkens after it, And grows erect, as that comes home.

Dissonance: A combination of harsh or jarring sounds, especially in poetry. Although such combinations may be accidental, poets sometimes intentionally make them to achieve particular effects. Dissonance is also sometimes used to refer to close but not identical rhymes. When this is the case, the word functions as a synonym for consonance. Robert Browning, Gerard Manley Hopkins, and many other poets have made deliberate use of dissonance.

Doppelganger: A literary technique by which a character is duplicated (usually in the form of an alter ego, though sometimes as a ghostly counterpart) or divided into two distinct, usually opposite personalities. The use of this character device is widespread in nineteenth- and twentieth- century literature, and indicates a growing awareness among authors that the "self" is really a composite of many "selves." A well-known story containing a *doppelganger* character is Robert Louis Stevenson's *Dr. Jekyll and Mr. Hyde,* which dramatizes an internal struggle between good and evil. Also known as The Double.

Double Entendre: A corruption of a French phrase meaning "double meaning." The term is used to indicate a word or phrase that is deliberately ambiguous, especially when one of the meanings is risque or improper. An example of a *double entendre* is the Elizabethan usage of the verb "die," which refers both to death and to orgasm.

Double, The: See *Doppelganger*

Draft: Any preliminary version of a written work. An author may write dozens of drafts which are revised to form the final work, or he or she may write only one, with few or no revisions. Dorothy Parker's observation that "I can't write five words but that I change seven" humorously indicates the purpose of the draft.

Drama: In its widest sense, a drama is any work designed to be presented by actors on a stage. Similarly, "drama" denotes a broad literary genre that includes a variety of forms, from pageant and spectacle to tragedy and comedy, as well as countless types and subtypes. More commonly in modern usage, however, a drama is a work that treats serious subjects and themes but does not aim at the grandeur of tragedy. This use of the term originated with the eighteenth-century French writer Denis Diderot, who used the word *drame* to designate his plays about middle- class life; thus "drama" typically features characters of a less exalted stature than those of tragedy. Examples of classical dramas include Menander's comedy *Dyscolus* and Sophocles' tragedy *Oedipus Rex.* Contemporary dramas include Eugene O'Neill's *The Iceman Cometh,* Lillian Hellman's *Little Foxes,* and August Wilson's *Ma Rainey's Black Bottom.*

Dramatic Irony: Occurs when the audience of a play or the reader of a work of literature knows something that a character in the work itself does not know. The irony is in the contrast between the intended meaning of the statements or actions of a character and the additional information understood by the audience. A celebrated example of dramatic irony is in Act V of William Shakespeare's *Romeo and Juliet,* where two young lovers meet their end as a result of a tragic misunderstanding. Here, the audience has full knowledge that Juliet's apparent "death" is merely temporary; she will regain her senses when the mysterious "sleeping potion" she has taken wears off. But Romeo, mistaking Juliet's drug-induced trance for true death, kills himself in grief. Upon awakening, Juliet discovers Romeo's corpse and, in despair, slays herself.

Dramatic Monologue: See *Monologue*

Dramatic Poetry: Any lyric work that employs elements of drama such as dialogue, conflict, or characterization, but excluding works that are intended for stage presentation. A monologue is a form of dramatic poetry.

Dramatis Personae: The characters in a work of literature, particularly a drama. The list of characters printed before the main text of a play or in the program is the *dramatis personae*.

Dream Allegory: See *Dream Vision*

Dream Vision: A literary convention, chiefly of the Middle Ages. In a dream vision a story is presented as a literal dream of the narrator. This device was commonly used to teach moral and religious lessons. Important works of this type are *The Divine Comedy* by Dante Alighieri, *Piers Plowman* by William Langland, and *The Pilgrim's Progress* by John Bunyan. Also known as Dream Allegory.

Dystopia: An imaginary place in a work of fiction where the characters lead dehumanized, fearful lives. Jack London's *The Iron Heel,* Yevgeny Zamyatin's *My,* Aldous Huxley's *Brave New World,* George Orwell's *Nineteen Eighty-four,* and Margaret Atwood's *Handmaid's Tale* portray versions of dystopia.

E

Eclogue: In classical literature, a poem featuring rural themes and structured as a dialogue among shepherds. Eclogues often took specific poetic forms, such as elegies or love poems. Some were written as the soliloquy of a shepherd. In later centuries, "eclogue" came to refer to any poem that was in the pastoral tradition or that had a dialogue or monologue structure. A classical example of an eclogue is Virgil's *Eclogues,* also known as *Bucolics.* Giovanni Boccaccio, Edmund Spenser, Andrew Marvell, Jonathan Swift, and Louis MacNeice also wrote eclogues.

Edwardian: Describes cultural conventions identified with the period of the reign of Edward VII of England (1901-1910). Writers of the Edwardian Age typically displayed a strong reaction against the propriety and conservatism of the Victorian Age. Their work often exhibits distrust of authority in religion, politics, and art and expresses strong doubts about the soundness of conventional values. Writers of this era include George Bernard Shaw, H. G. Wells, and Joseph Conrad.

Edwardian Age: See *Edwardian*

Electra Complex: A daughter's amorous obsession with her father. The term Electra complex comes from the plays of Euripides and Sophocles entitled *Electra,* in which the character Electra drives her brother Orestes to kill their mother and her lover in revenge for the murder of their father.

Elegy: A lyric poem that laments the death of a person or the eventual death of all people. In a conventional elegy, set in a classical world, the poet and subject are spoken of as shepherds. In modern criticism, the word elegy is often used to refer to a poem that is melancholy or mournfully contemplative. John Milton's "Lycidas" and Percy Bysshe Shelley's "Adonais" are two examples of this form.

Elizabethan Age: A period of great economic growth, religious controversy, and nationalism closely associated with the reign of Elizabeth I of England (1558-1603). The Elizabethan Age is considered a part of the general renaissance—that is, the flowering of arts and literature—that took place in Europe during the fourteenth through sixteenth centuries. The era is considered the golden age of English literature. The most important dramas in English and a great deal of lyric poetry were produced during this period, and modern English criticism began around this time. The notable authors of the period—Philip Sidney, Edmund Spenser, Christopher Marlowe, William Shakespeare, Ben Jonson, Francis Bacon, and John Donne—are among the best in all of English literature.

Elizabethan Drama: English comic and tragic plays produced during the Renaissance, or more narrowly, those plays written during the last years of and few years after Queen Elizabeth's reign. William Shakespeare is considered an Elizabethan dramatist in the broader sense, although most of his work was produced during the reign of James I. Examples of Elizabethan comedies include John Lyly's *The Woman in the Moone,* Thomas Dekker's *The Roaring Girl, or, Moll Cut Purse,* and William Shakespeare's *Twelfth Night.* Examples of Elizabethan tragedies include William Shakespeare's *Antony and Cleopatra,* Thomas Kyd's *The Spanish Tragedy,* and John Webster's *The Tragedy of the Duchess of Malfi.*

Empathy: A sense of shared experience, including emotional and physical feelings, with someone or something other than oneself. Empathy is often used to describe the response of a reader to a literary character. An example of an empathic passage is William Shakespeare's description in his narrative poem *Venus and Adonis* of: the snail, whose tender horns being hit, Shrinks backward in his shelly cave with pain. Readers of Gerard Manley Hopkins's *The Windhover* may experience some of the physical sensations evoked in the description of the movement of the falcon.

English Sonnet: See *Sonnet*

Enjambment: The running over of the sense and structure of a line of verse or a couplet into the following verse or couplet. Andrew Marvell's "To His Coy Mistress" is structured as a series of enjambments, as in lines 11-12: "My vegetable love should grow/Vaster than empires and more slow."

Enlightenment, The: An eighteenth-century philosophical movement. It began in France but had a wide impact throughout Europe and America. Thinkers of the Enlightenment valued reason and believed that both the individual and society could achieve a state of perfection. Corresponding to this essentially humanist vision was a resistance to religious authority. Important figures of the Enlightenment were Denis Diderot and Voltaire in France, Edward Gibbon and David Hume in England, and Thomas Paine and Thomas Jefferson in the United States.

Epic: A long narrative poem about the adventures of a hero of great historic or legendary importance. The setting is vast and the action is often given cosmic significance through the intervention of supernatural forces such as gods, angels, or demons. Epics are typically written in a classical style of grand simplicity with elaborate metaphors and allusions that enhance the symbolic importance of a hero's adventures. Some well-known epics are Homer's *Iliad* and *Odyssey*, Virgil's *Aeneid*, and John Milton's *Paradise Lost*.

Epic Simile: See *Homeric Simile*

Epic Theater: A theory of theatrical presentation developed by twentieth-century German playwright Bertolt Brecht. Brecht created a type of drama that the audience could view with complete detachment. He used what he termed "alienation effects" to create an emotional distance between the audience and the action on stage. Among these effects are: short, self-contained scenes that keep the play from building to a cathartic climax; songs that comment on the action; and techniques of acting that prevent the actor from developing an emotional identity with his role. Besides the plays of Bertolt Brecht, other plays that utilize epic theater conventions include those of Georg Buchner, Frank Wedekind, Erwin Piscator, and Leopold Jessner.

Epigram: A saying that makes the speaker's point quickly and concisely. Samuel Taylor Coleridge wrote an epigram that neatly sums up the form: What is an Epigram? A Dwarfish whole, Its body brevity, and wit its soul.

Epilogue: A concluding statement or section of a literary work. In dramas, particularly those of the seventeenth and eighteenth centuries, the epilogue is a closing speech, often in verse, delivered by an actor at the end of a play and spoken directly to the audience. A famous epilogue is Puck's speech at the end of William Shakespeare's *A Midsummer Night's Dream*.

Epiphany: A sudden revelation of truth inspired by a seemingly trivial incident. The term was widely used by James Joyce in his critical writings, and the stories in Joyce's *Dubliners* are commonly called "epiphanies."

Episode: An incident that forms part of a story and is significantly related to it. Episodes may be either self-contained narratives or events that depend on a larger context for their sense and importance. Examples of episodes include the founding of Wilmington, Delaware in Charles Reade's *The Disinherited Heir* and the individual events comprising the picaresque novels and medieval romances.

Episodic Plot: See *Plot*

Epitaph: An inscription on a tomb or tombstone, or a verse written on the occasion of a person's death. Epitaphs may be serious or humorous. Dorothy Parker's epitaph reads, "I told you I was sick."

Epithalamion: A song or poem written to honor and commemorate a marriage ceremony. Famous examples include Edmund Spenser's "Epithalamion" and e. e. cummings's "Epithalamion." Also spelled Epithalamium.

Epithalamium: See *Epithalamion*

Epithet: A word or phrase, often disparaging or abusive, that expresses a character trait of someone or something. "The Napoleon of crime" is an epithet applied to Professor Moriarty, arch-rival of Sherlock Holmes in Arthur Conan Doyle's series of detective stories.

Exempla: See *Exemplum*

Exemplum: A tale with a moral message. This form of literary sermonizing flourished during the Middle Ages, when *exempla* appeared in collections known as "example-books." The works of Geoffrey Chaucer are full of *exempla*.

Existentialism: A predominantly twentieth-century philosophy concerned with the nature and perception of human existence. There are two major strains of existentialist thought: atheistic and Christian. Followers of atheistic existentialism believe that the individual is alone in a godless universe and that the basic human condition is one of suffering and loneliness. Nevertheless, because there are no fixed values, individuals can create their own characters—indeed, they can shape themselves—through the exercise of free will. The atheistic strain culminates in and is popularly associated with the works of Jean-Paul Sartre. The Christian existentialists, on the other hand, believe that only in God may people find freedom from life's anguish. The two strains hold certain beliefs in common: that existence cannot be fully understood or described through empirical effort; that anguish is a universal element of life; that individuals must bear responsibility for their actions; and that there is no common standard of behavior or perception for religious and ethical matters. Existentialist thought figures prominently in the works of such authors as Eugene Ionesco, Franz Kafka, Fyodor Dostoyevsky, Simone de Beauvoir, Samuel Beckett, and Albert Camus.

Expatriates: See *Expatriatism*

Expatriatism: The practice of leaving one's country to live for an extended period in another country. Literary expatriates include English poets Percy Bysshe Shelley and John Keats in Italy, Polish novelist Joseph Conrad in England, American writers Richard Wright, James Baldwin, Gertrude Stein, and Ernest Hemingway in France, and Trinidadian author Neil Bissondath in Canada.

Exposition: Writing intended to explain the nature of an idea, thing, or theme. Expository writing is often combined with description, narration, or argument. In dramatic writing, the exposition is the introductory material which presents the characters, setting, and tone of the play. An example of dramatic exposition occurs in many nineteenth-century drawing-room comedies in which the butler and the maid open the play with relevant talk about their master and mistress; in composition, exposition relays factual information, as in encyclopedia entries.

Expressionism: An indistinct literary term, originally used to describe an early twentieth-century school of German painting. The term applies to almost any mode of unconventional, highly subjective writing that distorts reality in some way. Advocates of Expressionism include dramatists George Kaiser, Ernst Toller, Luigi Pirandello, Federico Garcia Lorca, Eugene O'Neill, and Elmer Rice; poets George Heym, Ernst Stadler, August Stramm, Gottfried Benn, and Georg Trakl; and novelists Franz Kafka and James Joyce.

Extended Monologue: See *Monologue*

F

Fable: A prose or verse narrative intended to convey a moral. Animals or inanimate objects with human characteristics often serve as characters in fables. A famous fable is Aesop's "The Tortoise and the Hare."

Fairy Tales: Short narratives featuring mythical beings such as fairies, elves, and sprites. These tales originally belonged to the folklore of a particular nation or region, such as those collected in Germany by Jacob and Wilhelm Grimm. Two other celebrated writers of fairy tales are Hans Christian Andersen and Rudyard Kipling.

Falling Action: See *Denouement*

Fantasy: A literary form related to mythology and folklore. Fantasy literature is typically set in non-existent realms and features supernatural beings. Notable examples of fantasy literature are *The Lord of the Rings* by J. R. R. Tolkien and the Gormenghast trilogy by Mervyn Peake.

Farce: A type of comedy characterized by broad humor, outlandish incidents, and often vulgar subject matter. Much of the "comedy" in film and television could more accurately be described as farce.

Feet: See *Foot*

Feminine Rhyme: See *Rhyme*

Femme fatale: A French phrase with the literal translation "fatal woman." A *femme fatale* is a sensuous, alluring woman who often leads men into danger or trouble. A classic example of the *femme fatale* is the nameless character in Billy Wilder's *The Seven Year Itch,* portrayed by Marilyn Monroe in the film adaptation.

Fiction: Any story that is the product of imagination rather than a documentation of fact. characters and events in such narratives may be based in real life but their ultimate form and configuration is a creation of the author. Geoffrey Chaucer's *The Canterbury Tales,* Laurence Sterne's *Tristram Shandy,* and Margaret Mitchell's *Gone with the Wind* arc examples of fiction.

Figurative Language: A technique in writing in which the author temporarily interrupts the order, construction, or meaning of the writing for a particular effect. This interruption takes the form of one or more figures of speech such as hyperbole, irony, or simile. Figurative language is the opposite of literal language, in which every word is truthful, accurate, and free of exaggeration or embellishment. Examples of figurative language are tropes such as metaphor and rhetorical figures such as apostrophe.

Figures of Speech: Writing that differs from customary conventions for construction, meaning, order, or significance for the purpose of a special meaning or effect. There are two major types of figures of speech: rhetorical figures, which do not make changes in the meaning of the words, and tropes, which do. Types of figures of speech include simile, hyperbole, alliteration, and pun, among many others.

Fin de siecle: A French term meaning "end of the century." The term is used to denote the last decade of the nineteenth century, a transition period when writers and other artists abandoned old conventions and looked for new techniques and objectives. Two writers commonly associated with the *fin de siecle* mindset are Oscar Wilde and George Bernard Shaw.

First Person: See *Point of View*

Flashback: A device used in literature to present action that occurred before the beginning of the story. Flashbacks are often introduced as the dreams or recollections of one or more characters. Flashback techniques are often used in films, where they are typically set off by a gradual changing of one picture to another.

Foil: A character in a work of literature whose physical or psychological qualities contrast strongly with, and therefore highlight, the corresponding qualities of another character. In his Sherlock Holmes stories, Arthur Conan Doyle portrayed Dr. Watson as a man of normal habits and intelligence, making him a foil for the eccentric and wonderfully perceptive Sherlock Holmes.

Folk Ballad: See *Ballad*

Folklore: Traditions and myths preserved in a culture or group of people. Typically, these are passed on by word of mouth in various forms—such as legends, songs, and proverbs—or preserved in customs and ceremonies. This term was first used by W. J. Thoms in 1846. Sir James Frazer's *The Golden Bough* is the record of English folklore; myths about the frontier and the Old South exemplify American folklore.

Folktale: A story originating in oral tradition. Folktales fall into a variety of categories, including legends, ghost stories, fairy tales, fables, and anecdotes based on historical figures and events. Examples of folktales include Giambattista Basile's *The Pentamerone,* which contains the tales of Puss in Boots, Rapunzel, Cinderella, and Beauty and the Beast, and Joel Chandler Harris's Uncle Remus stories, which represent transplanted African folktales and American tales about the characters Mike Fink, Johnny Appleseed, Paul Bunyan, and Pecos Bill.

Foot: The smallest unit of rhythm in a line of poetry. In English-language poetry, a foot is typically one accented syllable combined with one or two unaccented syllables. There are many different types of feet. When the accent is on the second syllable of a two syllable word (con-*tort*), the foot is an "iamb"; the reverse accentual pattern (*tor-ture*) is a "trochee." Other feet that commonly occur in poetry in English are "anapest," two unaccented syllables followed by an accented syllable as in in-ter-*cept*, and "dactyl," an accented syllable followed by two unaccented syllables as in *su*-i-cide.

Foreshadowing: A device used in literature to create expectation or to set up an explanation of later developments. In Charles Dickens's *Great Expectations,* the graveyard encounter at the beginning of the novel between Pip and the escaped convict Magwitch foreshadows the baleful atmosphere and events that comprise much of the narrative.

Form: The pattern or construction of a work which identifies its genre and distinguishes it from other genres. Examples of forms include the different genres, such as the lyric form or the short story form, and various patterns for poetry, such as the verse form or the stanza form.

Formalism: In literary criticism, the belief that literature should follow prescribed rules of construction, such as those that govern the sonnet form. Examples of formalism are found in the work of the New Critics and structuralists.

Fourteener Meter: See *Meter*

Free Verse: Poetry that lacks regular metrical and rhyme patterns but that tries to capture the cadences of everyday speech. The form allows a poet to exploit a variety of rhythmical effects within a single poem. Free-verse techniques have been widely used in the twentieth century by such writers as Ezra Pound, T. S. Eliot, Carl Sandburg, and William Carlos Williams. Also known as *Vers libre.*

Futurism: A flamboyant literary and artistic movement that developed in France, Italy, and Russia from 1908 through the 1920s. Futurist theater and poetry abandoned traditional literary forms. In their place, followers of the movement attempted to achieve total freedom of expression through bizarre imagery and deformed or newly invented words. The Futurists were self-consciously modern artists who attempted to incorporate the appearances and sounds of modern life into their work. Futurist writers include Filippo Tommaso Marinetti, Wyndham Lewis, Guillaume Apollinaire, Velimir Khlebnikov, and Vladimir Mayakovsky.

G

Genre: A category of literary work. In critical theory, genre may refer to both the content of a given work—tragedy, comedy, pastoral—and to its form, such as poetry, novel, or drama. This term also refers to types of popular literature, as in the genres of science fiction or the detective story.

Genteel Tradition: A term coined by critic George Santayana to describe the literary practice of certain late nineteenth-century American writers, especially New Englanders. Followers of the Genteel Tradition emphasized conventionality in social, religious, moral, and literary standards. Some of the best-known writers of the Genteel Tradition are R. H. Stoddard and Bayard Taylor.

Gilded Age: A period in American history during the 1870s characterized by political corruption and materialism. A number of important novels of social and political criticism were written during this time. Examples of Gilded Age literature include Henry Adams's *Democracy* and F. Marion Crawford's *An American Politician.*

Gothic: See *Gothicism*

Gothicism: In literary criticism, works characterized by a taste for the medieval or morbidly attractive. A gothic novel prominently features elements of horror, the supernatural, gloom, and violence: clanking chains, terror, charnel houses, ghosts, medieval castles, and mysteriously slamming doors. The term "gothic novel" is also applied to novels that lack elements of the traditional Gothic setting but that create a similar atmosphere of terror or dread. Mary Shelley's *Frankenstein* is perhaps the best-known English work of this kind.

Gothic Novel: See *Gothicism*

Great Chain of Being: The belief that all things and creatures in nature are organized in a hierarchy from inanimate objects at the bottom to God at the top. This system of belief was popular in the seventeenth and eighteenth centuries. A summary of the concept of the great chain of being can be found in the first epistle of Alexander Pope's *An Essay on Man,* and more recently in Arthur

O. Lovejoy's *The Great Chain of Being: A Study of the History of an Idea.*

Grotesque: In literary criticism, the subject matter of a work or a style of expression characterized by exaggeration, deformity, freakishness, and disorder. The grotesque often includes an element of comic absurdity. Early examples of literary grotesque include Francois Rabelais's *Pantagruel* and *Gargantua* and Thomas Nashe's *The Unfortunate Traveller,* while more recent examples can be found in the works of Edgar Allan Poe, Evelyn Waugh, Eudora Welty, Flannery O'Connor, Eugene Ionesco, Gunter Grass, Thomas Mann, Mervyn Peake, and Joseph Heller, among many others.

H

Haiku: The shortest form of Japanese poetry, constructed in three lines of five, seven, and five syllables respectively. The message of a *haiku* poem usually centers on some aspect of spirituality and provokes an emotional response in the reader. Early masters of *haiku* include Basho, Buson, Kobayashi Issa, and Masaoka Shiki. English writers of *haiku* include the Imagists, notably Ezra Pound, H. D., Amy Lowell, Carl Sandburg, and William Carlos Williams. Also known as *Hokku.*

Half Rhyme: See *Consonance*

Hamartia: In tragedy, the event or act that leads to the hero's or heroine's downfall. This term is often incorrectly used as a synonym for tragic flaw. In Richard Wright's *Native Son,* the act that seals Bigger Thomas's fate is his first impulsive murder.

Harlem Renaissance: The Harlem Renaissance of the 1920s is generally considered the first significant movement of black writers and artists in the United States. During this period, new and established black writers published more fiction and poetry than ever before, the first influential black literary journals were established, and black authors and artists received their first widespread recognition and serious critical appraisal. Among the major writers associated with this period are Claude McKay, Jean Toomer, Countee Cullen, Langston Hughes, Arna Bontemps, Nella Larsen, and Zora Neale Hurston. Works representative of the Harlem Renaissance include Arna Bon-

temps's poems "The Return" and "Golgotha Is a Mountain," Claude McKay's novel *Home to Harlem,* Nella Larsen's novel *Passing,* Langston Hughes's poem "The Negro Speaks of Rivers," and the journals *Crisis* and *Opportunity,* both founded during this period. Also known as Negro Renaissance and New Negro Movement.

Harlequin: A stock character of the *commedia dell'arte* who occasionally interrupted the action with silly antics. Harlequin first appeared on the English stage in John Day's *The Travailes of the Three English Brothers.* The San Francisco Mime Troupe is one of the few modern groups to adapt Harlequin to the needs of contemporary satire.

Hellenism: Imitation of ancient Greek thought or styles. Also, an approach to life that focuses on the growth and development of the intellect. "Hellenism" is sometimes used to refer to the belief that reason can be applied to examine all human experience. A cogent discussion of Hellenism can be found in Matthew Arnold's *Culture and Anarchy.*

Heptameter: See *Meter*

Hero/Heroine: The principal sympathetic character (male or female) in a literary work. Heroes and heroines typically exhibit admirable traits: idealism, courage, and integrity, for example. Famous heroes and heroines include Pip in Charles Dickens's *Great Expectations,* the anonymous narrator in Ralph Ellison's *Invisible Man,* and Sethe in Toni Morrison's *Beloved.*

Heroic Couplet: A rhyming couplet written in iambic pentameter (a verse with five iambic feet). The following lines by Alexander Pope are an example: "Truth guards the Poet, sanctifies the line,/ And makes Immortal, Verse as mean as mine."

Heroic Line: The meter and length of a line of verse in epic or heroic poetry. This varies by language and time period. For example, in English poetry, the heroic line is iambic pentameter (a verse with five iambic feet); in French, the alexandrine (a verse with six iambic feet); in classical literature, dactylic hexameter (a verse with six dactylic feet).

Heroine: See *Hero/Heroine*

Hexameter: See *Meter*

Historical Criticism: The study of a work based on its impact on the world of the time period in which it was written. Examples of post-modern historical criticism can be found in the work of Michel Foucault, Hayden White, Stephen Greenblatt, and Jonathan Goldberg.

Hokku: See *Haiku*

Holocaust: See *Holocaust Literature*

Holocaust Literature: Literature influenced by or written about the Holocaust of World War II. Such literature includes true stories of survival in concentration camps, escape, and life after the war, as well as fictional works and poetry. Representative works of Holocaust literature include Saul Bellow's *Mr. Sammler's Planet,* Anne Frank's *The Diary of a Young Girl,* Jerzy Kosinski's *The Painted Bird,* Arthur Miller's *Incident at Vichy,* Czeslaw Milosz's *Collected Poems,* William Styron's *Sophie's Choice,* and Art Spiegelman's *Maus.*

Homeric Simile: An elaborate, detailed comparison written as a simile many lines in length. An example of an epic simile from John Milton's *Paradise Lost* follows: Angel Forms, who lay entranced Thick as autumnal leaves that strow the brooks In Vallombrosa, where the Etrurian shades High over-arched embower; or scattered sedge Afloat, when with fierce winds Orion armed Hath vexed the Red-Sea coast, whose waves o'erthrew Busiris and his Memphian chivalry, While with perfidious hatred they pursued The sojourners of Goshen, who beheld From the safe shore their floating carcasses And broken chariot-wheels. Also known as Epic Simile.

Horatian Satire: See *Satire*

Humanism: A philosophy that places faith in the dignity of humankind and rejects the medieval perception of the individual as a weak, fallen creature. "Humanists" typically believe in the perfectibility of human nature and view reason and education as the means to that end. Humanist thought is represented in the works of Marsilio Ficino, Ludovico Castelvetro, Edmund Spenser, John Milton, Dean John Colet, Desiderius Erasmus, John Dryden, Alexander Pope, Matthew Arnold, and Irving Babbitt.

Humors: Mentions of the humors refer to the ancient Greek theory that a person's health and personality were determined by the balance of four basic fluids in the body: blood, phlegm, yellow bile, and black bile. A dominance of any fluid would cause extremes in behavior. An excess of blood created a sanguine person who was joyful, aggressive, and passionate; a phlegmatic person was shy, fearful, and sluggish; too much yellow bile led to a choleric temperament characterized by impatience, anger, bitterness, and stubbornness; and excessive black bile created melancholy, a state of laziness, gluttony, and lack of motivation. Literary treatment of the humors is exemplified by several characters in Ben Jonson's plays *Every Man in His Humour* and *Every Man out of His Humour.* Also spelled Humours.

Humours: See *Humors*

Hyperbole: In literary criticism, deliberate exaggeration used to achieve an effect. In William Shakespeare's *Macbeth,* Lady Macbeth hyperbolizes when she says, "All the perfumes of Arabia could not sweeten this little hand."

I

Iamb: See *Foot*

Idiom: A word construction or verbal expression closely associated with a given language. For example, in colloquial English the construction "how come" can be used instead of "why" to introduce a question. Similarly, "a piece of cake" is sometimes used to describe a task that is easily done.

Image: A concrete representation of an object or sensory experience. Typically, such a representation helps evoke the feelings associated with the object or experience itself. Images are either "literal" or "figurative." Literal images are especially concrete and involve little or no extension of the obvious meaning of the words used to express them. Figurative images do not follow the literal meaning of the words exactly. Images in literature are usually visual, but the term "image" can also refer to the representation of any sensory experience. In his poem "The Shepherd's Hour," Paul Verlaine presents the following image: "The Moon is red through horizon's fog;/ In a dancing mist the hazy meadow sleeps." The first line is broadly literal, while the second line involves turns of meaning associated with dancing and sleeping.

Imagery: The array of images in a literary work. Also, figurative language. William Butler Yeats's "The Second Coming" offers a powerful image of encroaching anarchy: Turning and turning in the widening gyre The falcon cannot hear the falconer; Things fall apart. . . .

Imagism: An English and American poetry movement that flourished between 1908 and 1917. The Imagists used precise, clearly presented images in their works. They also used common, everyday speech and aimed for conciseness, concrete imagery, and the creation of new rhythms. Participants in the Imagist movement included Ezra Pound, H. D. (Hilda Doolittle), and Amy Lowell, among others.

In medias res: A Latin term meaning "in the middle of things." It refers to the technique of beginning a story at its midpoint and then using various flashback devices to reveal previous action. This technique originated in such epics as Virgil's *Aeneid.*

Induction: The process of reaching a conclusion by reasoning from specific premises to form a general premise. Also, an introductory portion of a work of literature, especially a play. Geoffrey Chaucer's "Prologue" to the *Canterbury Tales,* Thomas Sackville's "Induction" to *The Mirror of Magistrates,* and the opening scene in William Shakespeare's *The Taming of the Shrew* are examples of inductions to literary works.

Intentional Fallacy: The belief that judgments of a literary work based solely on an author's stated or implied intentions are false and misleading. Critics who believe in the concept of the intentional fallacy typically argue that the work itself is sufficient matter for interpretation, even though they may concede that an author's statement of purpose can be useful. Analysis of William Wordsworth's *Lyrical Ballads* based on the observations about poetry he makes in his "Preface" to the second edition of that work is an example of the intentional fallacy.

Interior Monologue: A narrative technique in which characters' thoughts are revealed in a way that appears to be uncontrolled by the author. The interior monologue typically aims to reveal the inner self of a character. It portrays emotional experiences as they occur at both a conscious and unconscious level. images are often used to represent sensations or emotions. One of the best-known interior monologues in English is the Molly Bloom section at the close of James Joyce's *Ulysses.* The interior monologue is also common in the works of Virginia Woolf.

Internal Rhyme: Rhyme that occurs within a single line of verse. An example is in the opening line of Edgar Allan Poe's "The Raven": "Once upon a midnight dreary, while I pondered weak and weary." Here, "dreary" and "weary" make an internal rhyme.

Irish Literary Renaissance: A late nineteenth- and early twentieth-century movement in Irish literature. Members of the movement aimed to reduce the influence of British culture in Ireland and create an Irish national literature. William Butler Yeats, George Moore, and Sean O'Casey are three of the best-known figures of the movement.

Irony: In literary criticism, the effect of language in which the intended meaning is the opposite of what is stated. The title of Jonathan Swift's "A Modest Proposal" is ironic because what Swift proposes in this essay is cannibalism— hardly "modest."

Italian Sonnet: See *Sonnet*

J

Jacobean Age: The period of the reign of James I of England (1603-1625). The early literature of this period reflected the worldview of the Elizabethan Age, but a darker, more cynical attitude steadily grew in the art and literature of the Jacobean Age. This was an important time for English drama and poetry. Milestones include William Shakespeare's tragedies, tragi-comedies, and sonnets; Ben Jonson's various dramas; and John Donne's metaphysical poetry.

Jargon: Language that is used or understood only by a select group of people. Jargon may refer to terminology used in a certain profession, such as computer jargon, or it may refer to any nonsensical language that is not understood by most people. Literary examples of jargon are Francois Villon's *Ballades en jargon,* which is composed in the secret language of the *coquillards,* and Anthony Burgess's *A Clockwork Orange,* narrated in the fictional characters' language of "Nadsat."

Juvenalian Satire: See *Satire*

K

Knickerbocker Group: A somewhat indistinct group of New York writers of the first half of the nineteenth century. Members of the group were linked only by location and a common theme: New York life. Two famous members of the Knickerbocker Group were Washington Irving and William Cullen Bryant. The group's name derives from Irving's *Knickerbocker's History of New York*.

L

Lais: See *Lay*

Lay: A song or simple narrative poem. The form originated in medieval France. Early French *lais* were often based on the Celtic legends and other tales sung by Breton minstrels—thus the name of the "Breton lay." In fourteenth-century England, the term "lay" was used to describe short narratives written in imitation of the Breton lays. The most notable of these is Geoffrey Chaucer's "The Minstrel's Tale."

Leitmotiv: See *Motif*

Literal Language: An author uses literal language when he or she writes without exaggerating or embellishing the subject matter and without any tools of figurative language. To say "He ran very quickly down the street" is to use literal language, whereas to say "He ran like a hare down the street" would be using figurative language.

Literary Ballad: See *Ballad*

Literature: Literature is broadly defined as any written or spoken material, but the term most often refers to creative works. Literature includes poetry, drama, fiction, and many kinds of nonfiction writing, as well as oral, dramatic, and broadcast compositions not necessarily preserved in a written format, such as films and television programs.

Lost Generation: A term first used by Gertrude Stein to describe the post-World War I generation of American writers: men and women haunted by a sense of betrayal and emptiness brought about by the destructiveness of the war. The term is commonly applied to Hart Crane, Ernest Hemingway, F. Scott Fitzgerald, and others.

Lyric Poetry: A poem expressing the subjective feelings and personal emotions of the poet. Such poetry is melodic, since it was originally accompanied by a lyre in recitals. Most Western poetry in the twentieth century may be classified as lyrical. Examples of lyric poetry include A. E. Housman's elegy "To an Athlete Dying Young," the odes of Pindar and Horace, Thomas Gray and William Collins, the sonnets of Sir Thomas Wyatt and Sir Philip Sidney, Elizabeth Barrett Browning and Rainer Maria Rilke, and a host of other forms in the poetry of William Blake and Christina Rossetti, among many others.

M

Mannerism: Exaggerated, artificial adherence to a literary manner or style. Also, a popular style of the visual arts of late sixteenth-century Europe that was marked by elongation of the human form and by intentional spatial distortion. Literary works that are self-consciously high-toned and artistic are often said to be "mannered." Authors of such works include Henry James and Gertrude Stein.

Masculine Rhyme: See *Rhyme*

Masque: A lavish and elaborate form of entertainment, often performed in royal courts, that emphasizes song, dance, and costumery. The Renaissance form of the masque grew out of the spectacles of masked figures common in medieval England and Europe. The masque reached its peak of popularity and development in seventeenth-century England, during the reigns of James I and, especially, of Charles I. Ben Jonson, the most significant masque writer, also created the "antimasque," which incorporates elements of humor and the grotesque into the traditional masque and achieved greater dramatic quality. Masque-like interludes appear in Edmund Spenser's *The Faerie Queene* and in William Shakespeare's *The Tempest*. One of the best-known English masques is John Milton's *Comus*.

Measure: The foot, verse, or time sequence used in a literary work, especially a poem. Measure is often used somewhat incorrectly as a synonym for meter.

Melodrama: A play in which the typical plot is a conflict between characters who personify extreme good and evil. Melodramas usually end happily and emphasize sensationalism. Other literary forms that use the same techniques are often labeled "melodramatic." The term was formerly used to describe a combination of drama and music; as such, it was synonymous with "opera." Augustin Daly's *Under the Gaslight* and Dion Boucicault's *The Octoroon, The Colleen Bawn,* and *The Poor of New York* are examples of melodramas. The most popular media for twentieth-century melodramas are motion pictures and television.

Metaphor: A figure of speech that expresses an idea through the image of another object. Metaphors suggest the essence of the first object by identifying it with certain qualities of the second object. An example is "But soft, what light through yonder window breaks?/ It is the east, and Juliet is the sun" in William Shakespeare's *Romeo and Juliet.* Here, Juliet, the first object, is identified with qualities of the second object, the sun.

Metaphysical Conceit: See *Conceit*

Metaphysical Poetry: The body of poetry produced by a group of seventeenth-century English writers called the "Metaphysical Poets." The group includes John Donne and Andrew Marvell. The Metaphysical Poets made use of everyday speech, intellectual analysis, and unique imagery. They aimed to portray the ordinary conflicts and contradictions of life. Their poems often took the form of an argument, and many of them emphasize physical and religious love as well as the fleeting nature of life. Elaborate conceits are typical in metaphysical poetry. Marvell's "To His Coy Mistress" is a well-known example of a metaphysical poem.

Metaphysical Poets: See *Metaphysical Poetry*

Meter: In literary criticism, the repetition of sound patterns that creates a rhythm in poetry. The patterns are based on the number of syllables and the presence and absence of accents. The unit of rhythm in a line is called a foot. Types of meter are classified according to the number of feet in a line. These are the standard English lines: Monometer, one foot; Dimeter, two feet; Trimeter, three feet; Tetrameter, four feet; Pentameter, five feet; Hexameter, six feet (also called the Alexandrine); Heptameter, seven feet (also called the "Fourteener" when the feet are iambic). The most common English meter is the iambic pentameter, in which each line contains ten syllables, or five iambic feet, which individually are composed of an unstressed syllable followed by an accented syllable. Both of the following lines from Alfred, Lord Tennyson's "Ulysses" are written in iambic pentameter: Made weak by time and fate, but strong in will To strive, to seek, to find, and not to yield.

Mise en scene: The costumes, scenery, and other properties of a drama. Herbert Beerbohm Tree was renowned for the elaborate *mises en scene* of his lavish Shakespearean productions at His Majesty's Theatre between 1897 and 1915.

Modernism: Modern literary practices. Also, the principles of a literary school that lasted from roughly the beginning of the twentieth century until the end of World War II. Modernism is defined by its rejection of the literary conventions of the nineteenth century and by its opposition to conventional morality, taste, traditions, and economic values. Many writers are associated with the concepts of Modernism, including Albert Camus, Marcel Proust, D. H. Lawrence, W. H. Auden, Ernest Hemingway, William Faulkner, William Butler Yeats, Thomas Mann, Tennessee Williams, Eugene O'Neill, and James Joyce.

Monologue: A composition, written or oral, by a single individual. More specifically, a speech given by a single individual in a drama or other public entertainment. It has no set length, although it is usually several or more lines long. An example of an "extended monologue"—that is, a monologue of great length and seriousness—occurs in the one-act, one-character play *The Stronger* by August Strindberg.

Monometer: See *Meter*

Mood: The prevailing emotions of a work or of the author in his or her creation of the work. The mood of a work is not always what might be expected based on its subject matter. The poem "Dover Beach" by Matthew Arnold offers examples of two different moods originating from the same experience: watching the ocean at night. The mood of the first three lines—The sea is calm tonight The tide is full, the moon lies fair Upon the straights.... is in sharp contrast to the mood of the last three lines—And we are here as on a darkling plain Swept with confused alarms of struggle and flight, Where ignorant armies clash by night.

Motif: A theme, character type, image, metaphor, or other verbal element that recurs throughout a single work of literature or occurs in a number of different works over a period of time. For example, the various manifestations of the color white in Herman Melville's *Moby Dick* is a "specific" *motif,* while the trials of star-crossed lovers is a "conventional" *motif* from the literature of all periods. Also known as *Motiv* or *Leitmotiv.*

Motiv: See *Motif*

Muckrakers: An early twentieth-century group of American writers. Typically, their works exposed the wrongdoings of big business and government in the United States. Upton Sinclair's *The Jungle* exemplifies the muckraking novel.

Muses: Nine Greek mythological goddesses, the daughters of Zeus and Mnemosyne (Memory). Each muse patronized a specific area of the liberal arts and sciences. Calliope presided over epic poetry, Clio over history, Erato over love poetry, Euterpe over music or lyric poetry, Melpomene over tragedy, Polyhymnia over hymns to the gods, Terpsichore over dance, Thalia over comedy, and Urania over astronomy. Poets and writers traditionally made appeals to the Muses for inspiration in their work. John Milton invokes the aid of a muse at the beginning of the first book of his *Paradise Lost:* Of Man's First disobedience, and the Fruit of the Forbidden Tree, whose mortal taste Brought Death into the World, and all our woe, With loss of Eden, till one greater Man Restore us, and regain the blissful Seat, Sing Heav'nly Muse, that on the secret top of Oreb, or of Sinai, didst inspire That Shepherd, who first taught the chosen Seed, In the Beginning how the Heav'ns and Earth Rose out of Chaos. . . .

Mystery: See *Suspense*

Myth: An anonymous tale emerging from the traditional beliefs of a culture or social unit. Myths use supernatural explanations for natural phenomena. They may also explain cosmic issues like creation and death. Collections of myths, known as mythologies, are common to all cultures and nations, but the best-known myths belong to the Norse, Roman, and Greek mythologies. A famous myth is the story of Arachne, an arrogant young girl who challenged a goddess, Athena, to a weaving contest; when the girl won, Athena was enraged and turned Arachne into a spider, thus explaining the existence of spiders.

N

Narration: The telling of a series of events, real or invented. A narration may be either a simple narrative, in which the events are recounted chronologically, or a narrative with a plot, in which the account is given in a style reflecting the author's artistic concept of the story. Narration is sometimes used as a synonym for "storyline." The recounting of scary stories around a campfire is a form of narration.

Narrative: A verse or prose accounting of an event or sequence of events, real or invented. The term is also used as an adjective in the sense "method of narration." For example, in literary criticism, the expression "narrative technique" usually refers to the way the author structures and presents his or her story. Narratives range from the shortest accounts of events, as in Julius Caesar's remark, "I came, I saw, I conquered," to the longest historical or biographical works, as in Edward Gibbon's *The Decline and Fall of the Roman Empire,* as well as diaries, travelogues, novels, ballads, epics, short stories, and other fictional forms.

Narrative Poetry: A nondramatic poem in which the author tells a story. Such poems may be of any length or level of complexity. Epics such as *Beowulf* and ballads are forms of narrative poetry.

Narrator: The teller of a story. The narrator may be the author or a character in the story through whom the author speaks. Huckleberry Finn is the narrator of Mark Twain's *The Adventures of Huckleberry Finn.*

Naturalism: A literary movement of the late nineteenth and early twentieth centuries. The movement's major theorist, French novelist Emile Zola, envisioned a type of fiction that would examine human life with the objectivity of scientific inquiry. The Naturalists typically viewed human beings as either the products of "biological determinism," ruled by hereditary instincts and engaged in an endless struggle for survival, or as the products of "socioeconomic determinism," ruled by social and economic forces beyond their control. In their works, the Naturalists generally ignored the highest levels of society and focused on degradation: poverty, alcoholism, prostitution, insanity, and disease. Naturalism influenced authors throughout the world, including Henrik Ibsen and Thomas Hardy. In the United States, in particular, Naturalism had a profound impact. Among the authors who embraced its principles are Theodore Dreiser, Eugene O'Neill, Stephen Crane, Jack London, and Frank Norris.

Negritude: A literary movement based on the concept of a shared cultural bond on the part of black Africans, wherever they may be in the world. It traces its origins to the former French colonies of Africa and the Caribbean. Negritude poets, novelists, and essayists generally stress four points in their writings: One, black alienation from traditional African culture can lead to feelings of inferiority. Two, European colonialism and Western education should be resisted. Three, black Africans should seek to affirm and define their own identity. Four, African culture can and should be reclaimed. Many Negritude writers also claim that blacks can make unique contributions to the world, based on a heightened appreciation of nature, rhythm, and human emotions—aspects of life they say are not so highly valued in the materialistic and rationalistic West. Examples of Negritude literature include the poetry of both Senegalese Leopold Senghor in *Hosties noires* and Martiniquais Aime-Fernand Cesaire in *Return to My Native Land.*

Negro Renaissance: See *Harlem Renaissance*

Neoclassical Period: See *Neoclassicism*

Neoclassicism: In literary criticism, this term refers to the revival of the attitudes and styles of expression of classical literature. It is generally used to describe a period in European history beginning in the late seventeenth century and lasting until about 1800. In its purest form, Neoclassicism marked a return to order, proportion, restraint, logic, accuracy, and decorum. In England, where Neoclassicism perhaps was most popular, it reflected the influence of seventeenth-century French writers, especially dramatists. Neoclassical writers typically reacted against the intensity and enthusiasm of the Renaissance period. They wrote works that appealed to the intellect, using elevated language and classical literary forms such as satire and the ode. Neoclassical works were often governed by the classical goal of instruction. English neoclassicists included Alexander Pope, Jonathan Swift, Joseph Addison, Sir Richard Steele, John Gay, and Matthew Prior; French neoclassicists included Pierre Corneille and Jean-Baptiste Moliere. Also known as Age of Reason.

Neoclassicists: See *Neoclassicism*

New Criticism: A movement in literary criticism, dating from the late 1920s, that stressed close textual analysis in the interpretation of works of literature. The New Critics saw little merit in historical and biographical analysis. Rather, they aimed to examine the text alone, free from the question of how external events—biographical or otherwise—may have helped shape it. This predominantly American school was named "New Criticism" by one of its practitioners, John Crowe Ransom. Other important New Critics included Allen Tate, R. P. Blackmur, Robert Penn Warren, and Cleanth Brooks.

New Negro Movement: See *Harlem Renaissance*

Noble Savage: The idea that primitive man is noble and good but becomes evil and corrupted as he becomes civilized. The concept of the noble savage originated in the Renaissance period but is more closely identified with such later writers as Jean-Jacques Rousseau and Aphra Behn. First described in John Dryden's play *The Conquest of Granada,* the noble savage is portrayed by the various Native Americans in James Fenimore Cooper's "Leatherstocking Tales," by Queequeg, Daggoo, and Tashtego in Herman Melville's *Moby Dick,* and by John the Savage in Aldous Huxley's *Brave New World.*

O

Objective Correlative: An outward set of objects, a situation, or a chain of events corresponding to an inward experience and evoking this experience in the reader. The term frequently appears in modern criticism in discussions of authors' intended effects on the emotional responses of readers. This term was originally used by T. S. Eliot in his 1919 essay "Hamlet."

Objectivity: A quality in writing characterized by the absence of the author's opinion or feeling about the subject matter. Objectivity is an important factor in criticism. The novels of Henry James and, to a certain extent, the poems of John Larkin demonstrate objectivity, and it is central to John Keats's concept of "negative capability." Critical and journalistic writing usually are or attempt to be objective.

Occasional Verse: poetry written on the occasion of a significant historical or personal event. *Vers de societe* is sometimes called occasional verse although it is of a less serious nature. Famous examples of occasional verse include Andrew Marvell's "Horatian Ode upon Cromwell's Return from England," Walt Whitman's "When Lilacs Last in the Dooryard Bloom'd"— written upon the death of Abraham Lincoln—and Edmund Spenser's commemoration of his wedding, "Epithalamion."

Octave: A poem or stanza composed of eight lines. The term octave most often represents the first eight lines of a Petrarchan sonnet. An example of an octave is taken from a translation of a Petrarchan sonnet by Sir Thomas Wyatt: The pillar perisht is whereto I leant, The strongest stay of mine unquiet mind; The like of it no man again can find, From East to West Still seeking though he went. To mind unhap! for hap away hath rent Of all my joy the very bark and rind; And I, alas, by chance am thus assigned Daily to mourn till death do it relent.

Ode: Name given to an extended lyric poem characterized by exalted emotion and dignified style. An ode usually concerns a single, serious theme. Most odes, but not all, are addressed to an object or individual. Odes are distinguished from other lyric poetic forms by their complex rhythmic and stanzaic patterns. An example of this form is John Keats's "Ode to a Nightingale."

Oedipus Complex: A son's amorous obsession with his mother. The phrase is derived from the story of the ancient Theban hero Oedipus, who unknowingly killed his father and married his mother. Literary occurrences of the Oedipus complex include Andre Gide's *Oedipe* and Jean Cocteau's *La Machine infernale,* as well as the most famous, Sophocles' *Oedipus Rex.*

Omniscience: See *Point of View*

Onomatopoeia: The use of words whose sounds express or suggest their meaning. In its simplest sense, onomatopoeia may be represented by words that mimic the sounds they denote such as "hiss" or "meow." At a more subtle level, the pattern and rhythm of sounds and rhymes of a line or poem may be onomatopoeic. A celebrated example of onomatopoeia is the repetition of the word "bells" in Edgar Allan Poe's poem "The Bells."

Opera: A type of stage performance, usually a drama, in which the dialogue is sung. Classic examples of opera include Giuseppi Verdi's *La traviata,* Giacomo Puccini's *La Boheme,* and Richard Wagner's *Tristan und Isolde.* Major twentieth-century contributors to the form include Richard Strauss and Alban Berg.

Operetta: A usually romantic comic opera. John Gay's *The Beggar's Opera,* Richard Sheridan's *The Duenna,* and numerous works by William Gilbert and Arthur Sullivan are examples of operettas.

Oral Tradition: See *Oral Transmission*

Oral Transmission: A process by which songs, ballads, folklore, and other material are transmitted by word of mouth. The tradition of oral transmission predates the written record systems of literate society. Oral transmission preserves material sometimes over generations, although often with variations. Memory plays a large part in the recitation and preservation of orally transmitted material. Breton lays, French *fabliaux,* national epics (including the Anglo-Saxon *Beowulf,* the Spanish *El Cid,* and the Finnish *Kalevala*), Native American myths and legends, and African folktales told by plantation slaves are examples of orally transmitted literature.

Oration: Formal speaking intended to motivate the listeners to some action or feeling. Such public speaking was much more common before the development of timely printed communication such as newspapers. Famous examples of oration include Abraham Lincoln's "Gettysburg Address" and Dr. Martin Luther King Jr.'s "I Have a Dream" speech.

Ottava Rima: An eight-line stanza of poetry composed in iambic pentameter (a five-foot line in which each foot consists of an unaccented syllable followed by an accented syllable), following the abababcc rhyme scheme. This form has been prominently used by such important English writers as Lord Byron, Henry Wadsworth Longfellow, and W. B. Yeats.

Oxymoron: A phrase combining two contradictory terms. Oxymorons may be intentional or unintentional. The following speech from William Shakespeare's *Romeo and Juliet* uses several oxymorons: Why, then, O brawling love! O loving hate! O anything, of nothing first create! O heavy lightness! serious vanity! Mis-shapen chaos of well-seeming forms! Feather of lead, bright smoke, cold fire, sick health! This love feel I, that feel no love in this.

P

Pantheism: The idea that all things are both a manifestation or revelation of God and a part of God at the same time. Pantheism was a common attitude in the early societies of Egypt, India, and Greece—the term derives from the Greek *pan* meaning "all" and *theos* meaning "deity." It later became a significant part of the Christian faith. William Wordsworth and Ralph Waldo Emerson are among the many writers who have expressed the pantheistic attitude in their works.

Parable: A story intended to teach a moral lesson or answer an ethical question. In the West, the best examples of parables are those of Jesus Christ in the New Testament, notably "The Prodigal Son," but parables also are used in Sufism, rabbinic literature, Hasidism, and Zen Buddhism.

Paradox: A statement that appears illogical or contradictory at first, but may actually point to an underlying truth. "Less is more" is an example of a paradox. Literary examples include Francis Bacon's statement, "The most corrected copies are commonly the least correct," and "All animals are equal, but some animals are more equal than others" from George Orwell's *Animal Farm*.

Parallelism: A method of comparison of two ideas in which each is developed in the same grammatical structure. Ralph Waldo Emerson's "Civilization" contains this example of parallelism: Raphael paints wisdom; Handel sings it, Phidias carves it, Shakespeare writes it, Wren builds it, Columbus sails it, Luther preaches it, Washington arms it, Watt mechanizes it.

Parnassianism: A mid nineteenth-century movement in French literature. Followers of the movement stressed adherence to well-defined artistic forms as a reaction against the often chaotic expression of the artist's ego that dominated the work of the Romantics. The Parnassians also rejected the moral, ethical, and social themes exhibited in the works of French Romantics such as Victor Hugo. The aesthetic doctrines of the Parnassians strongly influenced the later symbolist and decadent movements. Members of the Parnassian school include Leconte de Lisle, Sully Prudhomme, Albert Glatigny, Francois Coppee, and Theodore de Banville.

Parody: In literary criticism, this term refers to an imitation of a serious literary work or the signature style of a particular author in a ridiculous manner. A typical parody adopts the style of the original and applies it to an inappropriate subject for humorous effect. Parody is a form of satire and could be considered the literary equivalent of a caricature or cartoon. Henry Fielding's *Shamela* is a parody of Samuel Richardson's *Pamela*.

Pastoral: A term derived from the Latin word "pastor," meaning shepherd. A pastoral is a literary composition on a rural theme. The conventions of the pastoral were originated by the third-century Greek poet Theocritus, who wrote about the experiences, love affairs, and pastimes of Sicilian shepherds. In a pastoral, characters and language of a courtly nature are often placed in a simple setting. The term pastoral is also used to classify dramas, elegies, and lyrics that exhibit the use of country settings and shepherd characters. Percy Bysshe Shelley's "Adonais" and John Milton's "Lycidas" are two famous examples of pastorals.

Pastorela: The Spanish name for the shepherds play, a folk drama reenacted during the Christmas season. Examples of *pastorelas* include Gomez Manrique's *Representacion del nacimiento* and the dramas of Lucas Fernandez and Juan del Encina.

Pathetic Fallacy: A term coined by English critic John Ruskin to identify writing that falsely endows nonhuman things with human intentions and feelings, such as "angry clouds" and "sad trees." The pathetic fallacy is a required convention in the classical poetic form of the pastoral elegy, and it is used in the modern poetry of T. S. Eliot, Ezra Pound, and the Imagists. Also known as Poetic Fallacy.

Pelado: Literally the "skinned one" or shirtless one, he was the stock underdog, sharp-witted picaresque character of Mexican vaudeville and tent shows. The *pelado* is found in such works as Don Catarino's *Los effectos de la crisis* and *Regreso a mi tierra*.

Pen Name: See *Pseudonym*

Pentameter: See *Meter*

Persona: A Latin term meaning "mask." *Personae* are the characters in a fictional work of literature. The *persona* generally functions as a mask through which the author tells a story in a voice other than his or her own. A *persona* is usually either a character in a story who acts as a narrator or an "implied author," a voice created by the author to act as the narrator for himself or herself. *Personae* include the narrator of Geoffrey Chaucer's *Canterbury Tales* and Marlow in Joseph Conrad's *Heart of Darkness*.

Personae: See *Persona*

Personal Point of View: See *Point of View*

Personification: A figure of speech that gives human qualities to abstract ideas, animals, and inanimate objects. William Shakespeare used personification in *Romeo and Juliet* in the lines "Arise, fair sun, and kill the envious moon,/ Who is already sick and pale with grief." Here, the moon is portrayed as being envious, sick, and pale with grief—all markedly human qualities. Also known as *Prosopopoeia*.

Petrarchan Sonnet: See *Sonnet*

Phenomenology: A method of literary criticism based on the belief that things have no existence outside of human consciousness or awareness. Proponents of this theory believe that art is a process that takes place in the mind of the observer as he or she contemplates an object rather than a quality of the object itself. Among phenomenological critics are Edmund Husserl, George Poulet, Marcel Raymond, and Roman Ingarden.

Picaresque Novel: Episodic fiction depicting the adventures of a roguish central character ("picaro" is Spanish for "rogue"). The

picaresque hero is commonly a low-born but clever individual who wanders into and out of various affairs of love, danger, and farcical intrigue. These involvements may take place at all social levels and typically present a humorous and wide-ranging satire of a given society. Prominent examples of the picaresque novel are *Don Quixote* by Miguel de Cervantes, *Tom Jones* by Henry Fielding, and *Moll Flanders* by Daniel Defoe.

Plagiarism: Claiming another person's written material as one's own. Plagiarism can take the form of direct, word-for-word copying or the theft of the substance or idea of the work. A student who copies an encyclopedia entry and turns it in as a report for school is guilty of plagiarism.

Platonic Criticism: A form of criticism that stresses an artistic work's usefulness as an agent of social engineering rather than any quality or value of the work itself. Platonic criticism takes as its starting point the ancient Greek philosopher Plato's comments on art in his *Republic*.

Platonism: The embracing of the doctrines of the philosopher Plato, popular among the poets of the Renaissance and the Romantic period. Platonism is more flexible than Aristotelian Criticism and places more emphasis on the supernatural and unknown aspects of life. Platonism is expressed in the love poetry of the Renaissance, the fourth book of Baldassare Castiglione's *The Book of the Courtier*, and the poetry of William Blake, William Wordsworth, Percy Bysshe Shelley, Friedrich Holderlin, William Butler Yeats, and Wallace Stevens.

Play: See *Drama*

Plot: In literary criticism, this term refers to the pattern of events in a narrative or drama. In its simplest sense, the plot guides the author in composing the work and helps the reader follow the work. Typically, plots exhibit causality and unity and have a beginning, a middle, and an end. Sometimes, however, a plot may consist of a series of disconnected events, in which case it is known as an "episodic plot." In his *Aspects of the Novel*, E. M. Forster distinguishes between a story, defined as a "narrative of events arranged in their time-sequence," and plot, which organizes the events to a "sense of causality." This definition closely mirrors Aristotle's discussion of plot in his *Poetics*.

Poem: In its broadest sense, a composition utilizing rhyme, meter, concrete detail, and expressive language to create a literary experience with emotional and aesthetic appeal. Typical poems include sonnets, odes, elegies, *haiku*, ballads, and free verse.

Poet: An author who writes poetry or verse. The term is also used to refer to an artist or writer who has an exceptional gift for expression, imagination, and energy in the making of art in any form. Well-known poets include Horace, Basho, Sir Philip Sidney, Sir Edmund Spenser, John Donne, Andrew Marvell, Alexander Pope, Jonathan Swift, George Gordon, Lord Byron, John Keats, Christina Rossetti, W. H. Auden, Stevie Smith, and Sylvia Plath.

Poetic Fallacy: See *Pathetic Fallacy*

Poetic Justice: An outcome in a literary work, not necessarily a poem, in which the good are rewarded and the evil are punished, especially in ways that particularly fit their virtues or crimes. For example, a murderer may himself be murdered, or a thief will find himself penniless.

Poetic License: Distortions of fact and literary convention made by a writer—not always a poet—for the sake of the effect gained. Poetic license is closely related to the concept of "artistic freedom." An author exercises poetic license by saying that a pile of money "reaches as high as a mountain" when the pile is actually only a foot or two high.

Poetics: This term has two closely related meanings. It denotes (1) an aesthetic theory in literary criticism about the essence of poetry or (2) rules prescribing the proper methods, content, style, or diction of poetry. The term poetics may also refer to theories about literature in general, not just poetry.

Poetry: In its broadest sense, writing that aims to present ideas and evoke an emotional experience in the reader through the use of meter, imagery, connotative and concrete words, and a carefully constructed structure based on rhythmic patterns. Poetry typically relies on words and expressions that have several layers of meaning. It also makes use of the effects of regular rhythm on the ear and may make a strong appeal to the senses through the use of imagery. Edgar Allan Poe's "Annabel Lee" and Walt Whitman's *Leaves of Grass* are famous examples of poetry.

Point of View: The narrative perspective from which a literary work is presented to the reader. There are four traditional points of view. The "third person omniscient" gives the reader a "godlike" perspective, unrestricted by time or place, from which to see actions and look into the minds of characters. This allows the author to comment openly on characters and events in the work. The "third person" point of view presents the events of the story from outside of any single character's perception, much like the omniscient point of view, but the reader must understand the action as it takes place and without any special insight into characters' minds or motivations. The "first person" or "personal" point of view relates events as they are perceived by a single character. The main character "tells" the story and may offer opinions about the action and characters which differ from those of the author. Much less common than omniscient, third person, and first person is the "second person" point of view, wherein the author tells the story as if it is happening to the reader. James Thurber employs the omniscient point of view in his short story "The Secret Life of Walter Mitty." Ernest Hemingway's "A Clean, Well-Lighted Place" is a short story told from the third person point of view. Mark Twain's novel *Huck Finn* is presented from the first person viewpoint. Jay McInerney's *Bright Lights, Big City* is an example of a novel which uses the second person point of view.

Polemic: A work in which the author takes a stand on a controversial subject, such as abortion or religion. Such works are often extremely argumentative or provocative. Classic examples of polemics include John Milton's *Aeropagitica* and Thomas Paine's *The American Crisis.*

Pornography: Writing intended to provoke feelings of lust in the reader. Such works are often condemned by critics and teachers, but those which can be shown to have literary value are viewed less harshly. Literary works that have been described as pornographic include

Ovid's *The Art of Love,* Margaret of Angouleme's *Heptameron,* John Cleland's *Memoirs of a Woman of Pleasure; or, the Life of Fanny Hill,* the anonymous *My Secret Life,* D. H. Lawrence's *Lady Chatterley's Lover,* and Vladimir Nabokov's *Lolita.*

Post-Aesthetic Movement: An artistic response made by African Americans to the black aesthetic movement of the 1960s and early '70s. Writers since that time have adopted a somewhat different tone in their work, with less emphasis placed on the disparity between black and white in the United States. In the words of post-aesthetic authors such as Toni Morrison, John Edgar Wideman, and Kristin Hunter, African Americans are portrayed as looking inward for answers to their own questions, rather than always looking to the outside world. Two well-known examples of works produced as part of the post-aesthetic movement are the Pulitzer Prize-winning novels *The Color Purple* by Alice Walker and *Beloved* by Toni Morrison.

Postmodernism: Writing from the 1960s forward characterized by experimentation and continuing to apply some of the fundamentals of modernism, which included existentialism and alienation. Postmodernists have gone a step further in the rejection of tradition begun with the modernists by also rejecting traditional forms, preferring the anti-novel over the novel and the anti-hero over the hero. Postmodern writers include Alain Robbe-Grillet, Thomas Pynchon, Margaret Drabble, John Fowles, Adolfo Bioy-Casares, and Gabriel Garcia Marquez.

Pre-Raphaelites: A circle of writers and artists in mid nineteenth-century England. Valuing the pre-Renaissance artistic qualities of religious symbolism, lavish pictorialism, and natural sensuousness, the Pre-Raphaelites cultivated a sense of mystery and melancholy that influenced later writers associated with the Symbolist and Decadent movements. The major members of the group include Dante Gabriel Rossetti, Christina Rossetti, Algernon Swinburne, and Walter Pater.

Primitivism: The belief that primitive peoples were nobler and less flawed than civilized peoples because they had not been subjected to the tainting influence of society. Examples of literature espousing primitivism include Aphra Behn's *Oroonoko: Or, The History of the Royal Slave,* Jean-Jacques Rousseau's *Julie ou la Nouvelle Heloise,* Oliver Goldsmith's *The Deserted Village,* the poems of Robert Burns, Herman Melville's stories *Typee, Omoo,* and *Mardi,* many poems of William Butler Yeats and Robert Frost, and William Golding's novel *Lord of the Flies.*

Projective Verse: A form of free verse in which the poet's breathing pattern determines the lines of the poem. Poets who advocate projective verse are against all formal structures in writing, including meter and form. Besides its creators, Robert Creeley, Robert Duncan, and Charles Olson, two other well-known projective verse poets are Denise Levertov and LeRoi Jones (Amiri Baraka). Also known as Breath Verse.

Prologue: An introductory section of a literary work. It often contains information establishing the situation of the characters or presents information about the setting, time period, or action. In drama, the prologue is spoken by a chorus or by one of the principal characters. In the "General Prologue" of *The Canterbury Tales,* Geoffrey Chaucer describes the main characters and establishes the setting and purpose of the work.

Prose: A literary medium that attempts to mirror the language of everyday speech. It is distinguished from poetry by its use of unmetered, unrhymed language consisting of logically related sentences. Prose is usually grouped into paragraphs that form a cohesive whole such as an essay or a novel. Recognized masters of English prose writing include Sir Thomas Malory, William Caxton, Raphael Holinshed, Joseph Addison, Mark Twain, and Ernest Hemingway.

Prosopopoeia: See *Personification*

Protagonist: The central character of a story who serves as a focus for its themes and incidents and as the principal rationale for its development. The protagonist is sometimes referred to in discussions of modern literature as the hero or anti-hero. Well-known protagonists are Hamlet in William Shakespeare's *Hamlet* and Jay Gatsby in F. Scott Fitzgerald's *The Great Gatsby.*

Protest Fiction: Protest fiction has as its primary purpose the protesting of some social injustice, such as racism or discrimination. One example of protest fiction is a series of five novels by Chester Himes, beginning in 1945 with *If He Hollers Let Him Go* and ending in 1955 with *The Primitive*. These works depict the destructive effects of race and gender stereotyping in the context of interracial relationships. Another African American author whose works often revolve around themes of social protest is John Oliver Killens. James Baldwin's essay "Everybody's Protest Novel" generated controversy by attacking the authors of protest fiction.

Proverb: A brief, sage saying that expresses a truth about life in a striking manner. "They are not all cooks who carry long knives" is an example of a proverb.

Pseudonym: A name assumed by a writer, most often intended to prevent his or her identification as the author of a work. Two or more authors may work together under one pseudonym, or an author may use a different name for each genre he or she publishes in. Some publishing companies maintain "house pseudonyms," under which any number of authors may write installations in a series. Some authors also choose a pseudonym over their real names the way an actor may use a stage name. Examples of pseudonyms (with the author's real name in parentheses) include Voltaire (Francois-Marie Arouet), Novalis (Friedrich von Hardenberg), Currer Bell (Charlotte Bronte), Ellis Bell (Emily Bronte), George Eliot (Maryann Evans), Honorio Bustos Donmecq (Adolfo Bioy-Casares and Jorge Luis Borges), and Richard Bachman (Stephen King).

Pun: A play on words that have similar sounds but different meanings. A serious example of the pun is from John Donne's "A Hymne to God the Father": Sweare by thyself, that at my death thy sonne Shall shine as he shines now, and hereto fore; And, having done that, Thou haste done; I fear no more.

Pure Poetry: poetry written without instructional intent or moral purpose that aims only to please a reader by its imagery or musical flow. The term pure poetry is used as the antonym of the term "didacticism." The poetry of Edgar Allan Poe, Stephane Mallarme, Paul Verlaine, Paul Valery, Juan Ramoz Jimenez, and Jorge Guillen offer examples of pure poetry.

Q

Quatrain: A four-line stanza of a poem or an entire poem consisting of four lines. The following quatrain is from Robert Herrick's "To Live Merrily, and to Trust to Good Verses": Round, round, the root do's run; And being ravisht thus, Come, I will drink a Tun To my *Propertius*.

R

Raisonneur: A character in a drama who functions as a spokesperson for the dramatist's views. The *raisonneur* typically observes the play without becoming central to its action. *Raisonneurs* were very common in plays of the nineteenth century.

Realism: A nineteenth-century European literary movement that sought to portray familiar characters, situations, and settings in a realistic manner. This was done primarily by using an objective narrative point of view and through the buildup of accurate detail. The standard for success of any realistic work depends on how faithfully it transfers common experience into fictional forms. The realistic method may be altered or extended, as in stream of consciousness writing, to record highly subjective experience. Seminal authors in the tradition of Realism include Honore de Balzac, Gustave Flaubert, and Henry James.

Refrain: A phrase repeated at intervals throughout a poem. A refrain may appear at the end of each stanza or at less regular intervals. It may be altered slightly at each appearance. Some refrains are nonsense expressions—as with "Nevermore" in Edgar Allan Poe's "The Raven"—that seem to take on a different significance with each use.

Renaissance: The period in European history that marked the end of the Middle Ages. It began in Italy in the late fourteenth century. In broad terms, it is usually seen as spanning the fourteenth, fifteenth, and sixteenth centuries, although it did not reach Great Britain, for example, until the 1480s or so. The Renaissance saw an awakening in almost every sphere of human activity, especially science, philosophy, and the arts. The period is best defined by the emergence of a general philosophy that emphasized the importance of the intellect, the individual, and world affairs. It contrasts strongly with the medieval worldview, characterized by the dominant concerns of faith, the social collective, and spiritual salvation. Prominent writers during the Renaissance include Niccolo Machiavelli and Baldassare Castiglione in Italy, Miguel de Cervantes and Lope de Vega in Spain, Jean Froissart and Francois Rabelais in France, Sir Thomas More and Sir Philip Sidney in England, and Desiderius Erasmus in Holland.

Repartee: Conversation featuring snappy retorts and witticisms. Masters of *repartee* include Sydney Smith, Charles Lamb, and Oscar Wilde. An example is recorded in the meeting of "Beau" Nash and John Wesley: Nash said, "I never make way for a fool," to which Wesley responded, "Don't you? I always do," and stepped aside.

Resolution: The portion of a story following the climax, in which the conflict is resolved. The resolution of Jane Austen's *Northanger Abbey* is neatly summed up in the following sentence: "Henry and Catherine were married, the bells rang and every body smiled."

Restoration: See *Restoration Age*

Restoration Age: A period in English literature beginning with the crowning of Charles II in 1660 and running to about 1700. The era, which was characterized by a reaction against Puritanism, was the first great age of the comedy of manners. The finest literature of the era is typically witty and urbane, and often lewd. Prominent Restoration Age writers include William Congreve, Samuel Pepys, John Dryden, and John Milton.

Revenge Tragedy: A dramatic form popular during the Elizabethan Age, in which the protagonist, directed by the ghost of his murdered father or son, inflicts retaliation upon a powerful villain. Notable features of the revenge tragedy include violence, bizarre criminal acts, intrigue, insanity, a hesitant protagonist, and the use of soliloquy. Thomas Kyd's *Spanish Tragedy* is the first example of revenge tragedy in English, and William Shakespeare's *Hamlet* is perhaps the best. Extreme examples of revenge tragedy, such as John Webster's *The Duchess of Malfi,* are labeled "tragedies of blood." Also known as Tragedy of Blood.

Revista: The Spanish term for a vaudeville musical revue. Examples of *revistas* include Antonio Guzman Aguilera's *Mexico para los mexicanos,* Daniel Vanegas's *Maldito jazz,* and Don Catarino's *Whiskey, morfina y marihuana* and *El desterrado.*

Rhetoric: In literary criticism, this term denotes the art of ethical persuasion. In its strictest sense, rhetoric adheres to various principles developed since classical times for arranging facts and ideas in a clear, persuasive, appealing manner. The term is also used to refer to effective prose in general and theories of or methods for composing effective prose. Classical examples of rhetorics include *The Rhetoric of Aristotle,* Quintillian's *Institutio Oratoria,* and Cicero's *Ad Herennium.*

Rhetorical Question: A question intended to provoke thought, but not an expressed answer, in the reader. It is most commonly used in oratory and other persuasive genres. The following lines from Thomas Gray's "Elegy Written in a Country Churchyard" ask rhetorical questions: Can storied urn or animated bust Back to its mansion call the fleeting breath? Can Honour's voice provoke the silent dust, Or Flattery soothe the dull cold ear of Death?

Rhyme: When used as a noun in literary criticism, this term generally refers to a poem in which words sound identical or very similar and appear in parallel positions in two or more lines. Rhymes are classified into different types according to where they fall in a line or stanza or according to the degree of similarity they exhibit in their spellings and sounds. Some major types of rhyme are "masculine" rhyme, "feminine" rhyme, and "triple" rhyme. In a masculine rhyme, the rhyming sound falls in a single accented syllable, as with "heat" and "eat." Feminine rhyme is a rhyme of two syllables, one stressed and one unstressed, as with "merry" and "tarry." Triple rhyme matches the sound of the accented syllable and the two unaccented syllables that follow: "narrative" and "declarative." Robert Browning alternates feminine and masculine rhymes in his "Soliloquy of the Spanish Cloister": Gr-r-r—there go, my heart's abhorrence! Water your damned flower-pots, do! If hate killed men, Brother Lawrence, God's blood, would not mine kill you! What? Your myrtle-bush wants trimming? Oh, that rose has prior claims— Needs its leaden vase filled brimming? Hell dry you up with flames! Triple rhymes can be found in

Thomas Hood's "Bridge of Sighs," George Gordon Byron's satirical verse, and Ogden Nash's comic poems.

Rhyme Royal: A stanza of seven lines composed in iambic pentameter and rhymed *ababbcc.* The name is said to be a tribute to King James I of Scotland, who made much use of the form in his poetry. Examples of rhyme royal include Geoffrey Chaucer's *The Parlement of Foules,* William Shakespeare's *The Rape of Lucrece,* William Morris's *The Early Paradise,* and John Masefield's *The Widow in the Bye Street.*

Rhyme Scheme: See *Rhyme*

Rhythm: A regular pattern of sound, time intervals, or events occurring in writing, most often and most discernably in poetry. Regular, reliable rhythm is known to be soothing to humans, while interrupted, unpredictable, or rapidly changing rhythm is disturbing. These effects are known to authors, who use them to produce a desired reaction in the reader. An example of a form of irregular rhythm is sprung rhythm poetry; quantitative verse, on the other hand, is very regular in its rhythm.

Rising Action: The part of a drama where the plot becomes increasingly complicated. Rising action leads up to the climax, or turning point, of a drama. The final "chase scene" of an action film is generally the rising action which culminates in the film's climax.

Rococo: A style of European architecture that flourished in the eighteenth century, especially in France. The most notable features of *rococo* are its extensive use of ornamentation and its themes of lightness, gaiety, and intimacy. In literary criticism, the term is often used disparagingly to refer to a decadent or over-ornamental style. Alexander Pope's "The Rape of the Lock" is an example of literary *rococo.*

Roman à clef: A French phrase meaning "novel with a key." It refers to a narrative in which real persons are portrayed under fictitious names. Jack Kerouac, for example, portrayed various real-life beat generation figures under fictitious names in his *On the Road.*

Romance: A broad term, usually denoting a narrative with exotic, exaggerated, often idealized characters, scenes, and themes. Nathaniel Hawthorne called his *The House of the Seven Gables* and *The Marble Faun* romances in order to distinguish them from clearly realistic works.

Romantic Age: See *Romanticism*

Romanticism: This term has two widely accepted meanings. In historical criticism, it refers to a European intellectual and artistic movement of the late eighteenth and early nineteenth centuries that sought greater freedom of personal expression than that allowed by the strict rules of literary form and logic of the eighteenth-century neoclassicists. The Romantics preferred emotional and imaginative expression to rational analysis. They considered the individual to be at the center of all experience and so placed him or her at the center of their art. The Romantics believed that the creative imagination reveals nobler truths—unique feelings and attitudes—than those that could be discovered by logic or by scientific examination. Both the natural world and the state of childhood were important sources for revelations of "eternal truths." "Romanticism" is also used as a general term to refer to a type of sensibility found in all periods of literary history and usually considered to be in opposition to the principles of classicism. In this sense, Romanticism signifies any work or philosophy in which the exotic or dreamlike figure strongly, or that is devoted to individualistic expression, self-analysis, or a pursuit of a higher realm of knowledge than can be discovered by human reason. Prominent Romantics include Jean-Jacques Rousseau, William Wordsworth, John Keats, Lord Byron, and Johann Wolfgang von Goethe.

Romantics: See *Romanticism*

Russian Symbolism: A Russian poetic movement, derived from French symbolism, that flourished between 1894 and 1910. While some Russian Symbolists continued in the French tradition, stressing aestheticism and the importance of suggestion above didactic intent, others saw their craft as a form of mystical worship, and themselves as mediators between the supernatural and the mundane. Russian symbolists include Aleksandr Blok, Vyacheslav Ivanovich Ivanov, Fyodor Sologub, Andrey Bely, Nikolay Gumilyov, and Vladimir Sergeyevich Solovyov.

S

Satire: A work that uses ridicule, humor, and wit to criticize and provoke change in human nature and institutions. There are two major types of satire: "formal" or "direct" satire speaks directly to the reader or to a character in the work; "indirect" satire relies upon the ridiculous behavior of its characters to make its point. Formal satire is further divided into two manners: the "Horatian," which ridicules gently, and the "Juvenalian," which derides its subjects harshly and bitterly. Voltaire's novella *Candide* is an indirect satire. Jonathan Swift's essay "A Modest Proposal" is a Juvenalian satire.

Scansion: The analysis or "scanning" of a poem to determine its meter and often its rhyme scheme. The most common system of scansion uses accents (slanted lines drawn above syllables) to show stressed syllables, breves (curved lines drawn above syllables) to show unstressed syllables, and vertical lines to separate each foot. In the first line of John Keats's *Endymion,* "A thing of beauty is a joy forever:" the word "thing," the first syllable of "beauty," the word "joy," and the second syllable of "forever" are stressed, while the words "A" and "of," the second syllable of "beauty," the word "a," and the first and third syllables of "forever" are unstressed. In the second line: "Its loveliness increases; it will never" a pair of vertical lines separate the foot ending with "increases" and the one beginning with "it."

Scene: A subdivision of an act of a drama, consisting of continuous action taking place at a single time and in a single location. The beginnings and endings of scenes may be indicated by clearing the stage of actors and props or by the entrances and exits of important characters. The first act of William Shakespeare's *Winter's Tale* is comprised of two scenes.

Science Fiction: A type of narrative about or based upon real or imagined scientific theories and technology. Science fiction is often peopled with alien creatures and set on other planets or in different dimensions. Karel Capek's *R.U.R.* is a major work of science fiction.

Second Person: See *Point of View*

Semiotics: The study of how literary forms and conventions affect the meaning of language. Semioticians include Ferdinand de Saussure, Charles Sanders Pierce, Claude Levi-Strauss, Jacques Lacan, Michel Foucault, Jacques Derrida, Roland Barthes, and Julia Kristeva.

Sestet: Any six-line poem or stanza. Examples of the sestet include the last six lines of the Petrarchan sonnet form, the stanza form of Robert Burns's "A Poet's Welcome to his love-begotten Daughter," and the sestina form in W. H. Auden's "Paysage Moralise."

Setting: The time, place, and culture in which the action of a narrative takes place. The elements of setting may include geographic location, characters' physical and mental environments, prevailing cultural attitudes, or the historical time in which the action takes place. Examples of settings include the romanticized Scotland in Sir Walter Scott's "Waverley" novels, the French provincial setting in Gustave Flaubert's *Madame Bovary,* the fictional Wessex country of Thomas Hardy's novels, and the small towns of southern Ontario in Alice Munro's short stories.

Shakespearean Sonnet: See *Sonnet*

Signifying Monkey: A popular trickster figure in black folklore, with hundreds of tales about this character documented since the 19th century. Henry Louis Gates Jr. examines the history of the signifying monkey in *The Signifying Monkey: Towards a Theory of Afro-American Literary Criticism,* published in 1988.

Simile: A comparison, usually using "like" or "as," of two essentially dissimilar things, as in "coffee as cold as ice" or "He sounded like a broken record." The title of Ernest Hemingway's "Hills Like White Elephants" contains a simile.

Slang: A type of informal verbal communication that is generally unacceptable for formal writing. Slang words and phrases are often colorful exaggerations used to emphasize the speaker's point; they may also be shortened versions of an often-used word or phrase. Examples of American slang from the 1990s include "yuppie" (an acronym for Young Urban Professional), "awesome" (for "excellent"), wired (for "nervous" or "excited"), and "chill out" (for relax).

Slant Rhyme: See *Consonance*

Slave Narrative: Autobiographical accounts of American slave life as told by escaped slaves. These works first appeared during the abolition movement of the 1830s through the 1850s. Olaudah Equiano's *The Interesting Narrative of Olaudah Equiano, or Gustavus Vassa, The African* and Harriet Ann Jacobs's *Incidents in the Life of a Slave Girl* are examples of the slave narrative.

Social Realism: See *Socialist Realism*

Socialist Realism: The Socialist Realism school of literary theory was proposed by Maxim Gorky and established as a dogma by the first Soviet Congress of Writers. It demanded adherence to a communist worldview in works of literature. Its doctrines required an objective viewpoint comprehensible to the working classes and themes of social struggle featuring strong proletarian heroes. A successful work of socialist realism is Nikolay Ostrovsky's *Kak zakalyalas stal* (*How the Steel Was Tempered*). Also known as Social Realism.

Soliloquy: A monologue in a drama used to give the audience information and to develop the speaker's character. It is typically a projection of the speaker's innermost thoughts. Usually delivered while the speaker is alone on stage, a soliloquy is intended to present an illusion of unspoken reflection. A celebrated soliloquy is Hamlet's "To be or not to be" speech in William Shakespeare's *Hamlet*.

Sonnet: A fourteen-line poem, usually composed in iambic pentameter, employing one of several rhyme schemes. There are three major types of sonnets, upon which all other variations of the form are based: the "Petrarchan" or "Italian" sonnet, the "Shakespearean" or "English" sonnet, and the "Spenserian" sonnet. A Petrarchan sonnet consists of an octave rhymed *abbaabba* and a "sestet" rhymed either *cdecde, cdccdc,* or *cdedce.* The octave poses a question or problem, relates a narrative, or puts forth a proposition; the sestet presents a solution to the problem, comments upon the narrative, or applies the proposition put forth in the octave. The Shakespearean sonnet is divided into three quatrains and a couplet rhymed *abab cdcd efef gg.* The couplet provides an epigrammatic comment on the narrative or problem put forth in the quatrains. The Spenserian sonnet uses three quatrains and a couplet like the Shakespearean,

but links their three rhyme schemes in this way: *abab bcbc cdcd ee.* The Spenserian sonnet develops its theme in two parts like the Petrarchan, its final six lines resolving a problem, analyzing a narrative, or applying a proposition put forth in its first eight lines. Examples of sonnets can be found in Petrarch's *Canzoniere,* Edmund Spenser's *Amoretti,* Elizabeth Barrett Browning's *Sonnets from the Portuguese,* Rainer Maria Rilke's *Sonnets to Orpheus,* and Adrienne Rich's poem "The Insusceptibles."

Spenserian Sonnet: See *Sonnet*

Spenserian Stanza: A nine-line stanza having eight verses in iambic pentameter, its ninth verse in iambic hexameter, and the rhyme scheme ababbcbcc. This stanza form was first used by Edmund Spenser in his allegorical poem *The Faerie Queene.*

Spondee: In poetry meter, a foot consisting of two long or stressed syllables occurring together. This form is quite rare in English verse, and is usually composed of two monosyllabic words. The first foot in the following line from Robert Burns's "Green Grow the Rashes" is an example of a spondee: Green grow the rashes, O.

Sprung Rhythm: Versification using a specific number of accented syllables per line but disregarding the number of unaccented syllables that fall in each line, producing an irregular rhythm in the poem. Gerard Manley Hopkins, who coined the term "sprung rhythm," is the most notable practitioner of this technique.

Stanza: A subdivision of a poem consisting of lines grouped together, often in recurring patterns of rhyme, line length, and meter. Stanzas may also serve as units of thought in a poem much like paragraphs in prose. Examples of stanza forms include the quatrain, *terza rima, ottava rima,* Spenserian, and the so-called *In Memoriam* stanza from Alfred, Lord Tennyson's poem by that title. The following is an example of the latter form: Love is and was my lord and king, And in his presence I attend To hear the tidings of my friend, Which every hour his couriers bring.

Stereotype: A stereotype was originally the name for a duplication made during the printing process; this led to its modern definition as a person or thing that is (or is assumed to be) the same as all others of its type. Common stereotypical characters include the absent-minded professor, the nagging wife, the troublemaking teenager, and the kind-hearted grandmother.

Stream of Consciousness: A narrative technique for rendering the inward experience of a character. This technique is designed to give the impression of an ever-changing series of thoughts, emotions, images, and memories in the spontaneous and seemingly illogical order that they occur in life. The textbook example of stream of consciousness is the last section of James Joyce's *Ulysses.*

Structuralism: A twentieth-century movement in literary criticism that examines how literary texts arrive at their meanings, rather than the meanings themselves. There are two major types of structuralist analysis: one examines the way patterns of linguistic structures unify a specific text and emphasize certain elements of that text, and the other interprets the way literary forms and conventions affect the meaning of language itself. Prominent structuralists include Michel Foucault, Roman Jakobson, and Roland Barthes.

Structure: The form taken by a piece of literature. The structure may be made obvious for ease of understanding, as in nonfiction works, or may obscured for artistic purposes, as in some poetry or seemingly "unstructured" prose. Examples of common literary structures include the plot of a narrative, the acts and scenes of a drama, and such poetic forms as the Shakespearean sonnet and the Pindaric ode.

Sturm und Drang: A German term meaning "storm and stress." It refers to a German literary movement of the 1770s and 1780s that reacted against the order and rationalism of the enlightenment, focusing instead on the intense experience of extraordinary individuals. Highly romantic, works of this movement, such as Johann Wolfgang von Goethe's *Gotz von Berlichingen,* are typified by realism, rebelliousness, and intense emotionalism.

Style: A writer's distinctive manner of arranging words to suit his or her ideas and purpose in writing. The unique imprint of the author's personality upon his or her writing, style is the product of an author's way of arranging ideas and his or her use of diction, different sentence structures, rhythm, figures of speech, rhetorical principles, and other elements of composition. Styles may be classified according to period (Metaphysical, Augustan, Georgian), individual authors (Chaucerian, Miltonic, Jamesian), level (grand, middle, low, plain), or language (scientific, expository, poetic, journalistic).

Subject: The person, event, or theme at the center of a work of literature. A work may have one or more subjects of each type, with shorter works tending to have fewer and longer works tending to have more. The subjects of James Baldwin's novel *Go Tell It on the Mountain* include the themes of father-son relationships, religious conversion, black life, and sexuality. The subjects of Anne Frank's *Diary of a Young Girl* include Anne and her family members as well as World War II, the Holocaust, and the themes of war, isolation, injustice, and racism.

Subjectivity: Writing that expresses the author's personal feelings about his subject, and which may or may not include factual information about the subject. Subjectivity is demonstrated in James Joyce's *Portrait of the Artist as a Young Man,* Samuel Butler's *The Way of All Flesh,* and Thomas Wolfe's *Look Homeward, Angel.*

Subplot: A secondary story in a narrative. A subplot may serve as a motivating or complicating force for the main plot of the work, or it may provide emphasis for, or relief from, the main plot. The conflict between the Capulets and the Montagues in William Shakespeare's *Romeo and Juliet* is an example of a subplot.

Surrealism: A term introduced to criticism by Guillaume Apollinaire and later adopted by Andre Breton. It refers to a French literary and artistic movement founded in the 1920s. The Surrealists sought to express unconscious thoughts and feelings in their works. The best-known technique used for achieving this aim was automatic writing—transcriptions of spontaneous outpourings from the unconscious. The Surrealists proposed to unify the contrary levels of conscious and unconscious, dream and reality, objectivity and subjectivity into a new level of "super-realism." Surrealism can be found in the poetry of Paul Eluard, Pierre Reverdy, and Louis Aragon, among others.

Suspense: A literary device in which the author maintains the audience's attention through the buildup of events, the outcome of which will soon be revealed. Suspense in William Shakespeare's *Hamlet* is sustained throughout by the question of whether or not the Prince will achieve what he has been instructed to do and of what he intends to do.

Syllogism: A method of presenting a logical argument. In its most basic form, the syllogism consists of a major premise, a minor premise, and a conclusion. An example of a syllogism is: Major premise: When it snows, the streets get wet. Minor premise: It is snowing. Conclusion: The streets are wet.

Symbol: Something that suggests or stands for something else without losing its original identity. In literature, symbols combine their literal meaning with the suggestion of an abstract concept. Literary symbols are of two types: those that carry complex associations of meaning no matter what their contexts, and those that derive their suggestive meaning from their functions in specific literary works. Examples of symbols are sunshine suggesting happiness, rain suggesting sorrow, and storm clouds suggesting despair.

Symbolism: This term has two widely accepted meanings. In historical criticism, it denotes an early modernist literary movement initiated in France during the nineteenth century that reacted against the prevailing standards of realism. Writers in this movement aimed to evoke, indirectly and symbolically, an order of being beyond the material world of the five senses. Poetic expression of personal emotion figured strongly in the movement, typically by means of a private set of symbols uniquely identifiable with the individual poet. The principal aim of the Symbolists was to express in words the highly complex feelings that grew out of everyday contact with the world. In a broader sense, the term "symbolism" refers to the use of one object to represent another. Early members of the Symbolist movement included the French authors Charles Baudelaire and Arthur Rimbaud; William Butler Yeats, James Joyce, and T. S. Eliot were influenced as the movement moved to Ireland, England, and the United States. Examples of the concept of symbolism include a flag that stands for a nation or movement, or an empty cupboard used to suggest hopelessness, poverty, and despair.

Symbolist: See *Symbolism*

Symbolist Movement: See *Symbolism*

Sympathetic Fallacy: See *Affective Fallacy*

T

Tale: A story told by a narrator with a simple plot and little character development. Tales are usually relatively short and often carry a simple message. Examples of tales can be found in the work of Rudyard Kipling, Somerset Maugham, Saki, Anton Chekhov, Guy de Maupassant, and Armistead Maupin.

Tall Tale: A humorous tale told in a straightforward, credible tone but relating absolutely impossible events or feats of the characters. Such tales were commonly told of frontier adventures during the settlement of the west in the United States. Tall tales have been spun around such legendary heroes as Mike Fink, Paul Bunyan, Davy Crockett, Johnny Appleseed, and Captain Stormalong as well as the real-life William F. Cody and Annie Oakley. Literary use of tall tales can be found in Washington Irving's *History of New York*, Mark Twain's *Life on the Mississippi*, and in the German R. F. Raspe's *Baron Munchausen's Narratives of His Marvellous Travels and Campaigns in Russia*.

Tanka: A form of Japanese poetry similar to *haiku*. A *tanka* is five lines long, with the lines containing five, seven, five, seven, and seven syllables respectively. Skilled *tanka* authors include Ishikawa Takuboku, Masaoka Shiki, Amy Lowell, and Adelaide Crapsey.

Teatro Grottesco: See *Theater of the Grotesque*

Terza Rima: A three-line stanza form in poetry in which the rhymes are made on the last word of each line in the following manner: the first and third lines of the first stanza, then the second line of the first stanza and the first and third lines of the second stanza, and so on with the middle line of any stanza rhyming with the first and third lines of the following stanza. An example of *terza rima* is Percy Bysshe Shelley's "The Triumph of Love": As in that trance of wondrous thought I lay This was the tenour of my waking dream. Methought I sate beside a public way Thick strewn with summer dust, and a great stream Of people there was hurrying to and fro Numerous as gnats upon the evening gleam,...

Tetrameter: See *Meter*

Textual Criticism: A branch of literary criticism that seeks to establish the authoritative text of a literary work. Textual critics typically compare all known manuscripts or printings of a single work in order to assess the meanings of differences and revisions. This procedure allows them to arrive at a definitive version that (supposedly) corresponds to the author's original intention. Textual criticism was applied during the Renaissance to salvage the classical texts of Greece and Rome, and modern works have been studied, for instance, to undo deliberate correction or censorship, as in the case of novels by Stephen Crane and Theodore Dreiser.

Theater of Cruelty: Term used to denote a group of theatrical techniques designed to eliminate the psychological and emotional distance between actors and audience. This concept, introduced in the 1930s in France, was intended to inspire a more intense theatrical experience than conventional theater allowed. The "cruelty" of this dramatic theory signified not sadism but heightened actor/audience involvement in the dramatic event. The theater of cruelty was theorized by Antonin Artaud in his *Le Theatre et son double* (*The Theatre and Its Double*), and also appears in the work of Jerzy Grotowski, Jean Genet, Jean Vilar, and Arthur Adamov, among others.

Theater of the Absurd: A post-World War II dramatic trend characterized by radical theatrical innovations. In works influenced by the Theater of the Absurd, nontraditional, sometimes grotesque characterizations, plots, and stage sets reveal a meaningless universe in which human values are irrelevant. Existentialist themes of estrangement, absurdity, and futility link many of the works of this movement. The principal writers of the Theater of the Absurd are Samuel Beckett, Eugene Ionesco, Jean Genet, and Harold Pinter.

Theater of the Grotesque: An Italian theatrical movement characterized by plays written around the ironic and macabre aspects of daily life in the World War I era. Theater of the Grotesque was named after the play

The Mask and the Face by Luigi Chiarelli, which was described as "a grotesque in three acts." The movement influenced the work of Italian dramatist Luigi Pirandello, author of *Right You Are, If You Think You Are.* Also known as *Teatro Grottesco.*

Theme: The main point of a work of literature. The term is used interchangeably with thesis. The theme of William Shakespeare's *Othello*— jealousy—is a common one.

Thesis: A thesis is both an essay and the point argued in the essay. Thesis novels and thesis plays share the quality of containing a thesis which is supported through the action of the story. A master's thesis and a doctoral dissertation are two theses required of graduate students.

Thesis Play: See *Thesis*

Three Unities: See *Unities*

Tone: The author's attitude toward his or her audience may be deduced from the tone of the work. A formal tone may create distance or convey politeness, while an informal tone may encourage a friendly, intimate, or intrusive feeling in the reader. The author's attitude toward his or her subject matter may also be deduced from the tone of the words he or she uses in discussing it. The tone of John F. Kennedy's speech which included the appeal to "ask not what your country can do for you" was intended to instill feelings of camaraderie and national pride in listeners.

Tragedy: A drama in prose or poetry about a noble, courageous hero of excellent character who, because of some tragic character flaw or *hamartia*, brings ruin upon him- or herself. Tragedy treats its subjects in a dignified and serious manner, using poetic language to help evoke pity and fear and bring about catharsis, a purging of these emotions. The tragic form was practiced extensively by the ancient Greeks. In the Middle Ages, when classical works were virtually unknown, tragedy came to denote any works about the fall of persons from exalted to low conditions due to any reason: fate, vice, weakness, etc. According to the classical definition of tragedy, such works present the "pathetic"—that which evokes pity—rather than the tragic. The classical form of tragedy was revived in the sixteenth century; it flourished especially on the

Elizabethan stage. In modern times, dramatists have attempted to adapt the form to the needs of modern society by drawing their heroes from the ranks of ordinary men and women and defining the nobility of these heroes in terms of spirit rather than exalted social standing. The greatest classical example of tragedy is Sophocles' *Oedipus Rex*. The "pathetic" derivation is exemplified in "The Monk's Tale" in Geoffrey Chaucer's *Canterbury Tales.* Notable works produced during the sixteenth century revival include William Shakespeare's *Hamlet, Othello,* and *King Lear*. Modern dramatists working in the tragic tradition include Henrik Ibsen, Arthur Miller, and Eugene O'Neill.

Tragedy of Blood: See *Revenge Tragedy*

Tragic Flaw: In a tragedy, the quality within the hero or heroine which leads to his or her downfall. Examples of the tragic flaw include Othello's jealousy and Hamlet's indecisiveness, although most great tragedies defy such simple interpretation.

Transcendentalism: An American philosophical and religious movement, based in New England from around 1835 until the Civil War. Transcendentalism was a form of American romanticism that had its roots abroad in the works of Thomas Carlyle, Samuel Coleridge, and Johann Wolfgang von Goethe. The Transcendentalists stressed the importance of intuition and subjective experience in communication with God. They rejected religious dogma and texts in favor of mysticism and scientific naturalism. They pursued truths that lie beyond the "colorless" realms perceived by reason and the senses and were active social reformers in public education, women's rights, and the abolition of slavery. Prominent members of the group include Ralph Waldo Emerson and Henry David Thoreau.

Trickster: A character or figure common in Native American and African literature who uses his ingenuity to defeat enemies and escape difficult situations. Tricksters are most often animals, such as the spider, hare, or coyote, although they may take the form of humans as well. Examples of trickster tales include Thomas King's *A Coyote Columbus Story,* Ashley F. Bryan's *The Dancing Granny* and Ishmael Reed's *The Last Days of Louisiana Red.*

Trimeter: See *Meter*
Triple Rhyme: See *Rhyme*
Trochee: See *Foot*

U
Understatement: See *Irony*

Unities: Strict rules of dramatic structure, formulated by Italian and French critics of the Renaissance and based loosely on the principles of drama discussed by Aristotle in his *Poetics*. Foremost among these rules were the three unities of action, time, and place that compelled a dramatist to: (1) construct a single plot with a beginning, middle, and end that details the causal relationships of action and character; (2) restrict the action to the events of a single day; and (3) limit the scene to a single place or city. The unities were observed faithfully by continental European writers until the Romantic Age, but they were never regularly observed in English drama. Modern dramatists are typically more concerned with a unity of impression or emotional effect than with any of the classical unities. The unities are observed in Pierre Corneille's tragedy *Polyeuctes* and Jean-Baptiste Racine's *Phedre.* Also known as Three Unities.

Urban Realism: A branch of realist writing that attempts to accurately reflect the often harsh facts of modern urban existence. Some works by Stephen Crane, Theodore Dreiser, Charles Dickens, Fyodor Dostoyevsky, Emile Zola, Abraham Cahan, and Henry Fuller feature urban realism. Modern examples include Claude Brown's *Manchild in the Promised Land* and Ron Milner's *What the Wine Sellers Buy.*

Utopia: A fictional perfect place, such as "paradise" or "heaven." Early literary utopias were included in Plato's *Republic* and Sir Thomas More's *Utopia,* while more modern utopias can be found in Samuel Butler's *Erewhon,* Theodor Herzka's *A Visit to Freeland,* and H. G. Wells' *A Modern Utopia.*

Utopian: See *Utopia*
Utopianism: See *Utopia*

V
Verisimilitude: Literally, the appearance of truth. In literary criticism, the term refers to aspects of a work of literature that seem

true to the reader. Verisimilitude is achieved in the work of Honore de Balzac, Gustave Flaubert, and Henry James, among other late nineteenth-century realist writers.

Vers de societe: See *Occasional Verse*

Vers libre: See *Free Verse*

Verse: A line of metered language, a line of a poem, or any work written in verse. The following line of verse is from the epic poem *Don Juan* by Lord Byron: "My way is to begin with the beginning."

Versification: The writing of verse. Versification may also refer to the meter, rhyme, and other mechanical components of a poem. Composition of a "Roses are red, violets are blue" poem to suit an occasion is a common form of versification practiced by students.

Victorian: Refers broadly to the reign of Queen Victoria of England (1837-1901) and to anything with qualities typical of that era. For example, the qualities of smug narrowmindedness, bourgeois materialism, faith in social progress, and priggish morality are often considered Victorian. This stereotype is contradicted by such dramatic intellectual developments as the theories of Charles Darwin, Karl Marx, and Sigmund Freud (which stirred strong debates in England) and the critical attitudes of serious Victorian writers like Charles Dickens and George Eliot. In literature, the Victorian Period was the great age of the English novel, and the latter part of the era saw the rise of movements such as decadence and symbolism. Works of Victorian literature include the poetry of Robert Browning and Alfred, Lord Tennyson, the criticism of Matthew Arnold and John Ruskin, and the novels of Emily Bronte, William Makepeace Thackeray,

and Thomas Hardy. Also known as Victorian Age and Victorian Period.

Victorian Age: See *Victorian*

Victorian Period: See *Victorian*

W

Weltanschauung: A German term referring to a person's worldview or philosophy. Examples of *weltanschauung* include Thomas Hardy's view of the human being as the victim of fate, destiny, or impersonal forces and circumstances, and the disillusioned and laconic cynicism expressed by such poets of the 1930s as W. H. Auden, Sir Stephen Spender, and Sir William Empson.

Weltschmerz: A German term meaning "world pain." It describes a sense of anguish about the nature of existence, usually associated with a melancholy, pessimistic attitude. *Weltschmerz* was expressed in England by George Gordon, Lord Byron in his *Manfred* and *Childe Harold's Pilgrimage,* in France by Viscount de Chateaubriand, Alfred de Vigny, and Alfred de Musset, in Russia by Aleksandr Pushkin and Mikhail Lermontov, in Poland by Juliusz Slowacki, and in America by Nathaniel Hawthorne.

Z

Zarzuela: A type of Spanish operetta. Writers of *zarzuelas* include Lope de Vega and Pedro Calderon.

Zeitgeist: A German term meaning "spirit of the time." It refers to the moral and intellectual trends of a given era. Examples of *zeitgeist* include the preoccupation with the more morbid aspects of dying and death in some Jacobean literature, especially in the works of dramatists Cyril Tourneur and John Webster, and the decadence of the French Symbolists.

Cumulative Author/Title Index

Barer, Marshall
   Once upon a Mattress: V28
Barnes, Peter
   The Ruling Class: V6
Barrie, J(ames) M.
   Peter Pan: V7
Barry, Philip
   The Philadelphia Story: V9
The Basic Training of Pavlo Hummel
   (Rabe): V3
Beane, Douglas Carter
   As Bees in Honey Drown: V21
The Bear (Chekhov): V26
Beautiful Señoritas (Prida): V23
Beauty (Martin): V31
Becket, or the Honor of God
   (Anouilh): V19
Beckett, Samuel
   Endgame: V18
   Krapp's Last Tape: V7
   Waiting for Godot: V2
Behan, Brendan
   The Hostage: V7
Behn, Aphra
   The Forc'd Marriage: V24
   The Rover: V16
Beim, Norman
   The Deserter: V18
The Belle's Stratagem (Cowley): V22
Bennett, Michael
   A Chorus Line: V33
Bent (Sherman): V20
Bernstein, Leonard
   West Side Story: V27
Beyond the Horizon (O'Neill): V16
BFE (Cho): V34
Biloxi Blues (Simon): V12
The Birthday Party (Pinter): V5
Black Nativity (Hughes): V32
Blank, Jessica
   The Exonerated: V24
Blessing, Lee
   Eleemosynary: V23
   A Walk in the Woods: V26
Blood Relations (Pollock): V3
Blood Wedding (García Lorca): V10
Blue Room (Hare): V7
Blue Surge (Gilman): V23
Blues for an Alabama Sky (Cleage):
   V14
Blues for Mister Charlie (Baldwin):
   V34
Boesman & Lena (Fugard): V6
A Bold Stroke for a Wife (Centlivre):
   V32
Bolt, Robert
   A Man for All Seasons: V2
Bond, Edward
   Lear: V3
   Saved: V8
Bonner, Marita
   The Purple Flower: V13

Both Your Houses (Anderson): V16
The Boys in the Band (Crowley): V14
Brand (Ibsen): V16
Brecht, Bertolt
   The Good Person of Szechwan: V9
   Mother Courage and Her
     Children: V5
   The Threepenny Opera: V4
Brighton Beach Memoirs (Simon):
   V6
Brooks, Mel
   The Producers: V21
The Browning Version (Rattigan): V8
Buero Vallejo, Antonio
   The Sleep of Reason: V11
Buried Child (Shepard): V6
Burn This (Wilson): V4
Burrows, Abe
   Guys and Dolls: V29
   How to Succeed in Business
     without Really Trying: V31
Bus Stop (Inge): V8
Bye-Bye, Brevoort (Welty): V26

C

Calderón de la Barca, Pedro
   Life Is a Dream: V23
Calm Down Mother (Terry): V18
Candida (Shaw): V30
Capek, Josef
   The Insect Play: V11
Capek, Karel
   The Insect Play: V11
   R.U.R.: V7
Carballido, Emilio
   I, Too, Speak of the Rose: V4
The Caretaker (Pinter): V7
Cariani, John
   Almost, Maine: V34
Cat on a Hot Tin Roof (Williams): V3
The Cenci (Artaud): V22
Centlivre, Susanna
   A Bold Stroke for a Wife: V32
The Chairs (Ionesco, Eugène): V9
The Changeling (Middleton): V22
Chase, Mary
   Harvey: V11
A Chaste Maid in Cheapside
   (Middleton): V18
Chayefsky, Paddy
   Marty: V26
Chekhov, Anton
   The Bear: V26
   The Cherry Orchard: V1
   The Seagull: V12
   The Three Sisters: V10
   Uncle Vanya: V5
The Cherry Orchard (Chekhov): V1
The Chickencoop Chinaman (Chin):
   V33

Children of a Lesser God (Medoff):
   V4
The Children's Hour (Hellman): V3
Childress, Alice
   Florence: V26
   Trouble in Mind: V8
   The Wedding Band: V2
   Wine in the Wilderness: V14
Chin, Frank
   The Chickencoop Chinaman: V33
Cho, Julia
   BFE: V34
A Chorus Line (Bennett): V33
A Chorus of Disapproval
   (Ayckbourn): V7
Christie, Agatha
   The Mousetrap: V2
Churchill, Caryl
   Cloud Nine: V16
   Far Away: V30
   Light Shining in Buckinghamshire:
     V27
   Serious Money: V25
   Top Girls: V12
Clark, John Pepper
   The Raft: V13
Cleage, Pearl
   Blues for an Alabama Sky: V14
   Flyin' West: V16
Cloud Nine (Churchill): V16
Coastal Disturbances (Howe): V32
Coburn, D. L.
   The Gin Game: V23
The Cocktail Party (Eliot): V13
Cocteau, Jean
   Indiscretions: V24
Collins, Wilkie
   The Frozen Deep: V28
Come Back, Little Sheba (Inge): V3
Congreve, William
   Love for Love: V14
   The Way of the World: V15
Connelly, Marc
   The Green Pastures: V12
Copenhagen (Frayn): V22
Corneille, Pierre
   Le Cid: V21
Coward, Noel
   Hay Fever: V6
   Private Lives: V3
Cowley, Hannah
   The Belle's Stratagem: V22
Crimes of the Heart (Henley): V2
Cristofer, Michael
   The Shadow Box: V15
The Critic (Sheridan): V14
Crossroads (Solórzano): V26
Crouse, Russel
   State of the Union: V19
Crowley, Mart
   The Boys in the Band: V14
The Crucible (Miller): V3

Shaw, George Bernard
  Arms and the Man: V22
  Candida: V30
  Major Barbara: V3
  Man and Superman: V6
  Mrs. Warren's Profession: V19
  Pygmalion: V1
  Saint Joan: V11
She Stoops to Conquer (Goldsmith):
  V1
Shear, Claudia
  Dirty Blonde: V24
Shepard, Sam
  Buried Child: V6
  Curse of the Starving Class: V14
  Fool for Love: V7
  True West: V3
Sheridan, Richard Brinsley
  The Critic: V14
  The Rivals: V15
  School for Scandal: V4
Sherman, Martin
  Bent: V20
Sherwood, Robert E.
  Abe Lincoln in Illinois: V11
  Idiot's Delight: V15
  The Petrified Forest: V17
The Shrike (Kramm): V15
Shue, Larry
  The Foreigner: V7
Side Man (Leight): V19
Simon, Neil
  Biloxi Blues: V12
  Brighton Beach Memoirs: V6
  The Governess: V27
  Lost in Yonkers: V18
  The Odd Couple: V2
  The Prisoner of Second Avenue:
  V24
The Sisters Rosensweig
  (Wasserstein): V17
Six Characters in Search of an Author
  (Pirandello): V4
Six Degrees of Separation (Guare):
  V13
Six Degrees of Separation (Motion
  Picture): V33
Sizwe Bansi is Dead (Fugard): V10
The Skin of Our Teeth (Wilder): V4
Slave Ship (Baraka): V11
Sleep Deprivation Chamber
  (Kennedy, Kennedy): V28
The Sleep of Reason (Buero Vallejo):
  V11
Sleuth (Shaffer): V13
Smith, Anna Deavere
  Fires in the Mirror: V22
  Twilight: Los Angeles, 1992: V2
A Soldier's Play (Fuller, Charles H.):
  V8
Solórzano, Carlos
  Crossroads: V26

Son, Diana
  Stop Kiss: V34
Sondheim, Stephen
  Into the Woods: V25
  Sunday in the Park with George:
  V28
  West Side Story: V27
Sophocles
  Ajax: V8
  Antigone: V1
  Electra: V4
  Oedipus Rex: V1
  Women of Trachis: Trachiniae:
  V24
Sorry, Wrong Number (Fletcher):
  V26
Soto, Gary
  Novio Boy: V26
The Sound of a Voice (Hwang): V18
Soyinka, Wole
  Death and the King's Horseman:
  V10
  The Trials of Brother Jero: V26
The Spanish Tragedy (Kyd): V21
Speed-the-Plow (Mamet): V6
Spike Heels (Rebeck): V11
The Square Root of Wonderful
  (McCullers): V18
Stanley (Gems): V25
State of the Union (Crouse and
  Lindsay): V19
Stein, Joseph
  Fiddler on the Roof: V7
Sticks and Bones (Rabe): V13
Stop Kiss (Son): V34
Stoppard, Tom
  Arcadia: V5
  *Dogg's Hamlet, Cahoot's
  Macbeth:* V16
  Indian Ink: V11
  The Real Thing: V8
  *Rosencrantz and Guildenstern Are
  Dead:* V2
  Travesties: V13
Strange Interlude (O'Neill): V20
Streamers (Rabe): V8
Street Scene (Rice): V12
A Streetcar Named Desire
  (Williams): V1
A Streetcar Named Desire (Motion
  picture): V27
Strindberg, August
  The Ghost Sonata: V9
  Miss Julie: V4
  The Stronger: V29
The Stronger (Strindberg): V29
The Subject Was Roses (Gilroy): V17
Sunday in the Park with George
  (Sondheim): V28
Sunrise at Campobello (Schary): V17
*Sweeney Todd: The Demon Barber of
  Fleet Street* (Wheeler): V19

*Sweeney Todd: The Demon Barber of
  Fleet Street* (Motion picture):
  V32
Sweet Bird of Youth (Williams): V12
Swerling, Jo
  Guys and Dolls: V29
Synge, J. M.
  *The Playboy of the Western
  World:* V18

T

Tagore, Rabindranath
  The Post Office: V26
Take Me Out (Greenberg): V24
Talley's Folly (Wilson): V12
Tamburlaine the Great (Marlowe):
  V21
Tape (Rivera): V30
Tartuffe (Molière): V18
A Taste of Honey (Delaney): V7
The Teahouse of the August Moon
  (Patrick): V13
Telling Tales (Cruz): V19
Terry, Megan
  Calm Down Mother: V18
That Championship Season (Miller):
  V12
The Theory of Everything
  (Gomolvilas): V34
They Knew What They Wanted
  (Howard): V29
This Is a Test (Gregg): V28
This Is Our Youth (Lonergan): V23
Thompson, Ernest
  On Golden Pond: V23
Thompson, Jay
  Once upon a Mattress: V28
Thompson, Judith
  Habitat: V22
A Thousand Clowns (Gardner): V20
Three Days of Rain (Greenberg): V32
The Three Sisters (Chekhov): V10
Three Tall Women (Albee): V8
The Threepenny Opera (Brecht): V4
Time Flies (Ives): V29
The Time of Your Life (Saroyan):
  V17
Tiny Alice (Albee): V10
'Tis Pity She's a Whore (Ford): V7
Tom Thumb (Fielding): V28
Topdog/Underdog (Parks): V22
Top Girls (Churchill): V12
Torch Song Trilogy (Fierstein): V6
The Tower (von Hofmannsthal): V12
Travesties (Stoppard): V13
Treadwell, Sophie
  Machinal: V22
The Trials of Brother Jero (Soyinka):
  V26
Trifles (Glaspell): V8
The Trojan Women (Euripides): V27

Cumulative Nationality/Ethnicity Index

Sunday in the Park with George:
V27
West Side Story: V27
Uhry, Alfred
Driving Miss Daisy: V11
Driving Miss Daisy (Motion
picture): V30
The Last Night of Ballyhoo: V15

Mexican

Carballido, Emilio
I, Too, Speak of the Rose: V4
López, Josefina
Real Women Have Curves: V33
Solórzano, Carlos
Crossroads: V26
Soto, Gary
Novio Boy: V26

Native Canadian

Highway, Tomson
The Rez Sisters: V2

Nigerian

Clark, John Pepper
The Raft: V13
Soyinka, Wole
Death and the King's Horseman:
V10
The Trials of Brother Jero: V26

Norwegian

Ibsen, Henrik
Brand: V16
A Doll's House: V1
An Enemy of the People: V25

Ghosts: V11
Hedda Gabler: V6
The Master Builder: V15
Peer Gynt: V8
The Wild Duck: V10

Puerto Rican

Rivera, José
Tape: V30

Romanian

Ionesco, Eugène
The Bald Soprano: V4
The Chairs: V9
Rhinoceros: V25

Russian

Chekhov, Anton
The Bear: V26
The Cherry Orchard: V1
The Seagull: V12
The Three Sisters: V10
Uncle Vanya: V5
Gogol, Nikolai
The Government Inspector: V12
Gorki, Maxim
The Lower Depths: V9
Swerling, Jo
Guys and Dolls: V29
Turgenev, Ivan
A Month in the Country: V6

Scottish

Barrie, J(ames) M.
Peter Pan: V7

South African

Fugard, Athol
Boesman & Lena: V6
A Lesson from Aloes: V24
"Master Harold"...and the Boys:
V3
Sizwe Bansi is Dead: V10

Spanish

Buero Vallejo, Antonio
The Sleep of Reason: V11
Calderón de la Barca, Pedro
Life Is a Dream: V23
García Lorca, Federico
Blood Wedding: V10
The House of Bernarda Alba:
V4

Swedish

Strindberg, August
The Ghost Sonata: V9
Miss Julie: V4
The Stronger: V29

Swiss

Frisch, Max
The Firebugs: V25

Ukrainian

Chayefsky, Paddy
Marty: V26

Venezuelan

Kaufman, Moisés
The Laramie Project: V22

Subject/Theme Index

WITHDRAWN

$159.00   5/17